To Set This World Right

TO SET ~THIS~ WORLD RIGHT

THE ANTISLAVERY MOVEMENT IN THOREAU'S CONCORD

Sandra Harbert Petrulionis

CORNELL UNIVERSITY PRESS
Ithaca and London

First published 2006 by Cornell University Press

Printed in the United States of America

Library of Congress Cataloging-in-Publication Date

Petrulionis, Sandra Harbert, 1959–
   To set this world right : the antislavery movement in Thoreau's Concord /
Sandra Harbert Petrulionis.
      p. cm.
   Includes bibliographical references and index.
   ISBN–13: 978–0–8014–4157–8 (cloth : alk. paper)
   ISBN–10: 0–8014–4157–9 (cloth : alk. paper)
   1. Thoreau, Henry David, 1817–1862.   2. Antislavery movements—
Massachusetts—Concord—History—19th century.   3. Abolitionists—
Massachusetts—Concord—History—19th century.   I. Title.

   E445.M4P48 2006
   973.7'114—dc22

2006023262

Cornell University Press strives to use environmentally responsible suppliers
and materials to the fullest extent possible in the publishing of its books.
Such materials include vegetable-based, low-VOC inks and acid-free papers
that are recycled, totally chlorine-free, or partly composed of nonwood fibers.
For further information, visit our website at www.cornellpress.cornell.edu.

Cloth printing   10 9 8 7 6 5 4 3 2 1 *for Joe and Laurel*

Contents

Acknowledgments

More than a decade ago, when researching Henry Thoreau's response to the arrest of fugitive slave Anthony Burns, I asked a senior Thoreau scholar what seemed at the time a simple enough question: "Where do I find all the details for Thoreau's antislavery involvement?" Bob Sattelmeyer suggested various biographies and local histories. Basically, I'd have "to piece the story together," he said, because *the* book on this topic didn't exist, a comment that inspired me to continue working on the subject. Like many before me, however, my initial direction changed course, and this book has evolved into something quite different from the one I set out to write. That project commenced in an optimistic desire to document the fugitive slaves who passed through Concord, Massachusetts, and with whom Henry Thoreau might have interacted. But it has become a story of influence and recovered lives—of little known women and men whose activism propelled Thoreau and others in this historic town to take a more public stand against slavery.

Portions of this book have been published in earlier versions in the following articles: "Editorial Savoir Faire: Thoreau Transforms His Journal into 'Slavery in Massachusetts,'" *Resources for American Literary Study* 25, no. 2 (1999): 206–31; and "'Swelling that Great Tide of Humanity': The Concord, Massachusetts, Female Anti-Slavery Society," *New England Quarterly* 74 (September 2001): 385–410.

During the past decade, many institutions, scholars, librarians, administrators, colleagues, friends, students, and family have contributed substantially to the shaping of this book. It is my pleasure to acknowledge them here.

For permission to cite from manuscript materials housed in their collections, I thank the following institutions and individuals: Abernethy Library of Middlebury College; American Antiquarian Society; Andover-Harvard Theological Library, Harvard Divinity School; Robert W. Woodruff Library, Atlanta University Center; Kent Bicknell; Boston Public Library/Rare Books Department, Courtesy of the Trustees; Boyd B. Stutler Collection, West Virginia State Archives; Chicago Historical Society; Division of Rare Book and

Manuscript Collections, Cornell University Library; Concord Free Public Library, Special Collections; Haverford College Library; The Huntington Library; Houghton Library, Harvard University; Kansas State Historical Society; Maine Historical Society; Phillips Library, Peabody Essex Museum; Pierpont Morgan Library; Smith College; Thoreau Society Collections, Thoreau Institute at Walden Woods; Clifton Waller Barrett Library, Special Collections, University of Virginia; Yale University Library; Arthur and Elizabeth Schlesinger Library on the History of Women in America, Radcliffe Institute for Advanced Study; and David T. and Hilda W. Sewall.

For support at two crucial stages of the project—a summer stipend to fund travel for initial research, and a one-year fellowship to complete and revise the entire manuscript—I am most grateful to the National Endowment for the Humanities. For three individual faculty grants, I thank Pennsylvania State University's Institute for the Arts & Humanities; and for a sabbatical leave and several research and development grants, I appreciate the ongoing support of Penn State Altoona.

For their valuable suggestions and clarifications, I would like to thank the two anonymous reviewers for the press. For their editorial expertise and advice, I am grateful to the editors and staff at Cornell University Press: Alison Kalett, Karen Laun, Nancy Ferguson, and Susan Barnett.

Fellow scholars of nineteenth-century American literature and history have been incredibly generous with their time and advice. Robert A. Gross has kindly shared archival materials as well as his vast knowledge of Concord history; he also read an early draft of the manuscript, much to its benefit. My indebtedness to his published and forthcoming work is reflected throughout the book. Gary Collison, Len Gougeon, and Bob Hudspeth encouraged and pointed me in the right directions at the inception of the project. Joel Myerson deciphered words on more than one perplexing manuscript letter; he and Ronald Bosco generously offered suggestions and provided copies of materials from their own research. Noelle Baker and Laura Dassow Walls each read a draft of the manuscript, and the final product has profited considerably from their insights. Others have shared research materials and given valuable guidance and support. My thanks to Bob Burkholder, Randall Conrad, Mary De Jong, Len Gougeon, Bob Sattelmeyer, and the entire staff at the Textual Center of *The Writings of Henry D. Thoreau*, especially Editor-in-Chief Elizabeth Hall Witherell, and Dianne Piper-Rybak, Mary Shelden, and Lihong Xie. A special debt of gratitude is also due to Bradley P. Dean, Thoreau scholar extraordinaire, whose recent and untimely death was a cruel setback for Thoreau scholarship. Like many others, I benefited tremendously from Brad's talent and largesse as a scholar and an archival sleuth; each chapter in this book reflects his advice and research.

Several librarians have educated me and responded patiently to my questions. Most especially, I thank Leslie Wilson of the Concord Free Public Library, who never tired of talking about Concord history and who nudged me to consider a broader scope to the project from the first day I sat in the crowded Special Collections room, which has now been beautifully—and spaciously!—renovated. Thank you also to Stacy Swazy Jones at the Robert W. Woodruff Library, Atlanta University Center; Eric Frazier at the Boston Public Library; Susan Halpert, Leslie Morris, and Jennie Rathbun at the Houghton Library, Harvard University; and Susan Hodson at the Huntington Library. The director and staff at Eiche Library, Penn State Altoona, have been patient and creative in securing nineteenth-century materials. Thank you to Head Librarian Tim Wherry and staff members Gale Biddle, Cindy McCarty, Jennifer Phillips, and Peggy Tromm.

In my experience, Pennsylvania State University has lived up to its promise of "one university, geographically dispersed" as colleagues from other campuses, especially Bob Burkholder, Phyllis Cole, Gary Collison, Richard Kopley, Beverly Peterson, and Gayle Smith have long shared my excitement for this topic. Penn State Altoona administrators and colleagues have given generously of their financial support and friendship even to joining me in zigzagging along country roads in quest of John Brown's Maryland compound. Thank you especially to Lori Bechtel, Brian Black, Mary De Jong, Marc Harris, Tom Liszka, Donna Lybecker, Ian Marshall, and Rebecca Strzelec.

I would also like to acknowledge many students and staff for microfilm reading, transcribing, proofreading, copying, and other research and administrative assistance: Robin Alford, Brittany Bovard, Dustin Brandt, Barbara Brunhuber, Jeannette Burgan, Joanna Clinich, Kristina Cole, Molly Cover, Willis Dell, Nicole Weaver Dodson, Sheila Evans, Amanda Freiwald, Danielle Garland, Aaron Heresco, Jason Hinkledire, Michele Kennedy, Brenda McCloskey, Jessica Sidler, Molly Slep, Clare Sutton, and Amy Wilkes.

For ten years, friends have enthusiastically solicited and patiently listened to regular updates of "where the book is now." A heartfelt thank you to Jana Argersinger, Noelle Baker, Ron Bosco, Kris Boudreau, Lisa Coffman, Mike Frederick, Linda Frost, Jayne Gordon, Bob Hudspeth, Joel Myerson, Mariane Schaum, Dan Shealy, Mary Shelden, and Laura Dassow Walls. Thank you also to Thoreau Society members for sharing a memorable weekend in and around Harpers Ferry, including an afternoon crouched in the attic of the Kennedy farm house just before we marched into town one cold night along the C & O Canal.

For their hospitality and friendship in sharing their Concord home, a special thanks to Lorna and the late John Mack. For their love and encouragement through the years, I am grateful to my parents, Gene and Margaret Harbert. Finally, this book is dedicated to my husband, Joe, and daughter, Laurel, without whose keen interest, sensible questions, multiple readings, and perpetual sense of humor this book would still be in progress.

To Set This World Right

Introduction

Before dawn on December 3, 1859, a day "suddenly quite cold" in Concord, Massachusetts, Henry David Thoreau walked quickly the half mile from his family's home on Main Street to Waldo and Lidian Emerson's house on the Cambridge Turnpike.[1] There, waiting and ready for him, he found a horse harnessed to a wagon; he stepped up to the driver's seat and headed back toward the center of town, soon passing the imposing First Unitarian Church, whose bells had remained silent the prior afternoon, town leaders declining to mark the hour John Brown was hanged. Thoreau nudged the mare onto Main Street, passing by the Middlesex Hotel and the county jail, perhaps remembering his stint there some thirteen years earlier, a one-night stand to protest slavery and the Mexican War. If so, the memory may have produced a chuckle as Thoreau realized that his morning's work made him a criminal once again. He drove by the milldam shops and the South Burying Ground, approaching neighbors likely just starting to stir that chilly morning—Ann and Francis Bigelow, Mary Merrick Brooks, William and Anne Whiting—any one of whom, he knew, would have taken his place if need be. Turning left at Brooks's home onto Sudbury Road, Thoreau came up promptly at seven o'clock to his destination, where Frank Sanborn's panic-stricken houseguest—"his name is Lockwood" Sanborn had told him—waited, breakfasted and ready.

Thoreau did not know the pale, dark-haired young man who emerged from the house, but he bade him sit on the back seat of the wagon and stay hidden. That he had arrived in Concord by accident the night before, that he must not be seen there, that he needed to board the train bound for Montreal, this much Thoreau knew. That "Lockwood" was not his real name, that he was one of the most wanted men in the country with a five-hundred-dollar bounty on his head, Thoreau certainly suspected. But as they proceeded back up Sudbury Road and turned onto Main Street, the

1

two men did not speak about these matters. Soon they veered right onto the Union Turnpike, en route to the South Acton train station, some four miles northwest.

Thoreau would recount this scene later that day in his journal, identifying his passenger only as "X." The young man had admitted to being "insane," a diagnosis Thoreau readily accepted, particularly when "X" jumped out of the wagon under the deluded fear that his driver meant to arrest rather than help him. Nonplussed, Thoreau had lugged the rattled man back in to the wagon, patiently responded to a flurry of questions, and reassured him that he was indeed being conveyed to safety. It was not the first time in recent years that Thoreau had helped a wanted man flee the country, although those fugitives from "justice" had been black.

Twenty-two years old, "Mr. Lockwood" had good reason to appear "insane." But that frigid December he vanished from Concord, bound for Montreal, where he disembarked the next day, the reward for his capture unclaimed. Thoreau arrived back in town at mid-morning, deposited the horse and wagon at Emerson's, and went home to a late breakfast. His mother and sister may not have questioned how he had spent the preceding hours, but their tacit approval, Thoreau knew, was assured.[2]

To understand how forty-two-year-old Henry Thoreau wound up the willing accomplice of a desperate criminal on the run from federal authorities, we must turn back nearly three decades to the early 1830s, to the first rumblings of antislavery sentiment in the celebrated town of Concord, Massachusetts. It is a story that encompasses most of this community's renowned literary figures, but perhaps none so intimately as Thoreau, whose fiery speeches sympathetic to the slave and to John Brown have long associated Concord with radical abolitionism. Initially, only a slim minority in this town espoused these views, but because Thoreau and his townsman Ralph Waldo Emerson ultimately championed the cause, Concord has gone into the historical record as an antislavery "hotbed."[3]

Through the years, scholars have extolled Thoreau for helping slaves via the Underground Railroad even as they have disparaged him for remaining on the sidelines until slavery came to Massachusetts via the Fugitive Slave Law in 1850. Many of these assessments, however, oversimplify. Thoreau was a philosopher, social critic, writer, and natural historian, but only a reluctant political reformer. He was and was not a radical abolitionist. He did, with his family, assist fugitive slaves. He denounced collective reform movements and abolitionist leaders, but on more than one occasion he also acted and spoke in concert with the local antislavery societies to which his mother, sisters, and aunts loyally belonged. Like nearly all northerners who opposed the "peculiar institution," Thoreau did respond more fervently to the slave's plight after federal laws delivered the crisis quite bodily to Massachusetts. And when this volatile issue overran his solitude, Thoreau frequently expressed frustration.[4]

Grassroots reform during the antebellum era was nearly always a communal effort, yet existing histories of this distinguished town and biographies of its illustrious authors have usually focused on the political ideals of Thoreau and Emerson rather than on the civic context in which their abolitionism evolved and took place. Although these works mention the handful of dedicated men and women who spearheaded local efforts, such individuals appear as peripheral figures.[5] *To Set This World Right: The Antislavery Movement in Thoreau's Concord* is the first book to recover the voices, events, and influence of this previously fragmented reform narrative. It frames the evolution of Thoreau's antislavery ideology as a product of his community's activism—from its emergence in the early 1830s, to gradual support for William Lloyd Garrison's immediatist and disunionist platforms, to the harboring of runaway slaves, to, finally, the unconditional embrace of John Brown's violent, revolutionary agenda by moderates and radicals alike. Most significantly, this book focuses on the extraordinary individuals who fostered such reform. Whenever possible, their voices tell this story. Henry Thoreau thus becomes an organizing rather than a main character in the broader narrative of a defining era in Concord's history.

This book examines fundamental questions about the origin and evolution of radical abolitionism in Concord, Massachusetts. When did antislavery activism begin here, and which factors contributed to its growth? Who were the primary instigators of these burgeoning efforts; what did they do, and when do they do it? What were the relationships between Concord activists and the nation's most prominent antislavery leaders next door in Boston? Through which strategies and means did these individuals exert their influence on town leaders, including America's foremost public intellectual, Ralph Waldo Emerson? When and why did Concord moderates finally embrace a radical antislavery agenda? On what basis has Henry Thoreau—who cherished nothing more than solitary tramps through his beloved woods and bogs—achieved lasting fame as an outspoken abolitionist? How active were his mother and sisters in the organized movement, and what sway did they exercise over Thoreau?

Partial answers to these inquiries lay scattered in a myriad of sources—biographies, histories, and anecdotal works. Too often, however, such sources cite each other with slight deference to primary documents and materials that reveal a far more imbricated reform narrative. The archival record contains regrettable gaps, but when examined with other evidence, it divulges an extraordinarily rich example of the diverse tactics exploited by a small coterie of committed individuals who provoked their neighbors to action, the moral urgency of abolishing slavery their sole objective. A sense of the strategic intent and collaborative nature of this behind-the-scenes activism is most striking in the voices of the women and men themselves. Thus, rather than paraphrase or excerpt from these documents, this book immerses readers in the primary sources.

Why Concord? Certainly, other northern communities can boast a record of antislavery activism as well as famous literary daughters and sons. In instructive ways, Concord serves as a microcosm of the evolution of antebellum abolitionism as well as of the complex nature of northern attitudes toward the vexing issues of slavery and race at this time, one that dispels the myth of the North as an egalitarian center of racial harmony and that reveals the dynamics at play between the women who brokered their moral influence into positions of political power with influential townsmen. In this historic locale, abolitionism crossed racial, class, and gender lines as a confederation of neighbors fomented a radical consciousness—as the Thoreaus, Emersons, and Alcotts worked in tandem with slave-owner's daughter and senator's wife Mary Merrick Brooks, harness maker William Whiting and his outspoken daughters Anne and Louisa, schoolteacher Mary Rice, and former slave John Garrison and his wife Susan. Here, Ann Bigelow and her blacksmith husband Francis fed and clothed fugitive slave Shadrach Minkins as he made his way to freedom. Here, the adolescent daughters of John Brown attended school and emotionally recovered after their father's notorious public hanging. Indeed, why Concord?[6]

Similar to his townsman Waldo Emerson, Henry Thoreau lingered on the sidelines of Concord's antislavery movement, yet ultimately he gravitated to the most extreme abolitionists, an evolution effected through years of persistent effort by determined neighbors around him—rich and poor, young and old, black and white, and most of all, female and male. The majority in their community maintained a practiced detachment from the plight of the enslaved, but these committed women and men at last prevailed on the philosophers of self-culture to accept the responsibility of their reputations. The story of "Henry Thoreau, Abolitionist" is, finally, inseparable from that of "Concord, Antislavery Town."

To Set This World Right progresses chronologically, beginning in chapter 1 with the inception of organized abolitionism in Concord, shortly after William Lloyd Garrison founded the *Liberator* in January 1831. Over the ensuing decade, antislavery organizers, including Garrison, Wendell Phillips, and Frederick Douglass spoke often to Concord audiences. Local reformers founded two organizations in the 1830s that would prove instrumental to their cause: the Middlesex County Anti-Slavery Society and the Concord Female Anti-Slavery Society. Long celebrated with nearby Lexington as the birthplace of the American Revolution, the generally quiet and provincial shire town of Concord now became a forum for Garrisonianism as key women and men acted in concert with state antislavery leaders, initiating petition drives, organizing fundraisers, and sponsoring lectures, including a controversial one by eloquent orator Wendell Phillips. The national "schism" that divided the organized movement was felt in Concord, but by 1843, the Garrisonians held sway here.

Chapter 2 opens in 1844, as ongoing mobilization efforts and an antiabolitionist backlash strengthened the alliance between Concord and Boston activists. Local reformers developed creative strategies and persevered despite being impeded in their efforts by conservative townsmen, including the clergy. On two memorable occasions, Wendell Phillips spoke again to conflicted Concord audiences; under the direction of Mary Merrick Brooks, the female antislavery society joined neighboring towns in hosting "celebrations" on August 1 to commemorate the anniversary of emancipation in the West Indies. The first of these events in 1844 marked a shift in Waldo Emerson's public commitment to the antislavery cause as Concord's leading intellectual addressed a gathering that included Frederick Douglass. Later that year, when the South Carolina government humiliated his intimate friend Samuel Hoar, Emerson responded even more stridently to the issue of slavery. Two years later, a recent inmate of the Concord jail, Henry Thoreau, followed up his antiwar protest by cohosting the August 1 event at Walden Pond, the second instance of his direct service to the female antislavery society. Also in this decade antislavery zealots in Concord, including Thoreau's mother and sisters, signed on to Garrison's most radical measure to date—disunion—northern secession from the slaveholding South. By the end of the 1840s, Wendell Phillips credited women's efforts in general and Mary Brooks's influence on Waldo Emerson in particular for the "gradual, silent, but steady, growth of reform in towns where a few women, all alone, have given their hearts to it." Nevertheless, despite these persistent efforts, and despite Henry Thoreau's memorable call in "Civil Disobedience" for "*one* HONEST man" to join him in jail, the decade ended with a vast, westward expansion of slavery—courtesy of the U.S. victory in the Mexican War—and the prospects for immediate abolition seemed dim indeed.[7]

Chapter 3 examines the beginning of the most turbulent era in the antebellum abolitionist crusade, the 1850s, a period in which southern legislators dominated Congress and a series of proslavery chief executives marshaled their majority forces to ensure the perpetuation of "the peculiar institution." The first legislative volley came in September 1850 when Congress passed a revamped Fugitive Slave Law as a key provision in the Compromise of 1850. In northern communities including Concord, tension heightened, and the Garrisonian tactic of "moral suasion" lost ground as abolitionists violently resisted this law. It was then that the Underground Railroad, an informal network used for years to aid escaping slaves, achieved its legendary stature, becoming more organized and far more busy. In varying degrees, Concord became caught up in all of the major fugitive slave cases that occurred in Boston in the early 1850s: William and Ellen Craft had lectured here; Shadrach Minkins arrived on a Concord doorstep en route to freedom; and Thomas Sims and Anthony Burns provoked Henry Thoreau to an unprecedented public alliance with the nation's most prominent abolitionists, giving a lecture in which he denounced the government and its leaders, proclaiming that his "thoughts" were "murder to the State."[8]

In chapter 4, antebellum abolitionism reaches its climax as Concord activists participated in the groundswell of support for "Free Kansas," a struggle that led many, especially a second generation of reformers, to abandon Garrison's doctrine of nonviolence. A new schoolmaster who chaired the state Kansas Committee, Franklin Benjamin Sanborn, ensured that Concord would play a leading role in this final phase of the antislavery struggle. Sanborn intensified the commitment of local activists, and as one of the "Secret Six" conspirators who financed John Brown's raid on Harpers Ferry, he linked the town to Brown's infamous move against slavery. It was Henry Thoreau, however, who in an impassioned speech first publicly backed Brown and his armed incursion. From his tentative remarks a decade earlier advocating the individual's duty to disobey an unjust government, Thoreau had now arrived, as had many in Concord, at an explicit acceptance of violence in the struggle to free 4 million people. The Slave Power's encroachment into Massachusetts, and personal encounters with desperate and courageous men and women, finally convinced Henry Thoreau that military action would likely be required—and certainly could be justified—to end the scourge of slavery, itself sustained by violence, in the United States.

As assessed by historians Jane H. and William H. Pease, a tense political atmosphere prevailed in the northern states by the 1850s such that "the reality of events [ran] counter to the moral imperative of an era," causing "reasonable men [to] join fanatics in rejecting quiet argument and compromise for more vigorous action."[9] Such a theory aids in understanding the radicalization of Concord, where by the eve of the Civil War, conservatives and moderates worked alongside former adversaries toward a common goal of immediate emancipation. A second wave of female abolitionists thrilled to the prospect of war, a sentiment in which they were encouraged by Harriet Tubman, who came to town a number of times during these years. Soon their harshest critics had rallied to the abolitionists' side. If ending slavery meant civil war, then Louisa Whiting; Lidian, Ellen, and Waldo Emerson; Abby and Louisa Alcott; Cynthia, Sophia, and Henry Thoreau—depending on his mood—considered it a fair exchange.

1

A Call to Consciousness, 1831–1843

In the year 1837, a few friends of the slave, two or three in number, held a meeting to see if a Society could not be formed in Concord for his benefit.

—"Annual Report of the Concord Female A. S. Society," *Liberator*, June 23, 1843

As thirty-six-year-old Mary Merrick Brooks glanced around at the crowd of women gathered in Susan Barrett's Concord home on October 18, 1837, she saw faces long familiar to her from childhood friendships and years of local charity efforts. Many had worked with her in the town's Female Charitable Society "to help the poor and needy of the town, to feed the hungry and clothe the naked." Today, however, these sixty-one women met to undertake a new and more overtly political project, one with far-reaching implications for them all, perhaps most for Susan Garrison, likely the lone black woman in the room, and soon to celebrate her silver wedding anniversary with a man who had spent much of his life as a slave. Little did Brooks and the others at this gathering imagine that in organizing a local antislavery society they had joined thousands of women across the country poised on the brink of social and political revolution. Over the next three decades, these women would transform what Lori Ginzberg has called an "ideology of benevolence," a largely private project, into public activism. At their behest, Concord, Massachusetts, would become an abolitionist stronghold; through their example, prominent townsmen would direct international attention to the plight of millions who subsisted as chattel property in the "land of liberty." Officers of the Concord Female Anti-Slavery Society would later characterize this formative meeting as "an event noticed but little by the inhabitants of the town, or noticed but to be ridiculed." In their own words, this organization was "destined . . . to do not a little towards swelling that great tide of humanity, which is finally to turn our world of sin and misery into a world of purity, holiness, and happiness."[1] Thus, from the society's inception, founders conceived their mission as social, political, and even global reform. Finally, radical abolitionism made a tentative appearance in the birthplace of the American Revolution.

It had been nearly six years since a brash young editor in Boston had proclaimed an intensified war on slavery. Taking the moral high ground that slavery was iniquitous in the eyes of God, William Lloyd Garrison issued on New Year's Day 1831 the inaugural four-page edition of a weekly newspaper dedicated to publicizing and ending slavery. From this first *Liberator* in which he proclaimed, "I am in earnest—I will not equivocate—I will not excuse—I will not retreat a single inch—and I WILL BE HEARD," to the final one of December 29, 1865, Garrison edited the longest-running, most influential antislavery periodical in America. In charged rhetoric that biographer Henry Mayer contends "made the moral issue of slavery so palpable that it could no longer be evaded," Garrison demanded that all slaves be emancipated without delay, an approach known as "immediatism." Further, Garrison insisted that freed slaves be accorded all rights of citizenship, an extremist agenda that horrified many whites; even several of those who shared his moral objections to slavery demurred when the editor promoted social and political equality for blacks.[2]

Some early nineteenth-century abolitionists had naively expected that the demise of the Atlantic slave trade in 1807 would signal the end of U.S. slavery, which had by then been abolished in most northern states, albeit primarily through gradual methods. Prior to Garrison's movement, antislavery efforts in the United States had, with some notable exceptions, produced few results, with religious objections to slavery countered by equally demonstrable biblical injunctions to the contrary. Through the auspices of the American Colonization Society, former American slaves had begun by the early 1820s to emigrate to the African nation of Liberia. Garrison, however, soon denounced such repatriation as inherently racist.[3]

Further disruptive to nascent abolitionism was a racism inseparable from the northern states' economic circumstances. Indeed, for most of its thirty-five-year run, the *Liberator* confronted a steadfastly antiabolition, if not proslavery, political climate in the North. The notion of white superiority persisted, sanctioned by most denominations of the Christian church and sustained by pseudoscience that fashioned existing stereotypes into "theories" of biological and racial hierarchies. But unquestionably central were financial considerations. Domestic slavery, sustained by the "Slave Power" dominating the legislative and executive branches of government, continued to be enormously profitable. As the British actress Fanny Kemble was told by a southern neighbor after she moved to coastal Georgia with her slaveholding husband in 1838, "abolition is impossible: because every healthy Negro can fetch a thousand dollars in the Charleston market at this moment." The burgeoning northern textile industry depended heavily on ready sources of raw cotton; likewise, agricultural processing interests counted on steady supplies of southern rice, sugar, and tobacco. As late as February 1861, a defender of slavery would write in the *New York Herald*: "Touch the negro, and you touch cotton—the mainspring that keeps the machinery of the world in motion." Intense "breeding" practices had fueled an enormously lucrative internal slave trade such that by the eve of the Civil War, the number of slaves in the United States had reached nearly 4 million, almost doubling over the previous thirty years. Despite these shocking statistics, most northerners had found it relatively easy to remain complacent about what southerners protectively referred to as their "peculiar institution." Now, however, Garrison's *Liberator* began arriving each Friday in northern parlors, graphically portraying beheadings, lynchings, and auctioned slave children. If readers continued to turn a blind eye to slavery after perusing the paper, they no longer did so ignorant of slavery's horrors.[4]

The cornerstone of Garrison's antislavery philosophy—the key weapon in his abolitionist arsenal—was nonviolent "moral suasion." Specific strategies for accomplishing his agenda soon followed. First, Garrison renounced the democratic process altogether since voting, to his mind, legitimized a proslavery government. Instead, he held that "political reformation is to be effected solely by a change in the moral vision of the people." Second, and initially more damaging to his movement's cohesion, Garrison encouraged women to participate fully in the abolitionist campaign. Added to these radical planks, by the early 1840s, Garrison would promote "disunion," northern secession from the slaveholding union. Although many of his initial allies eventually parted company with Garrison on one or more of these issues, his centrality to antebellum abolitionism is undisputed. He was, as fellow extremist Wendell Phillips later averred, "the first man to begin a *movement* designed to annihilate slavery."[5]

In addition to the *Liberator*, Garrison soon extended his reach through two influential organizations. In January 1832, he and eleven other men founded the New England Anti-Slavery Society, based in Boston; it was followed two years later by the American Anti-Slavery Society, formed in Philadelphia. Over the next three decades, antislavery "agents" proselytized the immediatist message on behalf of these groups throughout the free states, generating new societies each year. By 1839, Massachusetts alone boasted more than 240 local antislavery societies.[6]

Antipathy to Garrison predictably intensified after Nat Turner led fellow slaves on a murderous rampage in Southampton, Virginia eight months after the *Liberator* commenced. Although Garrison's publication had few subscribers south of the Mason Dixon line, papers there did run excerpts from it, evidence enough for proslavery zealots to accuse Garrison of inciting the rebellion. Garrison steadfastly denied any link to Nat Turner despite the fact that many issues of the *Liberator*, including the very first one, had promoted David Walker's incendiary treatise, *Appeal . . . to Coloured Citizens of the World*. In the fall of 1831, the Georgia legislature offered a five-thousand-dollar reward for Garrison's arrest; four years later, South Carolina Senator John Calhoun—slavery's most obdurate congressional champion—proposed a bill forbidding southern post offices from distributing antislavery propaganda.[7] But Garrison defied his accusers: "The slaves need no incentives at our hands. They will find them in their stripes." Back and forth, he bandied with his accusers, one of whom assured him, "Hell is gaping for you! the devil is feasting in anticipation!"[8]

In Concord, Massachusetts, where slavery had been abolished by state law in 1783, the *Yeoman's Gazette* reprinted southern reports of Turner's revolt, which portrayed the "heart-rending tale" and "the savage ferocity of these demons in human shape," as well as the clampdown that followed, including "the slaughter of many blacks without trial." Still, these and other accounts of the atrocities and inhumanities of slave life in the southern states figured merely as occasional news; the plight of the slave remained a remote, several days journey away, the antislavery cause an ideological abstraction to be debated over long winter evenings. By and large, white townsfolk in Concord remained comfortably aloof from the reformist fervor brewing some twenty miles away in Boston, a fact not lost on one newcomer from the city.[9]

When thirty-eight-year-old Prudence Ward and her mother moved from Boston to Concord in November 1833, their radical abolitionism, kindled by nearly three years of reading the *Liberator*, came with them. Concord had no organized abolitionist effort yet, although the next month a regional antislavery convention would take place there. The Wards took up residence in the center of town with their longtime friends Elizabeth, Maria, and Jane Thoreau, Henry David Thoreau's aunts. Just ahead of them, Rev. John and Mary Wilder, both also abolitionists, had relocated to the community when John took over as minister at the Trinitarian church. The Wilders rented from Cynthia Thoreau the rooms vacated when son Henry left that summer for Harvard College. At this time, the Thoreau household consisted of Cynthia and John Thoreau, and their four children—Helen (twenty-one years), John, Jr. (eighteen years), Henry (sixteen years), and Sophia (fourteen years)—in addition to Cynthia's sister, Louisa Dunbar. John Thoreau, Sr., made a modest living running a pencil manufactory, but paying boarders like the Wilders regularly supplemented the family's income. John Wilder would eventually steer a more moderate course than the Garrisonians, but his activism in Concord during this formative era—coupled with the Wards' influence on the extended Thoreau family—initiated a reformist sensibility that gave the orthodox church's sanction to radical abolitionism.[10]

The Concord in which the Wilders and Wards settled was a comfortable, prosperous town of some two thousand people, eighteen miles from Boston. In 1833, an average of forty stagecoaches per week brought passengers along a well-used route to what Robert A. Gross depicts as a "vital, bustling town." Agriculture still provided most of the town's income, but manufacturing and trade had expanded the economy over the last few decades. Christian congregants worshipped at one of two churches, the Unitarian First Church or the recently erected Trinitarian Second Church. In contrast to most northern clergy at this time, both of Concord's ministers promulgated an antislavery position. In fact, Wilder's predecessor at the Second Church, Rev. Daniel Southmayd, had been a founder of the American Anti-Slavery Society, while the venerable Ezra Ripley and his lieutenant, Barzillai Frost, tendered a cautious antislavery sentiment from the Unitarian pulpit. Town leaders, however—Samuel Hoar, Nathan Brooks, John Keyes—vigilantly upheld the status quo and avoided extremism of any kind, certainly abolitionism.[11] Civic pride notwithstanding, revolutionary ideology belonged to Concord's past.

In the early 1830s, slightly more than 1 percent of Concord residents were black—approximately thirty men, women, and children who with a few exceptions lived literally and figuratively on the margins of town. Some men, such as former slaves Thomas Dugan and John Garrison, owned property; along with butcher Peter Hutchinson, their names appeared on tax rolls. John and his wife Susan hosted antislavery meetings at their home and otherwise exchanged social courtesies with their white neighbors. More typical, however, were those on the other end of the socioeconomic spectrum, black men such as "Town pauper" Isaac Barrett, and Henry Marble, who died in the Concord jail.[12]

To Prudence Ward's way of thinking, her new home was absurdly behind the times. "There is a Lyceum here," she informed her brother shortly after arriving. "The speakers come very near saying hard things—on politics & religion—subjects, which by the laws of the Lyceum are not to be introduced." As intellectual community forums, New England lyceums sponsored debates and disseminated information to interested citizens—from social and political issues, to lectures on art, philosophy, history, and religion. The Concord lyceum had been established for five years when Ward arrived in town, but the questions recently considered there must have seemed insipid indeed to an abolitionist from Boston: "Ought the antislavery society to be encouraged?"; "Would it be an act of humanity to emancipate at once, all the slaves in the United States?"; "Are the intellectual qualities of the whites naturally superior to those of the negro race?"; and "Is the difference of Colour in the human Species particularly the difference betwe[e]n the African & the European races the effect of Climate or of other Causes?" While such inquiries at least reflected an awareness of anti-slavery, they hardly engaged with Garrison's immediatist agenda. When John Wilder argued the abolitionist side in these debates a month after moving to town, he came up squarely against local bigotry. Abolitionist Josiah Bartlett's son George later described the contention of this era as "a fierce battle . . . waged by the early supporters of the then unpopular cause."[13]

Concord's subscribers to the *Liberator* included many of those who led their community's earliest reform efforts—Dr. Josiah Bartlett, Samuel Barrett, William Whiting, Timothy and Maria Prescott, and the Thoreaus. The paper generated controversy and roused readers, but it also increased the general audience for antislavery lecturers who, thanks to John Wilder, now spoke regularly from the Trinitarian pulpit. With headlines blazing—"A BOSTONIAN SEIZED AS A RUNAWAY SLAVE!"; "the brig Tribune landed at New Orleans, from the District of Columbia, with 100 slaves for that market!"—the paper inspired one local subscriber to declare that "the *Liberator* has been the thunder cloud on high to agitate and purify the moral atmosphere."[14]

Just as close proximity to Boston had helped determine the town's historic role in the American Revolution, so Concord's strategic locale proved of tremendous advantage in connecting budding abolitionists with the leaders of the state and national organizations. Not only were three Concord men—John Wilder, William Whiting, and Josiah Bartlett—on hand when the Middlesex County Anti-Slavery Society formed in nearby Groton on October 1, 1834, but so was William Lloyd Garrison. At its next meeting, held at Concord's First Church on January 27, 1835, Samuel Barrett and Mary Merrick Brooks enlarged the town's representation in the society; soon Sophia and Helen Thoreau would also become involved. A portion of the preamble to its constitution reflected both the organization's purpose and affiliate status to the New England Anti-Slavery Society:

> Knowledge is power. To acquire and judiciously apply this power to the extinction of Slavery, requires extensive inquiry into the nature and circumstances of the Slave system. We the Subscribers have therefore associated under the title of the Middlesex Anti-Slavery Association auxiliary to the New England Anti-Slavery Society for the purpose of promoting knowledge on the subject of Slavery, and to use our influence for its extinction.

Despite the county society's ties to the state organization, however, this early meeting also reflects local abolitionists' distance from Garrison's promotion of racial integration. Among the resolutions passed that day was one decrying "amalgamation [which] ever has been and is a concomitant of

Slavery . . . those . . . endeavoring to sustain the institution are deserving the charge of promoting amalgamation."[15]

Concord's newspapers, the *Yeoman's Gazette* and the *Concord Freeman*, covered the advent of Garrison's notorious movement, with the *Gazette's* editorials easily outpacing the Democratic *Freeman's* more tentative stance. By the mid 1830s, although the volatile issue of freemasonry remained the essential litmus test for candidates, the question of antislavery had begun to exert a limited impact on the town's political mood. The piously conservative lawyer Samuel Hoar, who presided over Concord's semblance of a first family, had served twice in the state senate but was defeated for reelection in 1836 after one term in the U.S. Congress. Until this time, Hoar had confined his reformist impulses to the more staid social ills of temperance and sabbath restrictions. While antislavery in principle, in practice Hoar was, above all, anticontroversy. Congressman Hoar had cautiously defended abolitionists' right to petition—a position likely encouraged by his wife and daughter—but he had also criticized abolitionists for "error in their theory." In 1836, the *Concord Freeman* characterized Hoar as "not an abolitionist, but . . . so far friendly to abolitionists, as to defend them in his official capacity from the unguarded and reckless assaults, which southern representatives have made upon . . . THE RIGHT OF FREE DISCUSSION." His active membership in the American Colonization Society further distanced Hoar from the Garrisonians.[16]

That same year abolitionism weighed in as a corollary issue when two Concord men vied for Middlesex county treasurer. The incumbent, Postmaster John Keyes, a conservative and a Mason, was challenged by County Commissioner and farmer Timothy Prescott, an ardent Garrisonian. In endorsing Prescott, the anti-Masonic *Concord Freeman* declared Keyes "a thorough going, selfish, intriguing, insolent aristocrat, who respects the rights and feelings of no one." Despite such opprobrium, Keyes won this election, only to be defeated the following year.[17]

In 1838, the antislavery press grilled another moderate Concord candidate during a contentious congressional election. Nathan Brooks, the husband of abolitionist Mary Merrick Brooks, endeavored to remain unsullied by the mudslinging, but he received the full weight of Garrison's censure after he voted to approve the U.S. annexation of the independent republic of Texas. Nor, as a congressman, had Brooks ever voiced support for immediatism. In the months preceding the election, blistering attacks against him ran in the local papers as well as in the *Liberator*, which issued a special supplement—"Middlesex Awake!"—on the election: "He is deaf to the calls of the friends of humanity. Let them be deaf to his call for votes. . . . He refuses to give opinions. Don't give him votes. Count him a secret foe, and reject him openly. . . . He disregards your anxiety for the friendless slave. . . . He is for letting slavery alone—just now. Every real abolitionist will let him alone—just now." Since abolitionists equally disliked Brooks's rival, Democrat William Parmenter, they determined at a meeting in Concord to campaign against both men. Whether or not a result of this media barrage, Brooks lost the election.[18]

Ironically, at the same time the *Liberator* was vilifying her husband, Mary Merrick Brooks had positioned herself at the forefront of the local Garrisonian contingent. Yet this Concord native had likely not been raised to sympathize with the enslaved. Her father, Tilly Merrick, had grown up under the influence of his stepfather, Duncan Ingraham, a man who had not only owned slaves in Concord but whose business dealings included slave trading. After graduating from Harvard, Merrick sat out the Revolutionary War as an *"attaché"* in Holland; he and a stepbrother later became business partners in Amsterdam. Merrick subsequently settled in Charleston, South Carolina, and established "a large wholesale shipping trade" under the name Merrick & Course. There, in addition to this enterprise, he owned what his grandson would later describe as "large plantations at Eighteen Mile Creek, with the usual accompaniments of horses, hogs, negroes, and other cattle." Merrick returned to Concord after a severe business reversal, married a local woman, Sally Minot, and opened a small dry goods business. Over the years, their daughter Mary evolved from a flirtatious belle to a crusading moralist who once told her own son she regretted not having "strangled" him in his "cradle" when he admitted to drinking alcohol once with college friends. Mary Merrick Brooks must surely have deemed her father's slave-owning past abhorrent. Consciously or not, from the mid-1830s on, she epitomized a driven extremist who would spend her adult life atoning for "the sins of the father."[19]

During this formative era, another Concord family was at odds over the issue of slavery as young Boston attorney Charles Chauncy Emerson surpassed his older brother Waldo in espousing a radical antislavery position, although both men deplored the brazen aggressiveness of many abolitionists. Charles had been indecisive when confronted with slavery firsthand in Puerto Rico in the early 1830s, appraising slaves as "humanely treated" judging their situation "very tolerable." Troubled that "a slave is a slave, & is made to feel it," he nonetheless concluded that "self interest prevails with the master to treat them well." But further reflection brought Charles Emerson into the radical fold—"I am an abolitionist. And give me an hour & a half of your company, & I'll undertake you shall be one too," he declared to brother William in 1835—an alteration in sentiment that brought Emerson to admire men he had previously disdained: "They stand for principles: they are for justice."[20]

As antiabolition disturbance escalated in New England during the spring of 1835, Charles delivered a belligerent abolitionist speech in Duxbury, Massachusetts in which he pointed to the encouraging results of West Indian emancipation, granted by Great Britain the previous year, and countered the common objections for not following suit in the United States: "We must then have immediate emancipation if emancipation at all." The untimely death of Charles Emerson from tuberculosis in May 1836 cut short this combative voice, but his early commitment to immediatism conferred an influential legacy as the two women most devoted to him, his fiancée, Elizabeth Hoar, and his aunt Mary Moody Emerson, turned their attention to his brother Waldo, whom they pressured to take on the antislavery mantle.[21]

Regardless of the budding abolitionism underway when Waldo Emerson and his bride, Lidian Jackson, moved to Concord in September 1835, they both remained largely disengaged from the issue of slavery, a situation Mary Moody Emerson—in Concord for an extended stay—soon rectified by arranging for abolitionists Samuel Joseph May and George Thompson to visit them. May, the brother of Abigail May (Mrs. Bronson) Alcott, was an early and ardent supporter of William Lloyd Garrison; Thompson, the notorious British agitator, was nearing the end of a year-long American tour under the auspices of the Massachusetts Anti-Slavery Society. Mary Emerson herself had been won over to Garrisonianism earlier that year after an intense debate with abolitionist Charles Burleigh, who had recently lectured in Concord.[22] Hence, when she met Thompson at a county meeting that fall, Emerson invited him and May to meet her nephew, aware that she risked upsetting his new wife, to whom she explained: "At the first joy of seeing *May* so unexpectedly I asked him to call on yours & you & dine . . . he proposed breakfasting with you . . . in cool blood I believed it w^d be very pleasant to Mr. E. & he confessed a wish to see Mrs E. so he comes & Mr T. before 8 o'k expecting to breakfast at 8. Have I done you a favor? It would do me one if *you* could see the subject w'h agitates the Country as some do." Lidian Emerson was indeed irritated by the unexpected (and early) guest, but Mary urged her to prod Waldo toward antislavery: "Invite him to leave the higher Muses to their Elysian repose and with the higher genius of humanity enter those of living degraded misery and take the gauge of slavery." Phyllis Cole has explained that Mary Emerson soon became "a deep, long-term source of [Waldo Emerson's] idealist principles," her views ultimately strengthening the antislavery resolve of Lidian Emerson.[23]

In a brief journal entry about his breakfast visitors, Waldo Emerson noted that "Thompson the Abolitionist is incontrovertible," a conclusion surely not surprising to him, given the reputation Thompson had garnered during his New England appearances that year. Riots had erupted after many of his speeches; in fact, just weeks before they visited Emerson, Thompson and May had made hasty exits from both Haverhill, Massachusetts, and Concord, New Hampshire, when hostile crowds lobbed stones and eggs at them. Emerson respected May, but he judged accurately that

Thompson's ego bound him to a "Cause that men will bow to." Charles Emerson, however, inclined toward his aunt's more generous judgment of the British hothead: We should not "desert a Reformation because of the imperfections of the reformers."[24]

Two weeks later, the antiabolition faction again erupted, this time in Boston and brandishing weapons far more threatening than rotten eggs. "Patriotic citizens" posted handbills offering $100 for the first person who would lead "that infamous foreign scoundrel"—Thompson—"to the tar kettle before dark" after his scheduled address at a rally sponsored by the Boston Female Anti-Slavery Society. But when William Lloyd Garrison appeared on the scene, it was America's premier abolitionist rather than Britain's who was nearly lynched by a mob comprised of what one reporter dubbed "*gentlemen of property and standing from all parts of the city*."[25] Fourteen-year-old John Shepard Keyes of Concord, in Boston that evening, never forgot the terrifying sight: "I saw the famous Garrison mob, and frightened half to death clinging to my fathers hand I stood on the steps of a Court Street office and saw the sign over Garrison's paper pulled down and broken up, saw the men at the windows with a rope trying to hang him, and heard the howls of the mob. . . . It was terrible and troubled my dreams long after, tho not from any sympathy with Garrison." For his own safety, police put Garrison in the city jail overnight, where those keeping him company included Bronson and Abigail Alcott. For years, antislavery advocates would hark back to this incendiary night to defend their conversion to radical abolition.[26]

> Whose influence is so potent as Woman's?
>   —William Lloyd Garrison, March 4, 1833

By the time the Boston mob attacked Garrison, Mary Merrick Brooks had been active in the Middlesex County Anti-Slavery Society for nearly a year. She surely knew that antislavery women in Ohio had launched a national petition drive the year before, and that southern legislators had ridiculed both the documents and those who submitted them. As the petitions persisted, however, angry congressmen dealt with the paper deluge by passing a series of "gag rules" that effectively squelched debate on the floor, their refusal to accept the petitions shrouded in patriotic fear mongering: "Any attempt to agitate the question of Slavery in this House, is calculated to disturb the compromises of the constitution—to endanger the Union—and, if persisted in, to destroy, by a civil war, the peace and prosperity of the country." Such rhetoric merely increased the women's determination. By February 1837, after hundreds of petitions containing some thirty thousand signatures, half of which were women's, continued to flood Congress, Senator John Calhoun gave an extraordinary speech, not only demanding that "these insulting petitions" be refused, but defending the "fostering care," the "positive good" of slavery that had "so civilized and so improved" the lives of Africans. That summer, northern clergymen further enraged anti-slavery women with a communiqué denouncing their activism and advising Congregational ministers to remain mum about slavery from their pulpits.[27]

In May, seventy-one women from seven northern states defied this clerical advice and held the first American women's antislavery convention in Philadelphia. Two who attended this event were Senator Calhoun's fellow South Carolinians—Angelina and Sarah Grimké—who though they hailed from a slave-owning family, had relocated to Philadelphia and become outspoken abolitionists. In 1836, Angelina had published *Appeal to the Christian Women of the Southern States*, in which she pled with southern women to petition against slavery and to liberate any slaves within their control. Stimulated by the positive momentum generated at the Philadelphia convention, particularly with the reception to their lectures, the Grimkés embarked on a speaking tour little calculated to appease southern fury or ministerial ire. To northern audiences, their depictions of the horrors concomitant with slave life conferred instant credibility on the case for immediatism. With Garrison's backing, the women drew large crowds, despite the fact that many New Englanders were scandalized by their addressing audiences of both genders. Jeering men disrupted their appearances, clergymen forbore to share the pulpit, and some communities denied their meeting halls, but Garrison and other male abolitionists, such as New Hampshire editor Nathaniel Rogers, rebuked such critics: "Who are these men, that are so scandalized at Miss Grimké's speaking in public and that regard this unusual affair of a woman's speaking aloud with more apprehension than they do the enslavement of a sixth part of their nation?"[28]

The first week of September 1837, a warm welcome awaited Angelina and Sarah Grimké in Concord, Massachusetts. Both local newspapers announced their lectures, but the *Concord Freeman* particularly championed their right to speak in public:

> An outcry has recently been raised by some ministers, because *women* have undertaken to plead the cause of the poor slave. They seem to think, that if women are permitted to speak in behalf of the suffering, the clerical vocation is in danger. There is no help for men of such narrow, selfish views. . . . the people of New England will duly appreciate the moral and intellectual worth of these devoted women, such rude and vulgar attacks upon them to the contrary notwithstanding.

The Grimkés spoke three evenings in Concord, the second time to "a full house" at the Second Church. They were the guests of Mary Brooks and were also honored at dinners and receptions hosted by Mary Heywood and

Lidian Emerson.[29] As she related the town's enthusiastic welcome to her sister, Prudence Ward revealed that the Grimkés had won over at least some of the men predisposed against them:

> I found Miss Angelina exceedingly attractive in manner, with fine speaking eyes, & expressive countenance. She is lively, has a good deal of animation—& tho' at first you would not say she was handsome, yet she irresistibly attracts you. I couldn't withdraw my eyes from her. . . . She converses with readiness, & well. Mr. Hoar drew her out for the benefit of the whole. The next day she lectured again—& we had the satisfaction of hearing her—As a lecturer she will compare with most public speakers. She was perfectly at her ease, which of course made me so. She spoke to the purpose—reasonably—eloquently, & without declamation. . . . had much conversation with Mr. Hoar who is perfectly charmed with her. . . . their coming has awakened a greater interest in the subject than any previous lecturer. They stayed two nights with Mrs. Brooks & she accompanied them to Acton on Sunday where A[ngelina] was to deliver a lecture in the evening—Mr. Woodbury—who objected to her lecturing as a woman in his church—preached a sermon in which he recanted, & thought as southern women giving their testimony against slavery they ought to be allowed to speak. accordingly he went to hear her. The house was crowded.

That the moderate abolitionist Rev. James T. Woodbury made an about-face with regard to Angelina Grimké's speaking in his pulpit testifies to the striking impact of the women's lectures. Ward also noted that "the Misses Grimke proposed taking tea with Mrs. Garrison—'sister Garrison,'" seemingly pleased that in visiting Susan Garrison, these women practiced the racial equality they so earnestly preached.[30]

The *Yeoman's Gazette* reported that the lectures had "awakened an increased interest in this solemn and important subject among our citizens," while the *Concord Freeman* concurred with Ward as to Angelina Grimké's oratorical skill: "With an utterance at once strong, fluent, distinct and eloquent, she drew that picture of slavery—its injustice—its moral enormities, and its wide and evil influence upon our destiny as a nation, as must, and we believe did, satisfy every one who heard her, of the course it was the duty of the North to pursue, in view of its speedy and utter annihilation in this country." To this glowing endorsement, editor Francis Gourgas also discerned that "the truth is, *men* have faltered and have failed in their duty touching this matter of slavery," a pronouncement that must have provoked the *Freeman*'s more conservative readers even as it stoked the ambitions of Concord's antislavery women.[31]

Waldo Emerson grumbled that he accomplished no work that week because "we have had a great deal of company lately," but his wife felt otherwise. After the Grimkés left town, Lidian Emerson described to her sister a budding sense of purpose:

> I suppose [you] have heard of the Misses Grimké who [are going] about the country advocating [the freedom of] the slave. They have passed [this] week in Concord and been well received. They dined & took tea with [me] one day and it was a pleasure to entertain such angel strangers—pure & benevolent spirits are they. I think I shall not turn away my attention from the abolition cause till I have found whether there is not something for me personally to do and bear to forward it. I hope you will read any books or papers on the subject that you may meet with—if you can do nothing more for the oppressed after you have considered their case and become interested in it you can *pray* for them.

True to her word, Lidian Emerson attended a meeting that month at the First Church, held "to present a Constitution for an Anti-Slavery Society, in this town." The prospect that Waldo Emerson might address this group encouraged Prudence Ward:

> Yesterday it was announced . . . that the committee to whom was given the subject of forming an Antislavery Society would report on Tuesday evening, & Mr. Waldo Emerson would deliver an address. The citizens were invited to attend—Whether Mr. E. approves of societies—especially whether he will join one is uncertain—but I am rejoiced that he is coming out in this public manner on the subject of Abolitionism—We called this morning there. . . . I told Mrs. E. I was glad her husband was to lecture—She said she didn't think he would be lukewarm.

No evidence exists that Emerson addressed this or any other organizational meeting of the female society, although both local papers announced that he been requested to do so. Later that fall, however, Emerson disappointed Ward's expectations when he gave what Len Gougeon has characterized as a "tepid and philosophical" antislavery speech at the Second Church.[32]

The next month, Prudence Ward and her friends took matters into their own hands. On October 18, sixty-one Concord women—including Ward and her mother; Susan Garrison; Mary Brooks; Cynthia, Sophia, and Helen Thoreau; Mary Wilder; Susan Barrett; Maria Prescott; and Lidian Emerson—founded the Concord Female Anti-Slavery Society, one of eight local groups organized that year in the wake of the Grimkés' tour in the region. Wilder was chosen president and Brooks the secretary, but for all practical purposes, Brooks became the de facto director of the society's ceaseless endeavors over the next thirty years, particularly as she nurtured a crucial relationship with Maria Weston Chapman, the "tireless crusader" of Boston's female society. By the end of 1837, Prudence Ward proudly noted to her brother the altered mood in Concord from the prior year: "Our last Lyceum lecture was the 'History of St. Domingo' from Mr. Woodbury—A year since he wasn't allowed to deliver it, & this, he was requested to." What Ward did not presume to mention in this letter was her own considerable role in bringing about this significant change.[33]

From Cincinnati to Boston to Salem to Philadelphia and hundreds of smaller towns, women such as Ward and Brooks validated William Lloyd Garrison's prediction that "the destiny of the slaves is in the hands of the American women, and complete emancipation can never take place without their co-operation." Like their counterparts throughout the country, Concord women took to their work with a fervor, reveling in this sanctioned opportunity to formulate a political identity and become a cog in a grand national wheel. They met regularly to sew, strategize, and apprise each other of news from surrounding towns, in addition to disseminating anti-slavery propaganda, circulating and signing petitions, attending national conventions, and organizing local lectures. Philadelphia antislavery pioneer Mary Grew asserted that for these women, "*working* for the objects of their sympathy crystallized sentiment into principle."[34]

They targeted the conscience of their community and provided a congenial social outlet for each other, but society members also hawked their merchandise:

> The Concord Female Anti-Slavery Society will hold a FAIR, in Concord, (Mass.) on the 3d of August. A great variety of useful and ornamental articles, many of them from friends in Europe, will render the Fair attractive to all. Every description of children's clothing, worsted work, bags, caps, toys, paintings, engravings, books, &c., will be sold nearly or quite at cost. The refreshment table will be well supplied with ice creams, and other delicacies. There will be music in the Hall, at intervals, during the day and evening. . . .
> Will not the friends of the slave in Lexington, Littleton, Sudbury, Carlisle, Westford, and all the neighboring towns make an effort to attend, and induce others to come?

For this and other events, the society charged a sixpence admission fee because Mary Brooks insisted on wresting money from those who came merely to look: "If we have a good many beautiful things we can make a great trumpeting of them, and thus many will come and pay their entrance fee for the sake of seeing them if they do not intend to buy."[35]

Their proximity to Boston enabled Concord reformers to participate in the workload and events sponsored by that city's female society, particularly its annual merchandise fair, which after 1834 had become the most famous abolitionist fundraiser in the country. For several years, Mary Brooks, Prudence Ward, and the Thoreaus supplied items to sell and helped to staff this extravaganza. In 1839, their "skillfully executed housewifery" merited the compliments of Maria Weston Chapman in the *Liberator*. Prudence Ward described that her mother had started preparing months ahead: "We have been at work for the AntiSlavery Fair which is to be in Boston next month— & knitting being in mother's line, she has knit fourteen pairs of little socks for children, & we have been laughing this morning about sending them in to the show for a premium." Not only did the abolitionist faithful browse the goods at these events, but Boston's social elite were also drawn to them, a fact not lost on Garrison, who noted on seeing the wife of Chief Justice Lemuel Shaw that "her attendance shows that our cause is by no means so odious as it once was."[36]

Quite apart from their obvious fundraising value, these merchandising events—advertised in multiple outlets—fueled the public perception that abolition was indeed a legitimate concern for women. Women who would otherwise have been uncomfortable "overstepping the bounds of their 'sphere'" could now contribute to the antislavery cause through a time-honored venue. Their charity generated substantial revenues for Garrison's treasury as women transformed the ordinary, domestic tasks of sewing and baking into what Deborah Van Broekhoven judges "the radical and public work of antislavery fairs." Julie Roy Jeffrey elaborates further that this work provided an opportunity for women "to create a moral identity that was both rooted in and separate from her familial identity." Treasurers' Reports of the Massachusetts Anti-Slavery Society record the extent to which Concord women took part in a national phenomenon that translated into hundreds of dollars for abolitionist coffers. Such capital subsidized the *Liberator*, paid agents' salaries, and funded the costs of printing flyers and holding conventions. Antislavery newspapers regularly publicized the names of donors, thus allowing townswomen to track their giving in relation to neighboring communities. Viewed from a pecuniary perspective, Garrison's praise for women's antislavery groups is readily understood—they paid at least half his bills in any given year.[37]

Women's leadership in the abolitionist crusade complicates what scholars have referred to as "the ideology of separate spheres"—the antebellum social bifurcation that typically consigned men to the business and civic arenas, and women to the home, a domain that encompassed the spiritual and moral oversight of the family as well as domestic duties. In addition to slavery itself, northern women felt an imperative to protect black women from sexual abuse, however taboo the topic may have been for discussion. Such a sympathy surely informed the rationale of the antislavery women in Canton, Ohio, whose preamble maintained that "we are *not moving out of our proper sphere* as females when we assume a *public* stand in favor of our *oppressed sisters*."[38]

Southern politicians and many northern clergymen, however, persisted in vigorously opposing women's activism. To them, women's moral responsibilities in no way encompassed political action; on the contrary, they insisted that such behavior compromised the inherent femininity of all women. Virginia Congressman Henry A. Wise assessed that "woman in the parlor, woman in her proper sphere, is the ornament and comfort of man; but out of the parlor, out of her sphere, if there is a devil on earth, when she is a devil, woman is a devil incarnate!" In Boston, Rev. Nehemiah Adams, an apologist for slavery, went so far as to warn that women entering the public arena would "cease to bear fruit." Reverend Albert A. Folsom admonished his congregation in Hingham, Massachusetts, that a woman's involvement in abolition "poisons the soul, embitters the affections, and exasperates the feelings. She, who is naturally amiable and modest, by having her mind filled with the peculiar spirit which characterises the most clamorous among the Abolitionists, is imperceptibly transformed into a bigoted, rash, and morose being. Nor is this all. Self-sufficiency, arrogance and masculine boldness follow naturally in the train." His sermons, however, apparently had little effect on Folsom's parishioners—a few years later, Hingham townswomen donated their Sewing Circle proceeds to the state antislavery treasury.[39]

Angelina Grimké's rejoinder to such counsel did little to soothe tempers: "If it can be fairly established that women *can lecture*, then why may they not preach, & if *they* can preach, then woe! woe be unto that Clerical Denomination which now rules the world." Nor did male abolitionists pay any heed to the clergy's advice. Editor Nathaniel Rogers pled with women to join the fray: "Women . . . must agitate the conscience of the community. . . . It is her sphere. Slavery must be abolished at all sacrifices. You must see that it is done. You are as responsible for its being done, as men are. You are more responsible—for you have more moral influence. Be not too careful about keeping within any fashionable sphere. Do your duty. That is your sphere. . . . And shame on the ungenerous man, that will taunt and insult you, for doing his neglected duty." Words like these, coming from influential leaders, validated women's sense of moral obligation and provided them with ready rebuttals when neighbors criticized their increasingly radical, public sympathies.[40]

Not quite a month after the Concord female society came into being, the murder in Alton, Illinois, of abolitionist editor Elijah Lovejoy shocked the country. Antiabolition mobs in Missouri had repeatedly demolished Lovejoy's offices and printing presses; when he moved to southern Illinois and took delivery of a new press, yet another gang struck his operation. Because Lovejoy had been armed and attempted to defend himself, Garrison, nonresistant to the core, expressed "sorrow to learn, that he first took life before he lost his own." Concord reformers' attention to this issue mirrored the national debate. Waldo Emerson heroized Lovejoy, as did Boston abolitionist Wendell Phillips, whereas a well-informed Prudence Ward discerned both sides:

> Lovejoy perhaps didn't act the most wisely. There must be a difference of opinion with regard to this, among those who do not think resistance in all cases wrong—each one will judge for himself when is the right time to begin to fight—It is plain he was acting in accordance with the law, & with the consent of the magistrates—Have you seen Miss Grimke's letter on the subject? She condemns him & those with him, not only on her own ground of nonresistance, but thinks they were not consistent with their own doctrine—for they yielded at last, when if it was right to kill one man in defense of the press, it would be right to kill more, & they ought to have perished in its cause—but to her—fighting is altogether anti-Christian & forbidden.[41]

At this early juncture, Ward reveals that despite their agreement in principle, moral suasionists were thinking independently, and she seems to countenance armed resistance in self-defense.

The next year, two Concord women witnessed antiabolitionist aggression firsthand when Mary Brooks and her daughter, Caroline, attended the second Anti-Slavery Convention of American Women in Philadelphia. Attracting more than two hundred delegates, the gathering drew nearly three times the previous year's crowd, women decisively flouting pastoral injunctions to cease such affairs. While there, the Brookses listened to speeches by Maria Weston Chapman, Lucretia Mott, Angelina Grimké, and William Lloyd Garrison, among others. All convention participants had been warned to expect violence, especially when Grimké's provocative keynote address on the second day drew an unruly three thousand people, and when the women formally condemned the church for "implication in the sin" of slavery. That night a "*very* promiscuous assembly," apparently most angered by the delegates' interracial fraternization, heaved rocks and shattered windows before growing reckless enough to torch the brand new Pennsylvania Hall. According to various reports, Philadelphia Mayor John Swift "winked at the crowd," the city's fire unit did not respond, and the building burned to the ground. As one result of this hostile reception, conventioneers urged other abolitionists to abandon—to "come out" from—churches that refused to endorse antislavery, despite several women's vote against the divisive measure. The next day, delegates determined to stay on schedule and met in a makeshift location, leading one sympathizer to marvel at their "moral daring and heroism." When she returned to Concord after the harrowing experiences and uplifting camaraderie of this gathering, Mary Brooks surely had reason for recommitting to the antislavery effort.[42]

Since the female society's founding, Mary Brooks had pursued Waldo Emerson with a vengeance, convinced that his backing would lend critical weight to the immediatist cause. Brooks took every advantage of the tolerance Emerson accorded her as a neighbor and friend, and she exerted a decisive influence on his increasing engagement with antislavery. Len Gougeon has aptly characterized "the silent years" of 1838 through 1844, when Emerson struggled to revise his basic belief in the supposed inferiority of the African race and to determine the reform role most suited to him. In 1838, Emerson reflected sympathetically in his journal that "the Whole History of the negro is tragedy. By what accursed violation did they first exist that they should suffer always?" But at the same time, he reacted indignantly to a black family "riding in a coach": "I think they are more pitiable when rich than when poor. Of what use are riches to them?" Such private sentiments combined with a general disinclination to involve himself in the public turmoil over slavery. The absorbing studies of idealism and self-culture, of scientific and metaphysical speculation, consumed Emerson— political agitation of any stripe intruded on his time, and he was loathe to take up the banner of abolitionism.[43]

As the years wore on, however, four women fostered a domestic atmosphere of reform that ultimately compelled Emerson to a more central antislavery role: his wife, Lidian, his devoted friend Elizabeth Hoar, his aunt Mary Moody Emerson, and his neighbor Mary Brooks. To Lidian, Waldo Emerson was never fervent enough on the subject of slavery to suit, a disparity that was the longstanding public perception as well. Her membership in the female society as well as her reading of the *Liberator* and the continued influence of Mary Moody Emerson had provided Lidian with steady evidence of slavery's horrors, a reality she vocally and feelingly evoked to her husband's dismay. In contrast to Lidian and Mary Emerson's "temperamental excess," as Phyllis Cole has described his reaction to the women's emotional appeals, Waldo Emerson preferred reform rhetoric that tempered zeal with reserved legal discourse, after the fashion of his brother Charles. On the one hand, Emerson complained in his journal that "Lidian grieves aloud about the wretched negro in the horrors of the middle passage." Yet on the other, he depicted these same "horrors," as with this journal entry a few weeks later: "The fury with which the slaveholder & the slavetrader defend every inch of their plunder, of their bloody deck, & howling Auction . . . The loathsome details of the kidnapping; of the middle passage; six hundred living bodies sit for thirty days betwixt death & life in a posture of stone & when brought on deck for air cast themselves into the sea." Emerson simply did not comprehend that the women could transform their sentiment into effective political action, although this is exactly what they were doing. In fact, he need look no further than Concord (or his own parlor), where the female society was succeeding in many venues, including the orchestration of events at which Emerson himself would agree to be the keynote speaker. Moreover, other men noted approvingly his wife's activism, as when Wendell Phillips complimented Lidian Emerson for attending antislavery meetings "when her husband objected to her coming."[44]

Like his friend Waldo Emerson, in the late 1830s, Henry Thoreau was encircled by the antislavery fervor of the many women sharing his home. Indeed, Thoreau had been home only a few days after graduating from Harvard when the Grimkés lectured in Concord; by the time the female society formed in mid October, he had already resigned from teaching at the Center School. Similar to Emerson, the young Thoreau was critical of collective social action and favored individual conversion: "Nothing can be effected but by one man. . . . We must first succeed alone, that we may enjoy our success together. . . . In this matter of reforming the world, we have little faith in corporations." Thoreau's mother and sisters, however, were instrumental founders of the female antislavery society. Additionally, Sophia and Helen Thoreau subscribed to Nathaniel Rogers's antislavery paper, the *Herald of Freedom*, and disseminated it through Concord. They and the outspoken Cynthia Thoreau regularly attended antislavery conventions in Boston with Mary Brooks, Prudence Ward, and Susan Barrett; and Sophia and Helen both held various leadership posts in the county society. As Wendell Glick has pointed out, "a concentration of radical Abolitionist sentiment . . . must have overshadowed all other activities" in the Thoreau home.[45]

In 1838, Concord women circulated two antislavery petitions similar to those submitted to Congress the previous month by Josiah Bartlett and other townsmen. One protested the potential U.S. annexation of Texas and the other "pray[ed] for the abolition of slavery in the District of Columbia and of the slave trade throughout the U.S." A year later, Cynthia Thoreau and Elizabeth Barrett took the lead on two more petitions; in all, nearly two hundred women signed these four documents. The newly independent Texas loomed as one of the abolitionists' greatest fears—when brought into the union as a slave state, it would expand slavery dramatically into the western territories. Despite the female society's successful inroads with their townsfolk at this time, Prudence Ward was for the moment disheartened: "One almost despairs for the slave—when the community is so dead," she lamented.[46]

In 1839 and 1840, at the American Anti-Slavery Society's annual conventions in New York, a storm threatening for a few years split the abolitionist ranks. The rupture resulted primarily from two of Garrison's bedrock issues—refusal to use the political process to effect slavery's demise, and women's full participation in antislavery governance. From the beginning, the pragmatic Garrison understood that women would work relentlessly to achieve immediate and total emancipation, and he had encouraged them to take leadership roles in his movement. In 1840, at the first World Anti-Slavery Convention in London, he and other male abolitionists sat in the balcony alongside the women who were refused admittance to the proceedings; then Garrison returned to the United States recommitted to a public role in his movement for women. His refusal to exercise the elective franchise also appealed to women activists: They could not vote, and Garrison refused to do so. But the conservative faction, "the clerical snake . . . coiling in the grass for a spring," as Garrison characterized them, finally parted ways with the state society and formed assorted organizations, including the Massachusetts Abolition Society, the Liberty Party, and the American & Foreign Anti-Slavery Society, groups that would wield varying degrees of influence over the next decades. These men and their allies became known as the "new orgs," while Garrisonian "old orgs" or "ultras" now more blatantly incorporated women's rights into their original antislavery agenda. Focused as it was on women's status in the movement, this organizational schism cemented the bond between women's rights and radical abolitionism. The national controversy played itself out in local societies as well, a situation that challenged small societies to demonstrate their loyalty and to deliver their communities, particularly since the Boston female society remained staunchly "old org."[47]

From its founding, the Middlesex County Anti-Slavery Society had welcomed women members. Sophia and Helen Thoreau, and Mary Brooks regularly attended meetings, although none of them held an office in the organization until the 1840s. Whether women might *vote* on society resolutions, however, caused quite a stir at the meeting of July 23, 1839, held in Acton, when the men most opposed to this proposal, led by Rev. Joseph Warren Cross of Boxboro, stormed out to form their own society. Given Cross's recent appointment as a vice president in the "new organization," the disturbance probably surprised no one. Boston female society member Lucia Weston described William Lloyd Garrison girding for "the field of battle" as he set out for this meeting, with other old orgs in tow, "to save Middlesex County." Those members remaining after Cross and the others defected quickly passed two resolutions: One reversed the morning's decision to permit only "*gentlemen,* to participate in our proceedings"; the other "*affirm[ed]* the right of all members of this—the Am. & State Society—to participate in the business of said societies without regard to age, sex, clime, color, or condition." Weston explained that the "Boston folks brought up a resolution that all *persons* according to the words of the constitution should take part in the meeting."[48]

In the months following, the Middlesex County society's new officers endeavored to maintain a civil tone. Meeting announcements promised "free discussion of our principles—the interchange of friendly feeling." But despite such overtures, the rift became a permanent divide, and it was one that fully absorbed Concord abolitionists, particularly after combative newspaper editor and "old org" William S. Robinson moved back to his native town in 1839 to edit the *Yeoman's Gazette,* which he promptly renamed the *Republican.* In addition to blasting cautious politicians, Robinson soon took the *Concord Freeman's* editor to task for endorsing President Martin Van Buren for a second term: "It is too late in the day for the Freeman to force such doctrines down our throats. It cannot with all its cant and hypocrisy delude us into a belief that it is either just or democratic to swindle old revolutionary soldiers." Before long the editors' tirades consumed nearly as many column inches as the news stories they covered. Financially, Robinson managed to float the paper for little more than a year before bidding goodbye to Concord; as a parting shot, he deemed it "the best town in the world" even though "it has been going down hill pretty fast in these latter days." Years later, Robinson's wife, Harriet Hanson Robinson, expressed more severe judgments: "It is a dull old place, it is a narrow old place, it is a set old place. It is a snobbish old place, it is an old place full of Antedeluvian people and manners." Their characterizations, however, likely reveal more about the Robinsons' views of the conservative faction than with Concord itself.[49]

Others in town became caught up in the abolitionists' dispute, including Rev. John Wilder, whose influence had been vital to the development of immediatist sentiment in the community. On the issue of women's participation, however, Wilder broke with the Garrisonians and went wholly over to the "new orgs." His disaffection was evident as early as September 1838, when as Concord's lone representative to the national Peace Convention, Wilder withdrew from the proceedings "on account of the admission of women," a position taken by only a handful of the one hundred plus attendees. As the female society's first president and lead signatory of two antislavery petitions from Concord women, Mary Wilder shared her husband's dedication to abolitionism. She and her friend Maria Thoreau adopted his "new org" sentiments as well, exemplifying the divided nature of the community's abolitionism at this time. After the Wilders permanently moved from Concord in 1839, Thoreau kept Mary Wilder apprised of local friction and revealed her own reasons for aligning with the "new orgs": "Mrs. Brooks is as much engaged as ever in the Abolition cause, & goes all lengths with Garrison, for myself I can no longer follow such a leader. . . . a number have followed our example, we shall pay our money over to the female Emancipation society in Boston indeed Garrison's party are losing friends every day as you see by the papers I occasionally send you." Thoreau's greatest divergence from Garrison centered not on the issue of women's rights, but on the "sabbath" controversy. For the past several years, Garrison had encouraged "come-outerism" and had scorned traditional religious conventions, including the observance of a particular sabbath day. Her support for the "new orgs" not only put Thoreau at odds with Mary Brooks, but also ultimately dissociated her from the county society, whose leaders met in Concord on New Year's Day in 1841 to reaffirm their allegiance to Garrison and the "old orgs."[50]

Maria and her sister Jane Thoreau's support for the adversarial side was evident to "old org" ambassador Anne Warren Weston, who visited Mary Brooks in September 1841. Weston, the sister of Maria Weston Chapman, portrayed the Concord women she met in terms of their abolitionist sympathies:

> As for Mrs. Brooks . . . I *never* saw a woman more truly independent & conscienscous. She is . . . perfectly fearless, what the transcendentalists might hail as "the truest of women." . . . We spent the first evening abusing ministers and telling our own experiences. Mr. B. came in from his office about 9 & talked over the cause, non Resistance etc. for about an hour. He is . . . as good an abolitionist as his social standing will permit. . . . We had several calls, Mrs. & Miss Hoar & the Misses Thoreau, the first women very weak abolitionists of the old school, the second *new orgs*. I took them all for worldings & when the Thoreaus politely introduced Anti Slavery, it so happened that I in the most innocent manner gave some dabs at New Orgs, which greatly pleased Mrs. B.

Weston also met Cynthia Thoreau and the Alcotts, but without a doubt Mary Brooks most impressed her: "I have not ascertained how it is in Concord, but if any thing can be done rest assured Mrs. B. will do it." Her confidence in Brooks was well founded. Within two years, the female society boasted in its annual report to "have breasted the storm . . . the waves of new organization . . . have beat against us in vain."[51]

Among the stirring voices addressing Concord audiences in the early 1840s was a riveting young man who reinforced the "old org" resolve of local abolitionists. Escaped slave Frederick Douglass quite credibly and passionately refuted proslavery arguments. "I can tell you what I have seen with my own eyes, felt on my own person, and know to have occurred in my own neighborhood. . . . I can stand here and relate atrocities which would make your blood to boil at the statement of them," he thundered from the platform. Abolitionist Nathaniel Rogers reported his amazement on hearing Douglass:

> This is an extraordinary man. He was cut out for a hero. . . . As a speaker he has few equals. It is not declamation—but oratory, power of debate. He

watches the tide of discussion with the eye of the veteran, and dashes into it at once with all the tact of the forum or the bar. He has wit, argument, sarcasm, pathos—all that first-rate men show in their master efforts. : . . He is the chattel of some pale-faced tyrant. How his owner would cower and shiver to hear him thunder in an anti-slavery hall![52]

Douglass regularly attended Middlesex County society meetings over the next few years. In August 1841, the *Concord Freeman* noted his upcoming appearance in nearby Groton: "Mr. Douglass is a colored man, and has recently been a slave. It is said that he is very eloquent." Douglass first appeared in Concord on October 12 that year, along with Wendell Phillips, Samuel J. May, and others at the new Universalist meeting house. This day's topics included "the recent outrages" experienced by blacks in the North who refused to comply with segregated seating on the new rail cars. Douglass himself had been thrust to the "negro car" of a train in New Hampshire and thrown off one altogether in Massachusetts.[53]

At this county meeting in October, political "new orgs" wielded their slim influence by encouraging members to "throw off the shackles of party, & remember the *Slave* at the *ballot box*, voting for none but true abolitionists." William Lloyd Garrison, however, was also on hand and more than equal to the challenge. In the *Liberator*, he thanked Concord abolitionists for "their hospitality," but blasted the local clergymen—James Means, Wilder's replacement at the Second Church, and Barzillai Frost at the First Church—both of whom had barred "old orgs" from their pulpits:

> The ministers are not abolitionists—[they] occasionally mention the subject of slavery on particular days. . . . The influence of the churches is against the slave. 'The Orthodox church, under Mr. Wilder's administration, passed a vote, excluding slaveholders from communion; but, recently, they have 'voted to exclude all lecturers from the house, except those delivered by the minister, *or such as he approves*.' 'The Unitarian house, though heretofore granted for abolition purposes, it is understood is to be refused, after it is repaired, on the ground of its being too clean to admit impure subjects!'

As this backlash attests, Mary Brooks and her compatriots were indeed impacting the political landscape in Concord.[54]

Brooks had almost certainly met Frederick Douglass that summer at the Groton meeting and may have been responsible for his first appearance in Concord, since the prior week she had entreated Maria Weston Chapman to ensure that he would attend the fall meeting, along with other speakers:

> I do hope Wendell Phillips will come, as he will draw out more than any other person. I've got so as to feel somewhat fidgety, fearing he will not. I try to

trust in God when things go contrary to my wishes in abolition, and my abo-
lition trials are my hardest. . . . I want to be able to publish in the papers that
Wendell Phillips will deliver a lecture in the evening. I received a letter from
Edmund Quincy this morning, stating that he thought he should be here,
that a trifle should not prevent his coming. I have written to Mr. May but have
not received an answer—hope to see him. I want Douglass & Collins and
Garrison, and in short, feel the infinitinys of my nature by wishing the whole
Universe to be present.

Brooks may well have placed "trust in God," but when it came to orchestrat-
ing antislavery events in Concord, she relied on her own resources, which in
this as in many other cases, worked most effectively.[55]

Abby Alcott testified in her journal to the success of Brooks's labors by
billing the October county meeting as the "Great Anti-Slavery Convention."
The Alcotts welcomed Garrison as their guest as well as Alcott's brother,
Samuel J. May.[56] Presumably, like the other out-of-town speakers, Frederick
Douglass also stayed with a Concord host, most likely Cynthia Thoreau, who
typically lodged visiting abolitionists. Douglass's friendship with Helen
Thoreau, as evidenced in this letter, makes such a conjecture all the more
probable:

My kind Friend Helen, You may be somewhat interested to know the character of our contemplated meetings at Sudbury and Framingham. I have opportunity to send you a line by the kind hand of Mrs. Kimball.
   Our meeting or contemplated meeting at Sudbury—was a total failure,
we had no meeting—The clergy here as in Bedford arrayed themselves
against us, misrepresenting our views—maligning our characters and array-
ing against us the mob Spirit of the places. It was town meeting day you are
aware, I went into it. It was like going into a minagery. They *sneezed*, growled,
coughed and howled like so many hungry wild beasts I think I never went
into a town meeting where there was so many rum heads—rum noses as I
there beheld. It was amusing to see the harmony existing between the Rumis
and Rabbis in opposing our meeting—We found the same spirit here in Framingham—on the part of the clergy—Though we have a meeting. Br. Garrison
is here—in company with James Buffum—Dr. Farnsworth—Francis Jackson. . . . My regards to all the friends—Mrs. Brooks Bigilow your own family.

Possibly, the hostility Douglass confronted in the North was another factor
prompting Helen Thoreau to "come out" from the church, a step that further aligned her with Garrison and the "old orgs." Unquestionably, Douglass's frequent presence in Concord over the next few years added a palpable integrity to the immediatist argument.[57]

By December 1842, Concord's divisiveness over abolitionism had intensified. This time, Wendell Phillips set off the controversy, and twenty-five-year-old Henry Thoreau initiated the furor when as the curator coordinating the lyceum's winter lecture series, he announced that Phillips would speak that month on the subject of "Slavery." Conservative townsman John Keyes balked at this news and moved that "the vexed and disorganizing question of Abolitionism or Slavery should be kept out of" the lyceum. By majority vote, however, members tabled this resolution, and Phillips spoke as scheduled two nights later. The confrontationally eloquent Phillips had converted to Garrisonianism a few years earlier and rapidly become one of the most sought-after speakers on the antislavery circuit. A fringe benefit to his oratorical preeminence was an aristocratic pedigree—the young Boston Brahmin with a promising law career had thrown in his hat with the most seditious radicals. Like Garrison, Phillips also promoted an equal role in the movement for women; as a delegate to the World Anti-Slavery Convention, he had attempted to overturn the ruling that denied women seating on the convention floor.[58]

Likely, Thoreau's mother and sisters had recommended Phillips as a lyceum speaker since they and other female society members, including Mary Brooks and Prudence Ward, had heard him speak at several gatherings. Moreover, Lidian Emerson could have suggested Phillips, since Thoreau was then living in her household. His reading of the *Liberator* would also have acquainted Thoreau with Phillips's belligerent protest over the recent arrest of fugitive slave George Latimer: "My CURSE be on the Constitution of these United States," Phillips had threatened. At a time when abolitionism was still anathema, he castigated northerners for enabling the Slave Power: "But let us open our own bosoms, and ask ourselves by whom is slavery sustained. It is by the phalanx of the strength of numbers; by the force of public opinion—by the voice of the intelligent and the virtuous—by the voice of the church—by the consent of Christians—by the legislation of the country, and by our national policy." The fact that Concord lyceum members overrode Keyes and insisted on hearing Phillips evidences the measured change taking hold as immediatists cultivated a broader local audience. It had taken nearly ten years, but the same lyceum that in 1833 had denied antislavery societies' right to exist now welcomed one of their most combative agents. Another thirteen years would pass before Mary Brooks and her townswomen were granted voting rights in the lyceum; in the meantime they influenced its agenda through the townsmen who shared their views.[59]

True to form, Wendell Phillips proved a rousing draw for the "old orgs," and local abolitionists capitalized on the interest he generated as the year 1843 commenced. In early January, William Whiting organized a "Middlesex County Latimer Committee" to augment a "Great Mass Petition to the Legislature" then circulating in Boston. When presented to state lawmakers

in March, 15 percent of the sixty-four-thousand-plus signatures had origi-
nated in Middlesex County. In March, Mary Brooks reported for the *Liberator* on the recent county society meeting in Concord, which despite a poor
turnout, left her "full of hopes as to the results."[60] Her antislavery pen
worked the most magic, however, in frequent and dramatic appeals pleading for antislavery agents to speak yet again in Concord. Two months after
his lyceum appearance, Brooks beseeched Phillips to return, tempting him
by recounting the details of John Keyes's continued opposition:

> I have been hoping this morning that you are today in a most benevolent self
> sacrificing frame of mind, willing to lay your whole self on the AntiSlavery
> altar if you are not woe is me for I shall most justly lay myself open to your
> righteous indignation for I am about to request you to repeat your lecture
> which you delivered here in December. The facts which have induced me to
> repeat the invitation are these. The *Hon.* John Keyes a few weeks after you
> were here got up and made the most gross barefaced malignant misrepresen-
> tation of your lecture I have ever heard calling you all kinds of hard names
> saying you were a traitor to your country and deserved a traitor's fate. This
> has excited the curiosity of the Lyceum and many have expressed a strong de-
> sire to hear the lecture about which so much has been said. The curators
> have accordingly requested me to write you requesting you to come the
> Wednesday after the 22nd of March inst. Now can you, will you come. O I do
> hope you will I promise you that I will not again trouble you by asking you to
> come here to lecture. I do think much good can be done to the cause by your
> coming. Perhaps you can make a brief recapitulation of the leading parts of
> your lecture and fill it up with other matters.

Never one to put off until tomorrow a favor she could press today, Brooks
concluded, "If you cannot come at the time specified can you come the
week after. I feel that I must have you sometime."[61] Despite this impassioned
overture, Phillips would not appear at the Concord lyceum again until the
following year.

The Concord female society's intimacy with their sister organization in
Boston opened important venues that would prove vital to their mission
over the next twenty years. In the spring and summer of 1843, Brooks's missives to Maria Weston Chapman flew fast and furious—and ever more insistent—as Concord abolitionists faced increased resistance at home. The female society's strategies for an upcoming summer fair were central to this
correspondence, Brooks planning ice cream sales to boost the profits and
the turnout. And with a marketing eye, she apprised Chapman of the merchandise that would best sell:

> We think of having a Liberty tree, similar to your Christmas tree, if we can
> collect articles enough to put on it, for sixpence a piece, and for this purpose

we wish about 50 little dolls worth 3 cts a piece, and now I am going to beg the favor of you to purchase these for us, and send them up on Tuesday evening with the other things, as we have a meeting on Wednesday when we mean to dress them. We will pay you for the same soon. . . . I am troubling you a great deal and you have always worked like a giant in this cause . . . I don't know what is to set this world right it is so awfully wrong every where. I am sometimes strongly tempted to turn Millerite and have the business all done up quick.

Upset at any perceived slight, Brooks reacted testily to the fact that the Hutchinsons, popular antislavery balladeers, were apparently unavailable for the Concord fair:

Now I know there are many persons who would be present on that occasion were they advertised to be there. This, in addition to my own strong desire to hear them has induced me to write you, and feeling that you Boston folks who have had such frequent opportunities of hearing them, might not realize the importance to our cause of their appearance at that time I thought best to in- form you of the feelings of many with regard to them that you might make some efforts which you otherwise would not to secure their attendance.

Brooks paid attention to the buying habits of Concord's immigrant popula- tion and surmised that "caps and collars might sell I think if we had them. There are many Irish in town now if we had some clothing suitable for them we might sell it perhaps. I mean to stir round among these Irish and get them to the fair if possible."[62]

But despite these labors, the female society was forced to postpone its plans at the last minute "on account of our being unable to obtain the only Hall eligible for the sale." As Brooks informed Chapman in mid-July: "We are greatly surprised at the refusal, as it has been refused to no one before. We shall make an attempt to get another place as soon as possible." Evi- dently, the women did secure another location for a late summer fundraiser, since Helen Thoreau forwarded its proceeds to the state society treasury in September.[63]

Brooks regarded herself as Chapman's lieutenant and freely sought ad- vice and expressed gratitude even as she put forward a new appeal. As she rationalized to Chapman: "I have such a horrible dread of asking favors for myself or any body else that I did not feel boldness enough to do it without consulting you first. What do you think of it? Please tell me—I want to do something mighty, tremble and earthquake, burst a volcanoe, or do some- thing or other to attract attention to this said fair." Brooks also approached Chapman on behalf of friends, as when she recommended John and Susan Garrison's daughter, knowing her Boston friend's wealth of connections would open doors:

> Ellen Garrison, the bearer of this, is a coloured girl from our town who is going to Boston to obtain employment. She is a very intelligent girl for one of so few advantages, having born away the prize most frequently in our common schools for superiority of learning—She has met with us in our little Society and feels desirous to know something about the meetings of your Society in Boston, which she thinks of attending, if possible. She has written a letter for the post office at the fair, which shows some talent. I told her that you would be happy, I knew, to give her any requisite information and that I would write to you by her.

Brooks habitually defended her forwardness as vital to a shared cause, a tactic of apologetic importunity that usually succeeded. Such missionary zeal was but one example of a national phenomenon that William Lloyd Garrison did not take for granted: "The abolition men in this city are somewhat drowsy, but the women are, as usual, wide awake and the life of the cause," he had discerned years earlier. Whether or not Phillips and Garrison privately resented Brooks's unflagging claims on their time, they both consistently paid public tribute to antislavery women.[64]

Others letters reveal, however, that not all women in Concord valued Brooks's cause. After newlyweds Sophia and Nathaniel Hawthorne moved to town in 1842, Sophia bragged to her mother about exploiting the female society: "The ladies of the antislavery society take sewing in Concord and do it very cheaply. So shall I employ them, for I have no manner of scruple about making them take as little as possible; while I could not think of not giving full and ample price to a poor person, or a seamstress by profession." Both now and in later years, Sophia shared her husband's disdain for abolitionism, particularly when it entailed the (to her) indecorous entry of women into the public fray.[65]

A decade earlier Concord's lyceum and largest churches had hosted the first tentative discussions of antislavery in the community, but their doors were now closed to the Garrisonians; only the sustained mobilization of determined men and women would keep the issue alive over the next years. Fortunately, Mary Brooks—armed with charm and pushy persistence—battled on. As 1843 came to a close, she reminded Wendell Phillips that a year had passed since his last appearance in Concord:

> Our Lyceum is again about being opened, and again have I made a request to the curators that they should receive an antislavery lecture. Two of them, Mr. Hoar & Mr. Emerson, have consented, provided Mr. Phillips can be obtained. I could expatiate largely upon the advantages to our cause of having an antislavery lecture before a Lyceum, but you already know them. I do not need to urge you, for if you can come, you will, I know. I will only say that it is the dar-

ling desire of my heart to have you once fairly heard by the congregated wisdom of our famed liberty battle fighting town. Mr. Emerson says you may have the three months of December January & February to choose from, which week you will take, and it may be, if you prefer it, one week in November will be free for you.[66]

The fact that the conservative Samuel Hoar and the moderate Waldo Emerson jointly extended this invitation to Phillips reflects Brooks's remarkable success in enlisting town leaders to her side, despite her allegiance to the "old orgs." Phillips's acceptance of the invitation—and Hoar's regret that he extended it—would signal round two in the battle of the Concord lyceum curators. Most assuredly, the female society had earned the right to the self-congratulatory tone adopted in its annual report that year: "Never was there a time, since the commencement of our cause, when the American ear was so ready to hear our report. . . . God in his providence has placed this cause, in a great and unusual manner, in the hands of women."[67]

2

From Concern to Crusade, 1843–1849

> I want great names for this cause, for almost all the anti Slavery treas-
> ure is in earthen vessels, and though a diamond is as much a diamond
> in an old crockery bowl, as in a golden vase, yet men can much more
> readily be made to look for the diamond in the vase. If Mr. Emerson
> shall see fit to sign the petition, please ask him to put it at the head, it
> is seldom we get such coin, and when we do I am anxious to make it
> pass for all it is worth.
>
> —Mary Merrick Brooks to Lidian Emerson, [February 1846?]

Henry Thoreau had lived much of 1843 on Staten Island, New York, tutoring the children of William Emerson, Waldo's older brother. He returned to Concord in mid-December, just as lyceum members were again at odds over inviting Wendell Phillips to deliver another lecture on slavery. John Keyes had renewed his defamations, calling Phillips's prior address "vile, pernicious, and abominable," and he again demanded that Phillips speak on a nonpolitical topic. But the curators held firm. Phillips and his "bitter tongue" appeared before the lyceum on January 18, announced by the *Concord Freeman* in a notice that must have further incensed Keyes: "The distinguished talents of the Lecturer, and the vast importance of his subject, will undoubtedly draw a crowded audience."[1]

According to a resident identified only as "H. M."—perhaps female society member Harriet Minot—whose account of the confrontation appeared in the *Liberator*, Phillips spoke for an hour and a half to rapt listeners, despite uttering what the reporter satirically called "treason against Church and State." His blunt allegation that "the curse of every honest man should be upon its Constitution" so disturbed Keyes and Samuel Hoar that the two men scheduled time the following week for the community "to discuss the lecture." Unbeknownst to them, however, Phillips had been tipped off "that a resolution against him was to be introduced," and he showed up for the forum, took a seat in the back of the large First Church vestry, and quietly bided his time while first Keyes "talked an hour, quoting St. Paul, about leading captive silly women, &c. &c.," and then Hoar denigrated the "stripling" Phillips for his "arrogance." When they concluded, Phillips rose from his rear pew, "asked liberty to speak," and promptly took advantage of a second opportunity to proselytize in as many weeks before a Concord audience:

> I do not feel responsible for my manner. In a struggle for life, it is hardly fair for those who are lolling at ease to remark that the limbs of the combatant are not arranged in classic order. I agree with the last speaker, that this is a serious subject; otherwise, I should not have devoted my life to it. Stripling as I am, I but echo the voice of ages, of our venerated fathers, of statesman, poet, philosopher. The last gentleman has painted the danger to life, liberty, and happiness, that would be the consequence of doing right. That state of things is now legalized at the South. My liberty may be bought at too dear a price. If I cannot have it, except by sin, I reject it; but I would not so blaspheme God as to doubt the safety of obeying Him. . . . But our pulpits are silent. Who ever heard this subject presented, before the movement of the silly women and striplings? The first speaker accused me of ambitious motives. I should have chosen another path to fame. I would say to you, my young friends, who have been cautioned against excitement, and advised to fold your hands in selfish ease, throw yourselves upon the altar of some noble cause.[2]

"H. M." captured the entire imbroglio and pronounced the effect of Phillips's words "perfectly electrical," in addition to which she could not resist saluting Concord: "After all this, we are greatly encouraged that the old spirit of liberty is not yet quite extinct in our ancient town. Have we not reason?" A bit more subdued, the *Concord Freeman* nevertheless reported the tension: A "discussion has just closed on the propriety of admitting gentlemen to lecture before the Lyceum who advance sentiments similar to some embodied in Mr. Wendell Phillips's recent lecture. Without expressing an opinion on the value of the discussions in question, they can be said to have at least the one good effect of breaking the dull monotony of a country life, if not of rousing a spirit of inquiry among the people." That the local Democratic paper could concede "one good effect" had resulted from Phillips's lecture, and that its editor welcomed—albeit begrudgingly—"a spirit of inquiry" on the subject of abolitionism evidence the success of the radicals' perseverance. Even the reluctant in Concord were taking notice of the issue.[3]

A few weeks later, Mary Brooks reported to Phillips that his Concord critics seemed most upset by what they considered his negative influence over townswomen: "Mr. Frost says if the days of witchcraft had not passed he should think you had bewitched all our women, for he cannot find one who is not your advocate—and Mr. Hoar is much surprised that all the women

are in favor of such *stuff*, and he thinks it augurs badly for Concord people."
Their accusations flew in the face of facts that Keyes and Hoar simply could
not concede: that female society members had adopted a militant abolitionist sensibility on their own, that they had deliberately cultivated an atmosphere of reform in their community, and, perhaps most difficult to accept, that more than one respected townsman sympathized with and aided
the women's efforts. Brooks soon followed up her oblique compliment to
Phillips by urging him to speak in Concord again, particularly given that
"friends" had already raised money for the purpose. Phillips accepted, and
the *Concord Freeman* announced that he would lecture at the First Church on
February 20.[4]

By now, Mary Brooks had evolved into the undisputed leader of Concord's antislavery effort. To enact the society's goals, she fashioned a strategy dependent on presumption and persistence; emboldened by the
women's achievements as well as her own increasing stature among national
abolitionists, she showed little concern for their frenetic schedules as she repeatedly pressed Phillips, Garrison, and other prominent figures to speak
in Concord, quite accurately believing that their appearances kept the fervor alive. In her frequent correspondence with Phillips, especially, Brooks
merged boldness with duty. A letter to him in March 1844 opened tactically,
"as I am secretary of our Society I must obey orders even if I do trouble you
all the time." Phillips later praised Brooks for this very "bluntness" and
judged that "she never shrunk from speaking her whole thought; neither
did her tenderness of affection ever confuse her judgment. In the emergency of a great crisis she could see and rebuke the short-comings of those
she loved best." Brooks may have been overbearing at best and tyrannical at
worst, but this naturally aggressive character enabled her to succeed where
others, more circumspect and polite, would have failed.[5]

Discontented with his short-lived careers as a schoolteacher and a tutor,
twenty-six-year-old Henry Thoreau faced the plaguing question of vocation.
Perhaps it was witnessing Wendell Phillips overwhelm his conservative
townsmen in a debate, as well as a recent stopover at the utopian community
of Brook Farm that inspired Thoreau to refine his own reform ideology at
this time. Thus, when Waldo Emerson suggested that Thoreau join him in a
lecture series focusing on reform that winter, Thoreau accepted the opportunity. These "Sunday meetings" held over twelve weeks, February through
April, at Boston's Amory Hall attracted a motley set of ideologues. In addition to Emerson, Thoreau, Phillips, and Garrison, this year's lineup featured social utopian Charles Lane, Non-Resistance Society cofounder Adin
Ballou, and free thought leader and feminist Ernestine Rose. On March 3,
Emerson spoke on "New England Reformers"; Thoreau chose a similar
topic, "The Conservative and the Reformer," for his lecture on March 10.[6]

In his study of this lecture series, Linck Johnson points out that unlike the other speakers, Thoreau and Emerson challenged their listeners to inward self-reform rather than collective social action. For years, Emerson had disdained abolitionists as another in the disparate band of communal improvers: "The abolitionists with their holy cause; the Friends of the Poor; the ministers at large; the Prison Discipline Agents; the Soup Societies, the whole class of professed Philanthropists,—it is strange & horrible to say— are an altogether odious set of people." Individuals should heed the call of social reform, Emerson allowed, but only after perfecting themselves. In his Amory Hall address, Emerson disavowed the communitarian impulse underway at Brook Farm, Hopedale, and (the recently abandoned) Fruitlands, while, similarly, Thoreau in his lengthy remarks depicted organized reformers as "the impersonation of disorder and imperfection . . . seeking to discover the divine order and conform to it; and earnestly asking the cooperation of men." At this juncture only Thoreau's approach to social reform, not his position itself, differed from Emerson's. Like Emerson, Thoreau took issue with the plethora of reform mavens, yet he markedly excluded antislavery activists from censure. To Thoreau, these reformers directed their energies toward abolishing an immoral institution rather than exhorting others to embrace particular notions of social betterment. Thoreau therefore accommodated abolitionists' call to collective action within his own view that reform should be an individual enterprise. In Wendell Phillips, Thoreau had perceived a valid exemplar of civic improvement. No idle rhetorician stumping for a better world, Phillips demanded action from those who claimed to be morally outraged that more than 3 million people subsisted as slaves in the land of "Jefferson, Hancock, and Adams"; he hurled accusations at individual clergymen, politicians, and Concord's own naysayers in a bellicose style Thoreau would always admire.[7]

Later that year, another militant propelled Thoreau further toward immediatism. Indeed, the stirring words of Nathaniel P. Rogers, editor of the New Hampshire antislavery weekly, *Herald of Freedom*, gave rise to Thoreau's first published remarks on the subject. His sisters, who had subscribed to and circulated this paper through Concord, first brought Rogers to their brother's attention. In April 1844, in the last number of the Transcendentalist journal the *Dial*, Thoreau's brief paean to Rogers, entitled simply "Herald of Freedom," exhibits several of what would become Thoreau's political trademarks—the scathing wit, the moral umbrage, the outraged denunciations, the liberal exclamation marks and underlinings are all on display in this first antislavery piece. Thoreau admired Rogers's affinity for the New England wilderness and valued the editor's caustic tone, a "warwhoop," a "blast . . . 'on Fabyan's White Mountain's horn.'" As with Phillips, Thoreau likely also prized Rogers for his writings condemning the "selfworshipping clergy" and the "modern Church," which has relinquished its role as "the bride of Christ" in favor of being "the mistress of the military State . . . like all other harlots, enamored of the cockade and the scarlet coat of the soldier." Moreover, Rogers posed the questions that had begun to resonate most for Thoreau—"What is the moral effect of political effort?" he queried readers in April 1842.[8] Not surprisingly, Rogers delighted in Thoreau's "panegyric," which he published in the *Herald of Freedom* on May 10, 1844, prefaced by an appreciative acceptance of the compliments. Although uninformed about Thoreau himself—Rogers ventured he was "probably a German. He cannot have written much in this country, or his name would have reached me, from no farther off than Concord, Mass."—the editor reacted earnestly to Thoreau's words: "If he were a practiced writer, he could hardly have written so beautifully and freshly." Further, he encouraged Thoreau to "let Antislavery have the benefit of his beautiful pen." Characteristically mute in his journal about such matters, however, Thoreau did not comment on the essay's publication.[9]

By 1844, a dependable few townspeople—Samuel and Susan Barrett; Mary Brooks; Cynthia, Helen, and Sophia Thoreau; Anne Whiting—regularly attended state and national gatherings. But at the New England Anti-Slavery Convention that May in Boston, Concord delegates took a critical step with hundreds of other Garrisonians and adopted the following resolutions:

1. Resolved, That no equal union can exist between a slaveholding and a free community; that under any form of government, a large body of slaveholders must necessarily control the policy and character of the nation; and that it is the great fault of the United States Constitution, that it assists and facilitates this result.

2. Resolved, That for this reason, as well as for other reasons, no abolitionist can consistently swear to support the Constitution; that it is, in the opinion of this Convention, a gross departure from abolition principle for abolitionists to throw a ballot for any office under the State or United States Constitution, which requires such oath; and that we deem it a first duty for them to agitate for a dissolution of the Union.

Disunion—northern secession from the slaveholding states and the federal government—was a controversial move toward which Garrison had sidled for several months. The overwhelming affirmation of these resolutions (the vote of 250 to 24 included the "nay" of literary critic James Russell Lowell) demonstrates not only the support Garrison had marshaled for this extreme position, but also the abolitionists' desperation. The American Anti-Slavery Society followed suit the next year, resolving "to institute and promote a peaceful but vigorous agitation for the Dissolution of the existing political Union which binds the Slave and the Free in one intolerable chain." More than the practical considerations of how to effect such a move, Garrison enjoyed "the shock value" of the stratagem. "No Union with Slaveholders" became his new battle cry. Most of all, the slogan forced the question: On what basis did the northern states remain in a union with the slaveholding South?[10]

Although he expressed sentiments in this direction, it would be ten years before Henry Thoreau joined the disunion coalition. Not so with his mother and sisters, however. At the convention in May, Cynthia, Helen, and Sophia Thoreau voted in favor of the resolutions, their names appearing in the *Liberator* along with Mary Brooks's in a public display quite at odds with Henry Canby's depiction of the Thoreau women as "conventional." The *Concord Freeman* derisively reported the abolitionists' vote, although it did not name the local residents who endorsed it: "We have not heard from them since, but as they always perform what they promise, it is probable they have brought about the dissolution before this time." In her recent study of antebellum women's petitions, Susan Zaeske calls attention to the fact that most married women signed these resolutions with their own full names rather than their married signatures, a significant change as women began consciously to formulate their own political identity. Additionally suggestive of a radical turn is that women and men's names appear interspersed rather than in columns segregated by gender as had been the practice.[11]

Two weeks after this convention, Frederick Douglass and Charles Lenox Remond, a black abolitionist from Salem, addressed a poorly attended county society meeting in Concord, during which members disagreed over whether to endorse disunion. Secretary pro tem Helen Thoreau recorded the dispute, as well as a resolution condemning Massachusetts Senator Daniel Webster for favoring the rights of slaveholders. Mary Brooks exulted to Maria Weston Chapman that the women had valiantly stood their ground during the heated debates:

> Our Convention did not turn out well, our audience was not very large, and Mr. Frost, the Unitarian minister, ventured in and uttered some abominable sentiments. . . . The politicians are all in a fever and the abolitionists are all such. White took the anti dissolution side of the question and evidently carried the audience with him. Douglass and Remond answered him but they were neither of them in the best mood. . . . The women struck up "no union with slaveholders you followers of the free" and sang it with all the spirit they could muster, and I thought almost equalled the Hutchinsons.

Despite her frustration, the meeting concluded on the promising note that Brooks and Samuel Barrett took on the task of planning a "meeting to celebrate the anniversary of the Emancipation of the Slaves in the British West Indies, at Concord, on the coming first of August." Here would be an opportunity to seek redress for last summer's fair, postponed for lack of access to a public building.[12]

Brooks lost no time organizing what she resolved would be "a great gathering" to coincide with other local celebrations marking the tenth anniversary of West Indian emancipation, a day set aside for "all who love freedom, and hate slavery, [to] come together to testify their joy," as Garrison billed it. Brooks relayed to Chapman her vision of a huge paying crowd descending upon Concord, with as many key figures as she could ensnare:

> We are to have 25 cts per ticket for the dinner the profits to go to the National and State Anti Slavery Societies. I write to see whether you will not be present, and Boston friends generally. You know we shall have our railroad in full operation long before this time, and the ride from Boston to Concord will be for a mere nothing. White is to see Phillips and Garrison immediately, and secure Phillips if possible for the orators in the forenoon. Also will try and secure the Hutchinsons. Will you ascertain how many friends we may expect from Boston. . . . I shall write immediately to Pierpont lest he be engaged elsewhere. I do hope we shall make some money by our celebrations, besides the impression to be made on the minds of the people.[13]

Beginning July 5, the *Liberator* implored "the Friends of Freedom in Middlesex and the Neighboring Counties . . . to meet at Concord . . . to celebrate the anniversary of the emancipation of 800,000 slaves in the British West Indies." Festivities were scheduled to begin at 11:00 a.m.; for twenty-five cents, guests could enjoy a picnic excursion to Walden Woods. The *Concord Freeman*, though a good deal more reserved, announced the event as well: "There will be a gathering of the friends of freedom at Concord, on the 1st of August. . . . The occasion is a jubilee at which all can attend, whatever may be their peculiar views." Similar gatherings in other towns competed with theirs, but Concord's program testifies to Brooks's skilled recruiting: Frederick Douglass, John Pierpont, Samuel J. May, Walter Channing, and Waldo Emerson had all agreed to speak. A month before the occasion, Brooks sent out a plea for additional speakers to abolitionist agent Loring Moody:

> We have selected a spot about 3 quarters of a mile from the depot, before you arrive at Concord. Will you speak to Lewis Hayden, Channing, and as many others as you can to come. The idea of having a celebration with no speakers is not to be endured. Now do out of mercy to us poor women try and help us all you can, and help us a little more than this not on account of our being poor low women. The grove we have selected is not quite equal to Dedham, but very pleasant notwithstanding, and very near the rail road. . . . I hope Emerson will say a word think he will. But we want some good speakers whose souls are fired with genuine anti Slavery, whose souls are bowed to the earth

with the position of our country, and whose words shall burn into the very joints and marrow of pro Slavery.[14]

An example that Brooks did not hesitate to exploit her gender for the sake of the cause, this letter more significantly attests to her doubt that Waldo Emerson's "soul [was] fired with genuine anti Slavery." Boston abolitionists shared her reservations. Indeed, based on such concerns, Anne Warren Weston sought to persuade Wendell Phillips to attend Concord's rather than a similar celebration in Hingham: "But I hope *you* will go to Concord. . . . I see Waldo Emerson gives the oration. Did Mrs. Brooks write to you about it? If she did not, I hope it will not prevent your going. There will be a long summer afternoon to be improved, remember . . . as Concord will be Emerson & Pierpont & White & nobody knows what other trumpery. If you are there, all will go strait but if not dear sister Brooks may be grieved & great mischief done to the *holy cause of Disunion.* This is merely a word in season." Despite Maria Weston Chapman's having urged him to do likewise—"Mrs. Brooks . . . is *very* anxious that you & all the Boston Friends should be at Concord the 1st Aug."—Phillips apparently did not attend either the Concord or the Hingham celebrations.[15]

The weekly announcements preceding Concord's August 1 gathering had omitted one crucial detail. Each notice promised that "the place where the meeting is to be held" would be published the following week, but this information never appeared. Evidently, as with the prior summer, the Concord Female Anti-Slavery Society had coordinated a gala but not a location in which to hold it. Barzillai Frost, no doubt still smarting from Frederick Douglass's recent attacks on the clergy as well as Wendell Phillips's fusillade that winter, denied use of the First Church, as did the Trinitarian and the Universalist ministers. According to Sarah Alden Ripley, everyone in town knew of the crisis:

> Tomorrow is the anniversary of the West India Emancipation, Mr. Emerson is to deliver an address but we do not know where for they cannot get leave to open any of the churches. Mr. E thinks it will not be a record honourable in the annals of the town of his ancestors. George with his usual spirit of charity makes excuses for them with those who refuse. He says he does not think it so bad in them . . . for the abolitionists have acquired for themselves of late much odium in Concord by their attacks on the church and the Constitution. It is said that Mr. Emerson would have been allowed to speak in some public building, if it had not been understood that he was to be followed by other speakers.[16]

The society's dilemma brought out the neighborliness of even those unsympathetic to its cause when Nathaniel and Sophia Hawthorne offered the use of the Old Manse's expansive lawn for the luncheon. Ultimately, rain put an end to that option, and the crowd gathered in the courthouse—"we *took* the Court-house," female society member Anne Whiting boasted—setting the stage for Henry Thoreau, just returned that day from an excursion to the Berkshires, to star in a scene memorialized by Whiting for the *Herald of Freedom*:

> In passing I must recount to you an amusing circumstance. There was an unusual difficulty about ringing the bell of the Unitarian Meeting-house, and those who never hesitated before, now shrunk back, and did not dare to attempt it. Five or six individuals who were asked, declined for one or another reason. Your friend, David Henry Thoreau . . . seeing the timidity of one unfortunate youth, who dared not touch the bell rope, took hold of it with a strong arm; and the bell, (though set in its own way,) pealed forth its summons right merrily.—This reluctance among those timid gentlemen to ring the bell seems to me very amusing. One of them went to ask *leave* to ring it of one of the committee who take charge of the meeting-house, but not finding him at home, declined taking action on the subject.

Thirty-year-old Whiting makes it abundantly clear that she envied Thoreau his daring gesture:

> If I had been there, woman as I am, I would have *tried* to ring it, and do not doubt I should have succeeded. I should see my way clear to do so on this ground, if no other. No one asks leave to ring the bell for *fires*. Anti-slavery meetings have been distinguished for their "incendiary" character from the beginning. We should ring out the summons to Church and State to come and put out this fire which is doubly dangerous because it burns in the *hearts* of the people, and invariably makes its way through their pockets, so near and dear to the heart of New England![17]

Whiting then turned her descriptive powers to the day's speakers and marked the "sublime moment" when Waldo Emerson joined "our cause":

> Behold the speaker before you. He appears for the first time on the antislavery platform. You expect that he will look at his subject from an intellectual point of view merely; that he will give an impartial judgment on the merits & the faults of abolitionism, & stand on a clear eminence above the dust and turmoil of the movement. But not so.—Behold he has deceded among us.— —He grasps our hands with warm and earnest pressure and says,— "Brothers, I have come to enter with you into this holy war."

With this pronouncement, Whiting confirms Mary Brooks's belief as to the importance of Waldo Emerson's alliance with the antislavery "cause." Emerson had not spoken out against slavery since his brief remarks in November 1837, seven years prior. Since then, Mary Brooks and Lidian Emerson had steadily prodded him to accommodate abolitionism within his ideological framework of self-culture, an ongoing struggle he depicted in his journal that year: "My Genius loudly calls me to stay where I am, even with the degradation of owning bankstock and seeing poor men suffer whilst the Universal Genius apprises me of this disgrace & beckons me to the martyr's and redeemer's office." Despite having been the lead signatory on an anti-slavery petition earlier that year, Emerson remained doubtful about the effectiveness of collective reform: "Does not he do more to abolish Slavery who works all day steadily in his garden, than he who goes to the abolition meeting & makes a speech? The antislavery agency like so many of our employments is a suicidal business."[18]

Regardless of such misgivings, the two-and-a-half-hour speech that Emerson delivered at the female society's August 1 gathering is generally heralded as his first major antislavery address, marking a decided swing toward abolitionism. Emerson opened "An Address . . . on . . . the Emancipation of the Negroes in the British West Indies" appropriately enough by reviewing the turmoil that had finally convinced Great Britain to emancipate West Indian slaves a decade earlier. He "point[ed] to the bright example which England set . . . ten years ago" and proclaimed that the "conscience of the country" had now been similarly aroused in the United States. Slavery *will* be abolished here too, Emerson assured his listeners. Yet compared to Douglass and others who offered what Garrison applauded as "forcible addresses" that afternoon, Emerson's conviction seemed tame to the editor, "a very satisfactory and able performance."[19]

To prepare his speech, Emerson consulted various historical resources regarding both the slave trade and the success of British abolitionism, including Thomas Clarkson's *The History of the Rise, Progress, and Accomplishment of the Abolition of the African Slave Trade by the British Parliament,* James Thome and Horace Kimball's *Emancipation in the West Indies,* and other works documenting slavery's atrocities. Certainly, these authors detailed the abuses of slavery in the British colonies, but Emerson could have consulted sources much closer to home, such as Theodore Weld's acclaimed compendium *American Slavery As It Is* (1839) and Lydia Maria Child's *An Appeal in Favor of that Class of Americans Called Africans* (1833), a book still hailed as the "first full-scale analysis of the slavery question." Both works would have acquainted Emerson with the uniquely brutal conditions attendant with contemporary slavery in the United States as compared to past practices in other countries.[20]

Likely, Emerson limited his research in order to focus on the occasion, which was, after all, the anniversary of West Indian emancipation. Prior to prescribing Britain's example of abolition for the United States, however, Emerson had cited a few examples of the violence suffered by southern slaves, making it all the more curious that he avoided contemporary sources that could have provided a comprehensive overview of slavery in his own country. Margaret Fuller, who attended the August 1 celebration, offered flattery for "Waldo's oration . . . great heroic, calm, sweet, fair," but its import for her confirms the distant past and British rather than American slavery as its focus: "It was true happiness to hear him; tears came to my eyes. The old story of how the blacks received their emancipation: it seemed as if I had never heard before: he gave it such expression." Although similarly moved by Emerson's speech, another woman in the audience, Laura Hosmer, reflected on slavery closer at hand: "O may the glorious time soon arrive when we shall not only rejoice over West Indian Emancipation, but when all the sorrowing ones in our own country, may raise their heads, long bent low beneath the yoke of the oppressor, and join the general rejoicing." By August 1844, Waldo Emerson had indeed become convinced of the moral iniquity of slavery, but his message this day emphasized the steady, forward "progress in human society," as well as what Carolyn Sorisio argues was to him the inexorable fact of "racial difference" and "permanent racial victimization." To the slaves, despite admiring insurrectionary leader Toussaint Louverture, Emerson seemed to counsel patience rather than revolt: "I assure myself that this coldness and blindness will pass away. A single noble wind of sentiment will scatter them forever. . . . There is a blessed necessity by which the interest of men is always driving them to the right." From the immediatist position of Garrison and Brooks, he kept his distance.[21]

More important to Mary Brooks, however, than the words Emerson spoke this day was that *he* delivered them. Mary Moody Emerson felt similarly: "Here I am writing to the very Orator of this auspicious day to congratulate his condition." This odd accolade on Emerson's "condition" rather than on the speech itself underscores her belief that Waldo Emerson had appreciably altered his abolitionist perspective. Others apparently shared this view. In October, Mary Brooks presented Emerson with a medal on behalf of national abolitionists: "Emerson seems to have arrived, in what he says of the necessary disposition of heart for the prosecution of the cause (antislavery) to the same conclusion to which the American Society came when the idea was presented by Garrison, and which is so highly esteemed among us that it was the one selected for the medal." In conveying this honor, Brooks drove home to Emerson that the radicals now claimed him as one of their own.[22]

Female society members may have rejoiced that Emerson now shared their cause, but publicity of the August 1 event lambasted the town while complimenting his speech. The August 16 *Liberator* ran Emerson's address on the front page; the prior week, Garrison bewailed the poor turnout but applauded the women who brought off "a large and spirited meeting" in spite of the "disgrace" that "no meeting-house could be obtained. . . . This is *the* Concord of revolutionary renown—Concord 'in the year of our Lord one thousand eight hundred and forty-four, and in the sixty-eighth year of American Independence'! Its ancient patriotism has utterly perished." Garrison singled out Mary Brooks as the event's orchestrator in a public gesture that must have thrilled her:

> Yet, proud and obdurate as Concord is, there are some great and good spirits within its limits, whose fidelity to principle and devotion to the cause of bleeding humanity are worthy of universal fame. Among these it is not invidious to mention the honored name of a BROOKS—a lady who, for a number of years, has given herself to the work of emancipation with an unreservedness of spirit, a steadfastness of purpose, and a serenity and nobleness of soul, unsurpassed by any whose deeds are recorded on the scroll of Christian philanthropy.

Obviously, Garrison divined the source of reform power in Concord.[23]

Waldo Emerson remained conflicted about his West Indian address, nearly apologizing for it a few months later to his (proslavery) British friend Thomas Carlyle: "Though I sometimes accept a popular call, & preach on Temperance or the Abolition of slavery, as lately on the First of August, I am sure to feel before I have done with it, what an intrusion it is into another sphere & so much loss of virtue in my own." Still, Emerson did not object when the female society enlisted Henry Thoreau's help in arranging for the speech to be issued as a pamphlet. In a self-designation that calls into question the conventional view that Thoreau disparaged all organized reform, he signed himself "agent for the Society" when negotiating with publisher James Munroe.[24]

Before the year was out, circumstances touching those Emerson loved propelled him and other moderates closer to the radicals as Concord responded to a personal outrage from the Slave Power. At the end of November 1844, as emissary from the Massachusetts governor, Concord's Samuel Hoar traveled to Charleston, South Carolina, to register an official objection to the southern state's policy of imprisoning free blacks who entered Charleston aboard northern ships. Such laws had been on the books for years as southerners attempted to combat the frequency with which slaves escaped via the sea. Recently, however, not only were black sailors imprisoned, but South Carolina law now permitted these men to be auctioned as slaves if unable to validate their free status. Moreover, ship captains were now required to pay the expenses of their sailors' incarceration. Federal judges as well as northern legislators protested these practices to no avail; thus, Massachusetts lawmakers decided to dispatch agents to investigate before pursuing legal action.[25]

Samuel Hoar—known for conservative politics and a formal, restrained demeanor—seemed a perfect envoy for the mission. His daughter, Elizabeth, accompanied him, intending to visit family friends in Charleston. Once there, however, it became clear that ambassador Hoar would not be allowed to perform his official duties. Relations between North and South had been increasingly hostile for more than a decade, but with antislavery petitions still pouring in to Congress, headlines trumpeting "No Union with Slaveholders," and stepped up calls for slaves to flee their condition, the situation had grown dangerously tense. On his arrival, Samuel Hoar sent a letter to Governor James Hammond, explaining his mission and asking to meet, a preliminary missive that suggests Hoar expected a negative response: "The Governor of Massachusetts has appointed me an agent of that State, to execute the purposes above mentioned; and I arrived in this city this morning for that purpose. I do not know that your Excellency will consider it proper in any way to notice this subject, yet propriety seemed to require the communication." South Carolina's animosity toward northerners who ventured south to inspect its laws was such that neither the mayor of Charleston nor Governor Hammond could afford even to follow appropriate protocol with Hoar. A local sheriff put it bluntly: "It is considered a great insult on South Carolina by Massachusetts to send an agent here on such business. This city is highly incensed; you are in great danger, and you had better leave the city as soon as possible."[26]

Governor Hammond did relay Hoar's request to state legislators, who immediately branded Hoar "the emissary of a Foreign Government, hostile to our domestic institutions, and [who had come] with the sole purpose of subverting our internal police." South Carolina lawmakers further resolved that Hoar "is to be regarded in the character he has assumed, and to be treated accordingly"; they called on the governor "to expel from our territory the said agent," ensuring the full thrust of the affront. In the midst of these proceedings, both Samuel and Elizabeth Hoar faced threats and taunts from furious locals. Their friends in Charleston implored them to abandon the mission, but insulted to the core and honestly declaring he was "no abolitionist," Hoar initially refused to budge, insisting he would leave only after delivering his message to Governor Hammond in person. But a week of escalating intimidation forced him and Elizabeth to retreat to safer lodgings, and the obdurate New Englander finally realized the futility of carrying out his charge. Elizabeth bade a blunt farewell to their friends: "I find myself suddenly though not unexpectedly so occupied with the public hospitalities of Carolina that I am unable to acknowledge properly the kindness I have received from individuals. I must therefore beg you to accept my thanks for your politeness during our short visit, & hope that we may have an opportunity of renewing our acquaintance in free Massachusetts." After a week's stay, the Hoars were unceremoniously escorted from Charleston.[27]

Reports of their own esteemed emissaries so discourteously ushered from

South Carolina did not sit well in the North. Boston and New York newspapers reprinted the letters exchanged between Hoar, Governor Hammond, and South Carolina legislators, as well as the resolutions condemning Hoar's agency. The antislavery press naturally took the grimmest view of the affair, with related stories appearing in the *Liberator* for weeks. One letter to the editor characterized the incident as touching off "the final contest between the North and the South"; the Salem, Massachusetts, *Observer* reported that Hoar would likely "have been HANGED, but for the entreaties and protection of a few personal friends at Charleston." Once home, Hoar expressed his chagrin before a town meeting, his demeanor illustrating the patrician personality that Henry Thoreau once distinguished as "an unconquerable stiffness in a well-meaning & sensible man."[28]

The *Liberator* carried Hoar's report on the thwarted mission, including the fact that the investigation into the wrongful imprisonment of black Massachusetts sailors had been totally derailed. Except for this mention of his trip's sole objective, Hoar and other northerners were far more preoccupied with the personal insult of his expulsion than with the likelihood that free black men remained incarcerated in a slave state. Waldo Emerson's journal commentary likened the incident to a playground contest among bullies: "Every Carolina boy will not fail to tell every Massachusetts boy, whenever they meet, how the fact stands. The Boston merchants would willingly salve the matter over, but they cannot hereafter receive Southern gentlemen at their tables, without a consciousness of shame." Likewise, other northerners focused on the dishonor to Massachusetts: "The expulsion of Mr. Hoar from Charleston—how will Massachusetts bear the insult?" queried one *Liberator* correspondent. At the town meeting, Concord's Barzillai Frost, whose First Church was still closed to abolitionist speakers, offered "resolutions so fiery, so fiercely redolent of disunion, independency, and Massachusetts dignity, so sadly blood and thundrous that the committee, Mr. May, Secretary Palfrey, Mr. Emerson . . . would not report them." One abolitionist who attended the Concord town assembly did call attention to the misplaced outrage: "I did not expect much from the meeting," expressed William A. White in the *Liberator*, "for its anti-slavery was based on selfish principles. The people would not care, if all the slaves were murdered; but when the slaveholders begin to kick *them*, it is quite a different case, and something must be done."[29]

Apparently more effective than Mary Brooks's harangues, this offense to his friends brought Waldo Emerson to the brink of disunion—"Let us not pretend an union where union is not," he asserted—a stance he had rejected months earlier. Emerson especially bristled at suggestions that Hoar had retreated in disgrace:

> Mr. H. has behaved with the utmost temper, wisdom and firmness. . . . He steadily refused to leave the city, and declared to all parties his determination

to remain at every risk until he could execute the objects of his mission, and only left the city at last when the popular assemblage, of whose approach and intentions he had been formerly notified, came to his hotel "to conduct him to the boat"; go he must, and he had only the alternative to walk on his feet to the carriage which waited for him, or be dragged to it. . . . He has done all that man could do in the circumstances, and has put his own state in the best position which truth and honor required.[30]

Emerson continued to sulk over the next days: "If we could bring down the N. Eng culture to the Carolina level if we were cartwhip gentlemen it might be possible to retaliate very effectively, and to the apprehensions of Southerners. Shut up Mr Calhoun and Mr Rhett when they come to Boston as hostages for the mulattoes & negroes they have kidnapped from the caboose & the cabin of our ships. But the N. Eng. culture is not so low."[31]

Sarah Alden Ripley's version of the incident suggests that at least some in Concord had hoped that Hoar would refuse to leave Charleston:

Mr. Hoar is to stay and to test the constitutionality of the law by bringing a suit in the first case that shall occur. The papers of yesterday announce that the news of his mission was received with great demonstrations of violence on the part of the legislature, they declaring the interference of Massachusetts in the highest degree impertinent and that they shall maintain the law constitutional or not as a measure necessary to the public safety. I suppose you hear all this as I said before but one thing you do not read that Miss Elisabeth went with her father. That the abolitionists in Concord are exulting in the hope that Mr. Hoar unlike Elisabeth will be imprisoned to help along the good cause; but I rather think the Carolinians will not be so impolitic to gratify them so far.[32]

Even as he excited his community's sympathies, however, Hoar declined to associate closer with the abolitionists. When the state antislavery society invited him to recount his ordeal at its annual meeting in January, Hoar demurred on the grounds that such an appearance "might be imputed to a new-born zeal in the cause of liberty, produced by narrow and selfish considerations." With characteristic understatement, Hoar assured antislavery leaders of his continued commitment to end slavery: "Recent events have had no tendency to give me a more favorable opinion of this gigantic evil." Yet Hoar remained a generous donor to the American Colonization Society for years after the Charleston embarrassment.[33]

This humiliation of a local son roused antislavery passions, especially Waldo Emerson's, unlike any previous incident in Concord, a fact not lost on the radicals, who quickly exploited the episode to their own benefit. In January, the female society prevailed on lyceum curators to solicit another lecture by Wendell Phillips. Their refusal to invite Phillips this season had cost the lyceum Emerson's usual winter lectures; as Emerson explained in his journal: "The particular subject of Slavery had a commanding right to be heard in all places . . . the people must consent to be plagued with it from time to time until something was done, & we had appeased the negro blood so." Curator Samuel Barrett put Phillips's name forward once more at the end of February; his advance communiqué to Phillips reveals that abolitionists had laid their plans:

> I have been to see Mr. Emerson this evening and I find that he is somewhat anxious that an effort may be made next Wednesday evening to instruct the *acting curators* to invite you before the Lyceum to lecture on Anti-Slavery provided you can come as well any other time as next week. I told him we could not lose the opportunity of having you come to lecture if next week is the only time you can come next Friday evening Mr. Emerson will be at home and should you conclude not to wait until the Lyceum decides we should be glad to have you come at that time if it is agreeable—you will please to inform me before the next Wednesday evening that we may govern ourselves accordingly.[34]

As Barrett had anticipated—indeed had rather hoped—a coup took place at the next lyceum meeting. Lawyer John Shepard Keyes, carrying on the conservative mantle for his recently deceased father, objected to the invitation, but since Samuel Hoar had (not surprisingly) become noncommittal on the subject, Keyes found himself paired with Barzillai Frost as the lone dissenters. Frost may have been indignant over Hoar's treatment in South Carolina, but he loathed Wendell Phillips. Years later, Keyes blamed Mary Brooks, who joined the debate, for instigating the turmoil: "This time they didn't as they threatened to bring Phillips himself to put me down, but set Dr. Bartlett & Col. Whiting &c to advocate their cause. I always thought I had the better of that encounter, even if Mrs. Brooks their leader did contradict my statements in the open meeting with the words 'That's false Mr. Keyes.' "[35]

An exultant Barrett related to Phillips that the abolitionists' motion had carried:

> Although the clock has struck 12 I cannot defer longer of giving you a short account of the success which has attended our efforts to place the Lyceum on such free and liberal principles as to admit the subject of Anti-Slavery. At the close of the lecture I introduced the subject making a few remarks then moving that the members of the Lyceum request the Curators to invite you to lecture on Anti-Slavery. An amendment was offered by Doct Tewksbury that a committee be chosen to invite but wh[ich] would not accept the amend-

ment. A motion was then made by Doct Bartlett to dissolve the Lyceum he making a few remarks Also Frost & Keyes but the motion was lost. I then insisted upon my motion which brought Mr. Frost up and Oh! if you could have heard the charges brought against you after he had read some resolutions which were offered by you in May last at New-York you would probably have thought there was not much chance of your coming to Concord to lecture on Anti-Slavery.

The question was called for the vote was taken and resulted as follows *yeas 21* nays 15 I think—Mr. Keyes then resigned his office of Curator Mr. Frost did the same and so did Mr. Cheney the President A motion was then made to adjourn sine die and a vote was taken on the question those in favor were but very few while the president said the Lyceum was at end without taking a vote on the other side of the question although requested so to do. Thus ends my first chapter. My second will be much shorter—All those who were in favor of a free Lyceum were requested to tarry a few minutes A President pro tem was chosen and three Curators also consisting of Mr. Emerson Mr. Thoreau and myself—Mr. Thoreau declined—Mr. Emerson and myself I suppose are the curators to continue and end what Messrs Frost & Keyes did feel most like doing. Mr. Emerson asked me if I would write you and invite you to Lecture on next Wednesday evening before the Lyceum I consented—and will you please write an answer soon that we may make other arrangements if you cannot come. I should be glad were it not so late to tell you some things which were said by Mr. Frost. I will close by saying that if the friends of Annexation of Texas rejoice the Abolitionists of Concord have still more reason to that this question has been decided so favorably.

The next day, Emerson also dispatched an abrupt invitation to Phillips: "I am sorry if it annoy you, but excuse you the Concord Lyceum will not but awaits with erect ears the truth concerning Texas."[36]

The stage was thus set. On March 11, 1845, Phillips spoke to a Concord audience on the divisive topics of slavery and the annexation of Texas, an explosive situation over which abolitionists had worried for years, particularly since Tennessee slaveholder James K. Polk's election to president the past November. Later in 1845, over one hundred Concord women, led by Jane Thoreau, would submit an anti-Texas annexation petition; yet even as Phillips spoke, the subject was a fait accompli. Texas entered the union in December, the fifteenth state permitting slavery.[37]

Henry Thoreau was so roused by Phillips's speech in Concord that he fired off a letter, albeit anonymously, to the *Liberator*, which Garrison published on March 28 under the caption "Wendell Phillips Before Concord Lyceum." It opened by complimenting those who had insisted on hearing Phillips: "The admission of this gentleman into the Lyceum has been strenuously opposed by a respectable portion of our fellow citizens . . . and in each instance, the people have voted that they *would hear him.*" Thoreau also noted approvingly that one young woman "walked 5 miles through the snow from a neighboring town to be present on the occasion." As with Nathaniel Rogers, Thoreau most revered Phillips for bucking the tide of popular opinion. Indeed, as Thoreau portrayed him—with "few cracks or flaws in his moral nature," "unquestionable earnestness and integrity," and "freedom and steady wisdom"—Phillips embodied that most principled of individuals, a Transcendentalist: "He stands so distinctly, so firmly, and effectively, alone, and one honest man is so much more than a host, that we cannot but feel that he does himself injustice when he reminds us of 'the American Society, which he represents.' "[38]

In the public forum, Thoreau contended that Phillips had transformed the audience, but in his journal he comically recounted local opinion:

> "Well," says one; "He put it on to us poor Democrats pretty hard". "That's a severe dose" says another, "Well", responds the minister it's all true, every word of it." One of our most impartial and discriminating neighbors affirmed that he had perfectly demonstrated to his mind the truth of principles which he knew to be false. One elderly & sensible lady told us that she was much pleased—but as we inquired did you like it wholly every part of it—and she answered she must confess as she had heard but one antislavery lecture before she was not used to hearing the church so spoken of, but yet she liked it—and she was one of those who sit with honor under the very nave of the church.

This sketch reveals Thoreau's cognizance of a woman's open-mindedness versus the rigid preconceptions of his fellow townsmen. Helen Thoreau apprised Prudence Ward of the latest clash at the lyceum, reveling in the radicals' victory as well as her brother's moment in the spotlight: "Aunt Maria has, I suppose, kept you informed of our controversy with the Lyceum. A hard battle, but victory at last; next winter we shall have undoubtedly a free Lyceum. Mr. Emerson says that words cannot express his admiration for the lecture of Mr. Phillips. Did you receive the paper containing Henry's article about it?"[39]

. At the same time Henry Thoreau ventured into the public arena to extol Wendell Phillips, he had also committed himself to a self-improvement project that directed his attention inward. That spring he began to clear the pines, dig the root cellar, and erect the frame for what would become his private abode in the woods for the next two years. On July 4, 1845, Thoreau moved into a ten by fifteen foot cabin in the largely uninhabited environs adjoining Walden Pond on land recently purchased by Waldo Emerson, seeking there "to front only the essential facts of life." Among the many reasons for this move to solitude can be added a classic Thoreauvian withdrawal—Thoreau counterbalanced his attention to social reform with a pioneering experiment in individual improvement.[40]

Thoreau was not isolated from the outside world during his twenty-six months at Walden Pond. He frequently went into Concord; he stayed abreast of local and national events. Whether or not he attended a widely publicized antislavery meeting there that September, his family likely acquainted Thoreau with William Lloyd Garrison's blistering remarks that drew on Concord's historic setting. "I am for revolution," Garrison had cried: "Do not tell me of our past union, and for how many years we have been one. We were only one while we were ready to hunt, shoot down, and deliver up the slave, and allow the slave power to form an oligarchy on the floor of Congress! The moment we say no to this, the union ceases—the government falls." It was likely this speech that moved Waldo Emerson to pay a rare compliment to Garrison: "He brings his whole history with him, wherever he goes, & there is no falsehood or patchwork, but sincerity & unity." But surely no one was more elated than Mary Brooks by the editor's inflammatory words. To her mind, Garrison always revived the town's activism.[41]

Having succeeded, with Samuel Hoar's unwitting assistance, in bringing Emerson further into the fray, Mary Brooks now determined to keep him there. Thus, when she learned in November that curators of the New Bedford lyceum had passed a new policy seating blacks "in the North gallery," she took the news at once to Emerson, hoping he would call off his upcoming lecture there. This blatant racial segregation reversed the organization's accustomed practice and took New Bedford abolitionists by surprise. Their town boasted a sizeable black population and for years had been a generally welcoming port of entry for fugitive slaves. Months earlier, however, New Bedford resident Caroline Weston, sister of Maria Weston Chapman, had advised Wendell Phillips to speak there, discerning that "the public mind is charmingly disposed for an uproar." When lyceum curators voted two to one in favor of separate seating for blacks, Weston, advised by Phillips, made the strategic decision to contact Mary Brooks; as she informed Phillips, "I have written a full account of the matter to Mrs. Brooks & hope that Mr. E. may be disposed to refuse to lecture to the Lyceum under the circumstances—& if he will give his reasons in a letter to Mr. Greene."[42]

On learning of the new policy, Emerson rather mildly conveyed his objections to New Bedford lyceum secretary William Rotch: "This vote quite embarrasses me, and I should not know how to speak to the company. Besides, in its direct counteraction to the obvious duty and sentiment of New England, and of all freemen in regard to the colored people, the vote appears so unkind, and so unlooked for, that I could not come with any pleasure before the Society." Two days later, Brooks informed Caroline Weston that their maneuvering had succeeded according to plan:

I suppose it is about time to report to you the result of my missives to Mr. Emerson. I made him acquainted with the facts relating to the New Bedford Lyceum. . . . Mr. Rotch of your place wrote to Mr. Emerson, wishing him to appoint the time he would lecture before the Lyceum. Mr. Emerson replied, that he had received a statement of the expulsion of the coloured people from their accustomed privileges of being received as members, that if this statement were true, he could not lecture before this body. . . . I sincerely rejoice that Mr. Emerson has taken this stand and every friend of the coloured man will feel deeply grateful to him. I should not be surprised if they, the enemies of these poor despised ones, should endeavour to keep Mr. Emerson's refusal to lecture a secret. I apprize you of this that you may see that no false statement of the affair goes to Mr. E——, or if it does, keep me informed of the real truth.

Rotch countered that the new seating arrangements now permitted blacks to attend the lectures for free—"begging" Emerson to speak as scheduled, according to Weston—but Brooks assured her that Emerson would not renege: "You may say *from me* that Mr. E—will not lecture before the Lyceum." Further, Brooks encouraged Weston to spread the story:

I hope the report will go forth into every corner and crevice of New Bedford, that Mr. E. will not lecture before the Lyceum, because it treats those for whom it should care for above all others with scorn & contempt. I am amazed that those who pretend to believe in God's eternal law of righteous retribution could dare to do as they have done. And I am still more surprised that those whose hearts were so far penetrated with the wrong as to vote right, should not be willing to act consistently enough with that vote to sign the Protest and keep away from any participation in the doings of a body wh[ich] acts so wickedly and in a manner so despicably mean as they have acted. . . . I am sometimes selfish enough to regret ever having been an abolitionist, it has opened before me such a knowledge of injustice and wrong that my soul is at times crushed, and my reason reels, my faith in God is lost and I am for a while that most wretched of all beings an Atheist.[43]

More cogently than Emerson's circumspect note to Rotch did Brooks lay out the reasons for boycotting the lyceum. Her frustrations, however, remained private between the women. To Emerson, Brooks expressed only gratitude: "I wish the simple words I thank you, could be made to convey what I, as an individual feel for the part *you* have acted in this matter—sure I am I should impart to it a deeper meaning than it ordinarily conveys." For her part, Weston reported the women's triumph to Phillips: "This is what Ralph Waldo Emerson *has* done—I wrote to Mrs. Brooks as you advised . . . and kept them informed of the facts as they transpired. . . . Mr. Emerson replied that he had heard from friends & from common report that the Lyceum contemplated the expulsion of Colored people, &c.—& if this should be done *he* could *not* lecture." This epistolary flurry provides clear evidence that Brooks's sphere of influence in the antislavery movement now extended well beyond Concord. Her willingness to capitalize on her relationship with Emerson, and Weston's and Phillips's confidence that she wielded such influence with him, underscore a deliberate, tactical collaboration between these abolitionists. A few years later, Wendell Phillips paid homage to Brooks for her attentiveness to Emerson:

> I have wondered to see how the ablest and influential men are brought at last within the circle of this holy influence. There is Concord now, where Ralph W. Emerson lives, a man famous both sides of the ocean, and wielding by his pen a wide influence. I believe we owe all his interest in our cause to Mrs. Brooks and her half dozen friends. They have worked long, but lawyers, ministers, and all have been obliged sooner or later to bend to their influence.[44]

Interspersed with their victories, however, abolitionists were constantly reminded that most Concord residents, including friends and family, maligned their activities. In February 1846, Mary Brooks informed Maria Weston Chapman of her initial progress with a disunion petition she had been circulating at Chapman's request: "We have got between thirty & forty names to our petition. I have been labouring with Mr. Emerson. I ought to get him & S. Hoar, it is not decided yet in their minds. I have some hopes." What Brooks did not elucidate, however, was that she expected to persuade Emerson to sign after Samuel Hoar did so. But Hoar's refusal forced her to take another tack with Emerson. If she could not point to his townsmen's support for the petition, Brooks gambled that Emerson's abolitionist sympathies had progressed to the point where divine injunction and flattery might effect the desired end:

> I received the accompanying petition from the Boston friends, that I should obtain signatures to it in Concord. All the *I* which is in me rebelled, and I said "Lord send by whom thou will," but not by me. The command was, Obey! I went about it. Yesterday, Mr. Hoar being at home, I wrote him a note telling him that he had said again & again before the annexation of Texas, that in case that event took place, and was with all its horrors, or anything that might happen, would be greatly preferable to continuing in a union of robbery, perjury and extended oppression. That furthermore by his honorable endeavour, he had proved to Massachusetts, that wrongs & outrages offered to our citizens have no redress in the tribunes of this nation, that we are now slaves, and that there is great danger by our base submission to tyranny we

shall well merit our condition. And moreover that he knew well enough of the philosophy of reform to understand that men do not, in thus, move in masses, that the individual must first be sacrificed in order that there should be safety for the multitude. He answered that he could not sign the petition. Mr. Frost and Rockwood laughed about it. Mr. Brooks treats it with contempt, thinks his wife a very silly woman to have anything to do with it. Another minister to whom I applied, thinks it a foolish thing, in short every Whig instead of thinking it what it is, the plain dictate of common sense, and what even the instinct of self preservation would seem to point out pronounced it the most errant fanaticism. Now thought I, Mr. Emerson must be applied to. He is a man who has faith in moral principle, who believes that truth will subdue to itself principalities and powers, and moreover has the soul and courage, when he sees a thing to be right, to do it. Now if you, and a few like you, shall see what is demanded in this our nation's trial hour, we shall be saved. If on the contrary you do not, I shall comfort myself as I best may, by the inference which I shall draw, that God sees it yet necessary, by our destruction, to give to the world one more signal example of the awful consequences of injustice and oppression.

Apart from its illustration of Brooks's dramatic, soul-baring appeal to Emerson, this letter also evidences Nathan Brooks's "contempt" for both the antislavery crusade and his wife's leading role in it. That her husband joined his son-in-law Rockwood Hoar, the local clergy, and others in belittling her abolitionism had not, however, checked the activism of Mary Brooks. Indeed, as with her father's slaveholding past, such ridicule from her law-abiding spouse may have intensified her own commitment to antislavery action.[45]

When Emerson declined to sign the petition, Brooks next enlisted Lidian Emerson's help:

I think if he reads again the petition, his difficulty will be removed, for, as you will perceive, it asks men on coming out from the old government, to form one based on the self evident principles of the declaration of independence, and to carry out these principles fully. Now it seems to me, if these principles are thus carried out, the most extreme nonresistant would be a member of such a government, whether he joins it formally, or not for it would be a government "whose affairs would be peace, and whose exactors would be righteousness." . . . Please to present the petition to Mr. Bradford, your mother and Miss Ford, and any others of your family who are intelligent enough to do it.

Whether Emerson ultimately signed this petition is not known, but when the signatories appeared in the *Liberator* a few weeks later, they did include the names of twenty-four Concord residents, including Samuel Barrett.[46]

From his vantage at Walden Pond that first year, Thoreau watched his community register its objection to the Mexican War, "a naked grab for land cloaked in patriotic bombast," as Donald Yacovone has characterized it. Abolitionists were so dismayed by this military engagement—which had commenced in May 1846 and which they had been predicting since Texas won its independence from Mexico a decade earlier—that Garrison "wish[ed] success to the Mexicans, as the injured party, who are contending for their firesides and their country against enslaving and remorseless invaders." Abolitionist editor David Child avowed that the U.S. president "has no more right to enter Mexico, seize property, and slay inhabitants, whether Indians or others, than any citizen of the United States has to go into Great Britain and do it."[47]

A few weeks after the United States declared war on Mexico in May, a Concord delegation comprised of Helen and Sophia Thoreau, Mary Brooks, Anne Whiting, and Samuel and Susan Barrett attended the New England Anti-Slavery Convention in Boston. There they all signed an "Anti-War Pledge," promising "at all hazards, and at every sacrifice, to refuse enlistment, contribution, aid and countenance to the War." They did not possess the elective franchise that Henry Thoreau took for granted (although apparently never used), but his sisters nonetheless exercised their political clout in the public forums available to them. During his regular visits to town that year, Thoreau surely discussed the nation's turmoil with his family; perhaps he also mulled over the rhetoric of their antiwar pledge. He may have demurred from signing petitions and attending conventions, but Thoreau wholeheartedly shared his family's outrage over this unbridled military action. In *Walden*, Thoreau advocated "the unquestionable ability of man to elevate his life by a conscious endeavor," but the Mexican War obliged him to reconsider that goal in a new light: How should individuals "elevate" their own lives when injustices such as the Mexican War and slavery persisted? To what practical extent and in what specific manner should he "consciously endeavor" to resist such grievous moral wrongs?[48]

Thoreau's philosophy of individual reform was losing ground. In 1844, Nathaniel Rogers had been replaced as editor of the *Herald of Freedom* largely due to his increasing diatribes against organized abolitionism. Even Emerson, from whom Thoreau had absorbed the tenets of self-culture, now spoke more often, if not more fervently, to antislavery gatherings. Meanwhile, as his mother and sisters no doubt reminded him, slavery remained an economically thriving system with more than 3 million men, women, and children held captive. Walter Harding suggests that Thoreau may have sought examples of effective individual protest, finding inspiration in

Charles Lane's recent writings that justified nonpayment of taxes to a proslavery government. Perhaps prodded by the example of friends and the increased commitment of family, perhaps nudged by Prudence Ward or chastised by Mary Brooks, Thoreau may have concluded that his self-reform project at Walden could be mistaken for apathy. Whatever its motivation, Henry Thoreau's next action, at any rate, has become legendary.[49]

One evening in late July 1846, Thoreau walked in to Concord to pick up his shoes from the cobbler. Like his friend Bronson Alcott, Thoreau had refused on principle for the past few years to pay the $1.50 poll tax. Finally, the town jailer, Sam Staples, determined to serve him with a warrant for nonpayment of the tax, although Staples probably assumed Thoreau would pay up when faced with actually going to jail. When accosted, however, Thoreau (obligingly, as most enthusiasts have it) followed Staples to the imposing Middlesex County jail, a three-story stone edifice in the center of Concord, where he spent the night. Most sources credit a veiled Maria Thoreau with settling the debt for her nephew later that evening, although by then Staples was ensconced at home, bootless, and refused to go out again. How, exactly, the news of Thoreau's imprisonment traveled through town and reached the family is not certain, but Jane Hosmer recalled years later "that Mrs Thoreau went down to the aunts . . . and they were all concerned in the payment—Mrs.—Aunts Jane & Maria—though Maria was the one who went to the door, while the others waited near." Thoreau was reputedly angry when released the next morning that someone had paid the tax, but he completed his errand and returned to Walden Pond.[50]

An isolated happenstance, this jail stint became the framework on which Thoreau would construct a lucid argument for opposing an unjust government and illegitimate war. Regardless of the common perception, promulgated by John Shepard Keyes and other townsmen that Thoreau's protest— and Bronson Alcott's before him—was that of "silly, would-be martyrs," Thoreau would decisively posit the consequences that would result "if ten *honest* men only,—aye, if *one* HONEST man, in this State of Massachusetts, *ceasing to hold slaves*, were actually to withdraw from this copartnership, and be locked up in the county jail." At the time, Concord friends disagreed on the effectiveness of Thoreau's protest. Alcott, quite naturally, viewed the night in jail in a positive light—"a dignified non-compliance with the injunction of civil powers"—but Emerson deemed it "mean and skulking, and in bad taste," a condescension that undoubtedly speaks more to his disappointment with his young protégé at this time than to Thoreau's action itself. Emerson's own recent antiwar protest had been a brief Fourth of July speech in Dedham, where on the one hand, Emerson bemoaned "the political apathy of Massachusetts, and New England," and on the other reminded the audience that there were "other crimes than Slavery and the Mexican war." In his journal, Emerson waxed ambivalent about Thoreau's action:

"My friend Mr Thoreau has gone to jail rather than pay his tax. On him they could not calculate. The abolitionists denounce the war & give much time to it, but they pay the tax." Further, Emerson contended that "the abolitionists ought to resist & go to prison in multitudes on their known & described disagreements from the state." Nevertheless, Emerson's hypothetical debate with Thoreau concluded unsympathetically: "Refusing payment of the state tax does not reach the evil so nearly as many other methods within your reach. The state tax does not pay the Mexican War. Your coat, your sugar, your Latin & French & German book, your watch does. Yet these you do not stick at buying."[51]

The week following his night in jail, Thoreau extended his abolitionist identity as well as his relationship with the Concord Female Anti-Slavery Society by hosting its members and guests to his cabin site on August 1 for a second anniversary celebration of West Indian Emancipation. Thoreau did not mention this occasion in his journal, but he may be alluding to it in the "Visitors" chapter of *Walden*: "It is surprising how many great men and women a small house will contain. I have had twenty-five or thirty souls, with their bodies, at once under my roof." The *Liberator* announced the occasion's bucolic setting "in a fine grove about three quarters of a mile southeast of the Depot," and encouraged "all who love freedom and hate slavery" to turn out. Advertised speakers included William Henry Channing, Caleb Stetson, and Lewis Hayden, who had recently escaped from slavery in Kentucky and settled in Boston with his family. The *Liberator* also anticipated "that Ralph Waldo Emerson *will be heard*." True to Mary Brooks's earlier promise, the Fitchburg Railroad had transformed the three-hour stagecoach trip from Boston into an inexpensive hour. Moreover, passengers may have had her to thank for the marketing ploy that "reduce[d] the fare to Concord to half price, on the first of August, provided one hundred tickets can be sold."[52]

On August 7, an anonymous news account in the *Liberator* hailed the Concord event as "the best celebration ever had any where." The author's anxiety and pride suggest someone who helped organize the event, perhaps Anne Whiting or Harriet Minot, who had both previously reported on Concord's antislavery functions. From the warm, summer day to the like-minded reformers united by the shores of Walden Pond, the article depicted a scene of civic harmony: "The clouds in the morning, and the rain of the preceding day, made the air of the right temperature; the grove seemed the best of all groves. We had seats enough and to spare, plenty to eat, and a hogshead of good ice-water to drink. The very etherial would laugh at the latter enumerations; but never mind, we Abolitionists always attend to every thing, though we are people of but one idea." Absent neighbors were admonished:

The number present during the day was small; in the morning quite so. Concord people generally had to stay at home, for in common with the people of Massachusetts at large, they are obliged to abridge themselves of holidays, being busy in providing for the wants of their new sister Texas, and her interminable offspring. . . . Besides this, Concord people . . . have so lost all sense of that sacred word liberty, that you may shout it as loud as you please in their ears, and they will turn and give you a look, very similar to that of some superannuated person, from whose mind the memory of all those formerly dear has passed away.

The faithful who attended were cherished:

There were, however, a few who had yet some lingering sentiments of freedom beating in their bosoms—among them was seen the daughter of a signer of the Declaration of Independence, who by the irresistible law of sympathy is often drawn to gatherings like these, and who is yet to be drawn more and more. Then there were a very few farmers, who by the law were obliged to leave their hay, notwithstanding the bad weather we had had for so long a time previous; then there were about as many mechanics, one merchant, one lawyer, two physicians; and the ministers, much as has been said against them, on this occasion, God bless them! they did turn out well, particularly the Unitarians and the Universalists. The orthodox minister, though invited, did not attend; perhaps the same reason which made him desert last year, prevented his coming this, though the formidable name of Garrison did not once appear either in speech or on standard.

Although she favorably reviewed the day's speakers, including author and teacher Delia Bacon, Concord's Universalist minister Joseph Skinner, and Lewis Hayden, the reporter meted but tepid approval to "calm, philosophical Emerson, closely scrutinizing, nicely adjusting the scales, so that there should not be a hair too much in the one scale or the other, telling us the need be of all things."[53]

This pointed public censure toward townsfolk who stayed away, including the Trinitarian minister, reveals a more openly critical posture than in prior years toward the abolitionists' detractors, the reporter perhaps emboldened by the Mexican War's validation of the antislavery platform. But this account also underscores the fact that in Concord, radical abolitionism remained a minority effort. The men and women who called their community to task confronted hostility, racism, sexism, and—most predominantly—simple indifference. In contrast to the antislavery press, the *Concord Freeman* noted the low turnout for the occasion; quite behind the times, it exclaimed that William Henry Channing had advocated "the formation of a new Union and a new Constitution, and a dissolution of all fellowship with slaveholding!"[54]

As 1846 came to a close, abolitionists redoubled their labors despite the Mexican War that raged on. The Boston female society's fair that December was "more successful . . . than in any former year," the women raising more than four thousand dollars, a 25 percent increase over the prior year. That fall, responding to a fugitive slave's seizure from Boston harbor, abolitionists had convened a meeting, chaired by John Quincy Adams, to protest the possibility that this man would be returned to New Orleans. Invited to speak by an illustrious group that included Samuel Gridley Howe, Samuel Sewall, Charles Sumner, and Theodore Parker, Waldo Emerson apologized that he had nothing "useful or equal to the occasion" to say. As with his dominant emotion over the Hoars' expulsion from South Carolina, he seemed most disturbed by the "irreparable shame to Boston of this abduction." In mid December, Concord welcomed controversial husband and wife abolitionists Stephen and Abby Kelly Foster to speak. And at year end, the Alcott family provided refuge in their Lexington Road home to an escaped slave known only as "John."[55]

At the time, the Alcotts lived at "Hillside," not quite a mile east of the Emersons. According to Abby Alcott's journal, John had arrived late in December: "This month has been full of interest—Preparations for the 'Christmas tree' . . . The arrival of a Slave named for the present John—an inmate in my family untill some place where work can be provided—An amiable intelligent man just 7 weeks from the 'House of Bondage.'" On December 31, Alcott "rose early to give John his breakfast that he might go to his work by early dawn I was repaid for my effort by meeting God—the interview was short—but *real.*" A week later, Waldo Emerson noted a one dollar contribution "to runaway slave," almost certainly evidence that the Alcotts had solicited donations to help fund John's passage out of town. On January 13, Abby informed her brother that John had safely departed: "We have had an interesting fugitive here for 2 weeks—right from Maryland— He was anxious to get to Canada and we have forwarded him the best way we could—His sufferings have been great—his nature sickly—unparralleled."[56]

The next month, Bronson Alcott commenced his February journal with a lengthy entry on "Slavery," followed several pages later with details about a slave, presumably John, who had recently stayed with the family: "There arrives from the Maryland plantations a fugitive to sit at my table and fireside." Another week passed before Alcott disclosed further that "our friend the fugitive, who has shared now a week's hospitalities with us, sawing and piling my wood, feels this new taste of freedom yet unsafe here in New England, and so has left us for Canada." Alcott described this man as "scarce thirty years of age, athletic, dextrous, sagacious, and self-relying," and he appreciated the "impressive lesson to my children, bringing before them the wrongs of the black man." None of Bronson Alcott's several dated journal entries for January mentions this man, but critics have generally presumed that John, described by Abby in December and January, is the same escaped slave from Maryland whom Bronson describes in February.[57]

John's sojourn with the Alcotts gave rise to one of the most enduring stories about Henry Thoreau's service to the antislavery movement—that he hid runaway slaves at his Walden cabin. On Sundays this winter, Bronson Alcott trekked out to Walden Pond to spend the day with Thoreau; years later, Franklin Sanborn confidently stated that John had accompanied Alcott on one of these trips: "It was this slave, no doubt, who had lodged for a while in Thoreau's Walden hut." While certainly a plausible scenario, no other evidence corroborates Sanborn's claim, nor did Thoreau or Alcott mention John's visit to Walden. Yet Thoreau's own assertion in *Walden* that "one real runaway slave, among the rest, whom I helped to forward toward the northstar" has helped sustain the pervasive notion that fugitive slave(s) came to the Walden Pond cabin. Thoreau added this reference to the draft of *Walden* in 1852, when the number of runaway slaves passing through Boston and environs had increased dramatically. While the remote possibility exists that fugitives did seek Thoreau's help at Walden, this "real runaway" more likely represents the hundreds then fleeing north, some of whom Thoreau had definitely met by that time.[58]

As increased attention focused in the late nineteenth and early twentieth centuries on the figures of the antebellum American literary scene, the belief that Thoreau hid runaway slaves at Walden Pond persisted. In his 1878 biography, *Thoreau: His Life and Aims*, H. A. Page (the pseudonym of Dr. Alexander H. Japp) claimed that while at Walden, Thoreau "had, by his personal assistance, aided more than one slave 'towards the North star.'" Henry Salt made a similar assertion in 1890, but six years later, indignant "experts" convinced him to set the record straight: "I am informed . . . on good authority, that this is an error." Salt's retraction came at the insistence of physician and Thoreau enthusiast Samuel Arthur Jones, whose correspondence with Horace Hosmer, a contemporary of Thoreau, had persuaded him the story was a fiction. The irascible Hosmer dismissed as myth the idea that "there . . . was a 'Station' or a side track at Walden . . . it is *utter damned nonsense* to say so."[59]

But the next year another elderly memory complicated Hosmer's certitude. When Waldo's son, Edward Emerson, interviewed Concord Female Anti-Slavery Society stalwart Ann Bigelow, she reminisced that

> while Henry Thoreau was in the woods the slaves were sometimes brought to him there, but obviously there was no possible concealment in his house . . .

so he would look after them by day, and at night fall . . . get them to his mother's or (some) other house of hiding. . . . It was no part of his *plan* in making the Walden hermitage to make there a refuge for fugitives. That was only incidental. But when they came to him there, he acted more independently and by his own good judgment than while living in his mother's house. Then she had sway and he had only second place as helper.

Naturally, some fifty years after the facts, both Hosmer and Bigelow could have been partially if not wholly mistaken. Moreover, in a subsequent interview with Concord photographer Alfred Hosmer, a relative of Horace Hosmer, Bigelow maintained that Thoreau's "hut was *never* used as a station." Alfred Hosmer received additional confirmation to this effect from abolitionist Parker Pillsbury, a close friend of the Alcotts and Thoreaus, who responded in 1890 to Hosmer's query: "As to the Walden Cottage ever being in any sense; an *under ground Rail way Depot*, I must doubt it. We had Fugitive Slave lecturers like Fred. Douglass and Wm Wells Brown who would have called no doubt to see Thoreau at his Walden Cottage but no flying slave would ever have sought him there nor do I think Col. Whiting, or Mrs. Brooks, or Mr. & Mrs. Bigelow would ever have taken them there for concealment."[60]

While Thoreau scholars have not necessarily propounded this legend through the years, neither have they made the issue a matter of serious inquiry. Most investigators judge that Ann Bigelow's memory, however qualified by time and ill health, posits the more credible circumstances that Concord rather than Walden Pond "afforded infinitely more secure resting- and hiding-places for the fugitive slave," as Samuel Jones explained it. Nevertheless, Concord historian Allen French set down as fact in his 1915 book, *Old Concord* "that Henry hid slaves in his hut at Walden." Similarly, in her anecdotal *Memories of Concord,* published in 1926, Mary Hosmer Brown put forward "that many a runaway slave was hidden in the shack at Walden and driven under cover of darkness by Thoreau himself to the next safety post." In the mid-twentieth century, Wendell Glick and Walter Harding dismissed the tale as "fiction" and "tradition," yet as late as 1990, Paul Brooks cited Bigelow to propound once more the certainty that "at Walden, Thoreau helped to smuggle runaway slaves to his family's house."[61] The image of Thoreau rescuing desperate fugitives while living at Walden Pond has apparently proven too alluring to relinquish.

To be sure, the ghosts of Concord's racially bifurcated past did intrigue Henry Thoreau. In *Walden*, he reminisced about Cato Ingraham, a slave whose famous encounter with British Major Pitcairn at Concord's North Bridge on April 19, 1775 had become a local legend. Thoreau also admired Cato for bludgeoning to death a rabid dog who had terrorized the town and dispatched at least one respected townsman crying to the doctor after being bitten. Thoreau memorialized seamstress Zilpha White, who "led a hard life, and somewhat inhumane" on the outskirts of Walden Woods, and he benefited from the "apple-trees which Brister [Freeman] planted and tended." These "former inhabitants" permeate the environs in which Thoreau sauntered, yet by the time he moved to Walden in July 1845, he well knew that slavery's victims did not reside solely in the distant past. To some extent Thoreau's sentiments on race and slavery at this time reflect a condescension similar to Waldo Emerson's, as with this 1845 journal entry: "The degradation & suffering of the black man—will not have been in vain if they contribute thus indirectly to give a loftier tone to the religion and politics of this country."[62] Thoreau also frequently casts "slavery" in metaphorical terms, as for example with *Walden*'s pronouncement that "it is hard to have a southern overseer; it is worse to have a northern one; but worst of all when you are the slave-driver of yourself." But regardless of these similarities, Thoreau's few statements about race did not approach the complexity of Emerson's deliberations on the subject.[63]

By the autumn of 1847, after Henry Thoreau had left Walden Pond and returned to Concord, his more moderate townsmen had gradually but decidedly moved toward antislavery. Unlike their radical neighbors, however, these men trusted, as had the "new orgs" several years earlier, the political system to abolish slavery. By 1848, antislavery Whigs and Democrats came together, the old Liberty Party giving way to the Free Soil Party. The new party's convention that summer in Worcester, which attracted five thousand political abolitionists, was orchestrated by Samuel and Rockwood Hoar. The Free Soil Party made the antislavery platform more palatable to northerners, but Garrisonians still dismissed political solutions to slavery and held fast to their disunionist dogma, particularly in the wake of the Mexican War. But it was the disenfranchised immediatists who continued to dominate antislavery activities in Concord. William Whiting had circulated a disunion petition earlier that year and gathered nearly one hundred signatures, "42 legal voters, 50 non-voters," the latter being women. Nearly forty nearby locales submitted similar petitions, but Concord garnered a remarkably high number of signatories for a small town, offering a slight indication that the community's indifference to the antislavery cause was waning.[64]

A year later, in March 1849, a different kind of petition drive secured hundreds more Concord signatures when a free black man in Boston, Washington Goode, was sentenced to hang for the crime of murder. Allegedly, an intoxicated Goode had clashed with another black man over a woman. But Goode maintained his innocence, and his supporters alleged that the conviction rested solely on circumstantial evidence. They further contended that Goode had "been denied a trial by his peers, in consequence of a most cruel and murderous complexional prejudice."[65] Wendell

Phillips reminded audiences of reports contending that "had Goode been tried in some other countries, there would have been six black men on the jury." Given that no convicted prisoner had been executed in Boston for over a decade, and that no public hanging had occurred there in the past twenty years, those outraged over the racially motivated and biased sentencing felt hopeful that Goode's life would be spared.[66]

A statewide petition drive ultimately secured more than twenty thousand signatures calling for the governor to commute the sentence. In Concord, four hundred citizens affixed their names on a petition likely circulated by Anne Whiting. Signers declared the sentence "a crime in which we would under no circumstances participate, which we would prevent, if possible and in the guilt of which we will not by the seeming assent of silence, suffer ourselves to be implicated." Not surprisingly, many female society members signed the document, but so did moderates such as Nathan Brooks, and political naysayers such as Henry Thoreau, who exercised his right of petition at the very top of the document along with six other members of his family: Cynthia, Sophia, Helen, Maria, and Jane Thoreau, and Louisa Dunbar. Despite this overwhelming public opposition, Washington Goode—having failed in his attempt at suicide the previous day—was hanged on May 25 before "crowds of 'gaping idlers'" yelling racist epithets.[67]

During this agitated spring, Concord welcomed two lecturers new to the antislavery circuit. Fugitive slaves William and Ellen Craft, whose successful flight from south Georgia to Philadelphia the prior year brought instant credibility to the abolitionist message, had become celebrities at the state society meeting in January. The light-complected Ellen had disguised herself as a white man seeking medical treatment, bandages wrapped about her head, her arm bound in a sling so she would not be expected to sign hotel registers. William posed as her attentive servant, hovering constantly near his ailing "master." The couple's primary impetus for this risky thousand-mile escape was the fear that their children could be sold away from them. Their own lives assured them of this reality: At age eleven, Ellen Craft had been bestowed as a wedding gift to her white half-sister, while William and his sister had been mortgaged to a bank in reparation for the business losses of his owner.[68]

Former slave William Wells Brown introduced the couple at the state antislavery convention in late January 1849, a meeting Mary Brooks attended. Billed as "the Georgia fugitives," the Crafts embarked with Brown on a demanding lecture schedule, addressing New England crowds as often as five times per week. Maria Thoreau related their impending appearance in Concord in mid March to Prudence Ward, who was out of town: "Have you seen an account of a man and wife making their escape from slavery by the woman's enacting the master, and her husband the servant. I think their names are Crafts, Mrs. Brooks says their story is very interesting, and they are to come here tomorrow night to tell it." The couple no doubt received the same enthusiastic welcome in Concord as they had in surrounding towns; one listener reported that William Craft's "simple but graphic story drew forth repeated bursts of applause from the audience."[69]

Despite the warm welcome extended by some to such visitors, Concord was by no means free from race prejudice at this time. In November 1849, an astonished Maria Thoreau related this scene to Prudence Ward: "Last week some Indians from the Rocky Mountains exhibited here. . . . Sabbath P.M. the indian girl, which by the way was fine looking, went to Mr. Frost's church in company with a Miss Dodge, and was ushered into Mrs. Edmund Hosmer's pew, *who to* the surprise of many, immediately left it and took another, it was no sooner done than the Indian left the church and came over to ours, where she sat without any such demonstration." Thoreau obviously relished the tolerance of her Trinitarian congregants in contrast to the Unitarians' bigotry, but she also sought a motive to account for her neighbor's insulting behavior, perhaps the girl's "fantastical" clothing. Such an encounter makes more understandable Abby Alcott's appraisal of Concord in the late 1840s: "A cold heartless Brainless, Soulless place—It is very difficult to excite with thought, move into action, or warm with love, this stupid community."[70]

If his neighbors' were conflicted about race, Waldo Emerson remained just as divided. Increasingly drawn to antislavery ideas in principle, he nonetheless held to concepts that implied the superiority of Europeans and their cultures. In the mid 1840s, Emerson put forth this view of race:

> Ideas only save races. If the black man is feeble & not important to the existing races, not on a par with the best race, the black man must serve & be sold & exterminated. But if the black man carries in his bosom an indispensable element of a new & coming civilization . . . he will survive & play his part. So now it seems to me that the arrival of such men as Toussaint if he is pure blood, or of Douglas if he is pure blood, outweighs all the English & American humanity. . . . Here is the Anti-Slave. Here is Man; & if you have man, black or white is an insignificance.

Yet as late as 1848, Emerson penned this cryptic remark in his journal: "It is better to hold the negro race an inch under water than an inch over." Len Gougeon has plausibly interpreted this startling statement as a description of blacks' historical treatment rather than Emerson's own proscription, but the best attempts to contextualize this comment do not satisfy. A few lines below and under the heading "Races" on this journal page also appears the evolutionary bent of Emerson's thinking at the moment: "You cannot preserve races beyond their term. St. Michael pears have died out, and see what geology says to the old strata. Trilobium is no more except in the embryonic forms of crab & lobster." As a philosopher, Emerson clearly continued to grapple with questions of race and culture; as a social commentator he was less interested in the practical application of his theories, although he would stay marginally involved in the antislavery movement while privately sorting out what Laura Dassow Walls asserts was both a "biological" and "historical" conception of race.[71]

The antislavery community in Concord suffered the loss of a founding member when thirty-six year-old Helen Thoreau died of tuberculosis in June 1849. Although an account in 1970 portrayed her as "so quiet and unimposing that few seem to have remembered . . . this intelligent, humorless, homely member of the Thoreau family," William Lloyd Garrison felt otherwise. In a lengthy eulogy, he honored Helen's years of service:

> Our friend, Miss Thoreau, was an abolitionist. Endowed by nature with tender sensibilities, quick to feel for the woes of others, the cause of the slave met with a ready response in her heart. . . . She had the patience to investigate truth, the candor to acknowledge it when sufficient evidence was presented to her mind, and the moral courage to act in conformity with her convictions, however unpopular these convictions might be to the community around her. The cause of the slave did not come before her in its earliest beginnings; but as soon as it was presented, she set herself to inquire how it was, that a system which imbrutes man so cruelly, which tears asunder all the tenderest ties so ruthlessly, which puts out the life of the soul, by denying it the means of growth and progress so effectually, was supported. . . . she saw the church, almost universally, giving to the slaveholder or his abettor, the right hand of Christian fellowship—calling him dear brother in Christ. She saw the pulpits of the North open to Southern divines, while the advocates of the slave knocked in vain for admission at the door of almost every church in the land. She said to herself, Is this the church of Christ, and has it come down so low? She repudiated such a church. Immediately did she turn her back upon its communion, and if she went to the house of prayer, as she occasionally did, she went to see if the spirit of Christ and humanity might not be rising among them. Again and again she has called upon the writer of this notice, when returning from church, and said, with strong emotion, it is all darkness and gloom.

His testimonial closed with a sense of communal bereavement: "The abolitionists of Concord will mourn deeply her loss; for, few and feeble as they are, they can ill afford to lose one so intelligent and so true." Despite its scorn for the antiabolition contingent, this public praise reflected Garrison's regard for Thoreau, and once more positioned Concord women at the vanguard of local agitation.[72]

I quietly declare war with the State.

—Henry D. Thoreau, "Civil Disobedience," 1849

As they had predicted all along, the end of the Mexican War dealt a crushing defeat to the abolitionists. The Treaty of Guadalupe Hidalgo, brokered in February 1848, enlarged the United States by half a million square miles, southwestern territories into which slavery would almost certainly spread. Such was the charged climate that winter when Henry Thoreau twice delivered to an "attentive audience" at the Concord lyceum portions of an uncharacteristically political lecture, "The Rights and Duties of the Individual in Relation to Government," in which he decried the proslavery aegis of manifest destiny and contested the allegiance owed by individuals to an unjust government. At last, after a decade of immersion in the vocal abolitionism of family and community, Henry Thoreau now issued an urgent call to public action. No longer did he maintain that slavery could be abolished through self-reform. Nor, in a significant departure from Garrisonians, did he necessarily believe that slavery would be ended peacefully. Bronson Alcott took "great pleasure" in Thoreau's "well considered and reasoned" address, but when published the next year in the sole issue of Elizabeth Peabody's journal *Aesthetic Papers*—under the title "Resistance to Civil Government"—the essay generated scant and mostly negative attention. In fact, reviewers called "Civil Disobedience," as it is more commonly known, "crazy," "radically against our government," and more suited to the "Red Republicans" in France. Despite its eccentricity, a few readers did admire the essay's revolutionary nature; moreover, one reader exulted that "such a man as this breathes and lives in New England."[73]

Unlike Thoreau's previous tributes to abolitionists Nathaniel Rogers and Wendell Phillips, "Civil Disobedience" had not been hurriedly thrown together, but had been composed and refined since the incident that spawned it. Journal entries in the days following Thoreau's arrest in July 1846 contain a few sketchy notes railing against the state—"the only highway man I ever met"—but the essay did not fully take shape until Thoreau moved back to Concord, living again in the Emerson household while Waldo was abroad. In addition to Lidian Emerson's presumed influence, another likely impetus for "Civil Disobedience" may have been Thoreau's desire to balance the family reform scales. Thoreau did not share his mother and sisters' penchant for public activism, but he had never discounted its effectiveness. In fact, during the Concord lyceum's three debates in 1841 on the question "Is it ever proper to offer forcible resistance?", Henry and John Thoreau, Jr. had twice argued the affirmative position, joined, ironically enough, by Samuel Hoar as they sparred with Bronson Alcott, who took the opposing side. In "Civil Disobedience," Thoreau set forth his position on the current political unrest; he cited neither the disunion resolution signed by Cynthia, Helen, and Sophia, nor the antiwar pledge affirmed by both sisters, but his essay clearly endorsed the extremist stance of both documents. While, as most sources agree, Maria Thoreau paid the tax that sprang her nephew from jail, she and other female society members must have smiled when they heard Henry Thoreau deliver a condemnatory polemic so directly aligned with their own longstanding views.[74]

"Civil Disobedience" has easily rivaled *Walden* as the most read, most influential—and most misinterpreted—work of Henry Thoreau's literary canon. Its impact has been striking. In the twentieth century, both Mohandas K. Gandhi and Martin Luther King, Jr., cited the essay's influence on their respective crusades for civil rights. King contended "that what we were preparing to do in Montgomery was related to what Thoreau had expressed." As much as Thoreau inspired these courageous men in their campaigns of nonviolent social change, however, "Civil Disobedience" can simultaneously be construed to promote anarchy ("that government is best which governs not at all"); insurrection ("I think that it is not too soon for honest men to rebel and revolutionize"); violence ("I quietly declare war with the State"), and, assuredly, civil disobedience ("I say, break the law"). But too often, these and other pithy one-liners have been dislocated from the political context of 1849 in order to validate a range of agendas. Indeed, Jerome Lawrence and Robert E. Lee declared in their 1970 play, *The Night Thoreau Spent in Jail*, that "the man imprisoned in our play belongs more to the 1970's than to the age in which he lived." Further, Michael Meyer contends that scholars have also transferred their own ideologies to the author of "Civil Disobedience"—from the "thoroughgoing pacifist" of historian Arthur Schlesinger, Jr., to the "philosopher of freedom" acclaimed by Thoreau Society founder Walter Harding, to the principled rebel who inspired Danish resisters in World War II and freedom fighters in South Africa, to the "greatest American Anarchist," in the words of Emma Goldman.[75]

Howard Zinn has recently defined "civil disobedience" quite simply: "The deliberate violation of a law in pursuit of some social goal." The narrator of "Civil Disobedience" addressed readers directly: "What, for instance, it behoves a man to do here in America to-day with regard to slavery," to which he had already posited a response: "I answer that he cannot without disgrace be associated with it. I cannot for an instant recognize that political organization as *my* government which is the *slave's* government also." Thoreau does not yield; there is no middle ground: "If I have unjustly wrested a plank from a drowning man, I must restore it to him though I drown myself." Here, at last, was Henry Thoreau's antiwar pledge, his unique "immediatist" platform that echoed Garrison's castigation of the U.S. Constitution as "evil" and rejected common arguments for gradual emancipation: "This people must cease to hold slaves, and to make war on

Mexico, though it cost them their existence as a people." But in place of Garrison's symbolic "disunion," Thoreau articulated a personal dissolution and advised individuals to secede from the state: "Some are petitioning the State to dissolve the Union. . . . Why do they not dissolve it themselves,—the union between themselves and the State,—and refuse to pay their quota into its treasury? Do they not stand in the same relation to the State, that the State does to the Union?"[76]

Significantly, despite his own act of nonviolent resistance—refusing to pay his tax and going to jail—Thoreau did not rule out other modes of protest. Nancy Rosenblum correctly views Thoreau's act at this time as a "personal strategy, not principled opposition to returning force with force," a conclusion shared by others. In fact, even as he recommended his example of passive resistance, Thoreau recognized the improbability of attaining his idealistic goal. Examples of his conflicted deliberations appear throughout the essay. "The definition of a peaceable revolution" is succeeded by the caveat "if any such is possible"; to one rhetorical query, "but even suppose blood should flow?", Thoreau counters with another, "Is there not a sort of blood shed when the conscience is wounded?"; and although he "quietly declare[s] war with the State, after my fashion," he "will still make what use and get what advantage of her I can." These word choices— "revolutionize," "war," "refuse allegiance"—reflect that in 1848, Thoreau foresaw the eventuality when civil resistors might, and perhaps should, act forcefully. To be sure, "Civil Disobedience" presents a model of nonviolent civil protest. But at this phase of honing his political reform methodology, Thoreau has acknowledged—and does not condemn—the likelihood that his tactic will fail and other approaches succeed. And in true Thoreauvian fashion, he reserves the option to change his mind: "This, then, is my position at present."[77]

"Civil Disobedience" appeared in print at a time when abolitionists remained apprehensive about the prospects for immediate emancipation. Few achievements bore out Waldo Emerson's congratulatory spirit as he addressed an antislavery crowd in August 1849, gathered yet again to commemorate the anniversary of West Indian rather than American emancipation. The end of the Mexican War had vastly expanded the boundaries of chattel slavery; in January 1848, the discovery of gold in Sutter's Mill, California had, as Stephen Adams and Donald Ross assess, "made the spoils of war even more attractive." Abolitionists' paltry organizational advances paled against the sobering reality that another decade was ending with the institution of slavery still indelibly affixed on the national map—years of resolutions, petitions, conventions, speeches, and occasional "action from principle" had provoked tempers, aroused sentiment, and generated tangible aid for fleeing runaways—but they had not materially altered the enslaved status of more than 3 million people. On the contrary, the North's increasing industrialization, particularly in textiles, augured an increased market for southern cotton. At the end of the 1840s, despite the plantation agricultural system's various land-use concerns, slave labor had in fact never been more vital to the nation's economy, measured in net exports and outputs. To be sure, as Garrison had pledged eighteen years before, he was being heard. But abolitionists could point to more political setbacks than triumphs nearly twenty years after his movement commenced. During the next decade their situation would further erode.[78]

Late in 1849, a twenty-seven year-old woman slipped north into Pennsylvania from Maryland's eastern shore after hearing her owners discuss the impending sale of her person. Harriet Tubman worked in Philadelphia for a year before returning south on the first of her hazardous rescue missions—this time to spirit away her niece and two children, then on the auction block in Dorchester County, Maryland.[79] Tubman's vocation as a "conductor" on the notorious Underground Railroad would soon be taken up by Mary Brooks and her female society compatriots as a new law made Concord and all abolitionists criminal conspirators against the Slave Power.

Figure 1. Concord Center in the Early 1860s. Courtesy Concord Free Public Library.

Figure 2. Mary Merrick Brooks, 1852. By Alonzo Hartwell, Courtesy Concord Museum, Concord, MA., www.concordmuseum.org.

Figure 3. Prudence Ward. Courtesy Concord Free Public Library.

Figure 4. Sophia Thoreau. Courtesy Concord Free Public Library.

Figure 5. Cynthia Dunbar Thoreau. Courtesy Concord Free Public Library.

Figure 6. Helen Thoreau, 1849. Courtesy Concord Free Public Library.

Figure 7. Ralph Waldo Emerson. Courtesy Concord Free Public Library.

Figure 8. Lidian Jackson Emerson. Courtesy Concord Free Public Library.

Figure 9. Henry David Thoreau, 1856. Courtesy Concord Free Public Library.

Figure 10. Lewis Hayden, circa 1858. US 5278.36.25* v. 14.
By permission of the Houghton Library, Harvard University.

VOLUNTEERS IN THE ARMY OF JUSTICE, HUMANITY, PEACE AND LIBERTY.

ANTI-WAR PLEDGE.

We, the undersigned, desiring to show our utter abhorrence of slavery, and of every act either of the State or of the individual, which means to support it,—and to bind ourselves, before God and the world, to side with the oppressed, and not with the oppressor, *hereby pledge ourselves*, neither by act nor deed to aid, support or countenance the Government in the War with Mexico; but at all hazards, and at every sacrifice, to refuse enlistment, contribution, aid and countenance to the War.

Eliza H. Taft	W. W. Rich
Mary M. Brooks	Joseph A. Whitmarsh
Susan Barrett	Asa D. Hatch
Mary Danforth	Mary Ann Ford
Experience Nickerson	Mary T. S. Gunnison.
Susan Baker	Wm. H. Gunnison
Origen Bacheler	Anne M. Whiting
Wm. Sears	Lemuel Morton
Mary Sears	Alex. Harvey
Helen L. Thoreau	Francis L. Capen
Sophia E. Thoreau	D. S. Grandin
Uriah Ritchie	Geo. W. Lowell
Sally G. Andrews	Reuben H. Ober
Joseph W. Porter	Granville Homer
Polly D. Bradish	John Sawyer
Abby Torrey	D. M. Foster
Harriet A. Marston	Geo. W. Simonds
Marianne Cabot	John Russel
Lydia O. Lefavre	John Clement
Eliza J. Kenny	Sidney Hall
Hannah B. Spooner	Sam'l J. Hallowell
Hannah H. Perry	Simeon Dodge, Jr.
Sarah J. Davee	Wm. Shew
Ambrose Wellington	Charles Russell
Lucy J. K. Wellington	Robert B. Rogers.
Olive W. Bacon	Samuel G. Gilmore
H. G. Wallinbard	Lewis Ford
Mary Adams	Richard Plumer
Mary C. Sanger	Noah Jackman
N. Chesley	T. H. Bartlett
Geo. C. Leach	J. B. Kendall
Amory Parker	Adam Oswell
Anna K. Byron	Richard Brinkley
Caroline Foster	E. S. Walker
C. D. Barbour	Geo. J. Peterson
Angelina F. Wood	Charles Osgood
Betsey D. Holmes	George Evans
Lucy R. Browne	Samuel Henry

Figure 11. "Volunteers in the Army of Justice, Humanity, Peace and Liberty." Concord women sign an "Anti-War Pledge," *Liberator*, June 5, 1846. Others whose names appear on the list include William Lloyd Garrison, Wendell Phillips, Maria Weston Chapman, and William H. Channing. Courtesy General Research and Reference Division, Schomburg Center for Research in Black Culture, The New York Public Library, Astor, Lenox, and Tilden Foundations.

Figure 12. Ann Bigelow. Courtesy Concord Free Public Library.

Figure 13. Franklin Benjamin
Sanborn, 1855. Courtesy Harvard
University Archives (HUD
255.703A).

Figure 14. Louisa May Alcott.
Courtesy Concord Free Public Library.

Figure 15. Abigail May Alcott. Courtesy Concord Free Public Library.

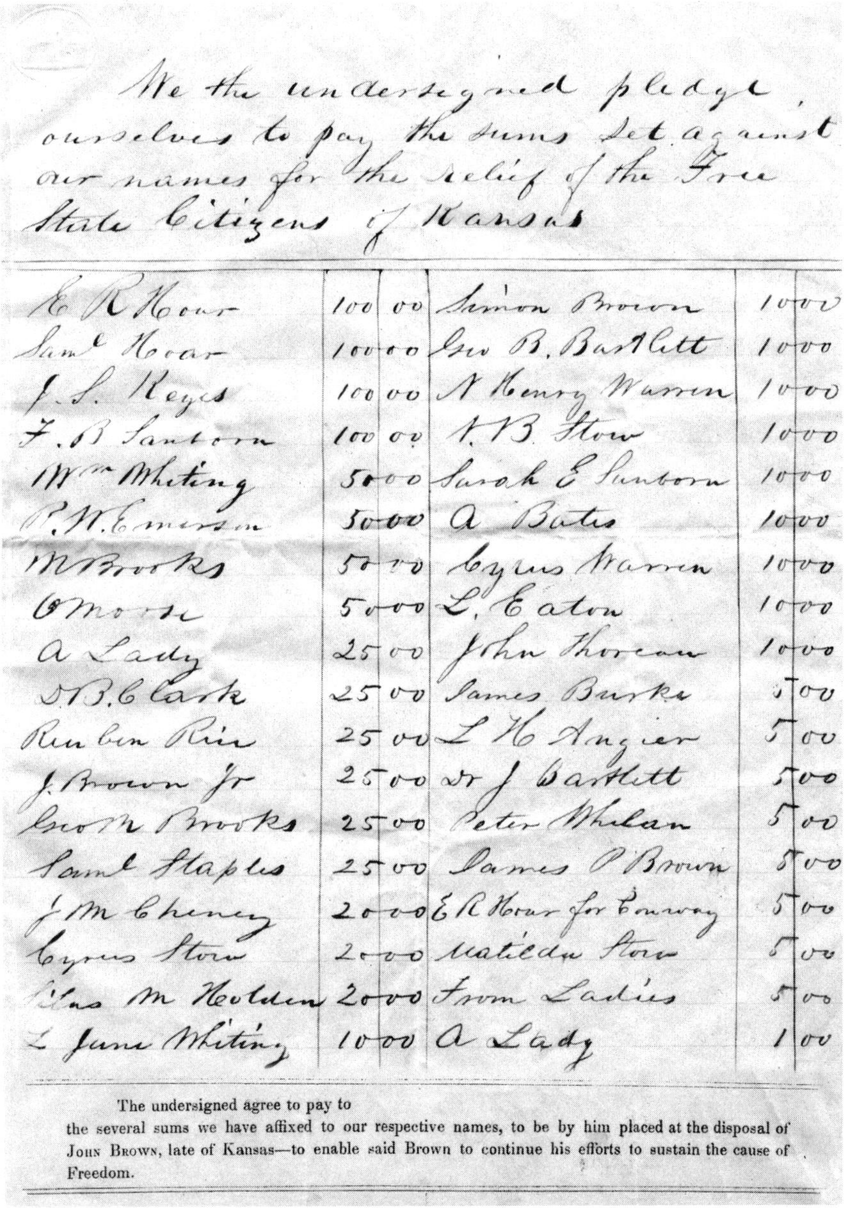

We the undersigned pledge ourselves to pay the sums set against our names for the relief of the Free State Citizens of Kansas

Name	Amount	Name	Amount
E R Hoar	100 00	Simon Brown	10 00
Saml Hoar	100 00	Geo. B. Bartlett	10 00
J. S. Keyes	100 00	N Henry Warren	10 00
F. B Sanborn	100 00	N. B. Stow	10 00
Wm Whiting	50 00	Sarah E Sanborn	10 00
R W Emerson	50 00	A Bates	10 00
N Brooks	50 00	Cyrus Warren	10 00
G Moore	50 00	L. Eaton	10 00
A Lady	25 00	John Thoreau	10 00
S B. Clark	25 00	James Burke	5 00
Reuben Rice	25 00	L H Angier	5 00
J. Brown Jr	25 00	dr J Bartlett	5 00
Geom Brooks	25 00	Peter Whelan	5 00
Saml Staples	25 00	James P Brown	5 00
J M Cheney	20 00	E R Hoar for Conway	5 00
Cyrus Stow	20 00	Matilda Stow	5 00
Silas M Holden	20 00	from Ladies	5 00
L Jane Whiting	10 00	A Lady	1 00

The undersigned agree to pay to
the several sums we have affixed to our respective names, to be by him placed at the disposal of
JOHN BROWN, late of Kansas—to enable said Brown to continue his efforts to sustain the cause of
Freedom.

Figure 16. Concord Subscription List for Relief of Free State Citizens of Kansas.
Courtesy Concord Free Public Library.

Figure 17. Ellen Tucker Emerson, 1872. Courtesy Concord Free Public Library.

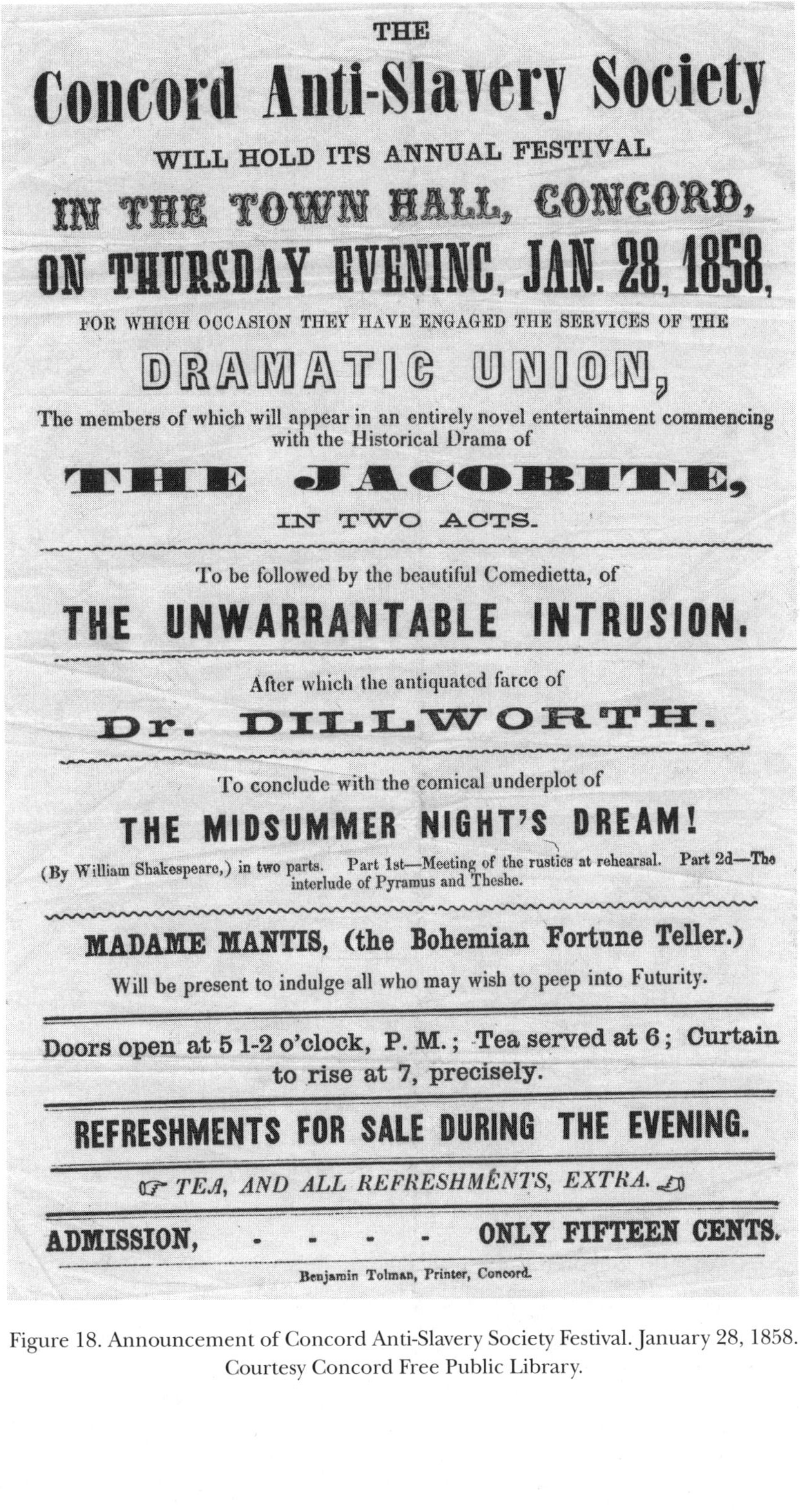

THE
Concord Anti-Slavery Society

WILL HOLD ITS ANNUAL FESTIVAL

IN THE TOWN HALL, CONCORD,
ON THURSDAY EVENING, JAN. 28, 1858,

FOR WHICH OCCASION THEY HAVE ENGAGED THE SERVICES OF THE

DRAMATIC UNION,

The members of which will appear in an entirely novel entertainment commencing with the Historical Drama of

THE JACOBITE,

IN TWO ACTS.

To be followed by the beautiful Comedietta, of

THE UNWARRANTABLE INTRUSION.

After which the antiquated farce of

Dr. DILLWORTH.

To conclude with the comical underplot of

THE MIDSUMMER NIGHT'S DREAM!

(By William Shakespeare,) in two parts. Part 1st—Meeting of the rustics at rehearsal. Part 2d—The interlude of Pyramus and Theshe.

MADAME MANTIS, (the Bohemian Fortune Teller.)

Will be present to indulge all who may wish to peep into Futurity.

Doors open at 5 1-2 o'clock, P. M.; Tea served at 6; Curtain to rise at 7, precisely.

REFRESHMENTS FOR SALE DURING THE EVENING.

☞ TEA, AND ALL REFRESHMENTS, EXTRA. ☜

ADMISSION, - - - - ONLY FIFTEEN CENTS.

Benjamin Tolman, Printer, Concord.

Figure 18. Announcement of Concord Anti-Slavery Society Festival. January 28, 1858. Courtesy Concord Free Public Library.

Figure 19. John Brown, May 1859. Courtesy Concord Free Public Library.

Figure 20. Francis Jackson Meriam, 1859. Courtesy Library of Congress, (LC-USZ61-747).

3

Upheaval in Our Town, 1850–1854

Here, in the humble recognition of the physical needs of humanity, we acknowledge our social ties also; and while smiles and words of good will and affection draw us together, a magnetic chain binds us, which forms the readiest and swiftest conductor for the lightning of true eloquence. If anti-slavery women earnestly desire to influence people who have hitherto remained passive, let them make these parties in every town throughout the State. A half dozen can set the ball in motion, and many a hand will afterwards help to roll it onward.

—Anne Whiting to William Lloyd Garrison, in the *Liberator*,
18 April 1851

The new decade opened with Concord abolitionists taking center stage at the Middlesex County Anti-Slavery Society meeting held in early March at the First Church—William Whiting was the organization's president, Minot Pratt served as secretary pro tem, Mary Brooks was appointed to the Nominating Committee, and Waldo Emerson addressed the gathering. Also on hand to advance several resolutions, including one that urged the "overthrow" of the Constitution, were William Lloyd Garrison and the fiery Parker Pillsbury. Tensions ran high this week and for good reason. Two days after this meeting, abolitionists throughout the country, but particularly in Massachusetts, would receive a severe blow when their cherished statesman, Daniel Webster, backed the reviled Fugitive Slave Law—the most divisive piece of proslavery legislation to date.[1]

In 1793, Congress had passed the first Fugitive Slave Law, which provided slave owners with rights in addition to those already granted by the Constitution to recover their escaped slaves. But as the antislavery campaign intensified in the early nineteenth century, some northern states had circumvented the older statute by enacting personal liberty laws, which among other things barred state judges from accepting fugitive slave cases, and prohibited state officials from helping to arrest runaways. By 1850, Senator

Henry Clay of Kentucky sought to diffuse these and other sectional tensions (resulting primarily from territorial acquisitions at the end of the Mexican War) by introducing an omnibus bill known as the Compromise of 1850, which included a revised Fugitive Slave Law that bolstered the penalties of the original law and made it far easier to recapture escaped slaves. If they could prove ownership, slaveholders could now pursue and capture their chattel property, none of whom could testify in their own behalf, from northern states. Specially appointed slave commissioners would preside over these cases, bringing to bear the federal government's enforcement arm and overriding existing precedent that state law alone regulated slavery. Moreover, these commissioners were handed an incentive to return rather than to free suspected runaways—ten dollars for every fugitive convicted, versus five for each case dropped for lack of evidence. Most galling to abolitionists, however, was the fact that any citizen could be compelled to aid in capturing slaves. Any person assisting or harboring an escaping slave faced "a fine not exceeding one thousand dollars, and imprisonment not exceeding six months." Twenty years after the *Liberator* had begun dispensing the horrors of slavery into northern homes, the Compromise of 1850 now made the paper's readers complicit with the Slave Power. Many who had heretofore trusted to the political system now converted to the immediatist ranks in earnest courtesy of the new Fugitive Slave Law.[2]

Although one resident later remembered the unpopularity of "antislavery sentiments" at mid-century, Bronson Alcott noted the altered climate in Concord by 1850: "Even Phillips and Garrison and Pillsbury are now listened to with some respect, and their doctrines and measures find favor from a very excellent body amongst us." The combative abolitionist Parker Pillsbury had lectured in Concord a few years earlier in company with fellow militant Stephen Foster, at which time Alcott had reported their small audience, not surprising given both men's flagrant contempt for the clergy and Foster's reputation for disrupting church services. But that Samuel Hoar, representing Concord in the state legislature in 1850, announced a goal of unifying northern political parties "in opposition to the further encroachment of the slave power" tellingly illustrates the immense sea change taking place as a result of the increasingly proslavery legislative climate. Hoar and other moderates, including his politically active son, Judge Ebenezer Rockwood Hoar (whose mother-in-law Mary Brooks most assuredly kept the abolitionist cause before him), maintained their erstwhile distance from the radicals, but these former adversaries now shared the objective of immediate emancipation. The principal difference between the two groups came down to strategy—the moderates persevered with the political machine, trusting that slavery could be abolished through the ballot, whereas the Garrisonians ratcheted up their calls for disunion. Regrettably, the extant records of Concord's antislavery leaders, particularly Mary

Brooks and other female society members, is more sparse during this decade than in previous years, evidence perhaps that the Fugitive Slave Law increased not only their activities but also their personal risk.[3]

Massachusetts's legendary senator, Daniel Webster, had served intermittently in the U.S. Congress since 1812. By the late 1840s, he was, according to biographer Irving Bartlett, "the most powerful single man in New England and one of the three or four most famous Americans in the world." Though always at odds with the Garrisonians, Webster had opposed the extension of slavery and, correspondingly, the annexation of Texas. He, like most Whig stalwarts, tolerated slavery as a flawed but obligatory compromise, the inescapable price of preserving the union—for whites. But when a substantial segment of his constituents aligned with portions of the immediatist platform and took to calling themselves "Conscience Whigs," the "Cotton Whig" Webster became increasingly isolated from his own party. By 1850, the senator's power had waned considerably.[4]

Senator Webster may have vacillated in the months since the Fugitive Slave Law had first been proposed, but on March 7, 1850, he threw his support to the bill in an address to Congress, "The Constitution and the Union," a rhetorical reversal that exhibited a glaring misjudgment of northern public opinion as well as Webster's ignorance of—or disinterest in—the political crisis fomenting in his own state. Many also surmised that Webster counted on the speech to conciliate southerners, whose votes he knew would be instrumental to a presidential bid. Thus, in his characteristically impassioned oratory, Webster affirmed that "a natural and original difference among the races of mankind, and the inferiority of the black or colored race to the white" justified the perpetuation of U.S. slavery. With his mantra—the union must be preserved—Webster concluded his remarks: "There can be no such thing as a peaceable secession," he foretold. Webster smugly chided northerners not to be "carried away by some fanatical idea," but to attend to their "constitutional obligations . . . to do all that is necessary for the recapture of fugitive slaves." Further, he urged "all the sober and sound minds at the North" to do their "duty," to consider the matter "a question of morals and a question of conscience." Webster realized that most northerners did not sympathize with the abolitionists, but this consummate politician miscalculated the extent to which they would resent a federal law authorizing slave owners to invade their state and reenslave their black neighbors and friends. At what Waldo Emerson termed "a fatal hour," Daniel Webster took a costly misstep from which his political career never recovered.[5]

Within days of the speech, public fury engulfed the North, decorum thrust aside as New Englanders condemned their treacherous senator. Wendell Phillips castigated Webster as one of "the greatest intellects God ever let the Devil buy," while Charles Sumner, soon to fill Webster's Senate seat, equated him with Judas Iscariot and Benedict Arnold. In Concord, Waldo Emerson vilified Webster's judgment as "the spray of a child's squirt against a granite wall," and for his small part, Henry Thoreau later inserted a caustic reference to "Webster's Fugitive-Slave Bill" into the draft of *Walden.* Yet not all of his constituents abandoned Webster. When the law passed, city officials sounded a one-hundred gun salute to him on Boston Common, while loyal clergymen reasserted biblical authority for the "divine sanction of Slavery," and defended Webster's "desire to cherish our Union as inviolable." But to most of his electorate, Daniel Webster never recovered from this ignominy. Certainly, state antislavery leaders shed no tears when he died two years later: "It is due to the Abolitionists and to the Slaves that it be known that they have no incense to burn before his shrine,—that Death has worked no change in their opinions of his acts and their detestation of his character."[6]

The Fugitive Slave Law took effect September 18, 1850. By mid October, approximately two thousand free blacks and fugitive slaves had left northern states; within six months, an estimated one hundred blacks had fled Boston; by the end of the year, the antislavery press in Canada welcomed thousands of new arrivals. Ninety percent of the alleged fugitives tried under the law during the 1850s would be remanded to slavery. The statute was flagrantly abused, but its lawful application led to the reenslavement of many blacks who had been living in free states for years, such as a Mr. Mitchum from Indiana who after living in that free state for nineteen years, was remanded to his "owner" and taken back to slavery in Kentucky, his wife and children left behind. Antislavery speeches now struck ever more incendiary chords, with exhortations to follow the "higher law" of conscience echoing Thoreau's call in "Civil Disobedience." When abolitionist William Bowditch lectured in Boston that fall, he queried his audience, "What is the highest test of moral truth? Is it to be found in the common consent of men?" To which Bowditch rejoined in Thoreauvian fashion: "It is the consciousness of each man's soul. Each man's soul is a law to himself."[7]

The month after the law passed, Mary Moody Emerson expressed dismay to Lidian Emerson at what struck her as Concord's silence about the new law: "Why have you not written to me anathamatising the odious *Bill* for returning the poor slave. . . . Are you all silent & acquiescent in Concord?!" Lidian shared Mary Emerson's bitterness that townsmen, including her husband, had earlier that year celebrated the seventy-fifth anniversary of the battles of Lexington and Concord on April 19 "without denouncing . . . our National Shame in standing on the neck of the enslaved black man while we shout aloud in praise of Freedom and pretend to love it on *principle.*" Lidian declared that Webster and his political cronies had violated "the Law of God . . . and on this glorious day of Jubilation not a hint was given that any thing was amiss in the Land—except the danger of Disunion!!! . . . let the

Slave groan or the Slave-Mother weep or the Slave Maiden shriek as they might." Perhaps to placate Lidian, and probably provoked by Mary Brooks, whose influence with him, as the following letter demonstrates, had increased appreciably, Waldo Emerson invited British abolitionist George Thompson, back in America for a second tour, to Concord later that year:

> I had the pleasure many years ago of detaining you on your journey for a short time at my house. I shall presume on that half hour's acquaintance to bring a request with which I am charged by an admirable woman, Mrs Nathan Brooks of this town,—a request which she & other ladies have warmly at heart,—that you will give us an evening, the earliest you please to name, when you will address the friends of liberty in this town.—I think, it goes far to make a thing right & important to be done,—that Mrs Brooks requests it.

Thompson spoke to the Concord lyceum on "British Politics" in January.[8]

In Boston, abolitionists took immediate measures to deal with the human crisis resulting from the Fugitive Slave Law. In the years after it passed, hundreds of at-risk men, women, and children were aided in their flight from the city by the reconstituted Vigilance Committee, a multiracial network originally formed in the 1840s to provide food, shelter, and other basic necessities to fugitives in Boston. Radical minister Theodore Parker, head of its Executive Committee, announced the organization's mission: "To be on the watch, and warn when an attempt is making to procure a warrant to arrest a fugitive; to see that he has knowledge of it; if brought before an officer, that he has counsel, and that all legal delays are made use of, and if he be adjudged a slave, then to alarm the town." The committee's efforts directly impacted Concord as abolitionists there contributed to this new wave of resistance. By the mid 1850s, among the committee's nearly two hundred (all male) members were Concordians William Whiting and George Minot; townsmen Waldo Emerson and George Bradford would soon contribute money to aid its work.[9]

The month after the Fugitive Slave bill became law, Massachusetts abolitionists took advantage of an opportunity to disabuse Daniel Webster of his optimism that "people will return to their sober senses, in due time, & Mass. be herself again." In mid October, two men from Macon, Georgia, arrived in Boston to claim William and Ellen Craft as the absconded property of Robert Collins. For nearly two years, this couple had lived safely in the city's black community; since the law enabled federal marshals to enlist city authorities, however, slave hunters Willis Hughes and John Knight took for granted the help of Boston officials. Instead, a Vigilance Committee contingent haunted their every move, tracking and harassing the two as relentlessly as they had intended to stalk the Crafts. The men even landed in jail on a myriad of charges, from "smoking in the street" to "running the toll," to slander, to attempted kidnapping. During these tense weeks, Boston abolitionists stood ready to implement their threats of armed defense, with William Craft vowing to "shoot any one, law officer or not, who should attempt to lay hold of him to carry him again into slavery." Committee members Theodore Parker and Ellis Gray Loring took turns hiding Ellen Craft in their homes, while her husband trusted to the brazen security methods of Lewis Hayden, who threatened to set off two kegs of dynamite in the basement of his Southac Street home rather than give up Craft or any other fugitive. Hughes and Knight stayed in Boston for more than a month trying to waylay the Crafts, but constantly thwarted, they returned home empty-handed. The Crafts then sailed immediately for England, where they remained until after the Civil War.[10]

A few days before the Crafts' safe departure, a woefully uninformed Daniel Webster observed that "the excitement caused by the Fugitive Slave Bill is fast subsiding, & it is thought that there is now no probability of any resistance, if a fugitive should be arrested." But he reacted quite differently on learning of the couple's getaway, especially since in his new position as secretary of state, Webster was now charged with enforcing the law he had so earnestly backed. Predictably, he blamed the "loss" of the Crafts on local authorities "not disposed to do their duty"; myopically, he still did not comprehend the intensity with which the law's opponents adhered to a sharply divergent concept of "duty." The "brawling abolitionist[s]," as Webster reviled them, frustrated his and other legislators' naïve hope that the Compromise of 1850 would, in fact, suit anyone North or South.[11]

This blatant attempt to reclaim the Crafts in the abolitionist stronghold of Boston radicalized a new cadre of activists, black and white, who parted company with Garrison's ideology of nonresistance. Instead, these men and women pledged to defy the Fugitive Slave Law violently as necessary. Rallies organized by free blacks attracted thousands, with militants such as former slave Henry Highland Garnet clamoring for fugitives to defend their liberty to the death. Following Lewis Hayden's example, black men in Boston formed a League of Freedom "to resist the law, rescue and protect the slave, at every hazard." Flanking Hayden were black caterer Joshua Bean Smith, radical Unitarian minister T. W. Higginson, Irishman Henry Kemp, and Cape Cod sailor Austin Bearse—committed Vigilance Committee members who armed themselves and patrolled Boston harbor on the lookout for incoming fugitives. Smith advised those who could little afford to buy a gun to "sell his coat for that purpose." Other abolitionists swathed their bravado in patriotic calls to arms. In what became a recurring motif in his speeches, Theodore Parker invoked his forebears and readied his historic arsenal—"the gun my grandfather fought with at the battle of Lexington . . . the musket he captured from a British soldier." Likewise, Waldo Emerson now spliced patriotism and abolitionism with his previous concern for "honor": "The Boston of the American Revolution . . . must bow its ancient honor in the dust, and make us irretrievably ashamed."[12]

Abolitionists who had been slaves themselves, such as Lewis Hayden and Frederick Douglass, especially pledged to combat the law at any cost. From the outset of his lecture career, Douglass had defended himself against violent crowds; by 1849, he announced he would "welcome" news of a slave insurrection. Douglass further fanned the flames at a convention in 1852, when he argued that "the only way to make the Fugitive Slave Law a dead letter is to make half a dozen or more dead kidnappers." By the middle of the decade, one of Douglass's most popular lectures was "Is it Right and Wise to Kill a Kidnapper?" Elsewhere, abolitionists also prepared for battle. Charles Lenox Remond, a regular speaker in Concord, condemned fugitives who fled to Canada, urging them to stay and confront their would-be captors. And in the central Massachusetts town of Springfield, one businessman-farmer formed a "League of Gileadites" among the free black men and women in his community, instructing them to resist the hated law as Gideon had done in the book of Judges: "Let the first blow be the sign for all to engage . . . make clean work with your enemies." Soon John Brown would heed his own advice.[13]

For some Concord abolitionists, the new militancy came as a welcome change from their steadfast adherence to moral suasion. The female society, still dominated by Mary Brooks, remained loyal Garrisonians; yet intimately connected as they were with Boston Vigilance Committee members, Concord reformers affirmed their readiness to defy the Fugitive Slave Law and aid runaway slaves. Although historian Larry Gara has convincingly argued that the renowned "Underground Railroad" was more a loose understanding than a systematic network of "stations," its efficiency was routinely extolled in the *Liberator* and other antislavery newspapers. One report from Canada in November 1853 announced that "within the last five days, several interesting little companies of fugitives have landed at this depot, on the invisible train of cars. Among them we have a man and his wife from New Orleans, several from Missouri, some from Kentucky, Virginia, and three from South Carolina."[14]

In Concord, abolitionists such as Vigilance Committee member William Whiting linked their community directly with the fugitive men and women aided by this organization, although, understandably, scant details of such activities remain. Yet between the lines of private correspondence and other documents are occasional glimpses of these probable, risky encounters. For instance, in a July 1850 note, Whiting sends his regrets to Samuel May, Jr., regarding an upcoming meeting:

I have just received your kind invitation to be present at the Anti Slavery Celebration tomorrow at Worcester. I regret exceedingly that it is not in my power to come. I had previously made an engagement to meet a man on some *special* business in Boston tomorrow, & as he is going away to some considerable distance, it will not be possible to defer it. I shall be with you in spirit; & I hope & trust you will have a good & profitable meeting. I am happy to believe that you are *alive* & *awake* too, in this noble & glorious cause. May God bless all the laudable undertakings, of every one who is striving for universal freedom.

The "*special* business" to which Whiting refers may have been assisting a fugitive slave to the "considerable distance" of Canada, a coded message that May would have understood.[15]

When interviewed in 1892 by Edward Emerson, Concord female society member Ann Bigelow confirmed that the town became a more active affiliate of the Vigilance Committee after the Fugitive Slave Law passed. According to her, during the turbulent decade of the 1850s "nearly every week some fugitive would be forwarded with the utmost secrecy to Concord to be harbored overnight," an almost certainly inflated claim that if true would place hundreds of runaway slaves here, versus the few documented cases. But the salient facts as Bigelow remembered them—that runaways typically stayed with her family, with the Thoreaus, or Mary Rice—do correspond with other evidence. Significantly, Bigelow did not mention to Emerson that his parents' home had hidden runaway slaves, an omission that militates against the time-honored rumor, still circulating, that Waldo "Emerson's home was a designated stop on the Underground Railroad." More than likely, this belief metastasized from Waldo and Lidian Emerson's 1854 pledge to shelter any fugitive needing help, or possibly it derived from the local story that the Emersons' next-door neighbor, Edmund Hosmer, hid slaves in the Emersons' barn. On several occasions, Waldo Emerson contributed financially to abolitionist endeavors, including the Vigilance Committee coffers, but no extant records document that he or Lidian ever sheltered fugitives in their Concord home. In 1893, Bigelow's niece, Ann Damon, also interviewed her aunt about the antislavery era in Concord. While Damon's findings essentially parallel Edward Emerson's, Bigelow added this enlightening comment: "Mr. Nathan Brooks & Mr. Ralph Waldo Emerson were always afraid of committal—we women never—they must obey the law." Such a remark reveals Bigelow's pride, several years after the facts, in the law-breaking spirit of female society members, risk-taking defiance that aligned these women with their militant counterparts in Boston.[16]

One notable instance when the clandestine network in Concord functioned as if well-rehearsed came in the predawn hours of Sunday, February 16, 1851, as a desperate knock on their door awakened Ann and Francis

Bigelow. The recent past of Shadrach Minkins had included many dramatic days, but surely none equaled the emotional rollercoaster of this weekend. Nine months earlier, the thirty-something man had made his getaway from a life of slavery in Norfolk, Virginia, arriving in Boston just before the Fugitive Slave Law became writ. Minkins secured a job waiting tables at the upscale Cornhill Coffee House and had begun to feel some measure of security in his life as a free man. Like many blacks in the city, however, he had grown uneasy after the law passed, knowing that his alleged owner, John De-Bree, could now more easily pursue and reenslave him. As it turned out, Minkins had good reason to worry: DeBree had sent an agent to Boston, whereupon city officials issued a warrant for his arrest. Late in the morning on February 15, deputies seized Minkins and whisked him to the courthouse, "in a manner the most sneaking, treacherous and dastardly," reported the *Liberator*.[17]

Word quickly spread through the city's abolitionist network that officials had arrested a man suspected of being a fugitive slave. By the time Minkins met with legal counsel and the U.S. slave commissioner for an initial hearing, the Vigilance Committee had mobilized hundreds of protestors to crowd outside the courtroom, at least half of them black activists bent on executing their recent oaths to die defending Minkins's right to be free. Despite calls for the room to clear after the hearing adjourned, the assembly verged on a breaking point, an even larger crowd massing outside. Then Lewis Hayden appeared. "Operated upon by a sudden electric thrill," as the *Liberator* later described it, the men rushed into the courtroom, shoved the guards away, and bodily propelled Minkins outside and onto the streets, disappearing with him into Boston's West End. Minkins hid in a friend's attic for a brief time, but later that afternoon, Hayden and John J. Smith, a black businessman and Vigilance Committee member, drove him in a wagon along what had evidently been settled on as the most prudent escape route that rainy night—from Rev. Joseph Lovejoy's home in Cambridge along " 'the underground railroad' for Concord," as Hayden later described, arriving at the Bigelows' home around 3:00 a.m.[18]

Ann Bigelow later recalled that she was not well that morning, so that when Hayden and Minkins appeared at their door, her husband "made a fire in the air-tight stove in her room to get the slave and his rescuer some breakfast, and meanwhile went over to get Mrs. Brooks," who, conveniently, lived across the street. Mary Brooks surprised Bigelow by bringing her husband, confronting the former congressman with, in Bigelow's words, "an abstract matter hitherto now presented to him in a most concrete form." Bigelow would later tell her niece that Nathan Brooks hesitated to break the law, but he nevertheless did so this morning by aiding and abetting Minkins. As the travelers rested and ate, the next phase of the escape came together. Francis Bigelow would drive Minkins the thirty miles west to

Leominster and turn him over to the safekeeping of Frances and Jonathan Drake, while Hayden and Smith returned to Boston. Mere days after the crisis began, Shadrach Minkins crossed the border from Vermont into Quebec, his fate no longer in the balance.[19]

Perhaps by midday on February 16, Ann Bigelow, Mary Brooks, and their husbands had whispered their predawn excitement to trusted compatriots. If so, the Whitings and Thoreaus just down the road would likely have been among the first to learn that the baffling disappearance of Shadrach Minkins had involved their town. An impromptu journal diatribe on slavery that day suggests that Henry Thoreau had been apprised of his neighbors' morning work: "What is it be born free & equal & not to live. What is the value of any political freedom, but as a means to moral freedom. Is it a freedom to be slaves or a freedom to be free, of which we boast. We are a nation of politicians—concerned about the outsides of freedom." The next day a townsman hinted to Nathan Brooks his suspicions that Minkins had come through Concord, but the conspirators' identities apparently remained unknown to all but a close circle for years to come, despite reports such as this one in the *New York Evangelist* a month later that speculated on Minkins's probable route to freedom: "Perhaps about midnight, he passed through the plains of Lexington and Concord." As Gary Collison has pointed out, several inaccuracies have grown up around Minkins's few hours in Concord, but one late-nineteenth-century synopsis totally elided the women's instrumental role. According to Samuel Drake, Minkins "was brought to Concord, at three o'clock in the morning of the 16th reaching the house of Francis E. Bigelow, by whom he was sheltered, fed, and before dawn driven [in] a stage on his way to Canada."[20]

First the Crafts, and now Minkins. A stunned Daniel Webster had not anticipated such contempt "in the city of Boston by a lawless mob." The majority of northerners shared his disgust, with several Boston papers denouncing the "mad Abolitionism" that had disgraced their city. Especially riled that "the rescue was made entirely by a rush of colored people," a New Hampshire Supreme Court justice warned Webster that more "scenes of outrage" were bound to follow. Unrepentant abolitionists, however, gloated in these signal victories against the loathsome Fugitive Slave Law. Former editor of the *Concord Republican*, William Robinson, boasted in the *Lowell American* of the real triumph "that the black men of Boston had the courage and humanity to attempt and successfully carry through that rescue, in spite of the majesty of law with which the United-States bloodhound commissioner had clothed himself." Theodore Parker again summoned the revolution's patriots: "I think it the most noble deed done in Boston since the destruction of the tea in 1773."[21] And in Concord, female society members rejoiced that Vigilance Committee operatives such as Lewis Hayden had put confidence in their town. The efficiency and secrecy with which they aided Minkins all but ensured that abolitionists there would be called on again.

The arrival of a young new Trinitarian minister in early 1851 intensified Concord's antislavery efforts this year. In the Reverend Daniel Foster, Mary Brooks met her equal in a fervent reformer whose advocacy of temperance and abolition had become the dominant causes in his life. The prior year, when Foster had preached as a guest in the pulpit there, Maria Thoreau advised that he lived "up to all the reforms of the day and is as radical as his cousin Stephen." Extremist views had mired Foster in one controversy after another for the past several years, and he struggled to make ends meet serving various small congregations. By the time Maria Thoreau heard him in Concord, Foster badly needed a job. Ultimately, the new minister's outspokenness would not play well in Concord either, but Foster's presence there at this critical juncture, with his stirring sermons and uncompromising immediatism, emboldened Mary Brooks and her colleagues. Foster would also inspire others in town, including Henry Thoreau, to attend more closely to the abolitionist cause.[22]

When he had been in Concord only a few weeks, Foster received a visit from a fugitive slave he had known in Boston, a man who now sought passage to Canada. Thomas H. Jones had escaped from slavery in 1849, and then joined his wife and children, whom he had sent ahead of him, in New York. Jones had purchased his wife's freedom, but he and his children remained slaves and were thus imperiled by the Fugitive Slave Law. In 1850, Jones had addressed delegates during the state society's annual meeting in Boston, and he validated claims "that the churches almost everywhere have shut their doors against the Slave and his cause, and gone into union with their oppressors." Foster sought help for Jones from his new neighbors:

> Brother Jones, a fugitive Slave, came this morning from Salem to see me & so I went round with him to solicit aid to fit him out for England to which country he is compelled to go for security from the hand of the pursuing oppressor. I have spent most of the day in this way, & collected for this poor brother $13.00. His gratitude & affection seemed to be very earnest indeed. He has returned home this evening happy in the warm welcome here given to him. I feel very happy also in having thus aided a poor suffering brother. Thank God for this precious opportunity of doing good.[23]

When Foster attended a female society get-together at Ann Bigelow's home some days later, he apparently related Jones's plight to Mary Brooks, since her husband contributed generously to Foster's solicitation: "On arrival home from Boston found Brother Jones here waiting to see me. He wanted ten dollars more to fit him out for England which sum I borrowed of Mr. Brooks for him. Then took Brother J. into a wagon with me & went on to Stoneham thirteen miles with him, got there about 9 oclock. Mr. Willard took him on the rest of the way to Salem." By week's end, Foster and other abolitionists in Concord would watch in horror as another black man met a much different fate. Instead of crossing north to Canada, fugitive slave Thomas Sims would be thrust aboard the *Acorn*, which waited in Boston harbor to return him to slavery in Savannah, Georgia. What Henry Thoreau castigated as "Webster's Fugitive-Slave Bill" would prevail in this year's second instance of a fugitive slave arrested in Boston.[24]

But on April 3, Concord abolitionists still felt triumphant. They had played a decisive role in Shadrach Minkins's escape, and thanks to Daniel Foster, the orthodox church not only welcomed abolitionist speakers once again, this day it actually hosted the quarterly meeting of the Middlesex County Anti-Slavery Society, whose Executive Committee and officers now included Mary Brooks and Sophia Thoreau.[25]

Concord abolitionists buzzed with excitement at hosting their Boston friends, particularly Lewis Hayden, then under indictment for his part in liberating Minkins. Despite the sarcasm of the *Middlesex Freeman*—"the speeches were characterized with the usual wildness of imagination"—the day came off as a grand success to the abolitionists' way of thinking. Days earlier, however, Mary Brooks had sent a frantic missive to Wendell Phillips lest an apparent scheduling error prevent him from showing: "Mrs. Green saw Miss Thoreau in Boston last week, and she told her that you supposed our Convention and tea-party was to be deferred a week longer. You may well suppose the trouble the information caused me, because, moreover, she said you were engaged on this Thursday. Now as to having a tea party without you it is impossible, so I trust the information is entirely without foundation."[26]

But Brooks need not have worried. On April 3, as Anne Whiting duly reported to Garrison, Phillips's "magical, electric eloquence" had reverberated in Concord prior to the female society's tea party, the organizing of which she recited at length:

Never was Tea Party arranged under more uncertainties. We had to work out an equation with *three* unknown quantities; and, what was hardest, to wait a month for the result. These quantities were, first, the state of public feeling towards our enterprise, a knowledge of which would enable us to calculate the number of guests to be expected; second, the amount of provisions which would be contributed by those who had not, hitherto, aided our efforts; and lastly, the kind of weather we should have on the eventful evening. The only known quantity was *faith*, and with that we worked out a triumphant result.

The morning of April 3d was not very promising, as you remember, but gradually the clouds parted, and at last the sun shone out and gladdened many an anxious heart. Meanwhile, busy hands and swift feet were engaged in preparing the tables for the evening. In the afternoon, the doors of the Orthodox meeting house were opened, for the first time, for the use of an anti-slavery meeting. How spacious, and airy and lofty it seemed, in comparison with the half buried, ill-ventilated vestry to which we have been limited for these many years, I leave you to imagine. But higher and broader, like the o'erarching heaven itself, seemed the spirit of that man by whose voice and influence alone its portals opened to receive us. Long may he remain, a *Foster*-father to his people, and a pillar of strength to the town, till he draw around him an impregnable phalanx of the true-hearted!

In epic and self-congratulatory proportions, Whiting then boasted of the women's lavish reception that followed the formal meeting:

It is time to go to the Tea Party. Arrived at the door, instead of the usual aspect of a lecture room, we beheld long tables spread, nicely arranged, and laden with a variety of tea-table luxuries, and at least a hundred people seated by them, while the buzz of merry voices reminded one of a hive of bees in swarming time. Soon the two hundred and twenty seats were filled, while many waited, supperless, for a vacancy. Swift-footed Hebes brought delicious, smoking tea and coffee, and the flow of 'almighty talk' swept on in resistless current. And here let me give one hearty hallelujah . . . for our 'domestic institution,' the Anti-Slavery Tea Table!

Her pride unmistakable, Whiting reveals that the female society's "tea table" had become a veritable "domestic institution." Moreover, she draws on the rhetoric of antebellum spiritualism, a movement that included a number of Concord practitioners—their shared reform sentiments "bind" the abolitionists, and their "influence" will spread like the "lightning of true eloquence." Daniel Foster, whose strident abolitionism had already provoked some in Concord, likewise raved about the women's hospitality: "This evening came the tea party or festival & truly it was a most delightful season. Besides the speakers of this afternoon we had this evening Russell & Hayden. Till 11 oclock we enjoyed a feast of reason & flow of soul. It was indeed good to be there."[27]

The next day's news, however, reversed this celebratory mood as Foster recorded in his journal the plight of Thomas Sims: "Learned the circumstances attending the arrest of Sims by the hellhounds of Boston in the employ of the slave power. . . . this terrible fact my brother is chained in Boston in the extremest peril from the accursed slave power." Little more than two weeks after Shadrach Minkins had been hustled out of the Boston courthouse, Sims had stolen in to the city, concealed aboard a ship just arrived from Savannah. A month later, the desperate twenty-three-year-old was seized on trumped up charges of theft; in reality, authorities suspected he was the escaped chattel of James Potter, a slaveholder recently arrived from Georgia to recover his "property."[28]

As with Minkins, Vigilance Committee members met at once to devise a rescue strategy. But this time the prisoner sat in a third-floor cell in a heavily barricaded courthouse. Federal officials, determined that Sims would not escape after the examples of the Crafts and Minkins, brought enormous pressure to bear on state and city leaders. A frantic nine days ensued in Boston—"a fiendish state of existence," Vigilance Committee member Dr. Henry Bowditch called it. From one day to the next, abolitionists vacillated as to the feasibility of freeing Sims. T. W. Higginson spoke contemptuously of his committee peers, men "extremely anxious not to be placed for one moment outside the pale of good citizenship." "If anything was done," Higginson knew, "it must be done by a very few." Although Lewis Hayden singled out a handful of trusted cohorts, he also cautioned Higginson that the ranks of black conspirators had drastically decreased as a result of the crackdown after Minkins's escape.[29]

Daniel Foster had hurried to Boston when he read of Sims's arrest. In addition to events unlikely to spring Sims from jail, such as prayer vigils, Foster also met with Vigilance Committee extremists, including Higginson and Bronson Alcott, as they ruminated over various rescue schemes. At the state antislavery convention that week, Foster joined Samuel Hoar—remarkably, a vice president of the proceedings—and thousands of others gathered to protest the Fugitive Slave Law at a rally that refueled hopes for Sims's liberation: "This has been a great day for Boston. The Anti fugitive Slave Bill Convention was a splendid affair. . . . There is great excitement in the city. The attempt will be made to rescue Simms if he is carried off in open day light no matter how many soldiers & police accompany to prevent. I shall be one in that attempt if it is made." Foster's optimism, however, was misplaced. Authorities alerted to the possibility that Sims could escape through his cell window had installed iron bars across it. By the time the slave commissioner decreed that Sims be remanded to James Potter's custody, most in the Vigilance Committee had relinquished hope.[30]

In what Henry Thoreau depicted as "the grey of the dawn" on April 12, hundreds of armed guards escorted Thomas Sims to the harbor, the first fugitive slave returned to slavery from Boston since 1770. Dazed and shouting abolitionists lined the streets; several more held vigil with Daniel Foster, who recounted the scene in his journal:

Some more than a hundred of us suspecting that Sims would be carried off in the night concluded to watch all night making the Liberator office our headquarters. Soon after midnight the police & military of Boston to the number of 500 thoroughly armed assembled around the Boston Bastille. They were drilled about two hours. Just as the moon set & before the day began to dawn Sims was brought out & placed in the center of this armed band. We saw him as he came out into the light of the lamp his face was bathed in tears yet he moved on as a martyr to his terrible fate. We accompanied the infamous band of Boston Tories who escorted a free man to slavery expressing our indignation & sorrow by cries of Shame &c &c which were repeated around the cowardly cavalcade to the very point of embarkation. By one impulse we were all moved to engage in some religious ceremonies to commemorate the departure of our missionary to the darkest land of heathendom. The friends called upon me to offer the prayer which I did. . . . & solemn time it was as deeply marked on memory's scroll as any event of life.

For this impromptu "prayer that touched all our souls," Foster received an outpouring of public gratitude over the next several days, sentiments shared by Henry Thoreau:

When I read the account of the carrying back of the fugitive into slavery, which was read last sunday evening—and read also what was not read here that the man who made the prayer on the wharf was Daniel Foster of *Concord* I could not help feeling a slight degree of pride because of all the towns in the Commonwealth Concord was the only one distinctly named as being represented in that tea-party—and as she had a place in the first so would have a place in this the last & perhaps next most important chapter of the Hist of Mass.

Thoreau rarely responded favorably to the clergy, but Foster's militant, impassioned certitude paralleled his own. Indeed, in his Fast Day sermon delivered the week of Sims's trial, Foster had urged global cataclysm upon those who continued to view blacks with race prejudice: "If so indeed it be, then Christ died in vain, and the sooner this crazy, selfish, cruel world is burned up, the better for the Universe." Foster and his wife, Dora, a close friend of Sophia Thoreau, left Concord the following year, church leaders choosing not to renew his contract, but his brief residence there had forged close ties as well as refocused public attention on Concord's antislavery activists.[31]

Like the rest of his family, Henry Thoreau attended closely to the crisis in Boston. Several virulent journal entries in late April rail against the Fugitive Slave Law, the strongest words he had yet written about slavery: "I hear a good deal said about trampling this law under foot—Why one need not go out of his way to do that— This law lies not at the level of the head or the reason— Its natural habitat is in the dirt. It was bred & has its life only in the dust & mire." Thoreau held in particular contempt the state and local officials, and their opportunistic politics, who authorized this travesty:

There is such an office if not such a man as the Governor of Massachusetts—What has he been about the last fortnight? He has probably had as much as he could do to keep on the fence during this moral earthquake. It seems to me that no such keen satire, no such cutting insult could be offered to that man, as the absence of all inquiry after him in this crisis. It appears to have been forgotten that there was such a man or such an office.

Thoreau likened the Slave Power's victim, in this case Sims, to Christ: "I wish you to consider this who the man was—whether he was Jesus christ or another—for in as much as ye did it unto the least of his brethren ye did it unto him Do you think *he* would have stayed here in *liberty* and let the black man go into slavery in his stead?" At one point in this diatribe, Thoreau resorted to the ridiculous, pointing out that reducing human beings to property was a tragic absurdity:

> I think that commonly we do not yet realize what slavery is—If I were seriously to propose to congress to make mankind into sausages, I have no doubt that most would smile at my proposition and if any believed me to be in earnest they would think that I proposed something much worse than Congress had ever done. But gentlemen if any of you will tell me that to make a man into a sausage would be much worse (would be any worse), than to make him into a slave—than it was then to enact the fugitive-slave law—I shall here accuse him of foolishness—of intellectual incapacity—of making a distinction without a difference.

Interestingly, that year Waldo Emerson similarly compared the Fugitive Slave Law to a hypothetical decree requiring that "every fifth [black] man-child should be boiled in hot water."[32] The outrageous reality of trafficking in human beings had finally become palpable to both men.

Thoreau especially decried the link between the corrupt political process and the press, judgments to which he would recur often in his antislavery tirades: "As for measures to be adopted among others I would advise abolitionists to make as earnest and vigorous and persevering an assault on the Press, as they have already made and with effect too—on the Church. . . . the press is almost without exception corrupt." Both proslavery and moderate editors heaped insult on injury during Sims's trial and after his rendition, many crediting Massachusetts officials for summarily performing their "duty," for "yield[ing] to the laws of the Union." Though he exempted the *Liberator* from censure, Thoreau accused most papers of "insult[ing] the common sense of the country": "Has not the Boston Herald acted its part well served its master faithfully—How could it have gone lower on its belly." Indeed, the *Boston Herald* crowed that "our city has been redeemed," while Concord's own *Middlesex Freeman* reported Sims's walk from the courthouse to the harbor with extraordinary insouciance: "We should not imagine his feelings to be of the most joyful description." A week later, the *Freeman*'s editor seemed relieved when Sims landed in Georgia: "The brig Acorn has arrived at Savannah, with Sims the Fugitive Slave, after a passage of five days— all well." For its part, the southern press relished reporting the news that upon disembarking, Sims had been flogged in the public square, a display unquestionably calculated to taunt the abolitionists.[33]

Sims's landing in Georgia relieved Daniel Webster. Seven months after it passed, he could finally boast to President Millard Fillmore that Massachusetts had complied with the Fugitive Slave Law: "You will have heard that the Negro Simms left Boston yesterday morng. On this occasion all Boston people appear to have behaved well." The president promptly applauded Webster "upon the triumph of law in Boston," but Webster's satisfaction with his state was short-lived. Before the end of April, Massachusetts voters elected abolitionist Charles Sumner, friend of Waldo Emerson and Henry Thoreau, to represent them in the U.S. Senate; further, Bostonians delivered a personal humiliation to Webster when city aldermen denied the use of Faneuil Hall for a rally supporting him.[34]

White Vigilance Committee members, meanwhile, increasingly pledged themselves to militant action alongside their black counterparts. Committee firebrands rebelled against the group's pacifist faction, some of whom (such as the wealthy Francis Jackson), had refused to consider even bribery in the attempt to free Sims. At the time, committee leader Theodore Parker defended those who "did all they could," sensitive to criticism from his friends that he "shrank in the wetting" and "preach[ed] peace" rather than developing a strategy to rescue Sims. Parker later admitted the state's weakness in handing Sims over without a fight and spoke contemptuously of nonresistants, once more conjuring up his revolutionary forebears: "I am no non-resistant, 'that nonsense never went down with me.' But it is no small matter which will compel me to shed human blood. But what could I do? I was born in the little town where the fight and bloodshed of the Revolution began."[35]

As Sims's trial was taking place, the Vigilance Committee initiated proceedings against the Suffolk County sheriff who had "refused to serve a writ of replevin" to Sims. William Whiting had hoped to enlist Waldo Emerson's support, but instead he relayed Emerson's concerns about such an action to Wendell Phillips:

> I recd a circular from the Vigilance Committee, petitioning for the removal from office of Sheriff Eveleth & hastened with it to Mr. Emerson, thinking that he would not hesitate to sign it, as his late lecture on the fugitive slave law showed him to be in a very healthy state on that subject. But he asked time to examine into the matter, & yesterday, told me that he had been informed

that a committee from the Senate, finding that Eveleth had consulted the Attorney General, on the proper course to be pursued, held him exonerated from censure. As another gentleman has made the same objection, and as the Vigilance Committee are probably prepared to meet it, you will do me a favor to suggest the proper reply to be made in the case. & I shall defer any attempt to get more signatures until I receive an answer from you.

Whiting refers in this letter to Emerson's speech against the Fugitive Slave Law, but it was not until early May that Emerson first delivered this address against the "filthy enactment," a statute he swore "not [to] obey."[36]

Perhaps her anticipation of Emerson's speech, coupled with pride at Whiting's and Daniel Foster's contributions to Vigilance Committee proceedings that month, prompted Mary Brooks to send Emerson this teasing and confident note in late April: "Years ago the ladies used to be admonished to leave off meddling with what did not belong to them and stay at home and mend stockings. I always replied that I would be very happy to do so when the men would fulfill *their* obligations. You will see by the accompanying letter that this is a case in point and the men seem gladly to perform their duties. As this is so, we ladies willingly withdraw and return with great pleasure to our ancient and *appropriate* employment." Unfortunately, the "accompanying letter" to which Brooks refers is no longer attached to hers; notwithstanding this assurance, however, Brooks by no means "withdrew" to the activist sidelines as the decade progressed.[37]

As he spoke to Concord citizens early in May, Emerson took up the radicals' cry, sounding Thoreauvian when he insisted that "an immoral law makes it a man's duty to break it." More direct and more personal than his preceding antislavery lectures, this address brought home the individual obligation to disobey the law. Emerson commenced with the rationale that "there seems to be no option. The last year has forced us all into politics, and made it a paramount duty to seek what it is often a duty to shun." At once he is saddened: "I wake in the morning with a painful sensation"; disgraced for his state: "I carry about all day . . . the odious remembrance of that ignominy which has fallen on Massachusetts"; and, selfishly, incommoded: "I have lived all my life in this State, and never had any experience of personal inconvenience from the laws, until now."[38]

Emerson's journal entries from this time, however, evidence an ongoing debate about the new law, to the point of indifference in its literal application: "The absence of moral feeling in the whiteman is the very calamity I deplore. The captivity of a thousand negroes is nothing to me." On the one hand, Emerson is impressed by slaves' resolve to be free: "You may say the slaves are better off as they are, & that nothing will tempt them to change their condition. This amiable argument falls to the ground in the case of the fugitive. He has certified, as distinctly as human nature could, his opinions."[39] But on the other hand, Emerson remained emotionally detached from the individual slave. Similar to his reaction when South Carolinians insulted Samuel Hoar, Emerson attended more to personal and civic dishonor in this speech than to the injustice perpetrated upon Thomas Sims, whose reenslavement did not elicit the same impassioned outcry as did the Boston mayor's capitulation to federal authority. In fact, when Emerson referred to Sims, he favored sentiment in this demeaning portrayal: "The poor black boy, whom the fame of Boston had reached in the recesses of a rice-swamp, or in the alleys of Savannah, on arriving here, finds all this force employed to catch him." Surely Emerson knew the details of Sims's capture and trial. In a host of news reports, he must have read how this resourceful man had survived hidden for two winter weeks aboard the boat that delivered him to freedom, how he had engineered his way out of the ship's brig when imprisoned there, how he had gouged his knife into one of the deputies (who always outnumbered the lone victim) as they attempted to seize him at nightfall on a side street in Boston. Nonetheless, Emerson depicted the daring Sims as a passive victim, "a poor black boy" depending on whites to liberate him.[40]

At least one member of the local audience was disappointed in Emerson's ninety minute speech. To Daniel Foster, "it wanted point & practicability. It was too much a dream, too little real, having hold of the victim of this great Diabolism with uncertain grasp." Although Emerson gave this lecture nine times locally over the next months as he campaigned for his friend John Gorham Palfrey, a Free Soil Congressional candidate, he eventually retreated from the abolitionist stage—"I have quite other slaves to free than those negroes," as he put it. Later, he clarified for Thomas Carlyle that the address had "clear[ed] my own skirts." The institution of slavery, however, continued to distress Emerson, and he would remain conflicted about it and abolitionism for years to come.[41]

Critics of the transcendentalists often note their slow move to a fundamental abolitionist position. Many have agreed, more or less, with the argument put forth in 1959 by Stanley Elkins that the transcendentalists did not truly regard slavery as "a social problem but a moral abstraction." To Elkins's way of thinking, these reformers bent on self-culture "were preoccupied with the natural essence of the slave, when they considered him at all." Proponents of such a view commonly distinguish the Fugitive Slave Law as evidence that only when Massachusetts became culpable with the Slave Power did Thoreau and Emerson truly become incensed over slavery. Emerson's first speech against this law in Concord, citing "personal inconvenience" as one reason he spoke out, certainly lends credence to such a view. Additionally, however, the humanized face of slavery—key to Garrison's strategy of moral suasion and to the continued mobilization of Concord's abolitionists—would propel both men from any residual hesitation to an unqualified endorsement of the militant abolitionism that had protected the Crafts and liberated Minkins.[42]

Just as Shadrach Minkins successfully eluded his slave owner's grasp with help from the Concord spur of the Underground Railroad, so did other slaves seek help in this community. On October 1, 1851, Henry Thoreau recounted in a surprisingly detailed journal entry that a slave on the run had spent the previous night with his family:

> 5 P m Just put a fugitive slave who has taken the name of Henry Williams into the cars for Canada. He escaped from Stafford County Virginia to Boston last October, has been in Shadracks place at the Cornhill Coffeehouse—had been corresponding through an agent with his master who is his father about buying—himself—his master asking $600 but he having been able to raise only $500.—heard that there were writs out for two Williamses fugitives—and was informed by his fellow servants & employer that Augerhole Burns & others of the police had called for him when he was out. Accordingly fled to Concord last night on foot—bringing a letter to our family from Mr Lovejoy of Cambridge—& another which Garrison had formerly given him on another occasion.
>
> He lodged with us & waited in the house till funds were collected with which to forward him. Intended to despatch him at noon through to Burlington—but when I went to buy his ticket saw one at the Depot who looked & behaved so much like a Boston policeman, that I did not venture that time.
>
> An intelligent and very well behaved man—a mullatto. . . . The slave said that he could guide himself by many other stars than the north star whose rising & setting he knew. They steered for the north star even when it had got round and appeared to them to be in the south. They frequently followed the telegraph when there was no railroad. The slaves bring many superstitions from Africa. The fugitives sometimes superstitiously carry a turf in their hats thinking that their success depends on it.

In addition to its details about Williams and Thoreau's vigilance for his security, this journal entry also confirms Thoreau's familiarity with Minkins—where he had worked in Boston, the network that brought him to Concord, and the name of deputy Frederick D. "Augerhole" Byrnes. It also evidences that during this anxious twenty-four hours with a man desperate for his freedom, Thoreau responded to Williams as an individual, sympathetically and respectfully. Rather than sentimentalizing Williams's plight or diverting to a general harangue against slavery, Thoreau was instead interested in his and other slaves' knowledge of navigation techniques as well as in their superstitions. The fact that Williams brought an introduction from Boston abolitionists suggests that he came alone rather than with Lewis Hayden or another Vigilance Committee member. Further, this letter may also indicate that the Thoreaus had served in this capacity on previous—and unfortunately undocumented—occasions, in addition to which it establishes that committee members placed the same trust in them as they did in the Bigelows and Brooks.[43]

Vigilance Committee records confirm Thoreau's account that Henry Williams had arrived in Boston a year earlier. For a time, he had lodged with Isabella S. Holmes, the daughter of black clergyman Samuel Snowden. Unfortunately, after Williams left Concord, he cannot be traced. Census records and city directories in Montreal list a mulatto waiter with this name in the city from 1859 until at least 1862, leaving a gap of eight years from the time he left Concord that could be accounted for if he had first lived elsewhere, or, simply, if the records are incomplete. By 1861, the Henry Williams in Montreal was forty years old, a husband and father.[44]

Thoreau's journal rarely affords such intimate glimpses; yet ironically, it provides the sole extant record documenting Henry Williams's brief sojourn in Concord. Two days after Williams had gone, Waldo Emerson recorded his fifty-cent contribution to "Miss Thoreau for a fugitive slave," likely Williams, although the intended recipient was not named. Williams took the train bound for Burlington, Vermont, a northwestern course that generally corresponds with the route Ann Bigelow later confirmed as standard for the fugitives leaving Concord for Canada: "They were escorted to West Fitchburg (never to Fitchburg, a large town) . . . where they got aboard the Northbound train." If Henry Williams did, as presumed, make it safely to Canada that fall, he added to the repute of the increasingly famous "Under-ground Railroad" which was "doing better business this fall than usual," according to headlines in the antislavery press. Canada's *Voice of the Fugitive* boasted this year that

> the Fugitive Slave Law has given it more vitality, more activity, more passengers, and more opposition, which invariably accelerates business. We have been under the necessity of tearing up the old strap rails, and putting down the regular T's, so that we can run a lot of slaves through from almost any of the bordering slave States into Canada, within 48 hours, and we defy the slaveholders and their abettors to beat that if they can.
>
> We have just received a fresh lot to-day of hearty looking men and women, on the last train from Virginia, and still there is room.

The week after Henry Williams left Concord, the *Liberator* carried news of multiple fugitive slave incidents—from "nine negroes" captured in Pennsylvania, to "servile disturbances" in North Carolina, to a Virginia slave arrested in New York.[45]

This scene repeated itself two years later, in the summer of 1853, when the Thoreaus looked after another runaway slave from Virginia. This time, however, it was not Henry Thoreau who recorded the encounter but Moncure Daniel Conway, a young abolitionist (also from Virginia) and Harvard Divinity School student living in Concord for the summer. Conway later explained that Thoreau had postponed their scheduled walk on July 27, as a result of this unexpected visitor:

> in the morning I found the Thoreaus agitated by the arrival of a coloured fugitive from Virginia, who had come to their door at daybreak. Thoreau took me to a room where his excellent sister, Sophia, was ministering to the fugitive, who recognized me as one he had seen. He was alarmed, but his fears passed into delight when after talking with him about our county I certified his genuineness. I observed the tender and lowly devotion of Thoreau to the African. He now and then drew near to the trembling man, and with a cheerful voice bade him feel at home, and have no fear that any power should again wrong him. That whole day he mounted guard over the fugitive, for it was a slave-hunting time. But the guard had no weapon, and probably there was no such thing in the house.
>
> The next day the fugitive was got off to Canada, and I enjoyed my first walk with Thoreau.

Thoreau's brief journal entry for this date notes the heavy rain, and the appearance of the autumnal dandelion, lilies, and pickerel weed. The next afternoon he walked "with Mr. Conway," with whom he talked about the shade-producing crabapple trees of Virginia. No clues, no interlined codes suggest that a fugitive slave had been with his family for the past day.[46]

Moncure Conway may also offer the most plausible explanation for another instance this year of the Thoreaus' aid to slave families, the details of which Henry Thoreau noted in his journal on November 1: "To night a free colored woman is lodging at our house whose errand to the north is to get money to buy her husband who is a slave to one moore in Norfolk vagina— She persuaded Moore though not a kind master to buy him that he might not be sold further south— Moore paid 600 dollars for him—but asks her 800." A few weeks earlier, Thoreau had noted that "a Mr Farquhar of Maryland came to see me," but he did not identify Farquhar or give any reason for this visit. Although seemingly unrelated, these two journal entries may be connected. Most likely, Thoreau's visitor was William Henry Farquhar, a Hicksite Quaker from Montgomery County, Maryland, who served as principal of the Fair Hill School for girls. Farquhar was an abolitionist friend of Moncure Conway as well as an active participant in Maryland's Underground Railroad. Some time this year or the next, according to Conway, Farquhar visited him in Cambridge; possibly, Conway took him then to meet his Concord friends. If so, Farquhar would certainly have been interested to learn of the Thoreaus' assistance to fugitive slaves. Perhaps the family agreed to help any slaves or family members who came to their home on Farquhar's recommendation, including, possibly, the woman who arrived on November 1. Neither Prudence Ward, nor Maria, Sophia, or Cynthia Thoreau recorded their impression of these enterprising and (surely) distraught houseguests. Yet such personal encounters, as Wendell Glick has claimed with regard to Henry Thoreau, undoubtedly strengthened the family's abolitionist sympathies and renewed their commitment to defy the Fugitive Slave Law.[47]

More frequent than fugitive slaves, however, were visitors much less to Henry Thoreau's liking. Dinner table conversation, with its complement of permanent and transient lodgers, ranged from those Thoreau admired to three abolitionists whose stay in June 1853 inspired one of his most derisive and comical journal entries:

> Here have been three Ultra Reformers Lecturers on Slavery—Temperance— the Church &c in and about our house & Mrs. Brooks' the last 3 or 4 days— A. D. Foss once a Baptist Minister in Hopkinton NH—Loring Moody A sort of traveling Patterer working Chaplain—& H. C. Wright, who shocks all the old women with his infidel writings. Though Foss was a stranger to the others—You would have thought them old and familiar cronies (they happened here together by accident—) They addressed each other constantly by their christian names—& rubbed you continually with the greasy cheeks of their kindness—They would not keep their distance, but cuddle up & lie spoon fashion with you no matter how hot the weather—nor how narrow the bed— chiefly Wright—I was awfully pestered with his benignity—feared I should get greased all over with it past restoration—Tried to keep some starch in my clothes—He wrote a book called A Kiss for a Blow—and he behaved as if one or the other was unavoidable—there was no alternative between these or as if I had given him a blow & the kiss was to be preferred. But would not a blow have been as good. He was bent on giving me the kiss when there was no quarrel & no agreement between us. I wanted that he should straighten his back—smooth out those ogling wrinkles of benignity about his eyes—& with a healthy reserve pronounce something in a down-right manner—It was difficult to keep clear of his slimy benignity with which he sought to cover you before he swallowed you & took you fairly into his bowels. It would have been far worse than the fate of Jona—I do not wish to get any nearer to a man's bowels than usual. They lick you as a cow her calf— —they would fain wrap you about with their bowels—W. addressed me as Henry within 1 minute from the time I first laid eyes on him—& when I spoke he said with drawling sultry sympathy Henry,—I know all you would say—I understand you perfectly—you need not explain any thing to me. & to another—I am going to dive into Henry's inmost depths—I said, "I trust you will not strike your head

against the bottom." He could tell in a dark room with his eyes blinded and in perfect stillness if there was one there whom he loved. One of the most attractive things about flowers is their beautiful reserve. The truly beautiful & noble puts its lover as it were at an infinite distance while it attracts him more strongly than ever. I do not like the men who come so near me with their bowels. It is the most disagreeable kind of snare to be caught in. Men's bowels are far more slimy than their brains—They must be ascetics who come near you with their bowels. . . . is it kindness to embrace a man? They lay their sweaty hand on your shoulder—or your knee—to magnetize you.

These "Ultra Reformers" were Loring Moody, Andrew Twombly Foss, and Henry Clarke Wright, a trio whom Michael Meyer has appealingly dubbed "ecclesiastical versions of used-car salesmen." All three were extremely visible agents on the Massachusetts antislavery circuit this year; the controversial Wright had lectured in Concord the prior month, while Moody had known Mary Brooks for a few years.[48]

Encounters with abolitionists of this ilk sustained Thoreau's predisposition against organized reform, an opinion further exacerbated that summer when William Lloyd Garrison rejected Bronson Alcott's overtures for employment. As Thoreau described the situation, Alcott

> had offered his services to the abolition society—to go about the country & speak for freedom as their agent, but they declined him. This is very much to their discredit—they should have been forward to secure him—Such a connexion with him would confer unexpected dignity on their enterprise. But they cannot tolerate a man who stands by a head above them. They are as bad, (Garrison & Philips &c), as the overseers & faculty of Harvard College— They require a man who will train well under them. Consequently they have not in their employ any but small men.

This angry pronouncement—and rare criticism of Phillips—no doubt resulted primarily from Thoreau's empathy for his friend's prolonged vocational and financial crisis, but the likes of Moody, Foss, and Clarke surely reinforced such a view.[49]

As 1854 commenced, the *Boston Daily Times* ridiculed Gerrit Smith and Joshua Giddings for their antislavery speeches to Congress, but other headlines—"The Nebraska Bill—Agitation in Prospect"—suggested the upheaval soon to consolidate abolitionist sentiment in the North. On January 25, William Whiting, now a vice president in the state antislavery society, attended its annual convention in Boston. Among the strident resolutions passed there was one pronouncing President Franklin Pierce "guilty of high treason against the cause of Liberty—of trampling under foot the provisions of the Constitution . . . the vilest of all the tyrants who now curse the nations of the earth." In March, Waldo Emerson reinserted himself into the fray and delivered, for the first time in three years, an antislavery speech at New York's Broadway Tabernacle. But despite abolitionists' sustained efforts, Congress had begun debating a bill that winter that would reignite the fury still smoldering from the Fugitive Slave Law.[50]

The Kansas Nebraska bill was the brainchild of Illinois Senator Stephen A. Douglas, who proposed it as a practical means to implement the next phase of manifest destiny. The bill effectively repealed the Missouri Compromise, which though far from acceptable to either North or South, had for the past thirty years balanced the Louisiana Purchase territories by permitting slavery south of latitude 36° 30', and prohibiting it north of that line, with the exception of the slave state of Missouri itself. The Kansas Nebraska Act, signed into law on May 30, mandated that "popular sovereignty" would instead determine whether new states came into the union free or slave. In the weeks after it passed, proslavery settlers—largely from Missouri and often with their slaves—rushed into the Kansas territory, touching off a series of hostile encounters that within a few years would burgeon to a localized civil war.[51]

Written in 1909, W. E. B. Du Bois's analysis of the act's intent and its ramifications for the antislavery movement is still one of the most cogent, if one-sided, elucidations of the causes central to the Kansas conflict:

> It was the secret understanding of the promoters of the bill that Kansas would become slave territory and Nebraska free, and this tacit compact was expressed in the formula that the people of each territory should have the right "to form and regulate their domestic institutions in their own way, subject only to the Constitution of the United States." But the game was so easy, and the price so cheap that the Southern leaders and their office-hunting Northern tools were not satisfied, even with the gain of territory, and so juggled the bill as virtually to leave all territory open to slavery even against the will of its people, while eventually they fortified their daring by a Supreme Court decision.
>
> The North, on the other hand, angry enough at even the necessity of disputing slavery north of the long established line, nevertheless began in good faith to prepare to vote slavery out of Kansas by pouring in free settlers.
>
> Thereupon ensued one of the strangest duels of modern times—a political battle between two economic systems: On the one side were all the machinery of government, close proximity to the battle-field and a deep-seated social ideal which did not propose to abide by the rules of the game; on the other hand were strong moral conviction, pressing economic necessity and capacity for organization.[52]

Predictably but to no avail, abolitionists denounced the bill at rallies throughout the North, labeling it further evidence that the Slave Power still dominated Congress. Henry Thoreau, busy this winter adding the finishing touches to the final draft of *Walden,* took time to comment on the news: "I read some of the the [*sic*] speeches in Congress about the Nebraska bill—a thing the like of which I have not done for a year . . . Your Congress Halls have an ale-house odor—a place for stale jokes & vulgar wit. It compels me to think of my fellow creatures as apes & babboons." Prudence Ward's friend Laura Harris was of the opinion that President Pierce and Senator Douglas should "*be skinned alive* . . . Do you not feel more excited against Northern than Southern slaveholders! I have never before felt so *personal* an interest in Abolition, as at present." To Mary Brooks, the law naturally called for an invitation to William Lloyd Garrison:

> Will it be in your power to come to Concord and talk to us on Slavery in general, and the Nebraska Bill in particular, next week on Thursday evening. There is to be something done about the Nebraska abomination in the Town Meeting on the 6th of March next. Our Society think it will be a good time to have a lecture. We have not much to offer you pecuniarily but we know you are always abounding in this work of the Lord and so we feel confident that if it possible you will come and strike a blow for freedom among us. Will you please send an answer as soon as convenient.

Although Garrison did attend to the "Nebraska Villany" in scores of news articles, a younger corps of abolitionists felt the forceful editor had begun to lose sight of the individual slaves themselves. T. W. Higginson complained years later that "Garrison . . . stood composedly by his desk preparing his next week's editorial, and almost exasperating the more hotheaded among us by the placid way in which he looked beyond the rescue of an individual to the purifying of a nation."[53]

Abolitionists were soon reminded, in an all-too-human example, of an earlier proslavery statute when another black man was arrested that May in Boston and arraigned as a fugitive slave. Twenty-year-old Anthony Burns had arrived in the city some weeks earlier, and had found work in a clothing store, going seemingly unnoticed. But when his alleged owner, Charles F. Suttle, from Alexandria, Virginia, traced Burns to Boston, he demanded that federal marshals arrest him, which they did on May 24—as with Thomas Sims, under cover of darkness and on the false pretense of jewelry theft. The propitious timing of Burns's capture—just two days after the House of Representatives had approved the Kansas Nebraska Act—mobilized abolitionists already crowding into Boston that week for two conventions, those of the Free Soil Party and the New England Anti-Slavery Society. As Anne Warren Weston judged, "the arrest of Burns coming as it did so immediately upon the passage of the Nebraska Bill has stirred up the hearts of all Massachusetts to a state of burning indignation." Like Sims, Burns was held in the Boston courthouse—"lawlessly converted into a prison, and filled with soldiers," described sixteen-year-old Charlotte Forten. Again, a legal team spearheaded by Richard Henry Dana, Jr., volunteered counsel, while Vigilance Committee zealots convened to devise a rescue. Simultaneously, Theodore Parker and black minister Leonard Grimes made behind the scenes inquiries to ascertain if Suttle would agree to sell Burns, a plan that almost worked.[54]

The intense week ended in disheartening failure, however, commencing on Friday, May 26, with what Higginson later called "one of the very best plots that ever—failed." That evening an estimated five thousand people amassed at Faneuil Hall to protest Burns's detention. Although Higginson, Parker, and Wendell Phillips had earlier decided on a strategy to spring Burns the next morning, their turbulent speeches that night worked the crowd to a predictable frenzy and derailed their own plans. As the meeting built to a climax, Phillips strode to the podium and demanded that Burns be "set free on the streets of Boston"; then Parker mockingly addressed the audience as "Fellow subjects of Virginia." The crowd began clamoring for Burns to be liberated that very night, and Higginson obligingly led the disorganized mob the few blocks to the courthouse, where they rammed the door and gained entrance, killing one guard in a scuffle that resulted in the immediate tightening of security around Anthony Burns. Henry Thoreau would valorize it as a "heroic attack," but the violent scene provoked the mayor to comply with federal orders that he quell the commotion. Boston was virtually under martial law.[55]

Over the next few days, some among the Vigilance Committee continued to hatch new ideas for rescuing Burns, but all such plans came to naught. Despite a moving, four-hour plea from defense attorney Dana, Commissioner Edward Greeley Loring carried out the bidding of the Slave Power and proclaimed Burns the property of Charles Suttle. City buildings were shrouded in black, some festooned with inverted American flags, the afternoon of Friday, June 2. Fifty thousand people thronged into the militarized streets to witness federal marshals escort Anthony Burns to the harbor, where the revenue cutter *Morris* waited to take him back to Virginia. City police had been directed "to fire upon the crowd" as necessary, and abolitionists watched in horror as an artillery regiment, three platoons of Marines (one with a cannon), and an armed posse of federal marshals ensured that Burns stepped aboard the boat. Even at the last minute, some who watched the largest "display of military force . . . since the Revolution" had believed Burns would be freed: "*If* the man is sent back there may be great difficulty. I cannot think he will be," a plaintive Anne Warren Weston had hoped. In the days that followed, most abolitionists vilified Commissioner Loring, but he was perhaps most dishonored by the gesture of the Woburn Female Anti-Slavery Society, whose members sent thirty pieces of silver to this modern day Judas.[56]

The fate of Anthony Burns revived abolitionists' shame over their similar failure to save Thomas Sims. But as before, it was not a black man's loss of freedom that provoked northerners to heed the abolitionist rhetoric many had resisted for decades, so much as personal humiliation and self-interest. Plainly, federal and state authorities would continue to enforce the Fugitive Slave Law. Further, courtesy of the Kansas Nebraska Act, slavery's westward expansion seemed assured, as did increased proslavery voting blocs and court appointments. In this discouraging climate Garrisonians once again confronted the futility of moral suasion. Their organization had gained little appreciable ground in its two decades of nonviolent abolitionism. In the days preceding the verdict rendering Burns to Virginia, Anne Weston and other Boston female society members assessed their dilemma: "We all sat down and talked about non-resistance. Mary R. maintained hers pretty well; mine was terribly poor. Ann Terry [Mrs. Wendell Phillips] had never had any. Mrs. Garrison's was of rather a traditional kind, but she kept saying in a rather aggravating manner how thankful she was that Garrison was a nonresistant."[57]

As with previous setbacks, their untenable situation in mid 1854 edged the moderates toward the radical abolitionist camp. One reporter summarized in the *Boston Daily Commonwealth* "that if we do not before long *resist*, there will be no liberty left for any man among us . . . now must the trial come between slavery and freedom." T. W. Higginson scoffed at those who argued that the antislavery movement had in fact made progress: "In spite of your Free Soil votes, your Uncle Tom's Cabin, and your New York Tribunes, here is the simple fact: *the South beats us more and more easily every time.*" He denounced the United States as "an oligarchy of Slaveholders," and defined the moment: "*A revolution is begun!* not a Reform, but a Revolution."[58]

The sensation of another fugitive slave held in Boston, and all of the news surrounding Burns's arrest, trial, and attempted rescue absorbed Concord abolitionists. Senator George Frisbie Hoar, Ebenezer Rockwood Hoar's younger brother, later described the communal despair, the "sense of gloom over the whole State," that pervaded these years following "the surrender of Anthony Burns and of Sims." Waldo Emerson began writing a new antislavery speech, and on June 22, Concord residents gathered to protest both the Fugitive Slave Law and the Kansas Nebraska Act. The abolitionists' erstwhile opponent, John Shepard Keyes, chaired the proceedings, compelling evidence of the momentous change in Concord's reform climate. The resolutions passed that day reflect the move toward resistance that had brought together many in Concord:

Resolved, That the passage of the Nebraska and Kanzas bills by the present Congress, is an unprovoked and wanton outrage upon the principles and feelings of the freemen of the North and West, and destroys all confidence in the integrity, good faith and honor of the national government.

Resolved, That the compromise of 1820 was in the nature of a compact between the slaveholding and the non-slaveholding States, and inasmuch as that compact has been repudiated by one party, the other party is thereby absolved from all the obligations supposed to be imposed by it.

Resolved, That the free States are at full liberty to resist the admission of any slave State into the Union hereafter, and that it is their solemn duty so to do.

Resolved, That the whole system of compromise measures has received a fatal stab in the house of its friends, and the Fugitive Slave Law of 1850 was a part of that system, and cannot stand without its support; therefore,

Resolved, That the Fugitive Slave Law must be repealed.

It had taken twenty years, but a last bastion of Concord's status quo had been inspired to antislavery action. This meeting ended with the tasking of a committee that included Samuel Hoar and Waldo Emerson to develop strategies for "arrest[ing] the alarming inroads of the Slave Power."[59]

On July 9, Waldo and Lidian Emerson attended another local protest, they and others pledging aid to any fugitive slaves who came to Concord. Many in this group—Mary Brooks, Mary Rice, William Whiting, Cynthia and John Thoreau—had for years been attending to such needs, but this public assembly secured the support of those previously unaffiliated with the radicals: Nathan Henry Warren, Stearns Wheeler, Nathan B. Stow, and James Weir, among others. The following week, invited by Emerson, Theodore Parker delivered in Concord his incendiary speech, "The Rights of Man in America," exclaiming that "the darkest periods of the American Revolution" did not compare with the "peril" that currently gripped the nation: "Then we were called to fight with swords. . . . Then our adversary was the other side of the sea, and wicked statutes were enacted against us in Westminster Hall. Now our enemy is at home; and something far costlier than swords is to be called into service."[60]

> The remembrance of the baseness of politicians spoils my walks—my thoughts are murder to the state— I endeavor in vain to observe Nature—my thoughts involuntarily go plotting against the state—I trust that all just men will conspire.
>
> —Henry D. Thoreau, June 16, 1854

The most visceral Concord reaction to Anthony Burns had thus far occurred privately as Henry Thoreau filled page after journal page in an impassioned outburst. Soon his rage over Burns's rendition would provoke Thoreau to an unprecedented public alliance with organized abolitionism. Five years after advising noncooperation with unjust laws, Thoreau had moved beyond abstractions and exhortations; he reviled the politicians who had capitulated to the Slave Power: "Why the U.S. Government never performed an act of justice in its life. . . . Of what use a governor or a legislature? they are nothing but politicians." Thoreau echoed his nation's profound sense of despair:

> Every man in New England capable of the sentiment of patriotism—must have lived the last three weeks with the sense of having suffered a vast indefinite loss. For my part my old & worthiest pursuits have lost I cannot say how much of their attraction, and I feel that my investment in life here is worth many percent less since Massachusetts—since Massachusetts last deliberately & forcibly restored an innocent man anthony Burns to slavery.
>
> I dwelt before in the illusion that my life passed somewhere only *between* heaven & hell—but now I cannot persuade myself—that I do not dwell wholly within hell—The site of that political organization called *Mass.* is to me morally covered with scoriae & volcanic cinders such as Milton imagined.
>
> If there is any hell more unprincipled than our rulers & our people—I feel curious to visit it.

Thoreau had planned to share these views at the Concord meeting on June 22, but frustrated with his neighbors for avoiding tyranny close to home he decided not to speak there: "I lately attended a meeting of the citizens of Concord, expecting, as one among many, to speak on the subject of slavery in Massachusetts; but I was surprised and disappointed to find that what had called my townsmen together was the destiny of Nebraska, and not of Massachusetts, and that what I had to say would be entirely out of order."[61]

Perhaps Thoreau felt out of step with his neighbors, but two weeks later, he did vent his anger, and to a larger and more diverse crowd than his Concord townsfolk. In a move extraordinary for him, Thoreau joined the nation's most provocative abolitionists as they gathered for the Massachusetts Anti-Slavery Society annual Fourth of July celebration in nearby Framingham. Before hundreds of people, upon a lecture platform decked with an inverted American flag, Thoreau reminded his fellow citizens that the issue at hand was a man's reenslavement. He condemned state and federal officials for capitulating to the Slave Power, advocated overthrow of the government, and in a move that surely gratified his mother and sister, embraced Garrison's call for disunion.[62]

Thoreau had likely decided at the last minute to address this rally. None of the advance notices carried his name except as he might be considered a miscellaneous other in this advertised lineup: "Wm. Lloyd Garrison, Wendell Phillips, Charles L. Remond, Stephen S. Foster, Lucy Stone, Edmund Quincy, Andrew T. Foss, &c." Possibly his neighbor William Whiting, an officer in the state society and a leader of the day's proceedings, urged Thoreau to come and offer the remarks he had not delivered in Concord. Or perhaps Moncure Conway, who also spoke that day, persuaded him to speak. Most recently, Thoreau had lectured on "Walking," "The Wild," "Economy," or on his excursions to Canada and Cape Cod. With the exception of the two lectures in Concord that were forerunners of "Civil Disobedience," Thoreau had not overtly addressed political topics, nor had he spoken at any event sponsored by an abolitionist group. The arrest of Anthony Burns, however, altered Thoreau's willingness to be an antislavery spokesman—at least temporarily. As he confided to his journal, "the state has fatally interfered with my just & proper business—It has not merely interrupted me in my passage through court-street on errands of trade—but it has to some extent interrupted me & every man on his onward & upward path in which he had trusted soon to leave Court street far behind." Additionally, Thoreau may have been discomfited by his own inaction. For the past month he had vented his temper privately while friends such as Bronson Alcott and T. W. Higginson had heeded his advice and acted from principle. Even his pedigreed Harvard classmate, Richard Henry Dana, Jr., had spoken out volubly as legal counselor to Minkins, Sims, and Burns. As Thoreau set off for Framingham at 8:00 a.m. that July 4, Lidian Emerson may already have been at work draping yards of "black cambric" over the "front gate and gate-posts," her Independence Day statement that the country was "wholly lost to any sense of righteousness."[63]

The day's festivities took place at the pastoral Harmony Grove amphitheater in South Framingham, a scene depicted in the *Liberator*: "The platform had upon it several mottoes, 'Virginia,' decorated with the ribbons and insignia of triumph, and 'Redeem Massachusetts' hung with the crape of servitude, while above them were two white flags bordered with black, bearing the names of 'Nebraska' and 'Kansas.' The American flag hung above the platform, Union down, draped in black." Garrison opened the meeting with a prayer and a fiery speech, but this day his actions surpassed even his rhetoric when in an exploit still characterized as a "most shocking staging of defiance," he set fire one document at a time to copies of Commissioner Loring's decision returning Burns to slavery, the indictment of Burns's would-be rescuers, the Fugitive Slave Law, and most disquieting to many in the audience, the U.S. Constitution itself—"a covenant with death and an agreement with hell"—Garrison decreed. Moncure Conway remembered Garrison holding the blazing Constitution aloft "until the last ash must have singed his fingers."[64]

It was in the sweltering mid-afternoon heat following Conway, Sojourner

Truth, Wendell Phillips, Stephen Foster, and Lucy Stone that Henry Thoreau stepped up to the platform and delivered an emotionally charged, blistering speech that matched the weather as well as Garrison's morning theatrics. By July 4, Anthony Burns had been reenslaved for a month, but Thoreau spoke with the immediacy of his journal's text: "Again it happens that the Boston Court House is full of armed men, holding prisoner and trying a MAN, to find out if he is not really a SLAVE. Does any one think that Justice or God awaits Mr. Loring's decision?" He professed indifference about recent political events—"There is not one slave in Nebraska; there are perhaps a million slaves in Massachusetts"—and he denigrated those who would be patriots: "Every humane and intelligent inhabitant of Concord, when he or she heard those bells and those cannons, thought not with pride of the events of the 19th of April, 1775, but with shame of the events of the 12th of April, 1851." In a fitting complement to Garrison's performance, Thoreau called for political leaders "who recognize a higher law than the Constitution." To him, the positivists who privileged such abstractions signified the widening gulf between proslavery sympathizers and abolitionists:

> They consider, not whether the Fugitive Slave Law is right, but whether it is what they call *constitutional.* Is virtue constitutional, or vice? Is equity constitutional, or iniquity? In important moral and vital questions like this, it is just as impertinent to ask whether a law is constitutional or not, as to ask whether it is profitable or not. . . . The question is not whether you or your grandfather, seventy years ago, did not enter into an agreement to serve the devil, and that service is not accordingly now due; but whether you will not now, for once and at last, serve God.

More insistent than in "Civil Disobedience," Thoreau called for "each inhabitant of the State [to] dissolve his union with her, as long as she delays to do her duty." He had "quietly declare[d] war" with his government five years earlier, but this day Thoreau brashly affirmed to the hundreds assembled that Fourth of July: "My thoughts are murder to the State, and involuntarily go plotting against her."[65]

In his conclusion, however, Thoreau shifted from this damning rhetoric and dispensed a transcendentalist's belief that human society would ultimately replicate the purity (justice) found in nature:

> But it chanced the other day that I scented a white water-lily, and a season I had waited for had arrived. It is the emblem of purity. . . . What confirmation of our hopes is in the fragrance of this flower! I shall not so soon despair of the world for it, notwithstanding slavery, and the cowardice and want of principle of Northern men. It suggests what kind of laws have prevailed longest

and widest, and still prevail, and that the time may come when man's deeds will smell as sweet. . . . If Nature can compound this fragrance still annually, I shall believe her still young and full of vigor, her integrity and genius unimpaired, and that there is virtue even in man, too, who is fitted to perceive and love it. It reminds me that Nature has been partner to no Missouri Compromise. I scent no compromise in the fragrance of the water-lily.

Lawrence Buell speaks for many in deeming this extended metaphor of a white lily "provocative . . . not because of any overt political radicalism, but rather because of its abrupt-seeming swerve *from* that." Yet interestingly, in the journal's version, the white lily precedes by several pages the "thoughts [that] are murder to the state," rather than immediately following that inflammatory pronouncement as it did in the speech. Thus when he spoke in Framingham, Thoreau purposefully juxtaposed "murder to the state" against the lily. Was he suggesting that violence might precede—might even bring about—the purity of justice? The author of "Civil Disobedience" had indeed finally acceded to the Garrisonians' disunionism, but he had also parted company with their faith that slavery would be abolished through moral suasion.[66]

However bemused some in the Framingham crowd that day were by Thoreau's Walden experiment (advance notices of the forthcoming book appeared in various newspapers that summer), at least some there knew of the family's service to Henry Williams and other fugitive slaves. Moncure Conway later described how favorably the audience received him:

> Thoreau had come all the way from Concord for this meeting. It was a rare thing for him to attend any meeting outside of Concord, and though he sometimes lectured in the Lyceum there, he had probably never spoken on a platform. He was now clamoured for and made a brief and quaint speech. . . .
> It was impossible to associate egotism with Thoreau; we all felt that the time and trouble he had taken at that crisis to proclaim his sympathy with the "Disunionists" was indeed important. He was there a representative of Concord, of science and letters, which could not quietly pursue their tasks while slavery was trampling down the rights of mankind.

In its annual report the next year, the Massachusetts Anti-Slavery Society corroborated this assessment and formally welcomed Thoreau into their fold: "In addition to the speakers whose names have become more familiar to Anti-Slavery ears and hearts, we had the pleasure, on the Fourth of July, to welcome HENRY D. THOREAU to the public advocacy of our cause."[67]

As the summer advanced, the press heralded Thoreau as one who extolled the sanctity of a "higher law," his address as "Words that Burn." The *Liberator* published the entire speech, captioned as "Slavery in Massachusetts," on July 21, but the most unqualified praise came from Thoreau's longtime literary promoter, editor Horace Greeley, who prefaced it with this paean in his *New York Tribune*.

> Thoreau is the Simon-Pure article, and his remarks have a rare piquancy and telling *point* which none but a man thoroughly in earnest and regardless of self in his fidelity to a deep conviction ever fully attains. The humor here so signally evinced is born of pathos—it is the lightning which reveals to hearers and readers the speaker's profound abhorrence of the sacrifice or subordination of one human being to the pleasure or convenience of another. A great many will read this speech with unction who will pretend to blame us for printing it; but our back is broad and can bear censure.

Abolitionist friends and strangers alike contacted Thoreau to ask for a copy of what T. W. Higginson pronounced "a literary statement of the truth, which . . . surpasses everything else." A New York woman he did not know, Sarah E. Webb, made a similar request, but Thoreau apologized for having no copy to send and referred her to the newspaper versions.[68]

"Slavery in Massachusetts" positioned Henry Thoreau in the summer of 1854 as a significant new voice in the organized antislavery movement; it unequivocally associated "the hermit of Walden" with the radical abolitionism of his mother, sister, aunts, and neighbors. But Thoreau wanted no part of the publicity and characteristically turned inward, even doubting the value of his remarks, as he confessed to a friend: "Methinks I have spent a rather unprofitable summer thus far. I have been too much with the world, as the poet might say." As with Emerson, public action was problematic for Thoreau, as he himself had recognized years earlier: "The struggle in me is between a love of contemplation and a love of action—the life of a philosopher & of a hero. The poetic & philosophic have my constant vote—the practice hinders & unfits me for the former." Later in 1854 Thoreau accepted an invitation from abolitionist Asa Fairbanks to lecture in Providence, Rhode Island, but Thoreau did not address slavery specifically in his speech there, and he complained the next day that he "would rather write books than lectures." Thoreau had ventured into the civic arena, had his say, and retreated from the front lines. His fall lecture tour, undertaken primarily to capitalize on *Walden*'s August publication, focused on "Moonlight," "The Wild," and "What Shall It Profit," subjects that absorbed him far more than slavery.[69]

Before the year was out, another fugitive slave slipped in and out of Concord, thanks to the Boston Vigilance Committee. One of that group's most daring partners, Austin Bearse, had liberated a man from Boston harbor and taken him to Lewis Hayden's, where he remained closeted for two weeks. Later, abolitionists feared Hayden's home was being watched; so, according to Bearse, he and William Bowditch drove the unidentified fugitive "to East Cambridge, thence to Somerville, from there to Medford, and finally to Concord—arriving at about one o'clock. We drove directly to Mr. Allen's house, by agreement—he being one of the Vigilance Committee." Interviewed in 1893, Bowditch remembered taking part in this or another similar scenario: "One person, I (with others) drove to Concord in a two horse carry-all, and deposited him with Mrs. Brooks, the mother of Judge Geo. M. Brooks." Unfortunately, neither of these retrospectives is corroborated by other extant documents, although both men accurately describe one of the routes used to convey other fugitives to Concord.[70]

The frenzy fueled by Anthony Burns and the Kansas Nebraska Act did not subside as the year 1854 wore on. Most lasting of this sensation in Concord were the bonds forged between former adversaries. When Samuel Hoar chaired a convention in Worcester that fall to organize the former Free Soilers into the new Republican Party, a key provision of its platform contested the new law. A veritable Concord task force had issued the circular enjoining men to attend this important assembly; along with Hoar's, the overture carried the signatures of Waldo Emerson, the soon-to-be lieutenant governor Simon Brown, and businessmen Addison Grant Fay and Daniel Shattuck. Those most consumed with abolitionist fervor in Concord, the female society members, may have been locked out of this political process, but their activism would intensify as they continued responding to the Kansas Nebraska Act. As the year 1854 ended, Henry Thoreau lectured widely on topics other than slavery, but his books were reviewed by an abolitionist editor, possibly Lydia Maria Child, in the *National Anti-Slavery Standard*. And on Christmas Day, Harriet Tubman liberated three of her brothers from slavery. Days later, these men ushered in the new year in St. Catherines, Ontario.[71]

4

Call to War, 1855–1868

Great is little Concord! Oh the finest town imaginable. When in May it gave 1360 dollars to Kanzas everybody said (out of Concord and in too) how much, how good. This autumn Miss Whiting going round to the people about her got 80 dollars, which was beyond her hopes.

—Ellen Emerson, September 1856

By 1855, the year after it became law, the Kansas Nebraska Act had fulfilled abolitionists' dire predictions of slavery's expanded dominion. "Squatter sovereignty" became the norm as thousands of heavily armed proslavery settlers—"border ruffians" the abolitionists scathingly called them—almost exclusively from Missouri and some accompanied by their slaves, massed over the border to settle in Kansas and vote for proslavery candidates. On their heels came antislavery colonizers proclaiming allegiance to a "Free Kansas." Neither group had compromise in mind.[1]

Immigrants from the Northeast, in contrast to those who crossed from Missouri into Kansas, faced a lengthy, costly journey via steamboat and stage to reach the western territory. To offset these expenses, educator Eli Thayer of Worcester, Massachusetts, organized the Emigrant Aid Company, through which he offered discounted travel arrangements, weapons, and other supplies to the parties emigrating west. Some critics disapproved of the company's speculative, for-profit basis, but many abolitionists, such as editor Horace Greeley, promoted the scheme, which raised thousands of dollars for the "Plan of Freedom." The Massachusetts legislature granted the company's charter early in 1855, enabling increased abolitionist strongholds in Kansas, particularly the cities of Topeka and Lawrence. Soon, antislavery émigrés had made enough of an impact that southern slave owners made death threats to any newcomers arriving in Kansas through the auspices of the Emigrant Aid Company.[2]

The "emigrant–train" bound for Kansas passed through Concord every Tuesday bearing money, supplies, and settlers to the embattled region. The town's abolitionists, who now included Samuel and Rockwood Hoar—enthusiastically raised money for the company, and Barzillai Frost advised First Church parishioners to contribute. It was the town's new schoolmaster, however, who kept "Free Kansas" central to Concord abolitionism during this era. At Waldo Emerson's suggestion, recent Harvard graduate Franklin Benjamin Sanborn had relocated to Concord early in 1855. With his sister, Sarah, Sanborn opened a coeducational school whose students soon included the Emerson and some of the Alcott children. Already a radical abolitionist, Sanborn became secretary of the State Kansas Committee the year after relocating to Concord.[3]

During the winter, Waldo Emerson delivered often the speech he had written after Anthony Burns's arrest. Emerson's exclamation that "one must write with a red hot iron to make any impression," must have made Garrison—composing type with such an iron for decades—smile, although Wendell Phillips deemed the address "one of the greatest and bravest ever made in the city of Boston, or in New England." Emerson spoke out this year in numerous cities about slavery, although he also turned down requests from abolitionists that he do so more often. The reaction of one Philadelphia listener, "surprised" to hear Emerson address "the politics of Antislavery," suggests that his renown as an antislavery orator was still limited.[4]

When Concord hosted the Middlesex County Anti-Slavery Society's meeting on June 29, 1855, Mary Brooks and William Whiting were especially pleased that William Lloyd Garrison and Wendell Phillips appeared. Whiting had shared with Samuel May, Jr., his hope that they would show up, since other speakers did not "draw out one fourth of the audience." Brooks had counted on her patriotic appeal in the *Liberator* to reel in bystanders: "It is earnestly desired that there may be a glorious turn-out on that occasion. There will be free speech and a free platform. Come one, come all, men, women and children! and make it manifest that the descendants of those who so bravely resisted British oppression in 1775, are not only *alive*, but *awake*, too, on the great subject of HUMAN FREEDOM!" Henry Thoreau invited his friend H. G. O. Blake to move up a scheduled visit so as to be in town when "Garrison & Phillips hold forth here." The *Liberator* reported that the Concord audience heard "the eloquent strains of the old pioneer of the anti-slavery cause, Wm. Lloyd Garrison, and to the soul-stirring words of Wendell Phillips, both of whom dwelt at length upon the criminality of the existing American Union, and the religious and political duty to effect a separation between the free and slaveholding States."[5]

Abolitionist Mary Grew was also on hand. Perhaps she and Brooks reminisced about the alarming night almost twenty years earlier when both had witnessed the torching of Philadelphia's Pennsylvania Hall at the second convention of women abolitionists. They may have exulted in the endurance of their movement's enthusiasm, what Grew would later distinguish as "a page of history," antislavery women's shared "consciousness of personal responsibility for the existence of that great national sin, and a consciousness of power to promote its overthrow." This dual "consciousness"—of "personal responsibility" and of "power" to effect radical social change—had evolved steadily since the 1830s, but Mary Brooks still relied on her sister reformers, as she made clear later that year to Maria Weston Chapman: "Well it is a comfort to feel that there are a few, O how few, who have put on the harness never to put it off while the slave treads our soil or humanity in any form is crushed and downtrodden. Of such are you. May God give you in abundance that peace and gladness of heart which always arises to those who care for the afflicted and distressed."[6]

This meeting also drew Concord's First Church minister Barzillai Frost back into the radicals' good graces, although William Whiting noted the reverend's unreadiness "to advocate a dissolution of the Union, (still hoping it might be preserved and slavery abolished)." Although some shared Frost's hesitation, by this summer, most northerners attending antislavery conventions were nodding their heads in tacit agreement as abolitionist leaders repeatedly denounced the U.S. Constitution and the union itself as contracts with slavery. On the same page as its report of the Concord meeting, the *Liberator* covered a more tangible example of extremist sentiment as convention participants in Syracuse, New York, responded to "an appeal . . . from a Mr. John Brown, who had five sons in Kansas, and who was desirous to join them. . . . A collection was taken up to aid the father in the objects, pistols and all." Soon, Concord abolitionists would themselves contribute to said Mr. Brown.[7]

By the mid-1850s, the Concord Female Anti-Slavery Society benefited from the labor of a second generation as many founders' daughters toiled in the reform trenches alongside their elders. Their adolescent engagement with abolition—two decades after the society formed—exemplifies how profitably their mothers had acted on Nathaniel Rogers's edict in 1837 that "women must . . . instill anti-slavery truth into the young mind." The Emigrant Aid Company and "Free Kansas" provided new venues in which these young women could forge their own identities as antislavery crusaders. Waldo and Lidian's elder daughter, Ellen, born in 1839, eagerly partook in the agitation; she was especially proud of local fundraising for Kansas emigrants, boasting to a friend that "in three days Miss Whiting's fund rose to 150, all of which goes for clothing, chiefly flannel underclothes which twice a week all women and girls of every age from all quarters come together to make up, and a subscription for money to furnish men and arms reached 400 dollars. . . . It is pleasant to have a whole town feeling all just the same, and these sewing times are I think, delightful. I never went to any sort of one before, so they are quite new to me." On behalf of these seamstresses, who "found it somewhat embarrassing to set a just valuation upon . . . plain sewing," Louisa Whiting sought help in determining "a scale of prices" from Maria Weston Chapman. Society member Harriet Hanson Robinson shared Emerson's pride in their work, but worried whether the women's aid would be enough: "The proslavery people seem determined to force slavery down the throats of the Kansas settlers, but I hope they won't succeed. We at the east must do all we can to prevent it."[8]

Ellen Emerson's zeal was matched by her neighbor and friend, Louisa May Alcott, whose family moved permanently back to Concord late in 1857. Six years earlier, at age nineteen, Alcott had expressed a desire to "do any-thing,—fight or work, hoot or cry" after listening to Wendell Phillips decry the reenslavement of Thomas Sims. Her family's intimacy with abolitionist leaders allowed Alcott to meet Phillips as well as Garrison and Theodore Parker—"great men," she reckoned them. She and Emerson both grew excited by the prospect of violence, even war, in the antislavery campaign, despite their mothers' steadfast adherence to the principles of moral suasion. Emerson delighted "to hear from any quarter that the North will be bold and leave the South. Twice lately very knowing people have said so and I always feel at once as if a civil war was a thing to be welcomed." Rather than youthful naïveté, Emerson's outlook corresponded to an increasing national senti-ment. As affairs in Kansas built to a boil, and as federal laws mandated north-ern collusion with the Slave Power, loyal Garrisonians—Angelina Grimké Weld, Lydia Maria Child, and Wendell Phillips included—renounced their former allegiance to nonviolence.[9]

Other Concord women broadened the scope of their activism during the 1850s, particularly Anne and Louisa Jane Whiting, both of whom took on wider public identities in their middle age. Louisa Whiting had lived for a time in South Carolina and Virginia; on her return home, she published a pamphlet in 1856 entitled *Influence of Slavery upon the White Population*, under the anonymous moniker "By a Former Resident of Slave States." In the same way that Lydia Maria Child and Frederick Douglass had called at-tention to the deleterious effect of slavery on white slave owners, Whiting contended that "a true understanding of the nature and influences of Amer-ican slavery forces the conviction that this system renders the master no less a 'victim' than the slave." Further, Whiting boldly confronted another "painful and delicate" subject, the frequency with which slave women were sexually abused. She "would gladly draw back" from the topic, Whiting claimed, but nevertheless asserted the "well-known fact that purity among southern men is almost an unknown virtue," pointing to "thousands of proofs" in the form of mulatto slaves who lived on nearly every slaveholder's estate. To substantiate the claim, Whiting deferred to a Virginia woman:

It is impossible to deny that this unnatural custom prevails to a fearful extent throughout the south. The testimony is of too positive and personal a character to be overcome. . . . The white mothers and daughters of the south have suffered under it for years, have seen their dearest affections trampled upon, their hopes of domestic happiness destroyed, and their future lives imbittered, even to agony, by those who should be all in all to them as husbands, sons, and brothers. I cannot use too strong language in reference to this subject, for I know that it will meet a heartfelt response from every southern woman. I would deal delicately with them if I could; but they know the fact, and their hearts bleed under the knowledge, however they may attempt to conceal their discoveries.[10]

That year Whiting also took pen in hand to excoriate South Carolina congressman Preston Brooks, whose violent beating in late May of Massachusetts senator Charles Sumner stunned the beloved senator's constituents. Whiting had met Brooks in South Carolina. On learning that she hailed from Concord, Massachusetts, he had proudly informed her of his part in the 1844 affair that thwarted Samuel and Elizabeth Hoar's mission in Charleston. Brooks had been an aide to South Carolina's governor and told Whiting that although careful to ensure the Hoars' physical safety, his orders had been to get them out of the city—without the chance to state their case. "*Right or no right*, Mr. Hoar must be silenced," Brooks had boasted to her. Now an incensed Whiting lashed out in a letter published in the *Liberator*. "The man who now, for the second time, bears the words of insult, and strikes the cowardly blow at Massachusetts! *This* is the sense of *justice* and *honor* which has felt outraged by those glorious words of imperishable Truth, which are now printed in Blood!" Like her neighbor Henry Thoreau, Whiting also took this opportunity to skewer the press, the politicians, and the clergy: "The cringing obsequiousness of even the most liberal divines . . . is painful to behold. . . . When Doctors of Divinity nurse monstrous crimes under its ample cloak, it is no longer charity, but a pharisaical pretence."[11]

As did Whiting, most northerners vilified Congressman Brooks after this assault, yet they were little surprised that Senator Sumner's insulting speeches had provoked such hostility. Elected to the Senate in 1851, the abolitionist Sumner had initially proceeded cautiously and avoided a belligerent antislavery position. In 1854, however, he directed Senate efforts to block the Kansas Nebraska Act. Then, thwarted in repeated attempts to debate slavery on the floor, Sumner ratcheted up the volume of his rhetoric and broadcast his intention to defy the Fugitive Slave Law. By 1856, most southerners regarded the forty-five-year-old Massachusetts senator as "the most dangerous adversary of slavery," a reputation that had in turn made him the darling of the North.[12]

It was a speech Sumner delivered to the Senate in the sweltering heat of May 19, 1856, however, that provoked Preston Brooks's near murderous attack three days later. In a three-hour address known as "The Crime against Kansas," Sumner confronted the deteriorating situation in the western territories, brought home to him when Kansas settlers and Massachusetts voters begged him to exercise legislative clout and halt the aid flowing there to help proslavery insurgents.[13] Sumner accused the Senate of authorizing the "rape of a virgin territory"; most offensive, he charged Senator Andrew Pickens Butler—a distant relative of Brooks—with making "a mistress" out of "the harlot Slavery," accusations that came uncomfortably close for any number of congressional slave owners and unacknowledged fathers. Sumner's words may have been a "thrilling illustration" to antislavery editors who published the entire speech in their papers, but southerners exploded.[14]

On May 22, Brooks accosted Sumner, alone and seated at his screwed-to-the-floor Senate desk, beating him in the head with the gold end of his cane until Sumner collapsed, bloody and unconscious. Brooks took refuge in personal and civic duty—to defend his family's sullied honor "and avenge the insult to my State."[15] Charged with assault, he went free on five hundred dollars bail, ultimately paying a three-hundred-dollar fine with no formal reprimand. Sumner, meanwhile, spent the next three and a half years recuperating. Conservative and moderate northerners may have opposed Sumner's abolitionist ideology, but they united with the radicals at this attack on their senator. Media stories fed the frenzy, particularly when a *New York Times* reporter who had happened on the scene claimed that another South Carolina Congressman had prevented him from coming to Sumner's aid. The *Albany Evening Journal* grieved that the "extreme discipline of the Plantation has been introduced into the Senate." Echoing many northern papers, the *Boston Evening Transcript* contended that the "cowardly and brutal assault" was nothing short of "attempted murder." Jubilant southerners, however, gloried in the nearly fatal insult, sending new canes to Brooks and chiding Sumner as a coward. One Richmond paper crowed that "at the first blow of the cane, he bellowed like a bull-calf."[16]

On May 26, Concord residents held an "Indignation Meeting," at which Sumner's longtime friend Waldo Emerson frankly acknowledged the irreconcilable differences between North and South: "I do not see how a barbarous community and a civilized community can constitute one state. I think we must get rid of slavery, or we must get rid of freedom."[17] On the verbal front at least, war had begun. Boston papers and the antislavery press carried Emerson's speech; from the central Pennsylvania health resort where he was convalescing, Senator Sumner thanked Emerson for "that most beautiful speech of yours." Once again, it was defending their own that inspired northerners to action. Here, then, was the injustice that would propel Emerson toward disunion, an injury to a friend and humiliation to a respected Massachusetts senator: "I am glad to see the terror at disunion & anarchy which I hear expressed disappearing. Massachusetts, in its great day, had no government: was an anarchy[;] every man stood on his own feet, & was his own governor. . . . Every man throughout the country was armed with knife & revolver & perfect peace reigned. Instant justice was administered to each offence." Like her friends in Concord, Louisa May Alcott paid homage to the injured senator and thrilled to see Sumner "pass up Beacon Street, pale and feeble, but smiling and bowing" when Bostonians held a "grand reception" for him in November.[18]

Frank Sanborn took advantage of the widespread rancor over the Sumner-Brooks affair to craft an alliance that would have been unthinkable a few years earlier. On July 4, 1856, he prevailed on several townsmen, including John and Henry Thoreau, Waldo Emerson, William Whiting, and John Shepard Keyes, to petition the governor to investigate reports that Massachusetts citizens had been "unlawfully seized, robbed, and held as prisoners" in Kansas. At a Concord fundraiser in June "for the relief of the Free State Citizens of Kansas," moderates had not only joined the radicals, they actually led the collection drive. Among those allied with Mary Brooks, William and Louisa Whiting, Frank and Sarah Sanborn, John Thoreau, and Waldo Emerson, were John Shepard Keyes, Nathan Brooks, Rockwood and Samuel Hoar, and Sam Staples—as treasurer of the effort, Nathan Brooks even collected the funds. Both Keyes and Emerson marveled that this appeal raised more than a thousand dollars in little more than an hour. Such partnerships affirm that the radicalizing of Concord's antislavery climate, intensified by the Fugitive Slave Law and Kansas Nebraska Act, would endure. Harriet Robinson later characterized the atmosphere in town at this time: "There was but one opinion with all true antislavery people as to the enormity of this attempt to force slavery upon the Kansas settlers."[19]

Sanborn set out that August to investigate for himself the state of western affairs. Although he turned around in Nebraska, never quite making it to Kansas, he came home so determined to devote his energies to the Kansas Committee that he turned his school over to Sarah Sanborn and a Harvard student. Eyewitness accounts of the front convinced Concord activists—as they did many abolitionists—that the west had become the focal point of the antislavery struggle, this despite Garrison's caution that such attention detracted from the goal of emancipation in *all* the slave states.[20]

This tension-filled summer, the newly formed Republican Party convened in Philadelphia where delegates passed an antislavery platform and nominated as their candidate for president the popular western explorer John Charles Frémont, son-in-law of longtime Missouri Senator Thomas Hart Benton. Campaign slogans for the new party exploited both the renewed hostilities in Kansas and the Brooks-Sumner uproar, as "Bleeding

Kansas and Bleeding Sumner" vied with "Free Kansas" and "Frémont for President." Frémont fervor enveloped the nation, Concord included, where the local Frémont Club boasted 150 members, and whose local townsmen, including Rockwood Hoar and William S. Robinson, addressed political rallies.[21] Prudence Ward solidly endorsed Frémont (despite her unenfranchised status) and hoped the nation would dispense with partisanship:

> We are all Freemont men & it is strange to find so many at such a crisis clinging to old parties or worse changing sides—instead of coming out & uniting on the only man who is fitted for the emergency. No matter whether a man has been, or is a Whig or a Democrat. The question now is, shall a stop be put to the incursions of the slave power & that men who *feel* its encroachments & have witnessed the ruffianly doings in Congress—in Kansas—indeed everywhere where any thing is done or said not agreeable to this power, can hold back, or throw the weight of their influence in an opposite direction is a marvel I can't understand. . . . I have strong hopes that Freemont will be chosen & if he is we shall have a President, that is a President. We have had shams long enough.

Although she agreed with Ward and Frank Sanborn that Frémont was "the *man* for this crisis," Harriet Robinson expressed the concern on all abolitionists' minds at the time: "If Fremont is not elected, what will become of us, the slaves and the Kansas people? I shall think the end is near."[22]

Throughout the fall of 1856, the election competed for the news spotlight with the residual upheaval from Sumner's assault and the worsening crisis in Kansas. But Garrison still disparaged the ballot box, regardless of influential endorsements for Frémont from nearly all northern newspapers as well as unprecedented political activism by women, spawned by Frémont's wildly popular wife Jessie, the first woman to campaign publicly with her presidential candidate husband. To Garrison, however, the Republican platform signified merely another compromise over slavery, in addition to which Frémont's judicious abolitionism did not suit. Wendell Phillips likewise viewed Frémont with suspicion and the Republican Party with disdain: "It is agitating for a political result, when the times demand revolution." Thus, yet another rupture among the abolitionists commenced, one that guaranteed the sectionalism of the nascent Republicans and that to some degree pitted Garrison against loyal friends such as Samuel J. May and Lydia Maria Child, who supported Frémont's bid. For their part, the Democrats had threatened to secede if Frémont won, a promise postponed when Frémont's proslavery opponent, James Buchanan, led in the close and contentious race, election results the *Liberator* reported as "the complete supremacy of . . . Border-Ruffian Democracy, and the continued rule of the Slave Power."[23]

Henry Thoreau may have shared his neighbors' hopes, but he had remained skeptical that Frémont could win. That winter, a committee of ultra abolitionists, including Frederick Douglass, who objected to the Republican platform, had solicited Thoreau to support "not merely Anti-Slavery Candidates, but thorough Abolition Candidates." The committee requested Thoreau to respond within weeks "if . . . willing that we should use your name," but no record exists to show whether he responded; later that year, however, while corresponding with his British friend Thomas Cholmondeley, Thoreau did confirm his backing for the radical options of disunion and even civil war:

> There has not been anything which you could call union between the North and South in this country for many years, and there cannot be so long as slavery is in the way. I only wish that Northern—that any men—were better material . . . that the north had more spirit and would settle the question at once, and here instead of struggling feebly and protractedly away off on the plains of Kansas. . . . all good people are praying that of the three candidates Fremont may be the man; but in my opinion the issue is quite doubtful. As far as I have observed, the worst man stands the best chance in this country. But as for politics, what I most admire now-a-days, is not the regular governments but the irregular primitive ones, like the Vigilance Committee in California and even the free state men in Kansas. They are the most divine.

Thoreau and Bronson Alcott spent the high-anxiety week of the presidential election in New York, where in addition to attending a church service led by the famed Henry Ward Beecher, they visited abolitionists Sarah Grimké and Angelina Grimké Weld, as well as Arnold Buffum and *New York Tribune* editor Horace Greeley.[24]

Abolitionists injected the dispute over western territorial sovereignty into the political campaign at every opportunity. Lecturing in Cambridge that September, Waldo Emerson referred to gruesome "details that have come from Kansas." He may have had in mind *The Reign of Terror in Kanzas*, a compilation that included a graphic account by Daniel Foster's brother, a Kansas veteran, who though he found "war . . . a terribly cruel thing," judged it "preferable to Slavery." This book depicted atrocities inflicted on antislavery émigrés to Kansas, such as a "Mr. Jennison" from Groton, Massachusetts, who had been "*killed and scalped!*" Emerson characterized the desperate climate where "the whole world knows that this is no accidental brawl, but a systematic war to the knife, and in loud defiance of all laws and liberties." Prudence Ward's friend Laura Harris not only trusted "the accounts from Kansas," but felt sure "that the slave power will triumph, because there are so many cravens at the North."[25]

Emerson's speech makes it clear that abolitionists were paying close attention to media reports about Kansas hostilities. Indeed, when a proslavery mob devastated the Free State city of Lawrence, Kansas, in late May the day before Brooks attacked Sumner, both stories dominated headlines for weeks, thereby reducing the column inches available to cover another particularly gruesome story out of Kansas that week. Despite scant knowledge then about the Pottawatomie Creek slayings, Concord's antislavery stalwarts, facing the prospect of yet another proslavery man in the White House, would soon welcome the ringleader of that bloody incident, a notorious veteran from the guerrilla war in Kansas—"old John Brown."

Fifty-five-year-old itinerant farmer and businessman John Brown had gone to southeastern Kansas late in October 1855 to join five of his sons and their families who had established themselves as "Free Staters" earlier that year in the border settlement of Ossawatomie. Brown's wife, Mary, and several other children remained behind at their home in North Elba, New York, on land provided by wealthy abolitionist Gerrit Smith. For Brown, the antislavery cause had since childhood been a moral and religious crusade. After multiple business failures, most notably in the wool trade, he had worked in the late 1840s to train the blacks living on Smith's compound to farm; later he had organized a black militia unit in western Massachusetts. Brown's most ambitious and unrealized goal, however, was to forge a "Great Black Way," a migration route for fugitive slaves that would extend north from Virginia over the Allegheny Mountains in Pennsylvania, and on to New York and Canada. But in 1855, his sons informed Brown of the critical need for personal and military supplies in Kansas, and he put other plans on hold. The younger Browns asked their father to bring along "pork, meal, and beans," and a stove, as well as "Colt revolvers, Minié rifles, and Bowie knives." Added to these essentials, the miscellaneous settlers desperately needed an organizational structure and combat training.[26]

Brown arrived in Kansas to find chaos—from his sons' squalid camp life of near starvation, to disorganized bands of Free Staters with varying degrees of antislavery conviction, to thousands of well-armed, marauding proslavery settlers backed by state legislators, courtesy of widespread election fraud. Shortly after Brown arrived, Emigrant Aid Company head Charles Robinson formed a small militia unit—the "First Brigade of Kansas Volunteers"—comprised of quickly commissioned "Captain" Brown, his sons, and another dozen men known as the "Liberty Guards." By December, Brown and his men had taken part in violent skirmishes, defending not only their "own" territories, but retaliating when other Free Staters came under attack.[27]

Most abolitionists had relinquished any hope of achieving a peaceful, legislative solution to the Kansas emergency, especially given presidents Pierce's and Buchanan's support for slavery's westward march. The new year had brought more and better armed abolitionists to the territory, leading to a series of brutal encounters near the Missouri border in early 1856. In Leavenworth, a Free State leader was brutally slain; near Lawrence, a sheriff was killed after arresting Free State settlers; and near the Missouri border, two Free Staters were murdered, and one was "tarred and cottoned" at the hands of a mob. Hundreds of new immigrants from the southern states rallied into Kansas, declaring white supremacy and "Alabama for Kansas." In late May, proslavery troops looted the Free State capital of Lawrence, burned the governor's home, and destroyed the Free State Hotel. Then, on May 24, Kansas residents learned with the rest of the nation that Congressman Brooks had nearly killed Senator Sumner.[28]

Biographers Stephen Oates and David S. Reynolds generally concur with earlier accounts that John Brown's next move was "violent retribution," a premeditated "radical retaliatory measure"—revenge—although chiefly, Brown sought to purge Kansas of proslavery forces in anticipation of an armed showdown. Reynolds further characterizes Brown's actions as "terrorism" instigated by "an explosion of vindictive rage."[29] For these and other reasons that will no doubt remain obscured, on the night of May 24, 1856, John Brown—prone to "*hurry up the fight*—always" according to son Salmon—ordered his company of eight men, including four sons, to ride with him to Pottawatomie Creek where Tennessee native James Doyle lived with his family.[30] He and his adult sons, members of the proslavery Kansas Law and Order Party, had for the past few months been involved in a war of words and intimidation with Brown and others. Doyle sat on the district's grand jury and had close ties to the proslavery legislature; moreover, he and others had threatened to "shoot and burn out their free-state neighbors," and he defended Kansans' right to hold slaves, although he owned none himself. The Doyles had, however, tracked runaway slaves with dogs, becoming, in Salmon Brown's estimate, "as low-down dogs themselves as men ever get to be." In John Brown's mind, the Doyles were proslavery foot soldiers in the border warfare of Kansas, insurgents Brown determined to strike.[31]

The horrendous executions at Pottawatomie Creek have assumed mythic proportions. What emerges after a century and a half is that Brown and his men forced Doyle and two grown sons, all unarmed, out of their home, and murdered them with broadswords. The group then reenacted similar scenes at two other cabins along the creek that night, killing Allen Wilkinson, a proslavery legislator, and William Sherman, a proslavery settler. More bothersome than the deliberate slaying of unarmed men is the possibility that Brown himself did not kill anyone that night—that instead, he commanded and watched as his sons and the other men carried out the attacks. In subsequent months, those close to Brown quoted him as stating, simply, "I did not myself kill any of those men at Pottawatomie, but I am as fully responsible as if I did." Inseparable from what happened here is Brown's trenchant Calvinism. Brown professed himself God's agent in the antislavery war, a devout conviction that went hand in hand, he often stated, with the biblical edict that "without shedding of blood is no remission." Even one as sympathetic to Brown as W. E. B. Du Bois deemed Pottawatomie Creek "bloody, relentless and cruel," notwithstanding that to him the "five twisted, red and mangled corpses" were "the cost of freedom" in Kansas.[32] David S. Reynolds adopts contemporary vernacular in viewing these killings as "a war crime committed against proslavery settlers by a man who saw slavery itself as an unprovoked war of one race against another."[33] Considerations of Brown's actions in Kansas have often eclipsed these salient arguments—that torture, sexual abuse, psychological trauma, and murder comprised a way of life for the nation's slaves, now nearly 4 million men, women, and children. Most abolitionists, including those in Concord, Massachusetts, would have been hard pressed to justify the slaughter of five unarmed men whose crimes were certainly in doubt—but on the troubled and turbid night of May 24, 1856, for a host of reasons that some of his own men found unconvincing, John Brown disagreed.

Brown and seven others were wanted men after Pottawatomie Creek, a moniker he carried proudly to Boston, Concord, and other northern cities the following year, as his quest for weapons and cash took him conveniently out of Kansas. Before leaving the West, he and his militia overwhelmed a proslavery posse at Black Jack, Kansas, but they also suffered a humiliating defeat at Ossawatomie, where Brown's son Frederick was killed. Brown would regale potential backers in the East, including Henry Thoreau, with tales of both fights.[34]

Brown checked in to his Boston hotel the first week in January in 1857, a time when abolitionists had reached an emotional nadir. He called on the state Kansas Committee office, where Frank Sanborn quickly appraised Brown's ability to reenergize the abolitionist campaign. What Brown most needed to conduct a protracted struggle for "Free Kansas," he told Sanborn, were guns and cash—"200 Sharps rifles and $30,000," to be exact. Sanborn's characterization of Brown to T. W. Higginson that week reveals that his reputation had preceded the Kansas soldier to the city: " 'Old Brown' of Kansas is now in Boston with one of his sons, looking for an object in which you will heartily sympathize." Within a few days, Sanborn opened doors that led to Brown meeting William Lloyd Garrison, Theodore Parker, and other abolitionists. They were poles apart in abolitionist methodology and biblical dogma, yet the New Testament nonresistant warmed to the Old Testament liberator in spite of himself. Garrison and Brown's debate absorbed the others, with Parker attempting to fuse the opposing views with his militant, patriotic Unitarianism. By now, Garrison understood that time on the Kansas front could drastically transform people, as it had his friend Charles Stearns, a pacifist from Connecticut who after months in the West had renounced nonviolence: "When I live with men made in God's image, I will never shoot them; but these pro-slavery Missourians are demons from the bottomless pit, and may be shot with impunity."[35]

Henry Thoreau visited Boston late that January, but no evidence points to his meeting Brown while there. He may, however, have heard about Brown in the weeks following, possibly from Theodore Parker, whom he encountered on the train returning from Fitchburg; or from T. W. Higginson, whom he visited in Worcester when there to lecture in mid February. Higginson had recently organized a Disunion Convention in Worcester, an event partially financed by at least one Concord abolitionist, Samuel Barrett. To Garrison's dismay, on this occasion Higginson had coupled civil war to disunion, contending that "two antagonistic nations could not live together any longer." Abolitionist Samuel May, Jr., exulted that moderates had finally acceded to the call for disunion: "The past six months have taught Northern men a great many lessons about the character of the Union, and the price we are paying for its continuance. The North is sick of the Southern *gas* on the subject. The Convention will do good!" Wendell Phillips, who had met John Brown by this time, did not attend the Worcester Convention due to a prior commitment—lecturing to the Concord lyceum on the (for once) uncontroversial topic of "European Street Life."[36]

Careless of his status as a wanted man, Brown refused to keep a low profile while in the Northeast. On February 18, he addressed a state legislative committee in Boston, reiterating his by now-familiar refrain that only weapons and money would secure the free statehood of Kansas. Lawmakers held fast to the purse strings, however, despite this dire forecast, forcing Brown to canvass the region further.[37] In early March he appealed "To the Friends of Freedom" in the *New York Tribune*, professing that "it is with *no little sacrifice of personal feeling* that I appear in this manner before the public." Brown's fundraising junket likely benefited that month from another stinging defeat for the antislavery cause—the Supreme Court ruling in "Dred Scott v. John F. A. Sandford." Native Marylander Chief Justice Taney may have freed his own slaves decades earlier, but he now set down as writ the premise that blacks "had no rights which the white man was bound to respect." The decision upheld racial inequality, but it also further emboldened black militants. "We owe no allegiance to a country which grinds us under its iron heel and treats us like dogs," exclaimed Charles Lenox Remond to a Philadelphia crowd a few weeks after this high court decision.[38]

John Brown carried his appeal to Concord early in March at the behest of the Female Anti-Slavery Society, an invitation issued by Sanborn: "Will it be possible for you to be present at the fair in Concord which I spoke to you about in New York, on Tuesday or Wednesday evening the 10th and 11th next? The ladies here would be very glad if you could, and I hope you will inform me as soon as you receive this, and I will send you word when to come." Sanborn later described Brown's first day in town: "I . . . took him with me at noon, across the street, to dine at Mrs. Thoreau's table, where I was then dining daily. . . . All Concord had heard the year before of Brown's fights and escapes in Kansas; and Thoreau . . . was desirous of meeting Brown. . . . at two o'clock I left Brown and Thoreau discussing Kansas affairs in Mrs. Thoreau's dining-room, or in the parlor. . . . Brown narrated in detail to Thoreau his most noted battle in Kansas—that of Black Jack." That afternoon, Waldo Emerson joined the enthralled party and invited Brown to his home the following night. Sanborn attests that these initial conversations led Emerson and Thoreau to an "intimate knowledge of Brown's character and general purpose," both men deciding "he was no common man."[39]

The next evening, Brown addressed a crowd at the Concord Town Hall prior to a reception for him at the Emersons. As in all his speeches during this eastern tour, Brown made the case for arming Kansas: "I propose, in order to make this meeting as useful and interesting as I can, to try and give a correct idea of the condition of things in Kansas, as they were while I was there, and as I suppose they still are, so far as the great question at issue is concerned." He tallied Free Staters' losses in wages and property, described gruesome scenes from the Kansas front, and to greatest effect, exploited his own personal grief: "I saw three mangled bodies of three young men, two of which were dead and had lain on the open ground for about eighteen hours for the flies to work at, the other living with twenty buckshot and bullet-holes in him. One of those two dead was my own son." Markedly absent from this heroic romance were the five "mangled bodies" Brown and his men had left scattered near Pottawatomie Creek, although Henry Thoreau did later remember Brown telling his Concord audience that "certain Border Ruffians . . . had a perfect right to be hung." Waldo Emerson, for one, found it a convincing argument:

> Captain John Brown of Kansas gave a good account of himself in the Town Hall, last night, to a meeting of Citizens. One of his good points was, the folly of the peace party in Kansas, who believed, that their strength lay in the greatness of their wrongs, & so discountenanced resistance. He wished to know if their wrong was greater than the negro's, & what kind of strength they gave to the negro?
>
> He believes on his own experience that one good, believing, strong-minded man is worth a hundred, nay twenty thousand men without character, for a settler in a new country; & that the right men will give a permanent direction to the fortunes of a state. For one of these bullying, drinking rowdies,—he seemed to think cholera, smallpox & consumption were as valuable recruits.

The first man who went in to Kansas from Missouri to interfere in the elections, he thought, had a perfect right to be shot. He gave a circumstantial account of the battle at Black-Jack, where 23 Missourians surrendered to 9 abolitionists.

Unlike Emerson, Thoreau did not record his first impression of Brown and contributed only a pittance to his cause, an indifference he later regretted.[40]

Concord abolitionists' trusting acceptance of Brown—who literally embodied the "Free Kansas" cause they had been subsidizing for years—has distressed many, especially as the punitive Brown dislodges reductive views of Thoreau the manifest pacifist or Emerson the indubitable moralist. Some critics charge that Concord's embrace of Brown reflected his hosts' penchant for violence, as in this recent analysis:

> His admirers thrilled to his stories of mayhem and bloodshed in the Border War of Kansas. Even in a hotbed of transcendentalism such as Concord, the American taste for violence was evident. But his hosts . . . and their guests heard only what they wished to hear. Brown was speaking the language of terror—arson, the slaughter of civilians, old and young, whereas they thought in terms of midnight rides, Minute Men, and Bunker Hill—scarcely the same level of action, with its possibility for the escalation of violence.

While such reasoning affords yet another opportunity to ridicule the naïveté of the transcendentalists, it begs to be contextualized. John Brown may indeed have exploited "the language of terror," but his Concord audience did not need selective hearing to be thrilled. For years they had listened to tales of terror whispered hurriedly in their homes by men such as Shadrach Minkins, Lewis Hayden, and Henry Williams, as well as a young woman desperate to "purchase" her husband for eight hundred dollars. Concord abolitionists may have welcomed Brown with open arms, but they did so from a need to believe that this fire-breather offered a convincing prospect to enact justice for millions living in terror rather than from a predisposition to "patriotic gore." As David S. Reynolds observes, at this juncture, "northerners [were] hungry for heroes." Whether abolitionists' faith in the fanatical John Brown was misguided is certainly a matter for continued debate, but such discussions must take into account the cynically realistic worldview of antislavery northerners in the late 1850s. The immense historiography on John Brown affirms that the diverse reactions to this sensational figure—in nineteenth-century Concord and since—resulted from a complex set of circumstances and cannot be reduced to cultural myths.[41]

Moreover, those abolitionists who did read sketchy reports about Brown's role in the Pottawatomie murders could easily dismiss such stories as half-truths, as proslavery cant, especially when Brown categorically denied involvement. In the weeks following the Pottawatomie killings, the *Liberator* had focused readers' attention on "Civil War in Kansas!" as well as on mob violence directed at abolitionists and widespread destruction of Free State settlements.[42] To Henry Thoreau's way of thinking, the violence in Kansas had to be offset against the ongoing devastation of human slavery—on this scale, millions of lives counterbalanced five victims, regardless how innocent. Many of the men and women funding Concord's "Free Kansas" campaign—and those doing likewise in other northern towns—had come to concede military conflict as the probable cost of abolishing slavery. Concord reformers would later judge Brown's atrocities in Kansas through the lens of heroism and border warfare, despite their best nonresistant principles.

Regardless how spellbound Brown had held them, supporters in Concord contributed only a trifle toward his financial goals. Yet all in, Brown returned to Kansas in late spring 1857 with one hundred Sharps rifles, promises of five thousand dollars in cash, and guarantees of more to come. Further generosity from wealthy abolitionists would keep the wolf from the door of Brown's family in New York. Most important, Brown had secured vital connections, not only with financiers of his Kansas plans, but with men who quietly encouraged his proposal for a more ambitious assault on slavery—a direct incursion into the slave states themselves.[43]

The following week, the Emersons' guest of honor diverged sharply from the riveting John Brown. Renowned Harvard zoologist Louis Agassiz, a close friend of the Emerson family, held court at their dinner table while in Concord to lecture at the lyceum. Eighteen-year-old Ellen Emerson characterized the company that afternoon, which included Henry Thoreau, as "thoroughly enchanted" with Agassiz. Perhaps at some point in the evening, particularly if the wine ran freely as it usually did when the Emersons entertained (particularly a European guest such as Agassiz), the conversation may have ranged to the illustrious scientist's speculations on polygenesis, an unsubstantiated "theory" proposing that multiple human "races" had evolved separately, and thus, were inherently unequal. But even if he did opine on the broader topic of racialist (pseudo)science, Professor Agassiz surely kept to himself his palpable loathing of African Americans, a sentiment he had expressed to his mother shortly after arriving in the United States in 1846:

> It was in Philadelphia that I first found myself in prolonged contact with negroes; all the domestics in my hotel were men of color. . . . I experienced pity at the sight of this degraded and degenerate race, and their lot inspired compassion in me in thinking that they are really men. Nonetheless, it is impossi-

ble for me to reprocess the feeling that they are not of the same blood as us. In seeing their black faces with their thick lips and grimacing teeth, the wool on their head, their bent knees, their elongated hands, their large curved nails, and especially the livid color of the palm of their hands, I could not take my eyes off their face in order to tell them to stay far away. And when they advanced that hideous hand towards my plate in order to serve me, I wished I were able to depart in order to eat a piece of bread elsewhere, rather than dine with such service. What unhappiness for the white race—to have tied their existence so closely with that of negroes in certain countries! God preserve us from such a contact!

In the decade since this "pronounced visceral revulsion"—to borrow Stephen Jay Gould's phrase for it—Agassiz had drawn on his stature as Harvard's reigning naturalist to promulgate polygenesis, thus emboldening proslavery advocates who argued that the existing hierarchy of race-based slavery was "natural." For such groundless "science," abolitionists and a few of Agassiz's peers, such as zoologist John Bachman, had condemned him. Theodore Parker, for example, criticized the scientist's "scheme of Classification" and "recent treatise of races," and claimed that Agassiz "has sold himself to the support of slavery."[44]

Some apologists for slavery had actually distanced themselves from the theory of polygenesis because it cast doubt on the biblical truism that all humans were created in perfect form and descended from one human ancestor. Other racist scientists, however, flocked to Agassiz, whose denials that he was proslavery rang hollow. Agassiz had argued in 1850 that compared with whites, Africans exhibited "a peculiar apathy, a peculiar indifference to the advantages afforded by civilized society." In the racist ethnology tome *Types of Mankind*, Josiah Nott cited Agassiz as the expert for "findings" that the black man's brain "never goes beyond that developed in the Caucasian in boyhood; and . . . it bears . . . a marked resemblance to the brain of the orang-outan." Additionally, Agassiz was close friends with America's other leading proponent of polygenesis, Dr. Samuel G. Morton, a proslavery anatomy professor at the University of Pennsylvania whose *Crania Americana* (1839) had presented his "research" findings, based on hundreds of skull measurements, that various human races had evolved separately. Professor Agassiz's views on race had been well disseminated by the time he lectured on "the different forms of animal life" in Concord that spring.[45]

Agassiz and Waldo Emerson had been friends and fellow members of the exclusive "Saturday Club" for a few years. In late 1855, Ellen Emerson had begun attending the Cambridge school run by Agassiz and his wife; she enjoyed the institution immensely, yet Ellen expressed reservations about Agassiz's reputation, insights that suggest his young pupil perhaps regarded the professor with more introspection than did her neighbors and family: "I

like him as I see him and yet I don't know him, and as to believing his theories, though it seems as if everything he says was true I remember I haven't
heard the other side." Although he later discounted some of his scientific
postulates, Henry Thoreau certainly esteemed Agassiz; in the 1840s he had
sent the professor several specimens (various fish, a turtle, snakes) for Harvard's collections, earning him public thanks in Agassiz's *Contributions to the
Natural History of the United States of America*. More than Emerson, Thoreau
had absorbed Agassiz's writings, especially *Principles of Zoology*. At the Emersons' dinner, Thoreau enjoyed one-upsmanship as he and Agassiz discussed
the egg-laying cycles of turtles among other subjects that Thoreau knew as
well or better than the guest of honor. Thoreau would disparage Emerson's
male-bonding antics with Agassiz during the Saturday Club's excursion to
the Adirondacks the following August, but he valued his own relationship
with the professor enough to visit him en route home from a lecture outing
the same year.[46]

Within days, Concord had feted Louis Agassiz and John Brown—as inspiring speakers, privileged guests, and friends. If the striking disparity between these men occurred to those gathered at the soiree, they recorded no
such misgivings. Laura Dassow Walls has no doubt surmised correctly that
Emerson (and, in this instance, several others) "valued whatever in Agassiz
corresponded with his own ideas, and the rest he simply ignored," just as he
had for years accommodated the belligerent racism of Thomas Carlyle,
whose views on slavery were inimical to Emerson's painstakingly derived
moral idealism. That evening as Agassiz enthralled the Emersons and their
guests, a townsman down the road may have been reflecting on a deed that
John Brown would have understood. William Whiting had that day contributed twelve dollars to help finance runaway slave Andrew Reason's getaway to Canada, but it would be six months before Reason's repayment of
the loan assured him that the fugitive had landed on free soil.[47]

John Brown had impressed many abolitionists during his foray to the
Northeast, but perhaps none so much as Concord's former Orthodox minister, Daniel Foster, who soon announced his imminent departure to join
John Brown and fight with him on the Kansas front. Foster, now chaplain of
the Massachusetts House of Representatives, had been working with Sanborn on Kansas Committee affairs; in early April 1857, he conveyed his
plans to head west to T. W. Higginson: "I go there fully believing that our
cause must receive a baptism of blood before it can be victorious. I expect
to serve in Capt. John Brown's company in the next Kansas war, which I
hope is inevitable & near at hand." By June, Foster had settled in Topeka as
a general agent for the Northeast Kansas Committee; by September, his was
among the names duly entered in John Brown's diary list of the "faithful."
Foster traveled back and forth from Kansas over the next few years trying to

convince the Unitarian hierarchy to sponsor western churches. His letters detailing life on the Kansas frontier appeared regularly in the *Liberator* during this time.[48]

In addition to Daniel and Dora Foster, other acquaintances amplified the Thoreaus' attentiveness to the ongoing crisis in Kansas. Quaker abolitionist John Otis Wattles, who had stayed with the Thoreau family when visiting Concord, corresponded with Henry Thoreau after he and his brother, Augustus, settled in Kansas in the mid 1850s. Both men professed the pacifist ethic customary to many Quakers, yet Augustus had often provided sanctuary to John Brown and his guerrillas. Such personal ties to Kansas, particularly after Concord abolitionists had personally befriended Brown, not only enlivened the newspaper headlines, but also underscored the risks that their own friends were taking to prevent slavery's expansion.[49]

Another friendship kept Henry Thoreau attuned to radical abolitionism during the late 1850s. Daniel Ricketson, an admirer of *Walden* from New Bedford, had become a frequent visitor to Concord since meeting Thoreau in 1854. One of Thoreau's first letters to him indicated that "mother & sister . . . know something about you as an abolitionist." When in town, Ricketson regularly "took tea" with Mary Brooks, whose "downright principles on the subject of slavery," as he phrased them, complemented his own. Visits to Ricketson in New Bedford occasionally coincided with antislavery events, as when Thoreau and Bronson Alcott listened to Garrison and Parker Pillsbury hold forth there just after John Brown's appearance in Concord. That year and the next the fiery Pillsbury came to Concord often, usually staying with the Thoreaus or Emersons, his caustic speeches endearing him to Abby Alcott: "He makes himself felt by all class of hearers—and the Politics of the day are his great theme He giving these time-serving politicians no quarter—He makes no pretence but hacks and tears at their roots and will have them down false and unprofitable as they are both to themselves and their cause . . . the Slave has no better friend."[50]

The Alcott family's permanent move back to Concord in late 1857 markedly enhanced the town's abolitionism. Early the next year, to the dismay of some residents, the four Alcott daughters put their acting and literary talents to work for the female society's annual festival by organizing a "Dramatic Union." Eldest daughter Anna shared with her father that "the other young ladies of our company being pro-slavery have withdrawn from the affairs & the Alcott girls alone remain to uphold the drama on this occasion." Despite these detractors, the festival came off on January 28, directed by Louisa May Alcott and with performances by Anna and May Alcott, Frank Sanborn, George Bartlett, and others. Theatrical sketches included Sanborn's "Prologue"—an allegory in verse—featuring "Slavery in a clerical dress with a bottle in his hand in form of a Bible," and "Manifest Destiny . . . [his] precious elder brother," who entered the stage whining for a bolt of whiskey. Similar to Thoreau's critiques of slavery, this biting satire emphasized the sordid state of the current political scene. The benefit raised more than fifty dollars for the state antislavery treasury, yet these dramatic performers would have been rebuked a generation earlier. Twenty-five years of ordinary women at the helm of the antislavery movement—from Mary Brooks's and Sophia Thoreau's leadership in the county society to Anne and Louisa Whiting's newspaper reporting—had paved the way for Concord's young thespians, of both genders, to collaborate as the main entertainment in a public forum. Despite some neighbors' disapproval of the Alcotts' abolitionism, within a few years, Louisa's political writings would receive accolades from Concord's leading townsmen.[51]

Frank Sanborn may have relished amateur theatricals, but work for "Free Kansas" consumed most of his time this winter. John Brown had returned to Kansas, but now he moved back and forth between Illinois, Wisconsin, Ohio, and Iowa, seeing Gerrit Smith at antislavery meetings and continuing to press Boston abolitionists for money to offset his plans and his family's needs. T. W. Higginson grew exasperated with the constant appeals and advised Brown that he was "always ready to invest money in treason" but simply did not have any to give. Yet when Brown began to unveil his strategy for "Rail Road business on a *somewhat extended* scale," he captured Higginson's full attention. In late January 1858, Brown returned east, holing up first with Frederick Douglass in Rochester, then going on to St. Catherines, Ontario, where in April he made the acquaintance of Harriet Tubman, whom he dubbed the "General." Brown assembled with other black fugitives at the "Chatham Convention" in May, and then met with Gerrit Smith, Sanborn, and other financial backers. He was still ostensibly soliciting funds for the war in Kansas, but Brown now unveiled an expanded battle plan—a slave uprising launched by a military incursion into "Virginia, the queen of the slave states." Sanborn later claimed to have questioned the plan's viability, but Brown was intransigent: "No argument could prevail against his fixed purpose; he was determined to make the attempt."[52]

Six abolitionists—Frank Sanborn, T. W. Higginson, Gerrit Smith, Theodore Parker, George Luther Stearns, and Samuel Gridley Howe—comprised a "secret Committee of Six" that continued to raise money for Brown at every opportunity, but keeping to itself the fact that donations no longer went solely to "Free Kansas." Appended to this contingent of white men should be a secret seventh, eighth, and ninth, since former slaves Lewis Hayden, Harriet Tubman, and Frederick Douglass each knew about and assisted in various means to further Brown's plans for the insurrection. Higginson was perhaps least likely of this cohort to be won over by personal magnetism or grandiose schemes. Skeptical when Sanborn had first introduced Brown, Higginson later provided his keen first impression: "I saw before me a man whose mere appearance and bearing refuted in advance some of the strange perversions which have found their way into many books, and which have often wholly missed the type to which he belonged. In his thin, worn, resolute face there were the signs of a fire which might wear him out . . . his talk was calm, persuasive, and coherent." Higginson explained (from the vantage of forty years), that the Secret Six had backed the scheme as Brown first proposed it—leading a raiding party into the southern states and methodically freeing slaves who would establish outposts along a northern route to Canada, Brown's "Great Black Way."[53]

It was the "Free State" of Kansas, however, that persisted in the minds of most abolitionists in 1858, especially as President James Buchanan moved ahead with plans to bring the western territory into the union as another slave state. Indeed, early that year, the president had declared that "Kansas is . . . as much a slave state as Georgia and South Carolina." In Boston, the Vigilance Committee persevered with its work of sheltering, feeding, clothing, and conveying fugitive slaves to safer locales. An occasional entry in the committee's records at this time serves as an explicit reminder of the hazards faced by those fleeing their situation. For example, the committee raised a hundred dollars in July 1858 to pay "for Artificial Leg for Johnson H. Walker, a fugitive slave, who in his flight from slavery in Maryland had his foot crushed by the car wheels at the Railroad Station in Wilmington, Delaware."[54]

In 1858, Waldo Emerson concluded that "it is impossible to be a gentleman, & not be an abolitionist." By 1859, his family welcomed Parker Pillsbury as their houseguest when the bellicose agent lectured again in Concord. Led by William Whiting, town activists submitted a petition this year to state legislators reasserting their demand for "a law to prevent the Rendition of any Fugitive Slave from Massachusetts." But it was the second visit of John Brown, passing his fifty-ninth birthday with them, that most invigorated Concord abolitionists that spring. Brown spent May 7, 8, and 9 here as Sanborn's guest; in addition to visiting once more with Emerson and Thoreau, he also called on Sarah Alden Ripley, her grandson later remembering Brown in the parlor of the Old Manse "spreading his coat tails before the fire like a pouter pigeon." Brown addressed a captive audience at Town Hall on the hot Sunday evening of May 8, when along with his habitual plea for money and weapons, he also regaled listeners with details of his recent "invasion of Missouri" that had freed eleven slaves and prompted President Buchanan to offer a $250 reward for Brown's arrest. The audience "applauded his successful deed," but Sanborn noted also the surprise of several who seemed "startled at this practical enforcement of the Golden Rule." Like Waldo Emerson two years before, Bronson Alcott was captivated by Brown's tale:

This evening hear Captain Brown speak at the Town Hall on Kansas affairs and the part taken by him in the late troubles there. He tells his story with surpassing simplicity and sense, impressing us all deeply by his courage and religious earnestness. Our best people listen to his words—Emerson, Thoreau, Judge Hoar, my wife—and some of them contribute something in aid of his plans without asking particulars, such confidence does he inspire with his integrity and abilities.

I have a few words with him after his speech, and find him superior to legal traditions and a disciple of the right, an idealist in thought and affairs of state. He is Sanborn's guest, and stays for a day only. A young man named Anderson accompanies him. They go armed, I am told, and will defend themselves if necessary. I believe they are now on their way to Connecticut and farther south, but the Captain leaves us much in the dark concerning his destination and designs for the coming months. Yet he does not conceal his hatred of slavery nor his readiness to strike a blow for freedom at the proper moment. I infer it is his intention to run off as many slaves as he can, and so render that property insecure to the master. I think him equal to anything he dares, the man to do the deed if it must be done, and with the martyr's temper and purpose. . . . Since here last he has added a flowing beard, which gives the soldierly air, and port of an apostle. Though sixty years of age, he is agile and alert, resolute, and ready for any audacity in any crisis. I think him about the manliest man I have ever seen, the type and synonym of the Just.

As Alcott noted, Brown held his plans close; Alcott also speculated correctly that Sanborn knew more about them than he shared. Sanborn continued to solicit for Brown that spring on the basis "of past services of that Capt— and the prospect of doing more," but he apparently told no one of Brown's modified plan.[55]

On the heels of this second call to arms from "Captain" Brown, Concord abolitionists were roused further when the notorious Harriet Tubman spoke there in May and again in June, both times invited by Sanborn, whom she had met the prior year. Sanborn relayed Tubman's schedule to T. W. Higginson in the hopes that he could meet her: "Harriet Tubman is here today to spend the Sunday—next Sunday she *may* be in Leicester with Mr. May. Tomorrow young Heywood is to speak here and to be the guest of Mrs. Brooks, while Harriet goes to Miss Whiting's." In addition to the Whitings and Brooks, Mary Peabody Mann and the Alcotts also entertained Tubman; before she left town, Waldo Emerson contributed five dollars to her fundraising appeal.[56] Having successfully liberated and settled her parents in the North, Tubman now hoped to raise enough money for their support so she could "resume the practice of her profession!" as Higginson declared when introducing her at a July 4 gathering in Framingham. Surely her Concord audience received Tubman as enthusiastically as the Independence Day crowd, where similar to Sojourner Truth, she spoke with a storyteller's charm, performing her story "in a style of quaint simplicity," according to a *Liberator* report. Another witness described Tubman's "great dramatic power; the scene rises before you as she saw it, and her voice and language change with her different actors." Regrettably, none of Tubman's Concord hosts recorded their impressions of this famous guest. Nor did Henry Thoreau, in Concord at the time, mention meeting or hearing Tubman, despite the fact that this intrepid woman would undoubtedly have impressed him as she had John Brown. Unfortunately, his co-conspirators did not always match Brown's egalitarianism. Even as Frank Sanborn pronounced Tubman "the heroine of the day" and "esteemed it an honor to know her," he also assessed this unparalleled woman as "a thorough 'nigger.' "[57]

As the summer of 1859 gave way to fall, memories of an undeclared war still lingered over Kansas, and abolitionists sensed they were poised on the brink of a national showdown over slavery. In Boston, Vigilance Committee members assisted fugitive slaves John Thompson and James Seymour to leave the city. Others circulated petitions demanding the removal of a Daniel Webster statue from the State House lawn. And in what Henry Thoreau described as the "Novemberish" cold of mid October, as reports trickled in about a shocking and violent occurrence at the confluence of the Potomac and Shenandoah Rivers in northern Virginia, Concord reformers passionately if not unanimously stood by "Old Brown."[58]

> An eventful year . . . to the world in its accession of a martyr to the cause of true liberty—a whole chapter of sublime prophecy for the cause of emancipation in America.
> —Abigail May Alcott to Samuel J. May, December 10, 1859

Henry Thoreau apparently first heard the news on October 19 in company with Bronson Alcott and Waldo Emerson. Soon, in spite of ample misinformation, including the erroneous report of Brown's death, all of Concord had discerned the bare facts—that on Sunday evening, October 16, John Brown and eighteen other men had walked quietly into the town of Harpers Ferry, Virginia, and had taken the federal arsenal; that by midday, October 17, the outside world had learned of the attack; that seventeen men, including ten of the raiders, had been killed; that, ultimately, thirty-six hours later, U.S. Marines commanded by Army colonel Robert E. Lee and assisted by Lieutenant J. E. B. Stuart had stormed the engine house where Brown was holed up, ultimately arresting him and four other raiders; and that, tragically, the first casualty of the mêlée had been Hayward Shepherd, a free black man.[59]

Concord abolitionists pored over newspaper coverage, glued to headlines that competed to sensationalize the events of Harpers Ferry. In a matter of days, as their own Frank Sanborn became publicly implicated in the affair, Concord friends paid still more attention to the news. While some stories were merely inaccurate, others so galled him that Henry Thoreau denounced even the *Liberator*, in which Garrison, quick to dissociate himself from the violence of the raid, had branded it "misguided, wild, and apparently insane." Waldo Emerson empathized with Garrison at this early juncture; he paid homage to Brown in his journal but confided to his brother that although "a true hero," Brown "lost his head" at Harpers Ferry. No evidence suggests that anyone in Concord other than Sanborn knew in advance of the plan to attack the federal arsenal, but abolitionists there had definitely known of Brown's desperation for money in the days preceding. On October 11, just five days prior to the raid, "Mrs. Thoreau & Miss Thoreau" gave five dollars to Emerson "for Capt. John Brown," a departure from earlier contributions to him that had been earmarked for "Free Kansas." Whether the Thoreaus or Emerson suspected just why Brown needed money in mid October is not clear; that they did, however, donate money for his discretionary use, which would have subsidized the Harpers Ferry operation had it gone as planned, seems certain.[60]

Frank Sanborn had not only been privy to details of the raid, but he, T. W. Higginson, George Luther Stearns, and Lewis Hayden had in fact orchestrated key phases of its final stages. After Brown's arrest, Sanborn— "amazed at the freedom with which" a jailed Brown granted interviews and admitted his plans—hovered in a state of nervous panic masquerading as bravado. An unapologetic Higginson refused to leave the country or go into hiding, but Sanborn fled twice to Quebec, the first time within days of Brown's capture. To Theodore Parker, conveniently abroad for health reasons, Sanborn rationalized his departure:

> I knew that I might be in their power if I staid at home; if not to be tried and punished for treason, yet to be annoyed by arrest and subpoena and forced to give evidence against my friends perhaps. If I were out of the way, I knew the evidence against them would be much less, and perhaps scarcely any, and in the uncertainty as to what Buchanan will do and how far public rage will go, I thought Canada the best place of refuge. I could not make preparations for flight without exciting suspicion; I therefore took advantage of a holiday, and was far away before any of my Concord friends knew of it—I shall be much blamed for it all, and that by many whose good opinion I value highly, but I believe I did what was best. The emergency was serious, and I knew it was no child's play I was going about.

As far as Ellen Emerson could accurately judge, "people who know Mr Sanborn are sure that it is all right, because he is not a coward." Her father, however, was "uneas[y] about Mr Sanborn's absence"; similarly, Wendell Phillips urged Sanborn to return.[61]

The historiography on John Brown and Harpers Ferry is voluminous, not surprising for an episode often touted as sparking the Civil War. But in the immediate aftermath of October 1859, apoplectic southerners and defensive northerners relied on misleading and incomplete news reports to discern the identity and objectives of this Kansas guerrilla. Southern papers considered Brown the forward element of an invading abolitionist army and warned readers to prepare for secession and war. Most northern editors condemned Brown and distanced their subscribers from his aggressive assault. Infuriated by this groundswell of public opinion, Henry Thoreau assailed the press: "They do not know the man. They must enlarge themselves to conceive of him. . . . They have got to conceive of a man of *ideas* and of *principle*, hard as it may be for them." From the moment he touched pencil to journal page in his opening salvo of October 19—"When a government puts forth its strength on the side of injustice, as ours (especially to-day) to maintain slavery and kill the liberators of the slave, what a merely brute, or worse than brute, force it is seen to be!"—to the last sentence that day several pages later—"Such a government is losing its power and respectability as surely as water runs out of a leaky vessel and is held by one that can contain it"—a spellbound Thoreau idealized John Brown as others demonized him. He had earlier taken issue with those who quibbled over the constitutionality of the Fugitive Slave Law; so now did Thoreau refute the charge that Brown's was a "treasonous" attack: "I do not complain of any tactics that are effective of good, whether one wields the quill or the sword, but I shall not think him mistaken who quickest succeeds to liberate the slave. I will judge of the tactics by the fruits." Initial bulletins inaccurately reporting Brown's death exacerbated Thoreau's rush to exalt the man and sanction his mission. Courtesy of John Brown and a mythmaking memory, Thoreau's antislavery fervor, nearly dormant for the past five years, had been resurrected.[62]

Supplementing news about the Harpers Ferry raid itself, journalists now dredged up tales of "the notorious Kansas outlaw" and "the scourge of Southern Kansas." Thoreau did not allude to the rampage at Pottawatomie Creek, but in his journal entries about Brown, he nonetheless deflected attention from it: "It galls me to listen to the remarks of craven-hearted neighbors who speak disparagingly of Brown because he resorted to violence, resisted the government, threw his life away!—what way have they thrown their lives, pray?—neighbors who would praise a man for attacking singly an ordinary band of thieves or murderers. Such minds are not equal to the occasion." Critical assessments of the news coverage at the time reveal just how selectively Thoreau read. He dismissed as antiabolitionist propaganda the accounts of Pottawatomie, choosing instead to credit the reports of James Redpath, an antislavery journalist for the *New York Tribune* who had happened on the scene in Kansas just after the killings, interviewed Brown, and wholly believed his protestation of innocence. Importantly, Thoreau also recognized that while every major paper in the country now detailed

Brown's gruesome past, news coverage of slavery's violence had for years appeared almost exclusively in antislavery papers. To those who professed horror at the mutilation of five white corpses in Kansas, Thoreau underscored the atrocities endured by slaves:

> The slave-ship is on her way, crowded with its dying hundreds; a small crew of slaveholders is smothering four millions under the hatches; and yet, the politician asserts that the only proper way by which deliverance is to be obtained is by "the quiet diffusion of sentiments of humanity," without any "outbreak!" And in the same breath they tell us that all is *quiet* now at Harper's Ferry. What is that that I hear cast overboard? The bodies of the dead, who have found deliverance. That is the way we are diffusing humanity, and all its sentiments with it.

With few pangs of conscience, Thoreau judged Brown by his intended ends rather than by his means. Only "they who are continually shocked by slavery have some right to be shocked by the violent death of the slaveholder," he avowed. If the tearful testimony of Mrs. Mahala Doyle, whose husband and sons had been Brown's victims at Pottawatomie Creek, troubled his conscience, Thoreau subscribed to no doubts about the justice of crushing the slave owner.[63]

Thoreau also thrilled to Brown as an elite military commander and credited him with the political victory of "Free Kansas" that had finally been achieved earlier in 1859: "I think that it was he more than any other who made Kansas as free as she is, who taught the slaveholder that it was not safe for him to carry his slaves thither." Thoreau did not denounce but in fact applauded the armed resistance of Harpers Ferry: "For once the Sharp's rifle and the revolver were employed in a righteous cause. The tools were in the hand of one who could use them." Several critics have noted that ultimately Thoreau confessed his own potential for violence: "I do not wish to kill or be killed, but I can foresee circumstances in which both of these things would be by me unavoidable." The intellectual posturing and nuanced oppositions of "Civil Disobedience" had given way. Like others who defended the Kansas vigilante, Thoreau "believed in John Brown because he wanted to believe in him."[64]

During Brown's trial, defense counselors briefly introduced the possibility that mental illness ran in the family, an allegation Brown immediately rejected, yet one still bandied about today. Again, however, Thoreau transferred this red herring back to the issue at hand, slavery itself: "Insane! A father and seven sons, and several more men besides,—as many, at least, as twelve disciples,—all struck with insanity at once; while the same tyrant holds with a firmer gripe than ever his four millions of slaves, and a thousand sane editors, his abettors, are saving their country and their bacon!

Just as insane as were their efforts in Kansas. Ask the tyrant who is his most dangerous foe, the sane man or the insane." Thoreau further dismissed the rumor by attacking those who spread it: "Of course, the mass of men . . . cannot conceive of a man who is actuated by higher motives than they are. Accordingly they pronounce him insane, for they know that they would never act as he does as long as they are themselves." Soon an imprisoned Brown offered his own rationale for his motives: "You know that Christ once armed Peter. So also in my case; I think he put a sword into my hand, and there continued it, so long as he saw best."[65] Sentenced at the end of October to hang on three counts—treason, inciting slaves to rebel, and murder—Brown affirmed that "it is a great comfort to feel assured that I am permitted to die *for a cause*," inspiring Thoreau to still grander accolades:

> He was a superior man. He did not value his bodily life in comparison with ideal things; he did not recognize unjust human laws, but resisted them, as he was bid; and now he is called insane by all who cannot appreciate such magnanimity. He needed no babbling lawyer, making false issues, to defend him. He was more than a match for all judges that American voters, or officeholders of whatever grade, can create. He could not have been tried by a jury of his peers, because his peers did not exist.
>
> When a man stands up serenely against the condemnation and vengeance of mankind, rising above them literally by a whole body,—though he were a slave, though he were a freeman, though he were of late the vilest murderer, who has settled that matter with himself,—the spectacle is a sublime one!—did n't ye know it, ye Garrisons, ye Buchanans, ye politicians, attorney-generals?—and we become criminal in comparison. Do yourselves the honor to recognize him. *He* needs none of your respect.

Garrison had long been friends with the family, but Henry Thoreau could not abide the editor's denunciation of Brown. Further, Thoreau surely appreciated that his own radicalism now exceeded that of the Garrisonians. Later in the winter, following Brown's execution, Thoreau mused that those who pronounced Brown crazy would have embraced him had his raid succeeded: "I have no doubt that, if he had gone with five thousand men, liberated a thousand slaves, killed a hundred or two slaveholders, and had as many more killed on his own side, but not lost his own life, such would have been prepared to call it by another name."[66]

In Thoreau's rendering, Brown transcended to the self-sacrificing divine, the state his executioner: "A government that pretends to be Christian and crucifies a million Christs every day! . . . A church that can never have done with excommunicating Christ while it exists." Subsequent journal entries echo this daring correspondence: "Some eighteen hundred years ago Christ was crucified; this morning, perhaps, John Brown was hung. These are the two ends of a chain which I rejoice to know is not without its links"; and, "Think of him,—of his rare qualities!—such a man as it takes ages to make. . . . You who pretend to care for Christ crucified, consider what you are about to do to him who offered himself to be the savior of four millions of men!" Ultimately, Thoreau bestowed upon Brown a compliment surpassing even Christian heroism: "A man of rare common sense and directness of speech, as of action; a Transcendentalist above all, a man of ideals and principles." The mythic edifice had been assembled. The Kansas fighter was "not Old Brown any longer" but "an Angel of Light."[67]

Before long, others joined Thoreau in deifying Brown. Theodore Parker, safely ensconced in Rome where his role as one of the "Secret Six" remained unknown even to friends, championed Brown, reiterating his previous rationale for violent abolitionism: "A man held against his will as a slave has a natural right to kill every one who seeks to prevent his enjoyment of liberty." Henry C. Wright, the houseguest whose "slimy benignity" had so revolted Thoreau a few years earlier, praised "God who giveth the victory over Slavery through *John Brown*." Even Garrison pronounced Brown "as faithful to truth as that of the most glorious of the Christian martyrs." But it was former slaves who especially treasured the grizzled warrior. To Frederick Douglass, "posterity will owe everlasting thanks to John Brown for lifting up once more to the gaze of a nation grown fat and flabby on the garbage of lust and oppression, a true standard of heroic philanthropy, and each coming generation will pay its installment of the debt." To Harriet Tubman, Brown was divine: "He gave up his life for our people, and how he never flinched, but was so brave to the end; its clar to me it wasn't mortal man, it was God in him."[68]

Some abolitionists remained conflicted, however. Samuel J. May praised Brown's willingness to act on behalf of the nation's (now nearly) 4 million slaves, but he deplored the violence enacted at Harpers Ferry. Lydia Maria Child disapproved of Brown's actions per se—"such violent attempts to right wrong are both injudicious and evil"—yet she valued his "generous intentions" and could not "help honoring the brave old man." This equivocating struck Thoreau as absurdly hypocritical. In contrast, Thoreau's other favorite radical, Wendell Phillips, unabashedly defended Brown in voicing southerners' worst fears: "The lesson of the hour is insurrection. Insurrection of thought always precedes the insurrection of arms. The last twenty years have been an insurrection of thought. We seem to be entering on a new phase of this great American struggle." Phillips affirmed slaves' "right to resist" in terms all Americans understood: "I will not argue that question to a people hoarse with shouting ever since July 4, 1776, that all men are created equal, that the right to liberty is inalienable, and that 'resistance to tyrants is obedience to God.'" Albeit he condemned the raid's violence, even Garrison had privately delighted in Brown's symbolic value: "John

Brown executed will do more for our good cause, incomparably, than John Brown pardoned." Thoreau's charges of hypocrisy seem right on the mark.[69]

Thoreau's autumnal saunters took place as usual throughout October, but by day's end most journal entries recur to Brown. Although the principled fury soon deteriorated into maudlin platitudes and Brown to a Puritan saint, the journal signaled only the beginning of Thoreau's tribute. On October 30, the day before Brown's conviction and sentencing, Thoreau gave his first public address about John Brown at First Church, becoming the first in Concord and among the first in the nation to begin constructing John Brown's iconic status. Waldo Emerson later recounted Thoreau's droll retort to those in town who had opposed this move: "I did not send to you for advice, but to announce that I am to speak." Replicating the composition process that had generated "Slavery in Massachusetts," Thoreau worked over his journal to create an address that soon became known as "A Plea for Captain John Brown." Many critics have focused on the deliberate choice of the word "plea." Indeed, Thoreau announced his intention "to correct the tone and the statements of the newspapers"; his goal was to reclaim John Brown's "character and actions." Media accounts had selectively focused on Brown's shortcomings in business and crimes in Kansas. So, too, did Thoreau posit a judicious biography. Rather than contend with Brown's actions, Thoreau erected a superior man, crafting a new "plea" on a span other than "guilty" and "not guilty." Arrayed in Thoreau's most impassioned rhetoric, the pike-wielding religious terrorist would apotheosize into a new breed of transcendentalist liberator.[70]

"A Plea" elicited conflicting opinions from Thoreau's Concord neighbors. Fifteen years old at the time he heard the speech, Edward Emerson later remembered Thoreau's "deeply stirred" delivery; Bronson Alcott judged it "a revolutionary Lecture," an "account . . . by which that martyr's fame will be transmitted to posterity," and Alcott relayed to Daniel Ricketson the "great favor" the speech elicited in town. Farmer Minot Pratt provided the most telling local reaction in a letter to his wife, female society member Maria Pratt, who missed hearing Thoreau herself:

> I have just returned (most 10 o'clock,) from hearing a sort of lecture from Henry Thoreau, on the subject of the affair at Harper's Ferry, or rather on the character of Capt. Brown. Henry spoke of him in terms of the most unqualified eulogy. I never heard him before speak so much in praise of any man, and did not know that his sympathies were so strong in favor of the poor slave. He thinks Capt. Brown has displayed heroic qualities that will cause him to be remembered wherever and whenever true heroism is admired. The lecture was full of Henry's quaint and strong expressions, hitting the politicians in the hardest manner, and showing but little of that venera-

tion which is due to our beloved President and all government officials, who are laboring so hard and so disinterestedly for the welfare of the dear people. The church, also, as a body, came in for a share of whipping, and it was laid on right earnestly.

Pratt reveals that the speech impacted him as Thoreau surely intended—instead of justifying the rationale for Harpers Ferry, the speech honored "the character of Capt. Brown." Although surprised by the denunciatory tone, unaware of Thoreau's fervent antislavery "sympathies," and a bit taken aback with the "unqualified" nature of the tribute, Pratt responded to the essence of Thoreau's message—"a man of *ideas* and *action*," Brown carried out his ideals. The moderate abolitionist Pratt was undoubtedly more receptive to "A Plea" than many in Thoreau's audience, but his analysis indicates nevertheless that at this early juncture there were some in the community who accepted the transcendent version of Brown that Thoreau put forward.[71]

It was Waldo Emerson, however, who so appreciated Thoreau's remarks that he recommended Thoreau deliver them in Boston as a stand-in for Frederick Douglass, who had hurriedly left the country in the wake of Harpers Ferry and would therefore not be in Boston to deliver his scheduled address. Emerson contacted the lecture series' organizer, Charles Slack, to tout Thoreau's "Plea":

> I understand there is some doubt about Mr. Douglass's keeping his engagement for Tuesday next. If there is a vacancy, I think you cannot do a greater public good than to send for Mr. Thoreau, who has read last night here a discourse on the history & character of Captain John Brown, which ought to be heard or read by every man in the Republic. He read it with great force & effect, & though the audience was of widely different parties, it was heard without a murmur of dissent.
>
> I wish it to be heard in Boston, &, if there is not room tomorrow night, can there not be next Sunday forenoon?

The recommendation obviously carried weight. On November 1, Thoreau offered his ardent testimonial to more than two thousand people gathered at Tremont Hall, the largest audience he had ever addressed. Two days later, he repeated the speech in Worcester, having asked friends there to arrange it: "I think that we should express ourselves at once, while Brown is alive," Thoreau urged.[72]

News reports of the speech berated Thoreau as "a thorough fanatic," with critics advising him to "imitate Brown and do good by rushing to the gallows." One abolitionist somewhat peevishly noted that "the exciting theme seemed to have awakened 'the hermit of Concord' from his usual state of

philosophic indifference," but William Robinson applauded Thoreau's re-
marks about Brown in the *Springfield Republican*.[73] New admirers, such as
Mary Jennie Tappan, daughter of an abolitionist family in Bradford, New
Hampshire, conveyed their regard directly:

> I wish to thank you for the utterance of those brave, true words in behalf of
> the noble Saint and self–forgetting hero of Harpers Ferry; just *the* words I so
> longed to have some living voice speak, *loud*, so that the world might hear—
> In the quiet of my home among the hills I read them tonight and feel that my
> thought has found a glorified expression and I am satisfied, and through the
> distance I reach forth my hand to thank you—bless you.

The speech's reception elicited no comment in his journal, but Thoreau
did remark on his inability to derive comfort from autumn's grandeur
"when my mind was filled with Captain Brown. So great a wrong as his fate
implied overshadowed all beauty in the world." Thoreau evinced surprise
"that the little dipper should be still diving in the river as of yore" in disregard of "Captain Brown's fate." Such comments contrast significantly with
the ability of the white water lily to buoy Thoreau's spirits following the rendition of Anthony Burns five years before. The usual solace Thoreau found
in nature eluded him now.[74]

Waldo Emerson's initial reaction to Harpers Ferry was more subdued
than Thoreau's, yet Emerson spoke out several times in support of Brown
this fall and winter, particularly at rallies to aid his family. He also joined
T. W. Higginson, Samuel E. Sewall, and Samuel Gridley Howe in soliciting
"contributions to aid in the defence of Capt. BROWN and his companions,
on trial for their lives in Virginia." Like Thoreau, Emerson soon venerated
Brown as "the rarest of heroes, a pure idealist," and he earned the contempt
of many with the audacious pronouncement that Brown would "make the
gallows glorious like the cross." Regrettably, however, in an observation
probably intended as a compliment, Emerson devalued three decades of
women's abolitionism in characterizing Brown's devotees: While "all gentlemen, of course, are on his [Brown's] side," he supposed that "all women are
drawn to him by their predominance of sentiment," a striking deviation
from Thoreau, who had observed "that the women of the land are where
the men should be." Thoreau came to this opinion practically, living as he
did with several women who shared his reverence for Brown.[75]

John Brown had deeply moved other Concord abolitionists as well.
Louisa May Alcott related her family's attitude to close friend Alfred Whitman, then living in Kansas:

> What are your ideas on the Harpers Ferry matter? If you are *my* Dolphus you
> are full of admiration for old Brow[n]s courage & pity for his probable end.

We are boiling over with excitement here for many of our people (Anti Slavery I mean) are concerned in it. We have a daily stampede for papers, & a nightly indignation meeting over the wickedness of our country, & the cowardice of the human race. I'm afraid mother will die of spontaneous combustion if things are not set right soon.

Abby Alcott validated her daughter's appraisal as she prophetically articulated Brown's legacy in her journal: "John Brown's martyrdom has perhaps been the event of /59.—The confederacy is shaken to its foundation The South have been made to believe that there are brave men in the North— The hour and the man both came at last to reveal to the South their sins— and to the Slaves their Savior—He came to them with a Sword, but he has slain thousands by his Word." Weeks before Brown was executed, Concord abolitionists had already envisioned the essence of his symbolic legacy— Brown's " 'Word' was mightier than his 'Sword.' "[76]

Abolitionists in Concord grieved over Brown as they would have a family member. On the unusually warm afternoon of December 2, just hours after Brown had ascended the gallows outside Charlestown, Virginia, more than two hundred attended a memorial service at Town Hall organized by Henry Thoreau, Waldo Emerson, Simon Brown, and John Shepard Keyes. Town leaders had refused permission for the First Church bells to mark the hour of Brown's execution, but Bronson Alcott found the occasion more solemn for its stillness: "It was more fitting to signify our sorrow in the subdued way, and silently." Simon Brown presided over the service; after a prayer by Rev. E. H. Sears of nearby Wayland, Thoreau prefaced the readings with these remarks:

So universal and widely related is any transcendent moral greatness—so nearly identical with greatness every where and in every age, as a pyramid contracts the nearer you approach its apex—that, when I now look over my commonplace book of poetry, I find that the best of it is oftenest applicable, in part or wholly, to the case of Captain Brown. Only what is true, and strong, and solemnly earnest will recommend itself to our mood at this time. Almost any noble verse may be read, either as his elegy, or eulogy, or be made the text of an oration on him. Indeed, such are now discerned to be the parts of a universal liturgy, applicable to those rare cases of heroes and martyrs, for which the ritual of no church has provided.

Perhaps no factor so epitomized the utterly transformed reform climate in Concord than John Shepard Keyes's partnership with Thoreau on this committee. Even so, an anxious Keyes had worried that participants might "giv[e] way to treasonable utterances if we allowed ourselves to speak our own sentiments" and therefore had "insisted" that no one read from his own writings. Thoreau's blatant disregard of this counsel earned Keyes's scorn: "D. H. Thoreau with his usual egotism broke the agreement and said some rambling incoherent sentences, that might have been unfortunate if they had not been unintelligible." But others who attended deemed the entire service a fitting tribute. Bronson Alcott's estimation—it was "distinguished by modesty, simplicity, and earnestness; worthy alike of the occasion and of the man"—was rendered more enthusiastically by his daughter Louisa: "The execution of Saint John the Just took place on the second. A meeting at the hall, and all Concord was there. Emerson, Thoreau, Father, and Sanborn spoke, and all were full of reverence and admiration for the martyr."[77] Thoreau learned later in the week that "certain persons disgraced themselves by hanging Brown in effigy" in Concord that day, but he scoffed at the rumored hundreds who condemned him for helping plan the commemoration: "A considerable part of Concord are in the condition of Virginia to-day,—afraid of their own shadows."

The *Boston Post* ridiculed Concord "abolitionists . . . insane attempt" to toll the bells for Brown and thought to belittle the entire occasion as "chiefly composed of ladies." Further, this reporter described the derisive "Last Will and Testament of Old John Brown" that someone had posted at the scene of Brown's effigy:

> I bequeath to Hon. Simon Brown my execution robe, the emblem of spotless purity and an unswerving politician.
>
> I bequeath to Hon. John S. Keyes my execution cord, made of material warranted to last to hang all the aiders and abettors of Old John Brown.
>
> I bequeath to H. D. Thoreau, Esq., my body and soul, he having eulogized my character and actions at Harper's Ferry above the Saints in Heaven.
>
> I bequeath to my beloved friend, Charles Bowers my old boots, and emblems of the souls of those I have murdered.
>
> I bequeath to Ralph Waldo Emerson all my personal property, and my execution cap, which contains nearly all the brains I ever had.
>
> I bequeath to Dr. Josiah Bartlett the superintending of the ringing of the bells, and flags at half-mast, union down.

This sketch lampoons all the memorial's organizers, although Thoreau's exaltation of Brown "above the Saints in Heaven" perhaps gave most offense.[78]

In January, "A Plea for Captain John Brown" reached a wider audience when included in James Redpath's *Echoes of Harpers Ferry*, a compilation of sermons, speeches, letters, and poems memorializing Brown and published to raise money for the families of the black Harpers Ferry raiders. That month, Redpath had sought Thoreau's permission to use "A Plea" in the book; he also confirmed Sophia Thoreau's admiration for Brown: "In a few weeks I shall be able to give Miss Thoreau a large number of duplicates of articles on J. B."[79] Concord abolitionists figured prominently in Redpath's collection, beginning with the title page, which displays the first stanza from Emerson's "Concord Hymn," the "shot heard round the world" taking on decidedly new significance. Added to Emerson's and Thoreau's speeches about Brown was Louisa May Alcott's poem, "With a Rose, That Bloomed on the Day of John Brown's Martyrdom," which had been published in the *Liberator* on January 20. Moreover, the entire proceedings of Concord's memorial service comprised the chapter "Death of Samson," a section introduced by Frank Sanborn: "The town which inaugurated the first American 'Insurrection' was faithful to its traditions in doing honor to the first martyr of the second and the grander Revolution." Later that year, Redpath further privileged Concord's centrality to Brown's vindication when he dedicated another book, his (and the first) biography of Brown, to the triad of "Wendell Phillips, Ralph Waldo Emerson, and Henry D. Thoreau, Defenders of the Faithful."[80] Such recognition, and in such company, must surely have gratified Thoreau.

Numerous works on Harpers Ferry cite Thoreau and Emerson's ringing endorsement of John Brown, thereby linking the intellectual legacy of antebellum reform with revolutionary abolitionism. David S. Reynolds argues categorically that "it was the Transcendentalists alone who rescued him from infamy and possible oblivion." Until the past decade or so, however, "A Plea for Captain John Brown" had not received the same critical attention as had "Civil Disobedience," which Michael Meyer has shown served through the 1970s as the foremost example of Thoreau's political ideology. Meyer maintains that critics "almost always . . . argued that Thoreau meant 'Civil Disobedience' more than he did 'A Plea for Captain John Brown,'" but recent emphasis has shifted. "A Plea" and "Slavery in Massachusetts" now appear regularly in anthologies alongside *Walden*, "Civil Disobedience," and the natural history essays. Not surprisingly, this attention to the more bellicose Thoreau has brought a new round of critical rebukes. Contemporary readers squirm, as did those in 1859, over Thoreau's brazen embrace of Brown and his violent means for pursuing the noble end of abolishing slavery; they wish at least that Thoreau had denounced the carnage of Pottawatomie Creek. Yet the uncompromising, combative tone of "A Plea" should surprise no one. It was, indeed, the next iteration of the reformist sensibility that had produced "Civil Disobedience." Its author may have viewed the political landscape of 1859 differently from that of 1848, but Thoreau's attitude toward injustice, particularly slavery, had never been one of nuance or conciliation. Deifying John Brown assuredly took Thoreau's antislavery passion to a more extreme level, but it did not convert a pacifist into a guerrilla. A rebellious fervor had always permeated

Thoreau's antislavery writings and actions—the moral life, from his vantage, was fraught with incongruous choices.[81]

The day after John Brown was hung, Henry Thoreau met with an unforeseen opportunity to do more than talk about the ongoing drama of Harpers Ferry. In fact, he became a criminal conspirator in the affair by aiding and abetting the most improbable of Brown's raiders, twenty-two-year-old Francis Jackson Meriam, the grandson of wealthy Boston Vigilance Committee treasurer Francis Jackson. Like many second-generation abolitionists in the turbulent 1850s, Meriam had parted ways with his grandfather's pacifism and hoped to put his considerable inheritance to work liberating fugitive slaves. In 1857, he had traveled extensively with journalist James Redpath—in the South, in Kansas, and to Haiti. In 1858, Redpath had connected him with John Brown; by the fall of 1859, Meriam was vaguely aware that Brown intended an operation in the slave states. Then, just days before the assault on Harpers Ferry, Meriam arrived on the scene, bearing what Brown always needed most—cash, in the form of six hundred dollars in gold. No one, Frank Sanborn and T. W. Higginson especially, judged him equal to the task—the young man suffered from poor health and had sight in only one eye—but Meriam provided the financial outlay that launched the Harpers Ferry campaign.[82]

Meriam was routed to Brown via Lewis Hayden, who after encountering him in Boston early in October, quickly assessed that Meriam's money could furnish the remaining supplies needed for the raid to commence. Hayden consulted with George Luther Stearns and then sent Meriam to meet Sanborn in Concord. Sanborn doubted Meriam's suitability for the mission, but he sought Higginson's opinion nonetheless: "Tomorrow or next day a Mr. Meriam of Boston . . . will call you, possibly tomorrow night—if not on Saturday A.M. on his way to N.Y. Perhaps you will have something to say to him, or some message for the shepherd." The next days passed in a blur for Meriam. Apparently, he met briefly with Higginson before heading to Brown, his family wired the money from Boston, he traveled to Philadelphia and Baltimore to purchase provisions, and, finally, on the eve of the attack, he came together with the others at Brown's compound in southeastern Maryland. The die now cast, Sanborn acknowledged to Higginson his severe reservations about Meriam: "I consider him about as fit to be on this enterprise as the devil is to keep a powder house; but everything has its use and must be put to it if possible." After all, Sanborn rationalized, "out of the mouths of babes and sucklings come dollars by the hundred, and what is wisdom compared to that?"[83]

Brown assembled his raiding party the night of October 16, and directed Meriam to stay behind with two others to guard the weapons cache. The next day, this group was to convene at a schoolhouse near the Potomac

River and arm the slaves who would be liberated in the attack. Instead, when the Harpers Ferry offensive failed, newspapers reported Meriam both alive and dead.[84] Finally, on November 3, a Richmond, Virginia, paper announced that four raiders, including Meriam, had escaped, a five-hundred-dollar reward posted for the capture of each man. This story gave a detailed physical description of Meriam, complete with the fact that "he has lost one eye—sometimes wears a glass eye." Three days later, however, the *National Anti-Slavery Standard* reiterated its earlier report that Meriam had "died of his wounds [and] been buried by his companions," but the following week, it too announced the reward for Meriam's capture, along with the fact that he and the other escapees had been "charged with the crimes of treason, murder, and conspiring and advising slaves to rebel." Family and friends thus remained ignorant of Meriam's status during these first intense weeks, although close friend William Lloyd Garrison, Jr., believed the worst: "This morning's telegraphic dispatch brings a confirmation of Francis Meriam's death. Where he died we know not yet. It is rumored that he was buried by some fugitive slaves in Pennsylvania. Poor fellow! he died in a noble cause."[85]

But the Richmond dispatch of November 3 had it right. Meriam had fled Maryland very much alive, in the company of four other frantic men— Owen Brown, John Cook, Barclay Coppoc, and Charles Plummer Tidd. Meriam's weak physical condition slowed everyone down as they scrambled north through the Appalachian Mountains, yet all except one ultimately made it, famished and cold, to safety. Cook refused to heed the others' warnings to keep away from populated areas and was captured outside Chambersburg, Pennsylvania, as he foraged for food. Shortly afterward, in what Owen Brown called an "affecting leave-taking," the remaining men put Meriam on a train bound for Philadelphia, where James Redpath helped him to continue north and sent word of his escape to relatives in Boston. By early November, Meriam had arrived in Chatham, Ontario, where he corresponded with Brown's family about the fate of other escapees.[86]

Yet on December 2, the day of John Brown's hanging, Meriam inexplicably showed up in Boston, throwing family and friends into a panic, as William Lloyd Garrison, Jr., explained: "It seems that Francis, under the insane idea that he must revenge Brown's death, came from Canada to Boston. . . . Francis was intensely excited and it was necessary that something should be done to get him out of the way forthwith." Frank Sanborn, who also saw Meriam then, accounted for his appearance a bit differently, although he concurred with Garrison as to Meriam's condition: Meriam "had left his safe retreat in Canada to urge upon Phillips, Wentworth Higginson, and myself the preparation of another attack on slavery, west of the Mississippi! It was a mad proposal, and the young man, almost broken down, physically and mentally, by the sufferings of his flight through Maryland and Pennsylvania, was little better than insane. I would listen to no such folly, and told him, as Phillips had, that he must return without delay to Montreal, a price of thousands being then set on his head." No doubt Sanborn also worried that if arrested, the unstable Meriam might divulge who had directed him to Brown the past October. Avenging Brown's pending execution may indeed have motivated Meriam to return, as perhaps did any guilt he felt at having hindered the others' escape—especially since John Cook now sat in a Virginia prison cell awaiting his hanging, scheduled for December 16.[87]

Regardless of his motives for turning up in Boston, friends and family implored Meriam to return to Canada. Finally he agreed, and Francis Jackson instructed him to take the Fitchburg train to South Acton, but Meriam mistakenly (according to Sanborn) boarded one bound only as far as Concord, one station short. He thus landed in alarm on the Sanborns' doorstep the evening of December 2, where Sarah Sanborn fed and hurried him upstairs and out of sight. When Frank Sanborn returned from Boston to find Meriam there, he turned to trusted friends who "asked no questions" to effect the young man's disappearance—first securing permission to borrow Waldo Emerson's horse and wagon, then requesting Henry Thoreau to drive "Mr. Lockwood" to the South Acton station early the next morning. Sanborn stressed that regardless of any wild talk, the passenger must be put on the train at all costs. In an elliptical journal entry on December 3, Thoreau documented his morning's drive:

> X was betrayed by his eyes, which had a glaring film over them and no serene depth into which you could look. Inquired particularly the way to Emerson's and the distance, and when I told him, said he knew it as well as if he saw it. Wished to turn and proceed to his house. Told me one or two things which he asked me not to tell S[anborn]. Said, "I know I am insane,"—and I knew it too. Also called it "nervous excitement." At length, when I made a certain remark, he said, "I don't know but *you* are Emerson; are you? You look somewhat like him." He said as much two or three times, and added once, "But then Emerson would n't lie." Finally put his questions to me, of Fate, etc., etc., as if I *were* Emerson. Getting to the woods, I remarked upon them, and he mentioned my name, but never to the end suspected who his companion was. Then "proceeded to the business,"—"since the time was short,"—and put to me the questions he was going to put to Emerson. His insanity exhibited itself chiefly by his incessant excited talk, scarcely allowing me to interrupt him, but once or twice apologizing for his behavior. What he said was for the most part connected and sensible enough.
>
> When I hear of John Brown and his wife weeping at length, it is as if the rocks sweated.

Mr. Lockwood's identity may have remained a secret, but Thoreau knew why the young man needed to vanish. Long after, Sanborn maintained that neither he, Thoreau, nor Emerson discussed the matter until a few years later, when, near death, Thoreau relayed the story to Sanborn "with some amusement," including the fact that at one point Meriam had "flung himself from the wagon":

> How Thoreau managed to get him back again he never told me; but I have always suspected some judicious force exercised on the slight youth, together with that earnest persuasive speech natural to the philosopher; for then they fell to discussing some moral question, and there was no more insurrection till they reached South Acton, where Thoreau saw his man on board the Canada train, and drove leisurely back to the Emerson house, returned Dolly [the horse] and the carriage to James Burke, and walked back to his own late breakfast. On the way he called at my door to say that "Mr. Lockwood had taken passage for Montreal,"—where he safely arrived the next morning.[88]

Other than T. W. Higginson, who may also have encountered the distraught young man at this time, apparently none of the other Secret Six conspirators learned of Meriam's fleeting emergence in Boston. But a communiqué Thoreau received during his final illness in 1862 suggests that another individual possibly knew of his aid to Meriam. Mary Stearns, wife of Secret Six financier George Luther Stearns and friend of Meriam's mother, Eliza Eddy, alluded to a favor Thoreau had unconsciously given her: "The spirit moves me, to send you some of my flowers—and I hope you will like to have them, because, it will be a satisfaction to do some pleasant thing for one, who has bestowed so liberally on me—unknown."[89] Stearns was the Emersons' houseguest the day before Thoreau drove Meriam to safety; the following summer, she and Meriam both attended a memorial service for John Brown in North Elba, New York. Perhaps she knew why Sanborn had borrowed the Emersons' horse and wagon; perhaps Meriam himself informed her of his inadvertent layover in Concord and safe conveyance out of town by an anonymous driver. As they listened at the July service to Richard Hinton read Thoreau's elegy, "The Last Days of John Brown," Meriam was presumably still oblivious that the author—who did not attend the ceremony—had been his rescuer, but Mary Stearns may have known otherwise.[90]

In "The Last Days of John Brown," Thoreau deems Brown's impact "meteor-like, flashing through the darkness in which we live"—"the *living* North . . . suddenly all transcendental." In this essay, Thoreau also mentions a letter that John Brown had sent to his wife and family in mid November, a missive reprinted widely in the *Liberator* and other papers;

Thoreau especially complimented Brown's advice "respecting the education of his daughters." Among other homilies, Brown had urged his wife to honor his belief that "plain but perfectly practical education" would best prepare the girls "to meet the stern realities of life with a good grace." Their daughter Annie, however, was less sanguine about other paternal counsel. At age fifteen, she and her sister-in-law Martha (whose husband, Oliver Brown, was killed at Harpers Ferry) had managed the household at the Kennedy Farm in Maryland for three months prior to the raid. Not only had these two teenagers handled the cooking, gardening, laundry, and cleaning for some twenty men, they also provided the necessary subterfuge when prying neighbors grew increasingly inquisitive. Albeit fiercely loyal to her father, Annie confided to T. W. Higginson just before Brown was executed that she could not honor his appeal "to become a *sincere, humble, earnest, & consistent Christian*":

> You wished a copy of my Fathers letter to me. (you shall have it.) In that letter he asks me to become a *Christian*. I am sorry that I cannot do as he wishes. I have several reasons (which are satisfactory to me) for not being what is commonly termed a *Christian*, one of which is, if there is another existence after this (and I believe there is.) I believe that *all* will finally be forgiven and *saved*. The notion of *eternal damnation* is contrary to all my ideas of justice, mercy, or benevolence, and I will not accept pardon on the terms offered. I choose to suffer individually for all the evil deeds done in this world by *me*.
>
> But enough of this. You will not thank me for giving you my religious views with out asking. But I did not want you to think that I was careless about my own welfare and did not know what kind of ground I was standing on.[91]

Concord welcomed this spirited young woman and her younger sister Sarah into their community in late February 1860 when abolitionists arranged for them to attend Sanborn's school. Sanborn related to Theodore Parker the circumstances that brought them to his classroom, diminishing as he did so Annie's key role preceding Harpers Ferry: "Two of Capt. Brown's daughters—one 16—the other 13—are to come to my school soon—probably next week. They are bright girls, tho' of course unused to the way of society. Anna is a woman already; she kept house for her father in Maryland."[92]

The Browns stayed with the Emersons for a short time until moving over to board with George and Julia Clark on Lexington Road, where Sanborn's assistant schoolteacher also lived. Ellen Emerson sympathized with their circumstances but still gossiped that although Sarah and Annie Brown were "not as homely as she expected," her friend Frank Preston Stearns found them "dreary." Others in town sympathized with the girls, as Emerson explained, "dressing them in Boston fashion, that they should look like the rest of the world when they go to school." Sanborn determined after a few days in his classroom that the Browns were "good and sensible, and will make fair scholars." But within weeks, Annie had succumbed to emotional distress and left for home in spite of her family's desire that she remain in Concord.[93]

Henry Thoreau almost certainly encountered Annie and Sarah Brown on several occasions during their stay in Concord, the first time likely at the welcome party Sophia and Cynthia Thoreau hosted for the girls shortly after they arrived in town. Bronson Alcott, who met them at the Thoreau home, maintained that Annie Brown told him Henry "reminded her of her father," although he did not elaborate. Thoreau surely would have known about Annie's critical role in the Harpers Ferry conspiracy; he would have prized her spirited loyalty to her father and valued her religious skepticism. Nevertheless, he left no record of these interactions with his hero's daughters.[94]

In late May, John Brown's widow, Mary, and her daughter-in-law, Belle, also visited Concord, staying with Sanborn and meeting with Boston friends to review ongoing efforts for their financial support. They were guests of the Alcotts at a reception following an antislavery meeting, an affair that drew an unexpected crowd, according to Louisa May Alcott: "The preparations had been made for twenty at the utmost, so when forty souls with the usual complement of bodies appeared, we grew desperate, and our neat little supper turned into a regular 'tea fight.' . . . I let the hungry *wait* and the thirsty *moan* for tea, while I picked out and helped the regular Antislavery set." Alcott especially doted on Belle's infant son: "He is named Frederick Watson Brown, after his murdered uncle and father, and is a fair heroic-looking baby, with a fine head, and serious eyes that look about him as if saying, 'I am a Brown! Are these friends or enemies?' "[95]

As part of the "Exhibition of the Schools of Concord" in March 1861, Louisa Alcott penned a song for the students to perform that unwittingly drew out local tensions still lingering over John Brown. Some Concordians were so "disturbed" by a verse honoring Brown that they advised Louisa to delete it—throwing her father, as superintendent of schools, into a quandary, and causing a "rabid" Abby Alcott to "denounce the whole town." Not only did the song remain intact, but Waldo Emerson read each stanza preceding the students' singing. John Shepard Keyes, now firmly in the radicals' camp, congratulated Louisa Alcott on "yr' fine song Miss Alcott the *second* verse especially." Alcott took the uproar in stride, pronounced the naysayers "a queer narrow minded set," and, overall, felt she had "won quite a little victory over the old fogies."[96]

Annie and Sarah Brown boarded with the Alcotts again in the spring and summer of 1861, this time to learn "housework," their stay a disgruntling prospect to Louisa, as her elder sister, Anna, noted: "The additional labor,

& care will be too much for mother and deprive *her* of all the leisure she so covets for her writing." Abby Alcott perceived, after the girls arrived, that Annie's condition had not visibly improved from the prior year: "The oldest has been dreadfully tried in her nervous system—She tries to study but her heart and thoughts are not in her books—She has had a terrible 'lesson for the day' its consequences may be most sad to *her* as well as fatal to her father—She lived 4 months at Harper's Ferry—Are we not beginning to reap in the Storm what was there Sown in the whirlwind." Time with the Alcotts, however, evidently proved restorative. By October, Annie Brown herself assessed the past several months: "At that time my mind and body were completely (or nearly so) over worked, and my nerves *unstrung* so that nothing but 'water cure doctoring' and quiet have restored me to my usual good health."[97]

Brown's Concord schoolteacher in part shared this emotional distress. Although Frank Sanborn had persevered with his teaching duties, he did so consumed with worry that he would be apprehended and forced to testify before the Senate committee investigating the Harpers Ferry conspiracy. The month after Brown was hanged, Sanborn had received—and ignored—a summons to appear in Washington, D.C., for that specific purpose. His predicament kept all of Concord on edge, his "doings" the town's "chief interest" according to Ellen Emerson. Even Henry Thoreau penned a cryptic journal entry about his friend's predicament. T. W. Higginson had disparaged his fellow conspirators for fleeing the country, yet Sanborn's alarm was, in fact, quite valid. On the night of April 3, 1860, federal marshals appeared at his home, setting the scene for Concord abolitionists to assume a starring role in the lingering drama of Harpers Ferry.[98]

When Sanborn answered a knock at the door late that evening, four deputies entered the room, presented a warrant for his arrest, clasped handcuffs on his wrists, and, in his words, "tried to force me from the house." The men then attempted to push him outside to their wagon, while Sarah Sanborn began "raising a constant alarm" through the neighborhood—"only think how well Miss Sanborn must have screamed," Ellen Emerson marveled the next day. Meanwhile, Sanborn himself, a tall, gangly man, hindered all attempts to place him into the carriage, in his own rendering:

> As they approached the door I braced my feet against the posts and delayed them. I did the same at the posts of the veranda, and it was some minutes before they got me on the gravel walk at the foot of my stone steps. . . . At the stone posts of the gateway I checked their progress once more, and again, when the four rascals lifted to insert me, feet foremost, in their carriage . . . I braced myself against the sides of the carriage door and broke them in. By this time it was revealed to them that my unfettered feet were making all this trouble, and one of the four, named Tarleton, wearing a long black beard,

grasped my feet and brought them together, so that I could no longer use them in resistance.

By now, the First Church bells were sounding the alarm, and a crowd had gathered on Sudbury Road. Some of Sanborn's students who boarded nearby with Ann and Francis Bigelow joined the action; one, Grace Mitchell, ran along the streets, summoning all the neighbors, including John Shepard Keyes.[99]

Many accounts of this seriocomic incident contain a generous measure of hyperbole, but nearly all witnesses credit townswomen most for depriving the marshals of their prey that evening. At one point, Sarah Sanborn "grasped the long beard" of one so firmly that he let go of her brother, both of them wrestling with the men as the neighbors came running. First to help were apparently William and Anne Whiting. Fifteen years after wishing that she instead of Henry Thoreau had rung the bells for the August 1 celebration in 1844, Anne Whiting now distinguished herself in the antislavery crusade, much to her friends' delight. Ellen Emerson bragged the next day that "Miss Anne Whiting got into the carriage and held the door and put herself in the way, and fought with a cane, and so prevented them from getting Mr Sanborn in, and gave the people time to collect. . . . The men hurt her and scratched her and tore her dress trying to get her out, but she stayed in and hindered them a long time." Louisa Alcott likewise exalted Whiting's courage: "Annie Whiting immortalized her self by getting into the kidnapper's carriage so that they could not put the long legged martyr in. One of the rascals grabbed her & said 'Get out.' 'I wont' said Annie. 'I'll tear your clothes.' 'Well tear away.' 'I'll whip up the horses & make them run away if you dont get out.' 'Let them run to the devil but I shant stir.' & the smart little woman didnt till the riot was over." The victim himself, Frank Sanborn, also heroized Whiting, who "climbed to the box beside the driver, and assured him that she was going as far as he and his horses went."[100]

Abbie May, the youngest Alcott daughter, summarized the evening's excitement for family friend Alfred Whitman:

> I must tell you all about the Sanborn kidnapping, which has kept the town in a perfect ferment ever since it happened & won't be forgotten in a hurry. Tuesday night about nine or after, just as we were going to bed we heard the town bell ringing tremendously & thinking it was fire merely looked out but not seeing any light went quietly to bed little dreaming what was really going on. Next morning Horace Mann came rushing in to tell us Mr. Sanborn had been arrested by officers, handcuffed, & would have been carried off but for the heroic conduct of Miss Sanborn & Anna Whiting. . . . as soon as Lu & I heard what Horace had to tell, we jumped out of bed, scrabbled on any clothing we get hold of & dashed off to town through mud & rain to Miss Whiting

who told us the whole affair . . . a great crowd had gathered & were knocking down the officers, right & left cutting the carriage to pieces & regularly rescuing poor S. who stood without hat or boots, till Judge Hoar arrived. . . . Altogether it's the greatest excitement we have had in Concord for a great while & is only the beginning of another revolution.[101]

Soon John Shepard Keyes arrived on the scene, the essence of level-headed thinking, in his estimation:

I ran to his house next to the high school house to find him handcuffed in the carryall with the 3 deputy marshals holding him, and an excited crowd of 30 men & women holding the horse and stopping the load in front. Sanborn terribly excited, and waving frantically his manacles and calling for help and then I enquired of the officers who recognized me their purpose and authority which they gave and then telling the crowd to detain them till I got back, rushed off to Judge Hoar's house. . . . I applied to him for a writ of Habeas Corpus for Sanborn and as soon as he understood the matter he granted it. I writing the petition therefore while he filled out the writ. Armed with this I hastened back to find the crowd swelled to a mob of hundreds. . . . My coolness and legal instinct alone prevented a dreadful row. . . . the officers were armed, and but for my prompt interference would have made sad work and a terrible result, instead of the quiet surrender I brought about by means of the writ. It was the best instance of presence of mind I can recall in my whole experience!

Armed "with a six-shooter," Sanborn then spent the night with a neighbor, while Henry Thoreau camped out in his home, on guard in case the deputies returned. Thoreau's is indisputably the most succinct of all the accounts: "Lodged at Sanborn's last night after his *rescue,* he being away."[102]

Abbie May Alcott's notion that "another revolution" had begun, similar to Thoreau's stress on "*rescue,*" affirms the abolitionists' sense of incredible triumph, a sentiment unabashedly on display when Mary Brooks exulted over Concord's moment in the limelight to Maria Weston Chapman later in the week:

How do you think I feel! In raptures I would be glad to be were it not that I am fearing, constantly, something else will be upon us that will not be met in the same determined manner. You never saw a more resolute set of people. One word from one they considered wise, and those wretches would have been torn to pieces in a moment. One of the officers told the deputy Sheriff that he had been in all kinds of mobs and in all kinds of danger, but he never felt in such fear before. . . . All the part I had in the affair was to run down street, in the first of it, crying murder, murder, help, help it is scholars, girls, run down the street, singing at houses, telling the people Sandborn was being carried off by United States Officers. . . . O if such a blow could be struck here that would thrust back the terrible usurpation which is fastening itself upon us, I should die content. We need Yankee wit and more than Yankee wisdom in this hour. . . . You don't know how anxious we feel. Do you think Massachusetts is ready to rebel, as she ought to do now? I can't think so. . . . Nonresistance principles are hard to abide by in this trial hour. If any thing new occurs I will apprise you of it as early as possible.[103]

The day after the arrest attempt, flanked by abolitionists and townsmen including, ironically, both John Shepard Keyes and Wendell Phillips, Sanborn appeared before the state Supreme Court in Boston, where Chief Justice Lemuel Shaw dismissed the warrant because there was "no legal authority to make the arrest." Sanborn returned to Concord a bona fide hero, met at the station by a cheering throng of hundreds and a cannon salute. He exuberantly hoisted his handcuffs in the air (why he still had them is anyone's guess), shouted that the marshals were lucky to be alive, and basked in the grandest moment of his life. Friends including Waldo Emerson, Henry Thoreau, and a somewhat dubious T. W. Higginson then gathered at Town Hall for what Abbie May Alcott called "an indignation meeting"—the heroic actions of "the brave Concordians" a sure sign of the revolutionary spirit of "old Concord." Thoreau—identified in the *New York Herald's* report as "a genius and a philosopher and reputed to be a man of practical sense and tact"—offered a few remarks to the crowd, calling the previous evening's excitement "the hottest fire he ever witnessed in Concord" and disparaging "the mean and sneaking method the United States officials took to accomplish their purpose." Multiple headlines in the *Liberator* heralded the sensation: "Great Excitement in Concord, Mass.—The Alarm Bells Rang—The whole Town turn out, and prevent Sanborn's being carried away." True to form, Garrison bestowed praise where he knew it due and singled out "The Women of Concord":

> The women, like the mothers of yore, were foremost in the affray, and by every possible means worried the officers. Miss Sanborn seized an officer by his beard, and compelled him to relinquish his hold of Mr. Sanborn. Miss Ann Whiting, daughter of Col. Whiting, approached officer Tarlton, raised his hat, and looking him steadily in the face, said, 'Let me see what kind of a looking man you are. You may come here again some day, and I shall want to know you!'
>
> Mr. Sanborn's sister, seeing the crowd surrounding the officers and her brother, and that she could do no more service there, seized the whip from the carriage and began belaboring the horses in good earnest, but one of the men took the whip from her. She then jumped into the carriage to prevent

her brother being put into it, but she was taken out with more force than politeness, having her clothes torn in the struggle.

The *New York Herald* likewise reported that "had it not been for two ladies—Miss Anna Maria Whiting and the sister of Sanborn—Sanborn would now have been on his way to Washington." The *Liberator* and other papers further noted that "as a token of their respect for her bravery," townsmen had presented Sarah Sanborn "one of the latest styles of Colt's revolvers." Additionally, she was appointed to a newly constituted Concord "vigilance committee," which also comprised Anne Whiting and Louisa Alcott.[104]

Other media accounts, however, such as this one in the antiabolitionist *New York Times*, encouraged officials' to force Sanborn's testimony: "What purpose those who sympathize with JOHN BROWN propose to serve by refusing to obey the subpoena of the Senate, except giving themselves a fleeting notoriety, we confess we are unable even to conjecture." Regardless of detractors, defending their own citizen had sealed the alliance between radical and moderate abolitionists. Once again an intrusive distant power—this time a domestic rather than a foreign tyrant—had been halted at Concord.[105]

> I've often longed to see a war, and now I have my wish. I long to be a man; but as I can't fight, I will content myself with working for those who can.
> —Louisa May Alcott, April 1861

On November 15, 1860, Waldo Emerson recorded a curious assortment of thoughts in his journal: "The news of last Wednesday morning (7th) was sublime, the pronunciation of the masses of America against Slavery. And now on Tuesday 14th I attended the dedication of the Zoological Museum at Cambridge, an auspicious & happy event, most honorable to Agassiz & to the State. On Wednesday 7th, we had Charles Sumner here at Concord & my house." With these three glimpses from his life's record that fall day, Emerson unconsciously denoted a partial spectrum of northern sentiment toward slavery at that time—from the long-awaited political victory for antislavery forces, to an enshrined Harvard professor whose writings legitimated slavery however much he denied that intention, to a rebelliously abolitionist senator whose speeches since his comeback had been more incendiary than ever. A year later, Sumner would go further yet: "People who ask for Peace should be told that peace is impossible while Slavery exists. Abolition is the Condition precedent." The time was near at hand when the nation would act on this standard.[106]

The preceding summer, talk of civil war in Concord had been inseparable from that of Abraham Lincoln's prospects. All but the most incorrigible Garrisonians believed the movement had edged closer to victory with the candidacy of this tepid antislavery Republican from Illinois, but local opinion on the homespun candidate was considerably mixed. Laura Harris reasoned to Prudence Ward that while she did "not feel the slightest interest in Mr. Lincoln . . . *if* he can obtain a large vote and rout the Democrats, it will be all right." But Sophia Thoreau held fast to disunionism, warning her cousin Mary Anne Dunbar not to "imagine that I am a Republican. My motto has long been 'no union with slaveholders' & I think prospects are brightening just now." When the Middlesex County Anti-Slavery Society met in Concord that July, members resolved that Lincoln was "a declared advocate of every pro-slavery compromise in the Constitution ever claimed by Calhoun or endorsed by Webster." The next day, Samuel Barrett succeeded William Whiting as the county society's president, retaining Concord leadership over local abolitionism. Henry Thoreau and Bronson Alcott were among those who addressed the meeting.[107]

Southerners had dreaded the prospect of a Lincoln presidency, but his election prompted unparalleled antiabolitionist violence in the North as well. On December 3, at a Boston rally marking the first anniversary of the "martyrdom" of John Brown, a mob shoved and insulted Frederick Douglass; raucous voices shouted down Frank Sanborn and James Redpath as they rose to speak; then "well-dressed rowdies," as the *Liberator* condemned them, completely took over the proceedings. William McFeely argues that this incident led Douglass to adopt a more deadly strategy than even John Brown: "We must make him [the slaveholder] feel that there is death in the air around him, that there is death in the pot before him, that there is death all around him." Similar violence threatened in Boston at the state society's annual meeting on January 24, where catcalls greeted Waldo Emerson when he denounced "the moral pestilence under which the country has suffered so long." Emerson persevered with his remarks despite rude interruptions throughout his speech, surely earning him the admiration of one Concord neighbor in the audience that day—Mary Brooks.[108]

The new year was distinguished by "events crowded upon each other," Harriet Robinson later recalled. At a benefit sponsored by the female society in February, Frank Sanborn entreated Wendell Phillips to speak: "The Antislavery ladies of Concord propose to hold a Festival on Friday evening the 15th inst. to raise money for the Massachusetts Society. . . . They will have speeches, refreshments, and probably a dance, and hope to attract a large company. Will it be in your power to be present and address them, for as long or as short a time as you please?" Phillips had lectured at the Concord lyceum weeks earlier and staunchly approved the bloody measures taken a half-century before by West Indian insurrectionist Toussaint Louverture: "The black man met the attempt, as every such attempt should be met, with war to the hilt. . . . to save his liberty, the negro exhausted every means, seized every weapon, and turned back the hateful invaders with a vengeance as terrible as their own." In the unlikely event that Concord abolitionists still viewed moral suasion as the sole viable option for ending slavery, Phillips insisted otherwise. "Slavery is a form of perpetual war," he declared, adding, "I prefer an insurrection which frees the slave in ten years to slavery for a century." Phillips spoke contemptuously of President Lincoln, "this [man] who does not know whether he has got any opinions."[109]

Some abolitionists at this juncture railed against what they regarded as a "*pro-slavery* war," but by now even Garrison had warmed in some measure to the likelihood of military combat, a prospect that seemed inescapable when the Confederate States of America formed in February. T. W. Higginson and John Brown had been right—slavery was "destined, as it began in blood, so to end." On April 12, General Pierre Beauregard's South Carolina unit fired on the federal garrison at Fort Sumter; less than a week later, Confederate troops took control of Harpers Ferry, Virginia "with no more authority than John Brown had had," asserts historian Merrill Peterson. Notwithstanding their remarks to the contrary, some abolitionists—even Frederick Douglass—were startled when hostilities broke out. But not in Concord, Massachusetts, where twenty-eight-year-old Louisa May Alcott characterized the momentous atmosphere after the first troops had marched out of town on another memorable April 19: "Of course the town is a high state of topsey turveyness, for every one is boiling over with excitement & when quiet Concord does get stirred up it is a sight to behold. All the young men & boys drill with all their might, the women & girls sew & prepare for nurses, the old folks settle the fate of the Nation in groves of newspapers, & the children make the streets hideous with distracted drums & fifes." Louisa's mother may have been more hesitant, but Abby Alcott was none the less ready for military engagement: "I dread a war—but is not a Peace based on such false compromises and compacts much more disastrous to the real prospects of the Country generally—and Freedom in particular—I think so."[110]

Lidian Emerson, her enthusiasm paralleling Alcott's, sensed in the war "the beginning of the end of slavery" and pronounced it the grandest day in Concord "for 86 years": "Now I begin to feel that I may love the Country and its Flag—it will before long be the sign of Freedom for all. 'Union' is *comparatively* dust in the balance." Lidian Emerson regarded the war as a battle exclusively to end slavery, "the only Holy War the earth has ever known except the war of Revolution—but exceeding that immeasurably in the grandeur of the result at which it aims." Her husband, however, who generally supported the war, shuddered at the "mortification that because a nation had no enemy, it should become its own." Though she rejoiced when war did break out, Lidian would not permit their son, Edward, to enlist until abolishing slavery became a cause for the military action.[111]

A month after the shots at Fort Sumter, Henry Thoreau departed for an excursion to Minnesota in a last effort to restore his failing health. He candidly assessed the potential gains of a war before leaving:

> As to the condition of the country, though Lincoln has been president for nearly a month, I continue to feel as if I lived in an interregnum, & we had no government at all. I have not heard that a single person, north or south, has as yet been punished for treason—stealing from the public treasury—or murdering on political accounts.
>
> If the people of the north thus come to see clearly that there can be no *Union* between freemen & slave-holders, & vote & act accordingly, I shall think that we have purchased that progress cheaply by this revolution. A nation of 20 millions of freemen will be far more respectable & powerful, than if 10 millions of slaves & slave holders were added to them.
>
> I am only afraid that they will still remember their miserable party watchwords—that Democrats will be Democrats still, & so by their concessions & want of patriotism, keep us in purgatory a spell longer.

But Thoreau soon tired of war talk and responded testily to Parker Pillsbury, who on a friend's behalf had asked Thoreau for a copy of his books but had also belittled their relevance in a time of national crisis: "How you can play with a 'bream' in the water when the Leviathan of Slavery is hourly threatening to swallow 'Old Abe' like Jonah." To such a restricted outlook, Thoreau replied: "As for my prospective reader, I hope that he *ignores* Fort Sumpter, & Old Abe, & all that, for that is just the most fatal, and indeed the only fatal, weapon you can direct against evil ever. . . . What business have you, if you are 'an angel of light,' to be pondering over the deeds of darkness. . . . I do not so much regret the present condition of things in this country (provided I regret it at all) as I do that I ever heard of it." Thoreau and his traveling companion, Horace Mann, Jr., heard little about the war while in Minnesota, "not enough to make us very excited," Mann relayed to his mother. But back in Concord that July, Thoreau had come around to Louisa Alcott's way of thinking, at least as Moncure Conway could sense his attitude. Conway described that though "sadly out of health . . . [Thoreau] was in a state of exaltation about the moral regeneration of the nation." His health continued to decline, and Thoreau died on May 6, 1862, never regaining vigor enough to undertake the biography of John Brown that Mary Stearns had thought him the most suited of all Brown's admirers to write: "I must venture to regret—— that you could not stay long enough, to write of 'Old John Brown.' I looked to you, for the worthy statement of his life, feeling sure you had penetrated its secret springs, and could tell what you had seen, and heard."[112]

Harriet Tubman had remained in touch with Frank Sanborn since her initial visit to Concord two years earlier; Sanborn publicized and solicited donations for her labors at every opportunity. She visited Concord again in 1860 and 1861, collecting for her continuous work to free slaves and to subsidize a black community that she had recently organized in St. Catherines, Ontario. Tubman had laid plans for her own John Brown style maneuver just before the war began, plans that Sanborn had hoped she would postpone since, as he explained to Wendell Phillips, "an insurrection might divide the North at this critical time; now the whole of the free states are good abolitionists." By the spring of 1862, Tubman had secured a position at Port Royal, South Carolina, working with the "contrabands" of war—the hundreds of freedmen, women, and children.[113]

Three decades of largely nonviolent activism had not abolished slavery, but a protracted military engagement soon would. F. G. De Fontaine argued in the *New York Herald* two months prior to Fort Sumter that abolitionists sought to "convert without compensation four millions of profitable and contented slaves into four millions of burdensome and discontented negroes," yet such had become a minority view in the North. The political sands had shifted. By the advent of the Civil War, abolitionism had become, if not mainstream, then nearly a fait accompli to most northerners. But faith competed with alarm for Abby Alcott, who at the end of 1861 described the nation's turmoil: "One of the most eventful years this country has experienced since 1812—600,000 troops are in the field ready for battle England threatens us—what another year will accomplish remains to be seen—May God in his infinite mercy overrule the wicked treachery of the South, and combine the North in wise and righteous action for the best good of the Country."[114] Abby may have shared Lidian Emerson's enthusiasm for the antislavery codicil to the impending "Holy War," but she was more apprehensive than previously about the costs of military action.

Abolitionists in Concord, Massachusetts, remained committed to improving their world, one citizen at a time, as the Civil War continued. Female society members now joined their countrywomen in shifting from antislavery to war-related tasks. Ellen Emerson bragged that her mother's bandages achieved a national reputation during the war: "When rolled, they were pinned with Mother's pins, stamped Concord, Mass. and packed. It is really incredible the fame those bandages won." In addition to sewing for the soldiers, townswomen went door-to-door for freedmen's relief—but not all in Concord shared their concern. Abby Alcott's assistance to Harriet Tubman earned her the scorn of some neighbors, as she explained to her brother:

> We have been collecting a bundle of clothing for Harriet Tubman—and indirectly we get the sense of the people—"Oh work for the soldiers let the niggers take care of themselves." I think everything should be done for the Blacks poor creatures, their fate is pathetic—If I was ten years younger I

would go down among them and help—I could not lead a raid as Harriet Tubman did with Montgomery but I could help somewhere these poor fugitives from tyranny and oppression.[115]

The community's racism also reared its ugly head in the gossipy missives of twenty-four-year-old Annie Keyes Bartlett, who kept her soldier brother, Ned, abreast of Concord's social scene. On the eve of the war's triumphant end, Bartlett ridiculed their sister's work to educate local blacks: "Martha told father she and Miss Andrews went out to Readville with Rip Monday and they taught the 'Nigs (to think of our Martha teaching the nigs tis too funny)." Ned Bartlett, a lieutenant in a black Massachusetts cavalry unit, probably found little humor in his sister's "joke."[116]

In 1862, two Concord women, Mary Rice and Mary Peabody Mann, sent a petition containing 350 schoolchildren's signatures requesting President Lincoln to link emancipation to the Union cause and "to free all slave children." But Lincoln offered them little hope. He advised Rice to remind the children that the president did not "have the power to grant all they ask," although they should "remember that God" did. Lincoln issued the Emancipation Proclamation only months later, however, leading to a long-imagined *Liberator* headline, "Glory, Hallelujah!"[117]

Several northern women headed south during and after the war to teach the freed slaves. Concord female society member Harriet Buttrick, teaching at a freedmen's school in Richmond, Virginia, enumerated the specific aid she expected from her townswomen:

Send the garments cut but *unmade*, together with some material for making yarn &c it will be much better than for you to make up what you send. . . . I know the Concord Society will aid me in this project. . . . I am ready to receive any garments you may have in readiness for me. Do you send them through the Boston Society? . . . I suppose you & Miss Richardson, the "indefatigable two" still meet at the Freedmans Aid rooms? . . . Remember me to all interested in me or the cause.

By 1863, nineteen-year-old Annie Brown had overcome her demons enough to venture south, where in almost unbelievable irony, she was assigned to teach freed slaves in the war-torn plantation estate of the man who had overseen her father's execution, former Virginia governor Henry A. Wise.[118]

Concord women continued to subsidize William Lloyd Garrison's work during the war years, but on December 29, 1865, the *Liberator's* final issue came off the press—emancipation achieved, the war ended. Even so, Mary Merrick Brooks remained vigilant, insisting to Wendell Phillips that "the work of the Abolitionists is not done, and will not be, until all God given rights are granted to the so called freedmen." But Brooks's extraordinary role in this struggle came to an end two and a half years later; fittingly, at her funeral, it was Phillips who paid homage to the woman who had kept Concord at the center of another American revolution:

> When, more than thirty years ago, I joined the Anti-Slavery movement, one of the first places I visited was Concord: Mrs. Brooks welcomed me to the old town. She was one—and a chief one—of half a dozen royal-minded women who represented the Anti-Slavery purpose of the place. The famous men who lived there turned then only a tolerant eye on the cause; standing themselves at a civil distance. In kindly deference to wife or friend, they showed their faces, now and then, at Anti-Slavery Meetings. Still it is but justice to say that it was the "continual coming" of those untiring women that "won or wearied" the noted names of Concord into sympathy with this great uprising for justice. If the town stands foremost among New England towns to-day—if its testimony has been earliest and most emphatic on many a great occasion—if, by THOREAU, it sent the first word of cheer to JOHN BROWN'S jail, and if, almost alone, it tolled its church bells when he was murdered—if in Burns and Sims days it drew all eyes to its fidelity; the parlors and vestry gatherings of those just endured women were the "upper chambers" of this Gospel. . . . We call others self-sacrificing and devoted; but she and her associates *lived* for their reform ideas.

Thus did Wendell Phillips honor three decades of antislavery reform that resulted when a few men and "a half dozen royal-minded women" in Concord, Massachusetts, determined, in Brooks's words, "to set this world right."[119]

The names of Henry Thoreau and Waldo Emerson are tantamount with well-examined lives, moral clarity, self-trust, "action from principle." Although Thoreau's advice to "live deliberately" and Emerson's call to "trust thyself" meant little to the individual slaves, for a century and a half now, their moving speeches against slavery have inspired many to battle injustice. Their lives prefigured and paralleled the nation's engagement with this divisive issue, yet these philosophers of reform turned their compelling rhetoric to the abolitionist cause only after an extremist fringe in their families and community persuaded them that the national emergency of slavery demanded unequivocal action.

Other names too seldom emerge from the archives and into the published record—Mary Merrick Brooks; Prudence Ward; John and Mary Wilder; Josiah Bartlett; Susan and Samuel Barrett; Susan and John Garrison; Timothy and Maria Prescott; Ann and Francis Bigelow; Cynthia, Helen, and Sophia Thoreau; Abby, Bronson, Anna, Louisa, and Abbie May Alcott;

Lidian and Ellen Emerson; William, Anne, and Louisa Whiting; Franklin and Sarah Sanborn; Harriet and William Robinson; Mary Rice. These women and men directed their community to right the national wrong of slavery inherited from those who had fired "the shot heard round the world" in their back yard.

Short Titles and Abbreviations for
Frequently Cited Works and Institutions

ABA, *J*   Odell Shepard, ed. *The Journals of Bronson Alcott.* 2 vols.
                    1938. Reprint, Port Washington, N.Y.: Kennikat, 1966.

AL   *American Literature.*

AME   Moncure Daniel Conway. *Autobiography Memories Experi-
                    ences.* 2 vols. Boston: Houghton Mifflin, 1904.

AmS   American Antiquarian Society, Worcester, Massachu-
                    setts.

Annual Report   *Annual Report of the Board of Managers of the Massachusetts
                    Anti-Slavery Society.* 1833–56. 24 vols. in 3. Westport,
                    Conn.: Negro Universities Press, 1970.

AQ   *American Quarterly.*

ATQ   *American Transcendental Quarterly.*

BBS   Boyd B. Stutler Collection, West Virginia State Archives.

BPL   Anti-Slavery Collection, Boston Public Library/Rare
                    Books Department, Boston, Massachusetts.

CFPL   Special Collections, Concord Free Public Library, Con-
                    cord, Massachusetts.

Corr   Henry David Thoreau. *The Correspondence of Henry David
                    Thoreau.* Edited by Walter Harding and Carl Bode. New
                    York: New York University Press, 1958.

CS   *Concord Saunterer.*

Days   Walter Harding. *The Days of Henry Thoreau.* 1962.
                    Reprint, Princeton: Princeton University Press, 1992.

D. S. Reynolds   David S. Reynolds. *John Brown Abolitionist: The Man Who
                    Killed Slavery, Sparked the Civil War, and Seeded Civil Rights.*
                    New York: Knopf, 2005.

EAS	Len Gougeon and Joel Myerson, eds. *Emerson's Antislavery Writings.* New Haven: Yale University Press, 1995.
ESQ	*Emerson Society Quarterly.*
Glick	Wendell Glick. "Thoreau and Radical Abolitionism: A Study of the Native Background of Thoreau's Social Philosophy." Ph.D. diss., Northwestern University, 1950.
ETE, *L*	Edith E. W. Gregg, ed. *The Letters of Ellen Tucker Emerson.* 2 vols. Kent, Ohio: Kent State University Press, 1982.
HL	Houghton Library, Harvard University, Cambridge, Massachusetts.
J	Henry D. Thoreau. *The Journal of Henry D. Thoreau.* Edited by Bradford Torrey and Francis H. Allen. 14 vols. in 2. 1906. Reprint, New York: Dover, 1962.
JER	*Journal of the Early Republic.*
JMN	Ralph Waldo Emerson. *The Journals and Miscellaneous Notebooks of Ralph Waldo Emerson.* Edited by William H. Gilman, Ralph H. Orth et al. 16 vols. Cambridge: Belknap Press of Harvard University Press, 1960–82.
JP	Henry D. Thoreau. *Journal.* Edited by John C. Broderick, Robert Sattelmeyer, Elizabeth Hall Witherell et al. 7 vols. to date. Princeton: Princeton University Press, 1981–.
Keyes	"Autobiography of Hon. John S. Keyes." Special Collections, Concord Free Public Library, Concord, Massachusetts.
LJE, *L*	Delores Bird Carpenter, ed. *The Selected Letters of Lidian Jackson Emerson.* Columbia: University of Missouri Press, 1987.
LMA, *J*	Joel Myerson, Daniel Shealy, and Madeleine B. Stern, eds. *The Journals of Louisa May Alcott.* Boston: Little, Brown, 1989.
LMA, *L*	Joel Myerson, Daniel Shealy, and Madeleine B. Stern, eds. *The Selected Letters of Louisa May Alcott.* Boston: Little, Brown, 1987.
Mass. Lyceum	Kenneth Walter Cameron, ed. *The Massachusetts Lyceum during the American Renaissance.* Hartford, Conn.: Transcendental Books, 1969.
Mayer	Henry Mayer. *All on Fire: William Lloyd Garrison and the Abolition of Slavery.* New York: St. Martin's, 1998.

MCASS	Middlesex County Anti-Slavery Society Records, Concord Free Public Library, Concord, Massachusetts.
McFeely	William S. McFeely. *Frederick Douglass.* New York: Norton, 1991.
MHi	Massachusetts Historical Society, Boston, Massachusetts.
NEQ	*New England Quarterly.*
Oates	Stephen B. Oates. *To Purge this Land with Blood: A Biography of John Brown.* New York: Harper & Row, 1970.
Recollections	Franklin Benjamin Sanborn. *Recollections of Seventy Years.* 2 vols. Boston: Gorham, 1909.
RP	Henry D. Thoreau. *Reform Papers.* Edited by Wendell Glick. Princeton: Princeton University Press, 1973.
RWE, *L*	*The Letters of Ralph Waldo Emerson.* 10 vols. Edited by Ralph L. Rusk and Eleanor M. Tilton. New York: Columbia University Press, 1939–95.
SAR	*Studies in the American Renaissance.*
SL	Schlesinger Library on the History of Women in America, Radcliffe Institute, Harvard University, Cambridge, Massachusetts.
Social Circle	*Memoirs of Members of the Social Circle in Concord.* Second Series. Cambridge, Mass.: Privately printed, Riverside, 1888; *Memoirs of Members of the Social Circle in Concord.* Third Series. Cambridge, Mass.: Privately printed, Riverside, 1907; *Memoirs of Members of the Social Circle in Concord.* Fourth Series. Cambridge, Mass.: Privately printed, Riverside, 1909.
TS	Thoreau Society Collections, Thoreau Institute at Walden Woods, Lincoln, Massachusetts.
TSB	*Thoreau Society Bulletin.*
Walden	Henry D. Thoreau. Edited by J. Lyndon Shanley. Princeton: Princeton University Press, 1971.
"*Warrington*"	Mrs. W. S. Robinson, ed. "*Warrington*" *Pen-Portraits: A Collection of Personal and Political Reminiscences from 1848 to 1876 from the Writings of William S. Robinson.* Boston: Mrs. W. S. Robinson, 1877.
WLG, *L*	*The Letters of William Lloyd Garrison.* 6 vols. Edited by Walter M. Merrill et al. Cambridge: Belknap Press of Harvard University Press, 1971–81.

Notes

Introduction

1. *J,* 13:3.

2. Details for these paragraphs derive from *J,* 13:3–4; Franklin Benjamin Sanborn, *The Personality of Thoreau* (Boston: Charles E. Goodspeed, 1901), 52–58; and Franklin Benjamin Sanborn, *The Life of Henry David Thoreau* (Boston: Houghton Mifflin, 1917), 290–94.

3. Several critics have described Concord's antislavery climate as a "hotbed." See, for example, Glick, 190.

4. A note about my use of the words *abolitionist* and *antislavery.* For years, scholars have distinguished between these terms, as did William Lloyd Garrison and his contemporaries. To Garrison, an abolitionist was one who shared his view that all slaves should be emancipated immediately; yet many who espoused antislavery did not support the extremes of Garrison's radical platform (Mayer, 364). Several historians preserve this distinction, while others posit definitions strikingly at odds with it. See, for example, James M. McPherson, *The Struggle for Equality: Abolitionists and the Negro in the Civil War and Reconstruction* (Princeton: Princeton University Press, 1964), 3; Lawrence Friedman, *Gregarious Saints: Self and Community in American Abolitionism, 1830–1870* (Cambridge: Cambridge University Press, 1982), 1–2; Alfred Bushnell Hart, *Slavery and Abolition 1831–1841* (1906; reprint, New York: Haskell House, 1968), 173–75; William E. Cain, Preface to *William Lloyd Garrison and the Fight against Slavery* (Bedford/St. Martin's, 1995), viii; and Mason Lowance, Jr., Introduction to *Against Slavery: An Abolitionist Reader* (New York: Penguin, 2000), xv–xvii. Given these disparate treatments, I have used "antislavery" and "abolitionist" somewhat interchangeably, although I also refer to "immediatist" and "Garrisonian" when discussing Garrison's movement and followers. Whether Henry Thoreau should be classified an "abolitionist" depends on which definition one adopts and which source one prefers. In the early 1930s, for example, Julian Hawthorne claimed Thoreau "was an abolitionist, though not of the shrieking variety." In 1939, Henry Seidel Canby countered that "Thoreau was never an Abolitionist," while in 1946, Nick Aaron Ford judged him "a true Abolitionist." In 1950, Wendell Glick argued against Ford's inclusivity, holding to the most restrictive sense of the word "abolitionist" and excluded Thoreau from "a label which he neither deserved nor wanted." Yet in 1962, Walter Harding comfortably used the term "abolitionist" to characterize Thoreau, as, more recently, have others such as Richard F. Teichgraeber and Kris Fresonke. See Edith Garrigues Hawthorne, ed., *The Memoirs of Julian Hawthorne* (New York: Macmillan, 1938), 110; Henry Seidel Canby, *Thoreau* (Boston: Houghton Mifflin, 1939), 383; Nick Aaron Ford, "Henry David Thoreau, Abolitionist," *NEQ* 19 (September 1946): 371; Glick, 6; *Days,* 344; Richard F. Teichgraeber III, *Sublime Thoughts/Penny Wisdom: Situating Emerson and Thoreau in the American Market* (Baltimore: Johns Hopkins University Press, 1995), 122; Kris Fresonke, "Thoreau and the Design of Dissent," *Religion and the Arts* 2, no. 2 (1998): 226.

5. One exception to this trend is Joan Trumbull, whose 1944 undergraduate thesis at Vassar College, "Concord and the Negro," called attention to the fact that women were the primary instigators of abolitionism in Concord (53–57). In several works, most notably *Virtue's Hero: Emerson, AntiSlavery, and Reform* (Athens: University of Georgia Press, 1990), Len Gougeon has traced the development of Ralph Waldo Emerson's abolitionist thought and public action, and he has noted the influence brought to bear on Emerson by community activists. In 1950, Wendell Glick assessed the relationship between Thoreau and organized antislavery, particularly examining the degree to which the ideology of Garrison and other activists such as Lydia Maria Child influenced Thoreau's thinking. Glick and other critics have found it significant that during his entire adult life, Thoreau was surrounded—in his home, at his dinner table, in his neighbors' parlor, at the local lecture podiums—by the charged topic of antislavery extremism (Glick, 7). In 1996, in *America's Bachelor Uncle: Thoreau and the American Polity* (Lawrence: University Press of Kansas, 1996), Bob Pepperman Taylor extended and updated Glick's focus in a study that broadly reinterprets Thoreau as a social critic and an antislavery polemicist. Finally, numerous studies of New England abolitionism acknowledge both Concord's and the transcendentalists' role in the antebellum antislavery effort. Most recently, David S. Reynolds in *John Brown, Abolitionist: The Man Who Killed Slavery, Sparked the Civil War, and Seeded Civil Rights* (New York: Knopf, 2005); Albert J. Von Frank in *The Trials of Anthony Burns: Freedom and Slavery in Emerson's Boston* (Cambridge: Harvard University Press, 1998); and Gary Collison in *Shadrach Minkins: From Fugitive Slave to Citizen* (Cambridge: Harvard University Press, 1997), have depicted Concord's contributions to specific moments in the antislavery struggle. Most historical treatments of Concord as well as biographies and other works on Thoreau mention his abolitionism. See especially "*Warrington*"; ABA, *J*; AME; *Days*; ETE, *L*; Canby, *Thoreau*; Barbara K. Elliott and Janet W. Jones, *Concord: Its Black History 1636–1860* (Concord, Mass.: Concord Public Schools, 1976); Edward Waldo Emerson, "Notes on the Underground Railway in Concord and the Concord Station and Officers thereof, with the Facts Concerning Henry Thoreau's Relations to It," typescript, 1892, CFPL; George Hendrick, ed., *Remembrances of Concord and the Thoreaus: Letters of Horace Hosmer to Dr. S. A. Jones* (Urbana: University of Illinois Press, 1977); Milton Meltzer and Walter Harding, *A Thoreau Profile* (1962; reprint, Lincoln, Mass.: Thoreau Society, 1998); Michael Meyer, *Several More Lives to Live: Thoreau's Political Reputation in America* (Westport, Conn.: Greenwood, 1977); Michael Meyer, "Thoreau, Abolitionists, and Reformers," *Thoreau among Others: Essays in Honor of Walter Harding*, ed. Rita K. Gollin (Geneseo, N.Y.: State University College of Arts & Sciences at Geneseo, 1983), 16–26; Sandra Harbert Petrulionis, " 'Swelling that Great Tide of Humanity': The Concord, Massachusetts, Female Anti-Slavery Society," *NEQ* 74 (September 2001): 385–418; Robert D. Richardson, Jr., *Henry Thoreau: A Life of the Mind* (Berkeley: University of California Press, 1986); Henry S. Salt, *Life of Henry David Thoreau*, ed. George Hendrick et al.(Urbana: University of Illinois Press, 1993); Sanborn, *Life of Thoreau*; Sanborn, *Personality of Thoreau*; Sanborn, *Recollections*; Taylor Stoehr, *Nay-Saying in Concord: Emerson, Alcott, and Thoreau* (Hamden, Conn.: Archon, 1979); and Teichgraeber, *Sublime Thoughts*, 1995).

6. Historian Richard D. Brown suggests that the value of "microhistory" is that it enables us to "recognize that every event embodies a kind of existential moment in which the course of history intersects with individual action." He contends further that "the glory of" such an approach "lies in its power to recover and reconstruct past events by exploring and connecting a wide range of data sources so as to produce a contextual, three-dimensional, analytic narrative in which actual people as well as abstract forces shape events" ("Microhistory and the Post-Modern Challenge," *JER* 23 [spring 2003]: 19, 18).

7. *RP*, 75; Wendell Phillips to Frances H. Drake, 11 Oct 1849, typescript, BPL.

8. *RP*, 108.

9. Jane H. Pease and William H. Pease, "Confrontation and Abolition in the 1850s," *Journal of American History* 58 (March 1972): 923.

Chapter 1. A Call to Consciousness, 1831–1843

1. *Concord Directory and Guide* . . . (Concord, Mass: E. H. Smith, 1892), 87; Lori D. Ginzberg, *Women and the Work of Benevolence: Morality, Politics, and Class in the Nineteenth-Century United States* (New Haven: Yale University Press, 1990), 1; *Liberator*, 23 Jun 1843. In addition to Ginzberg, for recent works on how women transformed their private charity into public action in antebellum America, see Anne M. Boylan, *The Origins of Women's Activism: New York and Boston, 1797–1840* (Chapel Hill: University of North Carolina Press, 2002); Debra Gold Hansen, *Strained Sisterhood: Gender and Class in the Boston Female Anti-Slavery Society* (Amherst: University of Massachusetts Press, 1993); Julie Roy Jeffrey, *The Great Silent Army of Abolitionism: Ordinary Women in the Antislavery Movement* (Chapel Hill: University of North Carolina Press, 1998); and Gayle T. Tate, *Unknown Tongues: Black Women's Political Activism in the Antebellum Era, 1830–1860* (East Lansing: Michigan State University Press, 2003). Since Susan Garrison hosted the society's meeting at her home on December 12, I am presuming that she also attended the founding meeting on October 18. For the first gatherings of the Concord Female Anti-Slavery Society, see Timothy Prescott diary, 18 Oct and 12 Dec 1837, HL, bMS Am 2312. In the *Liberator* of June 23, 1843, the society's annual report narrated the tensions and achievements of the organization's first years. Although the report's authorship is uncertain, the resolute, triumphant tone points to Mary Merrick Brooks.

2. *Liberator*, 1 Jan 1831; Mayer, 112. For background on the *Liberator*'s beginning, see Wendell Phillips Garrison and Francis Jackson Garrison, *William Lloyd Garrison 1805–1879: The Story of His Life Told by His Children*, 4 vols. (1885; reprint, New York: Negro Universities Press, 1969), 1:219–29; and Mayer, 106–20. For background on the abolitionists' earliest detractors, see Lorman Ratner, *Powder Keg: Northern Opposition to the Antislavery Movement, 1831–1840* (New York: Basic Books, 1968).

3. Mason Lowance, Jr., Introduction to *A House Divided: The Antebellum Slavery Debates in America, 1776–1865*, ed. Lowance (Princeton: Princeton University Press, 2003), xxx–xxxiii.

4. Gary B. Nash, *Forging Freedom: The Formation of Philadelphia's Black Community, 1720–1840* (Cambridge: Harvard University Press, 1988), 2–6, 172–74, 246–48; William E. Cain, Introduction to *William Lloyd Garrison and the Fight against Slavery* (Boston: Bedford/St. Martin's, 1995), 8–9; Catherine Clinton, ed., *Fanny Kemble's Journals* (Cambridge: Harvard University Press, 2000), 125; Walter Johnson, *Soul by Soul: Life Inside the Antebellum Slave Market* (Cambridge: Harvard University Press, 1999), 6; F. G. De Fontaine, *History of American Abolitionism; Its Four Great Epochs* . . . (New York: D. Appleton, 1861), 55. For a summary of gradual methods of abolition, including colonization, see Gerald Sorin, *Abolitionism: A New Perspective* (New York: Praeger, 1972), 38–43. For details of abolition in Massachusetts, see Elaine MacEacheren, "Emancipation of Slavery in Massachusetts: A Reexamination 1770–1790," *The Journal of Negro History* 55 (October 1970): 289–306.

5. WLG, *L*, 2:481; Mayer, 239, 250, 257, 313; Wendell Phillips, *Speeches, Lectures, and Letters*, second series (1891; reprint, New York: Arno, 1969), 462. For examples of early reports describing slavery's atrocities, see *Liberator*, 5 Feb and 29 Oct 1831, and 10 Nov 1832.

6. Mayer, 130–31, 174–77, 117, 120; *Annual Report*, 7:9.

7. Garrison and Garrison, *William Lloyd Garrison*, 1:239, 247, 232–33.

8. WLG, *L*, 1:134–35; quoted in Garrison and Garrison, *William Lloyd Garrison*, 1:235. For statistics on the extraordinary growth of the cotton industry during the antebellum era, see Stuart Bruchey, comp. and ed., *Cotton and the Growth of the American Economy: Sources and Readings* (New York: Harcourt, Brace & World, 1967). For a helpful discussion of how 19th-century (pseudo)science fostered a cultural mythology of race, particularly as it influenced Waldo Emerson, see Laura Dassow Walls, *Emerson's Life in Science: The Culture of Truth* (Ithaca: Cornell University Press, 2003), 181–87. Lawrence Friedman has called those agents who espoused Garrison's immediatism the "Boston Clique." See his *Gregarious Saints*, 43–67. It is important to remember, however, that throughout the antebellum era, Garrison's movement comprised only a minority of those who regarded themselves as antislavery. The *Concord Free-*

man took note of this irony: "The southerners complain; that the abolitionist is scattering fire-brands and the like amongst their slaves, and in their earnestness to censure they forget, that their own papers generally copy all the incendiary publications which appear at the north. . . . There is nothing in which the south can serve the abolitionist so well, as in copying and disseminating his sentiments" (10 Oct 1835). For more on Garrison's publicizing of Walker, see Mayer, 115.

9. *Yeoman's Gazette*, 3 and 17 Sep 1831.

10. *Liberator*, 30 Nov 1833; *Days*, 16–17, 22, 44, 73–74; Canby, *Thoreau*, 22–23; Mrs. Prudence Ward to George Ward, 21 Feb 1834, TS.

11. Lemuel Shattuck, *A History of the Town of Concord; Middlesex County, Massachusetts, from Its Earliest Settlement to 1832* . . . (Boston: Russell, Odiorne, 1835), 204–5, 211, 217–18, 192–94; Robert A. Gross, "Transcendentalism and Urbanism: Concord, Boston, and the Wider World," *Journal of American Studies* 18, no. 3 (1984): 371; John Wood Sweet, "The Liberal Dilemma and the Demise of the Town Church: Ezra Ripley's Pastorate in Concord, 1778–1841," *Proceedings of the Massachusetts Historical Society* 104 (1992): 79; Marc Harris, "The People of Concord: A Demographic History, 1750–1850," in *Concord: The Social History of a New England Town, 1750–1850*, ed. David Hackett Fischer (Waltham, Mass.: Brandeis University, 1983), 65. Two of Rev. Southmayd's parishioners were Maria and Jane Thoreau, both quite receptive to the Wards' abolitionism (see Robert A. Gross, "Faith in the Boardinghouse: New Views of Thoreau Family Religion," *TSB* 250 [winter 2005]: 1–5). Editor and Concord native William Robinson later contended that "Old Dr. Ripley was as slow as any of the Unitarian clergy to accept antislavery doctrines" (*"Warrington*," 71). Like many of her townswomen, Sarah Sherman Hoar, Samuel Hoar's wife, outpaced her husband in antislavery sympathies; before her marriage, she had opened a school for black children in New Haven, Connecticut (Ruth R. Wheeler, *Concord: Climate for Freedom* [Concord, Mass.: Concord Antiquarian Society, 1967], 167). For a discussion of how Concord evolved in its relationship to Boston's urban social and political milieu during the early and mid-nineteenth century, see Gross, "Transcendentalism and Urbanism."

12. Shattuck, *History*, 211; Harris, "People of Concord," 78; Concord (Mass.) Assessors' Records, 1826–1828, CFPL; Prescott diary, 12 Dec 1837, HL; "Plan of House Lot Concord Mass. Belonging to Daniel Shattuck . . . Nov. 13, 1860," Thoreau Land and Property Surveys 114, CFPL; *Concord, Massachusetts Births, Marriages, and Deaths 1635–1850* (Concord, Mass.: Printed by the Town, 1895), 348, 350. Among other jobs, John Garrison tended the garden at the Old Manse; in the summer of 1842, he and Henry Thoreau planted it as a wedding gift for newlyweds Nathaniel and Sophia Hawthorne (Franklin Benjamin Sanborn, *Hawthorne and His Friends: Reminiscence and Tribute* [Cedar Rapids, Iowa: Torch, 1908], 20). The Garrisons enjoyed warm relations with many white Concord families, as this 1836 diary entry of teenager Martha Prescott evidences: "Went to Mrs. Garrison's. . . . Mrs. G. is really quite agreeable. Her colour is all that draws the line between her & many of our aristocratic dames, for in sound sense she far surpasses many of them" (Leslie Wilson, " 'Treasure in My Own Mind': The Diary of Martha Lawrence Prescott, 1834–1836," *CS* n.s. 11 [2003]: 127). For more on the slaves who lived in eighteenth-century Concord, see Robert A. Gross, *The Minutemen and Their World* (New York: Hill and Wang, 1976), 94–98.

13. Prudence Ward to Dennis Ward, 7 Dec 1833, TS; Shattuck, *History*, 229; *Mass. Lyceum*, 132, 131, 130, 134; George B. Bartlett, "Concord Men and Memories," *Bay State Monthly* 3 (September 1885): 227. With an initial membership of fifty-seven, the Concord Lyceum was founded in January 1829, its open-ended purpose the "advancement of Popular Education, and the diffusion of useful information throughout the community generally" (*Mass. Lyceum*, 101–10). Robert A. Gross's forthcoming book, *The Transcendentalists and Their World*, will provide a detailed discussion of Concord's social, political, and religious milieu in the early nineteenth century.

14. E. R. Hoar, "Memoir of William Whiting," *Social Circle*, second series, 263; "Liberator, Mail Books," 1839, BPL; *Liberator*, 15 Feb 1839 and 17 Jan 1835; quoted in *Liberator*, 5 Apr 1839.

15. MCASS; WLG, *L*, 1:419; *Annual Report*, 3:6; *Liberator*, 17 Jan 1835. William Whiting owned a carriage and harness manufactory; Samuel Barrett was a farmer; Sophia and Helen Thoreau taught school intermittently; Mary Merrick Brooks was a Concord native and the wife of lawyer Nathan Brooks; and Dr. Josiah Bartlett had practiced medicine in Concord since 1820. See Shattuck, *History*, 218, 239; and Grindall Reynolds, "Memoir of Dr. Josiah Bartlett," *Social Circle*, second series, 174. Since the minutes of county society meetings do not reflect how individuals voted on the various resolutions, where Concord members stood on the subject of miscegenation is unknown. Although Garrison, Lydia Maria Child, and others insisted that emancipation be followed by racial equality, most abolitionists did not share their view, nor did they themselves always live up to their idealized rhetoric.

16. Robert A. Gross, "Squire Dickinson and Squire Hoar," *Proceedings of the Massachusetts Historical Society* 101 (1989): 15; *Concord Republican*, 11 Jun 1841; E. R. Hoar, "Samuel Hoar," *Social Circle*, third series, 37, 36; *Concord Freeman*, 19 Mar 1836. For a recent biography of the Hoar family, see Paula Ivaska Robbins, *The Royal Family of Concord: Samuel, Elizabeth, and Rockwood Hoar and Their Friendship with Ralph Waldo Emerson* ([Philadelphia]: Xlibris, 2003). For Hoar's membership from the 1830s until at least 1849 in the American Colonization Society, see the following editions of the *African Repository and Colonial Journal*: August 1836, April 1837, June 1843, January 1845, June 1846, July 1846, September 1846, April 1847, and March 1849. I am grateful to Robert Gross for alerting me to Hoar's colonizationism.

17. *Concord Freeman*, 5, 12, and 19 Mar 1836, and 11 Mar 1837; John S. Keyes, "Memoir of John Keyes," *Social Circle*, second series, 163. Editor Francis Gourgas acknowledged that Prescott was not his first choice, but that he had come to believe him "on the whole, perhaps as good a man as could have been selected" (*Concord Freeman*, 5 Mar 1836).

18. *Liberator*, "Middlesex Awake!" 1838; George M. Brooks, "Memoir of Nathan Brooks," *Social Circle*, second series, 204; *Liberator*, 14 Dec 1838; *Yeoman's Gazette*, 15 Dec 1838; *Concord Freeman*, 4 Jan 1839. Such campaigning seems to belie Garrison's claim to eschew the electoral process. For a discussion of Garrison's views on voting in the late 1830s, see Mayer, 256–57, 263–64. Waldo Emerson likely spoke for many in Concord when he blamed the abolitionists for Brooks's defeat: "You have not voted for Mr B because you have made so much of the slave question. You have ceased to be a man that you may be an abolitionist," he lamented in his journal (*JMN*, 7:223). Citations of Emerson's *Journals and Miscellaneous Notebooks* (*JMN*) are cited as clear text, with all editorial marks omitted.

19. Josiah Bartlett, "Duncan Ingraham," *The Centennial of the Social Circle in Concord March 21, 1882* (Cambridge: Riverside, 1882), 128; George M. Brooks, "Memoir of Tilly Merrick," *Social Circle*, second series, 59, 60, 61; Augustus Merrick Papers and Estate Papers and Tilly Merrick Papers, in the Nathan Brooks Family Papers, CFPL; George Brooks to Mary Merrick Brooks, 1 Mar 1844, Brooks Papers, CFPL. In addition to redressing her father's slaveholding, Brooks may have been inspired to her charity work by her mother, Sally Minot, who had served as treasurer of the Concord Female Charitable Society (Wheeler, *Climate*, 165–66). Other female antislavery society members had also descended from slaveholders. Lidian Emerson's grandmother had owned (and freed) at least one slave, "Phillis" (*JMN*, 5:281–82); Cynthia Thoreau's family, the Dunbars, had also owned slaves (Canby, *Thoreau*, 17). For more on Mary Brooks, see Sandra Harbert Petrulionis, "Selective Sympathy: The Public and Private Mary Merrick Brooks," *TSB* 226 (winter 1999): 1–3, 5; and Leslie Wilson, "Slaveholding and Abolition in One Concord Family," *The Concord Journal*, 27 Jun 2002, 11, as well as an 1836 letter in which Brooks expresses how "dreadfully degenerated" her family has become as compared to its "high minded Puritan" ancestors (Brooks to Maria Parker, 9 Feb 1836, Brooks Papers, CFPL).

20. Quoted in Ronald A. Bosco and Joel Myerson, *The Emerson Brothers: A Fraternal Biography in Letters* (New York: Oxford University Press, 2006), 163, 166, 174; Charles Chauncy Emerson to William Emerson, 7 Nov 1835, from transcript of the letters by Ronald A. Bosco and Joel Myerson in their electronic edition of the correspondence, forthcoming on the Ralph Waldo Emerson Society website at www.emersonsociety.org. I am grateful to Ron

Bosco and Joel Myerson for providing transcripts of the Emerson brothers' correspondence.

21. Charles Chauncy Emerson, "Lecture on Slavery," *ESQ* 16 (3rd quarter 1959): 15, 18. Previous reports that Charles Emerson delivered this lecture in Concord apparently derive from the fact that the dateline of the manuscript's first page also includes the word *Concord,* Emerson's location when he wrote the speech. Charles indicates to William Emerson that he will speak on "Slavery" the next day at Duxbury; no record exists of his having lectured on this subject in Concord.

22. *Concord Freeman*, 5 Apr 1835; Len Gougeon, "Abolition, the Emersons, and 1837," *NEQ* 54 (September 1981): 346–47; Phyllis Cole, *Mary Moody Emerson and the Origins of Transcendentalism* (New York: Oxford University Press, 1998), 233; Charles Chauncy Emerson to Elizabeth Hoar, 30 Mar [1835], Bosco and Myerson transcripts. Burleigh had held his Concord audience spellbound, but after the speech, he and Mary Emerson discussed Garrison's "conduct and character" for some time. By the end of the evening, she had converted to immediatism. Some have suggested that Burleigh's argument was assisted by his "tall figure, noble countenance, and unconventional dress, with sandy flowing beard and long ringlets" (Garrison and Garrison, *William Lloyd Garrison*, 1:476). See also Samuel J. May, *Some Recollections of Our Antislavery Conflict* (1869; reprint, New York: Arno, 1968), 62–66.

23. Nancy Craig Simmons, ed., *The Selected Letters of Mary Moody Emerson* (Athens: University of Georgia Press, 1993), 364; quoted in Cole, *Mary Moody Emerson*, 233; Phyllis Cole, "Pain and Protest in the Emerson Family," in *The Emerson Dilemma: Essays on Emerson and Social Reform*, ed. T. Gregory Garvey (Athens: University of Georgia Press, 2001) 68, 75. Lidian Emerson reacted as Mary had expected, exclaiming to her sister: "I have had this eve.g. a note from Aunt Mary saying she has knowing it would be pleasant to us invited Mr May & Mr Thompson the Abolitionists to breakfast with us tomorrow morning! And it is really not 'put-out' at all to me!" (LJE, *L*, 43).

24. *JMN*, 5: 90, 91, 73; Donald Yacovone, *Samuel Joseph May and the Dilemmas of the Liberal Persuasion, 1797–1871* (Philadelphia: Temple University Press, 1991), 60–63; Mayer, 199; Jane H. Pease and William H. Pease, "Samuel J. May: Civil Libertarian," *Cornell Library Journal* 3 (autumn 1967): 14; Charles Chauncy Emerson to William Emerson, 10 Oct [1835], Bosco and Myerson transcripts. For Waldo Emerson's fundamental dislike of abolitionists at this time, see Gougeon, "Abolition, the Emersons, and 1837." See also Samuel J. May, *Recollections*, 108–25.

25. *Concord Freeman*, 31 Oct 1835; quoted in Mayer, 206–7. Although Garrison well understood the serious threat posed by what he later called "the spirit of mobocracy," he shared George Thompson's view that anti-abolitionist violence "will do incalculable good to our cause" (WLG, *L*, 2: 365, 363).

26. Keyes, 42; WLG, *L*, 1: 542, n.1; Frederick C. Dahlstrand, *Amos Bronson Alcott: An Intellectual Biography* (Rutherford, N.J.: Fairleigh Dickinson University Press, 1982), 151. For details of this incident in which Garrison was very nearly killed, see especially Mayer, 200–209, and Lawrence Lader, *The Bold Brahmins: New England's War Against Slavery: 1831–1863* (New York: Dutton, 1961), 18–27.

27. Susan Zaeske, *Signatures of Citizenship: Petitioning, Antislavery, and Women's Political Identity* (Chapel Hill: University of North Carolina Press, 2003), 1, 69–85; Harry L. Watson, *Liberty and Power: The Politics of Jacksonian America* (New York: Hill and Wang, 1990), 203; quoted in *Concord Freeman*, 16 Jan 1836; *Annual Report*, 18:17; John C. Calhoun, "Speech in the U.S. Senate," in *Defending Slavery: Proslavery Thought in the Old South: A Brief History with Documents*, ed. Paul Finkelman (Boston: Bedford/St. Martin's, 2003), 55, 58, 59; WLG, *L*, 2:199–200. For congressional debate and passage of a series of "gag rules" in response to women's antislavery petitions, see Melvin I. Urofsky and Paul Finkelman, *A March of Liberty: A Constitutional History of the United States*, vol. 1, *From the Founding to 1890*, 2nd ed. (New York: Oxford University Press, 2002), 366–68. For statistics on antislavery petitions in 1837 and 1838, see Gerda Lerner, *The Feminist Thought of Sarah Grimké* (New York: Oxford University Press, 1998), 180–85. In 1837, approximately 70 percent of the Massachusetts signatures on

a petition to abolish slavery in the District of Columbia were female (Paul Goodman, *Of One Blood: Abolitionism and the Origins of Racial Equality* [Berkeley: University of California Press, 1998], 229). According to Irving Bartlett, although Senator Calhoun agreed that the Constitution guaranteed the right of petition, he did not believe that it mandated that these documents be accepted (*John C. Calhoun: A Biography* [New York: Norton, 1993], 223).

28. Lerner, *Feminist Thought*, 178–79; WLG, *L*, 2:185; Anne Warren Weston to Caroline Weston, 7 Aug 1837, BPL; Nathaniel Peabody Rogers, *An Address Delivered before the Concord Female Anti-Slavery Society, at Its Annual Meeting 25 Dec. 1837* (Concord, N.H.: William White, 1838), 19. For more on the Grimkés and the clergy's outrage toward them, see Samuel J. May, *Recollections*, 230–48.

29. *Concord Freeman*, 2 Sep 1837, and 12 Aug 1837; Prudence Ward to Caroline Sewall, 25 Sep [1837], Ellen Sewall Papers, The Huntington Library. Concord abolitionist Timothy Prescott recorded in his diary that the Grimkés lectured in town on September 4, 6, and 8. On September 5, he attended a reception for them at Mary Brooks's home; on the 7th, they spoke in Lowell, Massachusetts (Prescott diary, HL).

30. Prudence Ward to Caroline Sewall, 25 Sep [1837], Ellen Sewall Papers, Huntington. Ward was no doubt predisposed to think highly of the Grimkés since her sister, Caroline Sewall, had previously related her enjoyment of Angelina's *Appeal* (Caroline Sewall to Prudence Ward, 4 Nov 1836, Ellen Sewall Papers, Huntington).

31. *Yeoman's Gazette*, 9 Sep 1837; *Concord Freeman*, 16 Sep 1837.

32. RWE, *L*, 2:96; LJE, *L*, 60–61; *Yeoman's Gazette*, 23 Sep 1837; *Concord Freeman*, 23 Sep 1837; Prudence Ward to Caroline Sewall, 25 Sep [1837], Ellen Sewall Papers, Huntington; James Elliot Cabot, *A Memoir of Ralph Waldo Emerson*, 2 vols. (Boston: Houghton Mifflin, 1887), 2:425–26; Gougeon, "Abolition, the Emersons, and 1837," 364. According to Larry Ceplair, the time was ripe for the Grimkés—by May 1837, more than one third of adult, white women belonged to a reform organization (*The Public Years of Sarah and Angelina Grimké: Selected Writings 1835–1839* [New York: Columbia University Press, 1989], 135. See also Jean Fagan Yellin and John C. Van Horne, eds., *The Abolitionist Sisterhood: Women's Political Culture in Antebellum America* (Ithaca: Cornell University Press, 1994).

33. Lerner, *Feminist Thought*, 185; Jane H. Pease and William H. Pease, *Bound with Them in Chains: A Biographical History of the Antislavery Movement* (Westport, Conn.: Greenwood, 1972), 32; Prudence Ward to Dennis Ward, 27 Dec [1837], TS. The founding of the Concord Female Anti-Slavery Society is documented in the following: Prescott diary, 18 Oct 1837, HL; *Annual Report*, 6:xlii; *Annual Report of the American Anti-Slavery Society* (New York: American Anti-Slavery Society, 1838), 134; and *Liberator*, 20 Apr 1838. The female society's fragmentary records are housed in the Concord Free Public Library. For the number of female antislavery societies in America in the 1830s, see Goodman, *Of One Blood*, 207. According to abolitionist pioneer Mary Grew, the first female antislavery society in Massachusetts had been formed in Reading in March 1833 (Mary Grew, "Annals of Women's Anti-Slavery Societies," in *Proceedings of the American Anti-Slavery Society, at its Third Decade . . .* [1864; reprint, New York: Negro Universities Press, 1969], 124).

34. WLG, *L*, 1:208; Grew, *Annals*, 128.

35. Concord Female Anti-Slavery Society Records, CFPL; *Liberator*, 22 Jul 1842; Mary Merrick Brooks to Maria Weston Chapman, 27 Jun 1843, BPL.

36. Deborah Van Broekhoven, " 'Better than a Clay Club': The Organization of Anti-Slavery Fairs, 1835–60," *Slavery and Abolition* 19 (April 1998): 30, 38; Liberator, 8 Nov 1839; Prudence Ward to Dennis Ward, 30 Sep [1839], TS; Prudence Ward to Caroline Sewall, April n.y.; Ellen Sewall to Prudence Ward, [8] Jan 1841; Maria Thoreau to Prudence Ward, 17 Dec 1849, all in Ellen Sewall Papers, Huntington; Helen L. Thoreau to Maria Weston Chapman, 3 Dec 1845, BPL; WLG, *L*, 2:194. In 1877, Concord Female Anti-Slavery Society member Harriet Hanson Robinson explained that one of Mary Brooks's chief fundraising items, the "BROOKS CAKE," was served at all meetings. Robinson predicted that "when woman's work is recognized and valued as it should be, a new and good recipe will be as important a discovery as a new 'figure of speech' or a new poem." One hundred twenty-nine years later, I

take for granted we have reached that time: "One pound flour, one pound sugar, half-pound butter, four eggs, one cup milk, one teaspoonful soda, half-teaspoonful cream of tartar, half-pound currants (in half of it). This makes two loaves" ("*Warrington*," 73–74).

37. WLG, *L*, 2:449; Carolyn L. Karcher, *The First Woman in the Republic: A Cultural Biography of Lydia Maria Child* (Durham: Duke University Press, 1994), 219; Van Broekhoven, "Better than a Clay Club,'" 38; Jeffrey, *Great Silent Army*, 36. Typically, the *Liberator* listed the Concord female society collectively as a donor, but the $18 it raised in the fall of 1841 was credited to individual members: "From Concord, Helen Thoreean [Thoreau] 50, Abby Tolman 50, Susan Barrett 1, Francis Patten 50, Sarah Hosmer 50, Edwin Bigelow 50, Mrs. Tewksbury 25, Friend 25, Mrs. Prudence Ward 5, Miss Prudence Ward 3, Mrs. John Thurlo [Thoreau] 1, Mary Brooks 5" (*Liberator*, 15 Oct 1841). For more on the Boston female society and its antislavery fair, see Hansen, *Strained Sisterhood*; and Lee Chambers-Schiller, "A Good Work among the People: The Political Culture of the Boston Antislavery Fair," in Yellin and Van Horne, *Abolitionist Sisterhood*, 249–74.

38. Goodman, *Of One Blood*, 222; Karcher, *First Woman*, 185–86; quoted in Jeffrey, *Great Silent Army*, 57.

39. Quoted in Zaeske, *Signatures*, 128; quoted in Yacovone, *Samuel Joseph May*, 68; quoted in *Liberator*, 22 Sep 1837; *Annual Report*, 12:68.

40. Quoted in Zaeske, *Signatures*, 114; Rogers, *Address*, 18.

41. Mayer, 237; WLG, *L*, 2:329, 328; *JMN*, 5:437; Wendell Phillips, *Speeches, Lectures, and Letters* (1884; reprint, New York: Negro Universities Press, 1968), 1–10; Gougeon, *Virtue's Hero*, 38; Prudence Ward to Dennis Ward, 27 Dec [1837], TS. For abolitionists' disagreements over Lovejoy's right to self-defense, see John Demos, "The Antislavery Movement and the Problem of Violent 'Means,'" *NEQ* 37 (December 1964): 507–9; and Friedman, *Gregarious Saints*, 200–202. For Lovejoy's own defense of his right to free speech, delivered days before his murder, see "Elijah P. Lovejoy Defends His Right to Free Speech," in *The Abolitionists: A Collection of Their Writings*, ed. Louis Ruchames (New York: Capricorn, 1963), 139–41.

42. Ira V. Brown, "Am I Not a Woman and a Sister?': The Anti–Slavery Convention of American Women, 1837–1839," *Pennsylvania History* 50 (January 1983): 10, 9; *Proceedings of the Anti-Slavery Convention of American Women . . .* (Philadelphia: Merrihew and Gunn, 1838), 12, 8; WLG, *L*, 2:362; Mayer, 246; Ira V. Brown, "Cradle of Feminism: The Philadelphia Female Anti–Slavery Society, 1833–1840," *The Pennsylvania Magazine of History and Biography* 102 (April 1978): 158–60; Mayer, 242; quoted in *Liberator*, 25 May 1838. For an assessment of the increasing climate of racism at this time in the Northeast, see Nash, *Forging Freedom*, 246–79.

43. Gougeon, *Virtue's Hero*, 41–85; *JMN*, 7:58. See also *JMN*, 7:393, where Emerson writes: "Strange history this of *abolition*. The negro must be very old & belongs, one would say, to the fossil formations. What right has he to be intruding into the late & civil daylight of this dynasty of the Caucasians & Saxons? It is plain that so inferior a race must perish shortly like the poor Indians." In "Self-Reliance," Emerson counseled readers to ignore society's many claims on the individual, and he spoke dismissively of "the thousandfold Relief Societies" (Ralph Waldo Emerson, *The Collected Works of Ralph Waldo Emerson*, vol. 2, *Essays: First Series*, ed. Albert R. Ferguson and Jean Ferguson Carr [Cambridge: Belknap Press of Harvard University Press, 1979], 29, 31).

44. Cole, "Pain and Protest," 69, 72–73; *JMN*, 5:382, 440; quoted in ETE, *L*, 1:426.

45. *Days*, 52–54; Thoreau, *RP*, 42; Walter Harding, "Thoreau in Emerson's Account Books," *TSB* 159 (spring 1982): 1–3; Glick, 7. When the Thoreaus moved into a larger home in 1837, the Wards had moved in with them rather than continuing to board with Maria and Jane Thoreau (*Days*, 22, 73).

46. Petition of Josiah Bartlett and 69 others of Concord, Mass., 15 Jan 1838; Petition of Josiah Bartlett and 61 others of Concord, 16 Jan 1838; Petition of Mary W. F. Wilder and a number of other women of Concord, 12 Feb 1838; Petition of Mary W. F. Wilder and 192 other women of Concord, Massachusetts, 13 Feb 1838; Petition of Elizabeth Barrett and 182 other women of Concord, 7 Jan 1839, all in the Center for Legislative Archives, National

Archives, Washington, D.C.; Prudence Ward to Mrs. Joseph Ward, 13 Apr 1838, Abernethy Manuscripts, Julian W. Abernethy Collection of American Literature, Middlebury College Special Collections. I am grateful to Robert Gross for sharing the details of these petitions. Susan Zaeske shows that over the next twenty-five years, nearly 3 million women would sign petitions calling for an end to slavery (*Signatures*, 2). As the Massachusetts Anti-Slavery Society articulated it, "for the last ten years, the slaveholders of the South have been looking to the acquisition of Texas to the Union, with a burning thirst of avarice which nothing but human blood can allay, and a cannibal appetite for human flesh which nothing but hecatombs of sable victims can satisfy" (*Annual Report*, 5:42).

47. WLG, *L*, 2:553–54, 418; Mayer, 267, 277, 282. For a discussion of this tumult, see Mayer, 261–84; Pease and Pease, *Bound with Them in Chains*, 40–47; and *Liberator*, 18 Jan and 5 Apr 1839. The Massachusetts Abolition Society would eventually give way to the more successful Liberty Party. Ironically, one "new org" leader, Henry Stanton, had recently married Elizabeth Cady, whose views on women's enfranchisement beyond the antislavery movement would soon be well known.

48. MCASS; *Liberator*, 19 Jul 1839; Lucia Weston to Deborah Weston, Jul 1839, BPL.

49. *Liberator*, 6 Sep 1839; "*Warrington*," 18; *Concord Republican*, 14 Aug 1840, and 31 Dec 1841; Harriet Hanson Robinson journal, Sep 1858, SL.

50. *Liberator*, 28 Sep 1838; Thoreau to Wilder, 20 Mar 1841, Loomis-Wilder Family Papers, Manuscripts and Archives, Yale University Library; *Liberator*, 8 Jan 1841. See also Mayer, 226, 300–302. The First Church's relation to local antislavery efforts would have differed appreciably had an aspirant other than Barzillai Frost succeeded Ezra Ripley. One contender for the position, radical abolitionist Theodore Parker, had hoped for a job offer that never materialized (see Dean Grodzins, *American Heretic: Theodore Parker and Transcendentalism* [Chapel Hill: University of North Carolina Press, 2002], 77). When they left Concord, the Wilders first moved to Michigan, but eventually they relocated back to Massachusetts. I thank Robert Gross for bringing Mary Wilder's correspondence to my attention, and for sharing his transcripts of Harriet Hanson Robinson's journal. Through the years, Mary Wilder and Maria Thoreau remained close friends, but John Wilder's break with the Garrisonians was lasting. In the mid–1850s, he railed from his pulpit in Harwich, Massachusetts, against the time when "one-idea men, fanatics and infidels" had sundered the movement, a sermon that caused one listener to warn the *Liberator*'s readers: "I have never heard a more cunning and hypocritical address" (27 Jul 1855). For come-outerism and the abolitionist movement, see Pease and Pease, "Confrontation and Abolition," 923–24.

51. Anne Warren Weston to Deborah Weston, 16 Sep 1841, BPL; *Liberator*, 23 Jun 1843. For examples of other local female antislavery societies that suffered through the "schism" as well, see Abijah Allen to Francis Jackson, 21 Jul 1843, and Frances H. Drake to Maria Weston Chapman, 11 Jun 1843, both in BPL.

52. Philip S. Foner, ed. *Frederick Douglass: Selected Speeches and Writings* (Chicago: Lawrence Hill, 1999), 11–12; Nathaniel Peabody Rogers, *A Collection from the Miscellaneous Writings of Nathaniel Peabody Rogers*, 2nd ed. (Manchester, N.H.: William H. Fisk, 1849), 203–4. After meeting in 1841, Douglass and Garrison concurred that Douglass's life story and erudite telling of it would captivate audiences (McFeely, 83–90).

53. *Concord Freeman*, 27 Aug 1841; *Liberator*, 15 and 22 Oct 1841; McFeely, 92–93. Massachusetts abolished segregated railroad seating in April 1843; for more on this practice, see Charles Lenox Remond, "The Rights of Colored Citizens in Traveling," in Ruchames, *Abolitionists*, 179–84.

54. MCASS; *Liberator*, 29 Oct 1841. "New org" minister Rev. Joshua Leavitt lectured at the Second (Trinitarian) Church on 8 December 1842 (see Prudence Ward to Dennis Ward, 8 Dec 1842, TS; and WLG, *L*, 2: 216, n.4, 591–92). Since Ezra Ripley's death in September 1841, Rev. Barzillai Frost had backed away from the First Church's initial support for abolitionism.

55. *Liberator*, 17 Sep 1841; Brooks to Chapman, 4 Oct 1841, BPL.

56. Abigail May Alcott journal, 12 Oct 1841, Alcott Family Papers, HL, bMS Am 1130.14.

Abby Alcott, a founding member of the Philadelphia Female Anti-Slavery Society, was also active in the Boston and Concord societies. She and her husband, Bronson Alcott, were staunch Garrisonians, and radicals encircled her on many familial fronts. Her brother, Samuel Joseph May, had championed schoolteacher Prudence Crandall in 1833 when she faced opposition for opening a school for black girls in Canterbury, Connecticut; in 1851, he helped rescue fugitive slave Jerry McHenry from the Syracuse, New York, jail (see Samuel J. May, *Recollections*, 373–84; Yacovone, *Samuel Joseph May*, 43–55, 143–54; Mayer, 146–48; and Pease and Pease, "Samuel J. May," 276–307). Additionally, Abby Alcott's cousins, Samuel May, Jr. and Samuel E. Sewall, both served as agents of the Massachusetts Anti-Slavery Society.

57. Douglass to Helen [Thoreau], n.d., CAS Collection, CFPL. My thanks to Robert Gross for first bringing Douglass's letter to my attention. In March 1844, Douglass had called Sudbury, Massachusetts, "the darkest" of Massachusetts' locales, suggesting that this letter to Thoreau may have been written at that same time (*Liberator*, 15 Mar 1844). Henry Thoreau almost certainly met Douglass on one or more occasions in Concord, but no such record appears in his journal. Douglass addressed six meetings of the Middlesex County Anti-Slavery Society from 1841 to 1844, three of them in Concord (John W. Blassingame, ed., *The Frederick Douglass Papers*, series 1, *Speeches, Debates, and Interviews*, vol. 1, *1841–46* [New Haven: Yale University Press, 1979], lxxvii–xcv).

58. *Days*, 142; *Mass. Lyceum*, 156; James Brewer Stewart, *Wendell Phillips: Liberty's Hero* (Baton Rouge: Louisiana State University Press, 1986), 54–67; Mayer, 288–93. Garrison, who joined Charles Lenox Remond, Nathaniel Rogers, Lucretia Mott, and Elizabeth Cady Stanton in the "women's" balcony seating at the World convention, was astonished that George Thompson blasted the Americans for bringing the issue of women's rights into this forum (WLG, *L*, 2:654).

59. Quoted in *Liberator*, 20 May 1842; quoted in Mayer, 319. Thoreau had become secretary of the Concord lyceum on October 18, 1838; three weeks later, he was elected a curator (*Days*, 72). Women were finally permitted to join the Concord lyceum in 1837. To that time, women who did not have a male family member to admit them could attend "gratuitously." In 1854, women were granted voting rights in the organization (*Mass. Lyceum*, 148, 156, 146, 111, 169).

60. *Liberator*, 6 Jan and 17 Mar 1843. The protests were ineffectual, but Latimer's freedom was eventually purchased for $400. See Lois E. Horton, "Community Organization and Social Activism: Black Boston and the Antislavery Movement," *Sociological Inquiry* 55, no. 2 (1985): 193–94; James Oliver Horton, *Free People of Color: Inside the African American Community* (Washington: Smithsonian, 1993), 36; and John W. Blassingame, John R. McKivigan, and Peter P. Hinks, eds., *The Frederick Douglass Papers*, series 2, *Autobiographical Writings*, vol. 1, *Narrative* (New Haven: Yale University Press, 1999), 113.

61. Brooks to Phillips, 21 Feb [1843], Wendell Phillips Papers, HL, bMS Am 1953.

62. Brooks to Chapman, 8 May, 27 Jun, 20 May, and 30 Jun 1843, all in BPL. Brooks's plea evidently opened no doors; there is no record that the popular Hutchinsons ever performed in Concord (see Dale Cockrell, ed., *Excelsior: Journals of the Hutchinson Family Singers, 1842–1846* [Stuyvesant, N.Y.: Pendragon, 1989], 387–92).

63. Brooks to Chapman, 14 Jul 1843; Thoreau to Chapman, 4 Sep 1843, both in BPL; *Liberator*, 20 Oct and 22 Dec 1843.

64. Brooks to Chapman, 30 Jun 1843, and 10 Oct 1841, both in BPL; WLG, *L*, 2:180.

65. Quoted in Jean Fagan Yellin, "Hawthorne and the Slavery Question," in *A Historical Guide to Nathaniel Hawthorne*, ed. Larry J. Reynolds (New York: Oxford University Press, 2001), 140. As a young woman visiting Cuba, Sophia Hawthorne had been bothered by the sexual abuse of enslaved women, yet even then she had reacted with a white woman's privileged disdain, an attitude that prevailed throughout her life. See Megan Marshall, *The Peabody Sisters: Three Women Who Ignited American Romanticism* (Boston: Houghton Mifflin, 2005), 271–75; and Brenda Wineapple, *Hawthorne: A Life* (New York: Knopf, 2003), 118, 199. For more on Nathaniel Hawthorne's attitude toward slavery, see Larry J. Reynolds, "The

Challenge of Cultural Relativity: The Case of Hawthorne," *ESQ* 49 (1st–3rd quarters 2003): 129–47.

66. Brooks to Phillips, 4 Nov 1843, Phillips Papers, HL.

67. *Liberator*, 23 Jun 1843.

Chapter 2. From Concern to Crusade, 1843–1849

1. *Days*, 145–46; *Liberator*, 16 Feb 1844; Carl Bode, *The American Lyceum: Town Meeting of the Mind* (Carbondale: Southern Illinois University Press, 1968), 206; *Concord Freeman*, 12 Jan 1844. Phillips was originally slated to speak on January 17, but his talk was rescheduled for the next day.

2. *Liberator*, 16 Feb 1844; Sanborn, *Life of Thoreau*, 472–73; *Days*, 176. For the likelihood that "H. M." may be Harriet Minot, see "Notes and Queries," *TSB* 56 (summer 1956): 4. Years later, John Shepard Keyes described the senior John Keyes as "a good hater when his passions were roused"; and he proudly recalled his father's role in this second clash: "My father took up the objection that such topics as Abolition and Temperance were not proper in a literary course to which all parties went any more than political or sectarian addresses would be. Added to this was his disgust at Phillips attacks on the Constitution and Union, and there were hot debates at special meetings of the Lyceum over the question. I remember one where father most fiercely attacked Phillips' sentiments and expressions, and charged him with 'leading captive silly women' and foolish men, that made a buzzing like a hornets nest, and Phillips himself was got to the meeting to answer the attack; which he did eloquently I thought but not logically or effectively" ("John Keyes," *Social Circle*, second series, 166; Keyes, 110).

3. *Liberator*, 16 Feb 1844; *Concord Freeman*, 2 Feb 1844. Years later, in his depiction of Concord's activist women, Franklin Sanborn reordered the evening's remarks so that Phillips more conclusively bested the town's conservative ilk. Sanborn also presumed, with no apparent basis, that "H. M." might be Helen Thoreau, and he asserted that "the Thoreaus, Colonel Whiting, or some other abolitionist" had forewarned Phillips of the impending censure, an assertion that has become truncated in the retelling to "Thoreau informed Phillips of the plan" (Franklin Benjamin Sanborn, "The Women of Concord—IV. Mrs. Mary Merrick Brooks and the Anti-Slavery Movement," in *Transcendental Epilogue: Primary Materials for Research . . .* , vol. 3, ed. Kenneth Walter Cameron [Hartford, Conn.: Transcendental Books, 1982], 46; Gay Wilson Allen, *Waldo Emerson: A Biography* [New York: Viking, 1981], 427). But no evidence supports the argument that it was Henry Thoreau who contacted Phillips, although Thoreau undoubtedly relished his townsmen's discomfort as well as Phillips's concluding remarks: "To rise in the morning, to eat, and drink, and gather gold, is a life not worth having. Enthusiasm is the life of the soul" (*Liberator*, 16 Feb 1844).

4. Brooks to Phillips, 17 Mar 1844, Phillips Papers, HL; *Liberator*, 16 Feb 1844. Phillips's lecture at the First Church in February 1844 is at odds with the fact that later this year, Rev. Barzillai Frost again denied this building, as he had the prior year, to the Garrisonians. Perhaps the fact that Phillips lectured as an individual rather than on behalf of the state or county society caused Frost to alter his usual policy, or perhaps the *Concord Freeman*'s announcement of Phillips's upcoming lecture is in error (16 Feb 1844).

5. Brooks to Phillips, 17 Mar 1844, Phillips Papers, HL; *National Anti-Slavery Standard*, 11 Jul 1868.

6. For Thoreau's brief visit to Brook Farm late in 1843, see Sterling F. Delano, "George Bradford's Letters to Emerson from Brook Farm," *Resources for American Literary Study* 25, no. 1 (1999): 39–40. For a detailed discussion about Emerson's and Thoreau's participation in this lecture series, see Linck C. Johnson, "Reforming the Reformers: Emerson, Thoreau, and the Sunday Lectures at Amory Hall, Boston," *ESQ* 37 (4th quarter 1991): 235–89. Henry Mayer notes that "the series gained some luster by pulling in the cautious Ralph Waldo Emerson for what proved to be a wry and stand-offish address titled 'New England Reformers.'"

Mayer points out that Garrison was out of town and missed Emerson's lecture, which was therefore not reported in the *Liberator* (Mayer, 325).

7. Linck C. Johnson, "Reforming the Reformers," 237; *JMN*, 9:120; *RP*, 182, 184; *Liberator*, 16 Feb 1844. For Emerson's similar sentiments in the late 1830s, see also *JMN*, 7:204, 207. Thoreau had met millennialist William Henry Channing the year before and criticized him and others who "want faith and mistake their private ail for an infected atmosphere" (*Corr*, 147). See also Thoreau's irreverent review, published in 1843, of J. A. Etzler's idealistic reform treatise, *The Paradise within the Reach of All Men, without Labor, by Powers of Nature and Machinery* (*RP*, 19–47).

8. Harding, "Thoreau in Emerson's Account Books," 1–3; *RP*, 288, 49, 52; Rogers, *Miscellaneous Writings*, 219, 221–22, 220.

9. *Herald of Freedom*, 10 May 1844. For a discussion of Rogers's influence on Thoreau and the complete text of Rogers's preface to Thoreau's essay, see Wendell P. Glick, "Thoreau and the 'Herald of Freedom,'" *NEQ* 22 (June 1949): 198–99. (Note: This text contains a slight transcription error from the original essay as published in *Herald of Freedom*; the word "so" in the second line on p. 199 should read "no": "I read it with no small solicitude.") By the mid-1840s, even the come-outer Garrison had reservations about what he called Rogers's "speculative atheism" (WLG, *L*, 3:286), but this purported heresy met with a receptive auditor in Henry Thoreau.

10. *Liberator*, 14 Jun 1844; *Annual Report*, 13:30; Mayer, 328, 314–16; WLG, *L*, 3:288. For the meanings and ramifications of "disunion," see Pease and Pease, "Confrontation and Abolition," 930–37.

11. *Liberator*, 14 Jun 1844; Canby, *Thoreau*, 249; *Concord Freeman* 7 Jun 1844; Zaeske, *Signatures*, 109, 156.

12. MCASS; Brooks to Chapman, 16 Jun 1844, BPL; *Liberator*, 21 Jun 1844. For information on Remond, see William Edward Ward, "Charles Lenox Remond: Black Abolitionist, 1838–1873" (Ph.D. diss., Clark University, 1977).

13. *Liberator*, 5 Jul 1844; Brooks to Chapman, 16 Jun 1844, BPL. As Brooks predicted, the Concord station of the Fitchburg Railroad line opened that summer; a ride to or from Boston cost forty cents (*Concord Freeman*, 12 Jul 1844; *JMN*, 10:349). Observances of West Indian emancipation had been held since at least 1836, when female abolitionists in Philadelphia marked the occasion with speeches and banners hung through the city (see Patrick Rael, *Black Identity and Black Protest in the Antebellum North* [Chapel Hill: University of North Carolina Press, 2002], 63–65).

14. *Liberator*, 5 Jul 1844; *Concord Freeman*, 26 Jul 1844; Brooks to Moody, 7 Jul 18[44], BPL.

15. Weston to Phillips, 14 Jul 1844; Chapman to Ann and Wendell Phillips, 21 Jun [1844], both in Phillips Papers, HL.

16. *Liberator*, 5, 12, 19, and 26 Jul 1844; Ripley to George F. Simmons, 31 Jul 1844, SL.

17. *Herald of Freedom*, 16 Aug 1844; *Days*, 174. Walter Harding embellishes a bit, to Thoreau's advantage, upon Whiting's version: "Then Thoreau heard of the impasse. He rushed to the church, grasped the rope vigorously in his hands, and set the bell to ringing merrily until it had gathered a whole crowd for Emerson's speech" (*Days*, 175). An anonymous report of the occasion in the *Liberator* was also familiar with Thoreau's bell-ringing: "Some of the bolder sort made a rush to the Unitarian house at the time for commencing our services, and rung out a few peals from its steeple-top; but they were soon reminded of their audacity, by the key being speedily removed, lest the trespass should be repeated" (23 Aug 1844). Frank Sanborn later reprinted Whiting's letter but did not comment on Thoreau's feat (see Kenneth Walter Cameron, ed., *Table Talk: A Transcendentalist's Opinions on American Life, Literature, Art and People . . .* , Franklin Benjamin Sanborn[Hartford, Conn.: Transcendental Books, 1981], 224–25). For another contemporary account, see Gordon Milne, *George William Curtis and the Genteel Tradition* (Bloomington: Indiana University Press, 1956), 23.

18. *Herald of Freedom*, 16 Aug 1844; *JMN*, 9:62, 126; Petition of R. Waldo Emerson and 263 others of Concord, 6 Feb 1844, Center for Legislative Archives, National Archives, Washington, D.C.

19. Gougeon, Historical Background, xxx; *EAS*, 32, 26; *Liberator*, 9 Aug 1844. Critics remain sharply divided as to how firmly Emerson wore the mantle of "abolitionist" in the mid-1840s. Amy Earhart has pointed out that overall, the speech puts forth an economic rather than a moral rationale for emancipation ("Representative Men, Slave Revolt, and Emerson's 'Conversion' to Abolitionism," *ATQ* 13 [December 1999]: 299); but John Michael defends Emerson against critics who "have not taken the difficulties of the intellectual in a democratic society sufficiently into account" ("Democracy, Aesthetics, Individualism: Emerson as Public Intellectual," *Nineteenth-Century Prose* 30 [spring/fall 2003]: 196). Laura Dassow Walls has assessed Emerson's personal drive toward antislavery at this time as the response to lengthy considerations of utilitarianism, blended with the imperative for the universe to be moral. By examining the history, philosophy, and geology that Emerson read to prepare for his West Indian address, Walls makes the case that "for Emerson, the problem of race could not be approached apart from theories of development and their implications for types of mankind." Ultimately, she finds Emerson concluding that "one fought to free the slaves less for their sake than for one's own" (*Emerson's Life in Science*, 166, 75). See also Peter S. Field, "The Strange Career of Emerson and Race," *American Nineteenth Century History* 2 (spring 2001): 1–32; Len Gougeon, "Emerson's Abolition Conversion," in Garvey, *Emerson Dilemma*, 170–96; Michael Magee, "Emerson's Emancipation Proclamations," *Raritan* 20, no. 4 (2001): 96–116; Michael Magee, "The Motives of Emancipated Prose: Emerson and the Collaborating Reader," *ESQ* 47 (4th quarter 2001): 279–326; John Carlos Rowe, *At Emerson's Tomb: The Politics of Classic American Literature* (New York: Columbia University Press, 1997), 25–33; Martha Schoolman, "American Abolitionist Geographies: Literature and the Politics of Place, 1840–1861" (Ph.D. diss., University of Pennsylvania, 2005); Carolyn Sorisio, *Fleshing Out America: Race, Gender, and the Politics of the Body in American Literature, 1833–1879* (Athens: University of Georgia Press, 2002), 127–30; Teichgraeber, *Sublime Thoughts*, 90–103, 110–12; and Albert J. Von Frank, "Mrs. Brackett's Verdict: Magic and Means in Transcendental Antislavery Work," in *Transient and Permanent: The Transcendentalist Movement and Its Contexts*, ed. Charles Capper and Conrad Edick Wright (Boston: Massachusetts Historical Society, 1999), 385–407.

20. Gougeon, *Virtue's Hero*, 73–75; Gougeon, Historical Background, xxviii–xxix; Gougeon, "Abolition Conversion," 178–82; Karcher, *First Woman*, 183.

21. *EAS*, 23–24, 32, 33; Martha L. Berg and Alice de V. Perry, eds., " 'The Impulses of Human Nature': Margaret Fuller's Journal from June through October 1844," *Proceedings of the Massachusetts Historical Society* 102 (1990): 107; *National Anti-Slavery Standard*, 15 Aug 1844; Sorisio, *Fleshing Out America*, 128, 127. Weld's book, published in 1839, sold widely and had been enormously influential as abolitionist propaganda. Emerson and Child had met years earlier, and both were intimate friends of Boston abolitionist Ellis Gray Loring, who had lent Emerson some of the sources for the speech (Karcher, *First Woman*, 15; Gougeon, "Abolition Conversion," 180–82). Whether Loring recommended Child's *Appeal*, or whether Emerson chose not to accept such advice if offered, in either case resulted in an address largely uninformed by U.S. practices. The fact that Child had criticized Emerson's prescriptive views toward women in her 1843 "Letters from New York" may suggest an additional reason that Emerson would not have consulted her *Appeal*. See Karcher, *First Woman*, 323.

22. Nancy Craig Simmons, *Selected Letters*, 460; Brooks to Emerson, 17 Oct 1844, Letters to Ralph Waldo Emerson, HL, bMS Am 1280.

23. *Liberator*, 23, 16, and 9 Aug 1844. For additional reports of the speech, see also *Concord Freeman*, 2 Aug 1844; and *National Anti-Slavery Standard*, 15 Aug 1844.

24. Joseph Slater, ed., *The Correspondence of Emerson and Carlyle* (New York: Columbia University Press, 1964), 373; Thoreau to James Munroe & Co., 17 Sep 1845, Charles Roberts Autograph Letters Collection, Haverford College Library, Haverford, Pennsylvania.

25. Philip M. Hamer, "Great Britain, the United States, and the Negro Seamen Acts, 1822–1848," *Journal of Southern History* 1 (February 1935): 15–16, 22; "Samuel Hoar's Expulsion from Charleston," *Old South Leaflets* 6, no. 140 (1845; reprint, Boston: Directors of the Old South Work, [1903]), 315. Such a tragedy had almost occurred in 1834 when the papers

verifying the free status of Boston sailor John Tidd were stolen. Only when his landlord learned of the circumstances was Tidd saved from being sold as a slave in New Orleans (Lois E. Horton, "Community Organization," 187). For more information on these laws, see Hamer, "Great Britain."

26. "Samuel Hoar's Expulsion," 319; quoted in E. R. Hoar, "Samuel Hoar," *Social Circle*, third series, 40. The Hoars' Charleston friends included the author Caroline Gilman and her husband Samuel Gilman, a Unitarian minister and Harvard graduate who was not only a friend of Waldo Emerson but also the brother-in-law of abolitionist Ellis Gray Loring (Linda T. Prior, "Ralph Waldo Emerson and South Carolina," *South Carolina Historical Magazine* 79, no. 4 [1978]: 255; Robbins, *Royal Family*, 206, 208). Had Massachusetts Governor Briggs known better his southern peer, he may have realized the futility of Hoar's charge. A week after the Hoars left Charleston, the *Charleston Mercury* carried this response to abolitionists by South Carolina Governor Hammond: "Look at the Negro in Africa—a naked savage—almost a Cannibal, ruthlessly oppressing and destroying his fellows—idle, treacherous, idolatrous, and such a disgrace to the image of his God, in which you declare him to be made, that some of the wisest philosophers have denied him the possession of a soul. See him here— three millions at least of his rescued race—civilized, contributing immensely to the subsistence of the human family, his passions restrained, his affections cultivated, his bodily wants and infirmities provided for, and the Religion of his Maker and Redeemer taught him" (9 Dec 1844).

27. "Samuel Hoar's Expulsion," 320, 321, 323; Robbins, *Royal Family*, 211–13; Elizabeth Maxfield-Miller, "Elizabeth of Concord: Selected Letters of Elizabeth Sherman Hoar (1814– 1878) to the Emersons, Family, and the Emerson Circle (Part Three)," *SAR 1986*, ed. Joel Myerson (Charlottesville: University Press of Virginia, 1986), 143.

28. Quoted in *Liberator*, 20 Dec 1844; *Concord Freeman*, 27 Dec 1844; *JP*, 8:55.

29. *Liberator*, 27 Dec 1844; *JMN*, 9:161; quoted in Robbins, *Royal Family*, 218; *Liberator*, 31 Jan 1845.

30. *JMN*, 9:176, 75; RWE, *L*, 7:620–21.

31. *JMN*, 9:174.

32. Ripley to George F. Simmons, 12 Dec 1844, SL. On December 29, a rally was held at Faneuil Hall in Boston to protest "the expulsion of Mr. Hoar from South Carolina, and the proposed annexation of Texas" (*Liberator*, 17 Jan 1845). For a discussion of how this incident intensified the state society's calls for disunion, see also Garrison and Garrison, *William Lloyd Garrison*, 3:135.

33. *Annual Report*, 13:74; *African Repository and Colonial Journal (1825–1849)*, Jan 1845, 29; Jun 1846, 196; Jul 1846, 225; Apr 1847, 125; and Mar 1849, 83.

34. *JMN*, 9:102, Barrett to Phillips, 28 Feb 1845, Phillips Papers, HL. Despite his support for Phillips's appearances in Concord, Emerson harbored a mixed opinion of the fiery orator: "The first discovery I made of P[hillips] was that while I admired his eloquence I had not the faintest wish to meet the man. He had only an audience . . . and no personality" (*JMN*, 13:281–82).

35. Keyes, 110. Some accounts of this incident assume that the same John Keyes objected to all three of Phillips's lectures in Concord, but the elder Keyes had died at age 57 on August 29, 1844. For additional accounts of this contentious lyceum meeting, see *Mass. Lyceum*, 159– 60; and *Concord Freeman*, 7 Mar 1845. Later that year, the members voted to give the curators total authority in selecting lecturers and topics, removing the need for advance approval.

36. Barrett to Phillips, 5 Mar 1845, Phillips Papers, HL; RWE, *L*, 8:13.

37. *Mass. Lyceum*, 160; Allan Nevins, ed., *Polk: The Diary of a President 1845–1849: Covering the Mexican War, the Acquisition of Oregon, and the Conquest of California and the Southwest* (New York: Capricorn, 1968), xvii; Remonstrance of Jane Thoreau, 11 Dec 1845, Center for Legislative Archives, National Archives; Douglas V. Meed, *The Mexican War: 1846–1848* (New York: Routledge, 2003), 17.

38. *RP*, 59, 60, 61; *JP* 2:120. Revisions to his journal indicate that Thoreau had written portions of this tribute following Phillips's previous appearances in Concord.

39. *JP*, 2:123–24; quoted in Sanborn, "Women of Concord," 47.

40. *Days*, 181; *Walden*, 90. The multitude of personal and vocational reasons—including his brother's tragic and unexpected death in 1842, his disillusionment over career options, his desire to work uninterrupted on two book projects—that led Thoreau to undertake this Transcendentalist experiment at this time have been examined for decades. For the archaic view that his abode at Walden Pond allowed Thoreau to "escape from . . . the gossip of reform of his sisters and his aunts," see Canby, *Thoreau*, 225.

41. *Liberator*, 3 Oct 1845; *JMN*, 9:267.

42. *Liberator*, 28 Nov 1845; Brooks to Caroline Weston, 19 Nov 1845, BPL; Weston to Phillips, 9 Feb and 2 Nov 1845, both in Phillips Papers, HL. See also Len Gougeon, "Emerson and the New Bedford Affair," *SAR 1981*, ed. Joel Myerson (Boston: Twayne, 1981), 257–64.

43. *EAS*, 39; Brooks to Weston, 19 and 24 Nov 1845, BPL.

44. Brooks to Emerson, 24 Nov 1845, Letters to Ralph Waldo Emerson, HL; Weston to Phillips, 22 Nov 1845, Phillips Papers, HL; Phillips to Frances H. Drake, 11 Oct 1849, type-script, BPL. Although New Bedford abolitionists protested the lyceum's "cruel" and discriminatory policy, and although Rotch sounded chagrined in responding to Emerson's cancellation, the lyceum officers did not rescind the decision (*Liberator*, 28 Nov 1845). The next year, the state antislavery society formally thanked Emerson as well as Charles Sumner, who had also cancelled his lecture there (*Annual Report*, 14:92). New Bedford leaders, however, were not so generous; they invited Emerson to address their lyceum the following season but advised him not to repeat the "mistake" of "listening to the reports of the prejudiced who live on one idea & that exaggerated" (quoted in Gougeon, "New Bedford Affair," 261). For a discussion of the fugitive slave community in New Bedford during the antebellum era, see Kathryn Grover, *The Fugitive's Gibraltar: Escaping Slaves and Abolitionism in New Bedford, Massachusetts* (Amherst: University of Massachusetts Press, 2001).

45. Brooks to Chapman, 23 Feb 1846, BPL; Brooks to Emerson, Feb 1846, Letters to Ralph Waldo Emerson, HL.

46. Brooks to Lidian Jackson Emerson, [Feb 1846], Emerson Family Correspondence, HL, bMS Am 1280.226; *Liberator*, 13 Mar 1846.

47. Yacovone, *Samuel Joseph May*, 129; WLG, *L*, 3:489; David L. Child, "Letter to William Lloyd Garrison," in Ruchames, *Abolitionists*, 104–5.

48. *Liberator*, 5 Jun 1846; *Walden*, 90.

49. Friedman, *Gregarious Saints*, 59–60; *Days*, 201 .

50. *Days*, 202, 203–5; Fritz Oehlschlaeger and George Hendrick, eds., *Toward the Making of Thoreau's Modern Reputation: Selected Correspondence of S. A. Jones, A. W. Hosmer, H. S. Salt, H. G. O. Blake, and D. Ricketson* (Urbana: University of Illinois Press, 1979), 201. Thoreau's journal contains only a few notes about this episode (see *JP*, 2:262, 263). For a discussion of Alcott and Lane's influence on the development of Thoreau's political philosophy, see Glick, 203–6. Alcott had been arrested in 1843 for this nonpayment but was released when Samuel Hoar paid the tax. Though initially amused by Alcott's action, Thoreau also ceased to pay the poll tax in 1842 (John C. Broderick, "Thoreau, Alcott, and the Poll Tax," *Studies in Philology* 53 [1956]: 625). Some abolitionists had acted likewise on principle, but most, including Garrison, did pay their taxes (Gerald Sorin, *Abolitionism*, 75). See also *Days*, 200; Edward Waldo Emerson, "Alcott, Lane, Thoreau," *TSB* 175 (spring 1986): 6; and Taylor Stoehr, *Nay-Saying in Concord: Emerson, Alcott, and Thoreau* (Hamden, Conn.: Archon, 1979), 44–52. Walter Harding speculates that Staples, who was ready to retire, may have wanted to "clear the books" and erase Thoreau's residual backlog of nonpayment (*Days*, 202). For evidence that Maria Thoreau likely paid Henry's tax, see Oehlschlaeger and Hendrick, *Thoreau's Modern Reputation*, 197–202; and Samuel Arthur Jones, *Thoreau amongst Friends and Philistines and other Thoreauviana*, ed. George Hendrick (Athens: Ohio University Press, 1982), 63–66. For an argument that "non-payment of poll taxes was common a decade" later, see Broderick, "Thoreau, Alcott, and the Poll Tax," 619.

51. John S. Keyes, "Samuel Staples," *Social Circle*, fourth series, 137; *RP*, 75; ABA, *J*, 1:184, 183; *JMN*, 9:445, 446, 447; *EAS*, 43, 44. Critics through the years have shared Keyes's judg-

ment. In 1946, Stanley Edgar Hyman called "Thoreau's first great political gesture . . . largely ridiculous . . . both safe and imitative" ("Henry Thoreau in Our Time," in *Thoreau: A Collection of Critical Essays*, ed. Sherman Paul [Englewood Cliffs, N.J.: Prentice-Hall, 1962], 24). The night in jail has also spawned the fanciful scene of a paternalistic Emerson standing outside Thoreau's cell, shaking his head and asking Thoreau what he's doing in there, to which Thoreau smugly queries why his friend isn't in jail too. Linck Johnson characterizes this doubtful exchange as one that "casts Emerson . . . as a kind of straight man to Thoreau's passionate idealist" ("Emerson, Thoreau's Arrest, and the Trials of American Manhood," in Garvey, *Emerson Dilemma*, 35). Emerson's patronizing air must have especially rankled during the summer of 1846, when twenty-nine-year-old Thoreau was flush with the pleasure of his first full year at Walden, during which time he'd made steady progress on his writing. Since one half of a psychological dynamic usually generates and reacts to the other, Lawrence Buell's assessment that Thoreau "never quite passed beyond the rebellious pupil stage" in his relationship with Emerson suggests also that Emerson never transcended the expectant and disapproving teacher ("Emersonian Anti-Mentoring: From Thoreau to Dickinson and Beyond [in Honor of James McIntosh]," *Michigan Quarterly Review* 41 [summer 2002]: 356).

52. *Walden*, 140; *Liberator*, 31 Jul 1846. For a thorough discussion of this event, see Randall Conrad, "Realizing Resistance: Thoreau and the First of August, 1846, at Walden," *CS* n.s. 12/13 (2004/2005): 165–93.

53. *Liberator*, 7 Aug 1846. Emerson's speech from August 1, 1846, evidently does not survive, but if it resembled the one he delivered on the Fourth of July in Dedham, then the reporter's disappointment is understandable. See Gougeon, Historical Background, xxxv; and *EAS*, 41–44.

54. *Concord Freeman*, 7 Aug 1846.

55. *Annual Report*, 15:66–67; *Liberator*, 18 Sep and 11 Dec 1846; *EAS*, 45.

56. Abigail May Alcott, journal, undated entry Dec 1846 and 31 Dec 1846, Alcott Family Papers, HL; Emerson, Account Books, 7 Jan 1847, Ralph Waldo Emerson Journals and Notebooks, HL, MS Am 1280H; Abigail May Alcott to Samuel Joseph May, 13 Jan 1847, Amos Bronson Alcott Papers, HL, MS Am 1130.9. Based on the documentary trail of John's stay with the Alcotts, in 2001, the National Park Service designated 455 Lexington Road in Concord an official site on its "National Underground Railroad Network to Freedom" (see Molly Q. Eberle, "Wayside Joins Underground Railroad Network," *The Concord Journal* [4 Oct 2001], 2).

57. Amos Bronson Alcott journal, undated entry Feb 1847, Amos Bronson Alcott Papers, HL; ABA, *J*, 1:188, 190. Unless two different fugitives stayed with the Alcotts this winter—certainly a possibility—Bronson Alcott's February journal provides a retrospective of John's stay in December and January. See also Petrulionis, " 'Swelling that Great Tide,' " 401–3.

58. ABA, *J*, 1:186; Franklin Benjamin Sanborn, *Henry D. Thoreau* (Boston: Houghton Mifflin, 1883), 195; *Walden*, 152; Ronald Earl Clapper, "The Development of *Walden*: A Genetic Text," 2 vols. (Ph.D. diss., University of California Los Angeles, 1967), 1:31, 434.

59. H. A. Page [Alexander Hay Japp], *Thoreau: His Life and Aims* (1878; reprint, New York: Haskell House, 1972), 106; Salt, *Life of Thoreau*, 47; George Hendrick, ed., *Remembrances of Concord and the Thoreaus: Letters of Horace Hosmer to Dr. S. A. Jones* (Urbana: University of Illinois Press, 1977), 41, 43. Walter Harding cites Bronson Alcott's manuscript journal as evidence that Alcott took "an escaped Negro" to the Pond this winter (*Days*, 192), but I have not been able to find such an entry in Alcott's journal for the weeks before, during, or after John's stay in Concord. For correspondence back and forth on this subject between Samuel Jones, Henry Salt, and Alfred Hosmer, see Oehlschlaeger and Hendrick, *Thoreau's Modern Reputation*, 97, 113, 126, 136–38, 143, 165–66; and T. W. Higginson to Henry Salt, 6 Oct 1891, TS.

60. Edward Waldo Emerson, "Notes," 2–3; quoted in Oehlschlaeger and Hendrick, *Thoreau's Modern Reputation*, 143; Walter Harding, "Parker Pillsbury, the Walden Cabin, and the Underground Railroad," *TSB* 198 (winter 1992): 8. Bigelow's niece, Ann Damon, characterized her aunt in 1893 as "almost totally blind and deaf" (Damon to Wilbur H. Siebert, Dec

1893, Scrapbooks concerning the Underground Railroad 18—19—, HL, US 5278.36.25 v. 2). A hint that there may be more to learn about this rumor is suggested by Samuel May, Jr., who in 1893 advised that "Parker Pillsbury can tell you, better than I, of the help which that other Concord sage, Henry D. Thoreau, gave to the cause of freedom" (see Danvers Historical Society, *Old Anti-Slavery Days: Proceedings of the Commemorative Meeting Held by the Danvers Historical Society at the Town Hall, Danvers, April 26, 1893, with Introduction, Letters, and Sketches* (Danvers, Mass.: Danvers Mirror Print, 1893), 16.

61. Samuel Arthur Jones, "Thoreau and His Biographers," *Lippincott's Monthly Magazine* 48 (July to December 1891): 225; Allen French, *Old Concord* (Boston: Little, Brown, 1915), 12; Mary Hosmer Brown, *Memories of Concord* (Boston: Four Seas, 1926), 27; Glick, 3; *Days*, 195–96; Paul Brooks, *The People of Concord: One Year in the Flowering of New England* (Chester, Conn.: Globe Pequot, 1990), 76. Another archival note records logistics similar to Bigelow's recollection. Interviewed by Concord historian Allen French in 1935, Marion Barrett stated that "Samuel Barrett, the last Barrett who owned Barrett's Mill, was an abolitionist. If a slave was to be taken away, Thoreau would get Emerson's horse and carry the slave to Samuel Barrett, who took him to the next underground station" ("Statement of Miss Marrion M. Barrett," 11 Jul 1935, Allen French Papers, CFPL).

62. *Walden*, 257; *JP*, 7:177–79 (in press); Elliott and Jones, *Black History*, 30–31; *JP*, 2:122. I am grateful to Elizabeth Hall Witherell for making available the page proofs of the forthcoming *Journal 7: 1853*.

63. *Walden*, 7.

64. Frederick J. Blue, *The Free Soilers: Third Party Politics, 1848–54* (Urbana: University of Illinois Press, 1973), 1; "*Warrington*," 38; E. R. Hoar, "Samuel Hoar," *Social Circle*, third series, 45; Robbins, *Royal Family*, 248; *Liberator*, 19 Mar 1847, and 4 Feb 1848.

65. *Liberator*, 26 Jan 1849; Barry Kritzberg, "A Pre-Civil War Struggle against Capital Punishment: Charles Spear, Concord, and the Case of Washington Goode," *CS* n.s. 2 (fall 1994): 110, 106; *Liberator*, 4 May 1849.

66. Quoted in Kritzberg, "Pre-Civil War Struggle," 109.

67. *Liberator*, 4 May 1849; quoted in Ruth Wheeler, "Thoreau and Capital Punishment," *TSB* 86 (winter 1964): 1; "Protest of 400 Inhabitants of Concord against the Execution of Washington Goode," TS; quoted in Kritzberg, "Pre-Civil War Struggle," 110. For the likelihood that Anne Whiting led this petition drive, see Kritzberg, "A Pre-Civil War Struggle." Possibly because of his friendship with Governor Briggs, Samuel Hoar did not sign, although his daughter, Elizabeth, and daughter-in-law, Caroline Downes Brooks (Mary Brooks's daughter), did. Interestingly, although the manuscript petition clearly displays hundreds of signatures, a list of local petitions published in the *Liberator* on May 4, 1849, records only 51 signers from Concord, suggesting that more people signed after this issue of the *Liberator* went to press, or that perhaps two versions of the petition were circulated.

68. Barbara McCaskill, Introduction to William Craft, *Running a Thousand Miles for Freedom: The Escape of William and Ellen Craft from Slavery* (Athens: University of Georgia Press, 1999), ix, x; John Ernest, Introduction to William Craft, *Running a Thousand Miles for Freedom: Or, The Escape of William and Ellen Craft from Slavery* (Acton, Mass.: Copley, 2000), xi.

69. *Liberator*, 2 Mar, 27 Apr and 4 May 1849; Thoreau to Ward, 15 Mar 1849, Ellen Sewall Papers, Huntington.

70. Thoreau to Ward, 15 Nov 1849, Ellen Sewall Papers, Huntington; Abigail May Alcott to Samuel J. May, 10 Jul 1848, Alcott Family Papers, HL. Not even fifty years had diminished John Shepard Keyes's fear of the racial "other." In his autobiography, written at age eighty-eight, Keyes depicts "the great terror" of his childhood—his encounters with "Suke Cobb, a negro wench of about my age . . . How she would spring from the house and rush down the slope springing at a leap over the wall her scant single skirt flying out and her black legs!" (Keyes, 28). Keyes referred to Concord women's abolitionism as "niggering" (quoted in Robert A. Gross, "Young Men and Women of Fairest Promise: Transcendentalism in Concord," *CS* n.s. 2 [fall 1994]: 12); and his crude racism is also evident in his memoir of Sam Staples, whom Keyes describes as embarrassed when he unexpectedly ran into black female acquain-

tances one day in Boston—"black wenches" and "darkies," Keyes termed them ("Samuel Staples," *Social Circle*, fourth series, 138).

71. *JMN*, 9:125; *JMN*, 10:357; Gougeon, *Virtue's Hero*, 133; Walls, *Emerson's Life in Science*, 186. Emerson had shared a lecture platform in Concord with Frederick Douglass, but he evidently kept his distance and did not warm to this talented orator.

72. Michael Glenn Erlich, "Selected Anti-Slavery Speeches of Henry David Thoreau, 1848–1859: A Rhetorical Analysis" (Ph.D. diss., Ohio State University, 1970), 68; *Liberator*, 22 Jun 1849.

73. Sorin, *Abolitionism*, 133; David M. Potter, *The Impending Crisis: 1848–1861* (New York: Harper and Row, 1976), 1; Bradley P. Dean and Ronald Wesley Hoag, "Thoreau's Lectures After *Walden*: An Annotated Calendar," *SAR 1996*, ed. Joel Myerson (Charlottesville: University Press of Virginia, 1996), 360; ABA, *J*, 1:201; quoted in Gary Scharnhorst, *Henry David Thoreau: An Annotated Bibliography of Comment and Criticism Before 1900* (New York: Garland, 1992), 12, 13, 14, 18. See also Kent P. Ljungquist, "Thoreau in the Boston *Chronotype*," *TSB* 199 (spring 1992): 5. Scholars continue to debate which title is more authorial, but I have opted for the more common "Civil Disobedience."

74. *JP*, 2:262; *Mass. Lyceum*, 155. For background on Thoreau's reading as it may have influenced this essay, see Robert Sattelmeyer, *Thoreau's Reading: A Study in Intellectual History with Bibliographical Catalogue* (Princeton: Princeton University Press, 1988), 49–52.

75. M. K. Gandhi, *Non-Violent Resistance (Satyagraha)* (New York: Schocken, 1951), 3–4; Walter Harding, "Gandhi and Thoreau," *TSB* 23 (April 1948): 1–2; George Hendrick, "The Influence of Thoreau's 'Civil Disobedience' on Gandhi's *Satyagraha*," *NEQ* 29 (December 1956): 462–71; Martin Luther King, Jr., *Stride toward Freedom: The Montgomery Story* (1958; reprint, San Francisco: HarperCollins, 1986), 51; *RP*, 63, 67, 84, 73; Jerome Lawrence and Robert E. Lee, *The Night Thoreau Spent in Jail* (1970; reprint, New York: Bantam, 1972), vii; Meyer, *Several More Lives*, 89, 93; "Thoreau and the Danish Resistance: An Anonymous Memoir," in Hicks, *Thoreau in Our Season*, 20–21; Trevor N. W. Bush, "Thoreau in South Africa: A Letter from the Rev. Trevor N. W. Bush," in Hicks, *Thoreau in Our Season*, 27–28; Emma Goldman, *Anarchism and Other Essays* (New York: Dover, 1969), 56. King first read "Civil Disobedience" as a college student in the 1940s and was "fascinated by the idea of refusing to cooperate with an evil system." He reread it often and credited Thoreau with inspiring his sense of how to effect civil change (*Stride toward Freedom*, 91). Gandhi acknowledged Thoreau for coining the term "civil disobedience," but, importantly, he also realized that "Thoreau was not perhaps an out and out champion of non-violence" (*Non-Violent Resistance*, 3). In the 1950s, Senator Joseph McCarthy succeeded in banning an anthology of American literature because it contained "Civil Disobedience"; similarly in 1949, a writer expressed concern in the *New York Telegram* that the essay "might be too subversive for use in our high schools" (Walter Harding and Michael Meyer, *The New Thoreau Handbook* [New York: New York University Press, 1980], 209–10; ("Notes and Queries" *TSB* 30 [January 1950]: 3). Also amusing is the reaction of some Thoreau scholars in the 1960s when college "hippies" invoked Thoreau. In one instance, Raymond Adams, the first president of the Thoreau Society, was downright crotchety when students on his campus grew beards and quoted Thoreau : "Civil disobedience is one thing; the sit-in is another. The one is passive, like Thoreau's simply doing nothing about paying that tax; the other is more active, even aggressive, a kind of trespass" ("Thoreau's Return to Concord," *TSB* 96 [Summer 1966]: 1). Logically enough, this essay is usually examined in tandem with Thoreau's later antislavery essays, an approach however that often omits the momentous changes that would complicate the ideology and modus operandi of the radical abolitionists over the next decade. For the reception and influence of "Civil Disobedience" through the years, see Gary Scharnhorst, *Henry David Thoreau: A Case Study in Canonization* (Columbia, S.C.: Camden House, 1993), 50–53, 62–63, 74–75, 85–87; and Meyer, *Several More Lives*.

76. Howard Zinn, Introduction to Henry David Thoreau, "*The Higher Law*": *Thoreau on Civil Disobedience and Reform*, ed. Wendell Glick (Princeton: Princeton University Press, 2004), xiv; *RP*, 88, 67, 68, 72. For an argument that for Thoreau, "once the individual conscience

recognizes this [higher] law, its moral authority is binding and irrevocable on all matters," see Leigh Kathryn Jenco, "Thoreau's Critique of Democracy," *The Review of Politics* 65 (summer 2003): 360. For additional analyses of Thoreau's similarities to and differences with the Garrisonians, see Glick, 149–56; Peter J. Bellis, *Writing Revolution: Aesthetics and Politics in Hawthorne, Whitman, and Thoreau* (Athens: University of Georgia Press, 2003), 144; Carleton Mabee, *Black Freedom: The Nonviolent Abolitionists from 1830 through the Civil War* (New York: Macmillan, 1970), 263–67; and Teichgraeber, *Sublime Thoughts*, 126–34.

77. Nancy L. Rosenblum, Introduction to *Thoreau: Political Writings*, ed. Rosenblum (Cambridge: Cambridge University Press, 1996), xx; *RP*, 76, 77, 84. See also Michael J. Frederick, "Transcendental Ethos: A Study of Thoreau's Social Philosophy and Its Consistency in Relation to Antebellum Reform" (Master's thesis, Harvard University, 1998); William A. Herr, "Thoreau on Violence," *TSB* 131 (spring 1975): 2–4; Lewis Hyde, Introduction to *The Essays of Henry D. Thoreau* (New York: North Point, 2002), xxxv; Larry J. Reynolds, "The Cimeter's 'Sweet' Edge: Thoreau, Contemplation, and Violence," *Nineteenth-Century Prose* 31, no. 2 (fall 2004): 65; and Lawrence A. Rosenwald, "The Theory, Practice, and Influence of Thoreau's Civil Disobedience," in *A Historical Guide to Henry David Thoreau*, ed. William E. Cain (New York: Oxford University Press, 2000), 153–79.

78. *EAS*, 47; Stephen Adams and Donald Ross, Jr., *Revising Mythologies: The Composition of Thoreau's Major Works* (Charlottesville: University Press of Virginia, 1988), 217; *RP*, 72; Allan Kulikoff, *The Agrarian Origins of American Capitalism* (Charlottesville: University Press of Virginia, 1992), 236–37; Yacovone, *Samuel Joseph May*, 73; D. S. Reynolds, 441.

79. Kate Clifford Larson, *Bound for the Promised Land: Harriet Tubman, Portrait of an American Hero* (New York: Ballantine, 2004), 78–84, 89. At last, scholarly biographies of Harriet Tubman are available. Three studies of this extraordinary woman were recently published. See Larson, *Promised Land*; Jean M. Humez, *Harriet Tubman: The Life and the Life Stories* (Madison: University of Wisconsin Press, 2003); and Catherine Clinton, *Harriet Tubman: The Road to Freedom* (Boston: Little, Brown, 2004).

Chapter 3. Upheaval in Our Town, 1850–1854

1. *Liberator*, 12 Apr 1850.

2. Lois E. Horton, "Community Organization," 191; Thomas D. Morris, *Free Men All: The Personal Liberty Laws of the North, 1780–1861* (Baltimore: Johns Hopkins University Press, 1974), 114; Millard Fillmore, "The Fugitive Slave Bill," in *Annual Report*, 19:106. Historians have pointed to the irony that the Fugitive Slave Law's most vocal champions were southern proponents of "states' rights," who now insisted in a tacit expansion of federal power that the government protect their human property. See Larry Gara, "The Fugitive Slave Law: A Double Paradox," *Civil War History* 10 (January 1964): 229, 232–33.

3. Leslie Wilson, "A Concord Farmer Looks Back: The Reminiscences of William Henry Hunt," *CS* n.s. 10 (2002): 98; *ABA, J*, 1:227; Amos Bronson Alcott journal, Feb. 1847, Amos Bronson Alcott Papers, HL; Stacey M. Robertson, *Parker Pillsbury: Radical Abolitionist, Male Feminist* (Ithaca: Cornell University Press, 2000), 24, 82–83; Troy Duncan and Chris Dixon, "Denouncing the Brotherhood of Thieves: Stephen Symonds Foster's Critique of the Anti-Abolitionist Clergy," *Civil War History* 47, no. 2 (2001): 97; E. R. Hoar, "Samuel Hoar," *Social Circle*, third series, 45, 47. Other provisions of the law mandated that accused fugitives be remanded to their owners without trial, that they had no right to a writ of habeas corpus, and that they could not testify in any legal proceedings regarding their status (William W. Freehling, *The Road to Disunion*, vol. 1, *Secessionists at Bay, 1776–1854* [New York: Oxford University Press, 1990], 500–501).

4. Irving H. Bartlett, *Daniel Webster* (New York: Norton, 1978), 225, 226, 244. For the possibility that Concord's Rockwood Hoar coined the terms "Cotton" and "Conscience" Whig, see Edward W. Emerson, "Ebenezer Rockwood Hoar," in *Social Circle*, fourth series, 29. Irving Bartlett contends that "Webster's anti-slavery convictions were only part of a conservative view of the world which gave social and political stability a higher value than the eradication

of evil" (*Daniel Webster*, 244). Gary Collison argues, however, that "for the innumerable slaves . . . who yearned to find sanctuary there [in the north], questions of character and motive were beside the point. Daniel Webster's idea of 'American' did not include them" (*Shadrach Minkins*, 54).

5. Charles M. Wiltse and Michael J. Birkner, eds., *The Papers of Daniel Webster*, vol. 7, *Correspondence: 1850–1852* (Hanover, N.H.: University Press of New England, 1986), xiv; Charles M. Wiltse and Alan R. Berolzheimer, eds., *The Papers of Daniel Webster*, vol. 2, *Speeches and Formal Writings: 1834–1852* (Hanover, N.H.: University Press of New England, 1988), 519, 547, 541; *EAS*, 66. For Emerson's and other transcendentalists' immediate reactions to Daniel Webster after the speech, see Sam McGuire Worley, *Emerson, Thoreau, and the Role of the Cultural Critic* (Albany: State University of New York Press, 2001), 50–74. Worley contends that the March 7 speech "had shaken many of Webster's admirers more profoundly than we jaded moderns can easily appreciate" (53).

6. Phillips, *Speeches*, 45; Frederick J. Blue, *Charles Sumner and the Conscience of the North* (Arlington Heights, Ill.: Harlan Davidson, 1994), 54; *EAS*, 60; Thoreau, *Walden*, 232; Clapper, "Development of *Walden*," 2:621; Leonard W. Levy, "Sims' Case: The Fugitive Slave Law in Boston in 1851," *Journal of Negro History* 35 (January 1950): 40; John C. Lord, "*The Higher Law*," in *Its Application to The Fugitive Slave Bill. A Sermon on the Duties Men Owe to God and to Governments* (New York: Union Safety Committee, 1851), 10; M. Stuart, *Conscience and the Constitution . . .* (Boston: Crocker & Brewster, 1850), 7; *Annual Report*, 21:27. For a discussion of how Emerson and Thoreau differed in their views of Webster after the March 7 speech, see Leonard N. Neufeldt, "Emerson, Thoreau, and Daniel Webster," *ESQ* 26 (first quarter 1980): 26–37. Not everyone in Concord agreed with Emerson and Thoreau. John Shepard Keyes continued to support Webster after the speech and lamented the election of abolitionist Charles Sumner to fill the Senate seat vacated when Webster became secretary of state in 1851 (Keyes, 121).

7. Collison, *Shadrach Minkins*, 76; James Oliver Horton and Lois E. Horton, "A Federal Assault: African Americans and the Impact of the Fugitive Slave Law of 1850," in *Slavery and the Law*, ed. Paul Finkelman (Madison, Wis.: Madison House, 1997), 150, 151; *Voice of the Fugitive*, 9 Apr 1851; Freehling, *Road to Disunion*, 536; William I. Bowditch, *The Anti-Slavery Reform, Its Principle and Method* (Boston: Robert F. Wallcut, 1850), 6, 8. James O. Horton has explained that "no African American was safe from slavery. . . . Even legally free blacks were in danger from kidnappers selling them into slavery" (*Free People of Color: Inside the African American Community* [Washington: Smithsonian, 1993]), 58. He further notes that the Fugitive Slave Law "directly challenged Boston's reputation as a safe haven for fugitives" ("Defending the Manhood of the Race: The Crisis of Citizenship in Black Boston at Midcentury," in *Hope and Glory: Essays on the Legacy of the Fifty-Fourth Massachusetts Regiment*, ed. Martin H. Blatt, Thomas J. Brown, and Donald Yacovone [Amherst: University of Massachusetts Press, 2001]), 17.

8. Nancy Craig Simmons, *Selected Letters*, 525; LJE, *L*, 172–73; RWE, *L*, 8:265; *Mass. Lyceum*, 165. For the outline of the lecture that may have been the one Thompson delivered in Concord that year, see "Skeleton of a Lecture by George Thompson M.P. of England," Concord Antiquarian Society Collection, CFPL.

9. John Weiss, *Life and Correspondence of Theodore Parker*, 2 vols. in 1 (1864; reprint, New York: Arno, 1969), 2:94–95; [Francis Jackson], "Treasurer's Accounts. The Boston Vigilance Committee," Facsimile, Boston Public Library (Boston: Bostonian Society, [1924]), 23, 43, 69; Bearse, *Reminiscences*, 4–5. For details about the operations of the Vigilance Committee and its principal figures, see Jackson, "Treasurer's Accounts"; and Gary L. Collison, "The Boston Vigilance Committee: A Reconsideration," *Historical Journal of Massachusetts* 12 (1984): 104–16. During the 1850s, the Massachusetts Anti-Slavery Society ensured that fifty or more copies of the *Liberator* were delivered weekly to Congressional doors (*Annual Report*, 21:79, 24:20).

10. Wiltse and Birkner, *Correspondence*, 171; McCaskill, Introduction, xi–xiii; Ernest, Introduction, xiii–xiv; Boston Vigilance Committee, "Minutes, 28 October 1850," BPL; Weiss,

Life and Correspondence, 2:99, 96; Vincent Y. Bowditch, *Life and Correspondence of Henry Ingersoll Bowditch,* vol. 1 (Boston: Houghton Mifflin, 1902), 206; Stanley J. Robboy and Anita W. Robboy, "Lewis Hayden, from Fugitive Slave to Statesman," *NEQ* 46 (December 1973): 601; James Oliver Horton and Lois E. Horton, *Black Bostonians: Family Life and Community Struggle in the Antebellum North,* rev. ed. (New York: Holmes & Meier, 1999), 113; Horton and Horton, "A Federal Assault," 148. Hayden's residence at 66 Southac Street (since renamed Phillips Street) was renowned as a haven for runaway slaves. The home is now a historic site included on Boston's "Black Heritage Trail." See also Joel Strangis, *Lewis Hayden and the War against Slavery* (North Haven, Conn.: Linnet, 1999); and Harriet Beecher Stowe, *The Key to Uncle Tom's Cabin* (1854; reprint, New York: Arno, 1968), 303–5. Through the years of the Crafts' expatriation, the *Liberator* regularly reported on them, including the birth announcement of their first child (1 Apr 1853). Back in Georgia, Hughes was killed a year later in a brawl with Knight's brother (*Voice of the Fugitive,* 12 Feb 1851).

11. Wiltse and Birkner, *Correspondence,* 178, xiv, 181, 165.

12. Pease and Pease, "Confrontation and Abolition," 928; quoted in *Liberator,* 11 Oct 1850; Weiss, *Life and Correspondence,* 2:102; *EAS,* 54; Collison, *Shadrach Minkins,* 78–85. For a discussion of how northerners and southerners both invoked the American Revolution to defend individual liberty, see Eric J. Sundquist, "The Literature of Slavery and African American Culture," in *The Cambridge History of American Literature,* vol. 2, *1820–1865,* ed. Sacvan Bercovitch and Cyrus R. K. Patell (Cambridge: Cambridge University Press, 1995), 243–44. For a discussion of this tendency with regard to aristocratic notions of public discourse, see also Paul E. Teed, "The Politics of Sectional Memory: Theodore Parker and the *Massachusetts Quarterly Review,* 1847–1850," *JER* 21 (summer 2001): 320–29. According to John McWilliams, among Theodore Parker's most prized possessions were "the two muskets, which grandfather John Parker had carried home to Lexington after the retreat from Concord" (*New England's Crises and Cultural Memory: Literature, Politics, History, Religion, 1620–1860* [Cambridge: Cambridge University Press, 2004], 269). When fugitive slaves in Christiana, Pennsylvania, killed one of their pursuers before making it to Canada in the fall of 1851, the *Voice of the Fugitive* announced their arrival in similar rhetorical flair: "A nobler defence was never made in behalf of human liberty on the plains of Lexington, Concord, or Bunker Hill than was put forth by William Parker at Christiana" (quoted in *Frederick Douglass' Paper,* 24 Jun 1852). Lawrence J. Friedman argues that "a dual commitment to moral suasion and violent means was evident from the start," but he also contends that "most immediatists never relinquished their peace principles" (*Gregarious Saints,* 196–97). For the increasing radicalism of black abolitionists during the 1850s, including the origins of black nationalism, see Rael, *Black Identity,* 209–36. For an argument that "a willingness to undertake violence was a component of antebellum American concepts of manhood," see John R. McKivigan and Stanley Harrold, Introduction to *Antislavery Violence: Sectional, Racial, and Cultural Conflict in Antebellum America,* ed. McKivgan and Harrold (Knoxville: University of Tennessee Press, 1999), 3. For more about the resourceful Captain Bearse, see Sandra Harbert Petrulionis, "Fugitive Slave-Running on the *Moby Dick*: Captain Austin Bearse and the Abolitionist Crusade," *Resources for American Literary Study* 28 (2002): 53–81.

13. McFeely, 110, quoted in 192; Philip S. Foner, *Frederick Douglass,* 207, 277; Ward, "Charles Lenox Remond," 210; quoted in Oates, 73–74. Strained relations between Douglass and Garrison had existed since at least 1847. In 1851, Douglass opposed Garrison by judging that the U.S. Constitution was not necessarily a proslavery document, that it could "be made consistent" with freedom for all, black and white (quoted in McFeely, 169). For analyses of this regrettable falling out, see McFeely, 169–79; Mayer, 371–74; and C. Peter Ripley et al., eds., *The Black Abolitionist Papers,* 5 vols. (Chapel Hill: University of North Carolina Press, 1985–1992), 4:174–86. Gerald Sorin has argued that "black militancy not only preceded white militancy but it consistently gave abolitionism its hard edge and made it much more effective than it could otherwise have been" (*Abolitionism,* 105). See also Horton and Horton, "A Federal Assault," 152–55; and James H. Cook, "Fighting with Breath, Not Blows: Frederick Douglass and Antislavery Violence," in McKivigan and Harrold, *Antislavery Violence,* 128–63.

14. Larry Gara, *The Liberty Line: The Legend of the Underground Railroad* (1961; reprint, Lexington: University Press of Kentucky, 1996); *Liberator,* 25 Nov 1853. For other examples, see *Liberator,* 14 Nov 1851, 28 Oct 1853, 11 May 1855, and 4 Dec 1857. Late in the nineteenth century, historian Wilbur H. Siebert interviewed elderly abolitionists, pored over the few sources published on the subject and mapped out what he perceived to be the principal Underground Railroad routes used by the Vigilance Committee to funnel fugitives out of Boston. According to him, Concord figured as a stopover on two of these six primary systems. Siebert's research was fraught with errors, yet it established for years a basis for interpreting the Underground Railroad as a more organized and methodical system than was the case (*The Underground Railroad in Massachusetts* [Worcester: American Antiquarian Society, 1936]). Abolitionists likely did employ these and other routes, but such paths were by no means the only avenues to freedom. See also Gara, *Liberty Line,* 1–2, 17–18, 180; Benjamin Quarles, Foreword to William Still, *The Underground Railroad* (1871; reprint, Chicago: Johnson, 1970), v; and *Liberator,* 25 Nov 1853. Gara's work to demythologize the Underground Railroad has been applauded; recent studies have also pointed out, however, the degree of organization and collaboration that did exist among those who helped individuals fleeing slavery. See, for example, Stanley W. Harrold, *Subversives: Antislavery Community in Washington, D.C., 1828–1865* (Baton Rouge: Louisiana State University Press, 2003); and Collison, "Boston Vigilance Committee."

15. Whiting to May, 31 Jul 1850, BPL. For details of the Boston abolitionists who secured food, lodging, clothing, and means of escape to more than five hundred men, women, and children between 1850 and 1860, see Jackson, "Treasurer's Accounts." These records begin in October 1850, and therefore shed no light on Whiting's letter. Interestingly, although hundreds of fugitives left Boston after September 1850, the total number of blacks in the city actually increased over the next years as new runaways and free blacks continued to seek refuge there (see Peter R. Knights, *The Plain People of Boston, 1830–1860: A Study in City Growth* [New York: Oxford University Press, 1971], 31).

16. Edward Waldo Emerson, "Notes," 2; Magee, "Emerson's Emancipation Proclamations," 97; Hendrick, *Remembrances,* 41, 42; Damon to Wilbur H. Siebert, Dec 1893, Scrapbooks concerning the Underground Railroad, 18—19—, HL. For a record of Waldo Emerson's contributions to antislavery causes, see his Account Books for 1 Feb 1851, 19 Sep 1855, and 4 Jun 1857, Emerson Journals and Notebooks, HL.

17. Collison, *Shadrach Minkins,* 152, 13, 54–57, 61, 65–66, 110–15; *Liberator,* 21 Feb 1851.

18. *Liberator,* 21 Feb 1851; Collison, *Shadrach Minkins,* 115–33; *Boston Globe,* 7 Apr 1889; Edward Waldo Emerson, "Notes," 3. Gary Collison has examined the plethora of legends that relate to Minkins's early morning stopover in Concord, carefully sorting the probable from the unlikely. As he points out, Ann Bigelow left four slightly inconsistent accounts of what had clearly been a proud encounter for the female society (*Shadrach Minkins,* 153–57). No evidence indicates that Bigelow knew ahead of time that Hayden was on his way with Minkins to Concord. See also Gary L. Collison, "Shadrach in Concord," *CS* 19 (December 1987): 1–12; and *Boston Globe,* 7 Apr 1889. Two of the lawyers deliberating over the delay tactics for Minkins's defense were Abby Alcott's cousin Samuel E. Sewall and Waldo Emerson's friend Ellis Gray Loring.

19. Edward Waldo Emerson, "Notes," 3, 4; Collison, *Shadrach Minkins,* 153–65.

20. *JP,* 3:194; Edward Waldo Emerson, "Notes," 4; quoted in *Liberator,* 14 Mar 1851; Collison, *Shadrach Minkins,* 153; Samuel Adams Drake, *History of Middlesex County, Massachusetts . . . ,* 2 vols. (Boston: Estes and Lauriat, 1880), 1:399. Perhaps more informed than he let on, the editor of the *Middlesex Freeman* reported the following week that "the prisoner is no doubt by this time in some part of the British dominions" (21 Feb 1851). In one of history's lovely ironies, Francis Bigelow was seated on the jury the following year when Elizur Wright went on trial for helping rescue Minkins. For a discussion of those arrested (and all ultimately acquitted) for liberating Minkins, see Gary Collison, " 'This Flatigious Offense': Daniel Webster and the Shadrach Rescue Cases, 1851–1852," *NEQ* 68 (December 1995): 609–26.

21. Wiltse and Birkner, *Correspondence*, 206, 205; "*Warrington*," 191; Weiss, *Life and Correspondence*, 2:103.

22. Thoreau to Prudence Ward, 16 Jan 1850, Ellen Sewall Papers, Huntington; Bradley P. Dean, "Thoreau, Emerson, and the Reverend Daniel Foster," paper presented at the conference of the Modern Language Association (Philadelphia, Pa., December 2004), 3–4.

23. David A. Davis, Introduction to *The Experience of Rev. Thomas H. Jones, Who Was a Slave for Forty-Three Years*, in *North Carolina Slave Narratives: The Lives of Moses Roper, Lunsford Lane, Moses Grandy, & Thomas H. Jones* (Chapel Hill: University of North Carolina Press, 2003), 189–90; *Liberator*, 1 Feb 1850; *Annual Report*, 18:94, 98; Daniel Foster journal, 20 Mar 1851, Daniel Foster Papers, MHi.

24. Foster journal, 9 Apr 1851, Foster Papers, MHi; Thoreau, *Walden*, 232. In the *Liberator* later that spring, Jones relayed his safe arrival in New Brunswick (30 May 1851). For letters Jones wrote to his wife and other relatives while still enslaved, see Carter G. Woodson, ed., *The Mind of the Negro as Reflected in Letters Written during the Crisis, 1800–1860* (1926; reprint, New York: Russell & Russell, 1969), 545–51. Although Jones intended to go to England, he apparently never left Canada. Two years later, he served as the *Liberator*'s agent in New Brunswick (*Liberator*, 19 Aug 1853); by 1854, he was back in Boston, attempting to raise the purchase price of a son who remained enslaved. To that end, he dictated and published *The Experience and Personal Narrative of Uncle Tom Jones, Who Was for Forty Years a Slave*, a title deliberately chosen to trade on the fame of Harriet Beecher Stowe's *Uncle Tom's Cabin*. Several subsequent editions of this popular narrative, re-titled *The Experience of Thomas H. Jones, Who Was a Slave for Forty-Three Years*, appeared between then and 1885. It is also included in a recent anthology of slave narratives. See Andrews, *North Carolina Slave Narratives*, 189–279.

25. *Liberator*, 18 Apr 1851; MCASS.

26. *Middlesex Freeman*, 21 Mar and 4 Apr 1851; Brooks to Phillips, 31 Mar 1851, Phillips Papers, HL. Two years later, Brooks similarly appealed to Phillips: "We talk of a tea party here this month. Now will it be possible for you to come up to Concord, one night, and speak to us on the occasion. If so, will you write me soon, telling me the night it will be convenient for you to come" (Brooks to Phillips, 10 Mar 1853, Phillips Papers, HL).

27. *Liberator*, 7 Mar and 18 Apr 1851; Foster journal, 3 Apr 1851, Foster Papers, MHi. Anne Whiting had reported on the meeting and tea party in a personal letter to Garrison, which he published in the *Liberator* with a note indicating Whiting as the author. Spiritualism made inroads in Concord during the 1840s and 1850s, and was explored by a number of townspeople, including Prudence Ward, and Maria and Jane Thoreau (see Leslie Wilson, "'Taps in the Wall and Thumps in the Table-Drawer,'" *The Concord Journal*, 4 Jan 2001: 6; Thomas Blanding, "Rapping with the Thoreaus," *CS* 17 (March 1984): 1–6; and Harriet Hanson Robinson journal, 20 Aug 1856, SL).

28. Foster journal, 4 Apr 1851, Foster Papers, MHi; Levy, "Sims' Case," 43–44; Roger Lane, *Policing the City: Boston, 1822–1885* (Cambridge: Harvard University Press, 1967), 73. Sims had successfully escaped and hidden in the *M. & J. C. Gilmore* during the voyage from Georgia. He was discovered and locked up as the ship arrived in Boston, but he had managed to escape and elude recapture for weeks before Potter arrived and authorities tracked him down (see Nina Moore Tiffany, "Stories of the Fugitive Slaves. III. Sims," *New England Magazine* 8 [June 1890]: 385–88; and Levy, "Sims' Case"). Although his age has been reported as seventeen, Sims was apparently twenty-three years old (see Collison, *Shadrach Minkins*, 190).

29. Vincent Y. Bowditch, *Life and Correspondence*, 215; Horton and Horton, *Black Bostonians*, 115–16; Thomas Wentworth Higginson, *Cheerful Yesterdays* (1898; reprint, New York: Arno, 1968), 140, 143. Sims's incarceration in the city courthouse further enraged abolitionists since it violated a state law, passed in 1843, dictating that fugitives could not be held in public buildings (Morris, *Free Men All*, 114). Unitarian minister and political radical Thomas Wentworth Higginson was at the forefront of Vigilance Committee militance during the 1850s. Later, during the Civil War, he served in South Carolina as a colonel to the first black regiment comprised of freed slaves. See his *Army Life in a Black Regiment, and Other Writings*

(New York: Penguin, 1997); and Tilden G. Edelstein, *Strange Enthusiasm: A Life of Thomas Wentworth Higginson* (1968; reprint, New York: Atheneum, 1970).

30. Foster journal, 6, 7, and 8 Apr 1851, Foster Papers, MHi; ABA, *J*, 1:243–45; *Liberator*, 11 Apr 1851.

31. *JP*, 3:204–5; Theodore Parker, *The Slave Power*, ed. James K. Hosmer (1910; reprint, New York: Arno, 1969), 326; Foster journal, 14 Apr 1851, Foster Papers, MHi; Daniel Foster, *Our Nation's Sins and the Christian's Duty. A Fast Day Discourse* (Boston: White & Potter, 1851), 32; Vincent Y. Bowditch, *Life and Correspondence*, 223; Dean, "Reverend Daniel Foster," 7. For the words of Foster's prayer, see *Liberator*, 18 Apr 1851.

32. *JP*, 3:205, 203, 204; *JMN*, 11:360. Thoreau called Foster "a truer man" who didn't try to be "all things to all men" (*JP*, 4:289). After leaving Concord, the Fosters continued to correspond with and visit the Thoreaus.

33. *JP*, 3:206, 207, 208; quoted in Levy, "Sims' Case," 72; *Middlesex Freeman*, 18 and 25 Apr 1851. After his return to Georgia, Thomas Sims was sent to New Orleans, where he was then sold and taken to Mississippi. He escaped from slavery during the Civil War and obtained his freedom (see Lader, *Bold Brahmins*, 180; and Levy, "Sims' Case," 74).

34. Wiltse and Birkner, *Correspondence*, 232, 237, 233.

35. Deborah Weston to Anne Warren Weston, 15 Apr 1851, BPL; Parker, *Slave Power*, 361, 339; Theodore Parker, *The Rights of Man in America*, ed. F. B. Sanborn (1911; reprint, New York: Negro Universities Press, 1969), 151. Michael Fellman has explained that after 1850, "Garrison's nonresistant tactical stance became increasingly anachronistic . . . and yet the phenomenon of radical abolitionism . . . spread widely as a popularly shared ideological position" ("Theodore Parker and the Abolitionist Role in the 1850s," *Journal of American History* 61 [December 1974]: 666–67). John Demos observes that "non-resistance" had always presented a problem to the organized abolitionist movement; during the 1850s, he contends that it "completely collapsed" ("Antislavery Movement," 502–3). See also Horton and Horton, *Black Bostonians*, 125–38.

36. *Liberator*, 11 Apr 1851; Whiting to Phillips, 8 Apr 1851, Phillips Papers, HL; *EAS*, 65; *JMN*, 11:412.

37. Brooks to Emerson, 27 Apr 1851, Letters to Ralph Waldo Emerson, HL.

38. *EAS*, 57, 53.

39. *JMN*, 11:385, 411. Robert D. Richardson, Jr., argues that the return of Thomas Sims "snapped Emerson's equanimity" and converted Emerson into "an activist" (*Emerson: The Mind on Fire* [Berkeley: University of California Press, 1995], 496). For details about the context of this speech, see Linck C. Johnson, " 'Liberty Is Never Cheap': Emerson, 'The Fugitive Slave Law,' and the Antislavery Lecture Series at the Broadway Tabernacle," *NEQ* 76 (December 2003): 550–92. Johnson appraises Emerson's abolitionism at this time as "far more moderate" than the Garrisonians (554). See also Jeffrey B. Kurtz, "Condemning Webster: Judgment and Audience in Emerson's 'Fugitive Slave Law,' " *Quarterly Journal of Speech* 87, no. 3 (August 2001): 278–90.

40. *EAS*, 57, 53, 56, 69. For a discussion of how Emerson's "Fugitive Slave Law" address doubled as a campaign speech for Free Soil congressional candidate John Gorham Palfrey, see Len Gougeon, "Emerson and the Campaign of 1851," *Historical Journal of Massachusetts* 16, no. 1 (1988): 20–33. Barbara Packer has pointed out that his sentiments in the Fugitive Slave Law address "did not mean that Emerson had outgrown his prejudices or would never express them again, merely that he did not intend to let his conduct be determined by them." Historical Introduction to *The Conduct of Life*, in *The Collected Works of Ralph Waldo Emerson*, vol. 6, ed. Joseph Slater (Cambridge: Belknap Press of Harvard University Press, 2003), il. As late as March 1855, *Frederick Douglass' Paper* reported Emerson had recently "advocated what will be called compensation to the slaveholder, as the *most practical* and speediest method of abolishing slavery," a strategy opposed by most abolitionists (2 Mar 1855).

41. Foster journal, 4 May 1851, Foster Papers, MHi; *EAS*, 212; *JMN*, 13:80; Slater, *Correspondence*, 470.

42. Stanley M. Elkins, *Slavery: A Problem in American Institutional and Intellectual Life*, 3rd

ed., rev. (Chicago: University of Chicago Press, 1976), 170, 169; *EAS*, 53. For examples of critics who fault the transcendentalists for their slow move to antislavery, see Nancy L. Rosenblum, "The Inhibitions of Democracy on Romantic Political Thought: Thoreau's Democratic Individualism," in *Lessons of Romanticism: A Critical Companion*, ed. Thomas Pfau and Robert F. Gleckner (Durham: Duke University Press, 1998), 65; Barry Kritzberg, "Thoreau, Slavery, and Resistance to Civil Government," *Massachusetts Review* 30 (winter 1989): 548; and Alfred I. Tauber, *Henry David Thoreau and the Moral Agency of Knowing* (Berkeley: University of California Press, 2001), 191.

43. *JP*, 4:113–14.

44. Jackson, "Treasurer's Accounts," 8; Collison, *Shadrach Minkins*, 85. I am grateful to Gary Collison for providing these details from the 1861 Montreal census and city directory.

45. Emerson, Account Books, 3 Oct 1851, Emerson Journals and Notebooks, HL; Edward Waldo Emerson, "Notes," 2; *Voice of the Fugitive*, 5 Nov 1851; *Liberator*, 10 Oct 1851. By "Miss Thoreau," Waldo Emerson most likely referred to Sophia.

46. *AME*, 1:141; *JP*, 6:272–73. In her *Thoreau: His Home, Friends and Books*, Annie Russell Marble conflates the unidentified slave described by Conway in 1853 with Henry Williams's overnight stay with the Thoreaus in 1851. Marble claims that when Henry Williams, "whom [Thoreau] had so lovingly tended," returned from Canada, he presented Thoreau with a statuette of Uncle Tom and Eva, characters from Harriet Beecher Stowe's bestseller: "The negro spent his last penny for the gift, and walked from Boston to Concord to give it to his friend. Thoreau was deeply appreciative of the gratitude and always treasured the gift and its association." Marble's source for this information was George Tolman, then secretary of the Concord Antiquarian Society, whose catalog of Thoreau-related items in its collection identified a "Crockery Figure of Uncle Tom and Little Eva, given to Thoreau by a fugitive slave" (Tolman, 43). The statue is now housed in the Concord Museum. Tolman apparently left no other record about the statue's provenance. See Annie Russell Marble, *Thoreau: His Home, Friends and Books* (1902; reprint, New York: AMS, 1969), 198–99. For a photograph of the statue, see the Illustrations in *JP*, 4.

47. *JP*, 7:134–35, 103 (in press); *AME*, 1:103–9, 174–75; Glick, 154. Conway credits Farquhar and other Quakers with first causing him to question slavery's legitimacy. Neither this woman nor her enslaved husband have been identified. She may have come directly to Concord from Virginia, or she may have attempted to raise money in Boston (or elsewhere) before coming to Concord.

48. *JP*, 6:212–13; WLG, *L*, 1:570 n.5, 4:317 n.1; Meyer, "Thoreau, Abolitionists, and Reformers," 20.

49. *JP*, 6:294.

50. *Liberator*, 6 Jan 1854; *National Era*, 12 Jan 1854; *Annual Report*, 24:4–5, 16; *EAS*, 73–89. For details about the context of this lecture series and its other participants, see Linck C. Johnson, "'Liberty Is Never Cheap.'"

51. Mayer, 435–36; Nicole Etcheson, *Bleeding Kansas: Contested Liberty in the Civil War Era* (Lawrence: University Press of Kansas, 2004), 12, 5.

52. W. E. Burghardt Du Bois, *John Brown* (Philadelphia: George W. Jacobs, 1909), 135–36.

53. *JP*, 8:10; Harris to Ward, 18 Jun 1854, TS; Brooks to Garrison, 20 Feb 1854, BPL; *Liberator*, 24 Mar 1854; Higginson, *Cheerful Yesterdays*, 139.

54. Charles Emery Stevens, *Anthony Burns: A History* (1856; reprint, New York: Negro Universities Press, 1969), 17; Anne Warren Weston to Mary Weston, 30 Jul 1854, BPL; Brenda Stevenson, ed., *The Journals of Charlotte Forten Grimké* (New York: Oxford University Press, 1988), 63. The *National Anti-Slavery Standard* and the *Liberator* reported that Burns was located through a letter he sent to his brother in Virginia. Even though Burns sent the letter to Canada to be postmarked and mailed, he apparently had written "Boston" at the top of a page, along with the date (*National Anti-Slavery Standard*, 3 Jun 1854; *Liberator*, 2 Jun 1854). Anne Warren Weston believed that if Richard Henry Dana, Jr. and Wendell Phillips had not immediately become involved, Burns "would have been carried off with no stir" (Anne Warren Weston to "Folks," 30 May 1854, BPL). For the details of Burns's arrest, imprisonment, at-

tempted rescue, and rendition, see Von Frank, *Anthony Burns*; Stanley W. Campbell, *The Slave Catchers: Enforcement of the Fugitive Slave Law, 1850–1860* (Chapel Hill: University of North Carolina Press, 1968), 124–32; David R. Maginnes, "The Case of the Court House Rioters in the Rendition of the Fugitive Slave Anthony Burns, 1854," *Journal of Negro History* 56 (January 1971): 31–42; Samuel Shapiro, "The Rendition of Anthony Burns," *Journal of Negro History* 44 (January 1959): 34–51; and Jane H. Pease and William H. Pease, *The Fugitive Slave Law and Anthony Burns: A Problem in Law Enforcement* (Philadelphia: Lippincott, 1975). Boston abolitionists had not become complacent during the three years of relative calm since Thomas Sims's rendition. Vigilance Committee records reveal the steady, covert aid supplied to the city's fugitives by a reliable multiracial network who well understood how easily these men, women, and children could be seized. For details of the plan to purchase Burns's freedom, see Von Frank, *Anthony Burns*, 80–84; and Stevens, *Anthony Burns*, 61–79.

55. Higginson, *Cheerful Yesterdays*, 150–56; quoted in *National Anti-Slavery Standard*, 3 Jun 1854; *JP*, 8:175. Among the three hundred women crowded into Faneuil Hall that Friday evening was Anne Warren Weston, who judged that the rescue attempt failed at least partially because hundreds of disorganized agitators did not join the others at the courthouse (Weston to "Folks," 30 May 1854, BPL). Higginson's autobiography depicts "one of the most picturesque incidents" of the evening as Bronson Alcott, then living in Boston, came along after the excitement; walking up the courthouse steps, Alcott purportedly asked, "Why are we not within?" (*Cheerful Yesterdays*, 158). See also ABA, *J*, 1:272–73; and Dahlstrand, *Amos Bronson Alcott*, 235–36.

56. "Trial of Anthony Burns," *Proceedings of the Massachusetts Historical Society* 44 (January 1911): 324–26; Richard Henry Dana, Jr., *Speeches in Stirring Times and Letters to a Son*, ed. Richard H. Dana, 3d. (Boston: Houghton Mifflin, 1910), 210; Von Frank, *Anthony Burns*, 207–19; Stevens, *Anthony Burns*, 138, 143–50; *Liberator*, 9 Jun 1854; *Boston Daily Commonwealth*, 7 Jun 1854; Weston to "Folks," 30 May 1854, BPL; "*Warrington*," 208–9. The Vigilance Committee had called on Boston residents to "be present to witness the sacrifice . . . follow him in sad procession with your tears and prayers" (*National Anti-Slavery Standard*, 3 Jun 1854). Boston police captain Joseph K. Hayes, whose coincident membership on the Vigilance Committee had benefited its members when they needed extra security at meetings, now found his dual occupations incompatible; he resigned from the police force after telling his men: "I wish you distinctly to understand how much I shall help the U.S. in this business. If there is an attempt at a rescue, and it is likely to fail, I shall help the rescuers" (quoted in Stevens, *Anthony Burns*, 137). Von Frank points out that prior to his appointment as Slave Commissioner, Loring had written articles supporting the Fugitive Slave Law. A precedent for the women's "gift" to him had been established in 1851, when antislavery women in Syracuse, New York, sent thirty pieces of silver to the federal attorney who prosecuted the rescuers of fugitive slave Jerry McHenry. Despite their failure to free Burns, abolitionists did succeed in removing Loring from the bench in 1858 (Von Frank, *Anthony Burns*, 17, 241; Yacovone, *Samuel Joseph May*, 148). Charges were eventually dropped against Higginson, Parker, Phillips, and the others accused of attempting to rescue Burns and of causing the death of courthouse guard James Batchelder (Von Frank, *Anthony Burns*, 292–301). The man at the center of the ordeal, Anthony Burns, was soon sold at a slave auction in Richmond and taken to North Carolina. His freedom was purchased by Rev. Leonard Grimes in 1855, whereupon Burns entered Oberlin College in Ohio and studied to become a minister. Once free, Burns appeared at antislavery rallies in Boston and New York to narrate his story; he rejected, however, an offer to be paraded, as he deemed it, "like a monkey!" in P. T. Barnum's museum in New York (quoted in Stevens, *Anthony Burns*, 216). Burns later preached in Indiana and Canada, where he died in 1862. For more information about Burns's life after slavery, see John W. Blassingame, ed., *Slave Testimony: Two Centuries of Letters, Speeches, Interviews, and Autobiographies* (Baton Rouge: Louisiana State University Press, 1977), 109; Stevens, *Anthony Burns*, 188–216; Fred Landon, "Anthony Burns in Canada," Ontario Historical Society, *Papers and Records* 22 (1925): 3–7; and Anthony Burns to Wendell Phillips, 2 Aug 1856, Phillips Papers, HL. In the wake of their failure to rescue Burns, several of the most radical Vigilance Com-

mittee members formed "a secret oath-bound club" called the "Anti-man-hunting League," whose mission was to "capture and carry off to one of their places for concealment any slaveholder who should come to the State to hunt and reclaim a runaway slave ("Henry Ingersoll Bowditch," in *Proceedings of the American Academy of Arts and Sciences* n.s. 20 [Boston: University Press: John Wilson and Son, 1893], 314). Those who belonged to this organization included T. W. Higginson, Theodore Parker, Samuel May, Henry and William Bowditch, and Bronson Alcott (see "Boston Anti-Man-Hunting League" Records, MHi).

57. Weston to "Folks," 30 May 1854, BPL. For more on white abolitionists' reaction to the dishonor to Massachusetts, see Von Frank, *Anthony Burns*, 59–60.

58. *Boston Daily Commonwealth*, 7 Jun 1854; T. W. Higginson, *Massachusetts in Mourning. A Sermon, Preached in Worcester, on Sunday, June 4, 1854* (Boston: James Munroe, 1854), 10, 13, 12. The furor surrounding Burns renewed abolitionists' efforts to repeal the Fugitive Slave Law, but even as abolitionists submitted petitions demanding it be nullified, President Pierce instructed his attorney general to prosecute the law more effectively (*Boston Daily Commonwealth*, 7 Jun 1854; Pease and Pease, *Fugitive Slave Law*, 27). Burns's rendition also revived the fears of other Boston fugitives, and many took flight. The next week, Samuel May, Jr., sent two such women to the care of Caroline Healey Dall, then living in Canada: "Two women, one of them having a child, are to leave here without delay for Toronto. Both of them have been victims of the glorious institutions of our free and happy land. We pay their passage through. Their names are Houston and Johnson—both women in middle life, or even perhaps a little beyond. They have been in a state of the greatest trepidation for many days, and nothing can quiet them in the thought of remaining here" (May to Dall, 10 Jun 1854, Caroline Wells Healey Dall Papers, MHi).

59. George Frisbie Hoar, *Autobiography of Seventy Years*, 2 vols. (New York: Scribner's, 1903), 1:180; *EAS*, 217; *Liberator*, 30 Jun 1854. At times, Emerson still confessed to an abiding distaste for antislavery work: "If I may dare to say so, I have my own slaves to free, spirits in other prisons, whom no man visits, & whom I am sent to help, if I can. And in all my life, until the disastrous legislation three years ago on the Fugitive bill . . . the evil of slavery has been remote, & has never practically come to our doors. . . . Now, we have all been polluted by it" (*JMN*, 14:409–10).

60. Weiss, *Life and Correspondence*, 2:143; RWE, *L*, 4:452–53; Parker, *Rights of Man*, 343, 344.

61. *JP*, 8:164, 198; *RP*, 91. Thoreau's ire toward northern complicity with slavery was shared by his fellow Concord native, editor William Robinson, who wrote in the *Lowell American* that "slavery is stronger to-day in Massachusetts than it is in Georgia" ("*Warrington*," 192).

62. *Liberator*, 7 Jul 1854. Accounts differ as to the size of the Framingham crowd. The *New York Times* reported that "five or six hundred Abolitionists" attended (5 Jul 1854), while the *Boston Commonwealth* put the attendance at "about two thousand" (quoted in Bradley P. Dean, "More Context for Thoreau's 'Slavery in Massachusetts,' " *Thoreau Research Newsletter* 1 [July 1990]: 12).

63. *Liberator*, 23 Jun and 7 Jul 1854; *AME*, 1:184; Dean and Hoag, "Thoreau's Lectures," 360–61; *JP*, 8:198–99; *Days*, 39; Robert F. Lucid, *The Journal of Richard Henry Dana, Jr.*, vol. 2 (Cambridge: Belknap Press of Harvard University Press, 1968), 613–68; Ellen Tucker Emerson, *The Life of Lidian Jackson Emerson*, ed. Delores Bird Carpenter (Boston: Twayne, 1980), 125.

64. *Liberator*, 7 and 15 Jul 1854; Cain, Introduction, 35; *AME*, 1:185. See also Dean, "More Context," 12; *Liberator*, 16 Jun 1854; and Stephen W. Herring, "The Halcyon Days of Framingham's Harmony Grove," *TSB* 215 (spring 1996): 4.

65. *Liberator*, 14 Jul 1854; *RP*, 92, 91, 96, 104, 103, 108. "Slavery in Massachusetts" derived almost entirely from Thoreau's journal entries between May 29 and June 19, 1854, along with several that relate to Thomas Sims from April 1851. For a discussion of the substantive textual differences between the journal and speech, see Sandra Harbert Petrulionis, "Editorial Savoir-Faire: Thoreau Transforms His Journal into 'Slavery in Massachusetts,' " *Resources for*

American Literary Study 25, no. 2 (1999): 206–31. Notably omitted from Thoreau's public pronouncement of "murder to the state" was the journal's penciled phrase that followed it: "I am calculating how many miscreants each honest man can dispose of" (see Later Revision 200.30 in *JP*, 8:501).

66. *RP*, 108; Lawrence Buell, "American Pastoral Ideology Reappraised," *American Literary History* 1 (spring 1989): 6; *JP*, 8:195–96, 200. For a reading of the white lily "as Thoreau's turn back toward Reality in Eastern terms," see Larry J. Reynolds, "Cimeter's 'Sweet' Edge," 66. See Anne C. Rose, *Transcendentalism as a Social Movement, 1830–1850* (New Haven: Yale University Press, 1981), 222, for an argument that of all the transcendentalists, "only Thoreau was able to translate the spirit of Transcendentalist reform into an antislavery program pertinent to the 1850s, and he did so with extraordinary power." For a recent discussion that the white lily exposes "the pastoral as a faulty world-view," see Kris Fresonke, "Thoreau and the Design of Dissent," 232.

67. *AME*, 1:184–85; *Annual Report*, 24:27. *Walden* was published on August 9, 1854.

68. Scharnhorst, *Annotated Bibliography*, 23, 25, 28; *New York Daily Tribune*, 2 Aug 1854; quoted in "Thoreau and Horace Greeley," *TSB* 11 (April 1945): 3; *Corr*, 336, 337.

69. *Corr*, 330, 345–46; *JP*, 2:240; *J*, 7:79; Dean and Hoag, "Thoreau's Lectures," 361.

70. Austin Bearse, *Reminiscences of Fugitive-Slave Law Days in Boston* (1880; reprint, New York: Arno, 1969), 37–39; Bowditch to Wilbur H. Siebert, 5 Apr 1893, Scrapbooks concerning the Underground Railroad, 18—19—, HL. Bowditch's Brookline home had provided security for Lewis Hayden when he was sought for questioning after the failed attempt to rescue Anthony Burns (Von Frank, *Anthony Burns*, 118). For identification of Ephraim W. Allen, see WLG, *L*, 1:6; and Mayer, 22–27.

71. E. R. Hoar, "Samuel Hoar," *Social Circle*, third series, 47–48; D. W. Atwood to Samuel Hoar, C. C. Hazewell, Daniel Shattuck, A. G. Fay, Simon Brown, & R. W. Emerson, 1 Jul 1854, CFPL; Dean and Hoag, "Thoreau's Lectures," 361; Scharnhorst, *Annotated Bibliography*, 41; Larson, *Promised Land*, 302.

Chapter 4. Call to War, 1855–1868

1. Samuel A. Johnson, *The Battle Cry of Freedom: The New England Emigrant Aid Company in the Kansas Crusade* (Lawrence: University of Kansas Press, 1954), 7; Etcheson, *Bleeding Kansas*, 29, 50–68. Several scholars make the important point that not all Kansas émigrés were abolitionists. David M. Potter points out that Kansas's "great anomaly" was the fact that most Free Staters did not hold strong abolitionist convictions, but simply did not want to compete with slaveholders for their right to claim land (*Impending Crisis*, 202–3). See also Von Frank, *Anthony Burns*, 156; and Etcheson, *Bleeding Kansas*, 31. Proslavery settlers came to Kansas from states other than Missouri as well. In August 1856, the *Liberator* reported that twenty-six "South Carolinians . . . 'all armed to the teeth' " had set out for Kansas (1 Aug 1856).

2. Samuel A. Johnson, *Battle Cry*, 6, 7, 26–27, 33, 46; Etcheson, *Bleeding Kansas*, 35–40; Eli Thayer, *A History of The Kansas Crusade: Its Friends and Its Foes* (New York: Harper & Brothers, 1889), 48–51; Kenneth S. Davis, *Kansas: A Bicentennial History* (New York: Norton, 1976), 39, 40, 45.

3. "*Warrington*," 75; Harriet Hanson Robinson journal, 17 and 24 Apr 1855, SL; Samuel A. Johnson, *Battle Cry*, 126; *Mass. Lyceum*, 169; *Recollections*, 2:441–43, and 1:51.

4. Quoted in Gougeon, Historical Background, xliii; *EAS*, 91; *Annual Report*, 24:38; Linck C. Johnson, " 'Liberty Is Never Cheap,' " 591; *JMN*, 13:405. At this time, Emerson was also developing his most comprehensive discussion on the concept of "Race," published in *English Traits* in 1856.

5. Whiting to May, 8 Jun 1855, BPL; *Liberator*, 29 Jun and 6 Jul 1855; *Corr*, 376.

6. Liberator, 6 Jul 1855; Ira V. Brown, *Mary Grew: Abolitionist and Feminist (1813–1896)* (Selinsgrove, Pa.: Susquehanna University Press, 1991), 19; *Proceedings of the Anti-Slavery Convention of American Women*, 12; Grew, "Annals," 125, 124; Brooks to Chapman, 4 Nov 1855, BPL. Before long, however, Thoreau would lament the difficulty of forcing "Kansas out of

your head" (*J*, 9:36). In Grew's 1863 retrospective of women's activism, the Concord society was one of seven Massachusetts female societies recognized for its early work that created "a page of history" ("Annals," 124–25).

7. *Liberator*, 6 Jul 1855.

8. Rogers, *Address*, 18; ETE, *L*, 1:118–19; Whiting to Chapman, 13 Sep 1855, BPL; Robinson journal, 3 Sep 1856, SL. For a partial membership roster of the Concord Female Anti-Slavery Society in 1857, see "*Warrington*," 73.

9. LMA, *J*, 65, 79–80; ETE, *L*, 1:119; Mayer, 448; Demos, "Antislavery Movement" 523; Pease and Pease, "Confrontation and Abolition," 929. As early as 1852, Phillips had declared himself opposed to a strict policy of nonresistance: "The reason why I advise the slave to be guided by a policy of peace is because he has no chance. If he had one,—if he had as good a chance as those who went up to Lexington seventy-seven years ago,—I should call him the basest recreant that ever deserted wife and child if he did not vindicate his liberty by his own right hand" (*Speeches*, 86–87).

10. [Louisa Jane Whiting Barker], *Influence of Slavery upon the White Population* (New York: American Anti-Slavery Society, 1855), 1, 6, 8. Whiting quotes from *Margaret Douglass's Educational Laws of Virginia. The Personal Narrative of Mrs. Douglass, a Southern Woman, Who Was Imprisoned for One Month in the Common Jail of Norfolk . . .* (Boston: J. P. Jewett, 1854).

11. *Liberator*, 20 Jun 1856.

12. David Donald, *Charles Sumner and the Coming of the Civil War* (New York: Knopf, 1961), 288–89; Blue, *Charles Sumner*, 78–83. Manisha Sinha has recently argued that in fact many Boston Brahmins ostracized the junior senator Sumner as his radicalism increased. See her "The Caning of Charles Sumner: Slavery, Race, and Ideology in the Age of the Civil War," *JER* 23 (summer 2003): 238; see also Michael D. Pierson, " 'All Southern Society Is Assailed by the Foulest Charges': Charles Sumner's 'The Crime against Kansas' and the Escalation of Republican Anti-slavery Rhetoric," *NEQ* 68 (December 1995): 531–57.

13. Donald, *Charles Sumner*, 278; Blue, *Charles Sumner*, 88.

14. Quoted in Donald, *Charles Sumner*, 283; quoted in Blue, *Charles Sumner*, 90; *Liberator*, 23 and 30 May 1856.

15. Donald, *Charles Sumner*, 294–95; Blue, *Charles Sumner*, 93–94; quoted in Donald, *Charles Sumner*, 290.

16. Donald, *Charles Sumner*, 297, 308; Blue, *Charles Sumner*, 94–102; Beverly Wilson Palmer, ed., *The Selected Letters of Charles Sumner*, 2 vols. (Boston: Northeastern University Press, 1990), 1:448; quoted in *Proceedings of the State Disunion Convention, Held at Worcester, Massachusetts, January 15, 1857* (Boston: Printed for the Committee, 1857), 34. The nearsighted Sumner was not wearing his glasses at the time and therefore may not have recognized his attacker (Donald, *Charles Sumner*, 294). Brooks had a history of violent behavior and had been involved in two duels. Moreover, family connections had not saved him from being thrown out of South Carolina College after he threatened local police. Those who honor Brooks for his assault on Sumner are still with us today, awarding the "Preston Brooks Award" to contemporary secessionists (see Sinha, "Caning of Charles Sumner," 244, 261).

17. *JMN*, 14:92; *EAS*, 107, 108.

18. Palmer, *Selected Letters*, 1:465; *JMN*, 14:407; LMA, *J*, 80; LMA, *L*, 19.

19. Francis B. Dedmond, "Men of Concord Petition the Governor," *CS* 15 (winter 1980): 1; Emerson, Account Books, 13 and 16 Jun 1856, Emerson Journals and Notebooks, HL; *JMN*, 14:96; "Subscription List for Relief of Free State Citizens of Kansas," letterpress form with list of manuscript signatures attached, Sanborn Papers, CFPL; Keyes, 144; "*Warrington*," 76. Emerson's Account Books for 1856 reflect his payments toward Kansas relief that year on 19 Mar, 13 Jun, and 6 Sep. Interestingly, the $10 payment on March 19 was marked "for John Brown of Kansas to Mr. Sanborn," evidence that although Sanborn and Brown did not meet until January 1857, Concord abolitionists were already funding Brown's cause.

20. Jeffery Rossbach, *Ambivalent Conspirators: John Brown, the Secret Six, and a Theory of Slave Violence* (Philadelphia: University of Pennsylvania Press, 1982), 52–53; *Recollections*, 1:52, 73; Kenneth Walter Cameron, ed., *Young Reporter of Concord: A Checklist of F. B. Sanborn's Letters to*

Benjamin Smith Lyman, 1853–1867 . . . (Hartford, Conn.: Transcendental Books, 1978), 11; Mayer, 446.

21. Pamela Herr, *Jessie Benton Frémont: A Biography* (Norman: University of Oklahoma Press, 1987), 254; quoted in Blue, *Charles Sumner*, 101; Keyes, 144; Franklin Benjamin Sanborn to Theodore Parker, 8 Oct 1856, Sanborn Papers, CFPL; Harriet Hanson Robinson journal, 7 Aug and 11 Oct 1856, SL; ETE, *L*, 1:120; Allan Nevins, *Frémont: Pathmarker of the West*, vol. 2, *Frémont in the Civil War* (1939; reprint, Frederick Ungar, 1961), 439–58.

22. Ward to Mary Ward Counce, 20 Aug 1856, TS; Cameron, *Young Reporter*, 11; Robinson journal, 2 Nov 1856, SL. Election day fulfilled Robinson's worst fears: "Slavery reigns. . . . There is nothing to be said" (Robinson journal, Election Day 1856, SL.)

23. Nevins, *Frémont*, 443, 450, 455; Herr, *Jessie Frémont*, 273–74; Mayer, 454; Irving H. Bartlett, *Wendell Phillips: Brahmin Radical* (Boston: Beacon, 1961), 202–3; Edmund Ruffin, "Consequences of Abolition Agitation. No. 1," *Debow's Review* 22 (June 1857): 590; *Liberator*, 7 Nov 1856. An abolitionist, Jessie Benton Frémont also inspired many supporters of women's rights, including Lydia Maria Child: "What a shame *women* can't vote! We'd carry 'our Jessie' into the White House on our shoulders, *wouldn't* we?" (quoted in Herr, *Jessie Frémont*, 241). If Garrison had known Jessie Frémont better, he may have been more sanguine about the prospects for immediate emancipation under a Frémont presidency. She confided to a friend after her husband's defeat: "I do wish Mr. Frémont had been the one to administer the bitter dose of subjection to the South for he has the coolness & nerve to do it just as it needs to be done—without passion & without sympathy—as coldly as a surgeon over a hospital patient would he have cut off their right hand Kansas from the old unhealthy southern body" (Pamela Herr and Mary Lee Spence, eds., *The Letters of Jessie Benton Frémont* [Urbana: University of Illinois Press, 1993], 140). For more on Jessie Frémont's abolitionism, see also Blue, *No Taint of Compromise*, 238–64.

24. Smith, Tappan, et al. to Thoreau, 27 Feb 1856, Henry D. Thoreau Manuscripts, HL; *Corr*, 436, 438–40; ABA, *J*, 2:287–88. For a discussion of the Radical Abolition Party, see John Stauffer, *The Black Hearts of Men: Radical Abolitionists and the Transformation of Race* (Cambridge: Harvard University Press, 2002).

25. EAS, 111–12; *The Reign of Terror in Kanzas: As Encouraged by President Pierce, and Carried Out by the Southern Slave Power . . .* (Boston: Charles W. Briggs, 1856), 23, 18; Harris to Ward, 21 Sep 1856, TS. For a sample of the news coverage in the antislavery press devoted to the Sumner affair and the riots in Lawrence, Kansas, see the *Liberator*, 30 May 1856.

26. Oates, 97, 12, 15, 58–75, 84–93; D. S. Reynolds, 33–39, 66–94, 132–37; Du Bois, *John Brown*, 127.

27. Oates, 97–111; Etcheson, *Bleeding Kansas*, 53–61.

28. Oates, 114–19, 123–25; D. S. Reynolds, 139–51.

29. Oates, 385–86, n.3; quoted in Oswald Garrison Villard, *John Brown 1800–1859: A Biography Fifty Years After* (1910; reprint, New York: Knopf, 1943), 152; D. S. Reynolds, 158, 149.

30. Quoted in Oates, 119.

31. Oates, 119–23; D. S. Reynolds, 154–55; Salmon Brown, "The Pottawatomie Executions of May, 1856," typescript, 17 Nov 1911, Franklin B. Sanborn Papers, AmS., 3.

32. Oates, 134–37; D. S. Reynolds, 171–78; quoted in Franklin Benjamin Sanborn, ed., *The Life and Letters of John Brown, Liberator of Kansas and Martyr of Virginia* (1885; reprint, New York: Negro Universities Press, 1969), 260; Heb. 9:22; Du Bois, *John Brown*, 139, 144.

33. D. S. Reynolds, 8. The abolitionists who later supported Brown generally pled ignorance about Pottawatomie Creek, although a few initially defended it. Late in life, T. W. Higginson claimed to be unpersuaded of the justification for the Pottawatomie murders, although he also recalled that when in Kansas in late 1856, he "heard of no one who did not approve of the act, and its beneficial effects were universally asserted . . . it had given an immediate check to the armed aggressions of the Missourians" (*Cheerful Yesterdays*, 207–8). Sanborn rationalized that Brown's actions in Kansas "must not be judged by the every-day rules of conduct, which distinctly forbid violence and the infliction of death for private causes" (Sanborn, *Life and Letters*, 248). But others on the scene at the time, including Free State

Governor Charles Robinson, contended that the killings in fact thwarted Free Kansas efforts (Merrill D. Peterson, *John Brown: The Legend Revisited* [Charlottesville: University of Virginia Press, 2002], 63–64).

34. Oates, 151–54, 167–71; D. S. Reynolds, 185–88, 196–202.

35. Rossbach, *Ambivalent Conspirators*, 76–78, 79; Oates, 181–86; D. S. Reynolds, 208–9; Sanborn to Higginson, 5 Jan 1857, BPL; quoted in WLG, *L*, 2:562. For more on Garrison and Brown's contrasting abolitionism, see D. S. Reynolds, 51–65, and Mayer, 474–78.

36. *J*, 9:232, 237, 253–54; "The Committee of Arrangements of the Disunion Convention," Thomas Wentworth Higginson Letters and Journals, HL, MS 784; quoted in Rossbach, *Ambivalent Conspirators*, 88; Edelstein, *Strange Enthusiasm*, 200; May to T. W. Higginson, 14 Dec 1856, Higginson Letters and Journals, HL; Bartlett, *Wendell Phillips*, 208; *Mass. Lyceum*, 172.

37. Rossbach, *Ambivalent Conspirators*, 101; Oates, 194–95; D. S. Reynolds, 210–14.

38. *New York Daily Tribune*, 4 Mar 1857; Roger B. Taney, "Opinion of the Court in Dred Scott, Plaintiff in Error, v. John F. A. Sandford," in *A House Divided: The Antebellum Slavery Debates in America, 1776–1865*, ed. Mason I. Lowance, Jr. (Princeton: Princeton University Press, 2003), 459; *Liberator*, 11 Oct 1839; quoted in Horton, "Defending the Manhood of the Race," 7. See also Xi Wang, "The *Dred Scott* Case," in *Race on Trial: Law and Justice in American History*, ed. Annette Gordon-Reed (New York: Oxford University Press, 2002), 26.

39. Sanborn to Brown, 1 Mar 1857, John Brown Collection, Box 1, Folder 9, Robert W. Woodruff Library of the Atlanta University Center, Atlanta, Georgia; *Recollections*, 1:103, 104–5, 83. Rather than at the Emerson home, Brown actually stayed overnight at a room Emerson regularly reserved for guests in a farm house near his home (*Recollections*, 1:104).

40. *Recollections*, 1:108; Oates, 196–97; D. S. Reynolds, 214–15; Sanborn, *Life and Letters*, 243, 246; *JMN*, 14:125–26; *J*, 12:433, 437. Two laters years, after the Harpers Ferry raid, Thoreau downplayed Brown's inflammatory remarks in Concord: "He never overstated anything, but spoke within bounds. I remember particularly how, in his speech here, he referred to what his family had suffered in Kansas, never giving the least vent to his pent-up fire" (*J*, 12:432).

41. Bertram Wyatt-Brown, "'A Volcano Beneath a Mountain of Snow': John Brown and the Problem of Interpretation," in *His Soul Goes Marching On: Responses to John Brown and the Harpers Ferry Raid*, ed. Paul Finkelman (Charlottesville: University Press of Virginia, 1995), 23; D. S. Reynolds, 206.

42. *Liberator*, 13 and 20 Jun 1856.

43. Rossbach, *Ambivalent Conspirators*, 106; Frank Preston Stearns, *The Life and Public Services of George Luther Stearns* (1907; reprint, New York: Arno, 1969), 138, 139–40; George L. Stearns to Brown, 15 Apr 1857, Letters Received by Samuel Gridley Howe, MHi; Oates, 186; D. S. Reynolds, 212, 233, 237–38.

44. *Mass. Lyceum*, 172; ETE, *L*, 1:131; quoted in Stephen Jay Gould, *The Mismeasure of Man* (1981; rev. ed., New York: Norton, 1996), 76–77; quoted in *Liberator*, 26 May 1854; Theodore Parker to John Manley, 23 Feb 1860, Andover-Harvard Theological Library, Harvard Divinity School, Cambridge, Massachusetts. See also William Stanton, *The Leopard's Spots: Scientific Attitudes toward Race in America 1815–59* (Chicago: University of Chicago Press, 1960), 103–4.

45. Edward Lurie, *Louis Agassiz: A Life in Science* (Chicago: University of Chicago Press, 1960), 259, 265; Stanton, *Leopard's Spots*, 109; Jules Marcou, *Life, Letters, and Works of Louis Agassiz*, vol. 1 (New York: Macmillan, 1896), 293–94; Dana D. Nelson, *National Manhood: Capitalist Citizenship and the Imagined Fraternity of White Men* (Durham: Duke University Press, 1998), 274 n.16; quoted in Gould, *Mismeasure of Man*, 79; quoted in Walls, *Emerson's Life in Science*, 184; *Mass. Lyceum*, 172. In the midst of the Civil War, Agassiz would correspond with Samuel Gridley Howe, then working for the American Freedmen's Inquiry Commission, and advise strongly against the social integration of blacks and whites in postwar America, arguing among other racially motivated conclusions that blacks were incapable of "self-government" (see James M. McPherson, *The Struggle for Equality: Abolitionists and the Negro in the Civil War and Reconstruction* [Princeton: Princeton University Press, 1964], 145–46; and

Elizabeth Cary Agassiz, ed., *Louis Agassiz: His Life and Correspondence*, vol. 2 [Boston: Houghton Mifflin, 1885], 594–612). As do others, Laura Dassow Walls contends that "Agassiz knew that his arguments added the authority of science to the support of slaveholders" (*Emerson's Life in Science*, 183).

46. Edward Waldo Emerson, *The Early Years of the Saturday Club 1855–1870* (1918; reprint, Freeport, N.Y.: Books for Libraries, 1967), 30–38; ETE, *L*, 1:129; *Corr*, 177–83; "Notes and Queries," *TSB* 171 (spring 1985): 8; Sattelmeyer, *Thoreau's Reading*, 118; Joan Burbick, *Thoreau's Alternative History: Changing Perspectives on Nature, Culture, and Language* (Philadelphia: University of Pennsylvania Press, 1987), 126; *J*, 9:298–99; *J*, 11:119–20; *J*, 10:248. For more on Thoreau and Agassiz, see Laura Dassow Walls, *Seeing New Worlds: Henry David Thoreau and Nineteenth-Century Natural Science* (Madison: University of Wisconsin Press, 1995), 113–15, 132, 138, 144–45.

47. Walls, *Emerson's Life in Science*, 174; Neufeldt, "Emerson, Thoreau, and Daniel Webster," 34; Jackson, "Treasurer's Accounts," 52, 53. At this time, William Whiting also owned a part interest in the Boston Vigilance Committee's yacht, the *Flirt*, operated by Cape Cod sailor Austin Bearse for the purpose of rescuing fugitive slaves. In December 1857, shareholders decided to sell the boat in favor of "building a new and larger boat . . . which is to be used for the same purposes as the Flirt" ("Statement of Stockholders' Loss in Yacht Flirt," BPL). William Whiting's future son-in-law, Stephen Barker, who would marry Louisa Whiting, had decided years before that Agassiz's theory of polygenesis was morally flawed (see Barker to Franklin Benjamin Sanborn, 7 Feb 1853, F. B. Sanborn and William Ellery Channing Papers, HL, bMS Am 1898). For recent studies of racialist science in America, see Bruce Dain, *A Hideous Monster of the Mind: American Race Theory in the Early Republic* (Cambridge: Harvard University Press, 2002), and Rael, *Black Identity*, 237–78.

48. Quoted in Edelstein, *Strange Enthusiasm*, 204; Dean, "Reverend Daniel Foster," 10; Foster to Higginson, 2 Apr 1857, Kansas State Historical Society, Higginson Collection; Foster to Franklin Benjamin Sanborn, 1 and 3 Oct 1856, both in BBS; Foster to Samuel Gridley Howe, 10 Jun 1857, Howe Papers, MHi; John Brown, diaries, 11 Sep 1857, BPL; Charles Richard Denton, "The Unitarian Church and 'Kanzas Territory,' 1854–1861," *Kansas Historical Quarterly* 30 (fall and winter 1964): 483–87. For more information on Daniel Foster's Kansas activities, see Denton, "Unitarian Church," 477–89, as well as Foster's many letters to the *Liberator* preceding the Civil War (John W. Blassingame and Mae G. Henderson, eds., *Antislavery Newspapers and Periodicals*, vol. 2 [Boston: G. K. Hall, 1980]).

49. *Concord Republican*, 4 Jun 1841; Wattles to Thoreau, 5 Nov 1858, collection of David T. and Hilda W. Sewall; Oates, 177, 254–55, 262, 263; D. S. Reynolds, 270–71, 279, 280. In 1857, John and Augustus Wattles founded the town of Moneka, Kansas (WLG, *L*, 4:323 n.5).

50. *Corr*, 362; Ricketson journal, 20 Jun 1856, TS; Abigail May Alcott to Bronson Alcott, 24 Nov 1857; Anna Alcott to Amos Bronson Alcott, 21 Dec 1857, both in Amos Bronson Alcott Papers, HL; Abigail May Alcott journal, 15 [Apr] 1858, Alcott Family Papers, HL; ETE, *L*, 1:178; Cameron, *Table Talk*, 106. Through Pillsbury, Thoreau also became acquainted with Quaker abolitionist Jonathan Buffum, with whom he stayed when in Lynn, Massachusetts, to lecture in January 1858 (Thoreau to John Lewis Russell, 16 Jan 1858, Margaret W. Brooks Collection, Phillips Library, Peabody Essex Museum, Salem, Massachusetts; Thoreau to Jonathan Buffum, 16 Apr 1859, The Pierpont Morgan Library, New York, New York, MA 606, vol. XI). Thoreau may also have met Buffum at the state antislavery meeting in Framingham on the Fourth of July, 1854 (*Liberator*, 7 Jul 1854).

51. Sophia Thoreau to Mary Anne Dunbar, 31 Dec 1857, TS; Anna Alcott to Bronson Alcott, 1 Jan 1858, Amos Bronson Alcott Papers, HL; Kenneth Walter Cameron, ed., *Ungathered Poems and Transcendental Papers*, Franklin Benjamin Sanborn (Hartford, Conn.: Transcendental Books, 1981), 221–22; *Liberator*, 22 Jan and 12 Feb 1858. The *Liberator* published Sanborn's "Prologue" in its entirety on 19 Feb 1858.

52. Oates, 206–10, 224–34, 241–47; D. S. Reynolds, 248, 259–64; Higginson to Mr. N. Hawkins [John Brown], 8 Feb 1858; BPL; Rossbach, *Ambivalent Conspirators*, 137, 146; McFeely, 191–93; *Recollections*, 1:144–47. Douglass and Brown had first met in 1848. In Can-

ada, Brown familiarized Tubman with his scheme for the "Great Black Way"; her enthusiastic response, based as it was on an expert's knowledge of the Appalachian terrain, further motivated him. Biographer Kate Larson believes Tubman was possibly in Maryland on the day the Harpers Ferry raid began, rather than ill in New Bedford, Massachusetts, as is commonly thought. At the last moment Douglass had distanced himself from the plans, warning Brown that he was walking into a "perfect steel trap." William McFeely notes, however, that "at no point in the eleven years that he had known of Brown's hopes for an insurrection did Douglass repudiate the plan" (see Larson, *Promised Land*, 157–61, 169–76; McFeely, 186, 196, 195; Oates, 241–42; D. S. Reynolds, 259).

53. Edelstein, *Strange Enthusiasm*, 212–13; Oates, 238; Higginson, *Cheerful Yesterdays*, 219–21; Du Bois, 127.

54. Oates, 198; quoted in Jean H. Baker, *James Buchanan* (New York: Times Books, 2004), 102; Jackson, "Treasurer's Accounts," 56.

55. *JMN*, 14:198; ETE, *L*, 1:178; *Liberator*, 25 Mar 1859; *Recollections*, 1:163–65; Oates, 269, 262; D. S. Reynolds, 278–80, 290–91; Edward Simmons, *From Seven to Seventy: Memories of a Painter and a Yankee* (New York: Harper & Brothers, 1922), 3; *J*, 12:184; Cameron, *Ungathered Poems*, 66–67; ABA, *J*, 2:315–16, 317; Sanborn to Higginson, 6 Apr 1859, BPL. Brown was accompanied on this second visit to Concord by Jeremiah Anderson, a young man from Indiana who would be killed at Harpers Ferry (ABA, *J*, 2:315; Oates, 300).

56. Sanborn to Higginson, 30 May and 4 Jun 1859, both in BPL; Larson, *Promised Land*, 170; Kenneth Walter Cameron, ed., *Transcendental Youth and Age: Chapters in Biography and Autobiography*, Franklin Benjamin Sanborn (Hartford, Conn.: Transcendental Books, 1981), 151; Emerson, Account Books, 2 Jun 1859, Emerson Journals and Notebooks, HL.

57. Quoted in Larson, *Promised Land*, 172; Humez, *Harriet Tubman*, 35–38, 134, 135; *Liberator*, 8 Jul 1859; Sanborn to T. W. Higginson, 30 May 1859, BPL; Cameron, *Young Reporter*, 17. For T. W. Higginson's description of Tubman's visit ("We have had the greatest heroine of the age here"), see Mary Thacher Higginson, ed., *Letters and Journals of Thomas Wentworth Higginson 1846–1906* (Boston: Houghton Mifflin, 1921), 81–82. For another mention of Tubman's appearance at the Framingham rally on July Fourth, see the *National Anti-Slavery Standard*, 9 Jul 1859, a report that refers to her as "Harriet Garrison." Abolitionist Ezra Hervey Heywood spoke in Concord on 5 Jun 1860 (*Liberator*, 3 Jun 1859).

58. Jackson, *Treasurer's Acounts*, 62; *J*, 12:388; *Liberator*, 7 Oct 1859.

59. Sanborn, *Personality of Emerson*, 87–88; Oates, 290–302; D. S. Reynolds, 310–28. Thoreau did have Kansas, if not John Brown, on his mind two days before he learned about Harpers Ferry. In the midst of gathering cranberries, Thoreau reflected that "only absorbing employment prevails, succeeds, takes up space, occupies territory, determines the future of individuals and states, drives Kansas out of your head, and actually and permanently occupies the only desirable and free Kansas against all border ruffians" (*Wild Fruits: Thoreau's Rediscovered Last Manuscript*, ed. Bradley P. Dean [New York: Norton, 2000], 165). Hayward Shepherd's name has occasionally been transposed as Shepherd (or Shepard) Hayward, an error apparently first set down in 1910 (although corrected in later editions) by Oswald Garrison Villard in his biography of Brown (see Boyd B. Stutler to Eugene L. Delafield, 20 Dec 1949; and Boyd B. Stutler to Osward Garrison Villard, 22 and 31 Mar 1943, all in BBS).

60. Quoted in *J*, 12:407; *JMN*, 14:329–34, RWE, *L*, 5:178; Emerson, Account Books, 11 Oct 1859, Emerson Journals and Notebooks, HL. Garrison's fear that Brown would damage the credibility of the antislavery movement was well founded, at least initially. As one northern newspaper editor pointed out: "That John Brown and his associates are fanatics is plain enough, but that they are insane . . . cannot be for a moment pretended. They are just as insane as Garrison is" (quoted in Edward Stone, ed., *Incident at Harper's Ferry* [Englewood Cliffs, N.J.: Prentice-Hall, 1956], 170). The money Emerson collected was evidently not forwarded in time for Brown to use it, since in January 1860, he paid over to Sarah Sanborn "for Mrs. Captain John Brown" the amounts collected during preceding months (Emerson, Account Books, 12 Jan 1860, Emerson Journals and Notebooks, HL).

61. Sanborn to Phillips, 22 Oct 1859, Phillips Papers, HL; Sanborn to Higginson, 21 Oct

1859, BPL; Higginson, *Cheerful Yesterdays*, 224–26; Sanborn to Parker, 22 Oct 1859, Sanborn Papers, CFPL; ETE, *L*, 1:210–11; RWE, *L*, 5:179; Irving H. Bartlett, *Wendell Phillips*, 211–12. Of the "Secret Six," Stearns and Howe joined Sanborn in Canada, Theodore Parker was in Europe, and Gerrit Smith was institutionalized for a time after suffering a nervous breakdown. Higginson alone refused to flee, leading to harsh words and accusations among the compatriots (see Rossbach, *Ambivalent Conspirators*, 221–23, 226–32, 236; and, especially, Higginson to Sanborn, 3 Feb 1860, BPL).

62. Lorman A. Ratner and Dwight L. Teeter, Jr., *Fanatics and Fire-Eaters: Newspapers and the Coming of the Civil War* (Urbana: University of Illinois Press, 2003), 78; *J*, 12:413, 400, 410, 417. Thoreau began writing about Brown in his journal on October 19 and continued to do so for several weeks, during which time he kept pencil and paper under his pillow (*RP*, 118). David G. Fuller assesses the media coverage in the aftermath of Harpers Ferry to reveal "the explosive context in which Thoreau composed his lecture" (see "Correcting the Newspapers: Thoreau and 'A Plea for Captain John Brown,'" *CS* n.s. 5 [fall 1997]: 167). Several scholarly studies examine Thoreau's writings on and admiration for Brown. See, for example, Adams and Ross, *Revising Mythologies*, 228–39; Fuller, "Correcting the Newspapers"; Glick, 157–88; Hyde, Introduction, xxxvii–xlix; Michael Meyer, "Thoreau's Rescue of John Brown from History," *SAR 1980*, ed. Joel Myerson (Boston: Twayne, 1980), 301–16; Truman Nelson, "Thoreau and John Brown," in Hicks, *Thoreau in Our Season*, 134–53; Rosenblum, "Inhibitions of Democracy," 61–62; and Shawn St. Jean, "Thoreau's Radical Consistency," *Massachusetts Review* 39 (autumn 1998): 341–57.

63. *Boston Daily Evening Transcript*, 19 Oct 1859; *New York Times*, 20 Oct 1859; Meyer, "Thoreau's Rescue," 310; *J*, 12:401–2, 413, 418. By the time he traveled to Kansas, the young Redpath was already a radical abolitionist. His *The Roving Editor, or Talks with Slaves in the Southern States*, published in 1859, resulted from months of interviewing slaves. Abolitionists had for decades compared the violence suffered by innocent victims in the antislavery struggle to the unremitting atrocities of slavery itself. Bob Pepperman Taylor points out that in his graphic outburst, Thoreau "refuses to admit any image of slavery other than one that captures its full murderousness. . . . he is constantly struggling against the tendency of white Americans to think of slavery in more benign terms" (*Bachelor Uncle*, 109). Similarly, Barrie Stavis commented in 1970 he could not "understand why this deed [Pottawatomie Creek] has been *especially* singled out from a long history of violence and suppression occasioned by slavery, a history of vigilantism and lynchings" (*John Brown: The Sword and the Word* [South Brunswick, N.J.: A. S. Barnes, 1970], 51). In their studies of Brown, some historians have declined to acknowledge the violence inherent to slavery. In 1942, for example, James C. Malin lamented the "tendency among historians as well as readers to feel an obligation to decide who was the aggressor in the slavery controversy." Malin boasted that his own study offered "nothing of the sort," since "it is futile to assume that there is such a thing as an initial aggressive act" (*John Brown and the Legend of Fifty-Six* [Philadelphia: American Philosophical Society, 1942], 34). For Mahala Doyle's public letter to an imprisoned Brown, see *Liberator*, 16 Dec 1859.

64. *J*, 12:425, 422, 437; Charles E. Heller, *Portrait of an Abolitionist: A Biography of George Luther Stearns, 1809–1867* (Westport, Conn.: Greenwood, 1996), 83. After Thoreau's death, Waldo Emerson peremptorily referred to "somewhat military in his nature not to be subdued" (Joel Myerson, "Emerson's 'Thoreau': A New Edition from Manuscript," *SAR 1979* (Boston: Twayne, 1979), 39. For others who call attention to Thoreau's affinity for "military imagery," and for aggressive leaders such as George Washington, Oliver Cromwell, Sir Walter Raleigh, and, ultimately, John Brown, see D. S. Reynolds, 229–32; Sattelmeyer, *Thoreau's Reading*, 34; Linck C. Johnson, "Contexts of Bravery: Thoreau's Revisions of 'The Service' for *A Week*," in *SAR 1983*, ed. Joel Myerson (Charlottesville: University Press of Virginia, 1983), 281–96; Edward Wagenknecht, *Henry David Thoreau: What Manner of Man?* (Amherst: University of Massachusetts Press, 1981), 116–17; Nancy L. Rosenblum, "Thoreau's Militant Conscience," *Political Theory* 9 (February 1981): 81–110; Larry J. Reynolds, "Cimeter's 'Sweet' Edge"; and Wai Chee Dimock, *Through Other Continents: American Literature Across Deep Time*

(Princeton: Princeton University Press, 2006). Dimock claims that in responding to Brown, Thoreau was influenced by a "reproductive" reading of the *Bhagavad Gita*, in which Thoreau "gave . . . a new context of action" to this ancient text. Dimock believes that "Thoreau creates a political philosophy indebted to the *Bhagavad Gita* and opposed to it" (16, 20). Critics who subject Thoreau to psychoanalysis find it suggestive that his father died in early February, a few months before Brown's second visit to Concord. See Raymond Gozzi, "A Freudian View of Thoreau," in *Thoreau's Psychology: Eight Essays*, ed. Gozzi (Lanham, Md.: University Press of America, 1983), 14–16; and Lebeaux, *Thoreau's Seasons*, 325–31.

65. Oates, 324–25; D. S. Reynolds, 350–51; *J*, 12:413, 409; *Testimonies of Capt. John Brown, at Harper's Ferry, with His Address to the Court* (New York: American Anti-Slavery Society, 1860), 4.

66. Oates, 326–27; D. S. Reynolds, 353; Testimonies of Capt. John Brown, 12; *J*, 12:408; *J*, 13:18–19. Although Thoreau denounced Garrison in his journal, he toned this rhetoric down in his speech, eliding Garrison's name altogether: "Didn't ye know it, ye Liberators, ye Tribunes, ye Republicans?" (*RP*, 125). Nancy Rosenblum has argued that "Thoreau's political essays reflect his own progressively more radical position, worked out principally in relation to the Garrisonians" (Introduction, xvi). Indeed, in his 1840 essay "The Service," Thoreau may intentionally have taken aim at the recently founded New England Nonresistant Society, of which Garrison was cofounder: "We turn to meet mankind with its meek face preaching peace, and such nonresistance as the chaff that rides before the whirlwind. Let not our Peace be proclaimed by the rust on our swords, or our inability to draw them from their scabbards, but let her at least have so much work on her hands, as to keep those swords bright and sharp" (*RP*, 13). A century later, scholars still set down as fact the conviction that "Brown's family was riddled with insanity" (see, for example, Edmund Wilson, *Patriotic Gore: Studies in the Literature of the American Civil War* [1962; reprint, Boston: Northeastern University Press, 1984], 244; and Kenneth S. Davis, *Kansas*, 55). Historian James Oliver Horton, however, incisively cautions that "we should be very careful about assuming that a white man who is willing to put his life on the line for a black man is, of necessity, crazy" (Public Broadcasting Corporation). For recent discussions of how the charge of insanity continues to be entwined with the legend of John Brown, see Robert E. McGlone, "John Brown, Henry Wise, and the Politics of Insanity," in *His Soul Goes Marching On*, 213–52; and D. S. Reynolds, 350–51.

67. *J*, 12:404, 406, 424, 420; *RP*, 137. Like others, Robert Milder believes that in John Brown, Thoreau values "an idealized version of his own character" (*Reimagining Thoreau* [Cambridge: Cambridge University Press, 1995], 177).

68. Weiss, *Life and Correspondence*, 2:170; *JP*, 6:212; Wright to Wendell Phillips, 19 Nov 1859, Phillips Papers, HL *Liberator*, 9 Dec 1859; Philip S. Foner, *Frederick Douglass*, 374; quoted in Larson, *Promised Land*, 177. See also Philip Foner, "Douglass and John Brown," in *Blacks in the Abolitionist Movement*, ed. John H. Bracey, August Meier, and Elliott Rudwick (Belmont, Calif.: Wadsworth, 1971), 160–68.

69. Yacovone, *Samuel Joseph May*, 166; quoted in Milton Meltzer, *Tongue of Flame: The Life of Lydia Maria Child* (New York: Dell, 1965), 127; Milton Meltzer, Patricia G. Holland, and Francine Krasno, eds., *Lydia Maria Child: Selected Letters, 1817–1880* (Amherst: University of Massachusetts Press, 1982), 324; Phillips, *Speeches*, 263, 279; WLG, *L*, 4:665. Virginia governor Henry Wise miscalculated in allowing reporters access to the notorious prisoner, a situation that kept Brown in the headlines. Rather than a contrite prisoner awaiting his just execution, Brown preached that the nation verged on civil war. Henry Thoreau noted the irony: "Nothing could his enemies do but it redounded to his infinite advantage, the advantage of his cause. They did not hang him at once; they reserved him to preach to them. And here is another great blunder: they have not hung his four followers with him; that scene is still to come and so his victory is prolonged" (*J*, 13:6). For a summary of prevailing attitudes in Massachusetts at the time, see Betty L. Mitchell, "Massachusetts Reacts to John Brown's Raid," *Civil War History* 19 (March 1973): 65–79.

70. George W. Cooke, "The Two Thoreaus," in *Thoreau as Seen by His Contemporaries*, ed.

Walter Harding (1960; reprint, New York: Dover, 1989), 84; quoted in Myerson, "Emerson's 'Thoreau,'" 41; *RP*, 111. For an assessment of Thoreau's speech as "almost classic mythmaking," see Adams and Ross, *Revising Mythologies*, 228. Despite accounts that Thoreau delivered "A Plea" at Concord's Town Hall, the speech most likely took place at the First Church. See Dean and Hoag, "Thoreau's Lectures," 312; Sanborn, *Life of Thoreau*, 286; Edward Waldo Emerson, *Henry Thoreau as Remembered by a Young Friend* (1917; reprint, Mineola, N.Y.: Dover, 1999), 29; and ABA, *J*, 2:320. Similar to the journal entries from which "Slavery in Massachusetts" derived, the journal pages focusing on John Brown are heavily revised with many interlineations, cancellations, and revisions. For an evaluation of these textual differences from the speech, see Robert C. Albrecht, "Thoreau and His Audience: 'A Plea for Captain John Brown,'" *AL* 32 (January 1961): 393–402.

71. Edward Waldo Emerson, *Henry Thoreau* 29; ABA, *J*, 2:384; Richard L. Herrnstadt, ed., *The Letters of A. Bronson Alcott* (Ames: Iowa State University Press, 1969), 306; Harding, *Thoreau as Seen by His Contemporaries*, 158–59; Kenneth Walter Cameron, ed., *Transcendental Writers and Heroes . . .*, Franklin Benjamin Sanborn (Hartford, Conn.: Transcendental Books, 1978), 26. For a biographical sketch of Minot Pratt, see Kenneth Walter Cameron, ed., *Literary Comment in American Renaissance Newspapers . . .* (Hartford, Conn.: Transcendental Books, 1977), 84–85.

72. Emerson to Slack, 31 Oct 1859; and Thoreau to Slack, 1 Nov 1859, both in Charles W. Slack Papers, AmS; *Corr*, 563; Foner, "Douglass and John Brown," 164–67; Dean and Hoag, "Thoreau's Lectures," 314–15, 320–21. Douglass feared arrest despite the fact that no hard evidence linked him to the insurrectionary plot (see Frederick Douglass to Charles W. Slack, 28 Oct 1859, Slack Papers, AmS). For the critical reception of "A Plea," see Meyer, *Several More Lives*; Scharnhorst, *Annotated Bibliography*, 54–55; Scharnhorst, *Case Study*; and Dean and Hoag, "Thoreau's Lectures," 308–24.

73. Quoted in Dean and Hoag, "Thoreau's Lectures," 317; *Liberator*, 4 Nov 1859; "*Warrington*," 237.

74. Tappan to Thoreau, 7 Nov 1859, collection of David T. and Hilda W. Sewall; *J*, 12:443, 447.

75. Letterpress "Circular," S. E. Sewall, S. G. Howe, R. W. Emerson, Rev. T. W. Higginson, 2 Nov 1859, BPL; quoted in D. S. Reynolds, 366; *EAS*, 118, 123; *J*, 12:436. In January, Sophia Thoreau would organize female society members in making a quilt for Brown's family (see Annie Keyes Bartlett to Edward Jarvis Bartlett, 8 Jan 1860, Annie Keyes Bartlett Letters to Edward Jarvis Bartlett, CFPL).

76. LMA, *L*, 49; Abigail May Alcott journal, 31 Dec 1859, Alcott Family Papers, HL. For Concord contributions toward Brown's family, including ten dollars from Henry Thoreau, see Ralph Waldo Emerson, Account Books, 1 Nov, 29 Nov, 12 Dec, and 19 Dec 1859, and 12 Jan 1860, Emerson Journals and Notebooks, HL. For Emerson's importance to Brown's legacy, see D. S. Reynolds, 363–69.

77. *J*, 13:3–15; Oates, 351–52; *J*, 12:457–58; ABA, *J*, 2:323; James Redpath, *Echoes of Harpers Ferry* (1860; reprint, New York: Arno, 1969), 437; *RP*, 139; Keyes, 167, 168; LMA, *J*, 95.

78. Quoted in Michael Meyer, "Discord in Concord on the Day of John Brown's Hanging," *TSB* 146 (winter 1979): 2–3. Critics who see the interconnectedness of Thoreau's political and natural history writings find it especially fitting that Thoreau took notes for his "Dispersion of Seeds and Related Matters" on the back of an announcement for Brown's memorial service (see Lance Newman, "Thoreau's Materialism: From *Walden* to *Wild Fruits*," *Nineteenth-Century Prose* 31 [fall 2004]: 116). For Thoreau's leadership in planning the service, see also Franklin Benjamin Sanborn to T. W. Higginson, 28 Nov 1859, BPL; RWE, *L*, 5:182; ABA, *J*, 2:322; and Dean and Hoag, "Thoreau's Lectures," 324–31.

79. Redpath, *Echoes*, 3–5; Redpath to Thoreau, 5 Jan 1860, collection of Kent Bicknell. John Shepard Keyes strains credulity in this elderly reminiscence: "All of us knew Old John, all admired him, and many rejoiced in his attack on Slavery and there was a profound feeling of sorrow for his death. If I hadn't been Sheriff, I should have gone to the trial to defend him

I was so strongly moved by his courage and manliness" (Keyes, 168). Redpath had become an obsessive champion of Brown since meeting him in 1856; at the time he compiled *Echoes*, he was wanted for questioning about his involvement with Brown. Redpath also continued assisting fugitive slaves, as evidenced in this letter to T. W. Higginson in November 1859: "I was sent on a decidedly wild goose chase; but whatever it was possible to do for the fugitives, I *did*. *My own opinion* is, that they were *not* seen; &, if they were, that they are now further North than the region I was sent to. If I am mistaken, however, they will be found; a dozen blacks & abols are hunting for them" (Redpath to Higginson, 13 Nov 1859, BPL). In 1860, Redpath published the first biography of Brown, *The Public Life of Capt. John Brown* (Boston: Thayer and Eldridge, 1860), a book for which he had asked Henry Thoreau to help flesh out the details of Brown's triumph at the Battle of Black Jack (*Corr*, 574).

80. Redpath, *Echoes*, 437. In fact, David S. Reynolds has recently argued that "without the Concord Transcendentalists, John Brown would have had little cultural impact" (D. S. Reynolds, 4).

81. Potter, *Impending Crisis*, 381; D. S. Reynolds, 344; Meyer, *Several More Lives*, 160, 116, 152–62; Meyer, "Thoreau's Rescue," 301. The transcendentalists' exaltation of Brown has played a central role in historical understandings and contemporary revisionings of this controversial figure. Thoreau and Emerson's words are featured in scores of epigrams, introductions, and analyses. See, for example, Jules Abels, *Man on Fire: John Brown and the Cause of Liberty* (New York: Macmillan, 1971), 388–89; Richard O. Boyer, *The Legend of John Brown: A Biography and a History* (New York: Knopf, 1973), 1, 21–22, 23, 159; Scott John Hammond, "John Brown as Founder: America's Violent Confrontation with Its First Principles," in *Terrible Swift Sword: The Legacy of John Brown*, ed. Peggy A. Russo and Paul Finkelman (Athens: Ohio University Press, 2005), 61; Truman Nelson, *The Old Man: John Brown at Harper's Ferry* (New York: Holt, Rinehart and Winston, 1973), 186; Peterson, *John Brown*, 16–17, 23–24, 33; Zoe Trodd and John Stauffer, eds., *Meteor of the War: The John Brown Story* (Maplecrest, N.Y.: Brandywine, 2004), ii, 1, 4, 6; and Villard, *John Brown*, 273–74. In contrast to many, the dean of Thoreau studies, Walter Harding, always valued the John Brown writings. His otherwise favorable review of Carl Bode's 1947 *The Portable Thoreau* disapproved of their exclusion ("Additions to the Thoreau Bibliography: Notes and Reviews," *TSB* 19 [April 1947]: 4). Critics today typically examine Thoreau's political speeches in their entirety. Many hold that "Slavery in Massachusetts" and "A Plea for Captain John Brown" contradict Thoreau's advocacy of nonviolent resistance in "Civil Disobedience," while others insist that Thoreau never championed pacifism over other forms of "civil disobedience." Social activist Tom Hayden has recently urged that we celebrate the whole Thoreau, including the defender of John Brown; but others, such as Lewis Hyde, "part company with Thoreau when he gets to John Brown" (Tom Hayden, "The Conscience by the Pond" *Orion Online* (January/February 2005): 1–3, http://www.oriononline.org/pages/om/05–1om/Hayden.html; Hyde, Introduction, xlvi). Shawn St. Jean sees "*moral coherence*" as the link between Thoreau's political essays ("Radical Consistency," 342). Larry J. Reynolds has convincingly argued that the study of eastern scriptures had impressed on Thoreau that "heroic spiritual joy" can result from "bloody actuality," an "impasse," as St. Jean notes, at which many abolitionists—some more begrudgingly than others—had arrived by 1859 (Reynolds, "Cimeter's 'Sweet' Edge," 57; St. Jean, "Radical Consistency," 353). The moral dilemmas confronting antebellum America in the wake of Harpers Ferry have attained renewed relevance in the midst of the twenty-first century's "war on terror." As Sam McGuire Worley has recently argued, "Brown remains a disturbing figure not so much because of the specific danger he presented, but because of the possibility he raises of others who might be willing to act according to the imperatives of their own understanding of higher laws and on subjects about which there is far less consensus" (*Cultural Critic*, 100). For an extended discussion of Brown's relevance to contemporary conceptions of terrorism, see D. S. Reynolds, 500–506; and James N. Gilbert, "A Behavioral Analysis of John Brown: Martyr or Terrorist?" in Russo and Finkelman, *Terrible Swift Sword*, 107–17.

82. Richard J. Hinton, *John Brown and His Men* (1894; reprint, New York: Arno, 1968), 252–53; Edelstein, *Strange Enthusiasm*, 219; Francis Jackson to John Brown, Jr., 12 Feb 1860,

BBS. Meriam (whose name is often misspelled "Merriam") has been erroneously cited as Jackson's nephew rather than grandson, an error that may result from a letter in which Sanborn refers to him as Jackson's "*nepos*," Latin for grandson or nephew (see Sanborn to Higginson, 6 Oct 1859, BPL).

83. Hinton, *Brown and His Men*, 569–71; Lewis Hayden to Mary E. Stearns, 8 Apr 1878, BBS; Villard, *John Brown*, 420–24; Rossbach, *Ambivalent Conspirators*, 211–12; Edward Renehan, Jr., *The Secret Six: The True Tale of the Men Who Conspired with John Brown* (New York: Crown, 1995), 193–95; Sanborn to Higginson, 6 and 13 Oct 1859, BPL; Francis Jackson to John Brown, Jr., 12 Feb 1860, BBS. For evidence that Hayden was intimately acquainted with the Harpers Ferry plans, see Lewis Hayden to John Brown, Jr., 16 Sep 1859, published in the *New York Herald*, 25 Oct 1859. On October 15, Meriam sent a cryptic telegram to Hayden— "Orders disobeyed. Conditions broken. Pay S. immediately balance of my money. Allow no further expenses. Recall money advanced, if not sent"—a message that Richard Hinton believed alludes to a prearranged backup plan that Hayden would know to cancel once the raid began (quoted in Hinton, *Brown and His Men*, 267). Hinton describes Meriam "as absolutely fearless," but others commonly refer to his weak physical health and erratic emotional state (*Brown and His Men*, 568). Some go so far as to call Meriam "retarded," surely an overstated characterization, given that he had served as Redpath's translator in Haiti and had also begun writing a history, in French, of the West Indies (see "Notes on the History of Hayti," BPL). See, for example, Edelstein, *Strange Enthusiasm*, 220; and Oates, 287).

84. Oates, 288; D. S. Reynolds, 307; Hinton, *Brown and His Men*, 280; *Boston Courier*, 29 Oct 1859.

85. Quoted in Hinton, *Brown and His Men*, 548–49; *National Anti-Slavery Standard*, 5 and 12 Nov 1859; William Garrison, Jr., diary, 27 Oct 1859, Garrison Family Papers, Sophia Smith Collection, Smith College, Northampton, Massachusetts. Other friends sent consoling letters to Meriam's family (see, for example, Lydia Maria Child to Francis Jackson, 4 Nov 1859, William I. Bowditch Collection, Phillips Library, Peabody Essex Museum; Parker Pillsbury to Eliza Eddy, 2 Nov 1859, BPL; and Theodore Parker to Eliza Eddy in Octavius Brooks Frothingham, *Theodore Parker: A Biography* [Boston: James R. Osgood, 1874], 278–80).

86. Ralph Keeler, "Owen Brown's Escape from Harper's Ferry," *The Atlantic Monthly* 33 (March 1874): 345–47, 351, 354, 357–58; Hinton, *Brown and His Men*, 550–52, 572–74, 553; John R. McKivigan, "His Soul Goes Marching On: The Story of John Brown's Followers after the Harpers Ferry Raid," in McKivigan and Harrold, *Antislavery Violence*, 278; Annie Brown to T. W. Higginson, 4 Dec 1859, BPL. Cook was hanged in Virginia on December 16, 1859 (see Keeler, "Owen Brown's Escape," 354; and Hinton, *Brown and His Men*, 404–5). Possibly, the *National Anti-Slavery Standard*, whose associate editor Oliver Johnson was close friends with Francis Jackson, reported Meriam dead in early November to halt efforts for his capture. Charles Tidd, who made it to Canada after Meriam boarded the train near Chambersburg, wrote to T. W. Higginson in mid-December to ask if reports of Meriam's death were true (Tidd to Higginson, 18 Dec 1859, BPL).

87. William Lloyd Garrison, Jr., diary, 2 Dec 1859, Garrison Papers; Sanborn, *Personality of Thoreau*, 52–54. Sanborn incorrectly states that a reward of "thousands" had been posted for Meriam's capture; two thousand dollars were offered for all four escapees, five hundred for each (Hinton, *Brown and His Men*, 548–49).

88. Sanborn, *Personality of Thoreau*, 53–58; *J*, 13:3–4. Others also knew Meriam by the alias "Lockwood." George Luther Stearns freely admitted seeing "Mr. Lockwood" in Canada when testifying before the Senate committee investigating the raid ("Mason Report, Part XVI," BBS). If Sanborn can be believed, he did not interact with Meriam, who had eaten and was asleep by the time Sanborn returned home; when Thoreau arrived the next morning for "Mr. Lockwood," Sanborn claims he remained in his room (*Personality of Thoreau*, 54). See Higginson, *Cheerful Yesterdays*, 228, for his account of an "utterly demented" Harpers Ferry raider who showed up at his Worcester home that fall. If this visitor was Meriam, as seems likely, then he may have stopped in Worcester before coming to Boston. Higginson offered to provide refuge to him, but Francis Jackson explained that the family had sent Meriam

back to Canada "because his mind is so wrought up, & over excited about the scenes of Harpers Ferry; among friends, he dwells upon it continually, & with increasing ardor" (Jackson to Higginson, 6 Dec 1859, BPL).

89. Hinton, *Brown and His Men*, 575; Stearns to Thoreau, 23 Feb 1862, transcript of manuscript letter from files of *The Writings of Henry D. Thoreau*, University of California, Santa Barbara. I am grateful to Elizabeth Hall Witherell for permission to cite this transcript.

90. Stearns, *Life and Public Services*, 198; Ruth Brown Thompson to Mary E. Stearns, 10 Jun 1860, BBS; Hinton, *Brown and His Men*, 506; *RP*, 363; *Corr*, 582. The *Liberator* published "The Last Days of John Brown" in its account of the July Fourth service at North Elba. In 1860, Meriam returned to Haiti, hoping to recruit blacks there to help him lead an effort to free slaves in the southern U.S. During the Civil War, he recruited black soldiers in the Sea Islands to serve with him in the Third South Carolina Infantry. Meriam died in November 1865. See Hinton, *Brown and His Men*, 575–76; Francis J. Meriam to Wendell Phillips, 23 Aug and 11 Sep 1861; and Eliza Eddy to Wendell Phillips, 25 Apr 1866, all in Phillips Papers, HL. Hinton had prefaced his reading of Thoreau's accolade as follows: "I desire to read the manuscript I hold. It was handed to me at Concord, with a note, while on my way here, by one whom all must honor who know him—Henry D. Thoreau. . . . Mr. Thoreau's voice was the first which broke the disgraceful silence or hushed the senseless babble with which the grandest deed of our time was met" (quoted in *Liberator*, 27 Jul 1860).

91. *RP*, 145, 147, 150; "Words of John Brown," *Old South Leaflets* no. 84, vol. 4 (Boston: Directors of the Old South Work, 1897), 22; quoted in *Recollections*, 1:172; Villard, *John Brown*, 405, 416–20; John Brown to wife and children, 1 Oct 1859; and Annie Brown to Higginson, 28 Nov 1859, both in BPL.

92. Wendell Phillips to T. W. Higginson, 23 Jan 1860, BPL; *Recollections*, 1:207; Sanborn to Theodore Parker, 12 Feb 1860, Sanborn Papers, CFPL. Higginson, Wendell Phillips, and Parker Pillsbury were among the abolitionists who carried out Brown's wishes by seeing to his daughters' education. Sanborn waived tuition fees at his school, George Luther Stearns paid their board, and Phillips, Gerrit Smith, and others contributed money for clothing and other expenses (Stearns, *Life and Public Services*, 199; "Receipt for Miss Sarah Brown," Sanborn Papers, CFPL.) Annie Brown later related that her mother had refused to join the girls in Maryland for the domestic subterfuge: "It was a sorry disappointment to him [her father], her not going down to help him" (Annie Brown Adams, "Statement of Annie Brown," typescript, 1886, Chicago Historical Society, Chicago, Illinois, 2).

93. Sanborn to Wendell Phillips, 24 Feb 1860, Phillips Papers, HL; Annie Keyes Bartlett to Edward Jarvis Bartlett, 20 Feb 1860, Bartlett Letters, CFPL; Stearns, *Life and Public Services*, 199; Sanborn to Theodore Parker, 11 Mar and 1 Apr 1860, both in Sanborn Papers, CFPL. On the whole, Ellen Emerson regarded Annie Brown as a spectacle, "a girl brought up in the primitive spinning, weaving, sheep-tending, butter-making times" (ETE, *L*, 1:211). Brown later described these difficult weeks in Concord: "I made a trial last spring in order to prove to myself and others whether it were *best*, or *possible*, for me to do so. I gave it up because I thought it a harder task than my mind ought to bear, it was more than I ought to do. I do not think that I ought to knowingly *injure* myself even if I am called a *stubborn willful* girl by not doing so, by those who *do not know* that that would be the effect" (Brown to J. Miller McKim, 14 Oct 1861, Division of Rare and Manuscript Collections, Cornell University Library). For discussions of Annie's continuing emotional trauma, see Ruth Brown Thompson to Mary E. Stearns, 22 Apr 1860; and John Brown, Jr. to Mrs. George Luther Stearns, 1 May 1860, both in BBS.

94. Joel Myerson and Daniel Shealy, eds., "Three Contemporary Accounts of Louisa May Alcott, with Glimpses of Other Concord Notables," *NEQ* 59 (March 1986): 116; Amos Bronson Alcott, journal, 28 Feb 1860, Amos Bronson Alcott Papers, HL.

95. Franklin Benjamin Sanborn to Wendell Phillips, 22 May 1860, Phillips Papers, HL; LMA, *L*, 55–56, 57. Abby Alcott also mentioned this crowd in her journal: "Antislavery Society met here—42 present; My brother held a discussion on Non-resistance—Mr. Emerson—Sanborn—Miss Peabody—and Mr. Alcott the widows of John and Watson Brown were here—

with Watson's infant—10 months old" (24 May 1860, Alcott Family Papers, HL). The editors of her letters presume that Henry Thoreau is the "T." whom Louisa Alcott lists among the local friends attending this reception.

96. Anna Alcott Pratt diary, undated entry following 21 Mar 1861, Alcott Family Papers, HL; LMA, *L*, 62–63.

97. Anna Alcott Pratt diary, 26 Mar 1861, Alcott Family Papers, HL; Abigail May Alcott to Samuel J. May, 14 Apr 1861, Amos Bronson Alcott Papers, HL; Annie Brown to J. Miller McKim, 14 Oct 1861, Division of Rare and Manuscript Collections, Cornell University Library. Annie Brown later remembered the valuable housekeeping lesson she and her sister learned from the Alcotts: "They were the first persons I ever knew who advocated folding clothes and given them 'a b[r]ush and a promise' instead of spending so much useless time at the ironing board" (Myerson and Shealy, "Three Contemporary Accounts," 117). For more on Sarah Brown's continued studies at Sanborn's school, see Mary A. Brown to Sanborn, 6 Aug 1861; and Sanborn to Wendell Phillips, 11 Aug 1861, both in Phillips Papers, HL.

98. *Recollections*, 1:206–7; ETE, *L*, 1:210; *J* 12:445; Higginson to Sanborn, 3 Feb 1860, BPL.

99. *Recollections*, 1:208–10; ETE, *L*, 1:212–13; Cameron, "Sanborn's Preparatory School in Concord (1855–1863)," *American Renaissance Literary Report* 3 (1999): 67. For accounts of the arrest attempt, see *Recollections*, 1:208–18; Stearns, *Life and Public Services*, 215–16; *Liberator*, 13 Apr 1860. Some accounts maintain that at this time Sanborn still lived on Main Street across from the Thoreaus, but by now he had moved to Sudbury Road, just down from the Bigelows and Brooks (see Wheeler, *Climate*, 190; and Sanborn, *Personality of Thoreau*, 54).

100. *Recollections*, 1:210; ETE, *L*, 1:213; LMA, *L*, 53.

101. Alcott Nieriker to Whitman, 5 Apr 1860, Alcott Family Letters to Alfred Whitman, HL, bMS Am 1130.

102. Keyes, 168–69; *Recollections*, 1:211; *J*, 13:241.

103. Brooks to Chapman, 9 Apr 1860, BPL.

104. Keyes, 170; *Recollections*, 1:212–17; Sanborn to Theodore Parker, 8 Apr 1860, Sanborn Papers, CFPL; *New York Herald*, 7 Apr 1860; *Liberator*, 13 Apr 1860; Abbie May Alcott Nieriker to Alfred Whitman, 5 Apr 1860, Alcott Family Letters to Whitman, HL; Rossbach, *Ambivalent Conspirators*, 264.

105. *New York Times*, 6 Apr 1860. Surely Higginson took pleasure in remembering Sanborn's vow the previous November to "*refuse* . . . a writ of Habeas Corpus. . . . It is possible the anxiety of friends may induce me to modify this course, but I think not" (Sanborn to Higginson, 19 Nov 1859, BPL).

106. *JMN*, 14:363; Palmer, *Selected Letters*, 2:75. For Henry Thoreau's letter to Sumner praising his speech on the "Barbarism of Slavery," see *Corr*, 585. For news reports documenting the increasingly hostile behavior of southerners toward northerners at this time, see William Lloyd Garrison, *The "New Reign of Terror" in the Slaveholding States* (1860; reprint, New York: Arno, 1969).

107. Harris to Ward, 20 May 1860; Thoreau to Dunbar, 27 Dec 1860, both in TS; *Liberator*, 17 Aug 1860. Although antislavery in principle, Lincoln did not advocate racial equality, nor did he initially link the war with ending slavery. During his famous debates with Senator Stephen A. Douglas in 1858, Lincoln had stated unequivocally: "I am not, nor ever have been in favor of bringing about in any way the social and political equality of the white and black races. . . . while they do remain together there must be the position of superior and inferior, and I as much as any other man am in favor of having the superior position assigned to the white race" (quoted in Vincent Harding, *There Is a River: The Black Struggle for Freedom in America* [1981; reprint, New York: Harcourt Brace Jovanovich, 1992], 214). As war raged in December 1861, Lincoln cautioned those who advocated tying antislavery to the Union cause lest "the war . . . 'degenerate into a violent and remorseless revolutionary struggle' " (quoted in McPherson, *Struggle for Equality*, 94).

108. Merton L. Dillon, *The Abolitionists: The Growth of a Dissenting Majority* (DeKalb: Northern Illinois University Press, 1974), 250; *Liberator*, 7 Dec 1860; quoted in McFeely, 208, 211;

McPherson, *Struggle for Equality*, 42; *EAS*, 125, 126; *Liberator*, 1 Feb 1861. Likely irritated by this disturbance, Thoreau on this day defended John Brown against the arguments of two townsmen, including his former jailer, Sam Staples (see *J*, 14:291–92). The *Liberator* published Emerson's entire speech on February 1, 1861, complete with brackets indicating the numerous interruptions. See also *EAS*, 125–28.

109. "*Warrington*," 95; Sanborn to Phillips, 6 Feb 1861, Phillips Papers, HL; *Mass. Lyceum*, 176; Phillips, *Speeches*, 468, 475, 486; quoted in McPherson, *Struggle for Equality*, 35, 12. The Thoreaus were asked to host Phillips during his stay, but both Cynthia and Henry were ill and suggested he stay with Mary Brooks who "will be happy to entertain" him (*Corr*, 602). Like Garrison, Phillips had for years advocated northern disunion. Now that the South had instead seceded, he faced a dilemma that he resolved in a speech in Boston on April 21, 1861: "The only mistake that I have made, was in supposing Massachusetts wholly choked with cotton-dust and cankered with gold" (*Speeches*, 397).

110. Mayer, 520; Potter, *Impending Crisis*, 499, 582; quoted in Edelstein, *Strange Enthusiasm*, 211; Peterson, *John Brown*, 37; McPherson, *Struggle for Equality*, 46; LMA, *L*, 64; Abigail May Alcott to Samuel J. May, 14 Apr 1861, Amos Bronson Alcott Papers, HL. Louisa May Alcott in part fulfilled her wish by traveling to Washington, D.C., in December 1862 as a nurse at the Union Hotel Hospital. Unfortunately, she contracted typhoid fever and returned home in mid January. Later that year, James Redpath published *Hospital Sketches*, based on Alcott's nursing experiences (see LMA, *L*, 84 n.2, 86, 88 n.1). Louisa Whiting, now married to Rev. Stephen Barker, also nursed Civil War soldiers in Washington when her husband served as chaplain to the Fourteenth Massachusetts Infantry stationed there (see Frank Moore, *Women of the War: Their Heroism and Self-Sacrifice. True Stories of the Brave Women in the Civil War* [1866; reprint, Alexander, N.C.: Blue Gray Books, 1997], 263–66). Not all women abolitionists shared Alcott's enthusiasm for the war. Maria Weston Chapman, for one, bemoaned the sundering of "the moral sense" from the antislavery campaign (quoted in Friedman, *Gregarious Saints*, 217).

111. LJE, *L*, 220, 219; RWE, *L*, 9:51; Ellen Tucker Emerson, *Life*, 141.

112. Thoreau to George Thatcher, 31 Mar 1861, Maine Historical Society; Pillsbury to Thoreau, 9 Apr 1861, Thoreau Pillsbury Collection (#8197), Clifton Waller Barrett Library of American Literature, Special Collections, University of Virginia Library; *Corr*, 611; Walter Harding, *Thoreau's Minnesota Journey: Two Documents* (Geneseo, N.Y.: Thoreau Society, 1962), 51; *AME*, 1:335; Stearns to Thoreau, 23 Feb 1862, transcript of manuscript letter, files of *The Writings of Henry D. Thoreau*, University of California, Santa Barbara.

113. Cameron, *Young Reporter*, 33; Cameron, *Transcendental Youth and Age*, 151; Sanborn to Phillips, 30 Apr 1861, Phillips Papers, HL; Larson, *Promised Land*, 183, 192, 196, 203–5. Frank Sanborn's financial assistance to and friendship with Tubman continued throughout their lives; he wrote the first biographical sketch of this extraordinary woman, which appeared in the *Boston Commonwealth* on July 17, 1863 (Larson, *Promised Land* 219). For mentions of their relationship, see Larson, *Promised Land*, 161–62, 192, 218–20, 226, 269, 281. Despite this admiration, however, Sanborn always assessed Tubman in bigoted terms: "She was the type of her race, loyal to the death, secretive as the grave, but never with hatred in her heart for her worst oppressors. . . . Mercy and patience, those two qualities which the blacks display in excess, accompanied with deceit and indifference in moral matters, were Harriet's outstanding qualities" (Cameron, *Transcendental Youth and Age*, 152).

114. De Fontaine, *History of American Abolitionism*, 5; Abigail Alcott journal, 31 Dec 1861, Alcott Family Papers, HL. After the war, Abby Alcott added a postscript to this journal page: "(1865) as it has proved—success to the Righteous Cause—now if the Laws can protect the Emancipated Slaves establish Civil Rights then Peace will indeed prevail throughout this troubled nation."

115. Jeffrey, *Great Silent Army*, 212; Ellen Tucker Emerson, *Life*, 141; Abigail Alcott to Samuel Joseph May, 19 Jul 1863, Amos Bronson Alcott Papers, HL.

116. Annie Keyes Bartlett to Edward Jarvis Bartlett, 31 Mar 1864, Barlett Letters, CFPL.

117. Elliott and Jones, *Black History*, 84; *Liberator*, 2 Jan 1863. For more on Mary Rice, see

Steven R. Shelburne, "David E. Tenney's Reminiscences of Concord during the Early 1840s," *Thoreau Research Newsletter* 2 (October 1991): 1–7.

118. Buttrick to Mrs. Brooks, 17 Nov 1867, Letter File, CFPL; Brown to William Lloyd Garrison, 9 Jun 1863, BBS; Peterson, *John Brown*, 38. For more on Concord women who taught at freedmen's schools during and after the war, see Gladys E. H. Hosmer, "Yankee Schoolmarms in Dixie," typescript, CFPL. In 1864, Annie Brown and her mother moved to California. Annie married Samuel Adams in 1869; their family eventually included ten children. Calling herself "the last survivor" and "a relic of John Brown's raid on Harper's Ferry," she corresponded with Frank Sanborn in the early 1890s about the possibility of earning money by publishing memories of her father and her experiences at the Kennedy Farm, as well as her recollections of the (now famous) people she had known in Concord. In 1896, Adams's home was destroyed in a fire, and Sanborn solicited donations for the family in the *Springfield Republican*. For mention of Annie Brown's work with freed slaves in Virginia, see the *Liberator*, 29 Jan 1864. For letters describing her family's situation in the 1890s, see Annie Brown Adams to Franklin B. Sanborn, 25 Sep 1892, 24 Sep 1893, 28 Feb and 23 Dec 1894, all in BBS; and Cameron, *Transcendental Youth and Age*, 86.

119. Brooks to Phillips, 7 Dec 1865, Phillips Papers, HL; *National Anti-Slavery Standard*, 11 Jul 1868; *Liberator*, 23 Jun 1843. Prior to the final issue of the *Liberator*, Concord's Mary Rice conveyed her praise to Garrison: "My soul is filled with thanks to all the dear ones that have spoken a word, or lifted a finger to ameliorate the condition of the African race, bond and free. Of all persons upon earth, the Pioneer stands first" (Rice to Garrison, 25 Jun 1865, BPL).

Bibliography

Abels, Jules. *Man on Fire: John Brown and the Cause of Liberty*. New York: Macmillan, 1971.

Adams, Raymond. "Thoreau's Return to Concord." *TSB* 96 (summer 1966): 1–4.

Adams, Stephen, and Donald Ross, Jr. *Revising Mythologies: The Composition of Thoreau's Major Works*. Charlottesville: University Press of Virginia, 1988.

Agassiz, Elizabeth Cary, ed. *Louis Agassiz: His Life and Correspondence*. Vol. 2. Boston: Houghton Mifflin, 1885.

Albrecht, Robert C. "Thoreau and His Audience: 'A Plea for Captain John Brown.'" *AL* 32 (January 1961): 393–402.

Allen, Gay Wilson. *Waldo Emerson: A Biography*. New York: Viking, 1981.

Andrews, William L., et al., eds. *North Carolina Slave Narratives: The Lives of Moses Roper, Lunsford Lane, Moses Grandy, & Thomas H. Jones*. Chapel Hill: University of North Carolina Press, 2003.

Annual Report of the American Anti-Slavery Society. New York: American Anti-Slavery Society, 1838.

Baker, Jean H. *James Buchanan*. New York: Times Books, 2004.

[Barker, Louisa Jane Whiting]. *Influence of Slavery upon the White Population*. New York: American Anti-Slavery Society, 1855.

Bartlett, George B. "Concord Men and Memories." *Bay State Monthly* 3 (September 1885): 224-32.

Bartlett, Irving H. *John C. Calhoun: A Biography*. New York: Norton, 1993.

——. *Daniel Webster*. New York: Norton, 1978.

——. *Wendell Phillips: Brahmin Radical*. Boston: Beacon, 1961.

Bartlett, Josiah. "Duncan Ingraham." In *The Centennial of the Social Circle in Concord March 21, 1882*. Cambridge: Riverside, 1882. 127–30.

Bearse, Austin. *Reminiscences of Fugitive-Slave Law Days in Boston*. 1880. Reprint, New York: Arno, 1969.

Bellis, Peter J. *Writing Revolution: Aesthetics and Politics in Hawthorne, Whitman, and Thoreau*. Athens: University of Georgia Press, 2003.

Berg, Martha L., and Alice de V. Perry, eds. "'The Impulses of Human Nature': Margaret Fuller's Journal from June through October 1844." *Proceedings of the Massachusetts Historical Society* 102 (1990): 38–126.

Blanding, Thomas. "Rapping with the Thoreaus." *CS* 17 (March 1984): 1–6.

Blassingame, John W., ed. *Slave Testimony: Two Centuries of Letters, Speeches, Interviews, and Autobiographies.* Baton Rouge: Louisiana State University Press, 1977.

Blassingame, John W., et al., eds. *The Frederick Douglass Papers.* Series 1. *Speeches, Debates, and Interviews.* Vol. 1: *1841–46.* New Haven: Yale University Press, 1979.

Blassingame, John W., and Mae G. Henderson, eds. *Antislavery Newspapers and Periodicals.* Vol. 2: *1835–1865.* Boston: G. K. Hall, 1980.

Blassingame, John W., John R. McKivigan, and Peter P. Hinks, eds., *The Frederick Douglass Papers.* Series 2. *Autobiographical Writings.* Vol. 1: *Narrative.* New Haven: Yale University Press, 1999.

Blue, Frederick J. *Charles Sumner and the Conscience of the North.* Arlington Heights, Ill.: Harlan Davidson, 1994.

——. *The Free Soilers: Third Party Politics 1848–54.* Urbana: University of Illinois Press, 1973.

——. *No Taint of Compromise: Crusaders in Antislavery Politics.* Baton Rouge: Louisiana State University Press, 2005.

Bode, Carl. *The American Lyceum: Town Meeting of the Mind.* Carbondale: Southern Illinois University Press, 1968.

Bosco, Ronald A., and Joel Myerson. *The Emerson Brothers: A Fraternal Biography in Letters.* New York: Oxford University Press, 2006.

Bowditch, Vincent Y. *Life and Correspondence of Henry Ingersoll Bowditch.* Vol. 1. Boston: Houghton Mifflin, 1902.

Bowditch, William I. *The Anti-Slavery Reform, Its Principle and Method.* Boston: Robert F. Wallcut, 1850.

Boyer, Richard O. *The Legend of John Brown: A Biography and a History.* New York: Knopf, 1973.

Boylan, Anne M. *The Origins of Women's Activism: New York and Boston, 1797–1840.* Chapel Hill: University of North Carolina Press, 2002.

Broderick, John C. "Thoreau, Alcott, and the Poll Tax." *Studies in Philology* 53 (1956): 612–26.

Brooks, Paul. *The People of Concord: One Year in the Flowering of New England.* Chester, Conn.: Globe Pequot, 1990.

Brown, Ira V. " 'Am I Not a Woman and a Sister?': The Anti-Slavery Convention of American Women, 1837–1839." *Pennsylvania History* 50 (January 1983): 1–19.

——. "Cradle of Feminism: The Philadelphia Female Anti-Slavery Society, 1833–1840." *The Pennsylvania Magazine of History and Biography* 102 (April 1978): 143–66.

——. *Mary Grew: Abolitionist and Feminist (1813–1896).* Selinsgrove, Pa.: Susquehanna University Press, 1991.

Brown, Mary Hosmer. *Memories of Concord.* Boston: Four Seas, 1926.

Brown, Richard D. "Microhistory and the Post-Modern Challenge." *JER* 23 (spring 2003): 1–20.

Bruchey, Stuart, comp. and ed. *Cotton and the Growth of the American Economy: 1790–1860. Sources and Readings.* New York: Harcourt, Brace & World, 1967.

Buell, Lawrence. "American Pastoral Ideology Reappraised." *American Literary History* 1 (spring 1989): 1–29.

——. "Emersonian Anti-Mentoring: From Thoreau to Dickinson and Beyond (in

Honor of James McIntosh)." *Michigan Quarterly Review* 41 (summer 2002): 347–60.

Burbick, Joan. *Thoreau's Alternative History: Changing Perspectives on Nature, Culture, and Language.* Philadelphia: University of Pennsylvania Press, 1987.

Bush, Trevor N. W. "Thoreau in South Africa: A Letter from the Rev. Trevor N. W. Bush." In *Thoreau in Our Season.* Ed. John H. Hicks. Amherst: University of Massachusetts Press, 1967. 27–28.

Cabot, James Elliot. *A Memoir of Ralph Waldo Emerson.* 2 vols. Boston: Houghton Mifflin, 1887.

Cain, William E. Introduction to *William Lloyd Garrison and the Fight against Slavery: Selections from* The Liberator. Boston: Bedford/St. Martin's, 1995. 1–57.

——. Preface to *William Lloyd Garrison and the Fight against Slavery: Selections from* The Liberator. Boston: Bedford/St. Martin's, 1995. vii–ix.

Calhoun, John C. "Speech in the U.S. Senate." In *Defending Slavery: Proslavery Thought in the Old South. A Brief History with Documents.* Ed. Paul Finkelman. Boston: Bedford/St. Martin's, 2003. 54–60.

Cameron, Kenneth Walter. "Sanborn's Preparatory School in Concord (1855–1863)." *American Renaissance Literary Report* 3 (1989): 34–83.

Cameron, Kenneth Walter, ed. *Literary Comment in American Renaissance Newspapers . . .* Hartford, Conn.: Transcendental Books, 1977.

——. *Table Talk: A Transcendentalist's Opinions on American Life, Literature, Art and People . . .* Franklin Benjamin Sanborn. Hartford, Conn.: Transcendental Books, 1981.

——. *Transcendental Youth and Age: Chapters in Biography and Autobiography.* Franklin Benjamin Sanborn. Hartford, Conn.: Transcendental Books, 1981.

——. *Transcendental Writers and Heroes . . .* Franklin Benjamin Sanborn. Hartford, Conn.: Transcendental Books, 1978.

——. *Ungathered Poems and Transcendental Papers.* Franklin Benjamin Sanborn. Hartford, Conn.: Transcendental Books, 1981.

——. *Young Reporter of Concord: A Checklist of F. B. Sanborn's Letters to Benjamin Smith Lyman, 1853–1867 . . .* Hartford, Conn.: Transcendental Books, 1978.

Campbell, Stanley W. *The Slave Catchers: Enforcement of the Fugitive Slave Law, 1850–1860.* Chapel Hill: University of North Carolina Press, 1968.

Canby, Henry Seidel. *Thoreau.* Boston: Houghton Mifflin, 1939.

Ceplair, Larry, ed. *The Public Years of Sarah and Angelina Grimké: Selected Writings, 1835–1839.* New York: Columbia University Press, 1989.

Chambers-Schiller, Lee. " 'A Good Work among the People': The Political Culture of the Boston Antislavery Fair." In *The Abolitionist Sisterhood: Women's Political Culture in Antebellum America.* Ed. Jean Fagan Yellin. Ithaca: Cornell University Press, 1994. 249–74.

Child, David L. "Letter from Mr. Child." In *The Abolitionists: A Collection of Their Writings.* Ed. Louis Ruchames. New York: Putnam's, 1963. 103–9.

Clapper, Ronald Earl. "The Development of *Walden*: A Genetic Text." 2 vols. Ph.D. diss., University of California Los Angeles, 1967.

Clinton, Catherine. *Harriet Tubman: The Road to Freedom.* Boston: Little, Brown, 2004.

——, ed. *Fanny Kemble's Journals.* Cambridge: Harvard University Press, 2000.

Cockrell, Dale, ed. *Excelsior: Journals of the Hutchinson Family Singers, 1842–1846.* Stuyvesant, N.Y.: Pendragon, 1989.

Cole, Phyllis. *Mary Moody Emerson and the Origins of Transcendentalism: A Family History.* New York: Oxford University Press, 1998.

——. "Pain and Protest in the Emerson Family." In *The Emerson Dilemma: Essays on Emerson and Social Reform.* Ed. T. Gregory Garvey. Athens: University of Georgia Press, 2001. 67–92.

Collison, Gary. "The Boston Vigilance Committee: A Reconsideration." *Historical Journal of Massachusetts* 12 (1984): 104–16.

——. " 'This Flagitious Offense': Daniel Webster and the Shadrach Rescue Cases, 1851–1852." *NEQ* 68 (December 1995): 609–26.

——. *Shadrach Minkins: From Fugitive Slave to Citizen.* Cambridge: Harvard University Press, 1997.

——. "Shadrach in Concord." *CS* 19 (December 1987): 1–12.

Concord Directory and Guide . . . Concord, Mass: E. H. Smith, 1892.

Concord, Massachusetts Births, Marriages, and Deaths 1635–1850. Concord, Mass.: Printed by the Town, 1895.

Conrad, Randall. "Realizing Resistance: Thoreau and the First of August, 1846, at Walden." *CS* n.s. 12/13 (2004/2005): 165–93.

Cook, James H. "Fighting with Breath, Not Blows: Frederick Douglass and Antislavery Violence." In *Antislavery Violence: Sectional, Racial, and Cultural Conflict in Antebellum America.* Ed. John R. McKivigan and Stanley Harrold. Knoxville: University of Tennessee Press, 1999. 128–63.

Cooke, George W. "The Two Thoreaus." In *Thoreau as Seen by His Contemporaries.* Ed. Walter Harding. 1960. Reprint, New York: Dover, 1989. 81–87.

Dahlstrand, Frederick C. *Amos Bronson Alcott: An Intellectual Biography.* Rutherford, N.J.: Fairleigh Dickinson University Press, 1982.

Dain, Bruce. *A Hideous Monster of the Mind: American Race Theory in the Early Republic.* Cambridge: Harvard University Press, 2002.

Dana, Richard Henry, Jr. *Speeches in Stirring Times and Letters to a Son.* Ed. Richard H. Dana, 3d. Boston: Houghton Mifflin, 1910.

Danvers Historical Society. Old Anti-Slavery Days: Proceedings of the Commemorative Meeting, Held by the Danvers Historical Society at the Town Hall, Danvers, April 26, 1893, with Introduction, Letters, and Sketches. Danvers, Mass.: Danvers Mirror Print, 1893.

Davis, David A. Introduction to *The Experience of Rev. Thomas H. Jones, Who Was a Slave for Forty-Three Years.* In *North Carolina Slave Narratives: The Lives of Moses Roper, Lunsford Lane, Moses Grandy, & Thomas H. Jones.* Ed. William L. Andrews et al. Chapel Hill: University of North Carolina Press, 2003. 189–202.

Davis, Kenneth S. *Kansas: A Bicentennial History.* New York: Norton, 1976.

Dean, Bradley P. "More Context for Thoreau's 'Slavery in Massachusetts.' " *Thoreau Research Newsletter* 1 (July 1990): 12.

——. "Thoreau, Emerson, and the Reverend Daniel Foster." Paper presented at the conference of the Modern Language Association, Philadelphia, Pa., December 2004.

Dean, Bradley P., and Ronald Wesley Hoag. "Thoreau's Lectures after *Walden:* An Annotated Calendar." *SAR 1996.* Ed. Joel Myerson. Charlottesville: University Press of Virginia, 1996. 241–362.

Dedmond, Francis B. "Men of Concord Petition the Governor." *CS* 15 (winter 1980): 1–6.

De Fontaine, F. G. *History of American Abolitionism; Its Four Great Epochs . . .* New York: D. Appleton, 1861.

Delano, Sterling F. "George Bradford's Letters to Emerson from Brook Farm." *Resources for American Literary Study* 25, no. 1 (1999): 26–45.

Demos, John. "The Antislavery Movement and the Problem of Violent 'Means.'" *NEQ* 37 (December 1964): 501–26.

Denton, Charles Richard. "The Unitarian Church and 'Kanzas Territory,' 1854–1861." *Kansas Historical Quarterly* 30 (winter 1964): 455–91.

Dillon, Merton L. *The Abolitionists: The Growth of a Dissenting Majority.* DeKalb: Northern Illinois University Press, 1974.

Dimock, Wai Chee. *Through Other Continents: American Literature Across Deep Time.* Princeton: Princeton University Press, 2006.

Donald, David. *Charles Sumner and the Coming of the Civil War.* New York: Knopf, 1961.

Drake, Samuel Adams. *History of Middlesex County, Massachusetts . . .* 2 vols. Boston: Estes and Lauriat, 1880.

Du Bois, W. E. Burghardt. *John Brown.* Philadelphia: George W. Jacobs, 1909.

Duncan, Troy, and Chris Dixon. "Denouncing the Brotherhood of Thieves: Stephen Symonds Foster's Critique of the Anti-Abolitionist Clergy." *Civil War History* 47, no. 2 (2001): 97–117.

Earhart, Amy E. "Representative Men, Slave Revolt, and Emerson's 'Conversion' to Abolitionism." *ATQ* 13 (December 1999): 287–303.

Eberle, Molly Q. "Wayside Joins Underground Railroad Network." *The Concord Journal* (Oct. 4, 2001): 2.

Edelstein, Tilden G. *Strange Enthusiasm: A Life of Thomas Wentworth Higginson.* 1968. Reprint, New York: Atheneum, 1970.

Elkins, Stanley M. *Slavery: A Problem in American Institutional and Intellectual Life.* 3rd ed., rev. Chicago: University of Chicago Press, 1976.

Elliott, Barbara K., and Janet W. Jones. *Concord: Its Black History 1636–1860.* Concord, Mass.: Concord Public Schools, 1976.

Emerson, Charles Chauncy. "Lecture on Slavery." *ESQ* 16 (3rd quarter 1959): 12–21.

Emerson, Edward Waldo. "Alcott, Lane, Thoreau." *TSB* 175 (spring 1986): 6.

——. *The Early Years of the Saturday Club 1855–1870.* 1918. Reprint, Freeport, N.Y.: Books for Libraries, 1967.

——. *Henry Thoreau as Remembered by a Young Friend.* 1917. Reprint, Mineola, N.Y.: Dover, 1999.

Emerson, Ellen Tucker. *The Life of Lidian Jackson Emerson.* Ed. Delores Bird Carpenter. Rev. ed. East Lansing: Michigan State University Press, 1992.

Emerson, Ralph Waldo. *The Collected Works of Ralph Waldo Emerson.* Vol. 2: *Essays: First Series.* Ed. Albert R. Ferguson and Jean Ferguson Carr. Cambridge: Belknap Press of Harvard University Press, 1979.

Erlich, Michael Glenn. "Selected Anti-Slavery Speeches of Henry David Thoreau, 1848–1859: A Rhetorical Analysis." Ph.D. diss., Ohio State University, 1970.

Ernest, John. Introduction to William Craft, *Running a Thousand Miles for Freedom:*

Or, The Escape of William and Ellen Craft from Slavery. Acton, Mass.: Copley, 2000. vii–xxxiii.

Etcheson, Nicole. *Bleeding Kansas: Contested Liberty in the Civil War Era.* Lawrence: University Press of Kansas, 2004.

Fellman, Michael. "Theodore Parker and the Abolitionist Role in the 1850s." *Journal of American History* 61 (December 1974): 66–84.

Field, Peter S. "The Strange Career of Emerson and Race." *American Nineteenth Century History* 2, no. 1 (spring 2001): 1–32.

Finkelman, Paul, ed. *His Soul Goes Marching On: Responses to John Brown and the Harpers Ferry Raid.* Charlottesville: University Press of Virginia, 1995.

Foner, Philip. "Douglass and John Brown." In *Blacks in the Abolitionist Movement.* Ed. John H. Bracey, August Meier, and Elliott Rudwick. Belmont, Calif.: Wadsworth, 1971. 160–68.

———, ed. *Frederick Douglass: Selected Speeches and Writings.* Chicago: Lawrence Hill, 1999.

Ford, Nick Aaron. "Henry David Thoreau, Abolitionist." *NEQ* 19 (September 1946): 359–71.

Foster, Daniel. *Our Nation's Sins and the Christian's Duty. A Fast Day Discourse.* Boston: White & Potter, 1851.

Frederick, Michael J. "Transcendental Ethos: A Study of Thoreau's Social Philosophy and Its Consistency in Relation to Antebellum Reform." Master's thesis, Harvard University, 1998.

Freehling, William W. *The Road to Disunion.* Vol. 1: *Secessionists at Bay 1776–1854.* New York: Oxford University Press, 1990.

French, Allen. *Old Concord.* Boston: Little, Brown, 1915.

Fresonke, Kris. "Thoreau and the Design of Dissent." *Religion and the Arts* 2, no. 2 (1998): 221–41.

Friedman, Lawrence J. *Gregarious Saints: Self and Community in American Abolitionism, 1830–1870.* Cambridge: Cambridge University Press, 1982.

Frothingham, Octavius Brooks. *Theodore Parker: A Biography.* Boston: James R. Osgood, 1874.

Fuller, David G. "Correcting the Newspapers: Thoreau and 'A Plea for Captain John Brown.'" *CS* n.s. 5 (fall 1997): 165–75.

Gandhi, M. K. *Non-Violent Resistance (Satyagraha).* New York: Schocken, 1951.

Gara, Larry. "The Fugitive Slave Law: A Double Paradox." *Civil War History* 10 (January 1964): 229–40.

———. *The Liberty Line: The Legend of the Underground Railroad.* 1961. Reprint, Lexington: University Press of Kentucky, 1996.

Garrison, William Lloyd. *The New "Reign of Terror" in the Slaveholding States.* 1860. Reprint, New York: Arno, 1969.

———, Wendell Phillips, and Francis Jackson Garrison. *William Lloyd Garrison, 1805–1879: The Story of His Life Told by His Children.* 4 vols. 1885. Reprint, New York: Negro Universities Press, 1969.

Gilbert, James N. "A Behavioral Analysis of John Brown: Martyr or Terrorist?" In *Terrible Swift Sword: The Legacy of John Brown.* Ed. Peggy A. Russo and Paul Finkelman. Athens: Ohio University Press, 2005. 107–17.

Ginzberg, Lori D. *Women and the Work of Benevolence: Morality, Politics, and Class in the Nineteenth-Century United States*. New Haven: Yale University Press, 1990.

Glick, Wendell P. "Thoreau and the 'Herald of Freedom.'" *NEQ* 22 (June 1949): 193–204.

Goldman, Emma. *Anarchism and Other Essays*. New York: Dover, 1969.

Goodman, Paul. *Of One Blood: Abolitionism and the Origins of Racial Equality*. Berkeley: University of California Press, 1998.

Gougeon, Len. "Abolition, the Emersons, and 1837." *NEQ* 54 (September 1981): 345–64.

———. "Emerson and the Campaign of 1851." *Historical Journal of Massachusetts* 16, no. 1 (1988): 20–33.

———. "Emerson and the New Bedford Affair." *SAR 1981*. Ed. Joel Myerson. Boston: Twayne, 1981. 257–64.

———. "Emerson's Abolition Conversion." In *The Emerson Dilemma: Essays on Emerson and Social Reform*. Ed. T. Gregory Garvey. Athens: University of Georgia Press, 2001. 170–96.

———. Historical Background to *Emerson's Antislavery Writings*. Ed. Gougeon and Joel Myerson. New Haven: Yale University Press, 1995. xi–lvi.

———. *Virtue's Hero: Emerson, Antislavery, and Reform*. Athens: University of Georgia Press, 1990.

Gould, Stephen Jay. *The Mismeasure of Man*. 1981. Rev. ed. New York: Norton, 1996.

Gozzi, Raymond. "A Freudian View of Thoreau." In *Thoreau's Psychology: Eight Essays*. Ed. Gozzi. Lanham, Md.: University Press of America, 1983. 1–18.

Grew, Mary. "Annals of Women's Anti-Slavery Societies." *Proceedings of the American Anti-Slavery Society, at its Third Decade . . .* 1864. Reprint, New York: Negro Universities Press, 1969. 124–30.

Grodzins, Dean. *American Heretic: Theodore Parker and Transcendentalism*. Chapel Hill: University of North Carolina Press, 2002.

Gross, Robert A. "Faith in the Boardinghouse: New Views of Thoreau Family Religion." *TSB* 250 (winter 2005): 1–5.

———. *The Minutemen and Their World*. New York: Hill and Wang, 1976.

———. "Squire Dickinson and Squire Hoar." *Proceedings of the Massachusetts Historical Society* 101 (1989): 1–23.

———. "Transcendentalism and Urbanism: Concord, Boston, and the Wider World." *Journal of American Studies* 18, no. 3 (1984): 361–81.

———. "Young Men and Women of Fairest Promise: Transcendentalism in Concord." *CS* n.s. 2 (fall 1994): 5–18.

Grover, Kathryn. *The Fugitive's Gibraltar: Escaping Slaves and Abolitionism in New Bedford, Massachusetts*. Amherst: University of Massachusetts Press, 2001.

Hamer, Philip M. "Great Britain, the United States, and the Negro Seamen Acts, 1822–1848." *Journal of Southern History* 1 (February 1935): 3–28.

Hammond, Scott John. "John Brown as Founder: America's Violent Confrontation with Its First Principles." In *Terrible Swift Sword: The Legacy of John Brown*. Ed. Peggy A. Russo and Paul Finkelman. Athens: Ohio University Press, 2005. 61–76.

Hansen, Debra Gold. *Strained Sisterhood: Gender and Class in the Boston Female Anti-Slavery Society*. Amherst: University of Massachusetts Press, 1993.

Harding, Vincent. *There Is a River: The Black Struggle for Freedom in America.* 1981. Reprint, New York: Harcourt Brace Jovanovich, 1992.

Harding, Walter. "Additions to the Thoreau Bibliography: Notes and Reviews." *TSB* 19 (April 1947): 3–4.

——. "Gandhi and Thoreau." *TSB* 23 (April 1948): 1–2.

——. "Parker Pillsbury, the Walden Cabin, and the Underground Railroad." *TSB* 198 (winter 1992): 7–8.

——. "Thoreau in Emerson's Account Books." *TSB* 159 (spring 1982): 1–3.

——. *Thoreau as Seen by His Contemporaries.* New York: Dover, 1989.

——. *Thoreau's Minnesota Journey: Two Documents.* Geneseo, N.Y.: Thoreau Society, 1962.

Harding, Walter, and Michael Meyer. *The New Thoreau Handbook.* New York: New York University Press, 1980.

Harris, Marc. "The People of Concord: A Demographic History, 1750–1850." In *Concord: The Social History of a New England Town, 1750–1850.* Ed. David Hackett Fischer. Waltham, Mass.: Brandeis University, 1983. 65–138.

Harrold, Stanley. *Subversives: Antislavery Community in Washington, D.C., 1828–1865.* Baton Rouge: Louisiana State University Press, 2003.

Hart, Alfred Bushnell. *Slavery and Abolition 1831–1841.* 1906. Reprint, New York: Haskell House, 1968.

Hawthorne, Edith Garrigues, ed. *The Memoirs of Julian Hawthorne.* New York: Macmillan, 1938.

Hayden, Tom. "The Conscience by the Pond." *Orion Online* (January/February 2005): 1–3. http://www.oriononline.org/pages/om/05–1om/Hayden.html.

Heller, Charles E. *Portrait of an Abolitionist: A Biography of George Luther Stearns, 1809–1867.* Westport, Conn.: Greenwood, 1996.

Hendrick, George. "The Influence of Thoreau's 'Civil Disobedience' on Gandhi's *Satyagraha.* *NEQ* 29 (December 1956): 462–71.

——, ed. *Remembrances of Concord and the Thoreaus: Letters of Horace Hosmer to Dr. S. A. Jones.* Urbana: University of Illinois Press, 1977.

"Henry Ingersoll Bowditch." In *Proceedings of the American Academy of Arts and Sciences* n.s. 20. Boston: University Press: John Wilson and Son, 1893. 310–31.

Herr, Pamela. *Jessie Benton Frémont: A Biography.* Norman: University of Oklahoma Press, 1987.

Herr, Pamela, and Mary Lee Spence, eds. *The Letters of Jessie Benton Frémont.* Urbana: University of Illinois Press, 1993.

Herr, William A. "Thoreau on Violence." *TSB* 131 (spring 1975): 2–4.

Herring, Stephen W. "The Halcyon Days of Framingham's Harmony Grove." *TSB* 215 (spring 1996): 4–5.

Herrnstadt, Richard L., ed. *The Letters of A. Bronson Alcott.* Ames: Iowa State University Press, 1969.

Higginson, Mary Thacher, ed. *Letters and Journals of Thomas Wentworth Higginson, 1846–1906.* Boston: Houghton Mifflin, 1921.

Higginson, Thomas Wentworth. *Army Life in a Black Regiment, and Other Writings.* New York: Penguin, 1997.

——. *Cheerful Yesterdays.* 1898. Reprint, New York: Arno, 1968.

——. *Massachusetts in Mourning. A Sermon, Preached in Worcester, on Sunday, June 4, 1854.* Boston: James Munroe, 1854.

Hinton, Richard J. *John Brown and His Men.* Rev. ed. 1894. Reprint, New York: Arno, 1968.

Hoar, George F. *Autobiography of Seventy Years.* 2 vols. New York: Scribner's, 1903.

Horton, James Oliver. "Defending the Manhood of the Race: The Crisis of Citizenship in Black Boston at Midcentury." In *Hope and Glory: Essays on the Legacy of the Fifty-Fourth Massachusetts Regiment.* Ed. Martin H. Blatt, Thomas J. Brown, and Donald Yacovone. Amherst: University of Massachusetts Press, 2001. 7–20, 276–78.

——. *Free People of Color: Inside the African American Community.* Washington: Smithsonian, 1993.

Horton, James Oliver, and Lois E. Horton. *Black Bostonians: Family Life and Community Struggle in the Antebellum North.* Rev. ed. New York: Holmes & Meier, 1999.

——. "A Federal Assault: African Americans and the Impact of the Fugitive Slave Law of 1850." In *Slavery and the Law.* Ed. Paul Finkelman. Madison, Wis.: Madison House, 1997. 143–60.

Horton, Lois E. "Community Organization and Social Activism: Black Boston and the Antislavery Movement." *Sociological Inquiry* 55, no. 2 (1985): 182–99.

Humez, Jean M. *Harriet Tubman: The Life and the Life Stories.* Madison: University of Wisconsin Press, 2003.

Hyde, Lewis. Introduction to *The Essays of Henry D. Thoreau.* New York: North Point, 2002. vii–xlix.

Hyman, Stanley Edgar. "Henry Thoreau in Our Time." In *Thoreau: A Collection of Critical Essays.* Ed. Sherman Paul. Englewood Cliffs, N.J.: Prentice-Hall, 1962. 23–36.

[Jackson, Francis]. "Treasurer's Accounts. The Boston Vigilance Committee." Facsimile, Boston Public Library. Boston: Bostonian Society, [1924].

Jeffrey, Julie Roy. *The Great Silent Army of Abolitionism: Ordinary Women in the Antislavery Movement.* Chapel Hill: University of North Carolina Press, 1998.

Jenco, Leigh Kathryn. "Thoreau's Critique of Democracy." *The Review of Politics* 65 (summer 2003): 355–81.

Johnson, Linck C. "Contexts of Bravery: Thoreau's Revisions of 'The Service' for *A Week. SAR 1983.* Ed. Joel Myerson. Charlottesville: University Press of Virginia, 1983. 281–96.

——. "Emerson, Thoreau's Arrest, and the Trials of American Manhood." In *The Emerson Dilemma: Essays on Emerson and Social Reform.* Ed. T. Gregory Garvey. Athens: University of Georgia Press, 2001. 35–64.

——. " 'Liberty Is Never Cheap': Emerson, 'The Fugitive Slave Law,' and the Antislavery Lecture Series at the Broadway Tabernacle." *NEQ* 76 (December 2003): 550–92.

——. "Reforming the Reformers: Emerson, Thoreau, and the Sunday Lectures at Amory Hall, Boston." *ESQ* 37 (1991): 235–89.

Johnson, Samuel A. *The Battle Cry of Freedom: The New England Emigrant Aid Company in the Kansas Crusade.* Lawrence: University of Kansas Press, 1954.

Johnson, Walter. *Soul by Soul: Life inside the Antebellum Slave Market.* Cambridge: Harvard University Press, 1999.

Jones, Samuel Arthur. *Thoreau amongst Friends and Philistines and other Thoreau-viana.* Ed. George Hendrick. Athens: Ohio University Press, 1982.

———. "Thoreau and His Biographers." *Lippincott's Monthly Magazine* 48 (July–December 1891): 225.

Karcher, Carolyn L. *The First Woman in the Republic: A Cultural Biography of Lydia Maria Child.* Durham, N.C.: Duke University Press, 1994.

Keeler, Ralph. "Owen Brown's Escape from Harper's Ferry." *The Atlantic Monthly* 33 (March 1874): 342–66.

King, Martin Luther, Jr. *Stride toward Freedom: The Montgomery Story.* 1958. Reprint, San Francisco: HarperCollins, 1986.

Knights, Peter R. *The Plain People of Boston, 1830–1860: A Study in City Growth.* New York: Oxford University Press, 1971.

Kritzberg, Barry. "A Pre-Civil War Struggle against Capital Punishment: Charles Spear, Concord, and the Case of Washington Goode." *CS* n.s. 2 (fall 1994): 103–16.

———. "Thoreau, Slavery, and Resistance to Civil Government." *Massachusetts Review* 30 (winter 1989): 535–65.

Kulikoff, Allan. *The Agrarian Origins of American Capitalism.* Charlottesville: University Press of Virginia, 1992.

Kurtz, Jeffrey B. "Condemning Webster: Judgment and Audience in Emerson's 'Fugitive Slave Law.'" *Quarterly Journal of Speech* 87 (August 2001): 278–90.

Lader, Lawrence. *The Bold Brahmins: New England's War Against Slavery 1831–1863.* New York: Dutton, 1961.

Landon, Fred. "Anthony Burns in Canada." Ontario Historical Society, *Papers and Records* 22 (1925): 3–7.

Lane, Roger. *Policing the City: Boston 1822–1885.* Cambridge: Harvard University Press, 1967.

Larson, Kate Clifford. *Bound for the Promised Land: Harriet Tubman, Portrait of an American Hero.* New York: Ballantine, 2004.

Lawrence, Jerome, and Robert E. Lee. *The Night Thoreau Spent in Jail.* 1970. Reprint, New York: Bantam, 1972.

Lebeaux, Richard. *Thoreau's Seasons.* Amherst: University of Massachusetts Press, 1984.

Lerner, Gerda. *The Feminist Thought of Sarah Grimké.* New York: Oxford University Press, 1998.

Levy, Leonard W. "Sims' Case: The Fugitive Slave Law in Boston in 1851." *Journal of Negro History* 35 (January 1950): 39–74.

Ljungquist, Kent P. "Thoreau in the Boston *Chronotype*." *TSB* 199 (spring 1992): 5.

Lord, John C. *"The Higher Law," in Its Application to The Fugitive Slave Bill. A Sermon on the Duties Men Owe to God and to Governments.* New York: Union Safety Committee, 1851.

Lovejoy, Elijah P. "Elijah P. Lovejoy Defends His Right to Free Speech." In *The Abolitionists: A Collection of Their Writings.* Ed. Louis Ruchames. New York: Capricorn, 1963. 139–41.

Lowance, Mason, Jr. Introduction to *Against Slavery: An Abolitionist Reader.* New York: Penguin, 2000. xiii–xxxvi.

———. Introduction to *A House Divided: The Antebellum Slavery Debates in America, 1776–1865.* Ed. Lowance. Princeton: Princeton University Press, 2003. xxvii–lx.

Lucid, Robert F., ed. *The Journal of Richard Henry Dana, Jr.* Vol. 2. Cambridge: Belknap Press of Harvard University Press, 1968.

Lurie, Edward. *Louis Agassiz: A Life in Science.* Chicago: University of Chicago Press, 1960.

Mabee, Carleton. *Black Freedom: The Nonviolent Abolitionists from 1830 through the Civil War.* New York: Macmillan, 1970.

MacEacheren, Elaine. "Emancipation of Slavery in Massachusetts: A Reexamination 1770–1790." *The Journal of Negro History* 55 (October 1970): 289–306.

Magee, Michael. "Emerson's Emancipation Proclamations." *Raritan* 20, no. 4 (2001): 96–116.

——. "The Motives of Emancipated Prose: Emerson and the Collaborating Reader." *ESQ* 47 (4th quarter 2001): 279–326.

Maginnes, David R. "The Case of the Court House Rioters in the Rendition of the Fugitive Slave Anthony Burns, 1854." *Journal of Negro History* 56 (January 1971): 31–42.

Malin, James C. *John Brown and the Legend of Fifty-Six.* Philadelphia: American Philosophical Society, 1942.

Marble, Annie Russell. *Thoreau: His Home, Friends and Books.* 1902. Reprint, New York: AMS, 1969.

Marcou, Jules. *Life, Letters, and Works of Louis Agassiz.* Vol. 1. New York: Macmillan, 1896.

Marshall, Megan. *The Peabody Sisters: Three Women Who Ignited American Romanticism.* Boston: Houghton Mifflin, 2005.

Maxfield-Miller, Elizabeth. "Elizabeth of Concord: Selected Letters of Elizabeth Sherman Hoar (1814–1878) to the Emersons, Family, and the Emerson Circle (Part Three)." *SAR 1986.* Ed. Joel Myerson. Charlottesville: University Press of Virginia, 1986. 113–98.

May, Samuel J. *Some Recollections of Our Antislavery Conflict.* 1869. Reprint, New York: Arno, 1968.

McCaskill, Barbara. Introduction to William Craft, *Running a Thousand Miles for Freedom: The Escape of William and Ellen Craft from Slavery.* Athens: University of Georgia Press, 1999. vii–xxv.

McGlone, Robert E. "John Brown, Henry Wise, and the Politics of Insanity." In *His Soul Goes Marching On: Responses to John Brown and the Harpers Ferry Raid.* Ed. Paul Finkelman. Charlottesville: University Press of Virginia, 1995. 213–52.

McPherson, James M. *The Struggle for Equality: Abolitionists and the Negro in the Civil War and Reconstruction.* Princeton: Princeton University Press, 1964.

McWilliams, John. *New England's Crises and Cultural Memory: Literature, Politics, History, Religion, 1620–1860.* Cambridge: Cambridge University Press, 2004.

Meed, Douglas V. *The Mexican War: 1846–1848.* New York: Routledge, 2003.

Meltzer, Milton. *Tongue of Flame: The Life of Lydia Maria Child.* New York: Dell, 1965.

Meltzer, Milton, and Walter Harding. *A Thoreau Profile.* 1962. Reprint, Lincoln, Mass.: Thoreau Society, 1998.

Meltzer, Milton, Patricia G. Holland, and Francine Krasno, eds. *Lydia Maria Child: Selected Letters, 1817–1880.* Amherst: University of Massachusetts Press, 1982.

Meyer, Michael. "Discord in Concord on the Day of John Brown's Hanging." *TSB* 146 (winter 1979): 1–3.

——. *Several More Lives to Live: Thoreau's Political Reputation in America.* Westport, Conn.: Greenwood, 1977.

——. "Thoreau, Abolitionists, and Reformers." In *Thoreau among Others: Essays in Honor of Walter Harding.* Ed. Rita K. Gollin. Geneseo, N.Y.: State University College of Arts and Sciences at Geneseo, 1983. 16–26.

——. "Thoreau's Rescue of John Brown from History." *SAR 1980.* Ed. Joel Myerson. Boston: Twayne, 1980. 301–16.

Michael, John. "Democracy, Aesthetics, Individualism: Emerson as Public Intellectual." *Nineteenth-Century Prose* 30 (spring/fall 2003): 195–226.

Milder, Robert. *Reimagining Thoreau.* Cambridge: Cambridge University Press, 1995.

Milne, Gordon. *George William Curtis and the Genteel Tradition.* Bloomington: Indiana University Press, 1956.

Mitchell, Betty L. "Massachusetts Reacts to John Brown's Raid." *Civil War History* 19 (March 1973): 65–79.

Moore, Frank. *Women of the War: Their Heroism and Self-Sacrifice. True Stories of Brave Women in the Civil War.* 1866. Reprint, Alexander, N.C.: Blue Gray Books, 1997.

Morris, Thomas D. *Free Men All: The Personal Liberty Laws of the North, 1780–1861.* Baltimore: Johns Hopkins University Press, 1974.

Myerson, Joel. "Emerson's 'Thoreau': A New Edition from Manuscript." *SAR 1979.* Boston: Twayne, 1979. 17–92.

Myerson, Joel, and Daniel Shealy, eds. "Three Contemporary Accounts of Louisa May Alcott, with Glimpses of Other Concord Notables." *NEQ* 59 (March 1986): 109–22.

Nash, Gary B. *Forging Freedom: The Formation of Philadelphia's Black Community, 1720–1840.* Cambridge: Harvard University Press, 1988.

Nelson, Dana D. *National Manhood: Capitalist Citizenship and the Imagined Fraternity of White Men.* Durham, N.C.: Duke University Press, 1998.

Nelson, Truman. *The Old Man: John Brown at Harper's Ferry.* New York: Holt, Rinehart and Winston, 1973.

——. "Thoreau and John Brown." In *Thoreau in Our Season.* Ed. John H. Hicks. Amherst: University of Massachusetts Press, 1967. 134–53.

Neufeldt, Leonard N. "Emerson, Thoreau, and Daniel Webster." *ESQ* 26 (1st quarter 1980): 26–37.

Nevins, Allan. *Frémont: Pathmarker of the West.* Vol. 2: *Frémont in the Civil War.* 1939. Reprint, New York: Frederick Ungar, 1961.

——, ed. *Polk: The Diary of a President 1845–1849: Covering the Mexican War, the Acquisition of Oregon, and the Conquest of California and the Southwest.* New York: Capricorn, 1968.

Newman, Lance. "Thoreau's Materialism: From *Walden* to *Wild Fruits.*" *Nineteenth-Century Prose* 31 (fall 2004): 93–121.

"Notes and Queries." *TSB* 30 (January 1950): 3.

——. *TSB* 56 (summer 1956): 4.

——. *TSB* 171 (spring 1985): 7–8.

Oehlschlaeger, Fritz, and George Hendrick, eds. *Toward the Making of Thoreau's Modern Reputation: Selected Correspondence of S. A. Jones, A. W. Hosmer, H. S. Salt, H. G. O. Blake, and D. Ricketson.* Urbana: University of Illinois Press, 1979.

Packer, Barbara L. Historical Introduction to *The Conduct of Life*. In *The Collected Works of Ralph Waldo Emerson*, vol. 6. Ed. Joseph Slater. Cambridge: Belknap Press of Harvard University Press, 2003. xv–lxvii.

Page, H. A. [Japp, Alexander Hay]. *Thoreau: His Life and Aims*. 1878. Reprint, New York: Haskell House, 1972.

Palmer, Beverly Wilson, ed. *The Selected Letters of Charles Sumner*. 2 vols. Boston: Northeastern University Press, 1990.

Parker, Theodore. *The Slave Power*. Ed. James K. Hosmer. 1910. Reprint, New York: Arno, 1969.

——. *The Rights of Man in America*. Ed. F. B. Sanborn. 1911. Reprint, New York: Negro Universities Press, 1969.

Pease, Jane H., and William H. Pease. *Bound with Them in Chains: A Biographical History of the Antislavery Movement*. Westport, Conn.: Greenwood, 1972.

——. "Confrontation and Abolition in the 1850s." *Journal of American History* 58 (March 1972): 923–37.

——. *The Fugitive Slave Law and Anthony Burns: A Problem in Law Enforcement*. Philadelphia: Lippincott, 1975.

——. "Samuel J. May: Civil Libertarian." *Cornell Library Journal* 3 (autumn 1967): 7–25.

Peterson, Merrill D. *John Brown: The Legend Revisited*. Charlottesville: University of Virginia Press, 2002.

Petrulionis, Sandra Harbert. "Editorial Savoir Faire: Thoreau Transforms His Journal into 'Slavery in Massachusetts.'" *Resources for American Literary Study* 25, no. 2 (1999): 206–31.

——. "Fugitive Slave-Running on the *Moby-Dick*: Captain Austin Bearse and the Abolitionist Crusade." *Resources for American Literary Study* 28 (2002): 53–81.

——. "Selective Sympathy: The Public and Private Mary Merrick Brooks." *TSB* 226 (winter 1999): 1–3, 5.

——. "'Swelling that Great Tide of Humanity': The Concord, Massachusetts, Female Anti-Slavery Society." *NEQ* 74 (September 2001): 385–418.

Phillips, Wendell. *Speeches, Lectures, and Letters*. 1884. Reprint, New York: Negro Universities Press, 1968.

——. *Speeches, Lectures, and Letters*. Second Series. 1891. Reprint, New York: Arno, 1969.

Pierson, Michael D. "'All Southern Society Is Assailed by the Foulest Charges': Charles Sumner's 'The Crime against Kansas' and the Escalation of Republican Anti-slavery Rhetoric." *NEQ* 68 (December 1995): 531–57.

Potter, David M. *The Impending Crisis: 1848–1861*. New York: Harper and Row, 1976.

Prior, Linda T. "Ralph Waldo Emerson and South Carolina." *South Carolina Historical Magazine* 79, no. 4 (1978): 253–63.

Proceedings of the Anti-Slavery Convention of American Women Held in Philadelphia . . . Philadelphia: Merrihew and Gunn, 1838.

Proceedings of the State Disunion Convention, Held at Worcester, Massachusetts, January 15, 1857. Boston: Printed for the Committee, 1857.

Public Broadcasting Corporation. "John Brown's Holy War." Alexandria, Va.: PBS home video, 2002.

Quarles, Benjamin. Foreword to William Still, *The Underground Railroad*. 1871. Reprint, Chicago: Johnson, 1970. v–viii.

Rael, Patrick. *Black Identity and Black Protest in the Antebellum North*. Chapel Hill: University of North Carolina Press, 2002.

Ratner, Lorman. *Powder Keg: Northern Opposition to the Antislavery Movement, 1831– 1840*. New York: Basic Books, 1968.

Ratner, Lorman A., and Dwight L. Teeter, Jr. *Fanatics and Fire-Eaters: Newspapers and the Coming of the Civil War*. Urbana: University of Illinois Press, 2003.

Redpath, James. *Echoes of Harper's Ferry*. 1860. Reprint, New York: Arno, 1969.

——. *The Public Life of Capt. John Brown*. Boston: Thayer and Eldridge, 1860.

——. *The Roving Editor, or Talks with Slaves in the Southern States*. Ed. John R. McKivigan. 1859. Reprint, University Park, Pa.: Pennsylvania State University Press, 1996.

The Reign of Terror in Kanzas: As Encouraged by President Pierce, and Carried Out by the Southern Slave Power . . . Boston: Charles W. Briggs, 1856.

Remond, Charles Lenox. "The Rights of Colored Citizens in Traveling." In *The Abolitionists: A Collection of Their Writings*. Ed. Louis Ruchames. New York: Capricorn Books, 1963. 179–84.

Renehan, Edward J., Jr. *The Secret Six: The True Tale of the Men Who Conspired with John Brown*. New York: Crown, 1995.

Reynolds, Larry J. "The Challenge of Cultural Relativity: The Case of Hawthorne." *ESQ* 49 (1st–3rd quarters 2003): 129–47.

——. "The Cimeter's 'Sweet' Edge: Thoreau, Contemplation, and Violence." *Nineteenth-Century Prose* 31, no. 2 (fall 2004): 51–74.

Richardson, Robert D., Jr. *Emerson: The Mind on Fire*. Berkeley: University of California Press, 1995.

——. *Henry Thoreau: A Life of the Mind*. Berkeley: University of California Press, 1986.

Ripley, C. Peter, et al., eds. *The Black Abolitionist Papers*. 5 vols. Chapel Hill: University of North Carolina Press, 1985–1992.

Robbins, Paula Ivaska. *The Royal Family of Concord: Samuel, Elizabeth, and Rockwood Hoar and Their Friendship with Ralph Waldo Emerson*. Philadelphia: Xlibris, 2003.

Robboy, Stanley J., and Anita W. Robboy. "Lewis Hayden, from Fugitive Slave to Statesman." *NEQ* 46 (December 1973): 591–613.

Robertson, Stacey M. *Parker Pillsbury: Radical Abolitionist, Male Feminist*. Ithaca: Cornell University Press, 2000.

Rogers, Nathaniel Peabody. *An Address Delivered before the Concord Female Anti-Slavery Society, at Its Annual Meeting 25 Dec. 1837*. Concord, N.H.: William White, 1838.

——. *A Collection from the Miscellaneous Writings of Nathaniel Peabody Rogers*. 2nd ed. Manchester, N.H.: William H. Fisk, 1849.

Rose, Anne C. *Transcendentalism as a Social Movement, 1830–1850*. New Haven: Yale University Press, 1981.

Rosenblum, Nancy L. "The Inhibitions of Democracy on Romantic Political Thought: Thoreau's Democratic Individualism." In *Lessons of Romanticism: A Critical Companion*. Ed. Thomas Pfau and Robert F. Gleckner. Durham, N.C.: Duke University Press, 1998. 55–75.

——. Introduction to *Thoreau: Political Writings*. Ed. Rosenblum. Cambridge: Cambridge University Press, 1996. vii–xxxi.

——. "Thoreau's Militant Conscience." *Political Theory* 9 (February 1981): 81–110.

Rosenwald, Lawrence A. "The Theory, Practice, and Influence of Thoreau's Civil Disobedience." In *A Historical Guide to Henry David Thoreau*. Ed. William E. Cain. New York: Oxford University Press, 2000. 153–179.

Rossbach, Jeffery. *Ambivalent Conspirators: John Brown, the Secret Six, and a Theory of Slave Violence*. Philadelphia: University of Pennsylvania Press, 1982.

Rowe, John Carlos. *At Emerson's Tomb: The Politics of Classic American Literature*. New York: Columbia University Press, 1997.

Ruffin, Edmund. "Consequences of Abolition Agitation. No. 1." *Debow's Review* 22 (June 1857): 583–93.

Salt, Henry S. *Life of Henry David Thoreau*. Ed. George Hendrick et al. Urbana: University of Illinois Press, 1993.

"Samuel Hoar's Expulsion from Charleston." *Old South Leaflets* 6, no. 140. 1845. Reprint, Boston: Directors of the Old South Work, [1903]. 313–32.

Sanborn, Franklin Benjamin. *Hawthorne and His Friends: Reminiscence and Tribute*. Cedar Rapids, Iowa: Torch, 1908.

——. *Henry D. Thoreau*. Boston: Houghton Mifflin, 1883.

——. *The Life of Henry David Thoreau*. Boston: Houghton Mifflin, 1917.

——. *The Personality of Emerson*. Boston: Charles E. Goodspeed, 1903.

——. *The Personality of Thoreau*. Boston: Charles E. Goodspeed, 1901.

——. "The Women of Concord—IV. Mrs. Mary Merrick Brooks and the Anti-Slavery Movement." In *Transcendental Epilogue: Primary Materials for Research . . .* Vol. 3. Ed. Kenneth Walter Cameron. Hartford, Conn.: Transcendental Books, 1982. 44–47.

——, ed. *The Life and Letters of John Brown, Liberator of Kansas and Martyr of Virginia*. 1885. Reprint, New York: Negro Universities Press, 1969.

Sattelmeyer, Robert. *Thoreau's Reading: A Study in Intellectual History with Bibliographical Catalogue*. Princeton: Princeton University Press, 1988.

Scharnhorst, Gary. *Henry David Thoreau: An Annotated Bibliography of Comment and Criticism Before 1900*. New York: Garland, 1992.

——. *Henry David Thoreau: A Case Study in Canonization*. Columbia, S.C.: Camden House, 1993.

Schoolman, Martha. "American Abolitionist Geographies: Literature and the Politics of Place, 1840–1861." Ph.D. diss., University of Pennsylvania, 2005.

Shapiro, Samuel. "The Rendition of Anthony Burns." *Journal of Negro History* 44 (January 1959): 34–51.

Shattuck, Lemuel. *A History of the Town of Concord; Middlesex County, Massachusetts, from Its Earliest Settlement to 1832 . . .* Boston: Russell, Odiorne, 1835.

Shelburne, Steven R. "David E. Tenney's Reminiscences of Concord during the Early 1840s." *Thoreau Research Newsletter* 2 (October 1991): 1–7.

Siebert, Wilbur H. *The Underground Railroad in Massachusetts*. Worcester, Mass.: American Antiquarian Society, 1936.

Simmons, Edward. *From Seven to Seventy: Memories of a Painter and a Yankee*. New York: Harper and Brothers, 1922.

Simmons, Nancy Craig, ed. *The Selected Letters of Mary Moody Emerson.* Athens: University of Georgia Press, 1993.

Sinha, Manisha. "The Caning of Charles Sumner: Slavery, Race, and Ideology in the Age of the Civil War." *JER* 23 (summer 2003): 233–62.

Slater, Joseph, ed. *The Correspondence of Emerson and Carlyle.* New York: Columbia University Press, 1964.

Sorin, Gerald. *Abolitionism: A New Perspective.* New York: Praeger, 1972.

Sorisio, Carolyn. *Fleshing Out America: Race, Gender, and the Politics of the Body in American Literature, 1833–1879.* Athens: University of Georgia Press, 2002.

St. Jean, Shawn. "Thoreau's Radical Consistency." *Massachusetts Review* 39 (autumn 1998): 341–57.

Stanton, William. *The Leopard's Spots: Scientific Attitudes toward Race in America 1815–59.* Chicago: University of Chicago Press, 1960.

Stauffer, John. *The Black Hearts of Men: Radical Abolitionists and the Transformation of Race.* Cambridge: Harvard University Press, 2002.

Stavis, Barrie. *John Brown: The Sword and the Word.* South Brunswick, N.J.: A. S. Barnes, 1970.

Stearns, Frank Preston. *The Life and Public Services of George Luther Stearns.* 1907. Reprint, New York: Arno, 1969.

Stevens, Charles Emery. *Anthony Burns: A History.* 1856. Reprint, New York: Negro Universities Press, 1969.

Stevenson, Brenda, ed. *The Journals of Charlotte Forten Grimké.* New York: Oxford University Press, 1988.

Stewart, James Brewer. *Wendell Phillips: Liberty's Hero.* Baton Rouge: Louisiana State University Press, 1986.

Stoehr, Taylor. *Nay-Saying in Concord: Emerson, Alcott, and Thoreau.* Hamden, Conn.: Archon, 1979.

Stone, Edward, ed. *Incident at Harper's Ferry.* Englewood Cliffs, N.J.: Prentice-Hall, 1956.

Stowe, Harriet Beecher. *The Key to Uncle Tom's Cabin.* 1854. Reprint, New York: Arno, 1968.

Strangis, Joel. *Lewis Hayden and the War against Slavery.* North Haven, Conn.: Linnet, 1999.

Stuart, M. *Conscience and the Constitution . . .* Boston: Crocker & Brewster, 1850.

Sundquist, Eric J. "The Literature of Slavery and African American Culture." In *The Cambridge History of American Literature.* Vol. 2: *1820–1865.* Ed. Sacvan Bercovitch and Cyrus R. K. Patell. Cambridge: Cambridge University Press, 1995. 239–328.

Sweet, John. "The Liberal Dilemma and the Demise of the Town Church: Ezra Ripley's Pastorate in Concord, 1778–1841." *Proceedings of the Massachusetts Historical Society* 104 (1992): 73–109.

Taney, Roger B. "Opinion of the Court in Dred Scott, Plaintiff in Error, v. John F. A. Sandford." In *A House Divided: The Antebellum Slavery Debates in America, 1776–1865.* Ed. Mason I. Lowance, Jr. Princeton: Princeton University Press, 2003. 459–62.

Tate, Gayle T. *Unknown Tongues: Black Women's Political Activism in the Antebellum Era, 1830–1860.* East Lansing: Michigan State University Press, 2003.

Tauber, Alfred I. *Henry David Thoreau and the Moral Agency of Knowing.* Berkeley: University of California Press, 2001.

Taylor, Bob Pepperman. *America's Bachelor Uncle: Thoreau and the American Polity.* Lawrence: University Press of Kansas, 1996.

Teed, Paul E. "The Politics of Sectional Memory: Theodore Parker and the *Massachusetts Quarterly Review,* 1847–1850." *JER* 21 (summer 2001): 301–29.

Teichgraeber, Richard F., III. *Sublime Thoughts/Penny Wisdom: Situating Emerson and Thoreau in the American Market.* Baltimore: Johns Hopkins University Press, 1995.

Testimonies of Capt. John Brown, at Harper's Ferry, with His Address to the Court. New York: American Anti-Slavery Society, 1860.

Thayer, Eli. *A History of the Kansas Crusade: Its Friends and Its Foes.* New York: Harper & Brothers, 1889.

"Thoreau and the Danish Resistance: An Anonymous Memoir." In *Thoreau in Our Season.* Ed. John H. Hicks. Amherst: University of Massachusetts Press, 1967. 20–21.

Thoreau, Henry David. *Wild Fruits: Thoreau's Rediscovered Last Manuscript.* Ed. Bradley P. Dean. New York: Norton, 2000.

"Thoreau and Horace Greeley." *TSB* 11 (April 1945): 3.

Tiffany, Nina Moore. "Stories of the Fugitive Slaves. III: Sims." *New England Magazine* 8 (June 1890): 385–88.

Tolman, George. *Catalogue of a Portion of the Collection of the Concord Antiquarian Society.* Boston: Thomas P. Todd, 1911.

"Trial of Anthony Burns, 1854." *Proceedings of the Massachusetts Historical Society* 44 (January 1911): 322–34.

Trodd, Zoe, and John Stauffer, eds. *Meteor of the War: The John Brown Story.* Maplecrest, N.Y.: Brandywine, 2004.

Trumbull, Joan. "Concord and the Negro." Bachelor's thesis. Vassar College, 1944.

Urofsky, Melvin I., and Paul Finkelman. *A March of Liberty: A Constitutional History of the United States.* Vol. 1: *From the Founding to 1890.* 2nd ed. New York: Oxford University Press, 2002.

Van Broekhoven, Deborah. " 'Better than a Clay Club': The Organization of Anti-Slavery Fairs, 1835–60." *Slavery and Abolition* 19 (April 1998): 24–45.

Villard, Oswald Garrison. *John Brown 1800–1859: A Biography Fifty Years After.* 1910. Reprint, New York: Knopf, 1943.

Von Frank, Albert J. "Mrs. Brackett's Verdict: Magic and Means in Transcendental Antislavery Work." In *Transient and Permanent: The Transcendentalist Movement and Its Contexts.* Ed. Charles Capper and Conrad Edick Wright. Boston: Massachusetts Historical Society, 1999. 385–407.

——. *The Trials of Anthony Burns: Freedom and Slavery in Emerson's Boston.* Cambridge: Harvard University Press, 1998.

Wagenknecht, Edward. *Henry David Thoreau: What Manner of Man?* Amherst: University of Massachusetts Press, 1981.

Walls, Laura Dassow. *Emerson's Life in Science: The Culture of Truth.* Ithaca: Cornell University Press, 2003.

——. *Seeing New Worlds: Henry David Thoreau and Nineteenth-Century Natural Science.* Madison: University of Wisconsin Press, 1995.

Wang, Xi. "The *Dred Scott* Case." In *Race on Trial: Law and Justice in American History*. Ed. Annette Gordon-Reed. New York: Oxford University Press, 2002. 26–47.

Ward, William Edward. "Charles Lenox Remond: Black Abolitionist, 1838–1873." Ph.D. diss., Clark University, 1977.

Watson, Harry L. *Liberty and Power: The Politics of Jacksonian America*. New York: Hill and Wang, 1990.

Weiss, John. *Life and Correspondence of Theodore Parker*. 2 vols. in 1. 1864. Reprint, New York: Arno, 1969.

Wheeler, Ruth R. *Concord: Climate for Freedom*. Concord, Mass.: Concord Antiquarian Society, 1967.

——. "Thoreau and Capital Punishment." *TSB* 86 (winter 1964): 1.

Wilson, Edmund. *Patriotic Gore: Studies in the Literature of the American Civil War*. 1962. Reprint, Boston: Northeastern University Press, 1984.

Wilson, Leslie. "Slaveholding and Abolition in One Concord Family." *The Concord Journal* (June 27, 2002): 11.

——. "'Taps in the Wall and Thumps in the Table-Drawer.'" *The Concord Journal* (January 4, 2001): 6.

——. "'Treasure in My Own Mind': The Diary of Martha Lawrence Prescott, 1834–1836." *CS* n.s. 11 (2003): 93–152.

——. ed. "A Concord Farmer Looks Back: The Reminiscences of William Henry Hunt." *CS* n.s. 10 (2002): 65–123.

Wiltse, Charles M., and Alan R. Berolzheimer, eds. *The Papers of Daniel Webster*. Vol. 2: *Speeches and Formal Writings: 1834–1852*. Hanover, N.H.: University Press of New England, 1988.

Wiltse, Charles M., and Michael J. Birkner, eds. *The Papers of Daniel Webster*. Vol. 7: *Correspondence: 1850–1852*. Hanover, N.H.: University Press of New England, 1986.

Wineapple, Brenda. *Hawthorne: A Life*. New York: Knopf, 2003.

Woodson, Carter G., ed. *The Mind of the Negro as Reflected in Letters Written during the Crisis 1800–1860*. 1926. Reprint, New York: Russell & Russell, 1969.

"Words of John Brown. From His Account of His Childhood." *Old South Leaflets* no. 84. Vol. 4. Boston: Directors of the Old South Work, 1897. 25–28.

Worley, Sam McGuire. *Emerson, Thoreau, and the Role of the Cultural Critic*. Albany: State University of New York Press, 2001.

Wyatt-Brown, Bertram. "'A Volcano Beneath a Mountain of Snow': John Brown and the Problem of Interpretation." In *His Soul Goes Marching On: Responses to John Brown and the Harpers Ferry Raid*. Ed. Paul Finkelman. Charlottesville: University Press of Virginia, 1995. 10–38.

Yacovone, Donald. *Samuel Joseph May and the Dilemmas of the Liberal Persuasion, 1797–1871*. Philadelphia: Temple University Press, 1991.

Yellin, Jean Fagan. "Hawthorne and the Slavery Question." In *A Historical Guide to Nathaniel Hawthorne*. Ed. Larry J. Reynolds. New York: Oxford University Press, 2001. 135–64.

Yellin, Jean Fagan, and John C. Van Horne, eds. *The Abolitionist Sisterhood: Women's Political Culture in Antebellum America*. Ithaca: Cornell University Press, 1994.

Zaeske, Susan. *Signatures of Citizenship: Petitioning, Antislavery, and Women's Political Identity.* Chapel Hill: University of North Carolina Press, 2003.

Zinn, Howard. Introduction to Henry David Thoreau, *"The Higher Law": Thoreau on Civil Disobedience and Reform.* Princeton: Princeton University Press, 2004. ix–xxx.

Index

The Literature of Scotland

The Middle Ages to the Nineteenth Century

SECOND EDITION

Roderick Watson

First edition published in one volume 1984
Second edition published in two volumes 2007
PALGRAVE MACMILLAN
Houndmills, Basingstoke, Hampshire RG21 6XS and
175 Fifth Avenue, New York, N.Y. 10010
Companies and representatives throughout the world

PALGRAVE MACMILLAN is the global academic imprint of the Palgrave Macmillan division of St. Martin's Press, LLC and of Palgrave Macmillan Ltd. Macmillan® is a registered trademark in the United States, United Kingdom and other countries. Palgrave is a registered trademark in the European Union and other countries.

ISBN-13: 978-0-333-66664-7
ISBN-10: 0-333-66664-X

This book is printed on paper suitable for recycling and made from fully managed and sustained forest sources.

A catalogue record for this book is available from the British Library.

A catalog record for this book is available from the Library of Congress.

10 9 8 7 6 5 4 3 2 1
16 15 14 13 12 11 10 09 08 07

Printed and bound in CPD (Wales) Ltd, Ebbw Vale.

In memory of my mother and father

Contents

Preface

What is 'Scottish literature'? Is it writing *about* Scotland by anybody, or writing from authors currently living *in* Scotland, or is it literary production about anything by people born in Scotland or of Scottish descent living anywhere?

The critical and theoretical exploration of what we have understood 'Scotland' and 'Scottish identity' to mean, now and in the past, is the topic for a study in itself, but I have called this book *The Literature of Scotland*, rather than use the phrase 'Scottish Literature', in order to signal something of how I have chosen to understand these issues. The 'literature of Scotland' is intended to echo 'the matter of Scotland' in so far as the two volumes which constitute this study seek to trace the various versions of Scotland and engagements with Scotland that Scottish writers have undertaken over more than 700 years, during some of which time, of course, the very concept of 'Scotland' was either a new idea or under discussion in a debate that has continued until the present day.

National identity is a cultural and a political construction and 'the matter of Scotland' (after the Arthurian legends of 'the Matter of Britain') may well recall Barbour, or Blind Harry, or those medieval historians who constructed their own grandiose national genealogies to insist on Scotland's sovereign difference from whatever territories lay to the south. So it is no surprise that linguistic difference and literary production should have played key roles in this arena from the very start. Nor have such productions been slow to achieve cultural and then socio-political and historical impact, for the *representations* of reality (whatever their actual truth) quickly become a material factor in their own right. So the prejudices and passions of our poets and novelists in the supreme fiction of literature have contributed greatly to 'the matter of Scotland'.

There have been truly remarkable developments in the critical examination of Scottish literature and culture and in the number of specialist studies available since this book first appeared in 1984 in one volume. There has been an equally remarkable and enormously exciting growth in creative output and achievement in the field of contemporary Scottish writing. In this revised and expanded two-volume study, as with the first edition of *The Literature of Scotland*, the aim is to offer students and the general reader an introductory overview of the whole field of Scottish literature along with something of the biographical and historical background to the works at issue and the circumstances under which they arose.

This first volume of the new edition covers medieval to Victorian times and notable periods of great creative activity. The second volume recognises that the twentieth century has witnessed the richest and most diverse literary production in Scotland's long history. In the light of this wealth, and a growing international critical interest in Scottish studies, we have allocated an entire second volume to the writing and writers of the modern period. The separation is an artificial one, of course, for we can trace the immediately 'modern' back to at least the nineteenth century and have only to reflect, for example, on the continuing impact of James Hogg's *Justified Sinner* (1824) on contemporary authors to prove the point. Nevertheless, it seems appropriate – and hopefully both timely and useful – to allow more space for a critical overview of current Scottish literature in order to put contemporary writing into a wider and more detailed set of contexts and connections.

We know where we are by knowing where we came from, and it is hoped that readers will understand the present in the light of the past, and the past in the light of the present, by way of this narrative and chronological approach across two volumes, each of which stands alone as a text but should be best and most fully understood in the light of the other.

Of course no author's life can ever fully explain a work, and literary texts are inexhaustible in ways that transcend context and biography. But then again, no literary work can stand entirely apart from the conditions of its production and the political, philosophical, economic and cultural forces of its time. What were the literary conventions of the day? Does a writer's work accept or reject them, and how should we place it against the other arts of the period at home and abroad? Where does an author stand in relation to fellow authors, or the politics and cultural mores of the time? What are the circumstances that may or may not have shaped their imagination? How does their work fit, or not fit, the necessarily changing currents of Scottish literature? Which books have stayed the course in our collective memory, and which have disappeared, and why?

No true analysis or understanding can take place without this initial locating process, and it is hoped that these volumes with their timelines will provide just such a basic contextual grounding in advance of more specialised studies. Having said that, I have also sought to signal the links and affinities between creative artists by grouping writers and topics together in ways that reflect their generic, thematic and not just their chronological connections, while still staying close to the developing story decade by decade. Then again, I hope to offer descriptive, but also specifically critical and analytical responses to key works from key writers in each century, with an indication of the various critical debates that have arisen around those texts from one century, or even one decade, to the next.

While the book deals with a place called 'Scotland', we must not lose sight of the fact that the geographical boundaries of this small country have sustained many different histories and many authors writing in several different languages. And yet however various these writers have undoubtedly been, part of what this book will end up describing is their own engagement with this fascinating country and a series of understandings, growing and also changing, of what 'Scotland' might mean to them. So part of what this book traces is the slow growth of a Scottish canon, as writers and critics have perceived it over the ages. Nor can I pretend to stand outside my own times – or even my own preferences – in many of the critical assessments made in the following pages.

Beyond the tricky questions of canon formation, historical reception and current critical evaluation, a particular point of emphasis and acknowledgement should be declared here. I have been determined that literature in Gaelic – so often neglected in past literary histories – should take an uncontested place in the unfolding of Scotland's many different cultural expressions across the centuries. The Gaidhealtachd has been influential at every turn in Scotland's story and in how we have come to see ourselves. More detailed research into Gaelic literature and culture – and its many points of contact with and divergence from Irish, European, Classical and Lowland culture – is finally beginning in Scottish Studies today. Much work still remains to be done, but I owe a special debt to the translators who have made this work available to a much wider audience. Since many older translations of Gaelic poems adopted a rather tired poetic diction, I have used the most contemporary available English versions whenever possible. In this respect my thanks go to translations made by the late Iain Crichton Smith and the late Ian Grimble, and especially to Professor Derick Thomson and his book *An Introduction to Gaelic Poetry* (Gollancz, 1974). The exigencies of space argue against dual text quotation in a

study such as this, so for a fuller access to the originals readers are directed to my anthology *The Poetry of Scotland* (Edinburgh University Press, 1995); or more specifically to the following anthologies: Colm O Baoill's anthology of seventeenth-century Gaelic poems *The Harp's Cry/Gàir nan Clàrsach* (Birlinn, 1994); Derick Thomson's *Gaelic Poetry in the Eighteenth Century* (Association of Scottish Literary Studies, 1993); Donald Meek's edition of nineteenth-century Scottish Gaelic poetry, *The Wiles of the World/Caran An T-Saoghail* (Barbour Books, 2003); or Ronald Black's collection of twentieth-century Scottish Gaelic verse *An Tuil* (Polygon, 1999).

The four literary languages of Scotland – Gaelic, Latin, Scots and English – speak for a strongly polyphonic heritage whose implications are still with us, and indeed growing, as Scotland's citizens become more ethnically and culturally diverse. It is most certainly not this study's intention to reduce these many different voices to a single narrative of a single national identity. On the contrary, the plurality of Scottish culture – and indeed of all cultures – has been widely recognised in scholarly and theoretical circles in modern times, and has at last become a part of popular awareness. At the same time, I have sought to bring the many sides of Scotland's complex story together, while also leaving room for readers to draw their own conclusions. With this in mind I hope that this account of 'the literature of Scotland' will be found to be reliably informative and critically stimulating, as well as coherent, readable and entertaining.

Roderick Watson

Acknowledgements

Thanks are due to the University of Stirling and the National Library of Scotland for access to their holdings. It has been my preference to use modern translations of older Gaelic poems whenever possible, and in this respect I owe a special debt of appreciation to Ronald Black, Ian Grimble, Donald MacAulay, Donald Meek, William Neill, Iain Crichton Smith, and especially Derick Thomson for their translations of Gaelic poetry into English, some of which I specifically requested. The pioneer work of the Scottish Gaelic Text Society must also be acknowledged here, along with editors such as William Matheson, J. C. Watson, George Calder, Angus Macleod et al. The work of the Scottish Text Society has been equally invaluable. In particular, the author and publishers wish to thank Birlinn/Polygon for Ronald Black (ed.), *An Tuil* and Donald Meek (ed.), *The Wiles of the World/Caran An T-Saoghail*, who have kindly given permission for the use of translation material in copyright.

Every effort has been made to trace the copyright holders but if any have been inadvertently overlooked the publishers will be pleased to make the necessary arrangement at the first opportunity.

I must conclude by acknowledging colleagues, friends, students and the many scholars in Scottish history and literature whose researches continue to illuminate and to realign our understanding of Scotland's cultural history, never more so than in the last twenty years, which have seen a wealth of critical, historical and biographical analysis in the matter of Scotland and much first-rate theoretical and literary-critical analysis. Thanks are also due to the late Derry Jeffares who first brought this project to me; to the University of Stirling for its generous sabbatical provision; to all at Palgrave Macmillan for their enthusiasm and patience; to my wife Celia for her unfailing support.

Scotland

Scotland

Introduction:
renewals, revivals and revisions

How we see literature, or a cultural tradition, or even our own identity, depends upon an act of perception and hence of selection on our part. Different periods will make different selections from the available evidence according to the spirit of the times. Indeed, the music, literature and arts of the past are truly alive only because our understanding of them has to change in this way from generation to generation, or even during the course of a single life. Literary and cultural history is especially fluid, because persuasive theories about a nation's history and identity begin to influence how people think of themselves and hence, in turn, how writers express themselves, to be analysed by changing generations of literary critics. So goes the feedback loop. And contentious Scotland has certainly expended enough effort over the centuries defending and defining a sense of itself to itself, not least in the face of political or cultural pressures from a larger and more powerful neighbour to the south.

In the long narrative of Scotland there seem to have been three literary periods of outstandingly rich achievement. These would be the time of the 'makars', those great poets of the fifteenth century; the years from the eighteenth to the mid-nineteenth century, which saw the Enlightenment, a vernacular revival and a major engagement with Scottish history and identity; and the 'modern Scottish literary renaissance' and later productions of the twentieth century. These are not the only periods or points of interest, of course, but they are three particularly defining moments in how Scotland has come to be seen by others and to understand itself. This volume covers the first two periods while volume II is concerned with the last.

The process started at least as long ago as the wars of independence in the early fourteenth century and Barbour's *Bruce*, like Blind Harry's *Wallace* later, did much to define the 'idea' of Scotland and to establish an independent-minded and egalitarian outlook as a characteristic part of what was to be forged (the term is used advisedly) and reforged in later centuries as a sense of cultural and political commonality. The early fruits of this identification, together with close links to France and Europe and the flowering of the Scots language, came to full season in the poetry of Henryson, Dunbar, Douglas and Lindsay. Yet we should not forget that Henryson and Douglas in their own period, for example, would acknowledge a debt to and a sense of identification with Chaucer, their fellow poet from England and 'of makaris flour' as Dunbar put it.

It has often been supposed that such flowering was lost or damaged by the seventeenth century, and indeed later authors such as Edwin Muir and George Mackay Brown found nothing but desolation in the Reformation and blamed all the spiritual ills of early modern Scotland on Knox and Melville, pointing to the more extreme prohibitions on the staging of plays, and claiming that the reformers set out 'to crush the poet with an iron text'. This is to view the Reformation through the lens of a later agenda, and while the bloody excesses of the time can only be deplored, this account signally fails to recognise the extraordinarily widespread charge of intellectual energy and democratic debate that marked the period, even if much of that energy went into sermons, pamphlets and texts of instruction, rather than lyric verse. Too many popular histories tend to dismiss the importance of the Reformation in Scotland, just as the Puritan revolution and the tradition of dissent in the south has so often been misrepresented or marginalised in the construction of Royalist or conservative national narratives about England.

The next most productive and self confident period in Scottish cultural history was heralded by the 'Scottish Enlightenment' of the eighteenth century and the parallel literary productions of Ramsay, Fergusson and Burns. Contrary to the opinion of earlier historians who ascribed this flowering to the parliamentary union with England, the philosophical and scientific advances of the Enlightenment came from native stock, and should in fact be seen as a development of the best of the Reformation, for the Scots Presbyterian intellectual tradition had always valued instruction and debate and hence the place of philosophy, theory and analysis at the heart of the three stern graces of so much Scottish culture – education, law and religion. The Enlightenment produced figures of international standing such as David Hume and Adam Smith, and a wealth of talent in engineering and the physical sciences, very often among men who rose from humble backgrounds or merchant families like James Watt and Joseph Black. Clearly Scotland was flourishing and yet, paradoxically, an anxiety about national identity arose again, conjured up by the Union of 1707, the economic strength of England and the tendency of educated Scots to look to the metropolitan assumptions and opportunities of London.

In the face of such social change, in the face of political union and yet acute cultural difference, Scottish writers underwent a complex reaction that produced, in almost equal amounts, antiquarian interest, historical reflection, encyclopaedic and historiographical ambition, and the creatively dynamic validation of difference. In literary terms this resulted in a revival of writing in Scots, a new vernacular strength in Gaelic, the invention of the historical novel and then, in the following century, the psychological exploration of the divided self. The voice of the common people had been heard and in part redefined by the individual genius of Fergusson, Burns, Rob Donn and Duncan Bàn Macintyre. Nor was the matter of Scotland and Scottish identity forgotten, as Scott, Hogg, Galt and Stevenson made Scottish history and Scottish character the theatre for so many of their novels. Yet the vernacular mode and the pursuit of 'Scottishness' and Scottish 'character' eventually came to the point of exhaustion and decay. With industrialisation and the growth of cities, not to mention the spread of Scottish emigrants throughout the world, there was a huge demand for backward-looking and piously sentimental versions of the homeland leading to the growth and empire-wide success of 'kailyard' writing by the end of the century. The wit of Fergusson, the radical vision of Burns and the challenge and rigour of thinkers like Carlyle had little part to play in such developments. And yet the rise of Liberal and then Labour politics, the Home Rule question in Ireland and the grim aftermath of the First World War were beginning to stir a different sense of what Scotland was and what its future might be. Change was in the air.

So a 'Scottish Renaissance' happened again in the 1920s, as a political and critical effort to re-establish (or reinvent) the identity of a country that too many politicians, university professors and popular newspapers were coming to regard as merely 'North Britain'. And this period, which is discussed in depth in volume II, also marks the beginning of a wider recognition that global economic forces and the mass media were eroding everything that was most distinctive and hence of most value in *all* minority cultures in the modern world. The literary renaissance of the twentieth-century began with Scots, but soon came to recognise that the country's Gaelic inheritance was even more seriously in decline than the Scots one – much neglected and undervalued, indeed, by the Lowland Scots themselves. An understanding of hegemonic cultural forces and a sense of common purpose began to dawn. (MacDiarmid's essay from 1931, 'English Ascendancy in British

Literature', is a key early document in what would now be understood as postcolonial literary theory.)

So it was that many of the writers of the early twentieth-century renaissance aimed to reimagine a Scotland that could contribute something unique and valuable to the world at large. This agenda gave rise to works that sought to combine the personal with the national and indeed the global, as with MacDiarmid's emphasis on the rights of small nations and 'minority' languages combined with a universalising vision of political and scientific materialism; or the myth-building symbolisms of Neil Gunn, Edwin Muir and George Mackay Brown; or the identification that Lewis Grassic Gibbon, Sorley MacLean and George Campbell Hay made between the fate of their own people and that of oppressed cultures and individuals throughout the world.

The socio-political focus of Alasdair Gray and James Kelman can be seen to belong to the same tradition (although Kelman has no truck with questions of Scottish national identity as such) but as a general rule the Scottish writers of the second half of the century have been less persuaded of such system-building ambitions. In their place have come the exploration of personal identity and works of psychological interrogation related to issues of class, race, sexuality and gender at the hands of fine contemporary writers such as Liz Lochhead, Janice Galloway, A. L. Kennedy, Jackie Kay and Ali Smith. It is no accident that such a shift of focus should have come from women writers, inspired or irritated by those founding fathers, but in either case finally free of their shadow.

Of course the modern renaissance would have been stillborn without the talents of its remarkable writers, but scholars and academics have played a small part as well. To give a brief account of their production is to trace how Scotland's history and cultural identity has been subject to major revaluation in our times, and also to recognise the expansion of critical interest and scholarly study that has been particularly marked in the last twenty years of the twentieth century.

T. F. Henderson showed the way with his *Scottish Vernacular Literature* (1898), just as the Revd Nigel Macneill had dealt with Gaelic in *The Literature of the Highlanders* (1892) followed by the Revd Magnus Maclean with *The Literature of the Highlands* in 1903, updated in the 1920s. J. H. Millar ignored Gaelic but his exhaustive *Literary History of Scotland* (1903) is still a valuable (and acerbic) study. More recently in 1977 and again in 1992, Maurice Lindsay's *History of Scottish Literature* has taken a similarly inclusive approach (but still without Gaelic) from a modern point of view. By comparison with Millar's encyclopaedic book, Gregory Smith's *Scottish Literature:*

Character and Influence (1919) was much briefer but much more influential, too. Smith tried to define what might be called a national psychology, or at least national habits of expression, as manifested in Scottish literature over the centuries. Hugh MacDiarmid was much impressed and promptly incorporated some of these ideas into his own poetry to use as propaganda against the English cultural establishment. Following Gregory Smith (and similarly prone to essentialism) he proposed that the Scottish sensibility was characteristically extreme, containing a combination of opposite tendencies: a 'Caledonian anti-syzygy' that manifests itself in a delight in domestic realism and the accumulation of many small details on the one hand, and a love of excess and wild flights of fancy on the other. These were 'the polar twins of the Scottish muse' and MacDiarmid welcomed them as allies against the Victorian conception of the Scotsman as a dull, canny, parsi-monious peasant. By 1936, however, Edwin Muir's *Scott and Scotland* was suggesting that the 'Caledonian antisyzygy' was exactly what was *wrong* with the national psyche, for it would swing frantically from one extreme to the other without ever reaching rest or resolution. For better or for worse, Smith's new diagnosis of 'Scottishness' had entered the critical vocabulary and the creative resources of the nation.

The natural inheritor of Gregory Smith's thesis was Kurt Wittig, a German scholar whose work *The Scottish Tradition in Literature* (1958) pursued still further what he took to be the most unique and persistent features to be found in writing from Scotland. Twentieth-century accounts of the Scottish tradition have owed much to this and two further books, both from 1961. George Elder Davie's *The Democratic Intellect* stressed the philosophical and egalitarian ideals of traditional Scottish education, and David Craig's *Scottish Literature and the Scottish People, 1680–1830* makes a vigorous materialist analysis of the social conditions and assumptions that influenced Scottish writers and readers during a crucial period of their history. David Daiches also explored the special contradictions of eighteenth-century Scotland in his seminal study *The Paradox of Scottish Culture* (1964). Ten years later, on the Gaelic front, Derick Thomson offered his invaluable *Introduction to Gaelic Poetry* (1974).

In the years since *The Literature of Scotland* first appeared in 1984, there has been an explosion of writing on Scottish literary history. Between 1987 and 1988 Aberdeen University Press produced its four-volume *History of Scottish Literature* under the general editorship of Cairns Craig. With eighty essays from distinguished scholars and critics, this produced excellent accounts of specific authors. Its new insights into various areas of study and its specified further reading make it an indispensable reference, although the collected essay method can also leave historical and cultural lacunae. (As I write, another such scholarly project is forthcoming from Edinburgh University Press.)

More recent accounts of Scottish literary and cultural history have also followed this format, most notably in Paul Scott's editing of *Scotland: A Concise Cultural History* (Mainstream, 1993) with illuminating essays on literature, art, music, philosophy, sport, cinema, medicine, law, mathematics, education, etc. Christopher Whyte's editing of the essays in *Gendering the Nation* (Edinburgh University Press, 1995) made a crucial intervention in the debate about national identity from the point of view of the politics of gender, while *A History of Scottish Women's Writing*, edited by Douglas Gifford and Dorothy McMillan (Edinburgh University Press, 1997), has done a very great deal to reclaim cultural and critical territory for many writers whose contributions have been undervalued or just neglected in previous studies. In similar fashion, territory was reclaimed for Scottish Drama in the essays included in *A History of Scottish Theatre* (Polygon, 1998) edited by Bill Findlay, and in *Scottish Theatre since the Seventies*, edited by Randall Stevenson and Gavin Wallace (Edinburgh University Press, 1996). (The same editors also produced *The Scottish Novel since the Seventies* in 1993.) Marshall Walker's *Scottish Literature since 1707* (Longman, 1996), takes a more singular view, governed by a set of critical propositions and themes that allow him to analyse and compare the work of individual authors in their period. Finally, there is *Scottish Literature in English and Scots*, edited by Douglas Gifford, Sarah Dunnigan and Alan MacGillivray (Edinburgh, 2002). This mammoth volume draws on the collective teaching skills of the department of Scottish Literature at Glasgow University to operate as a combination literary history, encyclopaedia and literary companion with a wealth of suggested further reading.

Recent anthologies such as Catherine Kerrigan's *Scottish Women Poets* (Edinburgh University Press, 1991), Dorothy McMillan's *Modern Scottish Women Poets* (Canongate, 2003), and my own *The Poetry of Scotland: Gaelic, Scots, English, 1380–1980* (Edinburgh University Press, 1995) have helped to develop our understanding of the literary canon. Perhaps the most striking of these is Thomas Clancy's *The Triumph Tree: Scotland's Earliest Poetry AD 530–1350* (Canongate, 1998), which speaks for a period rarely anthologised in such terms (not least because the concept of 'Scotland' had yet to be born) in the languages of Latin, Welsh, Gaelic, Old English and Norse. In the introduction to his anthology of *Early Scottish Literature 1375–1707* (Mercat Press, 1997), R. D. S. Jack makes a passionate plea for a continuity in Scottish literary history, most especially in the Renaissance period via the rules of rhetoric and the poetic professionalism of verse production which prevailed from late medieval times to the seventeenth century. His interest in Scottish Literature's polymath origins and its early propensity for multi-vocal expression is entirely in keeping with the contemporary emphasis on these factors in Scottish literary histories from 1707 to the present day. Finally, the foundation of the Canongate Classics series in 1987, with support from the Scottish Arts Council, facilitated the republication and dissemination of over a hundred titles for both students and the general reader, in a conscious strategy to make available, to rethink, and even to change the Scottish literary canon.

Recent studies and essays have understood canonicity and the constructed nature of literary history much more clearly than earlier generations, and they have theorised the pressures of linguistic and cultural hegemony and the counter-narratives of national identity. Among the most influential of these is Robert Crawford's *Devolving English Literature* (Clarendon Press, 1992), which argues that Scotland has played a key part in the development of literary study in Britain, and also sees the Scottish experience in the wider perspective of American, Australian, Irish and Caribbean writing. Cairns Craig's *Out of History* (1996) and especially his study of *The Modern Scottish Novel: Narrative and the National Imagination* (Edinburgh University Press, 1999) make a related case for the fictional techniques and innovations that have been born out of Scottish writers' awareness of the tensions between their Calvinist inheritance and the dominance of English-language culture. For my own part, I have often argued for the modern Scottish literary renaissance as only one of many such devolutionary movements across the field of 'literatures in English' as opposed to the now contested hegemony of 'English Literature'. And I have argued, too, for the role played by Scottish literature, especially in its texts in Gaelic and its many varieties of Scots, as a significantly energetic, plural and polyphonic counterpole to the monological discourses of linguistic imperialism and 'high' culture.

In the last analysis, however, the present study is not intended to present a selective thesis in the vein of Wittig, Davie, Craig, Daiches, Craig or Crawford; nor can it quite lay claim to the detail of the four-volume *History of Scottish Literature*, or the study of *Scottish Women's Writing* edited by Gifford and McMillan. But there is still a need, as far as the student and the general reader is concerned, for a path somewhere between these two approaches – a critical and contextualised account of the lives, times and major works of Scotland's writers. The brief and selective historical summaries at the start of each chapter have been chosen to reflect those aspects of Scottish history that feature most frequently, or contentiously, in Scottish literature. Whenever appropriate, I have tried to recognise the relevance of critical concepts such as the 'democratic intellect', the 'vernacular revival' or the 'Caledonian antisyzygy' without proposing these as necessary or exclusive analytical tools. Having said this, however, it seems to me that there are at least two aspects of Scottish culture that have only occasionally received a proper recognition – although there are signs that this is changing. First, I would point once again to the co-presence of the Gaelic tradition and the mutual interactions between Highland and Lowland society and their conceptions and misconceptions of each other. And secondly, I believe that the best of what might be called the Presbyterian intellectual inheritance in Scotland has been undeservedly obscured or denied, because the popular imagination has been so easily distracted (and understandably repelled) by the worst excesses of Calvinism. Thus many Scots will tell enquiring visitors that the Reformation was the worst thing to happen in Scotland and that John Knox cast a permanent shadow on the Scottish face. This is a misleading myth not least because, for better or worse, it allows Scots to hide from the truth about themselves, and is just as sentimental in the end as that other mythical Scotland where the wicked English are perpetually chasing Flora MacDonald and Bonnie Prince Charlie across the heather.

Yet literature and history make lively and unscholarly bedfellows. And some of Scotland's most enduring images and myths (and misconceptions too) have been created by her greatest writers – which brings us back again to the consideration of how an author chooses their subject, why they choose to see it in a certain light and, from such works multiply reflected, how *we* choose to see ourselves.

1

The beginnings of Scotland: two cultures

SCOTLAND is a small place. Her population is no more than that of Greater London and she has been part of the United Kingdom for longer than the United States has been a nation. But Scotland is a distinctively different country, with a culture, a church, a tradition in education and a legal system of her own. Few visitors can have left the place without being told this and having met a prickly sense of difference expressed by the Scottish people. The national plant is a thistle, after all, whose motto, *Nemo me impune lacessit*, is translated as 'No one touches me with impunity', or, more vigorously, 'Wha daur meddle wi me?' The self-conscious assertion in these words reminds us that, as a small and often embattled country, Scotland has been much exercised over the centuries to protect a sense of identity, and this sense has regularly been stimulated or reflected or redefined and argued about in her literature. The thistle is a harsh talisman, and if it sometimes symbolises the libertarian Scottish ideal (as it does for the modern poet Hugh MacDiarmid), it can also be made to look like a skeleton in an endless history of internal dispute and failure. MacDiarmid is not the first Scottish writer to have felt himself impaled on the national plant.

Many elements go to influence the history and the culture of a people; in Scotland perhaps the single most significant factor has been the geography of the land itself. Scotland is divided by major mountain chains and chopped into odd elbow-shapes by an irregular coastline. Thus isolated areas such as Moray to the north of the Grampians, or Fife between the rivers Tay and Forth, or Dumfries and Galloway between Ayr and the Solway Firth, not to mention the Western Isles, were almost independent little kingdoms of their own for many centuries. The mountains divide the country's resources even more radically. The Lowlands comprise the more open and fertile lands, which follow the southern coasts up to the central belt (where most of the mineral deposits also lie); then they take in Edinburgh, Glasgow, Stirling, Perth and Dundee, and follow the east coast up to Aberdeen and round to the Moray Firth. By comparison the centre of the country is wild and bleak, dominated by the Grampian mountains and the North and West Highlands, which look out to even more remote islands and a rugged western coastline. Many parts of the Highlands were accessible only by sea or by difficult trails until as late as the eighteenth century, when a few strategic military roads were driven into the fastness after the Jacobite rebellions.

Scottish cultural history is equally divided because it has a native literary tradition in three languages – Gaelic, Scots and English – and there are a number of modern writers who still use at least two of these tongues to express themselves. Scots and English are cognate languages that belong to the dominant Lowland civilisation, which was agricultural, mercantile, urban, materialistic, literate and eventually industrial. Gaelic, on the other hand, belongs to an older and more warlike tradition of Highland clans, chiefs, boatmen, small crofters, herdsmen and hunters. These clans held strong family and regional loyalties and prided themselves on who they were, rather than on what they owned, and theirs was a sophisticated oral culture whose songs and poems and tunes were passed on from generation to generation usually without being written down. Not surprisingly, given such widely different values, these two cultures were often in conflict. But the densely populated Lowlands have encroached until Gaelic, once heard throughout the country, is now a minority language whose native-born speakers are largely confined to the north-west, the Western Isles and the Hebrides. The 2001 census shows that native speakers have declined to 58,600 (from 66,000 in 1991) even as more people in the towns are learning to understand something of the language. If a total of over 92,000 people have some basic language ability in Gaelic in 2001, this is still just under 2% of Scotland's population. Gaelic speaking in Scotland has declined by 75% since the first census thought to ask about the language in 1881. Yet everything that the casual visitor most usually associates with Scotland – kilts, bagpipes, mountains and clansmen – stems from this Gaelic minority, even if it is usually promoted by Lowland businessmen. This is not the only paradox that Scotland has to offer and, like the others, it springs directly from the nation's various and changing origins. So, although this literary history will not formally begin until the later fourteenth century, the roots of a Scottish identity take us back much further, at least as far as the Celts and the mysterious Picts.

The Celts

The Celts belonged to a major 'barbarian' culture, the oldest in Europe next to Latin and Greek, whose greatest sphere of influence by the fifth and fourth centuries BC included north-west Germany, France, northern Italy and the Spanish peninsula. Loosely linked by language, culture and custom, these tribes spread from the Danube, and reached their most westerly point in Ireland, Wales and Scotland. The Celtic languages belong to the Indo-European family and are commonly subdivided into two branches: the Goedelic or 'Q'-Celts, such as the Irish and Scottish Gaels, who retained the Indo-European 'qu' (later changed to 'c'); and the Brythonic or 'P'-Celts, such as the Welsh, the Cornish and the Bretons, whose language changes 'qu' to 'p'. Herodotus and the classical historians knew the *Keltoi* as tall warriors, fair-skinned, blue-eyed and moustached, who dressed in breeches, tunics and cloaks, wearing gold torcs and armlets with their hair stiffened and swept back like a horse's mane. They grew cereal crops, kept cattle and horses and valued hospitality, music, poetry, and feasts with plenty of fermented liquor to drink. Above all else they took pride in personal courage on the battlefield, where they favoured individual combats before the general mêlée and fought with spears, iron cutting-swords and light chariots. Indeed their skill with metalwork and metal weapons was a factor in the spread of their influence. Celtic society was patriarchal, based on tradition and status within the tribe as well as loyalty to the family and its elaborate ties of kinship. All in all, these warrior values are strikingly similar to the ancient heroic mores of Homer's Greece. Songs and epics were composed and recited by privileged tribal bards; a Druid caste carried out the ceremonies of their ritual year; and Celtic artists and craftsmen excelled in fine metalwork and the elaborate decoration of bowls, jewellery, weapons and chariots. Celtic ornamentation is at once organic and abstract, with complex coils of strapwork that often terminate in stylised animal or human heads with fierce or comic little faces. This art is most familiar to us today in its much later Christian manifestation – in the Celtic crosses of Ireland and Scotland, or in the elaborate illuminations on the pages of the Book of Kells or the Lindisfarne Gospels. The Celtic heritage was a strong one, and its influence can still be found in the living language, arts and social structures of Wales, Ireland and north-west Scotland. It lasted longest and changed least in these, the most isolated and far-flung outposts, because on the European mainland Celtic tribal culture eventually succumbed to the Roman Empire and evolved in different directions. Celtic place names in England testify to the once wider spread of Celtic culture.

The Picts

In almost 400 years of settlement in Britain the Romans rarely penetrated north of the Antonine Wall, which ran from the Clyde to the Forth, nor did they establish their influence in Ireland. Eumenius, a Roman writer of the late third century, referred to the tribes in the North as *Picti*, 'painted men', and in fact this was probably a common term for them among Roman soldiers. We know very little about these 'Picts'. The Gaels of Ireland called them *Priteni*, 'people of the designs', which may refer to their liking for body-paint or tattoos, and they were most probably descended from a native Bronze Age people who intermarried with later P-Celtic arrivals. Their original tongue may have been non-Indo-European, for some of their inscriptions are in a language unknown to us. Furthermore, this society of tribes and minor kingships seems to have been matrilineal, with precedence given to males descended through the female line, and this, too, may derive from an indigenous Bronze Age population. The Picts and their precursors left vitrified forts (where the stones are fused as if by fire) and distinctive hollow, tower-like brochs all over Scotland, especially in Caithness and the islands. Their skilfully carved symbol stones – many of them in the north-east – testify to their love of animal designs and Celtic-style elaboration. We know little more about the Picts, except that their customs and something of their identity lasted until the ninth century, when they seem to have been submerged under pressure from the Norse in the north and the Irish Gaels in the west.

The Gaels

The Gaels arrived from Ireland in the fifth century and established a kingdom of their own, called Dalriada, in Argyllshire and the south-west of Scotland. These Q-Celts – called *Scoti* by the Romans – are the ancestors of the Gaelic-speaking Highland Scots. Christianity also crossed the water from Ireland, and Bede's history tells how St Ninian first showed the way and then how St Columba and his successors brought the Church to Iona in the sixth century and went on to convert more and more of the Picts and the Scoti. These early men of

God were distinguished by their humble lives and by how humanely they accommodated Celtic mores and Celtic art to their Christian purpose. Works in praise of St Columba (*Colum Cille*) are among the very earliest Gaelic poems that survive. Dallán Forgaill in the late sixth century, for example, emphasises the scholarship, the nobility and the courage of Columba as a 'mighty warrior' of God, in a technically complex poem along lines not so very different from bardic praise of a chieftain. (Columba was descended from kings, after all, despite his peaceful name, which means 'dove'.) After the saint's death, Iona became a place of pilgrimage and it is said that forty-eight Scottish, eight Norwegian and four Irish kings are buried there – evidence of a cultural and political mobility which we would now call an international outlook. In the early twentieth century the cathedral building on Iona was restored and the Iona Community, founded by Revd George MacLeod (1895–1991) became a centre for interdenominational worship. The post-Reformation Protestant Church of Scotland has sought to associate itself with these humble beginnings on Iona, as a way of constructing its own ancient lineage, without seeming to depend on Rome.

Dalriada was not the only other kingdom within the Pictish sphere in the fifth and sixth centuries, for the Welsh-speaking Britons ruled Strathclyde, and Anglo-Saxon Angles from Northumbria held the south-east of Scotland, penetrating at one time as far as the Forth estuary. The epic Welsh (P-Celtic) battle-poem the *Gododdin* tells of a British raid out of Din Eidyn (Edinburgh) against the Angles, whom they fought near Catterick in Yorkshire about the year 600. But the Britons, like the Picts, gradually gave way to a Gaelic culture until the pattern of modern Scotland was finally set between the ascendant Gaels and the Old English-speaking Lowlanders from Northumbria – a minority whose time was yet to come. The Pictish kingdom was eroded by intermarriage with the Irish Gaels and still further in the eighth century when Norsemen came to colonise Orkney and Shetland and settled in the Western Isles and the north and west of Scotland.

The supremacy of Gaelic was finally assured in the ninth century when King Kenneth MacAlpin presented a legitimate claim to the Pictish throne and established himself as ruler of both Dalriada and Pictland, a kingdom later to be called Alba. The MacAlpin dynasty lasted almost 200 years, and when Malcolm II died in 1034 his country was called, for the first time, Scotia. There were struggles over the crown of Scotia, not least because MacAlpin's line had tried to favour direct succession instead of the Gaelic tradition of descent through brothers and uncles, or the Pictish preference for a matrilineal inheritance. Shakespeare's Macbeth (much maligned by the bard) was one of these claimants and he ruled for seventeen years before the rise of Malcolm III – Malcolm Canmore – established a dynasty that lasted for another two centuries.

A Scottish nation

The new kingdom of Scotland was forged between the presence of English Norman power to the south and the Norse occupation of the north and the Western Isles. Under the Canmores the monarchy began to follow Anglo-Norman feudal customs, for Malcolm's second wife came from the English royal line, who spoke Norman French. There were bloody wrangles over the disputed south-eastern parts of Scotland and northern England, and internal disputes, too, in the clash between Norman and Celtic mores. Still, the Norman influence gained strength as intermarriage and periods of peaceful trade consolidated the rule of King David I. Edinburgh was established as the seat of royal power; Norman forts, abbeys and monasteries were built throughout the kingdom and the Church became an increasingly feudal adjunct to the state. But Gaelic Scotland did not succumb easily, and the intransigently Celtic chiefs of the north-west reclaimed their territory from the Norsemen and established themselves as virtually autonomous Lords of the Isles. The Anglo-Norman Lothian influence continued to rise, however, and 'Inglis', the language at court, gradually prevailed over native Gaelic and spread through the Lowlands and up the east coast, taking the most fertile land and the most trade-worthy settlements into its sphere. Gaelic, the tongue of the original Scoti, was now called 'Scottis', or 'Ersche' (Irish). The line between Highland and Lowland Scotland was establishing itself slowly but surely, although Gaelic did survive in remoter parts of Galloway into the seventeenth century and in Perthshire and the north-east until modern times.

The reign of Alexander III in the second half of the thirteenth century was a period of exceptional peace, justice and prosperity in early Scotland, but this 'golden age' ended with his death. The succession was not obvious and there followed a protracted struggle between many contenders, not least the king's infant granddaughter, known as the Maid of Norway. Also in the running were two Border lords, John Balliol and Bruce of Annandale, and Edward I of England, who had recently subjugated Celtic Wales and had an old claim of his own to be

'Lord Paramount of Scotland'. It was this claim that persuaded the northern lords to call on Edward to settle what was a very complicated Norman feudal case. They eventually agreed on Balliol, who was crowned in 1292, swore fealty to Edward and promptly became his puppet. In the face of continuing unrest, however, and an alliance contracted between Scotland and France (the original 'Auld Alliance'), Edward reacted violently. He was at war with France, for he had feudal claims there himself, and he could not afford a threat from the north, especially since he was still faced with resistance in Wales. He took his army into Scotland in 1296 and penetrated to Perth, ravaging the Borders and killing thousands along the way. King John, ever since known as Toom Tabard ('empty coat'), ceded his realm to English governors and went south into comfortable captivity. Edward returned to London with much plunder, including the Stone of Destiny – the ancient Celtic throne-stone of Scotland – and the sworn allegiance of 2000 northern landowners. But he had behaved too savagely and left John de Warenne, an equally savage governor, in his wake and it was not long before active revolt broke out and a certain William Wallace, son of Sir Malcolm Wallace of Elderslie, killed the English Sheriff of Lanark in 1297 and made a name for himself during the subsequent uprising in Galloway. Over eighty years of fighting in what came to be known as the Scottish Wars of Independence had begun.

The Wars of Independence

Young William Wallace conducted a brilliant and ruthless guerrilla campaign and managed to join up with De Moray's Highlanders to control most of Scotland north of the river Tay. The great Scottish barons, the ruling Norman-feudal lords of the kingdom, had not as yet committed themselves, but Wallace was not leading a conventional Norman army, with emphasis on heavy troops, cavalry and siege-engines. In fact his forces were largely composed of foot soldiers and spearmen, made up from the Gaelic chiefs and their clansmen, middle-rank Lowland landowners with their followers. They could not attack castles, but they could move swiftly and control the countryside. Among men and women such as these a new sense of nationhood was growing – a sense that a country was defined by all those who lived in it and not just by the international family ties of a select few overlords with personal interests in Europe as well as north and south of the border. Wallace's hopes for Scotland were confirmed by a great victory at Stirling Bridge (1297), after which the English forces were driven beyond the border and several isolated garrisons surrendered. At the age of twenty-six he declared himself Guardian of Scotland on behalf of the exiled King John, but had to forfeit the title within a year when his forces were badly defeated at Falkirk, where they were overtaken by Edward at the head of a seasoned army shortly returned from the French campaign. The guardianship now passed to various members of the conventional nobility, and two in particular who had rival ambitions – John the Red Comyn and young Robert Bruce.

For the first five years of the new century Edward, 'the Hammer of the Scots', led a succession of campaigns across the border, determined to establish English control by pressing his claim to be feudal overlord to the Scottish barons. Wallace was betrayed in 1305 and taken to London, where his execution for 'treason' provided a ghastly public spectacle. Parts of his body were displayed in Newcastle, Berwick, Perth and Aberdeen, but the example of his short life proved to be more potent than his military successes. Wallace's and Scotland's cause was taken up early the next year by Robert Bruce, who killed his rival Comyn in a church at Dumfries and had himself crowned king at the traditional site in Scone. Comyn's murder was such an ill-timed and sacrilegious act that it was almost certainly unpremeditated, but the desperation of the moment committed Bruce to the larger challenge of the throne.

Bruce's fortunes did not go well at first, for he had to flee to the Highlands, where he sought support in the west – a perennial haven for disaffected causes. Edward, aging and ill and set on vengeance, led one more army into Scotland, but died by the Solway. His son was less eager to pursue the issue, and Bruce and his brother Edward Bruce were granted valuable time to consolidate themselves in fierce internal strife against the Scottish supporters of Balliol and Comyn. Bruce's 'Rape of Buchan' – Comyn country – was particularly terrible; it swept away many of the local Gaelic-speaking lairds, but it secured the north-east for his cause as he gradually established a hold over more and more of Scotland in a campaign based on mobility, ruthlessness and surprise. Perth, Linlithgow and Edinburgh were reclaimed, but the turning point came in 1314 in two days at the Bannock burn outside Stirling castle. Here Bruce met a huge English army, brought from the south by Edward II himself, committed to defend his key garrison at Stirling and thereafter to re-establish English power throughout the land. The overwhelming Scottish victory at Bannockburn was the beginning of the end in the struggle for independence, although hostilities were to drag on for many more years.

At last Bruce had gained the support of most of his kingdom, and the Declaration of Arbroath in 1320 made a striking assertion of Scotland's rights by appealing to the Pope not to side with the English against Bruce. This declaration, in Latin and signed by numerous earls and barons, is all the more unusual because it places an abstraction such as the nation itself as well as the freedom and liberty of individuals within it, above the rights of any monarch. The right of subjects to select their king was believed to be part of the Pictish tradition, but this was a new and even a dangerous idea in the feudal world and one that was to endure for a long time in the Scottish people's conception of themselves, although of course at this stage the declaration was speaking for the rights of landowners and not on behalf of the commons:

> Yet if he [the declared king] should give up what he has begun, and agree to make us or our kingdom subject to the King of England or the English, we should exert ourselves at once to drive him out as our enemy and a subverter of his own rights and ours, and make some other man who was well able to defend us our King; for, as long as but a hundred of us remain alive, never will we on any conditions be brought under English rule. It is in truth not for glory, nor riches, nor honours that we are fighting, but for freedom – for that alone, which no honest man gives up but with life itself.

The English did not formally recognise Bruce's kingship and the sovereignty of Scotland until a treaty was signed with Edward III in 1328. Worn and sick after years of war, Bruce died the following year, to be succeeded by his five-year-old son David. In no time at all the old Balliol faction had revived – encouraged by Edward, despite his treaty – and a succession of regents and David II himself were once again caught up in internal strife and renewed warfare against the English. By mid-century David was held hostage in England and the Black Death had arrived from Europe to ravage a land already laid waste by endless fighting. The absence of the king gave more power to the three Estates of barons, churchmen and burgesses – the very people who had insisted on their independence at Arbroath – but the sufferings of the peasants had completely disaffected them from feudal lords and all their doings. French knights on Scottish soil were horrified at the 'impudence' of the common people, who chased them with hoes when they rode through their crops. Perhaps they had little left to lose, and perhaps the spirit of that declaration was seeding itself even among the scorched grass-roots. David returned to his kingdom for the last fourteen years of his reign, to be succeeded by Robert II and Robert III, the 'Stewards' to his kingdom and the first, if undistinguished, members of a Stewart line which was to have more than enough problems in the centuries to come.

The Scots language

In Scotland, as in England and Europe throughout the Middle Ages, Latin was most commonly used for official purposes among the educated and governing classes. French was also used in England, but by the fourteenth century it had fallen out of use in Scotland and a new literature was growing up with original works and translations written in 'Inglis' – a version of Northern English speech which gradually took an even more distinctive character of its own. Within a hundred years this tongue was supplanting Gaelic (or 'Scottis') – and came to be called 'Scottis' in its stead. Although James IV could speak Gaelic himself, the poet Dunbar at his court could safely taunt his rival Kennedy for coming from 'inferior' Highland stock and for using 'Irish'. The old kingdom of Dalriada had slipped away.

Inevitably, in 400 years of development, Scots has very many words in common with English, although some are pronounced differently. Others come from older Anglo-Saxon forms that have dropped out of use in the south – words such as *dwine* (to decay or dwindle), *wersh* (insipid) and *thole* (to endure, suffer). Alternatively, Scots will take one form of a word from a Latin or French root when English takes another or leaves it altogether, as in *dispone* (dispose), or *dominie* (schoolmaster). Even common English words can be used in un-English ways, as in 'can I get to go' for 'may I go', or 'I doubt it's true' to mean 'I'm afraid it is true' – the opposite of what an English speaker might assume. Even for Scots themselves the writing, spelling and speaking of their language from the eighteenth century onwards can provide special problems, not the least of which is the number of apostrophes which are often added, quite wrongly, as if it were simply English with letters missing – thus a' for 'all' instead of the more correct *aa*, and fa' for *faa*, and so on. The guttural 'ch' is, of course, well known in Scots words such as *loch*, *licht*, *bricht*, and *nicht* and *heich* ('high'), but the Old English letter ȝ (yogh, the name combining its two main sounds) was also retained, although later printers had to use the standard Roman letters 'y', 'g' or even 'z' for it. (In quotations in this book, such 'z' spellings are avoided. Thus, where a text contains spellings such as *ze*, *zow*, the more familiar *ye*, *yow*, etc., are substituted.) Thus Scots words such as *tulzie* (brawl) and especially proper names such as

Menzies and Dalziel (and even MacKenzie) are often pronounced with an English 'z' when they should sound like 'toolye', 'Mingis', 'Dalyell' and even 'MacKingie'. By the same – mistaken – token, the unaccented syllables at the end of Scots words such as *pruvit* (proved) and *deavit* (deafened, bored) and *Scottis* itself, are often pronounced especially forcefully by modern readers, when they should be left relatively unstressed.

Some of the most distinctive and tricky features of Scots are to be found among the smallest words in its grammar. Among its pronouns Scots uses *ye* for 'you'; and *yon*, or *thon* as a variant of 'that' with *thae* for 'those'. English 'which' is usually rendered as *that* or *at* and the older form *whilk* (or *quhilk* – same pronunciation) is virtually obsolete. The indefinite article *a* and *an* is the same as English, but a scribal convention often writes them as *ane*, even although they should still be pronounced as usual. So Lindsay's play *Ane Pleasant Satyre of the Thrie Estaitis* should simply be called *A Pleasant Satyre*. On the other hand, *ane* in Scots is pronounced as it looks when used as an isolated numeral for 'one', as in *ane o them* (consider also *the tane and the tither*, for 'one and the other'); but when joined with a noun the form becomes *ae*, as in *ae weet forenicht* – one wet twilight. Finally, 'one' as an indefinite personal pronoun is not used as such, and the Scots idiom for 'if one thought so' is *gin a body thocht sae* ('if a person thought so'), or maybe *gin ye thocht sae*.

Scots developed differently from English in the pattern of its borrowings from other languages. Thus Gaelic has given many loan words, such as *loch, glen, ben, caber* (originally a roof beam), *sonsie* (jolly or plump), *crine* (to shrivel), *partan* (crab) and, of course, *whisky* – *usquebae*, from the Gaelic for 'water of life'. This influence is less than might be supposed, given how widespread Gaelic place names are throughout the country. Even so, Gaelic patterns of expression have entered the speech habits of Scotsmen, even when they think they are speaking English. Hence 'he's away to the fishing' for 'he has gone fishing', and 'Ian can't go to the school, he's got the measles', which follow Gaelic construction.

Old Norse made a particular contribution to Scots through Old English and its northern dialects, and then from the Viking settlement of the Northern Isles. Many common Scots words come from this source, such as *birk* (birch), *kirk* (church), *breeks* (breeches), and *skreich* (screech), as well as *big* (to build), *frae* (from), *gar* (to make, in the sense of persuade or cause to do), *tyne* (to lose), and so on. The original Anglo-Norman roots of Scots provided the language with a larger number of French-derived words, such as *douce* (quiet or gentle), *ashet* (dinner plate), *aumrie* (cupboard), *tassie* (cup), *houlet* (owl) and *mavis* (thrush), while later trade and the Auld Alliance brought further borrowings, such as *fash* (to bother) and *caddie* (originally *cadet*, a messenger). Finally, from the Netherlands, Scotland's other major source of foreign trade from the late fourteenth century onwards, came words such as *callant* (chap), *mutch* (a woman's cap), *kyte* (belly) and *dowp* (backside).

The literary Scots of the Makars was the dialect of mid-Scotland and this has been the basis of 'standard Scots', which developed as a versatile literary language from the fourteenth to the sixteenth century before meeting a renewed influx of English from south of the border. By the late seventeenth century the interface with English usage and the availability of old forms, new forms and regional variations made Scots spelling very fluid indeed. (English spelling was not yet standardised either.) The use of Scots itself came under threat when 'educated' people began to eradicate 'Scotticisms' from their writing – even if their accents remained resolutely Caledonian. There were many complicated reasons for this, and of course some shift in practice was inevitable after the two kingdoms were united. Then again, during the Reformation the Scots clergy had used an English translation of the Bible, and so an English form of spelling became associated with formal writing and high and serious matters.

It is important, however, to distinguish between issues of speech practice and those of orthographical convention, for it is certain that many apparently 'English' words would have been given full Scots pronunciation, and indeed the records of the Scottish Parliament continued to be written in full Scots up to the end of the seventeenth century. By the eighteenth and nineteenth centuries, however, broad Scots had gradually come to be linked with speech, with colloquial speech, and even with the common folk and rustic life. Thus William Alexander's north-east novel *Johnnie Gibb of Gushetneuk* (originally serialised in the *Aberdeen Free Press*, and published as a book in 1871) drew on its regional roots to deliver a rich discourse in Scots dialect. And in fact, as William Donaldson's researches have shown, Scots prose fiction continued to be published along these lines in the popular press right into the early twentieth century. It remains the case, however, that in the wider forum of literary publishing from the eighteenth century onwards, the Scots language became more and more associated with the 'speaking voice', as with Scott's characters or the 'narrators' of Galt's novels, or was featured mainly in the production of poetry.

Robert Burns's 'Lallans' was essentially mid-Scots from Ayrshire, but he introduced words from different dialects (his father came from the north-east, after all), and indeed he used anglified spellings for words that would still have been pronounced in the Scottish manner (e.g. 'ewes' for *yowes*). The nineteenth century saw many imitators of Burns and also a boom in sentimental dialect verses, often self-consciously rustic in manner, until the poets of the modern literary renaissance set out to change things in the 1920s. Hugh MacDiarmid in particular wanted to restore serious lyrical and intellectual status to the medium. He recognised that his language was a 'literary' construction to some extent, and in fact his early lyrics often drew direct inspiration from unusual dialect words that had long lain in the dictionary. Sydney Goodsir Smith's verses stayed a little closer to the Scots of the Makars, while Robert Garioch drew on his own north-east roots and his life in Edinburgh in order to validate contemporary spoken language. What exactly comprises 'standard Scots', after the eighteenth century or so, has become a debatable point, although common sense and common practice usually show the way. Scots is still potent in modern poetry and in the theatre – especially in what might be called working-class drama and in translations of classic European texts, but it is doubtful if the full weight of the language can be used again for discursive prose. Its gradual 'vernacularisation' towards the eighteenth century and its literary history since then have tended to keep it colloquial. 'Scots English', on the other hand, is a recognised linguistic category, and even if it lacks the formal stateliness of sixteenth-century Scots prose it survives and may indeed be spreading in the more general use of technical terms taken from Scots Law.

Latin literature

The arrival of the Latin language, with the Roman invasion, and later with the monks of Ireland crossing to Scotland, marks the beginnings of written literacy in the history of Gaelic, Irish and indeed Scottish and English literature in these islands. The spread of the Roman alphabet and written script – duly adapted – allowed much of the oral wealth of the Irish and Gaelic tradition, its epic poetry and its genealogies, to be recorded and carried down to us. The liturgical praise poems of Irish and Scottish monks followed a European delight in complex metres, alliteration and rhyme, and indeed many of these pieces would have been sung to music. There's no doubt that such virtuosity struck a happy chord with the native Gaelic tradition, and many makars of the period were equally skilled in both languages. Later Latin work took on the chronicling of history and battles, and among the greatest of these was Abbot Walter Bower's massive *Scotichronicon*, composed in Latin at the Abbey of Inchcolm in the Firth of Forth in the 1440s. This chronicle of the nation's history, like Barbour's *Bruce* before it, set out to make a case for a Scottish national identity in the aftermath of the Wars of Independence. It has been called the most substantial work of Scottish literature in the Middle Ages and it also serves as a source for Latin poems, epitaphs and sermons of the time, recorded (and perhaps 'improved') by the doughty Abbot, who concluded his magnum opus with the rhyming sentence *Non Scotus est Christe cui liber non placet iste*: 'Christ! He is not a Scot who is not pleased with this book.' It was, of course, like all works of its time, circulated in manuscript copies, and did not appear in print until 1759. The new nine-volume facing-text edition under the general editorship of D. E. R. Watt is the first time it has been translated entire.

Latin continued to be the international language of scholars and priests right up to Renaissance and Reformation times, and indeed George Buchanan, tutor to Montaigne in France and James VI in Scotland, was widely admired for his Latin verse and equally widely known as one of Europe's leading humanist scholars. In the seventeenth century, William Drummond of Hawthornden's polyglot Scots-English-Latin poem *Polemo-Middinia* looks back to a fifteenth century European tradition of 'macaronic' verse which mixes native language with Latin and 'Latinate' endings to broadly comic effect.

Gaelic literature

From the late twelfth century to the present day Gaelic has enjoyed a strong tradition of poetry, songs and prose tales, but its literature, whether memorised or written down, is most especially rich in poetry. This verse tradition falls into two main periods. The first stems from the bardic schools, a 'classical' and conservative tradition that followed old Irish models going back to the ninth century. Bardic verse was slow to change, but by the sixteenth century Gaelic songs were flourishing in a more vernacular form of the language, and in the next century poets such as Iain Lom and Mary MacLeod heralded the second great period by beginning to use this language in place of bardic formality. Thus the slow development of a specifically Scottish Gaelic vernacular poetry reached its greatest expression in the eighteenth century among poets such as Rob Donn Mackay, Alexander MacDonald and Duncan Bàn Macintyre. Then the doors of the Gaelic world were flung wider still by such poets as Sorley MacLean, George Campbell Hay, Derick Thomson and Iain Crichton Smith of the twentieth-century Scottish Renaissance. These writers take a specifically modern outlook, yet their work is never far from their heritage. The spirit of Gaelic literature, with its characteristic strengths and subjects, is still remarkably consistent.

Not much survives of early bardic verse in Scotland, and the recitation of genealogies and chronicles is of little specifically literary interest. In fact the classical schools were so stable that Gaelic verse from the fourteenth to the sixteenth centuries can be usefully summarised at this point. The most substantial single source of early Gaelic poetry comes down to us in the Book of the Dean of Lismore, a manuscript from 1512 that was only discovered and published in 1862. The Dean collected from oral sources in Argyll and Perthshire, and these included complex traditional praise poems along with much less formal satires, love lyrics, Christian poems and mildly obscene verses. Most notably this absolutely invaluable collection also includes Ossianic heroic ballads and verses in Irish, which demonstrate Scotland's continuing links with Ireland going back to their common roots and based on the free passage of poets between the two countries. Indeed, one of the very oldest surviving texts to deal with Scotland, the *Duan Albanach* (most probably by an Irish poet at the end of the eleventh century), uses a mixture of legend and oral history to tell how the Irish Gaels first came to settle in the north, and the two countries continued to exchange contacts through poets and poems and patrons well into the seventeenth century. The most striking example of the continuity of the Scottish bardic tradition must be the MacMhuirich dynasty who left Ireland around 1215 and served various branches of the MacDonald family for the next 500 years.

The Gaelic bardic system seems to have been firmly established by the thirteenth century. At first, this exclusive professional class produced learned and very highly wrought syllabic verses along classical Irish lines, and bardic colleges were set up to teach the conventions, including as many as 300 different and complex metrical schemes. At the highest level these (male) bards were fully literate and could aspire to the status of *filidh*. The task of the *filidh*, like the less exalted position of bard, was 'eulogy and elegy' – to sing his leader's praises, recite his genealogy, chronicle his times, describe victories in battle and lament his eventual death. The *filidh's* office was often hereditary, he had considerable prestige and could be a wealthy man in his own right, but he still depended on patronage and a stable aristocratic tradition. It is likely that the common folk preferred tales, ballads and love songs outwith this high-flown formal style and in this field women had their own role as poets and tradition bearers. More concerned to record the formal output of the *filidh*, however, later collectors had little interest in such 'lesser' art, and as a result much early colloquial work has, sadly, been lost to us.

Like all Celtic artists, the *filidhean* value impersonality and technical skill for their own sake and their verse is elaborate and conventional in its approach. Perhaps Dunbar's highly wrought aureate verses owe something to this heritage, despite his apparent contempt for things Gaelic. In any case, 'high-style' virtuosity was taken to be a professional benchmark in both Highland and Lowland cultures at this time. As late as 1695 Martin Martin (*A Description of the Western Isles of Scotland*, 1703) tells of a bardic school in the Highlands which followed the ancient Irish model of lying in a cold room, with a stone on the belly and eyes covered up, from which cell the trainee had to emerge in the morning with a long and complex composition committed to memory. Martin notes, however, that by his time the bardic class had largely lost the 'profit and esteem which was formerly due to their character . . . and are now allowed but a small salary'.

Traditional Gaelic praise poetry could contain many elements – praise of a horse, a bow, the chief's ancestry, his land, his valour or the beauty of his lady. Other poems strike a more elegiac note with a lament for a leader's death or for the passing of glory. Bardic verses used a highly formal literary language ('Classical Gaelic') based on the *rann*, a self-contained four-line stanza made up of two couplets of predetermined syllabic lengths and a variety of rhetorical and orna-mental devices, including linking patterns of internal rhyme, assonance and alliteration. *Brosnachadh* poems, or verses as an 'incitement' to war, were also written, and an early example, ascribed to Artur Dall MacGurcaigh and dating from about 1310, describes MacSween of Knapdale's fleet in terms which clearly show the parallels between Highland custom and the warriors and longboats of Scandinavia from 400 years before. (Gaelic chiefs from the north often boasted of their descent from Norse fighting-men.) In a later example from 1513, written for the Earl of Argyll before the Battle of Flodden, the unknown poet curses the English and asks the earl to punish their growing spite and power:

The roots from which they grow, destroy them,
their increase is too great,
and leave no Englishman alive after you
nor Englishwoman there to tell the tale.

Burn their bad coarse women,
burn their uncouth offspring,
and burn their sooty houses,
and rid us of the reproach of them.

Let their ashes float downstream
after burning their remains
show no mercy to a living Englishman
O chief, deadly slayer of the wounded.

(trs. K. H. Jackson)

Over 200 years later, the same bloodthirsty tradition was called up by Alasdair MacMhaighstir Alasdair (Alexander MacDonald), who wrote many poems in vernacular Gaelic to support the Jacobite rising of 1745.

Not all was war, however, and bardic metres were also used for laments or for gentler, more personal poems, such as the beautiful 'A phaidrín do dhúisg mo dhéar' ('O rosary that recalled my tear'), written in the 1460s by a non-professional poet, Aithbhreac Inghean Corcadail, in mourning for the death of her husband, Niall Og MacNeill:

O rosary that recalled my tear
dear was the finger in my sight,
that touched you once, beloved the heart
of him who owned you till tonight.

I grieve the death of him whose hand
you did entwine each hour of prayer;
my grief that it is lifeless now
and I no longer see it there.

(trs. D. Thomson)

When the geographical isolation and the autonomy of the clans began to pass during the sixteenth century, the bards passed, too. Nevertheless, later Gaelic poets retained a high prestige, even if they came from humble stock without classical training, and, in fact, aspects of bardic style, particularly set phrases and favourite epithets, were to survive in a looser and more vernacular form for centuries to come.

Literature in Scots in the fourteenth century

After the *brosnachadh* poems of the Gaelic poets, it is appropriate that
the first major literary achievement of the emerging Scots tradition
should be John Barbour's *The Bruce*, a Lowland poem of war and
victory. If Barbour had many predecessors, then they and their works
are shrouded by time or hidden in the smoke of scholarly dispute. The
oldest surviving fragment may date from the difficult years after 1286
and the end of Alexander III's 'golden age', but it comes to us as transcribed in 1424 by Andrew of Wyntoun from his *Oryginale Cronykil of
Scotland*:

Quhen Alexander our kynge was dede,	when
That Scotlande lede in lauche and le,	law and peace
Away was sons of alle and brede,	abundance of ale
Off wyne and wax, of gamyn and gle.	mirth
Our golde was changit into lede.	lead
Crist, borne in virgynyte,	
Succoure Scotlande, and ramede,	help
That is stade in perplexite.	beset

Also from Alexander's reign comes a long and relatively unskilled
metrical romance called *Sir Tristrem*, often ascribed to Thomas of
Ercildoune and later edited by Scott. But this, too, appears only in a
fourteenth-century transcription and the authorship is disputed.
Ercildoune is better known as 'Thomas the Rhymer' or 'True Thomas',
the poet in the later ballads who became the Queen of Elfland's lover
and was gifted with prophetic powers.

The *Awntyrs of Arthure* and *The Pistill of Susan* are two metrical
romances, each with rhymed and alliterative thirteen-line stanzas, that
survive in English transcriptions from the fifteenth century. The 'adventures' come from the stock of Arthurian tales, although they may be set
around the Borders; and the epistle about Susan goes to the Apocrypha
of the Bible for the moral tale of Susanna and the Elders. Andrew of
Wyntoun ascribed these to someone called 'Huchown off the Awle
Ryale' (although he puts 'Gawane' rather than Arthur in the title), and
it has been suggested that this Huchown is 'Sir Hew of Eglinton', a Scot
whom Dunbar lists among the dead poets of the past in his 'Lament for
the Makaris'. ('Awle Ryale' has been rendered as 'the King's palace'.)
Whether this connection holds or not, both poems belong to the same
literary mode as later Scottish verses such as *Rauf Coilyear* and *Golagros
and Gawane*, and these formed part of an 'alliterative revival' in the
poetry of the north, even if the names of their authors cannot be

convincingly established. 'Huchown' may or may not have been a Scot, but the nationality of John Barbour needs little proving.

John Barbour (1320?–95)

John Barbour was probably born in Aberdeen, and he is first mentioned in the records as Archdeacon there in 1357. In the next eleven years he travelled to study at Oxford and then to Paris on at least two occasions each. Thereafter he was given a post as clerk of audit and was one of the auditors of the Exchequer for Robert II's household. He wrote *The Bruce* during the years 1372–76 and two years later he was granted a royal pension in perpetuity, most probably in recognition of his poem, or perhaps because it was only finally completed then. A larger annual sum was awarded in 1388, and it is the cessation of this payment that marks his death in 1395.

From these slender details it can be seen that Barbour's long verse opus refers to events scarcely sixty years in the past, and it is likely that he had access to now lost sources, some of which might have been oral, for many of the details in the work. Many subsequent histories have drawn on the Archdeacon's narrative. The ubiquitous Wyntoun, a great admirer of *The Bruce*, confirmed its authorship and included 280 lines from it in his *Cronykil*. The poem survives in two manuscripts (Edinburgh and Cambridge) both transcribed in the late fifteenth century, and it was reprinted several times, the earliest known edition being in 1571. The original work was most probably recited at court, and its present division into books was done by Edinburgh lawyer and historian John Pinkerton in his 1790 edition. A. A. M. Duncan's edition of *The Bruce* (Canongate, 1997) provides a glossed text and a sustained commentary on where the poem matches or diverges from what we now take to be historical fact. The major part played by James Douglas in the poem suggests that a now lost history of the Douglas family was one of Barbour's sources. The poet's details can be more reliable than might be supposed, but the demands of his art tend to multiply the odds against the Scots for the sake of effect, and at one point the deeds of Bruce and his grandfather are conflated in order to minimise the hero's early connection with the English. In the same cause, Barbour's hero king is made of simpler stuff than the original, who suffered such divided Anglo-Norman loyalties and made a succession of broken promises to Edward and Balliol and Comyn. So *The Bruce* portrays a noble epic from the start, what Duncan calls a romance-biography, linking it to a Europe-wide genre of chivalric writing with a noble audience in mind, but privileging, in this case, a tale of freedom won (at least for the landed classes), rather than the values of courtly love. To this end the text strikes parallels with French romance literature, with episodes from the Bible or with the history of ancient Greece.

The English are allowed to be brave and chivalrous too, but they are never seen as less than prideful and acquisitive enemies. Even so, Barbour's patriotism (and an awareness of his royal patron), does not lead him into mere propaganda or far-fetched vaunting. In fact *The Bruce* is most striking for its unelaborated narrative: twenty books full of the dispositions of troops, the vagaries of the campaign and the speeches and deeds of individuals, all of which are recounted in forthright style combined with a clerkly eye for the circumstantial details of time, place and equipment:

> And went in hy towart the sea;   in haste
> Quhar Schir Nele Campbell thaim met   where
> Bath with schippis, and with meyte;   meat
> Saylys, ayris, and othir thing,   oars
> That was spedfull to thar passyng.
>
> (v, 570–4)

The same dispassionate and documentary approach even informs Barbour's account of the notorious 'Douglas larder', when Bruce's fiercest young lieutenant surprised the occupying English garrison at worship in the church of his family castle, and flung their bodies and surplus supplies (and the feast they had been about to eat) into the wine cellar:

> A foull melle thair can he mak;   mix
> For meill, malt, blude, and wyne
> Ran all to-gidder in a mellyne.
> That wes unsemly for to se;
> Tharfor the men of that cuntre,
> For sic thingis that mellit were,
> Callit it 'the Douglas Lardenere'.
>
> (v, 404–10)

Barbour tells us that this master of guerrilla terrorism was 'meyk and sweyt in cumpany' and spoke with a lisp. Douglas is a major character in the poem, and the tale ends with his death in battle against the Saracens twenty-four years later, while carrying Bruce's heart in a casket on a pilgrimage to the Holy Land – a journey the king had long promised himself, but did not live to make.

True stories are a double pleasure, as the author observes in his preface:

> The fyrst plesance is the carpyng,   telling
> And the tothir the suthfastnes,   truthfulness
> That schawys the thing rycht as it wes.
>
> (I, 6–8)

And one of the main things for Barbour, 'rycht as it wes', is the spirit of liberty, famously evoked in the very first book with lines which add a more than chivalric dimension to the tale:

> A! fredome is a noble thing!
> Fredome mayss man to haiff liking,   makes; pleasure
> Fredome all solace to man giffis: gives
> He levys at ess that frely levys.   lives at ease
> A noble hart may haiff nane ess,
> Na ellys nocht that may him pless,
> Gyff fredome failyhe; for fre liking   If freedom fail; love of liberty
> Is yharnyt our all othir thing.   yearned for over all
> Na he, that ay hass levyt fre,
> May nocht knaw weill the propyrte,
> The anger, na the wrechyt dome,   doom
> That is couplyt to foule thyrldome.   thraldom
> Bot gyff he had assayit it,   if he had tried it
> Than all perquer he suld it wyt;   by heart he should know it
> And suld think fredome mar to pryss   more to prize
> Than all the gold in the warld that is.
>
> (I, 225–40)

The unforced pace of such simple statement in Barbour's octosyllabic couplets pervades the whole poem as well as the character of its hero. Most notably, in comparison with Blind Harry's *Wallace* of a century later, Barbour's work is not suffused with blind hatred for the English. Strength, principle, loyalty and chivalric courage are what count, and the same virtues can be found even in the mouths of the common people who start to side with their king's cause:

> He com soyn in the houss, and fand   soon; found
> The gud wyf on the bynk sytand.   sitting on the bench
> Scho askit him soyn quhat he wes   She; what
> And quhyne he com, and quhar he gais.   when; where he goes
> 'A travelland man, dame', said he,
> 'That travalys heir throu the cuntre.'
> Scho said, 'All that travaland ere,   formerly

For saik of ane, ar welcom here.'
The King said, 'Gud dame, quhat is he
That garris yow have sic specialte   makes you have such
Till men that travalis?' 'Schir, perfay,'   [special liking
Quod the gud wif, 'I sall yow say;
Gud King Robert the Bruce is he,
That is rycht lord of this cuntre. . . .'
'Dame, lufis thou him sa weill?' said he.
'Yea, Schir,' scho said, 'sa God me se.'
'Dame', said he, 'Lo! Him here the by,   he is by you here
For I am he;' – 'Sa ye suthly?'   truly
'Yea, certis, dame;' – 'And quhar ar gane
Your men, quhen ye ar thus allane?'
'At this tyme, dame, I have no ma.'   more
Scho said, 'It may no wiss be swa;   no way be so
I have two sonnys wicht and hardy,   vigorous
Thai sail becum your men in hy.'   in haste
                    (VII, 237–64)

Not surprisingly, the natural climax of the poem – after the accounts
of Bruce's early sufferings – arrives with Bannockburn. Barbour's
lengthy description of that two-day battle includes the tactical manoeu-
vres of the troops, the speeches of the leaders and courageous deeds on
both sides; he also tells of the celebrated preliminary clash between
Bruce and De Bohun, and how the humble camp-followers, determined to fight for Scotland in their own way, formed an army with
sheets for banners, and convinced the faltering English that they were
new and deadly reinforcements. The sober simplicity of Barbour's
verses – and the occasional shafts of grim humour – perfectly convey
the purpose and the character of the Scottish cause as he sees it. Of
course, it is the 'great folk' who stand most in the foreground, but the
nobility of plain speech and simple dignity is shared by all. Thus
Bruce's chivalric idealism has a sturdily domestic and practical foundation, as he addresses his men before Bannockburn and reminds them
that, despite being outnumbered, they have three great advantages:

The first is, that we haf the richt;
And for the richt ilk man suld ficht.   every man should fight
The tothir is, thai are cummyn heir,
For lypnyng in thair gret power,   trusting
To seik us in our awne land,
And has broucht her, richt till our hand,   brought here
Richness in-to so gret plentee,
That the pouerest of yow sall be
Bath rych and mychty thar-with-all,
Gif that we wyn, as weill may fall.   may happen

The thrid is, that we for our lyvis
And for our childer and our wifis,
And for the fredome of our land,
Ar strenyeit in battale for to stand,   constrained/forced
And thai for thair mycht anerly . . .   only for their might
                 (XII, 235–49)

Professional knightly pride may have to give way in the face of men who are fighting to survive, but Bruce is king enough to know that the prospect of a little plunder helps, too.

Barbour concludes his account of Bannockburn with the understanding that a king must first earn and then maintain his people's loyalty, and be prays that 'thai that cummynge ar / of [Bruce's] ofspring, maynteyme the land, / And hald the folk . . . As weill as in his tyme did he!' Perhaps the poet had cause to worry, for Robert II was an aging and weak man when he came to the throne, and the Scots barons were, as always, ready to challenge his authority – not least the Douglases, who were fighting what was virtually a private war with England only three years after *The Bruce* had immortalised the loyalty of their most famous ancestor – 'that in his tyme sa worthy was'. The 'suthfast story' of Scotland was as complicated and bloody as ever.

Barbour's *Bruce* stands as a unique document to the efficacy of the vernacular in an extended mode incorporating chivalric romance, royal biography and verse chronicle. It also signals the War of Independence and the experience of English invasion as key elements in a growing sense of a national identity that went beyond the immediate interests of the aristocracy. One of the social factors in this development was the rise of the merchant class and also of a class of minor gentry who rented land from their lords, but employed others to work it, thus forming a bridge between high and low. A strong awareness of kinship connections and clan loyalties further tended to override differences of wealth or station, even as they celebrated the importance of blood descent. T. C. Smout has described the paradoxical nature of this growing sense of a common 'Scottishness' as 'compounded of both egalitarian and of patriarchal features, full of respect for birth while being free from humility'.

There was another and a grimmer factor in the shifting balance of social power in Scotland at this time, namely the various outbreaks of plague that devastated the country in the latter half of the fourteenth century. With the population more than decimated there was an increase in food supplies and a shortage of workforce, which meant that agricultural labour and skilled craftsmen began to come into their own. The same effects were felt in England and throughout medieval Europe.

2
The fifteenth century: the flowering

THE NATIONAL and cultural confidence of Scotland came to fruition in the fifteenth century, but it was neither easy nor peaceful. A succession of Stewart minorities aggravated the power balance between crown and barons and each king had to struggle to establish his rule. The Stewarts made some headway, but Douglas and Percy still ruled the Borders, while in the north-west the Clan Donald line claimed and held their own kingly rights as Lords of the Isles. Nevertheless, the royal right of succession gradually became established and accepted by almost all factions in Scotland. It was dearly bought: from James I to James IV no Stewart king lived beyond his prime and all of them died violently. Relationships with England were muted for the most part, but the capture of James I gave early notice that England still nursed hopes of suzerainty. Thus it was English policy to encourage malcontents in Scotland and to support the ambitions of the Lords of the Isles.

The Scottish connection with France was more cordial and from time to time the Auld Alliance was invoked to enlist Scotland's aid against her southern neighbour. But the end result was usually unhappy, especially when James IV died at Flodden in an entirely reluctant and futile bid to oblige French expectations by marching on England. Many Scotsmen travelled abroad to enlist as mercenaries in the armies of Europe: some fought for Joan of Arc and two of the elite corps in Charles VII's army were Scottish companies. In her turn, France's contribution was more cultural than military, and Pedro de Ayala noted how many young Scotsmen spoke French and made regular visits to the continent. The Scots pattern of education was based on the curriculum at Paris, and the universities of St Andrews (1412), Glasgow (1450) and Aberdeen (1494) were all founded along European lines. By the end of the century James IV had established at Aberdeen the first chair of medicine in Britain and had passed an act to require the sons of all barons and landowners to attend school from the age of eight for the study of Latin, law and the arts. In 1507 the same king established Walter Chepman and Andrew Myllar as printers in Edinburgh. They published poetry by Henryson and Dunbar as well as *Legends of the Saints* and the *Aberdeen Breviary* – a major project by the redoubtable Bishop Elphinstone of Aberdeen, whose intention was to preserve the Scottish form of worship against English influence.

By the second half of the century, in a period of peace with England, the burghs had gained in influence and wealth. Growing numbers of towns began to govern themselves in the pursuit of trade and to defend themselves too. Burgesses were obliged to provide weapons and to turn out for home-guard service if necessary. Royal burghs could send representatives to parliament, and their trading interests were another factor that maintained cultural links with Europe from Danzig to Spain. These connections, and especially the one with France, flourished in the architecture of this time. Falkland Palace, Linlithgow, the Border abbeys and the castles at Borthwick and Craigmillar show the full influence of northern 'perpendicular Gothic'. The Renaissance in Scotland could not match the glories of Italy – the cultural temperament, like the climate, tended to ruggedness rather than grace – but under James IV there was an energy and an excitement in the air.

The second half of the fifteenth century was a time of literary richness – one of the greatest that Scotland has seen. The outstanding poets were Robert Henryson and William Dunbar. Henryson has the finer spirit, but the period is characterised by Dunbar, although his poems actually date from the early 1500s. For this reason he has been included in the present chapter and also because the death of James IV and the psychological impact of his defeat at Flodden in 1513 makes a natural, if sad, conclusion to a century of high literary achievement.

The surface gorgeousness of Dunbar's poems contrasts with the wilder and more brutal extravagance of his imagination, and these, in turn, play against a darker and more singular spirit of pessimism. Dunbar speaks for professional virtuosity, he speaks of the prodigality of court life and he speaks of himself. Henryson, on the other hand, has a broader and less self-centred persona, a mature compassion for the spiritual plight of man and a practical sympathy for the common folk. He commends the values of peace and good order, values that were making difficult but discernible progress during his lifetime, and his poems frequently comment on how the common people are at the mercy of the rapacious and the powerful – a moral intended for the ears of those in power. There is a sense in which we hear the people in Henryson's version of Aesop's fables: a voice that later critics will come to claim as one of the defining characteristics of Scottish literature in the eighteenth and again in the twentieth century. The same voice can be heard in parts of *Rauf Coilyear* and 'Colkelbie's Sow' and also in the rougher folk energy of 'Peblis to the Play' and 'Christis Kirk of the Green'. Blind Harry's *Wallace* can also be seen as an expression of this proclivity, because of its narrative point of view and its sense that a nation is simply its people. Scotland had not yet achieved political stability, and schisms still existed between Lowlands and Highlands; but the prominence of such writers as Henryson and Dunbar, or the distinctively local colouring which was given to traditional European romance subjects, or the technical confidence and verve to be seen in aureate and ballad verse – all these point to what came to be known as the golden age of Scottish poetry.

Andrew of Wyntoun (1350?–1424?)

Inspired by the national spirit of *The Bruce*, the Prior at the island monastery of Loch Leven, **Andrew of Wyntoun** (1350?–1424?) ushered in the new century with a long history of Scotland written in dogged verse couplets over nine books, corresponding, the author informs us, to the nine orders of angels. *The Oryginale Cronykil of Scotland* (1424?) set out to establish the heritage of the Scots from 1408 right back to Adam and Eve, and woe betide any English monarch who will not recognise such a proud descent! It was Wyntoun's entirely fanciful account of Macbeth and the witches that gave Holinshed (1577) and hence Shakespeare the opening scenes of 'the Scottish play'. As a historian Wyntoun is more dependable nearer to his own times, and one of the last events recorded in his book tells how an eleven-year-old boy, newly crowned king of Scotland, fell into English hands.

James I (1394–1437)

Young James I was captured by the English in 1406 while being shipped to France – ironically, for his own safety. He spent the next eighteen years of his life as a political pawn in England, although no doubt his captivity was comfortable enough. He is said to have written *The Kingis Quair* (the King's Book) during 1424 – the last year of his sojourn – or 1425, and it seems likely that this ornate allegorical poem does, indeed, describe the circumstances under which he fell in love with his future wife, Joan of Beaufort. There is little reason to suppose, as some scholars have maintained, that James is not the author. Yet the poem was not really 'discovered' until the eighteenth century, and so it had little contemporary influence and James is not one of the poets mentioned in Dunbar's 'Lament for the Makaris'.

The Kingis Quair is an allegorical dream vision framed by the poet's imprisonment and his despair at a 'dedely life, full of peyne and penance'. There is no mention, however, that the protagonist is of royal blood, and his imprisonment has as much symbolic as literal force. As one might expect from the circumstances, the style is lightly Scotticised and markedly influenced by English models. It uses a seven-line rime-royal stanza similar to that of Chaucer's *Troilus and Criseyde*, and the mixture of realistic description and allegorical abstraction is reminiscent of Lydgate's *Temple of Glas*. The poet sees a beautiful woman outside his window and, rather in the manner of Palamoun in 'The Knight's Tale', he immediately falls in love with her. That night in a dream he presents his case to Venus before an emblematic assembly of all those who have felt the pangs of love. He meditates on free will in the manner of Boethius's *De Consolatione Philosophiae*, an influential and widely translated text in the Middle Ages.

Boethius, a fifth-century Roman philosopher and statesman, recommends a turn away from worldly attachments and the snares of fortune in favour of a life of the mind and the spirit. In the final analysis, however, James's poem gains most force from its physical descriptions and from the ironies inherent in its theme of love as a kind of captivity that offers escape from literal physical imprisonment. The bright images of birds and the garden of crystal waters and little fish convey the poet's sense of exhilaration, clarity and gratitude when he feels that his fortunes have turned. Although still incarcerated, he begins to feel free. By comparison, although the autobiographical element is very suggestive, his loved one remains a collection of rather abstract virtues. The poet's meditation on Fortune is especially poignant, for James had been hostage to that fickle wheel all his life and yet could win free only by submitting himself once more to her macabre influence. This time she smiles on him, but the narrator cannot help noticing that her wheel revolves over a hellish pit. In a delightfully original touch he has the goddess give him a tweak on the ear as they part, and this teasing nip wakes him from his dream and serves as a sardonic reminder of Fortune's incorrigible and potentially fatal playfulness. Nevertheless, the poet is now free – at least in spirit – and he can even bless the castle walls that keep him, because they provided the stage for his conversion to love.

It was not long before the king secured his release from Windsor and married Joan Beaufort. By 1424 he was restored to his throne in Scotland, where he determined to reassert his authority. But Fortune's wheel turned again, thirteen years later, when a discontented baron planned his assassination, and the author of *The Kingis Quair* met an ignominious death hiding in the privy of the royal bedchambers at Perth.

James's poem introduced the century with an allegorical work in courtly style. The literature that followed was, for the most part, less formal, less in the mode of Chaucer and Lydgate and closer to a more everyday vision of Scottish life. It was once the fashion to define the poets of this century as 'Scottish Chaucerians', but properly speaking only James owes the implied debt. The rest undoubtedly and frequently acknowledge Chaucer's greatness, but they draw as much from European and native influences as they do from the old master in England. At least three other poems have been ascribed to James I. 'Good Counsel' is a brief and sententious piece of advice to 'exil al vice and folow trewth alway', modelled after Chaucer's ballad of the same name, and there are few problems in accepting it as the king's work. It is not so, however, with 'Peblis to the Play' and 'Christis Kirk of the Green', and recent critical opinion favours a now unknown author for these pieces, from a time closer to the end of the fifteenth century.

Sir Richard Holland (fl. 1450)

If *The Kingis Quair* operates in the tradition of the dream vision and has moments reminiscent of 'The Knight's Tale', then Sir Richard Holland's *The Buke of the Howlat* (Book of the Owl) is a beast allegory after the fashion of Chaucer's *Parlement of Foules*. Holland's long poem was dedicated to Elizabeth Dunbar, wife to Archibald Douglas, Earl of Moray, and must have been written around 1450 as a panegyric to celebrate this powerful family and its history. The *Howlat* is written in the alliterative stanza earlier used in the north of England for *Gawain and the Green Knight*, but it is an allegory and also an entertaining satire rather than a romance tale. It is the first substantial poem of what was to become a Scottish revival of the use of alliteration in verse, seen also in the more conventionally chivalric *Rauf Coilyear*, *Golagros and Gawane* and the surviving English transcription of *Awntyrs of Arthure*.

Holland makes innumerable connections between the world of birds and the pomp and circumstance of papal and regal power. Thus the peacock is the pope of birds and the swallow is his herald, while cranes (cardinals), swans (bishops) and common sea-birds (monks) throng his holiness's court. In similar fashion the birds of prey represent temporal power, with the eagle as emperor and gerfalcons, goshawks and sparrowhawks as the dukes, captains and knights of his retinue. In the middle of the poem, while describing the heraldry at the eagle's court, the poet takes some twenty stanzas to recite the arms and the prowess of the Douglas family, starting with the tale of Bruce's heart.

This elaborate poem has a simple moral about the dangers of pride (Blind Harry's *Wallace* refers to it, to make a timely warning to Sir William), for the allegory is set in motion by the owl's desire to be more beautiful. On a traditional May morning, the poet overhears the howlat's complaint against Dame Nature, and he follows its course from the papal congregation of birds to the assembled might of the emperor's court, where a feast, with juggling and recitations, is being held. Finally, the company prays for Dame Nature to appear, and she orders each bird to give one of its feathers to the ugly howlat. But, as soon as he is arrayed in finery, the owl becomes insufferably proud ('pomposs, impertinat, and reprovable') and the other birds waste no time in asking Dame Nature to return him to his former state – 'hidowis of hair and of hyde'. This accomplished, they all fly off, leaving the howlat, and the poet, to contemplate a moral directed at the rich and powerful:

> Now mark yow mirour be me, all maner of man,
> Ye princis, prentis of pryde for penneis and prowe   images; pennies;
> That pullis the pure ay,   exploit; [profit
> Ye sall syng as I say,   [the poor
> All your welth will away,
> Thus I warn yow. . . .

The charm of *The Buke of the Howlat* lies in the way it miniaturises human society and dresses it in feathers, for neither the moral nor the celebration of the Douglases survives the test of time. Thus the Rook appears at the banquet as a Gaelic bard speaking gibberish, reciting genealogies, and demanding more food, all at the same time. It is a passage that Dunbar, with his prejudice against 'the ersche' tongue, would certainly have enjoyed:

> [shout and
> Sa come the Ruke with a rerd and a rane roch,   a rough rann
> A bard out of Irland with 'Banachadee'.   'blessing of God'
> Said: 'Gluntow guk dynyd dach hala mischy doch;   ('Gaelic' gibberish)
> Raike hir a rug of the rost, or scho sall ryme the.   Reach me[1] a chunk

Mich macmory ach mach mometir moch loch;   [of the roast or I'll
Set hir dovne, gif hir drink; quhat Dele alis the?'   satirise you.]
O Deremyne, O Donnall, O Dochardy droch;
Thir ar his Irland kingis of the Irischerye: These
O Knewlyn, O Conochor, O Gregre Makgrane;
The Schenachy, the Clarschach,   Gaelic bard; harp
The Ben schene, the Ballach,
The Crekery, the Corach,
Scho kennis thaim ilkane.   (I) know each one of them

The lapwing and the cuckoo, a pair of clowns, eventually drive off the harsh-voiced rook, but not before he has said his piece: 'Mony lesingis [lies] he maid; wald let for no man / To spek quhill [while] he spokin had, sparit no thingis'.

Although it has a broader and more humorous aspect, the *Howlat*, like *The Kingis Quair*, belongs to the world of formal literary genres. On the other hand, when Henryson uses animals in his versions of Aesop's fables, they are more fully and more humanely characterised and their milieu is recognisably the place of everyday life and common experience, rather than a theatre of courts, castles and enclosed gardens.

Robert Henryson (1435?–1505?)

We know very little about Robert Henryson. If we believe Dunbar's 'Lament for the Makaris' then death must have had his way with the elder poet sometime before 1508. The honorific 'master' says that he was a university man and a graduate, perhaps of an institution in Europe. Among others, the title page of the Bassandyne printing of *The Morall Fabillis* (done in 1571) refers to the author as a schoolmaster in Dunfermline. There is also evidence to suggest that he trained in law and operated as a notary public, and he does use legal terms and procedures in his poems. Henryson's fame rests on his fables and on *The Testament of Cresseid* – an extraordinary sequel to Chaucer's *Troilus and Criseyde*. Modern readers have come to value him highly and many would place his poetic achievement as second only to Chaucer, whom he acknowledged himself as the 'flower' of poets. Yet, although he shares something of the Englishman's compassion and sweet humour, Henryson has an occasional terseness and sometimes a grimness of outlook that belongs to a harsher northern clime, even although the

---

1   The bard refers to himself as 'she', a stereotypical convention in anglicising Gaelic.

spirit of *memento mori* was of course common throughout the Middle Ages. Dunbar shows this temperament even more clearly and it is worth pointing out that it was part of the nation's cultural expression long before John Knox and Calvinism arrived to give it a doctrinal dimension.

A poem such as 'The Bludy Serk' suggests that the oral tradition was well established in the Scots canon, and this supernatural tale of how a doomed knight rescues a maiden from a giant shows that Henryson could easily match the laconic edge of the ballad style, even if he does add a literary moral which explains that it is an allegory of Christ and man's soul. In similar fashion the poet takes the old French *pastourelle* genre and, with a light touch, creates the rustic dialogue of 'Robene and Makyne', where canny Robene is concerned more with the welfare of his sheep than with Makyne's passion for him. (When he finally does warm to the idea, she has changed her mind.) Henryson almost always works from established models and yet he so consistently transforms and vivifies his material that it seems as though Aesop's fables were always set in Scottish fields, or as though Troy were truly somewhere near Dunfermline. The poet's talent for realistic detail is expressed in succinct and unpretentious utterance, as though we were listening to the man himself speaking. These particular strengths, in Henryson and later poets, have done much to define the Scottish literary tradition even to the present day.

It is in his commitment to the human and the natural world that Henryson's Catholic faith and his wry and gentle imagination come together. 'Mane suld presume be ressoun naturall / To seirche the secreitis off the Trinitie', he writes in 'The Preiching of the Swallow': 'Yit nevertheles we may haif knawlegeing / Off God Almychtie be his creatouris / That he is gude, fair, wyis and bening.' Thus the separation of the physical from the spiritual seems artificial to Henryson, for in his view the natural world embodies the spirit quite plainly. When winter comes it is the effect on the animals that the poet visualises in his alliterated lines:

Than flouris fair faidit with froist man fall,	must
And birdis blyth changit thair noitis sweit	
In styll murning, neir slane with snaw and sleit.	
Thir dalis deip with dubbis drounit is,	dales; mud
Baith hill and holt heillit with frostis hair;	woods; hoar frosts
All wyld beistis than ffrom the bentis bair	heaths
Drawis ffor dreid unto thair dennis deip,	
Coucheand ffor cauld in coifis thame to keip.	coves/hollows

With the arrival of spring, man's work in the fields is celebrated until the land, the beasts upon it and the labouring folk are all equally present in the poet's eye and in the mind of God:

> Sum makand dyke, and sum the pleuch can wynd,   plough
> Sum sawand seidis fast ffrome place to place,   sowing
> The Harrowis hoppand in the saweris trace: sower's traces
> It wes grit Joy to him that luifit corne,
> To se thame laubour, baith at evin and morne.

'The Preiching of the Swallow' is one of thirteen poems in 'Eloquent and Ornate Scottish Meter' later compiled as *The Morall Fabillis of Esope the Phrygian* (most probably written around the 1460s), in which Henryson retells Aesop and other animal tales, drawing on popular tradition and the genre of beast epics throughout Europe such as the French *Roman de Renart*. He uses rime royal throughout – a seven-line stanza rhyming ababbcc with five strong stresses in each line – and his sense of humour, whether gently mocking, openly satirical or resolutely stern, is never absent. In 'The Taill How the Foxe Maid his Confessioun to Freir Wolf Waitskaith', the fox wants to salve his conscience and so he approaches Friar Wolf with these pious observations:

> 'Ye ar Mirrour, lanterns, and sicker way,   certain
> Suld gyde sic sempill folk as me to grace.
> Your bair feit, and your Russet Coull off gray,
> Your lene cheik, your paill pietious face.   pious
> Schawis to me your perfite halines.'

The wolf does seem surprisingly well versed in scriptural niceties, and for penance he forbids the fox to eat any meat. Temptation overcomes the sinner, however, and to escape the prohibition he catches a kid and 'christens' it a salmon by drowning it in the sea – 'Ga doun, Schir Kid, cum up Schir Salmond agane!' Stuffed with young goat the wily Tod lies dead to the world, musing idly in the sun that it only needs an arrow-shaft sticking out of his belly to complete the picture. Whereupon the goatherd comes along and obliges him. The fox has just enough time to give us his last words: 'allace and wellaway! . . . Me think na man may speik ane word in play / Bot now on dayis in ernist it is tane.' The moral of the tale is to beware the sudden stroke of death, lest it catch you unaware, but Henryson's wit gives it a crazier twist which even seems to comment on his own fabulation.

Many critics have remarked on the division between the humorous realism of the fables and the formal virtues that are extolled in the concluding morals. It is tempting to enjoy the fable and to dismiss the moral, but it must be stressed that both elements are equally central to the poem and to Henryson's vision. The *moralitas* may not always convince, but sometimes it can work with striking subtlety to give a broader, rather than a narrower account of the poem's meaning. In 'The Taill of the Cok and the Jasp', for example, *moralitas* and fable produce a kind of stalemate to trap the reader in real moral issues, quite different from simple maxims. A cock finds a precious jewel in the midden, but since he cannot eat it he leaves it there and goes his way:

> Thow hes na corne, and thairof haif I neid,
> Thy cullour dois bot confort to the sicht,
> And that is not aneuch my wame to feid.   enough; belly

In the fable the cock is a realist, yet the moral tells us he is a fool who prizes only his own ignorance, because the jewel symbolises knowledge and prudence – the only really enduring wealth – without which no one 'can Governe ane Realme, Cietie, or hous'. Alas, says the poet, the jewel is lost these days, still lying somewhere on a dunghill of disregard. While this allegory makes sense in its own terms, it does not mesh with the fable. The cock is not a swine that despises pearls because he knows only swill. On the contrary, he is aware of the Jasp's beauty and he recognises that it should be 'Exaltit in worschip and in grit honour' and set, perhaps, in a king's crown: 'Rise, gentill Jasp, of all stanes the flour, / Out of this midding, and pas quhar thow suld be'. But for himself, he observes that 'houngrie men may not leve on lukis'.

The reader is entirely convinced by this level-headed character and can scarcely blame him for leaving the stone, even if it does symbolise 'knowledge'. In fact, there need not be a contradiction between the two elements, and here again Henryson is using the moral to make his case more subtle. The final message which emerges from 'The Cok and the Jasp' is that knowledge and prudence belong in the first place with the king, and he must not expect too much of the common man, who has to struggle to find dry bread for his belly. If prudence is missing at court, why should it be valued in the farmyard? Moral and tale should not, therefore, be separated, for it is only through their conjunction that we reach the fullest insight into the frailties and contradictions of human existence.

In all aspects of his work Henryson's sympathies lie with the common folk. In 'The Taill of the Lyoun and the Mous' the king of the beasts spares an importunate mouse, but at a later date it is the tiny mouse and her relatives – the commoners – who gnaw through the nets to let the trapped lion escape. The *moralitas* extols mercy and vigilance in the great, not just as an abstract virtue, but as a matter of political prudence too, because 'Oftymis is sene' how 'ane man of small degre' can have his quittance of a nobleman. The message is clear: the mice may be small, 'wantoun' and 'unwyse', but they would have left the lion to die had he treated them too harshly at their first encounter: 'Bot King and Lord may weill wit quhat I mene'. The reader, too, will remember that the Declaration of Arbroath warned Robert Bruce that his subjects reserved the right to depose him if he betrayed their interests.

'The Wolf and the Lamb' makes the poet's position even more clear. The moral compares the lamb to the poor people and the wolf to those in power who pervert the laws to suit their own ends, particularly those feudal superiors who practise extortion on tenant farmers. Henryson provides details of how this is usually done and cries out at the plain injustice of a social and agricultural system which has the tenant labouring all day only to leave him 'lytill gude to drink or eit, / With his menye at evin quhen he cummis hame'. The abuse of power through the law is directly satirised in 'The Taill of the Scheip and the Doig', in which the poet observes all the technical niceties of legal procedure and places them in the mouths of a wolf as sheriff, a carrion-crow as beadle, a raven as coroner, a fox as clerk and a hawk as advocate. Little wonder, before such a court, that the sheep has to forfeit his fleece. This vivid and comic attack on the vested interests of authority does not hesitate to spell out its links with the human world and the darker implications of greed and folly.

The speech of the country sister in 'The Uponlandis Mous and the Burges Mous' is a model of native canny brevity, as when she is faced with the delicate titbits of her town sister's table and enquires:

> '. . . how lang will this lest?'
> 'For evermair, I wait, and langer to.'   know/expect
> 'Giff it be swa, ye ar at eis' (quod scho).   If it be so

Henryson shares her sense of caution as well as a countryman's taste for understatement, and he reminds us, with a straight face, of the part played by Fortune in the affairs of mice – 'Eftir joye oftymes cummis cair' – and then, when the steward discovers the two creatures at their feast in the cupboard, the poet pauses at just the most dramatic moment to comment dryly, 'Thay taryit not to wesche, as I suppose'. The fable's intimate expertise is entirely convincing in the accents of the country mouse – spokesperson for 'blyithnes in hart with small possessioun' – as she cries to her more sophisticated sister:

'I had lever thir fourty dayis fast,   rather
With watter caill, and to gnaw benis or peis,   cold water
Than all your feist in this dreid and diseis.'   unease

And with this she returns to her own humble home – undoubtedly situated somewhere in the kingdom of Fife.

The same voice gives unique colouring to Henryson's tale of 'Schir Chantecleir and the Foxe'. In 'The Nonne Preestes Tale' Chaucer's narrative style creates a brilliantly extended parody of rhetorical techniques and chivalric virtues, but the Scots poet's version retains the swift colloquial pace of the other fables. The code of *amour courtois* is exploded simply by reporting what the hens say about their fallen lover. At first, Pertok strikes a high-flown note by lamenting 'our dayis darling / Our nichtingall', but Sprutok – a more practical lady – reminds her that 'als gude lufe cummis as gais', and resolves to 'Chant this sang, "wes never wedow sa gay!"' As soon as Pertok is relieved of the burden of decorum, she too admits that the cock could not satisfy her and resolves to get within the week a fellow who 'suld better claw oure breik'. 'Schir Chantecleir' has been dismissed in three swift stanzas, and the hens' earthy honesty is a more telling judgement on his vanity than the main plot with the fox. Henryson's fables are full of such delights, demonstrating his ability to handle traditional materials as though the stories had never been told before.

Orpheus and Eurydice leaves the warmer world of the fables to make a grim Christian allegory out of that ancient myth, for the poet sees Orpheus's human and fleshly impatience as all too inevitable, despite his skill in the arts of celestial harmony and control. Here again, as with the Fables, the closing moral in strict favour of the sensible soul (Orpheus's musical skill), not being beglamoured by appetite (Eurydice) may be the best advice, but it is scarcely convincing to our own fallen and romantic natures –and the fact that we remain unconvinced may be the author's real point after all. Henryson's most famous poem, about Cresseid's downfall, is equally unrelenting at the end, although it also shows a stern kind of care.

The earliest printed version of *The Testament of Cresseid* was added to Chaucer's *Troilus and Criseyde* in a 1532 edition of the English poet's works. While Henryson's poem (also written in rime royal) is, indeed, a sequel to the longer tale, it demonstrates a very different point of view. Cresseid's failing is clear-cut: she is faithless and her sin is to blaspheme against Venus and Cupid, the fleshly deities to whom she has given her life. She has reason to be bitter in Henryson's version, for, having betrayed Troilus in favour of Diomede, she is herself discarded by her new lover. The Scots poet's view of the affair is sympathetic but clear-eyed and his spare introduction to her plight sets the mood for the whole poem:

> Quhen Diomeid had all his appetyte,
> And mair, fulfillit of this fair Ladie,
> Upon ane uther he set his haill delyte.

Henryson supplements the terse force of that phrase 'and mair' by noting that some men say that Cresseid became a common prostitute. She pays dearly for this and for her repudiation of Venus when the planets visit her in a dream trial, and Saturn and the Moon afflict her with leprosy. Cresseid's complaint is a passionate lament for the evanescence of worldly beauty and a warning about the fickleness of Fortune.

> 'Nocht is your fairnes bot ane faiding flour,   Nothing
> Nocht is your famous laud and hie honour
> Bot wind Inflat in uther mennis eiris.   ears
> Your roising reid to rotting sall retour: rosy skin; return
> Exampill mak of me in Your Memour!'

The familiar medieval theme of *ubi sunt* is evoked with a bitter power. Cresseid's good looks have become abominable and her very eyesight has been dimmed by disease, but Henryson's relentless and lucid fatalism makes her pay still more. Troilus passes one day and drops some alms in her leper's cup. He does not recognise her in her present state, but the pathetic figure somehow evokes memories of his erstwhile lover and prompts his charity. The moment is both dramatically and psychologically convincing. When Cresseid is told who her benefactor was, she finally accepts responsibility for her own failed honour, commends herself to chaste Diana and dies: 'O fals Cresseid and trew Knicht Troilus . . . Nane but my self as now I will accuse.' When he hears of her fate, Troilus erects a tomb over her grave.

The bare bones of the plot can give only a hint of the relentless concentration invested in the poem. It has the speed and the grim concision of a ballad, conveying beauty, terror and pity with masterly understatement. From the very start the *Testament* balances its setting with its subject matter – a formal rhetorical device – and gives it more than a hint of the Scottish climate, too. Thus the opening lines are set in springtime – a traditional beginning to a tale of love – but this fresh season has been symbolically countered by harsh and inclement weather:

Ane doolie sessoun to ane cairful dyte   A sad season to a sorrowful tale
Suld correspond, and be equivalent.
Richt sa it was quhen I began to wryte
This tragedie, the wedder richt fervent,
Quhen Aries, in middis of the Lent,
Schouris of haill can fra the north discend,
That scantlie fra the cauld I micht defend.

The poet himself, in the persona of an ageing and perhaps not too reliable narrator, wants to honour the star of Venus that night, hoping that 'My faidit hart of lufe scho wald mak grene', but the cold air drives him indoors to the fire, This wryly informal and domestic note allows Henryson to express his pity for Cresseid, and yet it never loses sight of the fact that she is a pagan character in a book with her fate already long established and inescapable.

I mend the fyre and beikit me about,   wrapped
Than tuik ane drink my spreitis to comfort,
And armit me weill fra the cauld thairout:
To cut the winter nicht and mak it schort,
I tuik ane Quair, and left all uther sport,   book
Written be worthie Chaucer glorious,
Of fair Cresseid, and worthie Troylus.

Of his distres me neidis nocht reheirs,
For worthie Chauceir in the samin buik
In gudelie termis and in Joly veirs
Compylit hes his cairis, quha will luik.
To brek my sleip ane uther quair I tuik,
In quihilk I fand the fatall destenie
Of fair Cresseid, that endit wretchitlie

Quha wait gif all that Chauceir wrait was trew?   Who knows if

Henryson meets the rhetorical conventions of narrative modesty by admitting that parts of the tale are not clear to him; this has the effect of distancing Cresseid's pain from us and yet, paradoxically, the method actually increases the emotional effect: 'Gif scho in hart was wa [sad] eneuch, God wait!'; and then: 'Sum said he maid ane Tomb of Merbell gray / And wrait her name. . . .' When Calchas sees his daughter's leprosy for the first time his lament is interrupted by the poet's curt comment, 'Thus was thair cair aneuch betwix thame twane'. The same succinct force can be found on Cresseid's lips, too, when she bewails the passing of her old life and realises her fate:

And for thy Bed tak now ane bunche of stro,
For waillit Wyne, and Meitis thou had tho,   choice
Tak mowlit Breid, Peirrie and Ceder sour: mouldy
Bot cop and Clapper, now is all ago.   Begging cup and
                                                    leper's clapper

Chaucer's version of the tale involves itself brilliantly and at length with
the sophisticated moods and trials of courtly love; but when Henryson
has Troilus reflect on the affair he sums it up with a stunning simplicity: 'Siching [sighing] full sadlie, said, "I can no moir, / Scho was
untrew, and wo is me thairfoir."' Such brevity is but the mask of feeling
and, indeed, there is a moving tenderness in how the characters treat
one another, as when Calchas welcomes his fallen daughter, or when
Troilus gives alms, or in how Henryson himself describes the leper folk
and how they receive Cresseid with a loving and practical concern:

'Sen thy weiping dowbillis bot thy wo,   Since; doubles
I counsail the mak vertew of ane neid.
To leir to clap thy Clapper to and fro,   learn
And leve eftir the law of lipper leid.'   leper people

The poet's narrative pace can be fast or lingering to equal effect, as
when Cresseid, newly afflicted with her disease, is summoned to dinner
by a serving-boy. She notices his good looks:

Quod scho: 'Fair Chyld ga to my Father deir,
And pray him come to speak with me anone'.
And sa he did, and said: 'Douchter quhat cheir?'

At other times the speed of the verse is greatly reduced, as the poet
draws on the older alliterative verse tradition and adds his talent for
domestic realism in order to convey the full terror of Saturn's presence:

His face fronsit, his lyre was lyke the Leid.   frozen; skin; lead
His teith chatterit, and cheverit with the Chin,
His ene drowpit, how sonkin in his heid,
Out of his Nois the Meldrop fast can rin,   drips
With lippis bla and cheikis leine and thin.   blue

'Robene and Makyne', 'The Bludy Serk' and the *Morall Fabillis* have
the same mastery of pace and ballad-like concision, but these qualities and
also the humane irony of Henryson's always direct and colloquial presence
reach their highest achievement in *The Testament*, giving us some of the
finest passages in European literature.

Sum said he maid ane Tomb of Merbell gray,
And wrait hir name and superscriptioun,
And laid it on hir grave quhair that scho lay,
In goldin Letteris, conteining this ressoun:
'Lo, fair Ladyis, Crisseid, of Troyis toun,
Sumtyme countit the flour of Womanheid,
Under this stane lait Lipper lyis deid.'

Henryson has the final word and the last line of the poem vibrates with his strong and tenderly fatalistic charity: 'Sen scho is deid, I speik of hir no moir.'

Blind Harry (1450–93)

If Barbour's *Bruce* reads like a lengthy biographical account of duty, chivalry and war in practice, written by a priest of the Church, then Blind Harry's *Wallace* is a popular thriller in which the reader is caught up by the narrative to ask 'What happens next?' through twelve books of verse. The *Wallace* is quite unlike *Golagros and Gawane* and other knightly romances of its time – for in place of the chivalric code it offers a crude but forceful character-study of its hero, full of circumstantial details and a heightened and bloody realism. *The Actes and Deidis of the Illustre and Vallyeant Campioun Schir William Wallace* must have been written around 1477 (170 years after the events it describes) and it is instructive to compare it with the nearly contemporary *Morte d'Arthur*. Malory's great prose work looks back to an imagined world of knights and ladies, and even as he describes the break-up of the Round Table he enshrines the values of chivalry and purity symbolised by the quest for the Holy Grail. Harry's *Wallace* has no such spiritual dimension and little time for the melancholy nobility of Malory's conclusion. On the contrary, the Scotsman's many descriptions of split brains and arms hewn away recreate the details of combat as if from a foot-soldier's point of view. For this reason the poem is much closer to the truth of warfare and the cruelty of the thirteenth, or indeed the fifteenth century. It is also closer to what we might assume to be the popular taste (then as now) for a succession of ever more gory effects.

We have few details about the author. He seems to have been a professional poet and it is known that on various occasions he appeared at court and received money from James IV. He is mentioned in the 'Lament for the Makaris' and probably died about 1492; and, although he is traditionally referred to as 'Blind Hary', it is not certain that he was born blind. At least one scholar has argued that the poet's grasp of military action and his descriptions of the weather and the lie of the landscape suggest that he lost his sight late in life. Harry describes himself as unlearned – 'a burell man' – and late-eighteenth-century critics were keen to support him in the role of rustic Homer – a blind peasant bard. This underestimates the skills available within the oral tradition and the conventional literary tropes of modesty. Nor does it accord with the plain and forceful versifying in Harry's heroic couplets, perhaps the earliest use of this measure in Scotland.

However composed, the *Wallace* became one of the nation's most widely read books and, until Burns came on the scene, the most often reprinted. Indeed, the poem virtually 'invented' the heroic figure of William Wallace as it is known today – right up to Mel Gibson's *Braveheart* (1995) – for although Harry claimed to be following a Latin original written by Wallace's chaplain, it seems as likely that he compiled the work himself from surviving tales, folk sources and his own imagination. His purpose was unashamedly nationalistic and anti-English. At a time when James III was attempting to make peace with his southern neighbours, Harry speaks for perpetual opposition, for keeping faith with France and for warlike virtues in a leader. Wallace would rather kill Englishmen than ransom them, and this is entirely in keeping with the facts of battle as they have always been for the mere troops. Indeed, this lack of knightly graces probably established him even more securely as a fully fledged folk hero.

The poem is long and in places merely tedious, but gradually a genuinely impressive picture emerges of a martyr swordfighter who will rescue Scotland on three different occasions before going – treacherously betrayed – to his own death. Robert Burns testified to the power of this figure to 'pour a Scottish prejudice' in his veins even in William Hamilton's shortened, paraphrased and highly popular version of the original. From the very start we gain a sense of Harry's Wallace as a fated person, rather like one of Marlowe's granitic heroes. Thus the young man has the misfortune to be bullied by a succession of arrogant (and ill-advised) Englishmen, as when he is fishing peacefully by a river and gets into an argument with five of Percy's men who demand his catch for their lord. The teenage Wallace, armed only with a net on a pole, and accompanied by a boy, is prepared to give them some but adds (too familiarly for the Englishmen), 'Gud frend, leiff part and tak nocht all away.' The retainer insists on having the lot and the vivid dialogue takes a more deadly turn:

'We serf a lord. Thir fische sall till him gang'.
Wallace ansuerd, said, 'Thow art in the wrang.'
'Quham dowis thow, Scot? In faith thow servis a   Whom do you
    blaw'   [address as 'thou';
Till him he ran and out a swerd can draw.   deserve a blow
Willyham was wa he had na wapynnis thar.   aghast
Bot the poutstaff the quhilk in hand he bar.   netpole
Wallas with it fast on the cheik him tuk
Wyth so gud will quhill of his feit he schuk.
The suerd flaw fra him a fut breid on the land.
Wallas was glaid and hynt it sone in hand,   glad and took it
And with the swerd ane awkwart straik him gawe,
Wndyr the hat his crage in sondir drawe.   under; neck
Be that the layff lychtyt about Wallas.   the rest set about
He had no helpe only bot goddis grace.
                                    (I, 397–410)

When two English survivors escape to tell Percy of the fight, the lord laughs at their discomfiture and refuses to pursue the Scot further. All the same, the hero flees the neighbourhood and Harry comments that he never left his sword behind again.

The poem's short sentences, terse dialogue and detailed violence make it particularly active and dramatic – the stuff of film-scripts, indeed. Although larger than life as a warrior, Wallace is not without some human qualities. He has a sense of humour (predictably grim) and his sufferings in battle and in sickness allow us to sympathise with him when his destiny and his own relentless will call him back to the practice of death after an all-too-brief spell of married happiness. At this point, the narrative takes a more tender and musical turn as it slips into *ballat royal*, an eight-line French stanza-form, to express a traditional farewell to life's comforts:

Now leiff thi myrth, now leiff thi haill plesance,   leave
Now leiff this blis, now leiff thi childis age,
Now leiff thi youth, now folow thi hard chance,
Now leiff thi lust, now leiff this mariage.
Now leiff thi luff, for thow sall los a gage   lose a pledge
Quhilk neuir in erd sall be redemyt agayne.
Folow fortoun and all hir fers outrage.   fortune
Go leiff in wer, go leiff in cruell payne,   live
                                    (VI, 81–8)

The tale soon returns to heroic couplets, however, as Wallace's wife is killed and he dedicates himself to further slaughter with a righteous and savage efficiency. If the tale dwells too much on killing Englishmen and general mayhem, it draws a veil over the manner of its hero's actual death, for William Wallace was hanged, cut down while still alive and disembowelled before his own eyes. Wallace was a hero and a martyr to his contemporaries, but Blind Harry's poem made him a legend, until even William Wordsworth intones the name as though it were talisman for a later revolution, synonymous with freedom itself:

> How Wallace fought for Scotland; left the name
> Of Wallace to be found, like a wild flower,
> All over his dear Country; left the deeds
> Of Wallace, like a family of Ghosts,
> To people the steep rocks and river banks,
> Her natural sanctuaries, with a local soul
> Of independence and stern liberty.
>
> (*The Prelude*, I, 213–19)

Wordsworth was not alone, and the myth of Wallace as a doomed freedom fighter of the common folk (he was actually the son of a knight) whose Christ-like death will liberate his people, has remained potent to the present day. His name was evoked by Mazzini and by Garibaldi's redshirts fighting for Italy in the nineteenth-century *Risorgimento*, and indeed Mel Gibson's wildly unhistorical film version of the tale was nothing less than the Americans' own War of Independence retold in kilts.

'Anonymous' poets

If we lack details of Blind Harry, there are poems from the latter half of the fifteenth century whose authors cannot now be traced at all. *The Knightly Tale of Golagros and Gawane* might have been written by Clerk of Tranent, cited in Dunbar's 'Lament' as the man who 'maid the Anteris [Adventures] of Gawane', but we cannot be sure. The poem is most likely contemporary with the *Wallace* but, quite unlike Harry's work, it is a courtly fiction which belongs to the fabled past with a plot of twelfth-century French origins in *Le Conte du Graal*. The climax involves a battle between rival champions Gawain and Golagros. To save his opponent's face, and because he cannot bear to kill him outright, Gawain pretends to lose the match. In the light of his gentlemanly discretion the two knights and their factions are soon reconciled. The poem uses the same thirteen-line stanza-form as *The Buke of the Howlat* – a favourite for alliterative romances. The same measure appears in *Rauf Coilyear*, and other similarities between the two romances suggest that the poet of *Rauf* was at least familiar with the Gawain piece. *Rauf Coilyear* goes back to the age of chivalry as well, but it gains a satirical or at least a humorous angle by making its short-tempered hero a collier (perhaps a charcoal-burner) by trade. Rauf becomes involved with Charlemagne when the king gets lost in a storm while out hunting. The collier offers shelter to the stranger but loses his temper with his anonymous guest when the latter's royal manners and polite hesitations make him slow to do his host's bidding. The great king receives buffets and a lecture on manners:

> 'Thow suld be courtes of kynd, and ane cunnand courteir.
>   Thocht that I simpill be,
>   Do as I bid the,
>   The hous is myne pardie,
>   And all that is heir.'

The host may be 'thrawin' but his table is generous with much game, taken, he explains, from the king's forest. Charles says he is one Wymond of the Queen's wardrobe and they part the next day with an agreement that Rauf will be paid to deliver a load of coal to the court on Christmas Day. The fiery collier is somewhat abashed when he discovers the true identity of his guest, but Charles gives him armour, a retinue and makes him a knight. All the same, he must still win his spurs by combat and this leads to further complications. But the tale ends happily and Rauf is made Marshal of France.

The two parts of Rauf Coilyear's tale almost certainly come from French sources, although stories of incognito kings were common in England, too. What begins as a rather pointed comment on manners, chivalry and the common man ends as an unlikely romance where everyone is rewarded with high office. Nevertheless, we appreciate the peppery Rauf of the earlier passages who proves with his fists the old French proverb that *'Charbonnier est maître chez soi'* and who might have been a model for the medieval understanding that to be a Scot was to have *piper in naso*, pepper in your nose.

The world of romance joins with the supernatural in poems such as 'King Berdok', 'The Gyre-Carling' and 'Lord Fergus' Ghost'. These pieces have an odd flavour, for they read less like magic and more like tall tales, and so they forfeit the sense of mystery and terror that the best of the great ballads have, not to mention that vital intimation of other planes of being. On the other hand, they take a matter-of-fact approach to the everyday, and couple it with an unusual sense of the instability of the physical world. It is a grotesque and striking combination. Hence Berdok, king of Babylon, lives in a cabbage-stalk in summer while a cockle-shell keeps him warm in winter, because, as the unknown author patiently explains, 'Kingis usit nocht to weir clayis in tha dayis.' The burlesque is grosser but the dislocating effect is the same in 'The Gyre-Carling', which, among other unlikely things, explains that the distinctive conical shape of the hill known as Berwick Law was produced by a witch who expelled it as a turd in her mirth.

While 'The Gyre-Carling' is outlandish, the scatological anti-Gaelic humour of 'How the First Helandman, of God was Maid', is closer to the realities of social and racial prejudice. (The poem is sometimes attributed to Montgomerie but is most likely to be an earlier production.) The author's position is clear from the start, for the title notes that the hero was made 'of ane horss turd, in Argylle, as is said', and no sooner is he created than he steals God's gully-knife and promises that, for as long as he can get gear thus, he will never work. The whole outrageous slander is expressed in the most good-humoured way, evincing a sturdy familiarity with the Supreme Being and his saints:

> God and Sanct Petir was gangand be the way,
> Heiche up in Ardgyle, quhair thair gait lay.   road
> Sanct Petir said to God in a sport word,
> 'Can ye nocht mak a Helandman of this horss turd?'
> God turned owre the horss turd with his pykit staff,
> And up start a Helandman blak as ony draff.   dregs
> Quod God to the Helandman 'Quhair wilt thow now?'
> 'I will down in the Lawland, Lord, and thair steill a kow.'

The economic foundations for Lowland Scottish prejudice could not be more succinctly put.

The failings of the priesthood provided equally popular material for broad comedy in verse, and 'The Freiris of Berwick' is sometimes attributed to Dunbar, although it lacks technical incisiveness and his acerbic spirit. This lively piece tells how two friars outwit the adulterous wife of an innkeeper and enjoy a luxurious meal at her expense. 'Colkelbie's Sow' also mixes the domestic, and the far-fetched (with a rather ponderous sense of humour), by playing on the disparity between its subject and a plot loosely based on the biblical parable of the talents, complete with *sententiae*, a 'prohemium' and apologies for its 'mokking meteris and mad matere'. Its three parts, in rather anglicised Scots, tell what became of the three pennies that Colkelbie got when he sold his pig. The author claims that he learned these tales and their moral implications from his toothless great-grandmother who had many such stories fresh in her mind. The poem's loose structure and its succession of ingenious events are, indeed, very reminiscent of oral fireside tales, although its use of 'literary' apparatus suggests a self-conscious and bookish side to the narrator as well.

A vivid and hilarious sense of country life characterises 'Peblis to the Play' and 'Christis Kirk of the Green', the best of the anonymous poems of this period. They have been ascribed to James I, but a later author is much more likely. Both poems give a light-hearted account of the antics that took place on two holiday occasions. 'Peblis' happens at Beltane (the old Scots fire festival that ushers in the summer), and the description of the 'play' – of the wooing and dancing and drinking and fighting – is undoubtedly true to the life and spirit of that festival. 'Christis Kirk' sets out to cap even Peebles's distinction, with extravagant behaviour described at a local fair-day:

> Was never in Scotland heard nor seen
>   Sic dauncing nor deray,   disturbance
> Neither at Falkland on the green,
>   Nor Peblis at the play
> As was of wooeris, as I ween,   suitors
>   At Christ Kirk on ane day:
> There come our kitties washen clean
>   In their new kirtillis of grey,
>   Full gay,
> At Christis Kirk of the green.

Both poems are remarkable for their rollicking rhythms, and this pattern of the 'Christ's Kirk stanza' has been much copied, with variations, in later Scots verse. The stanzas have ten lines each, the first eight of which rhyme abababab on alternate iambic tetrameter and trimeter. This provides a 'headlong' pace further emphasised by alliteration and the recurrence of the rhyme. Then there comes a 'bob-wheel' line of only two syllables to be clinched by a six-syllable refrain, which is the title of the piece repeated at this point throughout the poem. The 'bob' line gives a most distinctive catch at the end of each stanza before precipitating the reader on to the next. The effect is especially well suited to recitation or singing and it does much to enhance the broad wit of the poems and to further their irresistible comic progress.

Fergusson and Burns learned much from these patterns and both use nine-line versions of them (without the 'bob') for their own accounts of the people at play: Fergusson in 'Hallow-Fair' and 'Leith Races' and Burns in 'The Ordination' and 'The Holy Fair'. What the later poets gain in satirical and social comment, their unknown predecessor makes up for with a boisterousness that recalls a Flemish Kermess by

Brueghel, full of fierce dancing, willing women, brawling men and some pretty wild play with bows and arrows:

A yaip young man that stude him neist   keen
　Loused off a shot with ire:
He ettled the bern in at the breist,   aimed at the man's breast
　The bolt flew owre the byre;   over the cowshed
And cryit Fy! he had slain a priest
　A mile beyond ane mire;
Than bow and bag fra him he kest,   cast
　And fled as fierce as fire
　　Off flint,
At Christis Kirk of the green.

'Symmie and his Bruder' is yet another of those popular verses about merry friars – also notable for its use of the 'Christis Kirk' stanza – but 'The Thrie Tailes of the Thrie Priests of Peblis' is a longer and more conscientious affair, probably dating from the 1480s and commenting on the social ills and political failings in the reign of James III. It is a modest satire mainly concerned with telling its tales – and stories within the stories – as recounted by three priests after a particularly satisfying and worldly supper. Its cheerful vernacular uses homely couplets based on a pentameter line, and the tales, borrowed from older models or *fablieux*, have a simple domestic realism. It is possible to see an underlying unease in some of them about the growing power of money and the burgess class in the fifteenth century. In the last analysis, however, they remain a series of moral fables, and one has to look to Dunbar for the excitements of witty and acid criticism and to David Lindsay in the next century before social satire becomes a fully sharpened political weapon.

William Dunbar (1460?–1520?)

The fifteenth century ended with a 'second golden age' and a contemporary report from one Don Pedro de Ayala paints a picture of James IV as a gifted Renaissance prince. De Ayala was commissioned to his task because of Spain's eagerness to make an alliance with Scotland, and so in 1498 he sent off a document in cypher that described the king and his country. Doubtless the report is somewhat idealised, but Ayala had no reason to flatter or to lie outright. He tells of a well-read man with several languages, generous, handsome, popular and valiant to the point of recklessness in physical combat. He describes a country which is prosperous but not rich and a people who are extremely hospitable, bold, proud of appearances and quick to take offence. There is a contradictory side to the monarch, however, which de Ayala does not report, although it makes James even more a man of his times as a Renaissance prince whose temperament and whose kingdom, too, still retains something of a darker medieval past. The king was haunted by remorse all his life, perhaps for the part he felt he had played in his father's death, when, on the side of the Border lords he stood against the unpopular James III at the battle of Sauchieburn after which his father was killed. Only fifteen when he came to the throne (the father himself was only thirty-six), James went on religious retreats and was given to bouts of melancholy. He chose to wear an iron chain around his waist in penance and yet he also enjoyed an extravagant life, devoted to magnificent pageants, gambling, making love, good clothes and music. He shared these passions with equally strong intellectual pursuits, having an act passed in 1496 to make education compulsory for the offspring of men of substance and sending his own two illegitimate sons to be educated in Italy, where they studied for a while under Erasmus. By the end of his reign, however, the extent of these enthusiasms and his practical excitement with artillery, alchemy, medicine, surgery and mighty warships had left the crown almost bankrupt. (Launched in 1511, the *Great Michael* was the largest and most expensive war vessel of its day, displacing 1000 tons with a crew of nearly 300.) James was considerate and generous to religious orders and equally open-handed to passing musicians, jugglers and mountebanks. All his life he hoped to lead a crusade to the Holy Land, but at home he rewarded the most unsuitable men with powerful ecclesiastical positions. He was the last Scots ruler to speak Gaelic and he encouraged the commons to approach him and give him their opinions freely. In his strengths and failings, James is not unique among monarchs of his time, but the generous scope of his involvements and the number of his contradictions make him an especially charismatic, headstrong and romantic figure – one of Scotland's most popular kings.

William Dunbar is the most significant literary figure of the late fifteenth and early sixteenth century, a poet whose technical skill is second to none. He mastered English stanza-forms from Chaucer and Lydgate and he was equally at home with French style, especially in the use of refrain. (His particular forte is to use refrains supported by strong alliteration carried over into two or three lines of the verse.) Despite his technical brilliance, his humour can be harsh and pessimistic at times, or wildly Rabelaisian – closer to the late medieval mood than to that of the Renaissance. And yet, in moments of personal doubt, he seems much more modern – a spirit from the seventeenth or even the twentieth century. Because of these contradictions he epitomises more than any other writer the brilliance, the materialistic confidence and the spiritual unease of James's court and the onset of the Renaissance in Scotland.

We know little of Dunbar's life except that he was born around 1460 and educated at St Andrew's University; he may have become a Franciscan novice and he probably travelled a fair amount, visiting Paris and Oxford. For the last ten years of the century he seems to have served James as a notary and an ambassador, particularly in connection with the king's various plans for marriage. We know that Dunbar wanted a benefice as recompense for his services, but he had to settle for a series of pensions instead, probably given to him for his skill as a poet. Most of the poems that have survived date between 1490 and 1510 and they give a vivid picture of the court and its doings, unequalled in their colour and frankness.

Dunbar's commitment as a professional bard can be seen in formal, ceremonial works such as the poem which has come to be known as 'The Thistle and the Rose', commemorating the political marriage which James made with Margaret Tudor of England, in 1503. It uses the dream-vision convention to tell how the Thistle is crowned king of plants before celebrating its marriage to the red and white (English) rose. It is not above warning the king against letting his affections stray. In the same functional vein, 'Blyth Aberdeane' records the pageants with which this 'beryl of all touns' greeted Queen Margaret when she visited the north-east in 1511. The more ornate alliteration of 'Renounit, ryall, right reverend and serene' is a flattering address to Barnardus Stewart, who arrived at court in 1508 as ambassador from King Louis XII of France: 'B in thi name betaknis batalrus, / A able in field, R right renoune most hie' and so on: a public poem doing what is expected of it.

Dunbar admired Chaucer for his 'fresch anamalit termes celicall', but the Scotsman's aureate verse has no equal and his work abounds in brilliant and highly coloured descriptions. He shows us less of the natural sphere than Henryson, whose poems are closer to the world of fields and seasons, but his images have a hard elaborate and jewel-like intensity that has impressed many readers over the centuries. This richness is especially evident in the divine poems, such as the address to the Virgin Mary, 'Hale sterne superne, hale in eterne', where the verse achieves a music-like abstraction wholly given over to bright, clashing metallic

effects of alliterative and assonantal virtuosity – the verbal equivalent of
a page from the Book of Kells:

Empryce of prys, imperatrice,	Empress
Brycht polist precious stane,	
Victrice of vyce, hie genetrice	
Of Jhesu, lord soverayne:	
Our wys pavys fra enemys	shield
Agane the feyndis trayne,	Against; fiend's followers
Oratrice, mediatrice, salvatrice,	
To God gret suffragane:	
Ave Maria, gracia plena,	
Haile sterne meridians,	
Spyce, flour delyce of paradys	
That baire the gloryus grayne.	seed

When the poet dreams of Christ's passion on Good Friday ('Amang
thir freiris within ane cloister'), it is the physical details of the torment
that immediately engage him, and he even imagines that the soldiers let
the cross fall deliberately, to hurt the saviour more, before they raise
him above Calvary. The poem concludes with abstractions and the
dreamer is assailed by personifications such as Compassion, Contrition,
Ruth and Remembrance. In another poem it is the Resurrection on
Easter Sunday and the harrowing of Hell that stir Dunbar to announce,
'Done is a battell on the dragon blak', where the lines resound like a
gong with military triumph as the murk of the pit is suddenly penetrated by crystal-clear light:

The grit victour agane is rissen on hicht	
That for our querrell to the deth wes woundit;	
The sone that wox all paill now schynis bricht,	
And, dirknes clerit, our fayth is now refoundit:	
The knell of mercy fra the hevin is soundit,	
The Cristin ar deliverit of thair wo,	
The Jowis and thair errour ar confoundit:	Jews
Surrexit dominus de sepulchro.	
The fo is chasit, the battell is done ceis,	
The presone brokin, the jevellouris fleit and flemit . . .	gaolers fled
	and banished

The exalted orchestration of language and sound in these religious
poems leaves little scope for empathy or a more personal approach to
God despite its great artistic power, yet this achievement reveals quite
a lot about Dunbar's sensibility. It has been suggested that the

complexity of his verse may also owe something to a Gaelic bardic tradition and perhaps he did have an affinity with the Celtic love of complex and elaborate organic patterns developed to the point of pure abstraction.

'The Goldyn Targe' demonstrates Dunbar's aureate and emblematic imagination at work in a secular vein. In a dream allegory of a tournament the golden shield of the poet's reason is eventually, inevitably, overcome by a congregation of all the feminine virtues, seasons and goddesses. The players are borrowed from the *Roman de la Rose* and the stanza from Chaucer's 'Compleynt of Faire Anelida'. (The same pattern crops up at the start of Book II of the *Wallace*.) The poem is set traditionally in the month of May. The sunlight becomes 'clear', 'purified', 'crystalline', an effect typical of Dunbar's vision, and reminiscent, too, of parts of *The Kingis Quair*:

The rosis yong, new spreding of thair knopis,	buds
War powderit brycht with hevinly beriall droppis	beryl
Throu bemes rede birnying as ruby sperkis	
The skyes rang for schoutyng of the larkis;	
The purpur hevyn, outscailit in silvir sloppis,	overflowing;
Ourgilt the treis, branchis lef, and barkis	gilded over

Henryson's animals and plants have an individual existence as well as a place in the wider domestic ecology; but, for Dunbar, fish, fowl and flowers are turned to enamelled emblems of nature and set in a brilliant and Byzantine mosaic.

In a less elevated mode, the poet's skill with appearances provides a uniquely lively record of domestic behaviour at the court of King James. He describes a dance in the Queen's chamber ('Sir Jhon Sinclair begouthe to dance') and delights in exposing the antics of her retinue. Court physician Robert Shaw staggers like a hobbled cart-horse; Dunbar himself capers like a wanton colt until he loses his slipper; and in the extremity of the jig the Queen's almoner breaks wind 'lyk a stirk stackrand in the ry' [bullock staggering in the rye]. 'A mirrear dance mycht na man se', and Dunbar gleefully exposes the vulgar, mortal clay beneath the rich clothes and the pompous behaviour. From the evidence of such poems it becomes apparent that Dunbar's relationship with the court was at times a mixed and uneasy thing. He reminds the king that he has not yet received his expected advancement and begs him to listen to a petition from the Queen on his behalf ('Schir, for your grace bayth nicht and day'). Or he tells of his ambition to gain a benefice – 'Schir, yit remember as of befoir' – and presents James, and the reader, with a curious amalgam of slyly comic pathos and painful need: 'Jok that wes wont to keip the stirkis / Can now draw him ane cleik of kirkis . . . Worth all my ballatis undir the birkis [birch trees] / Exces of thocht dois me mischief.' With the same wry mixture he portrays himself in another poem as an old grey horse, poorly clad and cast aside without a decent stall to winter in ('Schir lett it nevir in toun be tald'). Yet this is not Dunbar's only persona, and the mask of a faithful old steed is cast aside to reveal sharper teeth and a less venerable nature when he pays off old scores by attacking James Dog, or Doig, the keeper of the Queen's wardrobe, who was rash enough to deny him a new doublet ('The wardraipper of Venus boure' and 'O gracious princes, guid and fair').

Flyting and the Gaelic influence

Dunbar's acid and brilliant technique is given traditional scope under the guise of flyting. Literary flyting – 'scolding' – was a popular mode in fifteenth- and sixteenth-century Scotland. It is a disputation in verse between poets, and a licence for inspired and absurd invective. Sheer expressive extravagance and technical ingenuity is the thing and, like a bout of professional wrestling, the contestants need not actually dislike each other before or even after the exercise. There are analogues in Greek, Arabic, Italian and Provencal literatures, but the genre owes more to oral contests in medieval Gaelic verse than it does to the European canon, and its heavily patterned hyperbolic abuse and its delight in the grotesque show the other side of the bardic praise poems. Indeed, the Gaelic bard's skill with words was truly a weapon in an oral society and he could threaten his enemies or a backsliding benefactor with verses that would confer on them an uncomfortable notoriety. A poet's curse was best avoided, and popular belief held that it could even raise blisters. The Bannatyne Manuscript contains examples of flyting such as 'The Flytting betwix the Sowtar and the Tailyar' – shoemakers and tailors being traditional enemies. Or again, 'The cursing of Sir Johine Rowlis upon the steilaris of his fowlis' offers no less than 261 lines of horrendous malediction upon presumptuous hen rustlers. As late as the 1580s Alexander Montgomerie and Sir Patrick Hume of Polwarth produced and delivered between them the 'Polwart and Montgomerie Flytting' and the story is that King James VI pronounced Montgomerie the victor. 'The Flyting of Dunbar and Kennedy' is the earliest surviving example of this genre in Scots. The two poets take turns at blast and counterblast, and it is likely that these originally went round the court as manuscripts or they may even have been performed as a verbal duel. Either way, they provide an outlet for the popular delight in grotesquerie already found in 'King Berdok' and 'The Gyre-Carling', a tradition carried into the twentieth century in aspects of the verse and prose of Hugh MacDiarmid, Sydney Goodsir Smith and even Irvine Welsh.

Walter Kennedy (1460?–1508?), of noble descent, was a contemporary of Dunbar, and in his time he was almost as well known a poet as his adversary. He came from the Carrick district of Ayrshire, and Dunbar takes the opportunity to mock his knowledge of Gaelic and to accuse him of country manners: 'Thy trechour tung hes ane Heland strynd; / Ane Lawland erse wald make a bettir noyis'; and 'The gallowis gaipis eftir thy graceless gruntill, [snout] / As thow wald for an haggeis, hungry gled' [hawk]. Regarding himself as a more sophisticated figure, Dunbar concentrates his attack on Kennedy's personal appearance and on the supposed gaucheness of the stereotypical Highlander when he appears in the capital: 'Stra wispis hingis owt quhair that the wattis [welts] ar worne . . . Than rynis thow down the gait [street] with gild of boyis, / And all the toun tykis hingand in thy heilis'. The poem gains force like a terrible spell – 'I conjure the, thow hungert heland gaist' – and ends with a veritable snare-drummer's paradiddle of internal rhyme and alliteration:

> Baird rehator, theif of natur, fals tratour, feyindis gett;   Bard enemy;
> Filling of tauch, rak sauch, cry crauch, thow art oursett;   [offspring
> Muttoun dryver, girnall ryver, yadswyvar, fowll fell the;
> Herretyk, lunatyk, purspyk, carlingis pet,   old woman's
> Rottin crok, dirtin dok, cry cok, or I sall quell the.

Lines two, three and five might be glossed as: 'Tallow-stuffed [one], [gallows] rope-stretcher, cry "give up", you are overthrown; Sheep-rustler, meal-robber, mare-buggerer – may ill befall you;' concluding with: 'Diseased ewe, dirty arse, admit defeat, or I shall quell you.'

Such virtuosity was not limited to flyting, of course, for it appears as a kind of choral music in Dunbar's holy poems, such as 'Hale sterne superne, hale in eterne', and indeed Henryson's 'Prayer for the Pest' concluded with just such a flourish:

> Superne / Lucerne/ guberne / this pestilens,
> preserve/ and serve/ that we not sterve thairin.
> Declyne / that pyne / be they Devyne prudens.

Internal rhyme was a popular device on both sides of the border in medieval Latin verse and hymns, but its special density in Scottish poetry, especially in the work of Dunbar, and in the later poems of Alexander Scott and Alexander Montgomerie, suggests a cultural predilection for such effects. In fact the Gaelic *filidhean* delighted in the most complex preset patterns of internal rhymes and alliterations, usually set out in syllabic couplets and four-line stanzas. Whether Dunbar knew Gaelic well or not, it seems very likely that he and his audience responded to such effects, because they were already present as a familiar part of Scotland's Latin and especially its Celtic heritage. After all, his rival Kennedy and the practice of flyting itself both came from Highland roots, and we know that James could speak Gaelic and rewarded Gaelic poets for recitals at court. On the other hand, Dunbar's overwhelming use of strong initial stresses, and the harsh and explosive consonants in his lines belong to the Lowland Scots tradition, with its links to Old English and Scandinavian sounds. By comparison, Gaelic verse lays greater emphasis on the softer chiming of assonance among internal vowels.

Despite his Gaelic heritage, Kennedy cannot quite rise to Dunbar's virtuosity in verse; on the other hand, it does lead him to attack his enemy's genealogy by giving his family a long tradition of cowardice and treachery and connivance with the English. He defends Gaelic as 'the gud language of this land' that 'sould be all trew Scottis mennis leid'. Such national feeling is significant, and we remember that Gaelic was still being spoken at this time in Galloway, Perthshire and the north-east, even if it was no longer the language of Lowland power.

Flyting is a hectic and specialised form, and Dunbar's comic gift is better displayed, at least to modern tastes, in his skill with burlesque and parody. In 'Ane Ballat of the Fenyeit Frier of Tungland' he satirises John Damian, an alchemist and 'sham friar' whom James had made abbot of Tungland in Galloway, much to Dunbar's envy and disgust. Damian literally fell from royal grace, however, when he attempted to fly like Icarus from the battlements of Stirling Castle, only to plummet into a dunghill and break his thigh. In vain did he explain that he only failed because he had glued too many hen feathers among the eagle's plumes on his wings, and that hen feathers 'covet the mydding and not the skyis'. Dunbar tells the tale with undisguised glee and the same colloquial gusto with which he scolds the merchants of Edinburgh for the noisy, crowded and smelly streets of their city ('Quhy will ye marchantis of renoun'). In other poems he follows French and Latin models by parodying the office of the dead in order to satirise a drunken court physician ('I, Maister Andro Kennedy'), or to persuade the king to stop doing penance with the Franciscans at Stirling, which is 'purgatory' compared to the heavenly delights of holding court in the capital ('We that are heir in hevins glory').

James was a part of this contradictory milieu, surrounded by brilliant men and importuned by place-seekers and charlatans. Dunbar hated the scene and yet he loves to depict it in poems that were written, after all, for the entertainment of the principal players. In 'Schir ye have mony servitouris' he points out that his own work will last as long as anything done by the king's company of diviners, philosophers, ship-builders and 'uther gudlie wichtis'. Furthermore, he complains that other, much less worthy types seem to thrive at court – the 'fenyeouris, fleichouris, and flatteraris' [pretenders, coaxers and flatterers], the 'fantastik fulis bayth fals and gredy, / Of toung untrew and hand evill diedie', the gossips, spongers, parasites, shovers and pushers, jostlers and thrusters who scurry and crowd in the corridors of power and who respect learning in no man. Here is the darker side of the life described by Don Pedro de Ayala, and in a characteristically devastating use of the catalogue Dunbar assembles it for our delectation and conveys his contempt in a *tour de force* of accumulating alliterative epithets:

Cryaris, craikaris, and clatteraris,	
Soukaris, groukaris, gledaris, gunnaris,	
Monsouris of France, gud claret cunnaris,	wine connoisseurs
Inopportoun askaris of Yrland kynd,	Irish petitioners
And meit revaris lyk out of mynd,	meat rustlers
Scaffaris and scamleris in the nuke,	snackers; pot-lickers
And hall huntaris of draik and duik,	
Thrimlaris and thristaris as thay war woid,	Hustlers,thrusters; mad
Kokenis, and kennis na man of gude,	Rogues
Schulderaris and schowaris that hes no schame,	
And to no cunning than can clame,	knowledge
And can non uthir craft nor curis	know; office
Bot to mak thrang, schir, in your duris,	crowd round; doors
And rusche in quhair thay counsale heir,	
And will at na man nurtir leyr	learn breeding

The poet's heart nearly bursts when all these creatures reap favour and he is ignored. He is just at the point of crying 'fy on this fals world', when an outrageous afterthought prompts him to conclude that he might be more patient if he, too, had some reward with the rest:

Had I rewarde among the laif:	others
It wald me sumthing satisfie	

And les of my malancolie,
   And gar me mony falt ouerse   make; overlook
That now is brayd befoir myn e . . .

The comic effrontery of this offer to write fewer satirical attacks if he is rewarded more is breathtaking, and yet curiously touching as well. We are moved because we sense that he probably means it. Dunbar's eye is unsparing when he regards the court; he mocks, chastises and derides it with all his considerable wit and technical dexterity, but ultimately his work needs it, and he himself belongs to it body and soul.

Perhaps it is his dependence on the court that makes Dunbar's forays against it so successful; but there is a wilder, demonic side to his imagination, and this, too, must play a part in giving his work its special edge. 'The Dance of the Sevin Deidly Synnis' conjures up personifications of Pride, Anger, Envy, and so on, and sets them cavorting to the latest steps from France in a nightmarish version of that dance in the Queen's chamber. The seven sins were a common motif in medieval literature and art, but Dunbar's vision of their awful Scotch reel in Hell seems to be an original twist. They are brilliantly and specifically characterised, simultaneously comic and disgusting:

And first of all in dance wes Pryd,
With hair wyld bak and bonet on syd . . .
Than Yre come in with sturt and stryfe,   Wrath; feud
His hand wes ay upoun his knyfe,
   He brandeist lyk a beir;   swaggered; bear
Bostaris, braggaris, and barganeris
Eftir him passit in to pairis . . .
Syne Sweirnes, at the secound bidding,   Sloth
Come lyk a sow out of a midding,
   Full slepy wes his grunyie . . .   snout

Each of them leads his human followers in a wretched babble of 'harlottis' and 'prestis', 'druncharts' and 'bakbyttaris in secreit placis', enough to grace the court of any king. The prideful skip in burning fires, the creatures of anger stab and cut each other with knives, the covetous vomit hot molten gold and the lecherous go through the dance leading each other by the penis.

Than the fowll monstir Glutteny,
Off wame unsasiable and gredy,   belly; insatiable
   To dance he did him dres;   begin
Him followit mony fowll drunckart
With can and collep, cop and quart,   flagon

In surffet and excess;
Full mony a waistles wallydrag   fat weakling
With wamis unweildable did furth wag   unmanageable
In creische that did incres.   blubber
'Drynk', ay thay cryit with mony a gaip;
The feyndis gaif thame hait leid to laip,   hot lead
Thair lovery wes na les.   portion

The whole terrible carnival continues until the Highlanders arrive,
whereupon they take up so much room in Hell and make such a noise
with their clatter in 'Ersche' that the Devil smothers the lot with smoke
and ends the dance.

The poem has stunning verbal and imaginative force – a wild
goliardic drive in the halfway house between horror and farce. The
same capacity for eldritch extravagance and all-too-specific physical
realism characterises the cultural tradition which produced 'Tam o'
Shanter' and *A Drunk Man Looks at the Thistle*. It is this precipitous
imagination that gives a particularly furious barb to Dunbar's technical
virtuosity, whether he is sending up the Office for the Dead or
burlesquing the medieval *débat* on love.

'The Tretis of the Tua Mariit Wemen and the Wedo' begins in high
style when the poet overhears three ladies discussing love in a garden
on Midsummer Eve. The setting, the aureate terms and the alliterative
blank verse all prepare the reader for a courtly poem on a matter of
sophisticated interest. It is noticeable, however, that their enjoyment at
table as they 'wachtit at the wyne' is just a little heartier than their
dainty white fingers might lead one to expect. These suspicions are
confirmed and the vision is shattered when they speak. One of the
wives wants to be as free as the birds to show herself 'At playis and at
preichingis and pilgramages', to move among men and 'cheis and be
chosen, and change quhen me lykit'. Like May in Chaucer's
'Merchant's Tale', she is married to a crabbed old man: 'Ane bumbart,
[dolt] ane dron bee, ane bag full of flewme, / Ane skabbit skarth
[cormorant], ane scorpioun, ane scutarde [shitten] behind'. Unlike
Chaucer, however, Dunbar allows no room for compassion at the
plight of this 'amyable', so bawdily does she describe the chains of her
condition. In response, the widow advocates utter hypocrisy: she has
had two husbands and like the Wife of Bath she is a woman of broad
experience and appetite. She advises the ladies to keep a lover and to
dominate their husbands if they can; but widowhood is best of all –
'My mouth it makis murnyng, and my mynd lauchis'. Like Henryson's
Sprutok, she has a lively sexual preference and, as she describes how she

comforts and flirts with several men at once, it slowly becomes apparent to the reader that her 'fair calling' is to run a brothel. Yet her speech throughout is larded with the terms of courtly love while she talks of her honour and advocates mercy as a 'meckle vertu' in women, just in case some pining (and no doubt paying) youth should die for want of her. Finally, the poem slips back into its ideal and aureate setting, as Dunbar distances his audience from what the ladies are actually saying and returns to 'silver schouris' and 'the sweit savour of the sward and singing of foulis'. It is a gay and coarse exposure of womankind, very much in the tradition of medieval anti-feminist literature, but without the subtlety and sympathy of the 'marriage cycle' in *The Canterbury Tales*. The Scots poet explodes the romance conventions, but his poem is essentially a cruel laugh at the gullibility of men.

The highly coloured scenes and the sometimes brutally reductive eye at work in Dunbar's poetry have their source in a darker aspect of his vision. He is never far from the 'malancolie' that stems from a strong sense of his own impending dissolution. This shadow provides a contrast that even further heightens the glitter of his wit and the enamelled elaboration of his style. 'Mutability' – the evanescence of man's earthly life – is a constant theme in late medieval literature, finding particularly fine expression in Villon's *Testament* from 1461, where the general pathos of the refrain from one of the ballades – '*Mais où sont les neiges d'antan?*' [but where are the snows of yester year?] – mingles with Villon's macabre but defiant awareness of the decay of the physical flesh. Dunbar's work, too, follows this vein of *memento mori*, but he is also prone to moods of highly personal anguish, and these moments of despair give his poems a more modern, even an existential aspect. 'I seik about this warld unstabile' begins by admitting that despite all his wit he has failed to find even one thought that is not ultimately deceitful:

> For yesterday I did declair
> Quhow that the seasoun soft and fair
>   Com in als fresche as pako fedder;   peacock
>   This day it stangis lyk ane edder,   adder
> Concluding all in my contrair.

All existence seems to offer him this personal affront, and he judges life to be a violent succession of absolute contrasts: 'Yisterday fair up sprang the flouris, / This day thai are all slane with schouris'. Not even in the closing stanza is there any hint of Christian comfort or eternal assurance:

So nixt to summer winter bein,
Nixt eftir confort cairis kein,
    Nixt dirk mednycht the mirthefull morrow,
    Nixt eftir joye aye cumis sorrow:
So is this warld and ay hes bein.

The masterly use of repetition makes its point and the contrasts are
stark and inescapable.

Dunbar's poems in this mood show little of the bitter-sweet pathos
of the medieval sense of mutability, nor do they show the fully Catholic
compassion for erring man seen in Henryson's 'Preiching of the
Swallow'. Instead, his pessimism has a misanthropic and sometimes a
curiously triumphant note. His certainty may be unpalatable, but it is
certainty, and he has found 'ane sentence convenabille' after all. He
writes of despair with great intensity, but such moments are almost
always prompted by mental or physical weaknesses with little hint of a
solely spiritual or moral dimension. He is a materialist and the images
he chooses are telling. When his spirit is utterly forlorn and 'no ladeis
bewtie' nor 'gold in kist [chest], nor wyne in coup' can help him, it is
not because he misses his saviour, but rather it is 'for laik of symmer
with his flouris' ('In to thir dirk and drublie dayis'). When he muses on
Fortune's wheel and on how we must always be ready to leave this
short life, ('Full oft I mus'), he concludes that we should enjoy
ourselves – 'For to be blyth me think it best' – and yet this last refrain
is repeated so often in the poem that it begins to lose all sense of
conviction. When Dunbar commends spiritual love over fleshly love in
'Now culit is dame Venus brand', he sees it entirely as a matter of age
over youth, made possible only because 'Venus fyre' within him is
nowadays 'deid and cauld'. The closing stanzas accept that, left to itself,
youth will never consider spiritual matters in the face of 'this fals dissa-
vand warldis blis'. The poet commends Christ's cause, but again he
sounds revealingly hesitant about it: 'He suld be luffit agane, think me'.
Finally, as an expression of Christian morality, the poem's continuing
refrain has an oddly determinist and physiological bias: 'Now cumis
aige quhair yewth hes been / And trew lufe rysis fro the splene.' Even
if we grant that the theory of humours would seem more apposite in
Dunbar's time than it does now, these lines still seem strangely, even
grotesquely indecorous, undoubtedly suggesting a certain unease in
the speaker's spirit.

Dunbar's discontent and his materialistic cast of mind have resulted
in some poems that seem almost modern, at least to post-Romantic
eyes. The poet has suffered a migraine in 'My heid did yak yester nicht';

he can scarcely look on the light and he cannot find words to express his thoughts, trapped somewhere in his memory, 'Dullit in dulnes and distres'. He may rise in the morning but his spirit is still sleeping and it seems that nothing can stir it:

> For mirth, for menstrallie and play,
> For din nor danceing nor deray,
> It will nocht walkin me no wise.

The spirit of this poem is worthy of Coleridge, with its despair at a loss of imaging power, its inability to face the light, source of all illumination, and its failure to 'dyt thought'.

A conventional Christian note is allowed to appear at the very end of the famous poem 'Lament for the Makaris', but it seems like an abrupt and unconvincing afterthought:

> Sen for the deid remeid is none,   Since; death
> Best is that we for dede dispone   prepare
> Eftir our deid that lif may we:
> *Timor mortis conturbat me.*

If this is hope, it is quite outweighed by the force of the previous twenty-four stanzas, not to mention the internal rhyme 'remeid' and the repetition of 'deid' in each of the last three lines. Every stanza ends with that solemn Latin refrain from the Office for the Dead – 'the fear of death disturbs me' – conveying a personal terror which strikes like a funeral bell. By comparison, Henryson's 'Prayer for the Pest' is devoutly Christian, making supplication to God's mercy and power in every stanza. Death by plague was a familiar visitor at the beginning of the fifteenth century, yet Henryson's prayer shows no personal anguish and accepts it utterly in true 'medieval' humility as the justice of God: 'our syn is all the cause of thiss'. In contrast, Dunbar draws on the medieval *danse macabre* for his poem (Lydgate before him had used the same Latin line) as well as a list of type-figures of those who must inevitably come to die: 'Princis, prelotis, and potestatis, / Baithe riche and pur of al degre' – all are mortal, not forgetting the intellectuals of James's court, 'Rethoris, logicianis and theologgis, / Thame helpis no conclusionis sle' [cunning]. Death even takes 'on the moderis breist sowkand, / The bab full of benignite'. For, with that thin and relentless 'ee' rhyme echoing down the poem, there can be no suggestion of acceptance. Indeed, from the very first verse the poem generates a personal cry – 'I that in heill wes and gladnes /Am trublit now with gret seiknes' – and this note is confirmed when Dunbar begins to name all the other poets who have played their part in the pageant and gone to the grave. The toll contains twenty-four makars – a most useful record for the literary historian, although some remain unknown to us or only a few lines by them survive. They and their works have, indeed, been devoured by that 'strang unmerciful tyrand':

I se that makaris amang the laif	rest
Playis heir ther pageant, syne gois to graif;	grave
Sparit is nocht ther faculte:	
Timor mortis conturbat me.	

He hes done petuously devour
The noble Chaucer of makaris flour,
The Monk of Bery, and Gower, all thre:
Timor mortis conturbat me.

. . .

In Dunfermelyne he hes done roune	
With Maister Robert Henrysoun.	
Schir Johne the Ros enbrast hes he:	embraced
Timor mortis conturbat me.	

And he hes now tane last of aw	
Gud gentill Stobo and Quintyne Schaw,	
Of quham all wichtis hes pete:	whom; beings; pity
Timor mortis conturbat me.	

Gud Maister Walter Kennedy
In poynt of dede lyis veraly:
Gret reuth it were that so suld be:
Timor mortis conturbat me.

Sen he hes all my brether tane	
He will nocht lat me lif alane;	
On forse I man his nyxt pray be:	Perforce; must
Timor mortis conturbat me.	

Sen for the deid remeid is none,
Best is that we for dede dispone
Eftir our deid that lif may we:
Timor mortis conturbat me.

Starkly and unforgettably, the 'Lament' expresses the greatest imponderable of human existence. In this context the capacity to make poems was all-important to Dunbar, for, when it fails, as in 'My heid did yak yester nicht', or when he foresees his extinction as a man, he is left with nothing else. Except, of course, that his work has given him a special kind of life after death – perhaps the immortality that meant most to him after all. The darker poems are the antithesis of Dunbar's commitment to the glitter of court life. His technical bravura, his satirical wit, his worldly cynicism and his inner terror make a potent and disturbing combination, and perhaps this is why he speaks so powerfully to modern readers.

James IV and the brilliance of Scotland's first steps into the Renaissance were soon to be swept away. The Scottish king had treaties with both England and France, but Henry VIII's increasingly hostile acts against France and a recent raid on Scottish shipping finally committed James to the Auld Alliance and led him, reluctantly but guided, perhaps, by a notion of chivalric honour, to invade England. The Scots army was catastrophically defeated at the Battle of Flodden in 1513, where some 10,000 men were killed on Branxton Hill in Northumberland. James himself died in the thick of the fighting along with members of his retinue, many nobles and hundreds of the lesser gentry and yeomanry. The English retired, the king's infant son succeeded to the throne for yet another Stewart minority, and a peace was concluded the following year. The battle had served no military or political purpose whatsoever, and Scotland was shattered by the loss of her most popular king. Most households of note counted one or more members among the dead and Flodden Field passed into the folk memory, and remains to this day, a traumatic symbol of failure and grief, later commemorated in the song 'The Flowers of the Forest' and a pipe tune of that name too. Dunbar lived on for another seven years at least, but we hear nothing more from him or about him, and we do not even know where he was buried.

Writing in prose

The works of James I, Henryson, Holland and Dunbar reach a high order of accomplishment. In fifteenth-century Scotland such powers of imagination and technique are solely the province of the poet, and vernacular prose remains in its infancy. The literature of most countries shows the same pattern, although in this respect the prose romances of France and Malory's *Le Mort d'Arthur* are more advanced. **Sir Gilbert Hay** (1400?–1499?) provides the earliest known literary prose in Scots

with his translations from French and Latin originals. Hay is also credited with the *Alexander*, a lengthy verse translation from the French,
and he is mentioned as a poet in Dunbar's 'Lament'. His career also
emphasises the French connection, because he was at one time
Chamberlain to Charles VII. Back in Scotland in 1456, he made his
manuscript translations at the request of his host, the Earl of Orkney
and Caithness. *The Buke of Armys*, *The Buke of the Order of Knychthood*
and *The Buke of the Governaunce of Princis*, all from the French, have
to do with noble models of philosophy, behaviour and belief. Caxton
was to publish his own translation of the *Livre de l'Ordre de Chevalrie*
almost thirty years later, so the taste for such topics survived for quite
some time and, of course, long after the chivalric order itself.

The only other prose writer of note is **John of Ireland**
(1440?–1496?), who, like Hay, had been to France, spending thirty
years there and ending up as confessor and counsellor to Charles's
successor, Louis XI. He produced an original piece of Scots prose
(again in manuscript only) for the edification of the nineteen-year-old
James IV. *The Meroure of Wysdome* (1490) is a lengthy treatise (seven
books) on political and personal wisdom linked to theological and
philosophical discussion, in which the author is at pains to legitimise his
position by referring to the authority of holy writ and to the scholarship of Paris. John reveals something of the status of vernacular prose
among academics in his time by being anxious to point out that, for
writing, he knows Latin better than he does the 'commoune langage'
of his country. Nevertheless, a considerable tradition in vernacular
historiography was soon to evolve in Scotland, and the undistinguished
verse of Wyntoun's *Oryginale Cronykil* of 1424 was followed by a
number of prose historians in the next era and then by a host of doctrinal historians in the seventeenth century. In the meantime, John of
Ireland defends his use of the vernacular, even although he knows that
'mony errouris agane the faith and haly doctrine of iesu and of the kyrk
ar writtin in this tounge and in inglis, at a part of the pepil of thi realme
ar infekit with it'.

It is not too fanciful to detect here already the rumblings of
approaching Reformation and the major part that vernacular prose was
to play in it.

3
The sixteenth century:
John the Commonweill

WHEN the Renaissance came to Scotland it came as a spirit from abroad gradually making itself felt in the harsher climate of a northern country. The spirit flowered until Flodden left the crown on the head of a two-year-old boy. Then, within only fifteen years, a new factor was added to the perennially shifting balance of power between king and barons. The scale was tipped in 1528 when a 24-year old priest, Patrick Hamilton, a pupil of Erasmus and of Luther, was burned as a heretic at St Andrew's for preaching that man stands alone before God and is justi-fied only by his faith. Hamilton argued that this faith is God's gift only and cannot be earned by good works, or interpreted or ameliorated by the hierarchy of any church. Soon this bare philosophical light, with all the hard clarity of the north, quite outshone the Mediterranean sunshine of that late spring at the court of King James IV. Nor was it simply a matter of religious belief, for kings, too, are only men before their maker, and soon the new church was reminding them of that fact and resisting all attempts at royal control. By the end of the century Andrew Melville was speaking for the very spirit of Scottish Presbyterianism when he reminded his ruler that 'there is twa kings and twa kingdomes in Scotland. Thair is Chryst Jesus the King, and his kingdome the Kirk, whose subject King James the Saxt is, and of whose kingdome nocht a king, nor a laird, nor a heid, bot a member.' This exhilarating and dangerous insight was to engage the intellectual and creative energy of the country for the next 200 years. It gave the Reformation a more revolutionary and democratic cast than it had in England, where the monarch remained as head of the Church, yet its fiercer elements would propose a far more total control over the indi-vidual spirit than any mere king could ever hope to achieve.

James V, 'the gudeman of Ballengeich', died in ineffectual despon-dency, yet at the beginning of his reign he had vigorously advanced the influence of the crown by taxation and military action. He provided funds for the Court of Session, annexed the power of the Lords of the Isles and led expeditions into the Borders to control the reivers there. In those debatable lands the barons still ruled like minor kings, doing nothing to discourage bandit families from raiding property and burning churches in England and Scotland alike. (One of these wild men, Johnny Armstrong, is remembered in tales and ballads: he and forty-eight of his men were hanged in 1530.) When Henry VIII split from Rome he was eager to make an alliance with his northern neighbour, but James sided instead with Catholic Europe through a French marriage, although his sickly bride died within a year. His second wife was made of stronger stuff, and Mary of Guise, destined to be the mother of Mary Queen of Scots, was an especially staunch supporter of both the old religion and the absolute power of monarchs. This alignment established a tension between Scotland, England and France that was to dominate the century and make it impossible to separate the issues of religion and politics. Thus Protestant reformers would be supported by England against their own sovereign, while Scottish nobles took first one and then the other side according to their conscience and their sense of personal advantage. In such a context there was little hope that more moderate Catholic reformers would prevail, and the fiasco of the battle at Solway Moss further disillusioned both commons and nobles against the notion of military action in the French Catholic cause. 'It cam wi a lass, and it'll pass wi a lass', James is said to have murmured about the Stewart succession when he heard of his daughter Mary's birth as he lay on his death bed at the age of thirty. For the next eighteen years Mary of Guise acted as queen regent. Henry pressed his plans to make an English marriage with the infant Scottish queen and when all else failed he tried brutal persuasion by ordering his armies to make deliberately destructive raids on southern Scotland, 'sparing no creature alyve'. But Henry's 'rough wooing' and his boast that he was the 'very owner of Scotland' only strengthened the Auld Alliance, and the child Mary fled first to Inchmahome Priory and then was sent to France, where she was betrothed to the Dauphin. They married in 1558. She was 16 and he was 14. He succeeded to the throne within a year and died the year after that, leaving Mary at the mercy of his mother Catherine de Medici.

In the meantime, the queen regent had been steadfastly resisting the gathering changes of Reformation. She had a potent ally in Cardinal David Beaton, but he only spurred on the Reformers' cause and ensured his own death when he burned another Lutheran reformer, the young George Wishart at St Andrew's in 1546, thus launching an aging

John Knox into brief exile and a stormy career. Knox returned from Europe inspired with Calvin's doctrinaire vision of a fighting faith. He motivated a Protestant pressure-group among the nobles, calling themselves the Lords of the Congregation of Jesus Christ, and his passionate preaching around the country encouraged his followers to see themselves as the Children of Israel, engaged against an oppressor no less harsh than Pharaoh himself. The country almost came to civil war before the Treaty of Leith and the queen regent's death brought about the first Reformation parliament in 1560, whereupon the Confession of Faith and *The First Book of Discipline* set out the Scottish ideals for a new Protestant kirk. When Mary Queen of Scots returned from France in 1561, she found her mother's religion out of favour and her own priest intimidated at court. The first years of her reign passed off well enough, but hers was a fraught existence, for in the eyes of Catholic Europe she, and not Elizabeth I, was the legitimate heir to the English throne. The young queen was soon submerged in a rising tide of political, religious and sexual intrigue which her own headstrong nature did nothing to quell. After the murder of her favourite, Rizzio, and the assassination of her effete husband Darnley, she allowed herself to be abducted by Bothwell (who was suspected of complicity in Darnley's death), and then, most ill-advisedly, she married him in 1567 only a week after he divorced his own wife. In the ensuing uproar Bothwell had to flee the country and Mary was forced to abdicate in favour of her infant son. After a last desperate throw of the dice, she retreated to exile in England, where her cousin Elizabeth kept her in effective captivity for nineteen years before finally resolving the threat of Catholic succession with the edge of the headsman's axe.

James VI's inheritance was not an auspicious one, and his early love of culture and his own pretensions to literature were pursued in an uneasy and isolated context. In the Ruthven raid of 1582 the sixteen-year-old king was actually kidnapped by nobles who feared that his infatuation with the young lord of Aubigny, the Duke of Lennox, would lead to dangerous Catholic influence at court. Lennox fled and James escaped to wage his long but circumspect tug-of-war with Presbyterianism at home, while keeping an eye abroad on his prospects for the throne of England.

After Knox's death in 1572 it was **Andrew Melville** (1545–1622) who consolidated Scottish Presbyterianism and developed the aims in Knox's *First Book of Discipline*. Melville was a graduate of St Andrews and Paris and a scholar and theologian of European reputation who held chairs in Geneva and Glasgow and became moderator of the

General Assembly. The Presbyterian ideals were noble in many ways, although not always fully realised. The new church was to be based on a democratic hierarchy beginning with each congregation and working up to the General Assembly, a kind of church parliament that was answerable only to God. At the grass roots, ministers had to be elected by their own congregations and no landowner could put his own man in the pulpit. At the same time the clergy were an independent and influential moral authority in the parish and could mete out punishments in public for the social misdemeanours of their flock. The new kirk set great store on the Bible as the full expression of God's will, and so preaching and educating the masses became a worthy priority. Every householder was to read the Bible to his family; there was to be a schoolmaster skilled in the classics in every parish; bursaries were to be made available for the talented poor, while there were to be colleges in every large town, and divinity was to be taught at the universities along with medicine and law. There was already a good foundation for this work and the University of Edinburgh was founded in 1582 to join St Andrews, Glasgow and two universities in Aberdeen to aid the project. Unusually for this time, Edinburgh University was established by a Royal rather than a Papal charter and was funded by the town council to make it, in effect, the first civic university. This practical concern with the status and welfare of the common man, both spiritual and temporal, was radical and humane, yet, as so often happens, the revolutionary ideal contained the seeds of authoritarianism. The Calvinist doctrine of the elect also led to exclusiveness, and in some circles a narrow literalism in the reading of the Scriptures produced fanaticism and intolerance.

James VI was not slow to see the political implications of such a structure, nor was Melville afraid to point them out, famously calling his monarch 'God's sillie vassal'. The king duly noted that 'Presbytery agreeth as well with a monarch as God and the Devil', and gradually set about regaining a degree of royal control. Preaching the absolute separation of Church and State, Melville was threatened with prison and had to flee to England for a couple of years, studying at Oxford and Cambridge, before returning to Scotland to take up the struggle again. At the end of March in 1603 the news arrived in Edinburgh that Queen Elizabeth had died. A week later, King James set off for the south and the throne of England.

Melville and James were to clash again in 1606, when he was called south to advise on the new (King James) translation of the Bible. Melville's opposition to episcopacy in general and to English services in particular got him imprisoned for five years, before being allowed to spend the rest of his life in exile as a professor of the University of Sedan in France. The Scottish Reformation's radical distinction between Church and monarch, between a conception of God as absolute and of the state as limited, was to be a cause of dispute, in one form or another, right into the nineteenth century.

Gavin Douglas (1475?–1522)

In both his work and his life, standing divided between the Renaissance and the late Middle Ages, Gavin Douglas demonstrates something of the contradictions to be found in sixteenth-century Scotland. His greatest achievement was the translation of Virgil's *Aeneid*, and, although it is distinctly medieval in setting and interpretation, its commitment to the classical world and its concern to speak to a broader audience undoubtedly belongs to the new age. Douglas was born into the 'Red Douglases', the earls of Angus, who, with the 'Black Douglases' of Lanarkshire, were among the most powerful and ambitious families in Lowland Scotland, both boasting descent from the line of Robert Bruce's great champion and both with remote claims to the Scottish throne. Gavin, or Gawin, was the third son of the fifth Earl of Angus, Archibald 'Bell the Cat', who earned his nickname when he hanged seven of James III's special but 'low-born' court favourites from the Bridge at Lauder. Young Gavin Douglas went to St Andrew's University in 1490 at the usual age of fifteen. He graduated after four years' study (conducted in Latin) of typical subjects such as grammar, rhetoric, Aristotle, mathematics, music and astronomy.

It is likely that he also went to Paris and visited the continent at least once more before settling in his native land with a career in the Church, established as Dean of Dunkeld in 1497 and securing a place about six years later at the church of St Giles in Edinburgh and also the Scottish court, where he must have crossed paths with William Dunbar. It was during these years that he wrote his poetry, completing the *Eneados* in 1513, scarcely two months before the Battle of Flodden. After the death of James IV all Douglas's energies were directed towards political affairs and to seeking an ecclesiastical appointment commensurate with his family's rank. He was eventually granted a bishopric at Dunkeld, but the French-connected factions of the regent Albany suspected him of political alignment with England. Matters came to a head and the poet had to resort to bribes and threat of arms to retain his place at Dunkeld and his standing in the tangled pattern of influence. But in the end he still had to flee to England, where he spent his days at court trying to arrange his return to the north. He died of the plague in 1522, exiled in London and a victim of the family influence that had promised so much.

Douglas's first poem, *The Palis of Honoure* (1501), is wholeheartedly within the medieval dream-allegory tradition. Dedicated to the king, the piece follows a French vogue for such subjects and expounds, in three books, the various ways in which honour may be obtained in the life of a gentleman. In his dream the poet has various encounters with the allegorical representatives of Wisdom and Love; he is taught proper humility and sees famous writers from all times (including Dunbar); and he has a confrontation with the world's pain and the hope of salvation. When the poet finally does gain the palace of honour, guarded by Patience, organised by Charity, he is led to a keyhole where he glimpses Honour himself, only to faint before his blinding glory. The style of the poem is aureate and 'enamelled' along the lines of Dunbar's near-contemporary pieces 'The Goldyn Targe' and 'The Thrissil and the Rois'. Thus Douglas delights in using an elaborate polysyllabic diction to 'amplify' or extend his descriptions, and he encourages the formal complexities of his craft by choosing a difficult nine-line stanza that depends on only two rhymes. These factors, the author's fluent Latinity and a wealth of learned allusions to history, myth, the Bible and the classics, make the poem something of a young man's *tour de force*, a dish worthy indeed of being set before the king.

Douglas is often credited with another allegorical poem, called 'King Hart', but much doubt must remain about the attribution since it appears only once, in the Maitland Manuscript, added by a later hand. Such allegories belong to an earlier age, and it is Douglas's translation of the *Aeneid* that kept his name alive in the seventeenth and eighteenth centuries when greater makars were all but forgotten. It also contains, in the form of the prologues to each book, the best of his own original poetry and memorable reflections on the use of the vernacular and the art of translation itself.

Douglas worked on his *Eneados* for a year and half before setting literature aside in favour of his political career. Next to the *Wallace* it was the longest piece of verse yet sustained in Scots. It circulated in various manuscript copies, at least five of which have survived, but it was not published until 1553, thirty-one years after its author's death. (This was in an unsatisfactory edition made in London, anglicised and 'Protestantised'.) Nevertheless, it was common practice at the time for books to be copied by hand, for Chepman and Myllar's press – established in Edinburgh in 1507 – had not yet had time to fulfil the growing demand for Scottish books. Virgil's works were particularly popular throughout Europe, with over a hundred Latin editions printed by the beginning of the century and many others copied by hand. Some classical authors were also being translated and, indeed, in 1509 Octavien de Saint Gelais published an edition of the *Aeneid* in French. Whether Douglas saw the French version or not, he felt himself to be in the forefront of the movement to make the classics available to a wider audience, and in the 'Conclusio' to his labours he encouraged fault-finders to do something more useful, such as translating Ovid.

Douglas's was the first full-length translation of a major classical text to be made anywhere in Britain and it earns him a deserved place in the cultural history of the Northern Renaissance. He was not unaware of the importance of his achievement. Accordingly, he castigates Caxton for inferior passages in his version (1490), which was based on a French paraphrase, and prides himself on keeping close to the 'fixt sentens or mater' of his original, so that 'all thocht my termys be nocht polisht alway, / Hys sentence sall I hald, as that I may'. Nevertheless, the poem is not exactly Virgil's, for the Latin hexameters have been rendered into heroic couplets and the text is expanded and explained in places with the aid of Ascensius's commentary as attached to his Latin edition of Virgil, first published in Paris in 1501. Furthermore, Douglas prefaces the thirteen books (one by Maphaeus Vegius) with original prologues of his own. In six of these (I, III, V, VI, IX and XIII), he gives serious attention to the problems of translation, which he solves by choosing contemporary equivalents in weapons, clothes, ships and manners. He asks for help if he has made errors, and warns against those who would spy out every 'falt and cruyk', even if he admits that he can see very few faults himself: after all, 'the blak craw thinkis hyr awin byrdis quhite'. This running commentary adds great charm to Douglas's version of the classical poem. Indeed his narrative couplets and Scottish settings provide a robust immediacy which may well be better suited to the primitive world of Aeneas than the decorous circumlocutions chosen by Dryden and later neoclassical translators. (This was certainly Ezra Pound's opinion, who even preferred Douglas to the original.)

Some of Douglas's finest poetry comes from the descriptions of the natural world that introduce Books VII, XII and XIII. These passages have become part of poetic history by anticipating James Thomson's *The Seasons* (1730) and hence something of the natural and informal descriptions of weather and landscape later realised by the English Romantics.

The Prologue to Book XII describes dawn on a May morning. It starts conventionally enough when Phoebus's chariot appears above the sea, dame Flora scatters flowers, and the poet creates a literary landscape of blossoms, animals and young people in a scene reminiscent of the more formal *Palis of Honoure*. Yet there is physical particularity too, as every detail is brilliantly etched in the sun's early light:

Towris, turettis, kyrnellis, pynnaclys hie	battlements
Of kyrkis, castellis and ilke fair cite,	each
Stude payntit, euery fyall and stage,	little tower and storey
Apon the plane grund, by thar awyn umbrage.	shadow

Plants and flowers are described with botanical specificity. Giddy young lovers pine and tease each other with whispered, oblique phrases:

Smyland says ane, 'I couth in previte	know how to
Schaw the a bourd', 'ha, quhat be that?' quod he	jest
'Quhat thyng?' 'That most be secrete', said the tother.	

Here and everywhere Douglas catches a sense of movement with telling and realistic detail: 'So dusty pulder upstouris in euery streit, / Quhil corby [crow] gaspit for the fervent heit.' It was just this quality that Thomas Warton admired when he praised the passage for being 'the effusion of a mind not overlaid by the descriptions of other poets, but operating, by its own force and bias, . . . on such objects as really occurred' (*The History of English Poetry*, 1774–81).

If Douglas begins Book XII with a welcome to the May dawn, the Prologue to the following book describes a sunset in June – a luminous northern evening declining slowly into silence and darkness. In the night the poet dreams that Maphaeus Vegius chides him for not having translated his supplement to Virgil. Convinced by the ghost's argument (and the blows it rains on his head) Douglas agrees to satisfy his querulous visitor. Waking in the half-light before dawn he sees the stars quenched one by one – 'That to behald was plesans and half wondir' – until the workaday world gets under way and the spell is broken by a farm steward shouting to his men 'Awaik! On fut! Go till our husbandry.'

The poet's delight in natural settings, described almost for their own sake, is most striking of all in his account of a northern winter in the Prologue to Book VII. In a scene reminiscent of the opening to *The Testament of Cresseid* we see the translator composing himself for sleep, wrapped in three layers 'fortil expell the peralus persand [piercing] cald', while outside, under the watery light of the moon, he hears 'the geiss claking eik by nyghtis tyde / Atour [around] the cite fleand'. In the morning he peeps from the window at the 'scharp hailstanys . . . hoppand on the thak [thatch] and on the causay by' before withdrawing to the fireside to take up again the burden of his verses. Outside his window a typically northern countryside wrestles in the grip of the 'schort days', ruggedly evoked in harsh alliterative lines:

Thik drumly skuggis dyrknyt so the hevyn,	shadows
Dym skyis oft furth warpit feirful levyn,	hurled; lightning
Flaggis of fire, and mony felloun flaw,	deadly blast
Scharpe soppys of sleit and of the snypand snaw.	biting
The dolly dichis war all donk and wait,	dismal; dank
The law valle flodderit all with spait,	spate (flood water)
The plane stretis and euery hie way	
Full of floschis, dubbis, myre and clay.	pools; puddles

Warton was right to find an almost Romantic spirit in such passages, but the poet was still a man of his time, and keen to draw acceptably Christian conclusions – 'ful of sentence' – from the 'pagan' world of classical literature.

Douglas affects to distrust learned Latinate terms, preferring them 'haymly playn' and 'famyliar' without 'facund rethoryk' so that his text will be 'braid and plane, / Kepand na sudron [southern speech] bot our awyn langage, / And spekis as I lernyt quhen I was page'. Indeed, he is the first of the makars to refer to 'Scottis' and 'the langage of Scottis natioun' to describe the tongue which Blind Harry would have called 'Inglis' (to distinguish it from Gaelic, or 'Erse', the original 'Scottis') and, although at times Douglas refers to the limitations of his chosen speech, he is prepared to use some 'bastard Latin', French or English to help out. By these means Douglas's language substantially extended the range of the vernacular, using coinages of his own to make his Scots richer and denser still.

Douglas is consistently aware of the radical significance of his humanist project and of the task of translation itself. At the close of the thirteenth and final book he expresses the modest desire that his labour shall be a 'neidfull wark', especially 'to thame wald Virgil to childryn expone'. He hopes that the classics will not belong only to 'masteris of grammar sculys . . . techand on . . . benkis and stulys', but that Virgil will now be available to 'euery gentill Scot' – even to those who cannot read: 'And to onletterit folk be red on hight / That erst was bot with clerkis comprehend'. Such an outlook characterises the Renaissance and what was to be the best aspect of the slowly growing spirit of Reformation in Scotland.

Sir David Lindsay (1490–1555)

Like Dunbar and Douglas, but with somewhat more success, David Lindsay spent most of his life at the Scottish court. He was most likely born in 1490, probably on his father's estate in Fife. By 1511 he was part of the royal household, employed as 'Keeper of the Kingis Grace's Person' – attendant and companion to the infant James V. He tells us in his poems how he used to sing to the royal baby and carry him on his back. In 1522 he married Janet Douglas also in royal service. Lindsay's association with the young king was broken for four years when Archibald Douglas, nephew to Gavin and sixth Earl of Angus, became chancellor and assumed total power by holding the twelve-year-old James captive in Edinburgh Castle. In 1528, however, the king escaped to lead an army against his captor, and the Red Douglas had to forfeit his estates and go into exile in England.

It is not certain what formal education Lindsay had, but he was undoubtedly an able man and his career prospered. (A David Lindsay graduated from St Andrews in 1508, but in the same year 'one called Lindsay' is also mentioned as a groom at court.) In the 1530s he began to produce poems that presumed to advise the king, making satirical comments on the state of the nation and especially on the failings of the Church. James must have had some sympathy with these views, for he used the first performances of *The Thrie Estaitis* as a warning to some of his recalcitrant bishops to reform themselves. Lindsay was made a royal herald and later he was knighted to become Lyon King-at-Arms, responsible for Scottish heraldry and the arranging of pageants, plays and farces for state occasions and the entertainment of the court. Schir Dauid Lyndesay of the Mount, as he was called, also served as an ambassador abroad, visiting Brussels, Paris and perhaps Italy in his travels.

At home his views on the failings and the misconduct of the clergy inevitably involved him with the cause of reform (he knew John Knox and is said to have encouraged him to take up preaching) but his early criticisms are based on a distaste for bad practice rather than fundamental doctrinal difference. In 1546 he acted as intermediary between the king and the group who had killed Cardinal Beaton and taken over St Andrew's Castle. (He called on them to surrender, but they held out until the following year.) 'The Tragedie of the Late Cardinal Beaton' does not leave Lindsay's sympathies in doubt, for the ghost of Beaton effectively condemns himself by describing his own career. The poem is a 'tragedy' only in the old sense that it concerns the fall of a powerful man:

My gret ryches, nor rentis proffitabyll
My Syluer work, Jowellis inestimabyll,
My Papall pompe, of gold my ryche threasure,
My lyfe, and all, I loste in half ane hour.

Lindsay concentrates in some detail on Beaton's great political influence and particularly on the commitments to France and Rome that would not allow him to countenance peace with England despite the high cost to everyone else:

Had we with Ingland kepit our contrackis,
Our nobyll men had leuit in peace and rest,
Our Marchandis had nocht lost so mony packis,
Our commoun peple had nocht bene opprest. . . .

On theological issues Lindsay has the cardinal admit that he did not read the Bible and did not encourage the teaching of it to the common folk, putting to great torment, indeed, the 'fauoraris of the auld and new Testament'. The poet does not mention the fire that consumed Wishart and directly fuelled Beaton's own death, although he does have a line where the ghost confesses to having destroyed many men, 'sum with the fyre'. This may seem a striking omission, but it was probably a well-considered one, for not even the Lord Lyon could challenge the authority of the spiritual arm with impunity. Douglas Hamer has suggested that the printer of 'the Tragedie' had to flee from arrest and that this was the poem of Lindsay's that we know to have been burned by the ecclesiastical authorities in 1549. Nevertheless, Lindsay's work does not bear an overtly Protestant doctrine, but is fired, rather, by a hatred of unearned privilege, most especially in the established Church. He seems to have remained a Catholic, albeit a severely critical one who wished to see the Church give up wealth and temporal powers and return to its simple role as teacher of the Testaments to the people.

Beyond all matters of Christian doctrine, Lindsay's morality is founded on his sense of natural justice and his sympathy with the feelings and prejudices of the common people. In the spirit of *Rauf Coilyear* his hatred of oppression, his lurid anti-clericalism, and his ribald sense of humour have guaranteed a lasting and general popularity to his work. These forces find early expression in 'The Dreme' and 'The Papyngo' and come to fruition in *Ane Pleasant Satyre of the Thrie Estaitis*. It is a measure of Lindsay's influence that he managed to stay at court during these turbulent times, for his views must have made him powerful enemies. Although he continued to write until just before his death at the age of sixty-five, his other work never matched the achievement of *The Thrie Estaitis*. His poems were published and republished in subsequent years and a popular collected edition appeared in 1568, but *The Thrie Estaitis* itself was not printed until 1602, over sixty years after its first performance.

Lindsay's purpose was clear from the start. 'The Dreme of Schir David Lyndesay' was probably written around 1528, when James V attained the throne. The Prologue describes how the poet used to play the lute and act the fool for his infant sovereign. Then the dream takes him on an elaborate tour of the cosmos from Hell to Heaven and back to Scotland again. 'Why are the people so poor', the poet asks, 'when they live in so pleasant a place?' The answer, of course, is misgovernment, and at this point John the Commonweill arrives in rags to describe how he has fled from oppression in the Borders and Highlands alike, without justice from the king or comfort from the Church, nor will he return until Scotland is better governed. The dreamer awakes to point out the moral to his king.

'The Complaynt of Schir David Lindesay' celebrates James's escape from the bad influence of the Douglas family. It allows the poet to offer yet more advice to his monarch and to remind him along the way that he would appreciate a gift of money, or even a loan – 'Off gold ane thousand pound, or tway'. Clearly the poet enjoyed good relations with the king, and James was not above flyting his old companion in verses of his own, and tolerating a reply too, which warns him explicitly against his sexual adventures ('The Answer to the Kyngis Flyting', 1536). Lindsay wrote a number of other pieces satirising life at court, such as 'In Contemptioun of Syde Taillis' (*c.*1540) or 'The Confessioun of Bagsche' (*c.*1534) which has the king's old hound complain about the scuffling for preference, the backbiting and the dogfights that go on in the presence of power. Now that Bagsche is old and despised, he regrets his cruelty when he was on top. 'Belief weill', he reminds the current favourites, 'ye ar bot doggis.' The animal analogy provides Lindsay with further scope for satire in *The Testament and Complaynt of the Papyngo* (1530), in which the king's parrot, wounded by a fall from a tree, makes her last will and testament after setting down two epistles full of advice to the king and her fellow courtiers. The garrulous bird expounds on the follies of climbing too high, on good government, on the fate of the Stewart kings and on the mutability of human affairs – all with awesome fluency. The 'Papyngo' takes its place in a tradition of animal satire, debate or epistle, running from the Howlat to Henryson's fables, to Hamilton of Gilbertfield's 'Last Dying Words of Bonny Heck' and

Burns's 'Twa Dogs'. Notwithstanding the charms of his preaching parrot, Lindsay's finest satire remains *The Thrie Estaitis*.

It is possible that it was a short version of this play that was performed in 1540 at the palace of Linlithgow on 6 January, the Feast of Epiphany, before James V and the court. Yule at the Scottish court was kept after the French fashion with the election of an 'Abbot of Unreason' to ensure entertainment for all. The ceremonies of Twelfth Night belonged to this tradition, with the choosing of a mock sovereign – the King or Queen of the Bean – to direct dances, games and burlesques. Great licence was allowed on such occasions, and it was in this context that Lindsay's merry exposure of folly and weakness amongst the powerful of this world was first performed. This is not to underestimate the author's seriousness, or his openly political intention, for when *The Thrie Estaitis* was next performed, in Fife, at the Castle Hill in Cupar in June 1552, the text had been developed closer to what we know today: its satirical force had been strengthened and further elements of popular comedy, energetic caricature and vulgar farce were directed towards an audience in which, this time, the commons outnumbered the nobility. The third performance of the *Satyre* was equally public, on the sunny slopes of the Calton Hill in Edinburgh in 1554 in the presence of Mary of Guise, Queen Regent of Scotland. It had been fourteen years since the first performance, during which time James V had died shortly after Solway Moss; Wishart and Beaton had both perished in windy St Andrew's; and Henry VIII's troops had crossed the Border and even reached Edinburgh in their destructive zeal to persuade Scotland into an English marriage alliance. In this period of reform and counter-reform Lindsay's play must have been a potent instrument. It was not to be performed again until 1948, when Tyrone Guthrie's memorable production at the Edinburgh International Festival rediscovered Lindsay's dramatic flair and the popular comic vigour of his verse. The play has been revived at least five times since; a modern adaptation has fired a shaft at the Press (*The Four Estates*), and the poet Alan Spence has done a contemporary version.

The final version of *The Thrie Estaitis* is in two parts separated by an interlude in which the 'rude mechanicals' provide comic relief by making comments on what has gone before. This was a common device between the acts of the early morality plays, and, since the whole performance must have taken many hours, it would have allowed the nobility some leeway to finish lunch and return to the play proper. Here and elsewhere Lindsay displays a shrewd stagecraft, derived no doubt from his experience of pageants, English morality plays and allegorical masques as well as a theatrical tradition in France that mixed morality, farce and fools' plays on the one stage. The work's roots in morality and masque can be seen, for example, when the Estates return to the stage in Part Two, being led backwards by their ruling vices in a procession; or, at the end, when Falsehood comes to be hanged, his final speech summons all oppressors to follow him into death, until the rope tightens around his neck and a black crow is released to symbolise his soul. There are equally memorable scenes when the Pauper 'invades' the stage from the audience during the interlude and demands that his complaints be heard, despite the efforts of the players to stop him. At every turn, anarchic moments such as this are used, along with what must have been topical local references, to play against the more allegorical set pieces.

Lindsay also manages a number of sophisticated verse-forms and modes of address. The play's formal speeches are made in iambic pentameters with an eight-line stanza and a linking rhyme scheme, a form used in Latin and French verse and in some early English mystery plays. There are swift-moving passages when single lines rhymed in couplets are exchanged between speakers (*stychomythia*), and moments when a jogging bob-wheel is used to set a three-stress line against a four-stress norm – a familiar effect and already a favourite with Scots poets:

> I haue sic pleasour at my hart,
> That garris me sing the treble pairt: makes
> Wald sum gude fellow fill the quart
>   It wald my hairt reioyce.

> Howbeit my coat be short and nippit,
> Thankis be to God I am weill hippit   padded
> Thocht all my gold may sone be grippit
>   Intill ane pennie pursse.

When John the Commonweill first speaks, his diction is appropriately plain and forceful: 'Out of my gait, for Gods saik let me ga', and 'Gude maister I wald speir at you ane thing, / Quhair traist ye I sall find yon new cumde King?' But when he accuses the Estates and their special sins, his couplets ring out in longer and sterner lines: 'And as ye se Temporalitie hes neid of correctioun, / Quhilk hes lang tyme bene led by publick oppressioun'. Such vigour and variety is remarkable for 1540, it is uncommon in contemporary morality plays and predates by at least twenty years the main body of notable pre-Shakespearean plays in England.

Lindsay's drama opens by showing how the young Rex Humanitas, encouraged by his minions, Wantonness, Placebo and Solace, is ensnared by Sensuality, the beautiful natural daughter of Venus. At such a court the aged adviser Good Counsel is ignored, while the vices of Flattery, Falsehood and Deceit dress up as friars and thrive as 'Devotion', 'Sapience' and 'Discretion'. The whole is played out in front of symbolic groups representing the assembled three Estates. Leaders of the Catholic Church, or the 'Spirituality', comprise the first Estate, the second is that of the lords and barons – the 'Temporality' – while the third Estate consists of established burgesses and merchants. Ordinary working folk without property or power have no place in this parliament and they are represented by the Pauper, who 'interrupts' the play, and by John the Commonweill, who comes forward in Part Two and testifies against all three arms of the establishment. Such an abstract gives little impression of the earthy nature of the satire, for the three vices are hilariously and broadly scurrilous and Flattery is a role for a leading comedian, who takes several disguises in the course of the play. Court and Church are his stamping-grounds, while Deceit reigns over merchants, and Falsehood thrives among the craftsmen. The first part of the play follows the promotion of these villains and parallels it with the misfortunes of the two maidens Verity and Chastity, who arrive on the scene only to be spurned by each Estate in turn. (Verity carries the New Testament 'in English toung' and is greeted with horror by the Spirituality and condemned as a heretic and a 'Lutherian'.) Before long, however, Divine Correction arrives to free the maidens from the stocks and assemble a parliament of all the Estates, at which he makes an examination of the condition of the kingdom. Correction strikes an old and familiar Scottish chord by asking 'Quhat is ane King?', and by giving the answer that he is 'nocht bot ane officiar, / To caus his Lieges liue in equitie'. Armed with God's truth, however, there is a new and thrilling resonance to his authority:

I haue power greit Princes to doun thring,	throw down
That liues contrair the Maiestie Divyne:	
Against the treuth quhilk plainlie dois maling	malign
Repent they nocht I put them to ruyne.	

The political and philosophical impact of this insight must have been heady stuff for the commons in the audience, and one notices how often the word 'reformatioun' is repeated in the text.

The interlude provides a vulgar satire on the abuses of mendicant friars and the selling of remissions and relics, made all the more pointed because the audience knows that the corrupt Pardoner is Flattery in disguise. The second movement of the play presents John the Commonweill's case against the three Estates and its parliamentary model heralds a more directly political direction for the work. The barons and the merchants submit to correction without demur, but the Spirituality resists and the parliament turns into a trial against corruption in the Church. Here Lindsay makes a vivid piece of propaganda drama in which many social and ecclesiastical abuses are specifically described, along with their painful effects on the commons and the country in general. The message is driven home at every turn, for the interlude and the epilogue repeat the arguments in burlesque terms; a 'learned Doctor' actually preaches a sermon from the stage and, towards the end of the play, no less than fifteen acts of proposed reformation are read out formally and at length to the assembled audience. Such complaints are not unfamiliar – Chaucer's Pardoner led the way, after all – but Lindsay's case is outstanding because he links specific suggestions to his talent for drama and comedy.

From the very start *The Thrie Estaitis* establishes a stirring and potentially democratic truth about the nature of man, and the audience is brought to realise it on two radically different levels. All men are equal before God (a not unfamiliar theme in religious doctrine, but here the Pauper has a voice, too); and all men are equal before their appetites. Thus Dame Sensuality speaks to the Estates:

> Paipis, Patriarks, or Prelats venerabill,
> Common pepill and Princes temporall,
> Ar subject all to me Dame Sensuall.

The play's impact depends on us being able to feel the essential truth of these and the following lines, even while we know that such feelings are sinful:

> Quhat vails your kingdome and your rent,
>   And all your great treasure,
> Without ye haif ane mirrie lyfe,
> And cast asyde all sturt and stryfe . . .
>   Fall to and tak your pleasure.

And that pleasure is convincingly portrayed:

Behauld my visage flammand as the fyre.
Behauld my papis of portratour perfyte.
To luke on mee luiffers hes greit delyte.

In just the same way, Lindsay shows that Divine Correction applies to
all classes – 'To rich and puir I beir ane equall hand' – and that Verity,
a simple maid armed only with the New Testament, can dare to counsel
kings.
These recognitions are at the heart of Lindsay's purpose. He is no
puritan (as witness the bawdiness of his verses and Correction's
approval of hunting and lawful merriness), but he believes in what
would now be called public accountability. Good Counsel points out
that, while cobblers and tailors are skilled workers at their trade, there
are bishops and parsons who can neither read nor preach. Surely the
Church should be no less craftsmanlike than the laity? It should recruit
its members on merit alone: 'Cair thou nocht quhat estait sa ever he be,
/ Sa thay can teich and preich the veritie'. But the Spirituality's only
defence is to attack the presumption of its critics – 'it is heresie, / To
speik against our law and libertie' – until even the merchants see the
weakness of such an argument from those who 'will correct and nocht
be correctit'. Good Counsel, that shrewd courtier, adds that it is only
common sense for a king to look after his humbler subjects, for 'the
husband-men and commons thay war wont, / Go in the battell formest
in the front', while John the Commonweill quotes from St Paul to
make a nobler case for the dignity of 'men that labours with thair
hands':

Qui non laborat no manducet.
This is in Inglische toung or leit: language
Quha labouris nocht he sall not eit.

John, Good Counsel, the merchants and the lords all agree that the
first duty of churchmen should be to teach the people, and to clarify
the Scriptures.
Confronted by Divine Correction and King Humanity, the
Spirituality is made to discard its power and its rich robes, as Bishop,
Abbot, Parson and Prioress all stand nakedly revealed as 'verie fuillis'.
They do not leave the stage, however, without a final telling shot – 'We
say the Kings war greiter fuillis nor we / That us promovit to sa greit
dignitie' – and these lines must have produced a moment of gleeful
recognition among the groundlings. John the Commonweill takes his
seat in parliament, and in a sequence of light-heartedly brutal vignettes

Theft, Deceit and Falsehood make their final speeches and are hanged. Flattery alone survives (by having testified against his fellows) and his escape serves as a reminder that the principle of duplicity and the appetite for fair words will never be extinguished from human society. As though to emphasise the point, the Epilogue reminds us that there is a kind of democracy among dunces, for 'the number of fuillis ar infinite' – and they thrive in every class.

Lindsay's other works are something of an anticlimax, although 'The Historie of Squyer Meldrum' (*c.*1550) is an enjoyable and rollicking account of the loves and valiant doings of a Fifeshire laird, probably written shortly after the real William Meldrum died. By comparison, *Ane Dialogue betwix Experience and ane Courteour, Off the Miserabyll Estait of the Warld* scarcely moves faster than a crawl. The four books of this poem, also known as *The Monarche*, were probably written between 1548 and 1553, and their extended disquisition on the Catholic Church's failings suggests that in Lindsay's later years his didactic impulse had become merely pedantic. With *The Thrie Estaitis*, however, he had created a unique form of propaganda drama, fully committed to the public forum, not too extreme in its doctrinal views, acceptably liberal and practical in its proposed reforms of the Catholic Church and, above all, brilliantly tailored to influence the audience by the communal delights of laughter, anger and debate. This was to prove an influential model for Scottish theatre in the 1970s.

The theatre in Scotland

It seems certain that there were precursors to *The Thrie Estaitis* and Lindsay's grasp of stagecraft suggests as much; but very few dramatic texts or reputations have survived. The older observances of folk festivals and folk dramas associated with May rites (regularly denounced by the Church), and the popularity of guild processions, clerk plays and passion plays associated with religious festivals, and the performance of elaborate pageants at court – all these contributed to the growth of a theatrical understanding and indicate the power and the popularity of dramatic performance. The Bannatyne Manuscript preserves a fragment from the early part of the century, sometimes attributed to Dunbar, and known as the 'Littil Interlude of the Droichis Part of the Play'. Dorothy Riach has argued that 'The Passion of Christ', a long poem by Walter Kennedy (he of Dunbar's flyting), might have first seen the light as a liturgical Passion Play for Easter. It is known that

John Knox was mentioned in an anti-Catholic piece, *Historye of Christis Passioun*, written by a Dominican friar called John Kyllour and performed for James V at Stirling in 1535. The play accuses a corrupt priesthood of betraying Christ to the mob and to Pilate, and four years later Kyllour paid for it with his life when Cardinal Beaton ordered him burned at the stake in Edinburgh. The Dundee merchant James Wedderburn, whose two brothers were responsible for the Lutheran *Gude and Godlie Ballatis*, is reported to have written anti-Catholic comedies and tragedies in Scots around 1540, and had to flee for his life, dying in exile in Dieppe. It is known that the minor poet Robert Sempill had a play performed in 1568. (He also wrote a violently anti-Papist verse attack on the Archbishop of St Andrews in 1584 – 'The Legend of the Lymmaris Lyfe'.)

It seems likely, then, that there was a young dramatic tradition in Scotland and the propaganda value of popular public performance was not lost on the early reformers. (Knox himself attended such a play in St Andrews in 1571.) In the course of the Reformation, however, the Kirk sessions came to oppose dramatic performances on feast days and religious festivals, which they associated with Catholicism, and although at first they remained content to ban only clerk plays based on interpretation of the Scriptures, they gradually came to suspect all plays as 'slanderous and undecent'. In 1599 the Kirk attempted to prohibit people from attending a comedy performed in Edinburgh by a group of English players led by Laurence Fletcher, but James VI (who had already sponsored a performance at Holyrood) stepped in and assured his subjects that they could go to the show. The same company returned in 1601, once again under the king's protection, and went on to tour successfully in Aberdeen and Dundee. Popular belief has it that Shakespeare may have been one of the players. Even so, James alone could not make the theatre flourish in post-Reformation Scotland, and of course he was soon to leave for London.

A lively, ribald and short verse comedy in Scots called *Philotus* was published in 1603 and went into two editions (the second of which anglified the spelling), but the author is unknown, although Robert Sempill, William Montgomerie and James VI have all been proposed. Most likely performed at court and based on an English tale which also provided the bones of Shakespeare's *Twelfth Night*, *Philotus* is a comedy of errors after the Italian manner on sexual disguise, mistaken identity and the marriage between age and youth. As drama it doesn't compare with Lindsay's play, much less with a contemporary English piece such as *All's Well that Ends Well*, but the plot has its own dark humour, moving from comic complexity to violence, obscenity and a wild sexual confusion, all in a vigorous colloquial verse scheme, rhyming aaabcccb, dddefffe, and at other times ababbcbc etc. The contentious temper of the times in Scotland was not sympathetic to a theatre still in its infancy, and the wide success of the *Gude and Godlie Ballatis* speaks for a fairly unsophisticated public taste. The final factor was that Edinburgh, unlike London, did not support a regular popular playhouse nor any settled professional group of actors. Whether this was due to a lack of public interest or to the presence of public 'morals' it is difficult at this distance in time to tell. In either case, the early promise of *The Thrie Estaitis* was not fulfilled, and when the court moved to London with the Union of the Crowns in 1603, an important source of dramatic patronage was lost to Scotland, not to be recovered until after the Restoration. If the theatre never became a popular art in Scotland, the same cannot be said for songs and ballads, however. Of course the great ballads were born out of an oral tradition, as we shall see in the next chapter, and so their creators and the date of their first appearance cannot be identified in the usual way, but they would have been circulating through the sixteenth and seventeenth centuries, and in their own way they brought considerable colour and drama to the folk.

Writing in prose

David Lindsay's hopes that his verse would speak to 'Jok and Thome', like Gavin Douglas's concern for 'onletterit folk', reflect what was to be a growing commitment among prose writers of this period. Latin was still the tongue of learned discourse, and **John Major**, or **Mair** (1467–1550), a school-man of the old order who was educated at Cambridge and Paris, used it for his philosophical commentaries and for his influential *History of Greater Britain both England and Scotland* (1521). Major was distrustful of humanistic culture, but he numbered George Buchanan and John Knox amongst his pupils and something of his scholastic severity in disputation coloured the outlook of both men. Notwithstanding the continued use of Latin at the universities, the spread of printing and the unfolding of the Reformation soon made both Protestant and Catholic writers acutely aware of the public power of their mother tongue. Some, such as Buchanan, retained a strong affinity with Latinate constructions, while others, such as Bellenden or Pitscottie, produced a more natural vernacular style. The most influential example was set by John Knox, who anglicised his fierce Scots prose, with his eye on new readers south of the Border. This tendency was reinforced at the end of the century by James VI's move to London in 1603 and by the literary excellence of English writers such as Francis Bacon and Sir Thomas Browne. Back in Scotland, however, chronicles, pamphlets and theological disputations were more common, and by these means a nation was instructed about its individuality and how that manifested itself geographically, politically and spiritually.

The translation of the Bible into English, linked as it was with the spread of Protestantism, had a profound effect on the development of Scots vernacular prose. Murdoch Nisbet is credited with a Scots version of Wycliffe's fourteenth-century New Testament translation, but the work remained in manuscript and was not printed until 1901, so by far the most potent influence on the northern reformers came from testaments published in English. These began with the work of William Tyndale, undertaken at some personal risk (1525–34); officially tolerated versions followed, with Miles Coverdale's (1535) and the so-called Matthews Bible (1537), which was revised into Cromwell's Great Bible of 1539. The Calvinist Geneva Bible from 1560 came to hold a special place in Scottish hearts, and finally, of course, the Authorised Version appeared in 1611. Thus it was prose in English that spoke to Protestant Scotland for the next three centuries, exerting an enormous cultural influence on a people who laid such emphasis on the reading and teaching of Scripture. (We should not forget, all the same, that a Scots pronunciation would most likely have prevailed in any public recitation.)

It was at James V's request that **John Bellenden** (1495–1550?), the archdeacon of Moray, undertook a free translation of Hector Boece's *Historia gentis Scotorum*, intended, no doubt, for the edification of the king's own barons and courtiers. *The History and Chronicles of Scotland*, in vigorous and straightforward Scots, was completed in 1533 and printed in Edinburgh no fewer than three times within the next fifteen years. Indeed, the current interest in history encouraged one William Stewart in 1535 to versify Boece into Scots. Bellenden also translated the first five books of Livy's *History of Rome* (1532) and prefaced the work with a rhymed prologue of his own.

The Complaynt of Scotland, sometimes ascribed to Robert Wedderburn, was printed and published in 1549 as an account of 'this affligit realme quhilk is my native countre'. The author's patriotism and his anti-English feeling can be explained by remembering that Solway Moss and Henry VIII's 'rough wooing' were still fresh and bitter memories. It is the most colourful early prose in vernacular Scots, and the nearest to imaginative writing in that it follows the allegorical-verse tradition by including a dream vision and using ornate descriptive language. Like Douglas before him, the writer adjusts his mother tongue to meet his needs and asks readers to forgive him if he has, in places, 'myxt oure langage witht part of termis dreuyn fra lateen, be rason that oure scottis tong is nocht sa copeus as is the lateen tong'. He claims that his intention is to speak as plainly as possible:

> For I thocht it nocht necessair til hef fardit ande lardit this tracteit witht exquisite termis, quhilkis are nocht daily usit, bot rather I hef usit domestic Scottis langage, maist intelligibil for the vulgare pepil.

In spite of its distrust of 'exquisite termis' and its purpose as propaganda, *The Complaynt* parades Latinate diction, high-brow prognostication and classical allusions across its pages as if to assure both author and reader of its intellectual respectability. Its main message is conveyed by an extended allegory in which the dire state of the country is explained through Dame Scotia's confrontation with her three errant sons, representing Church, nobles and the common people. This scheme was adapted from the original French prose of Alain Chartier's *Quadrilogue Invectif* (1422) – the most notable of several borrowings in the text – but *The Complaynt* still has a distinctively Scottish flavour of its own. It begins by philosophising on the fate of the nation, the mutability of temporal power and the forthcoming end of the world; then, fatigued by his efforts, the author repairs to the countryside for rest and relaxation. Strictly speaking, this 'Monolog Recreative' has nothing to do with the book's main purpose, but the author launches himself into a descriptive blizzard of detail like some forewarning of Sir Thomas Urquhart's own encyclopaedic muse. At dawn the sounds of the countryside begin to make themselves heard in this manner:

> For fyrst furth on the fresche feildis, the nolt [cattle] maid noyis witht mony loud lou. Baytht horse and meyris did fast nee, and the folis nechyr. The bullis began to bullir, quhen the sheip began to blait, be cause the calfis began tyl mo, quhen the doggis berkit. Than the suyne [swine] began to quhryne quhen thai herd the asse rair quhilk gart [made] the hennis kekkyl quhen the cokis creu. The chekyns began to peu quehn the gled [hawk] quhissillit. The fox follouit the fed geise, and gart them cry claik. The gayslingis cryit quhilk, quhilk, and the dukis cryit quaik . . .

When the cacophony is finally documented, the author visits the seashore to witness a complicated naval engagement between two warships; he takes breakfast with a group of shepherds and reports on the joys of pastoral life and its contributions to science and astronomy; when the rustic company turns to recreation, the indefatigable scribe lists by name the forty-seven tales, thirty-eight songs and thirty dances they performed! Having survived this marathon, he wanders among the meadows and eventually falls asleep to have the allegorical dream vision, which is, after all, his main subject – but not before he has made an inventory of all the flowers and herbs and their medicinal properties. Over the centuries this recurring enumerative exhaustiveness has a mad charm of its own in Scottish literature. But the sheer garrulousness of *The Complaynt* must have been something of a trial for the 'vulgar pepil' who were supposed to be reading it, even if future scholars have cause to bless its documentary zeal.

The most entertaining of the vernacular histories is by **Robert Lindsay of Pitscottie** (1532–90?). His *Historie and Cronikles of Scotland* was completed in the mid 1570s, but not published until 1782, when it went through three more editions at twenty- to thirty-year intervals. Many of the more colourful anecdotes in Scots history – from James II to James VI – come from Pitscottie, for although his chronology is as uncertain as his sense of relevance, he has a splendid, gossipy journalist's eye for domestic detail, personal dramas and curious events. He knew men who had served at court or gone to war and so it seems likely that their reported experiences are not too far from the truth, even if they gained a little in the telling. Certainly the Scottish tapestry would be paler without the colour of Pitscottie's account of how James II was killed by a bursting gun, or the tragedy at Flodden, or the dying words of Border reiver and Stewart king, or the confusion and panic at the battle of Pinkie in 1547, or dynastic betrayals and escapes, a ghost at Linlithgow, Siamese twins, strange portents, royal hunting-parties and all the fascinating details of courtly fashion and behaviour. By comparison with Pitscottie, Bishop John Leslie (1527–96) is more austere and accurate, but much less interesting. His ten-volume *History of Scotland* was written in Latin during the 1570s, published in Rome in 1578, and translated into Scots by Father James Dalrymple eighteen years later. Both at home and in France, Leslie remained a faithful ally to Mary Queen of Scots throughout her life.

A more contentious servant was **George Buchanan** (1506–82), almost all of whose works were in Latin. Born to an old but poor family near Killearn, Buchanan was educated at an uncle's expense, attending university at St Andrews and Paris where he lived for several years as a teacher and then as a tutor to a Scots nobleman, which connection brought him to the attention of the king who bade him return to Scotland. Buchanan had taken up the cause of Reformation while he was in Europe and, encouraged by James V, he produced a satire against the Franciscans, which led to a charge of heresy and the personal and enduring enmity of Cardinal Beaton. So Buchanan had to flee to Europe where he spent twenty years at various universities, including a spell as tutor to Montaigne at Bordeaux (who acted in his dramas) and a scrape with the Inquisition in Portugal, where he was imprisoned from 1550 to 1552, spending his time on a Latin translation of the Psalms of David. Eventually Buchanan returned to Scotland to become an adviser to Mary Queen of Scots, a friend of John Knox's and a severe authority on education and reformation, becoming the first Moderator of the General Assembly of the Church of Scotland in 1567. Dismayed by the murder of Darnley, he prepared scathing charges against the queen and, for the last twelve years of his life, acted as tutor to the young James VI.

Buchanan was famous throughout Europe as scholar of the new humanism and was regarded as the finest Latin poet since classical times. As a scholar with a European constituency Latin was his principal medium, and he produced, among other pieces, translations from the Greek of Euripides, the verse paraphrase of the Psalms, biblical and classical masques for the court, and much admired metrical poetry of his own. In the 1550s he wrote two tragedies in the Senecan style: *Jephthah* and *John the Baptist*. Rhetorical, formal and highly moral, these plays were scarcely aimed at the groundlings. Nevertheless they continued to be performed in Europe – often in translation – for the next hundred years, being particularly well received in France and proving influential in the evolution of French drama.

A lengthy history of Scotland, *Rerum Scoticarum Historia* (1582), reminded Buchanan's royal charge that the people of ancient Gaeldom had had the right to depose unsatisfactory kings. This was erroneous, but not by any means irrelevant, and *De Jure Regni apud Scotos* (1579) had pursued the same issue in contemporary terms through seven editions, with translations in English, German and Dutch, before the king suppressed it in 1586 and produced his own *Basilikon Doron*, as a counter-claim for the divine right of monarchs. Buchanan's Scots vernacular prose includes a propaganda-piece against the Hamiltons, and *The Chamaeleon* (1570), a short satirical attack on William Maitland of Lethington, the devious secretary to the queen, who was accused of changing colours and religions daily. Buchanan's polemical style in the vernacular is impeded rather than helped by his fluency in Latin, and it cannot match the simpler and more forceful prose of his contemporary John Knox.

John Knox (1505–72) was born near Haddington, educated at the universities of Glasgow and St Andrews, ordained as a priest and employed as a notary and tutor in his home district. He was in his forties before he joined himself to the Reformation movement in Scotland. A gradual intellectual commitment was catalysed by his meeting with George Wishart, who returned to Scotland from Switzerland to propose a new church, protected by the state but acknowledging only Christ as its leader. Knox carried a two-handed sword to protect the young preacher, but could not forestall Wishart's trial for heresy, within the year, at St Andrews, where he was strangled and burned at the stake. Thenceforth Knox was caught up in the conflict. He only began to preach at the insistence of his fellows, and spoke his first sermon to the men who occupied St Andrews after the revengeful murder of Beaton. When the castle finally surrendered in 1547, Knox was condemned with the other commoners to the French galleys, where he sat at an oar for almost two years before a petition from the English government brought about his release. He served in England as chaplain to Edward VI, but the accession of Mary Tudor in 1553 renewed the persecution of Protestants and Knox planned to go abroad, having married the young woman who was to bear him two sons before her death in 1560. He spent the next four years in Frankfurt and Geneva, where his early thoughts on election were powerfully influenced by Calvin's doctrines. Thus began his politico-religious war on behalf of a revolutionary democratic Theocracy, a 'godly discipline' of behaviour to be guided at every turn by reference to the text of the Bible. He toured Scotland briefly in 1555 and savoured the public effectiveness of his preaching. During these years he also produced several pamphlets addressed to the people of Scotland and England, including a violent attack on 'bloody Mary': *A Faythful Admonition unto the Professours of Goddis Truthe in England* (1554), which did little to quench the fires of persecution in the South. His famous *First Blast of the Trumpet against the Monstruous Regiment of Women* (1558) had an equally backhanded effect. This treatise is informed with the misogyny of the times and coloured again by Knox's own cantankerously patriarchal views about the female sex. (These did not stop him from marrying again in 1564 and, at the age of fifty-nine, taking a girl scarcely seventeen years old to be his wife. The disparity in their ages caused some talk, but Knox ignored it and eventually became the father of two daughters.) The *First Blast* turned out to be a rather loud tactical error, however, for although it was directed at the political and religious policies of Mary Tudor in England and the queen regent in Scotland, it caused costly offence to Elizabeth I, who was, after all, a champion of Protestantism in her way, and a potential ally.

In 1559 Knox returned to Scotland and made another great preaching-tour – joining in what was now open conflict between the Lords of the Congregation and the forces of Mary of Guise. Each faction sought armed support from outside, the Protestants from England and the Catholics from France. Mobs rioted in Perth for two days after one of Knox's sermons and a situation of virtual civil war was only averted by the military impasse at Leith and by the death of Mary of Guise from dropsy. The spokesman for Christian Reformation was pleased to hail her painful end as a judgement from God. After the Treaty of Leith, the Reformation Parliament of 1560 and the Confession of Faith placed religious authority firmly in the hands of the new church and, as author of a treatise on predestination (1560) and as one of the writers of *The First Book of Discipline* (1560), it was John Knox whose vision helped to set the pattern for intellectual, social and religious life in Scotland, an iron mould which has endured, at least in some circles, virtually until modern times. The arrival of Mary Queen of Scots heralded a turbulent seven years, and Knox had several private and public clashes with her, preaching that one Mass was more fearful to him than 10,000 armed enemies landed in the realm to suppress the whole religion. Events and eyewitnesses alike testify to the intemperate power of his rhetoric as he smote the pulpit as though to 'ding it in blads and fly out of it'. All the same, Knox found it prudent to retire from the court for a spell, during which time (1566–67) he completed *The Historie of the Reformation of Religioun within the Realm of Scotland*, which was only published seventy-two years after his death. 'Here lies ane', said Morton at his graveside 'who never feared the face of man.'

It is impossible to warm to Knox's harsh, authoritarian nature, but it is equally difficult not to admit the forcefulness of his prose in *The Historie of the Reformatioun*. The energetic violence of his certainty, his grim sense of humour, his fluency in plain un-Latinate English and Scots colloquial speech, his eye for physical detail and his use of dramatic dialogue – all these testify to what must have been a truly powerful physical and political presence. He is an agitator rather than a philosopher, biased in his judgements and dogmatic in his opinions,

yet there is something awesome in his unswerving adherence to what he saw as his duty. 'Madam,' he said to his queen, 'I am not master of myself, but must obey him who commands me to speak plain, and to flatter no flesh upon the face of the earth.' Carlyle saw him as a hero of private judgement, comparing him to some 'Old Hebrew Prophet', with the 'same inflexibility, intolerance, rigid narrow-looking adherence to God's truth, stern rebuke in the name of God to all that forsake truth', and he admired how Knox refused to do reverence to an image of the Virgin Mary when he was a prisoner in the galleys:

> Mother? Mother of God? said Knox, when the turn came to him: This is no Mother of God: this is 'a pented bredd [board] – a piece of wood, I tell you with paint on it! She is fitter for swimming, I think, than for being worshipped', added Knox, and flung the thing into the river. It was not very cheap jesting there: but come of it what might, this thing to Knox was and must continue nothing other than the real truth; it was a pented bredd: worship it he would not.
>
> ('The Hero as Priest', *On Heroes and Hero-Worship*, 1841)

Knox's metaphysical audacity and grim-humoured, hard-nosed facticity speak for something in Scottish culture, and at least his prose is a stylistic advance on the laboured diction of *The Complaynt*. Here is his account of Cardinal Beaton's end:

> And so he [James Melven] stroke him twyse or thrise trowght with a stog sweard;and so he fell, never word heard out of his mouth, but 'I am a preast; fy, fy: all is gone.'
> Whill they war thus occupyed with the Cardinall, the fray rises in the toune, The Provost assembles the communitie, and cumis to the fowseis [moats] syd, crying 'What have ye done with my Lord Cardinall? Whare is my Lord Cardinall? Have ye slayne my Lord Cardinall'? Let us see my Lord Cardinall.' Thei that war within answered gentilye, 'Best it war unto yow to returns to your awin, houssis; for the man ye call the Cardinall has receaved his reward, and in his awin persons will truble the warld no more.' But then more enraigedlye thei cry, 'We shall never departe till that we see him.' And so was he brought to the East blokhouse head, and schawen dead ower the wall to the faythless multitude, which wold not beleve befoir it saw: How miserably lay David Betoun, cairfull Cardinall. And so thei departed, without *Requiem aeternam* and *Requiescat in pace*, song for his saule. Now, becaus the wether was hote (for it was in Maij, as ye have heard) and his funerallis could not suddandly be prepared, it was thowght best, to keep him frome styncking, to geve him great salt ynewcht, [enough] a cope of lead, and a nuk in the boddome of the Sea-toore [tower] (a place whare many, of Goddis childrene had bein empreasoned befoir) to await what exequeis his brethrene the Bischoppes wold prepare for him.
> These thingis we wreat merrelie.

'This is superb,' wrote J. H. Millar dryly, 'if not distinctively Christian', and, indeed, John Knox has remained patron saint and domestic demon in the Scottish psyche for over 480 years. Knox's 'passion for truth', so admired by Carlyle, was really a passion only for his vision of the truth, with no patience for others or for the balanced judgement of philosopher or scholar. Yet his absoluteness could not have thrived had Scotland not been fertile ground for passionate personal conviction, and a delight in what MacDiarmid later called the 'hard fact', 'the inoppugnable reality'. It is one of history's ironies that equally uncompromising attitudes should be so much a part of left-wing commitment in modern Scotland, and that one of its popular manifestations should be to blame Knox alone for all the puritanical and constricting aspects of national culture.

James VI (1566–1625) should be mentioned as a prose writer, although his work had far less political influence than that of his fiercest preacher. As patron of the poets who came to be known as the 'Castalian band', and at the tender age of seventeen, James produced sonnets of his own prefaced by a short treatise on poetic forms. Three years later he wrote *Daemonologie* as a proof of the dangerous existence of witchcraft. He is no less than a man of his time in this belief, but it is a shameful fact that the persecution and the burning of 'witches' – mostly female commoners – reached appalling heights in post-Reformation Scotland. These epidemics of social hysteria used to break out for a few years at a time, lasting into the mid-seventeenth century. In 1588 and 1589 James produced two theological essays – 'meditations' – on verses from the Bible, while the *Basilikon Doron* (1599) was a defence of kingship written for the instruction of prince Henry and informed by James's determination not to allow the Presbyterian Church to dictate to him. About this time, he began to write only in English, as in *A Counterblaste to Tobacco* (1604) in which he preaches against the newly fashionable addiction as 'a custom loathsome to the eye, hateful to the nose, harmful to the brain, dangerous to the lungs, and in the black stinking fume thereof nearest resembling the horrible stygian smoke of the pit that is bottomless'. A collection of James's works was published in London in 1616 and a comparison with earlier texts shows that where possible the king replaced Scots words with the English equivalents. This process will characterise the development of Scots prose from now on.

Minor poetry of the Reformation

Doctrinal conflict, disputatious pamphleteering, Knox's unyielding personality, the puritanism and religious persecution of subsequent years, all these darken our view of the early Reformation in Scotland. It is easy to miss the revolutionary exhilaration of a new movement that proposed a return to fundamentals, to the philosophical importance of individual judgement and to the surprising, unasked for, unearned, unacquirable descent of God's grace upon the faithful. Something of this Lutheran spirit of celebration is caught in a collection of hymns and lyrics directed to the Protestant cause, mostly collected and composed by **Robert Wedderburn** (1510?–1557), a priest of Dundee, assisted by his older brothers John, also a priest, and James, a merchant. *Ane Compendious Buik of Godlie Psalms and Spirituall Sangs* contains a calendar, the catechism, and metrical psalms and hymns in the Lutheran style, some translated from German. The collection, usually known as the *Gude and Godlie Ballatis*, is mostly notable, however, for the way it rearranges popular and courtly material – 'changeit out of Prophane Sangis in Godlie Sangis, for avoyding of sin and harlotrie'. The lively spirit of many of these pieces, and doubtless their thinly concealed worldliness too, made them a considerable popular success. Editions (also commonly called the *Dundee Psalms*), were published in 1567, 1578, 1600 and 1621. Along with the list of shepherds' songs in *The Complaynt*, they provide useful evidence of a vigorous musical tradition, except that the perennial themes of love, courting and the chase have been assimilated into a spiritual context. The process is not exactly one of bowdlerising or parody, but more like a mimicry of popular airs, especially directed at 'young personis . . . as are not exercisit in the Scriptures':

> Quho is at my windo, quho, quho?
> Go from my window, go, go,
> Quha callis thair so lyke ane stranger,
> 　　Go from my windo, go.

> Lord I am heir ane wratcheit mortall
> That for thy mercy dois cry and call
> Unto the my Lord Celestiall,
> 　　Se quho is at my windo, quho.

If these lines look rather thin, it must be remembered that they would have been set and sung to old tunes. A certain parallel suggests itself with Gospel songs or modern spirituals:

Downe be yone Riuer I ran,
Downe be yone Riuer I ran,
        Thinkand on Christ sa fre,
That brocht me to libertie,
        And I ane sinful man.

The practice of 'spiritualising' secular lyrics was not confined to
Protestantism, for an earlier Roman Catholic version of the following
old love-song also survives, and would have been sung in church on
selected occasions.

My lufe murnis for me, for me,
My lufe that murnis for me, for me,
I am not kynde, hes not in mynde
My lufe that murnis for me.

Quha is my lufe, bot God abufe,
Quhilk all this world hes wrocht;
The King of blis, my lufe he is,
Full deir he hes me bocht.

Other pieces are considerably less lamb-like, as in this rowdy attack on
God's vicar, an original song, if scarcely original in sentiment:

The Paip, that Pagane full of pryde,
He hes us blindit lang,
For quhair the blind the blind dois gyde
Na wounder baith ga wrang;
Lyke Prince and King he led the Regne
Of all iniquitie:
Hay trix, tryme go trix, under the grene wod tre.

The *Godlie Ballatis* have little in the way of literary merit, but they do
convey an often-forgotten side to the Reformation, evoking as they do
a hint of the revivalist meeting, with its willing submergence of the self,
and perhaps of the critical faculties too, in cheerful congregational
singing. Calvin's conception of the elect and his absolutist arrogance
have not yet dampened this group celebration. And the stiff
respectability of the Victorian kirk is still a long way off.

The rowdier side to the Reformation continued to be expressed in
verse, and numerous political and ecclesiastical broadsheets were circu-
lating in the second half of the century, mostly published by Robert
Lekpreuik's Press in Edinburgh. The most notable of these satirists is
Robert Sempill (1530–95), who wrote secular pieces such as
'Margaret Fleming' and 'Johnet Reid', as well as satirical attacks on the

Old Church, including a famously abusive diatribe against the Archbishop of St Andrews: 'The Legend of the Lymmaris Lyfe'.

It is a pleasing paradox that 'godlie' versions may have helped to save 'prophane' originals from oblivion, but two other major verse collections of the period deliberately set out to record and preserve old Scottish poetry. Without the Bannatyne and Maitland manuscripts, the store of fifteenth- and sixteenth-century Scots verse would be tragically impoverished, for they contain poems by Henryson, Dunbar and Douglas as well as many anonymous or disputed pieces that would otherwise have been lost.

George Bannatyne (1545–1608) was an Edinburgh merchant who returned to his home in Forfarshire in 1568 to escape an outbreak of plague in the capital. During his year's sojourn he transcribed many poems from old and tattered copies and prints (long since lost) and even included in the collection some unremarkable verses of his own. Containing over 400 items, this is a crucial source for Henryson's *Fables* and almost all the work of Alexander Scott. Allan Ramsay drew on this manuscript for his *Ever Green* collection in 1724, and editors, scholars and readers ever since have had cause to be grateful for the fruits of Bannatyne's enforced retreat. A complete edition of the Bannatyne MS was edited by the Scottish Text Society (1928–34). The original ended up in the Advocates Library in Edinburgh and is now held in the National Library of Scotland.

Sir Richard Maitland of Lethington (1496–1586) was a legal judge of noble birth and long-standing service who also collected old poems over the years and arranged to have them compiled in a manuscript anthology. This collection favoured Dunbar's poetry in particular. There are two Maitland manuscripts, known by the size of their paper: Sir Richard's Folio; and the Quarto that was later compiled by his daughter Marie. They can be found at Magdalene College, Cambridge. Maitland was himself a poet (a better one than Bannatyne) and also included his own work in the collection. But he did not start composing until he was in his sixties, suffering from failing eyesight and ill at ease with the Reformation and changing times. 'Quhair is the blyithnes that hes bein, / Baith in burgh and landwart sene, / Amang lordis and ladyis schene, / Daunsing, singing, game and play?' His verses are seldom cheerful.

The next most important collection in Scottish letters, the Asloan manuscript, is the earliest, dating from the start of the sixteenth century. It is a collection made in 1515 by an Edinburgh scribe or notary called John Asloan, which ended up in the library of Sir

Alexander Boswell of Auchinleck, a song writer, a song collector, an antiquarian of note and the son of James Boswell, the biographer of Dr Johnson. The manuscript is now held in the National Library of Scotland.

Alexander Scott (1525?–1584?) did not share Maitland's personal and political gloom, although his poems date from the 1560s and the turbulent years of the Reformation Parliament and Mary Stewart's reign. Scott's only political poem, 'Ane New Yeir Gift to the Quene Mary quhen scho Come First Hame, 1562', is full of dull advice and reflections, but it includes the worthy wish that the queen will ban all disputations on holy writ by anyone other than qualified scholars, for these days even 'lymmer lawdis and little lassis lo / Will argun bayth with bischop, preist, and freir'. 'The Justing and Debait up at the Drum betwix Wa. Adamsone and Johine Sym' has these two worthy commoners in a burlesque of knightly combat and shares both its earthy vivacity and its metre with the older 'Christis Kirk' and 'Peblis' poems. With the exception of a couple of psalms, the rest of Scott's work (or what was preserved of it in the Bannatyne Manuscript), consists of love lyrics. Some of these follow a medieval ethos by giving a coarse recital of the sexual weaknesses of women ('Ane Ballat Maid to the Derisioun and Scorne of Wantoun Wemen'), while others are more sophisticated in a playfully cynical, Ovidian way, as in 'Of Wemenkynd', where the poet begins by posing himself a problem:

> I muse and mervellis in my mind,
> Quhat way to wryt, or put in vers,
> The quent consaitis of wemenkynd . . . .

Scott's verse is technically various: he can use short, simple lines, rather in the manner of Skelton, or metrical gymnastics reminiscent of Dunbar. The following lines from 'A Rondel of Luve' use the old French rondel form, with a fine epigrammatic succinctness:

> Lufe is an fervent fyre
> Kendillit without desyre:
> Schort plesour, lang displesour;
> Repentance is the hyre;
> Ane pure tressour without mesour:
> Lufe is an fervent fyre,

In all cases Scott's muse explores the pain of sophisticated love affairs expressed in a worldly manner, not unlike Wyatt's love poems, but technically more polished. It is physical attraction that Scott pursues, and if there is little sense of the ideal in his work, he can still rise to a fine erotic directness.

The Castalian band

The poetry of the sixteenth century closes with Alexander Montgomerie and James VI's 'Castalian band'. When the boy king escaped from the Protestant nobles who had kidnapped him on the 'Ruthven Raid', he re-established himself at court (in 1583) surrounded by more sympathetic lords. His mother Mary had written sonnets in French, and James produced his own poems in *Poetical Exercises* (1591) having started, at the age of seventeen, with the *Essayes of a Prentise in the Divine Art of Poesie* (1584). This latter volume was prefaced by the 'Reulis and Cautelis [cautions] to be observit and eschewit in Scottis Poesie' which set out precepts for good practice in technique (how to write 'flowingly' in rhyme and metre, how to use figurative language) and also in subject matter, with advice on appropriate forms, originality and the avoidance of clichés. James's ambitions allowed him to style himself as 'Apollo' ruling a court where poetry and song were to prevail, and he warned against assuming that love was the only fit subject for poetry, proposing the equal importance of a moral and a metaphysical dimension. The play *Philotus* was probably a part of the court's entertainment during these years, but the little group could not support a wider theatrical tradition. Among these courtly practitioners of the muse, Alexander Montgomerie is the most distinguished, having taken the king's fancy by challenging another writer – Patrick Hume of Polwarth – to a flyting-match and sinking him with floods of ingenious invective. The other poets remain relatively minor, including James himself. The king came to call his circle 'brothers of the Castalian band', after the fountain of Castalia, sacred to Apollo and muses. During this special decade of music and poetry, models were sought and works translated from France and Italy, many Petrarchan-style love sonnets were written in the English manner or after Ronsard, and always the qualities of smoothness and sophisticated lightness were prized.

Although not Castalian 'brothers', Robert Sempill and 'old Alexander Scott' would have visited the court and had a ready audience there, while another poet of the period, **Alexander Hume** (1557–1609), grew tired of seeking royal favour and withdrew to become a minister of the church at Logie, near Stirling. Hume renounced his early secular work in favour of worthier themes and pref-

aced his collection *Hymns and Sacred Songs* (1599) with the sour
remark that 'In princes' Courts . . . the chief pastime is to sing
prophane sonnets, and vaine ballads of love.' Despite this moral tone,
his best-known poem, 'Of the Day Estivall', is a beautiful description
of a Midsummer's Day, celebrating domestic, rural observances and
every natural detail bathed in heat and a brilliant light:

> What pleasour were to walke and see
> Endlang a river cleare,
> The perfite forme of everie tree,
> Within the deepe appeare?

> The Salmon out of cruifs and creels
> Up hailed into skowts,　　　　　　　　cobles (fishing boats)
> The bells, and circles on the weills,
> throw lowpping of the trouts.　　　　jumping

> O: then it were a seemely thing,
> While all is still and calme,
> The praise of God to play and sing,
> With cornet and with shalme.

Alexander Montgomerie (1555?–97?) met the favour of his king –
he was a distant blood relation – and came to prominence in his mid
thirties. He had quite a large poetic output, although much of his work
was not published until relatively modern times. The seventeen-year-
old monarch enjoyed Montgomerie's poetry, hailed him as a master in
the craft and awarded him a pension in 1583 (although it took the poet
some ten years of manoeuvring to collect it). For his part,
Montgomerie took care to admire his royal patron without fear of
excess, even if, at times, he saw quite clearly what life at court entailed:
'First thou mon preis thy Prince to pleiss, / Thoght contrare
Conscience he commands'. Montgomerie left Scotland in 1586,
perhaps on business for James, which took him to Flanders, France and
Spain. He was a Catholic involved with Catholic interests at court, and
this connection may explain his mission and the fact that he got into
unspecified trouble abroad and was imprisoned there for some years.
He returned to Scotland in 1591, but by this time his fortunes were
ebbing, for he had slipped from James's favour. When he was implicated in a Catholic plot in 1597 – apparently to do with a Spanish invasion – he more or less disappeared from public ken. The dates for both
his birth and his death remain obscure.

Montgomerie wrote many love sonnets showing the influence of
Scott, Ronsard and the English models of Wyatt and Sidney. Although

he affects the conventional pose of complaint both as a man of affairs and as a lover, there is at times a genuinely pessimistic and irritable cast to his poems, a note that the affliction of gout and the instability of his financial status probably did nothing to dispel. A coarser and wilder delight, reminiscent of Dunbar's technique, informs the 'Flyting betwixt Montgomerie and Polwart', a sustained and lengthy exercise in the old-fashioned duel of invective 'by ryme' – 'anger to asswage, make melancholy lesse.' Montgomerie begins in relatively mild terms:

POLWART, yee peip like a mouse amongst thornes;
Na cunning yee keepe; POLWART, yee peip;
Ye look like a sheipe an ye had twa hornes:
POLWART, ye peip like a mouse amongst thornes.

In due course Polwarth replies, and forcefully, too. Enraged that he should be 'bitten' in verse by another, and especially bitten by such 'a duck' as Polwarth, Montgomerie promises to drive him from the 'kings chimney nuike', but not before his adversary delivers a few raspberries more:

Thou was begotten, some sayes mee,
Betwixt the devil and a dun kow,
An night when that the fiend was fow.   drunk

Since Montgomerie seems to have spent part of his youth in Argyll, Polwarth chides him for having Highland connections, showing, like Dunbar, a courtier's contempt for life in the west. Tradition has it that James gave the victory to Montgomerie, but it is Polwarth who has the exhaustive last word, sustained for sixty-six lines in a torrentially lavatorial strain:

Fond flytter, shit shytter, bacon byther, all defyld!
Blunt bleittar, paddock pricker, puddin eiter, perverse!
Hen plucker, closet mucker, house cucker, very vyld!
Tanny cheeks, I think thou speiks with thy breeks, foul-erse!

In complete contrast to the rude extravagances of the flyting, Montgomerie's aureate lines in 'The Bankis of Helicon' celebrate the beauty of the poet's lady; but they, too, suggest echoes of Dunbar and really belong to an earlier mode of writing. The same stanza-form (invented by Montgomerie) and the same somewhat antique mode of expression are seen to far better effect in *The Cherrie and the Slae*, Montgomerie's longest and most famous work. It is likely that it would have been recited at court and it was not published until 1597, but by the end of the eighteenth century it had gone through twenty-two editions, making it the most widely read Scots poem next to *The Wallace* and the verses of Burns. Allan Ramsay included it in his *Ever Green* and copied the form for his own 'The Vision', while Burns later adopted the complex fourteen-line 'quatorzain' stanza for his 'Epistle to Davie' and the recitative parts of the 'The Jolly Beggars'.

The Cherrie and the Slae opens on a May morning whose crystal clear light beams down on a landscape typical of the old dream allegories. Although Montgomerie uses some 'enamelled' terms and peoples the scene with classical references, he also draws on images from nature and manages to imbue the scene with a sense of idyllic freshness. In this setting, the poet accidentally wounds himself with one of Cupid's darts and finds himself possessed not only by Courage, Desire and Hope, but also by their counterparts, Dread, Danger and Despair. Too late he realises that his peace of mind has left him:

> To late I knaw quha hewis too hie
> The spail sall fall into his eie,   chips; eye
>   To late I went to Scuillis:
> To late I heard the swallow preiche,
> To late Experience dois teache,
>   The Skuil-maister of fuillis:
> To late to fynde the nest I seik,
>   Quhen all the birdis are flowin:
> To late the stabill dore I steik,   shut
>   Quhen all the steids are stowin:
>   To lait ay, their stait ay,
>   All fulische folke espye:
>   Behynd so, they fynd so,
>   Remeid and so do I.

Montgomerie's quatorzain is at its best with these wry and *triste* epigrams. In this state of mind the poet comes to a stream before a precipitous crag with a cherry tree growing at the top, while below, on his side of the water, a bush of sloe berries offers itself to any passer-by. He is divided between a sweet, impossible ideal, and the humbler, sourer, more attainable fruit of expediency. As a love allegory the symbols ask him to choose between a high-born lady and a common mistress, and the young lover's divided feelings engage in a symbolic debate before he finally decides to seek the cherries. No sooner has the allegorical company arrived at the unclimbable cherry tree, than the ripe fruit drops into the poet's hands. When he tastes the cherries he finds himself relieved of every care and offers up praises to God. The descriptive opening scenes are detailed, charming and in the familiar love-allegory mode, but the debate that follows is lengthy, abstract and rather tedious, despite classical allusions and many familiar proverbs done in telling rhyme. Indeed some critics have maintained that the argument is an addition prompted only by an impulse to moralise, The allegory, too, is undoubtedly odd, for it conveys a fable about erotic experience with all the conventional trappings of the *Roman de la Rose*, and then turns into an extended sermon. Helena Shire explains the predominance of the *débat* by making the convincing case that at one level the choice between cherry tree and sloe bush is, for Montgomerie, a choice between the Catholic and the Reformed churches. This fits what we know of the poet's sympathies and it certainly explains why the option is discussed at such length and in such weighty terms. Whatever the complexities of the allegory, the poem most probably earned its wide popularity through the freshness of those opening scenes and because of the epigrammatical impact of dozens of quotable saws, such as 'Quhat can thou losse, quhen honour lyvis?', or 'Brunt bairn with fyre the danger dreidis', or 'als guid drinking out of glas, /As gold in ony wise' and the marvellously 'oratorious' 'Tak time in time or time be tint [lost] / For tyme will not remaine' – worthy of Polonius at his most lugubrious. Montgomerie has been called the 'last of the makars', but, notwithstanding the successes of *The Cherrie and the Slae*, he cannot really match the earlier work of Henryson, Dunbar, Douglas or Lindsay, and with him the golden age of Scottish poetry undoubtedly declines and comes to a close.

The contest between Montgomerie and Polwarth reminds us that in flyting, at least, Gaelic forms were still present in court life, although the wildness of the mode was granted a special tolerance by the sophisticates of the 'Castalian band' and James had recommended short words and a tumbling headlong delivery for it in his 'Reulis and Cautelis'. In the oral tradition of Gaeldom at large, bardic measures were still as formal as anything in the classical canon of the Renaissance, but it is not clear if this was ever fully appreciated by that courtly group of musicians and writers with their sights set on England, Italy and the humanism of du Bellay, Ronsard and the *Pléiade* in France. In fact the period from the sixteenth to the eighteenth centuries was particularly rich in Gaelic music and songs and it was the songs indeed that introduced a shift towards a more vernacular Gaelic that began to penetrate formal bardic practice later in the following century. A popular tradition in Scots songs and ballads was underway as well, but it seems appropriate to end this chapter with a closer look at something of the Highland culture that Montgomerie must have left behind him in Argyll.

Gaelic song and music

Gaelic songs and folk poetry derive from the community in the most direct way, and all their values, in both technique and outlook, stem from a conservative society, isolated, clan-based and bound by strong family ties and an enduring sense of place. Thus there are many songs celebrating place – islands, hills and favourite glens – and traditional themes and approaches prevail even in accounts of human relationships. The song-style often uses the first person and offers many striking details and yet it retains an objective and unselfconscious dignity, more elevated than the voice of the Scots ballads but similarly impersonal in its progress, even when involved (as in the Scots tradition too) with songs of betrayal and longing and supernatural encounter. Such work was not part of the formal bardic tradition and many early examples have been lost to us because they were not deemed sufficiently grand to be worth transcribing and collecting. The Fernaig Manuscript (*c.*1690) is an exception, but as Derek Thomson has pointed out, this common oral tradition was not actively sought out until much later – when Macpherson's *Ossian* generated a vogue for all things Highland in the eighteenth century.

Many Gaelic songs take a 'functional' context. For instance, the *iorram* or rowing-songs use the rhythms of the oars to deal with battles or laments – for the clans often sailed to war, and a dead chieftain would be carried to burial in his boat. Some of the earliest surviving vernacular songs deal with fighting, and the Jacobite risings ensured that this particular genre was heard well into the nineteenth century, even if its expression was to vary from direct incitement to romantic nostalgia. On the distaff side there are innumerable songs connected with the tasks of reaping, spinning, weaving, waulking and milking, not to mention love songs, lullabies, and ballads from the point of view of the jealous woman. Early examples of these show all the signs of an oral art by which songs are retained in the memory, performed and transmitted with the help of repetition, traditional images and more or less stock epithets. At the same time, such 'work songs' or songs for partic-

ular occasions became a recognised mode within which poets could
seek a more literary expression.

The *oran luadhaidh*, or waulking song, was sung by women, often in
a call-and-response pattern, while they 'waulked' lengths of wet cloth by
pulling and rubbing on it to thicken the fibres. One such early Gaelic
waulking song, 'Seathan Mac Righ Eireann' ('Seathan, Son of the King
of Ireland'), may date from the sixteenth century, and in one version at
least, is almost 200 lines long. The singer of 'Seathan' laments the death
of her lover in long rhyming paragraphs in which her memories and
desires accumulate extraordinary emotional force by way of repetition
and a host of details:

> But Seathan is in the lonely chamber,
> without drinking of cups or goblets,
> without drinking of wines from splendid silver tankards,
> without drinking of ale with his cronies and gentlemen,
> without drinking to music, without kiss from seductive woman,
> without music of harp, without listening to melody,
> but strait bands on his shoulders,
> and looped bands on the bier poles.
>
> I am a sister of Aodh and yellow-haired Brian,
> I am a kinswoman of Fionn son of Cumhall,
> I am the wife, of brown-haired Seathan, the wanderer,
> but alas! for those who said I was a joyous wife,
> I am a poor, sad, mournful, sorrowful wife,
> ful of anguish and grief and woe. . . .
>
> If Seathan could be but redeemed
> The ransom could be got like rushes,
> silver could be got like ashes,
> gold could be got on the fringe of meadows,
> wine could be got like spring water,
> beer could be got like a cool verdant stream;
> there would not be a goat in the rock or stony upland,
> there would not be a young she-goat in meadow,
> there would not be a sheep on rocky shelf or mountain top,
> there would not be cattle on plain or in fold,
> there would not be pig or cow in pastures;
> the salmon would come from the seas,
> the trout would come from the river-banks,
> the geldings would come from the rushes;
> there would not be a black or white-shouldered cow
> high or low in the fold,
> at the edge of the township or in stall,
> that I would not send, my love, to redeem thee,
> even to my green plaid,

though that should take the one cow from me,
and it was not the one black cow of my fold,
but herds of white-shouldered cattle,
of white-headed, white-backed, red-eared cattle.

But Seathan is to-night in the upper town,
neither gold nor tears will win him,
neither drink nor music . . .

> (trs. Alexander Carmichael; rev. J. C. Watson, A. Matheson)

(The use of exhaustive catalogues in this way has been a powerful and common device in Gaelic and Irish literature through the ages. The same penchant appears in Scots work such as *The Complaynt of Scotland*, or even Urquhart's *Rabelais*, as well as in the modern world-language poems of MacDiarmid, or in the prose of Irish writers such as James Joyce and Samuel Beckett, who take a similar delight in presenting the reader with lengthy and all-inclusive lists.)

The Gaelic songbook has ballads, religious verses, nonsense pieces, drinking songs and lullabies, but it is especially rich in love songs and laments – *cumha*. Many love songs celebrate courting and physical beauty; others have a more melancholy edge of loss or betrayal. The ritual practice of keening over the dead body of a loved one has produced a context for some particularly moving songs, and sometimes chilling images. 'Ailein Duinn, shiubhlainn leat' ('Brown-haired Allan, I would go with you') is a lament in this vein, although it comes from as late as the eighteenth century, composed by Ann Campbell of Scalpay in Harris, and like 'Seathan' it uses long rhymed verse-paragraphs of irregular length. It was made for the death of her fiancé, who was lost at sea on his way to their wedding:

It is a sad tale I have tonight,
not of the death of the cattle in want,
but of the wetness of your shirt,
and of the porpoises tearing at you.
Brown-haired Allan,
I heard that you had been drowned,
would that I were beside you,
on whatever rock or bank you came ashore,
in whatever heap of seaweed the high tide leaves you.
I would drink a drink, whatever my kin say,
not of the red wine of Spain
but of your breast's blood, I would prefer that . . .

> (trs. D. Thomson)

If song and music can be said to thrive in Scotland from the sixteenth to the eighteenth centuries, then there is particular genius to be found in the essentially folk-based traditions of Gaelic and the Scots ballads. By comparison, the songs of James VI's Castalian poets belong to a more urbane genre that looks to European models in form and music and never achieves the penetrating cry of the Gaelic *cumha*, or the grim concision of the Border ballads. And, of course, the full effect of these native songs is not felt until their haunting melodies are heard with all the incisive delivery of the traditional singer, whose sense of timing and use of grace notes far transcend in passion and power the politer classical training of the salon.

Gaelic songs can be sung on their own, like the ballads, or they can be accompanied by the little Celtic harp, the *clarsach* – also a solo instrument in its own right for quiet melodies. The clarsach goes back to the early society of aristocratic Gaeldom; Highland bards would be sent to Ireland to learn its use, and chiefs of the old style would keep a harper in their entourage, along with a bard, a piper and even a fool. Among the last of these minstrels in Scotland was Roderick Morison (1656–1713?) – *an Clàrsair Dall*, 'the blind harper' – from Lewis, who lived in Lochaber and Skye in the seventeenth century under the protection of the Clan MacLeod. Airs to his songs have survived, but little of his purely instrumental work remains. In general the fiddle took over from the harp in succeeding generations, and indeed some harp tunes were only preserved through fiddle adaptations, until the nineteenth century saw a revival of interest in the clarsach as an instrument for ladies in the drawing room.

As though reflecting the fiercer side of the Highland sensibility, the bagpipe is a more disturbing and warlike instrument. Like the harp, its origins are too ancient to be specifically Scottish, and in the Middle Ages it was widely known throughout Europe. In the isolation of the Highlands, however, pipe music continued to develop well into the nineteenth century, and thrives today in marches and dances (strathspeys, reels and jigs) as well as the more melodic slow airs. The finest pipe music is not to be found with the massed bands and tartans of modern times, but with the solo pipes playing *ceòl mór* ('the big music') – unique to Scotland and originally called simply 'pipe-playing' (*piobaireachd*, or, in English, pibroch). This, the 'classical music' of the bagpipe, first states a simple theme as the *urlar*, or ground, and moves to *siubhal*, or variation, the variations increasing in complexity until *crunluath*, the climax, is reached and the progression ends with a return to the bare ground. The rules of construction and variation are highly developed, and pipe tunes and their proper fingering can be passed on only by personal tuition, so a system of mimetic syllabic chanting called *canntaireachd* was evolved as a level of aural notation – although it could also be written down as 'words'. Conventional musical notation only came to be used in the mid-nineteenth century and it still cannot give a complete account of the subtleties of the grace notes and how the instrument should be fingered. Like Celtic carving or the art of the Book of Kells, pibroch favours complication and technical virtuosity as the tune is gradually embellished with repetition or variation through the multiplication of notes, all within a fixed framework. Yet the melody too is vital, for these deceptively simple pentatonic lines are the ground or 'floor' upon which everything else is built. Tunes from the pipe-tradition can equal the finest melodies in European music, and it has been suggested that Dvořák first heard the slow movement of the 'New World' symphony in the beautiful air of 'MacIntosh's Lament'. Pibrochs can be stirring war-tunes, or boasts and challenges in the *brosnachadh* vein, but some of the finest tunes of glory have been the laments, poignant and strong, sad and yet somehow exultant.

We know little about early pipe music except that it existed, and even the development of pibroch is unclear until the sixteenth century, when an almost legendary family called **the MacCrimmons** appeared as hereditary pipers to the Macleods of Skye, where they are reputed to have run a piping college at Boreraig. Some of the finest pibrochs were composed by MacCrimmons during the seventeenth and eighteenth centuries, when pibroch really came into its own, and the same family had pipers in it for another hundred years. Other families made significant contributions too, often beginning with MacCrimmon tuition, and two in particular stand out. The Mackays of Gairloch were descended from Iain Dall MacKay (1656–1754), the blind piper whose masterpiece, 'Lament for Patrick Og MacCrimmon', was composed in honour of his old teacher. The MacKays of Raasay, on the other hand, stem from John MacKay (1767–1845), who mastered about 250 tunes in *canntaireachd* and passed on a large part of the MacCrimmon heritage. In turn his son Angus (1813–58) recorded over 180 tunes in manuscript, to make a link with piping in modern times. Perhaps it is in pibroch, more than in any other art from a relatively remote Highland society, that the autonomy and the sophisticated intensity of Gaelic culture developed to its furthest and purest expression.

It is a sad reflection that the century was to end with James VI's attempts (like his grandfather before him) to subdue Gaelic culture and the power of the clans. Chiefs who could not provide documentary evidence for their lands were forced to surrender them by an act of Parliament in 1597. When the MacLeods of Lewis fell foul of this edict, Lowland settlers were sent off to colonise the island – a colonial adventure in keeping with the Plantation of Ulster in 1606, with the same end in view: – that of breaking down Highland allegiances and the 'Celtic connection' with Ireland. The Lewis scheme did not succeed, but the model for it (and for Ulster) was described in James's textbook on the art of monarchy, *Basilikon Doron*, which speaks of his determination to 'civilize the best inclined among them, rooting out or transporting the barbarous and stubborne sort and planting civilitie in their roomes'. In 1609, twelve West Highland chiefs, tricked into captivity in Edinburgh, were forced to sign the Statutes of Iona designed, in Colm Ó Baoill's words, 'to contribute to the civilisation and deGaelicisation of the Highlands, as well as to further the Reformation there'. (The first book to be printed in Gaelic was Bishop John Carswell's translation of the Book of Common Order, also known as Knox's liturgy in 1567.) Among other things the Statutes of Iona also tried to ban bards and required Highland chiefs to send their eldest sons to Lowland schools 'quhill thay may be found sufficientlie to speik, reid, and wryte Inglische'.

4

The seventeenth century: crown and Covenant; the ballads

AFTER the union of the crowns, Scotland was disrupted by conflict for almost ninety years as the struggle between Presbyterians, Episcopalians, Catholics and extreme dissenters continued. For the people in the northern part of the kingdom, the Civil War, the Restoration and the Revolution Settlement were only further episodes in a cause that had started, as far as they were concerned, with the triumph of the Kirk in Mary's reign and the Declaration of Faith in 1560. These disputatious years consumed the intellectual and creative energies of two generations to the exclusion of almost everything else. Thus although there were no Scots writers to equal Donne and Marvell (although Drummond and Urquhart are of note) there was a powerfully analytical prose tradition in the work of Hume, Mackenzie, Dalrymple and Rutherford. Perhaps the best poetic expression of the turbulent times came from the biting verses of Iain Lom, who used a more vernacular Gaelic than the old *filidhean* had favoured, and whose work looks forward to the flowering of Gaelic verse in the next century. In Scotland's other language the traditional Scots ballads continued to circulate with the common people, producing some of the finest oral poetry in Europe and laying down a literary treasure for future generations.

From the vantage point of his new throne in London, James VI and I began to reconsolidate his authority and the principle of divine right, making a speech to parliament in which he informed the nation that 'Kings are not onely GODS lieutenants upon earth, and sit upon GODS throne, but even by GOD himselfe they are called gods'. (Henceforth the old line of 'Stewards' was to spell its name 'Stuart'.) He used his powers to restore episcopacy in Scotland, and when Charles I acceded in 1625 he continued his father's policy by reclaiming for the crown all those Church lands which had been redistributed by the Reformation. After the coronation at Edinburgh in 1633, Charles passed acts of parliament to establish Anglican forms of worship – on pain of excommunication. The communion table was turned back into an altar, confession was restored and a new prayer book imposed. Popular unrest spread and in 1637 a famous riot broke out in St Giles' Cathedral, when a band of serving-women attacked the priest for following the new ways. At a more responsible level a plebiscite was organised to declare support for the 1560 Confession of Faith. This 'National Covenant' was drawn up at Greyfriars' Churchyard in 1638 and signed by thousands of people from all classes amid scenes of delirious fervour. The Covenant declared loyalty to the king, but requested him to re-establish the goals of Presbyterianism and not to interfere with the proper business of a free parliament and the General Assembly. The next two years saw the spasmodic 'Bishops' Wars' until Montrose's tactics with the volunteer Covenanting armies eventually persuaded Charles to make concessions to the Scots by calling an English parliament – only to have that parliament take away his right to terminate it. (Indeed, the 'Long Parliament' was eventually to depose him.)

When the Civil War broke out in the south the Scottish extremists pressed their case and the 'Solemn League and Covenant' was drawn up in 1643 to force the king to stamp out Catholicism and Episcopacy throughout Britain. At this point Montrose's conscience led him to side with Charles, and he was not alone in his belief that the Solemn League had gone too far. The Highlands had never been too enthusiastic, even about the relatively mild National Covenant, and so Montrose found support there to wage a brief and brilliant military campaign. His forces began to dwindle, however, and after defeat at Philiphaugh in 1645 he had to escape into exile. Inspired by their ministers' battle cry of 'Jesus and no quarter!', the unforgiving Covenanters massacred the beaten clansmen and all their wives and children for days.

Despite his defeat, when it finally came at Naseby, Charles still refused to sign the Solemn League and Covenant and by this time the Independents in the New Model Army had become equally uncomfortable with the notion of universal compulsory Presbyterianism. Nevertheless, the Covenanters were still convinced that their faith could be imposed by royal decree, and after Charles's execution in 1649 they took their cause to his nineteen-year-old exiled son. He too refused, and once again Montrose was prevailed upon to take up arms on behalf of kingship and his king, only to be betrayed and captured within a few months. 'Arrayed like a bridegroom' in fine linen and ribbons, he was executed at the Mercat Cross in Edinburgh in 1650 – and only a month later his young Stuart prince signed the Covenant after all. With a bloody reversal only too typical of the times, the Scots Presbyterian forces duly marched south to fight against Cromwell on behalf of what was now the Royalist cause. They were defeated at Worcester in 1651; Charles escaped to France, and Scotland was subdued under English judges and troops commanded by General Monck. Peace prevailed for the next eight years, although after two decades of civil and religious turmoil it had an air of exhaustion about it.

The Restoration in 1660 was welcomed by the Scots – after all, Charles was still a Stuart monarch; but the more radical Presbyterians from the south-west (called 'Whiggamores' during the Civil War) resented the return of bishops, not to mention the king and his favoured lords. Some 300 dissenting ministers left their parishes and held services with their congregations on the open hillsides, despite attempts by troopers to disperse them. It was not long before an armed rising of dissenters from Galloway declared for the Covenant and marched on Edinburgh, only to be routed at Rullion Green in the Pentlands by Sir Thomas Dalyell of the Binns. Many were transported to Barbados and a few were hanged at the gibbet, but the hillside conventicles continued to grow – even after it was made a capital offence to attend them. These were 'the Killing Times', when radical preachers carried weapons and their congregations were harried by the mounted dragoons of Dalyell and John Graham of Claverhouse, who noted that 'there were as many elephants and crocodiles in Galloway as loyal or regular persons'. Walter Scott's novel *Old Mortality* (1816) deals with what happened after 1678 when Archbishop Sharp of St Andrews was brutally murdered by a party of Covenanters who came across his coach outside the city. Scott was not sympathetic to the assassins' cause. The dissenters' ambitions were further aroused by a confused engagement at Drumclog, during which an armed conventicle put the dragoons of 'bluidy Clavers' to flight. Flushed with success, but divided by internal disputes, the Covenanters raised an army of 5000 that was eventually defeated by the king's forces at Bothwell Brig. Yet every death was a martyrdom that added to their resolve. Militant working-class groups such as Richard Cameron's 'Society Folk' refused to make allegiance to any ruler other than Christ himself, and so they were outlawed and persecuted. Some Cameronians were killed on the spot for refusing to acknowledge the king, and, although such brutal acts were not widespread, they provided powerful moral and political ammunition that the Covenanters were not slow to use in comparing themselves to the Children of Israel under the oppression of a godless Pharaoh. John Galt's novel *Ringan Gilhaize* (1823), tells the story of these troubled times from the point of view, not unsympathetically, of one of the Covenanters.

Paradoxically, the cause of Presbyterianism was best served by James II when he came to the throne in 1685 and proceeded, against advice, to restore Catholics to power throughout the realm. In both England and Scotland this amounted to political suicide, and within three years, faced with widespread revolution, James had to forfeit the crown to his sister Mary and her husband from Protestant Holland, William of Orange. John Graham of Claverhouse ('Bonnie Dundee' to his supporters) came out for James's cause and led some of the clans to victory at Killiecrankie, but he himself was killed on the field. Without Graham's leadership his dispirited forces were finally defeated at Dunkeld at the hands of a Protestant 'Cameronian' regiment who had so recently been outlaws themselves, fleeing from 'Clavers' when he, in his turn, had been the arm of established authority. A similar rising in Ireland was defeated by King William and his army at the Battle of the Boyne, and to this day the date '1690' and the epithet 'King Billy' have been rallying-cries for intransigently anti-Catholic 'Orangemen' in Ulster and Scotland.

William's next step was to bring the Highlands into line and to 'extirpate' those who resisted. Accordingly, the clans were required to sign an oath of fealty to the crown and, when the MacDonalds of Glencoe were late to do so in 1692, John Dalrymple, the Secretary of State in Scotland, decided to make an example of them. In due course Campbell soldiers descended on winter-bound Glencoe and sought hospitality from the MacDonalds. After several days of food and shelter, the soldiers turned on their hosts in an act of planned terrorism, killing nearly forty MacDonalds and driving the rest out into the snow. The 'Massacre of Glencoe' outraged public opinion, and, although it encouraged other chiefs to recognise William, they did not forget the matter, nor the treachery of the Campbells. Nor was the Jacobite question resolved, for, when James II died in exile in 1701, his son James (the 'Old Pretender' and father to 'Bonnie Prince Charlie') was recognised by Louis XIV as the rightful and Catholic heir to the British throne.

The rest of Scotland returned to a semblance of stability, with the wheel of prejudice now turned against the Episcopalians as the General Assembly recovered its influence and restored the heritage of Knox and

Melville. In material terms the last twenty years of the century saw a growth in trade and prosperity and Scots capital began to look for investments abroad. Plans were made for expansion to Africa and the East Indies, but, when these were blocked by the influence of the East India Company, Scottish businessmen came up with the optimistic 'Darien Scheme' (1698) to form a trading company of their own in Central America. The chosen site was ridden with fever, however, and when things began to go wrong the English trading interests in Jamaica refused to help, and even hindered the project. The Darien adventure ended with many deaths, a catastrophic commercial loss to the country and much bitterness against the English.

The seventeenth century seemed determined to end badly as a series of poor harvests brought poverty and famine to Scotland and most of northern Europe. But Scotland's hardship had been more than material, and, after almost a hundred years of civil, constitutional and religious strife, the cost in psychological and cultural terms can scarcely be calculated. On the one hand the Presbyterian ideal enhanced the status of every individual citizen as he or she stood, literate and alone, before God and the word of God in the Bible. On the other hand, the Kirk could not allow such freedom to lead to licence and unorthodoxy, and so the parish minister and his elders played an influential part in social and moral guidance and control. When narrow Calvinism was in the ascendancy, as it was from 1690 until about 1720, such men had the baleful power of commissars in a one-party state and, indeed, in 1696 an Edinburgh student was actually executed for the crime of blasphemy. In cultural terms, the humane spirit of the makars had all but disappeared. Many Scots intellectuals were turning to London, to English and to long-established Latin for their models, and gradually Scots was becoming regarded as the vernacular speech of country people. This process of 'vernacularisation' continued into the next century, but its results were not entirely negative. If Scots was associated with 'vulgar' directness, then it also spoke with the very voice of the people – vigorous, swift, violent, earthy, realistically in touch with hardship and the seasons and yet capable, too, of romance and a sense of wonder. James's 'Castalian band', pursuing French styles and European humanist links, had not been concerned with such forces, but they were burgeoning nonetheless without need of courtly patronage in the great Scottish ballads – some of the finest and most popular examples of the oral tradition to be found anywhere in the world. It was not until the end of the century and the beginning of the next that this colloquial energy was to flourish again in a more peaceful world of books and publishing.

Poets at court

When King James took the road to London in 1603 he retained his role as patron of the muse and was soon joined by a number of Scottish poets. William Alexander and Robert Ayton received knighthoods and positions of favour; Sir David Murray (fl. 1620) later joined the short-lived Prince Henry's retinue, and the sonneteer Robert Kerr (1578–1654) received an earldom from Charles I and became an intimate of the London literati. **Sir William Alexander** (1577?–1640) wrote sonnets in the fashion of a gentleman of the day. An admirer of Spenser, he knew Drummond in the north and befriended Michael Drayton in England, but there is little of lasting value in *Aurora*, his collection of sonnets published in 1604. A venture into Jacobean verse drama – most likely closet texts for reading rather than acting – resulted in four lengthy *Monarchicke Tragedies* (1603–7) outlining the perils of ambition in the ancient world, featuring Darius, Croesus, Alexander the Great and Julius Caesar. An equally sustained exercise in verse, *Doomesday* (1614), produced over 10,000 moral and unexciting lines on the vanity of worldly ambition. Alexander was a moving figure in a succession of (ultimately unsuccessful) schemes to colonise Nova Scotia in the 1620s. He rose to be Secretary of State for Scotland in 1628, and was made Earl of Stirling in 1632, developing the fine Argyll's Lodging as his home when he came north. But he was an unpopular and profit-seeking politician who eventually lost everything and died in poverty.

Sir Robert Ayton (1569–1638) was a better poet with a degree of skill in English verse as well as in Latin, French and Greek. Ayton, from a prosperous Fife family, joined the court shortly after the king's arrival in London, and within eight years he had been knighted and made a member of the royal household. He made friends of Ben Jonson and Hobbes and appears in Aubrey's *Brief Lives*. In common with many of his accomplished contemporaries, however, he was not published in his own lifetime, nor did he consider himself to 'affect the name of a poet'. His best work is probably to be found in songs for the lute rather like Thomas Campion's, and it is possible that he was the author of the original version of the piece that Burns turned into 'Auld Lang Syne'. Almost half his output was in Latin and only a few of his early poems were in Scots. He addressed verses to the king on all the issues of the day, including some lines on the Gunpowder Plot of 1605.

Many contemporary Scottish writers were similarly fluent in Latin, and they too chose to eschew the vernacular tradition in favour of the scholarly example of George Buchanan. Among these were the gallant James Crichton (1560–83), later hailed by Sir Thomas Urquhart as 'the admirable Crichtoun', and Arthur Johnston (1587–1661) who edited and contributed to an anthology of many other Scottish Latin poets, *Delitiae Poetarum Scotorum* (1637). **James Graham, the Marquis of Montrose** (1612–50) is mainly remembered for the brilliance of his brief military career, but he too produced civilised verses. The best known of these is addressed to his mistress as 'My Dear and Only Love', but four lines from it could well apply to the author's own grim end:

> He either fears his Fate too much,
>   Or his Deserts are small,
> That puts it not unto the Touch,
>   To win or lose it all.

William Drummond of Hawthornden (1585–1649)

Unlike his friend Montrose, William Drummond tried to avoid public life and religious dispute. Educated in Edinburgh and a student of law in France, he inherited his father's estate at Hawthornden near Lasswade, just outside Edinburgh, and decided to settle there at the age of twenty-four on his own terms as a man of letters. He collected books avidly and expanded Hawthornden's already substantial library; he read widely in French and Italian and showed a taste for epigrams, anagrams, ephemera and curiosities of all sorts. Drummond's first poem, 'Teares, on the Death of Moeliades' (1612), was a conventional lament on the death of Prince Henry, James's eldest son, infused with the influence of Sir Philip Sidney. Before long he had compiled a collection of songs and a sequence modelled on *Astrophel and Stella*, with other sonnets translated or adapted from French and Italian, all in a sad neo-Platonic vain. This romantic colouring does seem to have been a genuine part of Drummond's temperament, later reinforced by the early death of his fiancée in 1616. Drummond's collection was first published probably in 1614 and then again in 1616, finely bound and expensively set, just as he insisted all his works should be.

Drummond was especially keen to be appreciated in England, and his manuscripts show his many literary debts and the care he took to excise all Scoticisms of expression and spelling from his verse. Within formal modes his elegant lines aim for a smooth and decorative flow of sound (a general characteristic of James's circle), rather than for the strenuous dialectic of Donne or the wit of Marvell. Drummond's fellow writers thought highly of his erudition and, like them, we can admire his particular penchant for sweet and sensuously melancholy accounts of loneliness:

> Sound hoarse sad *Lute*, true Witnesse of my Woe,
> And striue no more to ease self-chosen Paine
> With Soule-enchanting Sounds, your Accents straine
> Vnto these Teares vncessantly which flow.
> Shrill Treeble weepe, and you dull Basses show
> Your Masters Sorrow *in a deadly Vaine*,
> Let neuer ioyfull Hand vpon you goe,
> Nor Consort keepe but when you doe complaine.
> Flie Phoebus Rayes, nay, hate the irkesome Light,
> Woods solitarie Shades for thee are best,
> Or the black Horrours of the blackest Night,
> When all the *World* (saue Thou and I) doth rest:
> Then sound sad Lute, and beare a mourning Part,
> Thou *Hell* may'st mooue, though not a Woman's *Heart*.
>
> (Sonnet XXVIII of 'The First Part')

Despite his declared preference for Hawthornden, the 'sweet solitarie Place, / Where from the vulgare I estranged liue', Drummond was not a complete recluse. He corresponded with Michael Drayton in England and with Alexander and Kerr, his fellow Scots at court in London. Ben Jonson particularly admired Drummond's work, visiting Scotland late in 1618 to stay at Hawthornden for three weeks. The host made notes on his guest's table talk and his *Conversations with Ben Jonson* (1711) have become well known and widely quoted, not least for the portrait they paint of the bibulous playwright as a 'contemner and Scorner of others' and a 'great lover and praiser of himself'.

Drummond developed the melancholy of his earlier poems to produce *Flowres of Sion* (1623), a collection of madrigals, sonnets and hymns all of which reflect on human frailty, on the instability of the world and on the 'contemplation of invisible excellences above by the visible below' (Sonnet XVIII).

> O Sunne invisible, that doest abide
> Within thy bright abysmes, most faire, most darke,
> Where with thy proper Rayes thou dost thee hide;
> O euer-shining neuer full seene marke,
>   To guide mee in Lifes Night, thy light mee show,
>   The more I search of thee, the lesse I know.
>
> (Sonnet XVII)

Once again the poet praises the lonely life, but now his sonnets have a more philosophical dimension, named after spiritual solitaries and outcasts – 'For the Prodigal', 'For the Magdalene' and 'For the Baptists'. Drummond's best poems are in this mode, including translations from European sources whose spirit has been well and fully assimilated into the poet's own character. In the same volume he developed his theme in prose with *A Cypresse Grove*, a meditation on death derived from Italian models and especially from the French of Montaigne's *Essais*. Written almost twenty years before Sir Thomas Browne's *Religio Medici* was published, *A Cypresse Grove, or Philosophical Reflections Against the Fear of Death* anticipates and matches the latter's achievement with a musical and weighty prose written largely for poetic effect. Perhaps Drummond is the more sober of the two, for he lacks the conjurer's adroitness with which the Norwich man makes to dance the heavy furniture of his style.

Notwithstanding the melancholy of *A Cypresse Grove*, 'wormewood' was not Drummond's only food, nor 'Teares his Drinke', and during the course of his life he produced satirical and sexually comic verses as well as various proverbs and epigrams. He is usually credited with a Macaronic jest called 'Polemo-Middinia', where Scots and English words are mixed with dog Latin and given Latin endings to lampoon a countryside quarrel over rights of way on a footpath. He had a mistress and three children and at forty-five he married and fathered another large family. In 1627 he had invented and patented plans for numerous ingenious weapons of war and by 1633 he had become well enough known to be put in charge of the pageant for Charles I's visit to Edinburgh. He found politics uncongenial and had little sympathy with the more extreme Presbyterians, although he had signed the National Covenant in 1638. His pamphlets in favour of peace and toleration on all sides were not published during his lifetime. *Irene, A Remonstrance for Concord, Amitie and Love amongst His Majesties Subjects* (1638) praises Charles I for making concessions to the Covenant and lectures the commoners on the virtues of obedience: 'Good Princes should be obeyed, yea evill Princes should be tollerated . . . they are not to be judged by their Subjectes.'

Perhaps the author's peaceful seclusion on the banks of the North Esk would not have survived the broadcasting of such sentiments; but, in any case, events moved on without Drummond. A lengthy *History of Scotland* covering the period 1423–1542 was published six years after his death and has little to distinguish it. Drummond ended his days at Hawthornden with his wealth greatly reduced, engaged in litigation and embittered by the times in which he lived. He left an unfinished satire about a country 'latlie turned most part Mad' by the worshipping of a golden 'calfe anant' (Covenant) which was really only made of paper after all. His youthful taste for solitude had turned a little sour in the mouth, and, as a conservative who looked back to the Elizabethan England of Sidney and Spenser for his literary values, his isolation in the Scotland of the turbulent 1640s was never more poignantly acute.

Writing in prose

Alas, the music of *A Cypresse Grove* is not typical, and for the most part Scottish prose in the seventeenth century consists of treatises on religious doctrine, church politics, histories, memoirs, letters, or contumacious and wordy mixtures of all these. Whatever their sectarian views, almost everyone followed Knox's example in avoiding overtly Scottish expressions. The Latin poet and historian **David Hume of Godscroft** (1558–1630?) argued in favour of a union between Scotland and England in his Latin study *De Unione Insulae Britanniae* (1605) with a vision of a moderate civic society, tolerant of cultural and political differences, that almost anticipates the Enlightenment, while still seeking to sustain a Scottish identity. In the same spirit he supported the use of Scots prose, accounting it 'a mean study to learn to speak or read English', even though he had to confess that he had sometimes 'yielded . . . to the tyranny of custom and the times' by 'not seeking curiously for words, but taking them as they came to hand'. As secretary to Archibald Douglas, 8th earl of Angus, Hume's monumental study of *The History of the House and Race of Douglas and Angus*, (Edinburgh, 1644) is self-confessedly partial to that family's interpretation of events and is the source of a number of memorable vignettes from Scottish history, including the incident with Bruce and the spider – observed by Douglas, according to Hume, and told to Bruce as a parable. Hume's writing is forceful and clear. He was one of the stout reformers who sought to limit the power of kings under the eye of God and the Church and indeed when he was implicated in the Ruthven Raid that sought to free the young King James from Catholic influence, he had to flee to England for a spell. He associated his Calvinist sentiments with the hardy virtues of ancient Rome and linked these to what he took to be the honest plainness of Scots:

> For the language, it is my mother-tongue, that is, Scottish: and why not, to Scottish men? why should I contemne it? I never thought the difference so

great, as that by seeking to speak English, I would hazard the imputation of affectation. Every tongue hath its own vertue and grace. Some are more substantiall, others more ornate and succinct. They have also their own defects and faultinesses, some are harsh, some are effeminate, some are rude, some affectate and swelling. The Romanes spake from their heart, the Grecians with their lips only, and their ordinary speech was complements; especially the Asiatick Greeks did use a loose and blown kind of phrase. And who is there that keeps that golden mean? For my own part, I like our own, and he that writes well in it, writes well enough to me.

Even so, there's not much Scots evident in this passage and his not unequivocal feelings about the language's sturdy roots may be gathered from the fact that he changed the name of his house from 'Gowkscroft' (Cuckoo farm) to 'Godscroft'.

The grammarian Alexander Hume (1558–1631?) was no relation, but he used a diluted Scots to propound his theories on orthography in *Grammatica Nova* (1612); nevertheless the title of one of his later pamphlets refers only to 'the Britan Tongue'. Scots was used, again rarely, by Abacuck Bysset (fl. 1610) for a catalogue of ancient historical sites called *The Rolement of Courtis* (1622), in which he defended his 'awin . . . mother tung' as 'pithie and schorte'; although it must be admitted that his own practice does not always attain brevity:

I haue nocht bene copius in langaig be far drevin, uncouth evill placed termis, and multiplicatioun of wordis be paraphraces of circumlocutioun of speich, silogismes, and refutatioun of argumentis be, parablis or compareso-nis; nor haue I adhered to auld proverbis or bywordis, fair, flattering, fenzeit [invented], and counterfuit fictionis, uttered be archadicienis, maid up, counterfuit, and phrasing langaige; neither haue I . . . used minzeard [mincing] nor effeminate tantting invective nor skornefull wordis, vane, saterick, or louse wowsting and wanting [boasting and vaunting] speeches; nor haue I . . . .

Most prose at the time was characterised by exactly this tendency to be 'copius'. John Brown (d. 1679), for instance, an exiled Covenanter, could produce a 'pamphlet' of 400 pages on the sufferings of godly ministers in Scotland, while the even more extreme Alexander Shields (d. 1700) produced 700 pages of his *Hind Let Loose* for the Cameronian viewpoint in 1687, including an argument for the assassination of uncovenanted and unrightful authority. On the other hand, **Sir George Mackenzie of Rosehaugh** (1636–91), defended national eloquence in his *Preface to Pleadings* (1673) by claiming that Scots was best suited for arguing in the law court, because 'our pronunciation is like ourselves, fiery, abrupt, sprightly and bold'. As Lord Advocate,

Mackenzie founded the Advocates' Library in Edinburgh (now part of the National Library) and produced several more books on the law, noted for the clarity of their argument in English prose, as well as political studies, a novel (*Aretina*, 1660) poems, moral essays and *Religio Stoici* (1663), which contained his reflections on the schisms within the Church. He was a gifted man who abhorred fanaticism and was strongly opposed to the obscene witchcraft trials in his time. He was equally forcefully in favour of the proper authority of the king, and his prosecution of dissenting Covenanters, although legal and humane by his lights, earned him the nickname of 'bluidy Mackenzie'. His *Memoirs of the Affairs of Scotland from the Restoration* was not published until long after his death.

The other famous name in Scots Law, but this time a sympathiser with the Covenanters, was **Sir James Dalrymple** (1616–95), later Viscount Stair, known for his *Institutions of the Law of Scotland* (1681). 'Stair's Institutions', or just 'Stair', set the future mould for Scots Law as an independent system of jurisprudence with a strongly argued logical bias and close links to European practice. Dalrymple acted as a Commissioner for the Cromwellian government, and was respected enough by both parties to take a hand in the restoration of Charles II, but his firmly Protestant principles would not let him swear not to take up arms against the king. At a later point his refusal to take the Test Oath forced him to live in Holland before being allowed to return in the reign of William and Mary, who made him a Viscount in 1690. The arranged marriage of Dalrymple's daughter Janet and her tragic early death became the subject of Scott's novel *The Bride of Lammermuir*, but his other children and their descendants made distinguished careers for themselves. Actually, as Secretary of State, his son John's career ended in scandal because of his part in arranging the massacre of Glencoe. Sir James's great-grandson was the eighteenth-century judge and historian Sir David Dalrymple, Lord Hailes.

All four of the ancient Scots Universities had a strong commitment to Law, Logic, Philosophy, Science and Medicine, and the writings of such men as Mackenzie and Dalrymple – both equally if differently engaged in religious and political issues – paved the way for open discussion and the rigorous application of rational argument to ethical matters that was later to become the hallmark of the Scottish Enlightenment. The Enlightenment's debt to the previous century's turbulent disputes, and its appetite for debate, should not be underestimated.

If the legal training of Mackenzie and Dalrymple made them shun casuistry, the same cannot be said of most of the religious controversialists who took it upon themselves to expound the words of God. Yet there were some divines of great expressive ability and the church-going public relished their demonstrations of dialectical eloquence, whether simple and passionate, or decked in the sesquipedelian flowers of classical rhetoric. Godly debate was as 'forensic' as any lawyer could desire. Men such as Robert Bruce and the unfortunately named Andrew Cant were famous for the power of their preaching, while others were noted more for erudition. Best regarded of all was the extempore composition of complex arguments, redolent with learned references and cunning strophes. Publications in both Latin and English abounded, with titles such as *Instructiones Historico-Theologicae* (1645), by John Forbes, a moderate Episcopalian who was the professor of Divinity at Aberdeen University, or *Aaron's Rod Blossoming* (1646), by George Gillespie, a member of the Presbyterian camp. Then there was *Lex Rex* (1644) by **Samuel Rutherford** (1600–61), who argued against the king in a work 'stuffed with positions, that in the time of peace and order, would have been judged damnable treasons'. Indeed, seventeen years later (after the Restoration), the pamphlet was burned in public by the hangman at Edinburgh and again at St Andrews, under the old author's college windows. He died in the same year. Rutherford was no extremist but a notable teacher and a moving preacher. He became Professor of Divinity at New College and latterly Rector at St Andrews, and had declined the offer of a chair at two universities in Holland. His religious writing, such as *Christ Dying and Drawing Sinners to Himself* (1647), is passionately metaphysical, drawn to the unknowable nature of infinity. His copious correspondence strikes a more personal note and was published as *Joshua redivivus* after his death.

Among the outstanding divines of the day, **Robert Baillie** (1599–1662) was a man of shrewd and moderate temper who possessed a 'golden' Latin style and became known for his intellectual excellence in twelve or thirteen languages. He was a determined Presbyterian, an ecclesiastical diplomat with some service abroad and several publications in defence of his beliefs; but it is his *Letters and Journals* (1637–62) that provide an invaluable insight into the contemporary world of political and ecclesiastical affairs. They begin in 1637, the year of the riot in St Giles' against the Anglican prayer book. Baillie was equally opposed to 'Laud's liturgy', but he feared the worst for Scotland:

> What shall be the event, God knows: there was in our Land ever such ane appearance of a sturr; the whole people thinks Poperie at the doores; the scandalous pamphlets which comes daily new from England adde oyl to this

flame; no man may speak any thing in publick for the King's part, except he would have himself marked for a sacrifice to be killed one day. I think our people possessed with a bloody devill, farr above any thing that ever I could have imagined. . . . For myself, I think, God, to revenge the crying sinns of all estates and professions . . . is going to execute his long denounced threatnings, and to give us over unto madness, that we may every one shoot our swords in our neighbours hearts.

Within a year the National Covenant was signed to make, in effect, a direct challenge to the power of kings.

A vivid picture of subsequent events can be found in other diaries and memoirs, such as those of Sir John Lauder and Sir James Turner – Presbyterians who gradually came to support the king, or at least the cause of the crown. (Turner was one of the models for Walter Scott's Dugald Dalgetty in *A Legend of Montrose*.) Henry Guthrie (?1600–76), whose opinion of *Lex Rex* has already been heard, was a moderate Episcopalian, and, although he had signed the Covenant, like Montrose he eventually took the king's side. The waters of dissent were certainly muddy enough, and Guthrie maintains that the 'spontaneous' St Giles' riot had actually been planned three months in advance, so that women 'might give the first affront to the book, assuring them that men should afterwards take the business out of their hands'. The diaries of John Nicoll (1590–1667) testify to the confusions of the day in a different sense, for he left blanks in his pages so that he could adjust his views in retrospect and insert 'God save the King!' at appropriately prophetic points! Nicoll's accounts of the passing scene are more reliable, but his belief in witches and his interest in witch trials testify to troubled times and a thoroughly unlikeable character.

History and doctrinal dispute became inseparable, and many chroniclers were intent only on a vindication of their particular church. John Spottiswoode (1565–1639), the Bishop of St Andrews, had to flee for London when his cause was defeated, but his *History of the Church of Scotland* (1655) shows a relatively generous recognition that 'popular fury once roused can keep no measure, nor do anything with advice and judgment'. The Episcopalian historian Gilbert Burnet (1643–1715) was amazed by another side to the common people when he toured the country in the 1660s to meet:

a poor commonality, so capable of arguing upon points of government, and on the bounds to be set on the power of Princes, in matters of religion: upon all these topicks they had texts of scripture at hand; and were ready with their anssers, to anything that was said to them. This measure of knowledge was spread even among the meanest of them, the cottagers and their servants.

David Calderwood (1575–1650) shows a Presbyterian bias, and his *History of the Kirk of Scotland* (1678) is vividly anecdotal, as when he describes how Bishop Spottiswoode (the rival historian) deprived reformer David Dickson of his ministry:

> 'The will of the Lord be done', said Mr David. 'Though you cast me off, yit the Lord will take me up. Send me where ye please. I hope my Master sall goe with me; and as He hath beene with me heirtofore, He will be with me still as with His owne weake servant.'
>
> 'Sweith away!' said the bishop, as if he had been speaking to a dogge; 'Pack, you swinger!' and crying to the doorekeeper, he sayes, 'Shoote him out!'

It is difficult not to sympathise with the bold Spottiswoode in the face of Dickson's pious complacency, and we shall let him have the last word.

Witchcraft and superstition

The persecution of witches and heretics had been part of Catholic Europe since medieval times and was particularly common in Germany in the later fifteenth century. In Scotland, however, it was the Presbyterian extremists 200 years later who were to prove the most committed to the discovery and extirpation of witchcraft, as if the righteous fear of the Lord had also brought with it a paranoid terror of the Devil. Perhaps, too, the Kirk's insistence on rigid patriarchal authority led to barely submerged resentments against the implications of female knowledge in traditional herbal healing, and especially of female sexuality, for witches' covens were widely suspected of the most promiscuous behaviour. James VI's treatise on *Daemonologie* had pursued these various anxieties in 1597, spurred by the North Berwick trials of 1590 at which he heard a coven confess under torture that they had tried to raise a storm to drown him on his return from Denmark.

Mass hysteria and the use of torture to exact confessions and to implicate others meant that fears and fantasies spread like wildfire. T. C. Smout has estimated that between 3000 and 4500 people were executed as witches in Scotland between 1560 and the end of the seventeenth century. There were particularly disgraceful epidemics of witch burning in the 1590s, the late 1620s, the 1640s (when Covenanting fervour was at its height and the General Assembly declared war on witchcraft) and then again in the 1660s. Some male warlocks were indicted, and trials based on personal revenge or political advantage were not unknown, but by far the most part of the persecution was against female witches who were almost always country people or drawn from the poorer classes. By the end of the century legal doubts about the validity of forced confession finally began to restrain the wilder excesses of the witch prickers and the insanity of tests that proved witches innocent only if they drowned. Nevertheless, the belief in witches was sustained for years to come and its irrational roots can be seen in the work of George Sinclair (1618–87), one-time professor of Philosophy at Glasgow, who produced studies on engineering and hydrostatics, as well as *Satan's Invisible World Discovered* (1685), in which he set himself, equally scientifically, to recount all the instances he could gather of supernatural events and apparitions, including the evidence heard at contemporary witchcraft trials.

The Secret Commonwealth of Elves, Fauns, and Fairies (1691), written by Robert Kirk (1644–92), was quite another matter. Like his father before him, Kirk was a minister at Aberfoyle, then an entirely Gaelic-speaking area. This led Kirk, a learned man, to translate the Psalms into Gaelic in 1684 and then to oversee the production of a Bible in Gaelic which he transliterated himself from a version in Irish orthography. He also made a small Gaelic dictionary and helped to distribute 'Kirk's Bible', which he completed in 1690. In *The Secret Commonwealth* Kirk's next task was to write a 'natural history' of Celtic fairy lore. The *Sidh* (pronounced 'Shee') are not like the gauzy-winged creatures of Victorian sentiment, but are more likely to appear as full-sized good-looking beings dressed as mortals, though with a preference for wearing green and silver. Nevertheless, they are capricious folk with supernatural powers, so it is not safe to speak ill of them and they are best referred to as 'the good people':

> [They] are said to be of a midle Nature betwixt man and angel, (as were daemons thought to be of old); of intelligent studious spirits, and light changable bodies, (lik those called astral) they are sometimes heard to bake bread, strike hammers, and to do such like services within the little hillocks where they most haunt. They remove to other Lodgings at the beginning of each quarter of the year. . . . 'Tis one of their tenets that nothing perisheth, but (as the sun and the year) everything goes in a circle, less or greater, and is renewed or refreshed in its revolutions.

James's *Daemonologie* had been less sympathetic to the Sidh, referring to them as 'one of the sortes of illusiones that was rifest in time of Papistrie', when the Devil 'illuded the senses of sundry simple creatures, in making them beleeve that they saw and hearde such thinges as were nothing so indeed'. Without doubt, the king regarded himself as the voice of reason in this matter, yet more suffering was caused in James's kingdom by Christian belief in the power of the Devil than can ever be laid at the feet of the fairies.

As a seventh son, Robert Kirk was reputed to have second sight, and, when he collapsed of a stroke at the age of fifty-one on the Hill of the Fairies in Aberfoyle, the tale went round that he was not really dead, but finally captured by the 'good people'. Walter Scott records how his likeness was reputed to have been seen after the funeral on two occasions. The spiriting away of mortals is the very stuff of the popular supernatural ballads, and these songs of beauty and awe, and also Kirk's book, which is a repository of folk belief in itself, make a refreshing change from the blighted fields of dogmatic theology.

Ballads and ballad-collectors

The Scots ballads derive from an oral tradition in narrative songs that flourished during the sixteenth and seventeenth centuries. Since they were not published or regarded as 'literature', it is difficult to establish their authorship or when they first appeared, and these matters have led to much speculation ever since. Whatever their origins, the ballads were 'discovered' by antiquarians and literary enthusiasts in the eighteenth century, when many examples were collected and transcribed, often from women who were the tradition bearers in family and community. In Scotland this appetite for old songs and a vernacular identity was given a special charge after the union of parliaments in 1707, and a key part was played by their appearance in Allan Ramsay's *Tea Table Miscellany* anthologies (1724–37). As early as 1711, Joseph Addison had praised 'Chevy Chase' in the *Spectator* for its 'majestic simplicity', while Bishop Thomas Percy's collection *Reliques of Ancient English Poetry* (1765 et seq.) did even more to create the pre-Romantic craze for 'old, unhappy far-off things and battles long ago'. Percy's interest was aroused when he found a manuscript collection of ballads being used by servants to light fires in a friend's house. He saved the sheets and began to gather ballads from enthusiasts around the country, although it can be difficult to distinguish between songs recorded verbatim and pieces 'improved', or patched from older fragments, or specially written for the occasion.

Others soon followed. David Herd published *Ancient and Modern Scottish Songs* in 1776, and in the 1780s John Pinkerton produced two collections of old Scottish ballads, although he was not above including forgeries of his own. The irascible Joseph Ritson was a better scholar and his many volumes stressed the importance of recording the melody as well as the words. Sir Walter Scott tells of his excitement at the age of thirteen when he first came across Percy's *Reliques* and how this youthful delight led him to become a collector himself. The two volumes which he called *Minstrelsy of the Scottish Border* (1802–3) contain some unscholarly editorial improvements that he came to regret in later years (he may even have composed most of 'Kinmont Willie') but nevertheless his work was not unsympathetic and very influential. Jamieson's *Popular Ballads and Songs* followed in 1806, and Motherwell's *Minstrelsy Ancient and Modern* (1827) took Ritson's line by insisting that collectors should seek authenticity. What the tradition bearers themselves thought of these scholarly pursuits might be another matter, as in James Hogg's story of the meeting between his mother and Walter Scott: Old Margaret Laidlaw was a repository of traditional songs and folklore but she was less than impressed by the young Sheriff's antiquarian zeal, remarking that the songs he had collected from her 'war made for singing, an' no for reading; and they're nouther right spelled nor right setten doun', adding, 'ye hae broken the charm now.'

The modern study of ballads owes most to the long dedication of an American scholar, Francis J. Child, whose life's work, *The English and Scottish Popular Ballads*, appeared from 1882 to 1898 in five volumes. Alas, Child died before he could produce the critical introduction that was to summarise his findings. Child accumulated and numbered 305 ballads and many variants, which he classified with letters, so that it is now usual, for example, to refer to the twenty-seven different versions of 'The Twa Sisters' as 'Child 10A, B, C', and so on. (In fact there are even more versions of this tale than Child printed.) In Aberdeenshire the local poet and folklorist Gavin Greig (1856–1914) spent the last ten years of his life gathering ballad tunes with the assistance of the Revd J. B. Duncan (1848–1917), who collated the texts. When it was finally published and edited by modern scholars at the School of Scottish Studies in Edinburgh, the eight volumes of the Greig–Duncan collection (1981–2002) contained over 3000 traditional tunes and ballads. In Denmark, Grundtvig and Olvik made a similarly extensive gathering of Danish ballads in *Danmarks Gamle Folkeviser* (6 vols, 1853–1920) and the groundwork was laid for what has now become a subject of international expertise, drawing on philology, anthropology, comparative literature and folk-life studies. Thus, if doubts exist about the authenticity of 'Edward' as it appeared in the *Reliques*, these can be dispelled by the realisation that the same tale is told in Swedish, Danish and Finnish ballads. The spelling of Percy's version (got from Lord Hailes in Edinburgh) may be contrivedly 'antique', but its narrative patterns clearly belong to authentic tradition. 'Lord Randal' (Child 12), is an equally famous ballad, first collected in Edinburgh in 1710; but versions of it are found in Czechoslovakia, Hungary, Sweden and, a hundred years earlier, in Italy. Thus although there is not enough information to chart when or where the 'Lord Randal' tale first appeared in Scotland, it is clear that the oral tradition can prove to be surprisingly robust and far-travelled.

In a more esoteric structuralist vein, Stith Thompson classified the motifs which appear in folk tales from many countries (*Motif-index of Folk Literature*, 6 vols, 1932–6), and it can be shown that many of these motifs are, indeed, international, and that some of them also occur in a few Scottish ballads. Recent theories on the nature of oral composition and transmission have derived from work done by Milman Parry and Albert Lord on Yugoslavian folk epic (Lord, *The Singer of Tales*, 1960), and comparisons have been established between Yugoslavian composition and that of Homer's ancient epic verse. It is also recognised that the ballad-singer her- or himself is of primary importance in any study of the form, and modern students give full attention to these sources. Thus an early and invaluable contribution to Child's collection was provided by Mrs Anna Brown of Falkland (1747–1810), who came from the north-east and knew thirty-eight ballad stories, no less than one-eighth of all the 'classic' Anglo-Scottish themes ever recorded. Today, the School of Scottish Studies in Edinburgh (founded in 1951) has a huge archive of material gathered from traditional singers over the years, and the advent of the tape-recorder has added a vital dimension to the collection of ballads, songs and tales. The oral tradition still survives in Scotland, especially among the 'travelling people', who lead their itinerant, gipsy-like lives despite society's attempts to make them conform. Some of the finest traditional singers have come from these families, most notably the late Jeannie Robertson (1908–75), a 'sweet and heroic voice', and her daughter Lizzie Higgins (1929–93).

Since few ballads were written down or published when they first appeared, problems immediately arise about the date and the 'authenticity' of their eventual texts. In fact the very notion of an 'authentic text' is misguided, and such literary considerations cannot apply to an oral tradition in which the bare bones of the tale remain more or less constant while settings, proper names and other such details vary according to circumstances. The Robin Hood tales come from some of the oldest known ballads, circulating in the fifteenth century, and in this case a link can be made back to the late medieval minstrels who sang and recited the long narrative works so popular in the fourteenth century. Carols, religious lyrics, riddles and folk songs joined the canon and began to disseminate among the people, and it seems likely that the ballad-forms as collected by Child, with their distinctive quatrains and their use of refrain and repetition, had began to appear by the sixteenth century. The author of *The Complaynt of Scotland* (1549) names many tales, dances and old songs as performed by shepherds, and his list includes what must have been versions of 'The Battle of Harlaw' (Child 163), and 'The Battle of Otterburn' (Child 161), and 'The Hunting of the Cheviot' or 'Chevy Chase' (Child 162), which date from at least the beginning of the century and tell about a border conflict which took place as long ago as 1388. Sir Philip Sidney testified to the power of 'Chevy Chase' in 1595, writing in his *Apology for Poetry* that it moved his heart 'moore then with a trumpet: and yet it is sung by some blinde crouder'. *The Complaynt* also mentions the 'dance' called 'Johnne Ermistrang', and, from the 1570s, Pitscottie's *Historie and Chronicles of Scotland* gives an account of that reiver's fate (only forty years before) which uses phrases identical to those found in the ballad of 'Johnie Armstrong' (Child 169) as transcribed nearly a hundred years later in the 1650s. The conclusion to be drawn is that the oral tradition can be remarkably stable, despite our contemporary and literate lack of confidence in the powers of memory and recitation. By the seventeenth century the professional minstrel class was disappearing and ballads had become the property of singers among the common people, and very often it was women who proved to be the most effective tradition bearers in this field. At the same time these ballads were beginning to appear more frequently in print and manuscript and, indeed, the old folio which provided Bishop Percy with so many of his 'reliques' was just such a collection, copied out in the 1650s from other written and perhaps some oral sources.

The nature of ballads

If the literary history of the ballads cannot help but be obscure in places, then the question of how they were composed has been in the past a matter of outright disagreement. 'Communalists' held that a ballad is evolved by accretion from tales and the folk consciousness; while 'individualists' made a case for a single 'begetter', at least at first, whose composition might then be gradually disseminated and changed by others – recreated or re-remembered – as time passes. A version of the latter view has prevailed among modern scholars, although it is not necessary to suppose, as some 'individualists' did, that the process of transmission is always one of decline. On the contrary, it has been held that ballads are sustained by a process of re-creation and not just by simple feats (or lapses) of memory. Thus a singer will reconstruct the song from his or her knowledge of the key moments of the tale, as well as from a deep familiarity with the patterns of ballad expression and their many stock phrases and rhymes. Perhaps that singer's 'best' version of the song would tend to become fixed in his or her repertoire, but the process of oral re-creation would still play a part between singers, down the generations, or from district to district. Inevitably, some versions are thinner than others and the spread of literacy and printed copies must also be a factor; nevertheless the theory of oral re-creation does help to explain the variations which occur in different versions of a ballad, and how these differences can sometimes be equally effective, sustaining the tale and its artistic impact over the generations. It follows that the 'typical ballad' contains many elements that are of structural help to the singer in remembering and telling the tale effectively, and, by the same token, these features lend themselves to dramatic and poetic results.

The ballad is a song that tells a tale by letting the events and the characters speak for themselves. It focuses on a single crucial dramatic situation; the narrator almost never makes a personal comment, and little time is spent in setting the scene or explaining motives. Even the longest ballad is comparatively brief when compared to verse romance or folk epic, and, of course, it is sung to a distinctive melody. The Scottish ballads tell of fated lovers, or battles and blood feuds or visitations from the other world – the very stuff of popular taste; and yet their presentation of this romantic, violent or uncanny material is realistic, objective and concise. In fact it is just this trenchant impersonality that produces effects of great emotional power. Ballad melodies are often appropriately stately and plaintive, repeating themselves hypnotically with each short verse, but they manage to avoid monotony by the singer's use of variations and grace notes at suitably expressive points. A typical stanza uses four lines, with a rhyme scheme such as abcb, often alternating between four and three strong stresses:

The king sits in Dumfermling toune,   (4)
Drinking the blude-reid wine: (3)
'O whar will I get a guid sailor,   (4)
To sail this schip of mine?'   (3)
('Sir Patrick Spens', Child 58A)

Another common form uses a constant refrain or refrains in lines three and four:

There was three ladies playd at the ba,
With a hey ho and a lilie gay
There cam a knight and played oer them a',
As the primrose spreads so sweetly.
('The Cruel Brother', Child 11A)

These opening stanzas from two different ballads show how quickly the songs get to the point as they unfold their tales with a characteristic mixture of immediacy and artful delay, a movement well named 'leaping and lingering'. Here the demands of art and those of oral performance compliment each other most fruitfully, and the ballads are full of stock phrases such as 'then up and spak' or 'loud, loud lauched [or cried] he'; colours come with traditional epithets, such as 'blude-reid', 'milk-white' or 'berry-brown'; and numbers are usually 'magic' quantities such as three and seven. Antithetical sets of questions and answers accumulate in the songs, or whole phrases recur in an incremental repetition that makes the tale 'linger' and yet at the same time produces a sense of steadily advancing inevitability. All these devices bear witness to the ballad's origins, in which an act of oral re-creation meets with an act of memory to recognise the dramatic and performative need for a telling delay before surrendering to sudden and inevitable denouement.

The Scottish ballads

The Scottish ballads are among the finest. While it is true that the tale may be internationally familiar, the particular form it takes within the genre will be dictated by the cultural and historical forces that shaped the singer. The forces in Scotland up until the sixteenth and seventeenth centuries were particularly well suited to songs about violent, romantic and eerie encounters, all told with succinct wit and an enduring sense of fatalism. Such qualities were already established within Scottish literary expression, from the warlike celebration of Barbour and Blind Harry to the grimly tender understatement of Henryson when he describes how Cresseid's father discovers her leprosy – 'then was thair care enough betwixt them twain'; or, again, to the terrible, witty cruelty of Knox's account of the death of Beaton. The courtly poetry of the early seventeenth century and the studied melancholy of Drummond had parted company from these tough roots, and it is thanks to the many anonymous singers and the female tradition bearers that the voice of the ballads has been carried over: from the makars to the vernacular revival in the eighteenth century, and ultimately to Scottish poets of more modern times.

Although the divisions are fluid, the Scottish ballads are concerned with three perennially popular topics – violent history, tragic romance and the supernatural. All of these elements, like the songs themselves, belong in special measure to the Border country – from Edinburgh and Newcastle in the east to Dumfries and Penrith in the west. It is a wild, rolling, convoluted landscape scattered with old battlefields, castles, towers and fortified houses. Loyalties were fiercely local, and Border barons had long regarded themselves as rulers of their own small kingdoms with no allegiance to politics or boundaries or even the king himself. Equally independent lesser lairds, with notorious family names such as Armstrong, Ker and Scott, sallied forth as reivers to capture cattle and horses – the wealth of the district – from the English or, with equal facility, from their Scottish neighbours. James V led an expedition against the Borders in 1530 (when he hanged Johnie Armstrong), before having to move north to pacify the equally troublesome clans. It is no accident that the great songs of fighting, loving and terror should have arisen from such conditions: they occur again in the northeast of Scotland, where Lowlands and Highlands met along a different border, but the true crucible of the ballad tradition lies to the south and particularly towards the centre and west of the country. Here the more open ground of Teviot and Tweed (and the route from Berwick to Edinburgh) begins to give way to the pass at Carter Bar in the hills above Jedburgh, to the tangled outlawed valleys of the 'debatable lands' at Eskdale and Liddesdale above Carlisle, and to the treacherous boglands of Solway Moss. The 'historical' ballads in particular are full of names, places and events from this part of Scotland.

Tales of violent history

'The Battle of Otterburn' (Child 161) and 'The Hunting of the Cheviot' or 'Chevy Chase' (Child 162), both tell of a raid the Scots made on Northumberland in 1388 and of how the Scotsman Sir Hugh Douglas perished on the sword of Sir Harry Percy, who was in his turn killed or captured by Douglas's nephew Montgomerie. 'Chevy Chase' tells the story from the English point of view, and 'Otterburn' favours the Scots. The latter was sent to Walter Scott by James Hogg, and is best known for the lines in which Douglas has an eerie premonition that the battle will be won only after his own death:

'My nephew bauld,' the Douglas said,
  'What boots the death of ane?
Last night I dreamed a dreary dream,
  And I ken the day's thy ain.
I dreamed I saw a battle fought
  Beyond the isle of Sky,
When lo, a dead man wan the field,
  And I thought that man was I.'
                    (Child 161C)

The Battle of Harlaw was fought north-west of Aberdeen in 1411, between Donald of the Isles and Lowland forces from Angus and the Mearns. The ranting ballad of the same name (Child 163), with its parodies of the Highland accent ('Yes, me cam frae ta Hielans, man'), must date from considerably after the conflict. On the other hand, 'The Battle of Philiphaugh' (Child 202) is probably contemporary with the defeat of Montrose, 'our cruel enemy', outside Selkirk in 1645. 'The Bonny Earl of Murray' (Child 181) laments how, in 1592, James Stewart of Doune was killed by his old enemy the Earl of Huntly, who had been instructed to convey him to the king without harm. As with almost all the ballads, this tale of the doings of great people is seen from the point of view of the common folk. In fact Murray was burned out of his mother's house and killed while trying to escape, but one version of the song has him admit his 'brother' Huntly in a trusting way, only to be stabbed in his bed like King Duncan in *Macbeth*. The best-known version has a beautiful melody, simultaneously rousing and tender, which opens with the verses:

Ye Highlands, and ye Lawlands,
  Oh where have you been,'
They have slain the Earl of Murray,
  And they layd him on the green.

'Now wae be to thee, Huntly!
  And wherefore did you sae?
I bade you bring him wi you,
  But forbade you him to slay.'

He was a braw gallant,
    And he rid at the ring;
And the bonny Earl of Murray,
    Oh he might have been a king.
                        (Child 181A)

In the ballads, historical accuracy always takes second place to heroic figures and dramatic events, and so John Armstrong's deserved execution at the hands of James V is retold as a treacherous betrayal, and one version (copied, according to Allan Ramsay, from a descendant of Armstrong's) even manages to be patriotic:

John murdered was at Carlinrigg,
    And all his galant companie:
But Scotlands heart was never sae wae,
    To see sae mony brave men die

Because they savd their country deir
    Frae Englishmen; nane were sae bauld,
Whyle Johnie livd on the border-syde,
    Nane of them durst cum neir his hald.
                        (Child 169C)

Another version ends more convincingly, on a note chillingly reminiscent of revenge plays by Tourneur or Webster:

O then bespoke his little son,
    As he was set on his nurses knee:
'If ever I live for to be a man,
    My father's blood revenged shall be.'
                        (Child 169B)

In more recent years an equally unlikely folk hero has been made of a small American murderer called William Bonney, but we still listen with pleasure to tales of Billy the Kid, and we thrill to Armstrong's grim and cutting retort when his sovereign refused to spare his life:

To seik het water beneth cauld yce,
    Surely it is a great folie.
I half asked grace at a graceless face,
    But ther is nane for my men and me.

The memorable history behind 'Mary Hamilton' (Child 173), is equally cloudy when it comes to facts. There are nearly forty variants of the tale, also known as 'The Queen's Marie' and 'The Four Maries', and almost all of them have the poignant lines:

Last nicht there was four Maries,
    The nicht there'l be but three;
There was Marie Seton, and Marie Beton,
    And Marie Carmichael, and me.

(Child 173A)

The tale has it that Mary Hamilton was executed because she drowned
her illegitimate baby, whose father was Darnley, 'the hichest Stewart of
a' and the queen's unworthy husband. Mary Queen of Scots did,
indeed, have four Marys attending her, but they were ladies of gentle
birth from the families of Seaton, Beaton, Fleming and Livingston.
And there was a scandal at court in 1563, but it involved an apothecary
and a French lady of the chamber, with no mention of any Mary
Hamilton. In fact, there *was* a Mary Hamilton who suffered a fate
similar to that recounted in the ballad, but she was an attendant to the
wife of Peter the Great of Russia at the end of the seventeenth century.
All these names and events have merged in the popular imagination to
fit a sad and lilting melody full of memorable lines and images.
Consider how Mary goes to her death in the following verses, in which
the action is typically heightened and delayed by the incremental repetitions of statement and reply, and by the antithesis between laughter
and tears:

'O Marie, put on your robes o black,
    Or else your robes o brown,
For ye maun gang wi me the night,
    To see fair Edinboro town.'

'I winna put on my robes o black,
    Nor yet my robes o brown;
But I'll put on my robes o white,
    To shine through Edinboro town.'

When she gaed up the Cannogate,
    She laughd loud laughters three;
But whan she cam doun the Cannogate
    The tear blinded her ee.

When she gaed up the Parliament stair,
    The heel cam aff her shee;   shoe
And lang or she cam doun again
    She was condemned to dee.

Atmosphere, setting and intense feeling are all conveyed in these lines,
but only through direct speech and direct action. Her bold decision to
wear virginal white, and the ill omen of her broken heel – these are

exactly the kind of details at which the ballads excel, and they strike the listener with the simple force of a bolt of electricity.

The creative versatility of oral tradition can be gauged by comparing what is functionally the same stanza, drawn from five different versions of the song:

> 'Last night I washed the queen's feet,
>   And gently laid her down;
> And a' the thanks I've gotten the nicht
>   To be hangd in Edinboro town.'
>   (Child 173A)

> 'Yestreen I wush Queen Mary's feet,
>   And bore her till her bed;
> This day she's given me my reward,
>   This gallows-tree to tread.'
>   (Child 173B)

> 'Yestreen I mad Queen Mary's bed,
>   Kembed doun her yellow hair.'
> Is this the reward I am to get,
>   To tread the gallows-stair.'
>   (Child 173C)

> 'Seven years an I made Queen Mary's bed,
>   Seven years an I combed her hair,
> An a hansoms reward noo she's gien to me,
>   Gien me the gallows-tow to wear!'
>   (Child 173N)

> 'O wha will comb Queen Mary's heed?
>   Or wha will brade her hair?
> And wha will lace her middle sae jimp,   slender
>   Whan I am nae langer there?'
>   (Child 173W)

It is not possible to advance critical reasons for preferring any one version over the others: structurally speaking they all focus on past services as compared to present fate, and, although the details change, each stanza is effective in its own way.

An equally poetic power, and something of the same historical uncertainty, is at work in 'Sir Patrick Spens' (Child 58). In typical 'leaping and lingering' fashion, the singer goes directly to the beginning and then to the end of the ill-fated voyage, pausing only to record Sir Patrick's reactions, and an old sailor's premonition of disaster:

> The first line that Sir Patrick red,
>   A loud lauch lauched he;
> The next line that Sir Patrick red,
>   The teir blinded his ee.

. . .

> 'Late late yestreen I saw the new moone,
>   Wi the auld moone in her arme,
> And I feir, I feir, my deir master,
>   That we will cum to harme.'

(Child 58A)

When the storm has had its way, the ballad focuses on small details in a series of poignantly understated 'snapshots':

> O our Scots nobles wer richt laith
>   To weet their cork-heild shoone;
> But lang owre a' the play were playd,
>   Thair hats they swam aboone.
>
> O lang, lang may their ladies sit,
>   Wi thair fans into their hand,
> Or eir they se Sir Patrick Spence
>   Cum sailing to the land.
>
> O lang, lang may the ladies stand,
>   Wi their gold kems in their hair
> Waiting for thair ain deir lords,
>   For they'll se thame na mair.
>
> Haf owre, haf owre to Aberdour,
>   It's fiftie fadom deip,
> And thair lies guid Sir Patrick Spence,
>   Wi the Scots lords at his feit.

(Child 58A)

If the functional reason for such repetition in oral art is by now understood, it still remains to point to the extraordinarily moving symbolic effects which it creates at the same time. Our attention is seized by those fashionably cork-heeled shoes, by the fans and gold combs and all the genteel accoutrements of a privileged class. The physical movement of the ladies, when they switch from sitting to standing, has an equally dramatic eloquence, and this is matched in turn by a contrasting vision of Sir Patrick Spens under fifty fathoms of water with their drowned husbands laid at his feet – like those sleeping stone dogs carved at the end of a knight's tomb.

Tales of tragic romance

'Mary Hamilton' and 'Sir Patrick Spens' could almost belong to the 'tragic romance' category of ballads, except that the latter are more fiercely suffused with the passions of love, jealousy or betrayal. 'The Dowie Howms of Yarrow' (Child 214) tells how a Border laird is killed by his brother-in-law after a drunken quarrel, and the first two stanzas, when the tale is 'leaping' at its swiftest, provide an extraordinary example of ballad concision:

> Late at een, drinkin the wine,
>   Or early in a morning,
> They set a combat them between,
>   To fight it in the dawin'.
>
> 'O stay at hame, my noble lord!
>   O stay at hame, my marrow!   partner (spouse)
> My cruel brother will you betray,
>   On the dowie houms o' Yarrow.   dreary low river banks
>   (Child 214E)

Jealous brothers, sisters and mothers abound in these tales and, not surprisingly, there are many international variants on the same themes. 'The Twa Sisters' (Child 10) exists in over sixty versions from Scotland, England, Denmark, Norway, Iceland, the Faeroes and Sweden. In most of these versions a musical instrument is made from the bones of the drowned girl, and when it is played it reveals that she was murdered by her sister – clearly a folk tale of wide and enduring force. In another ballad, it is a brother who kills his sister because, although others in the family were consulted, his particular consent to her marriage was not asked. Like so many of its kind, 'The Cruel Brother' (Child 11) ends with a dying person leaving their goods to those around them, until the final bequest is made:

> 'What will you leave to your brother, John?'
>   *With a hey ho and a lillie gay.*
> 'The gallows-tree to hang him on!'
>   *As the primrose spreads so sweetly.*
>   (Child 11A)

The world of the ballads revolves around sudden contrasts between tears and laughter, peace and war, love and hatred, marriage and death; and contrast is found again in the juxtaposition of the dying girl's curse and the sweet refrain that has accompanied the grim narrative from the start. 'Lord Randal' (Child 12) and 'Edward' (Child 13), are among the best-known ballads to use the device of a surprise last bequest, and they too have many international variations. In each case a heavily structured and repetitiously patterned duologue is set up between the hero and another person, until it produces a sense of inevitable process, a painful journey towards death or a final, ghastly revelation. Lord Randal leaves 'hell and fire' to his true love, who has poisoned him, while Edward curses his mother for persuading him to kill his father. Incremental repetition and the melody's slow pace are vital to the overall effect, and in 'Lord Randal' only the first half of the third line in each stanza actually advances the plot, while everything else, rhymes and line-endings included, is said over and over again:

'O where ha you been, Lord Randal, my son?
And where ha you been, my handsome young man?'
'I ha been at the green wood; mother, mak my bed soon,
For I'm wearied wi hunting, an fain wad lie down.'

'An wha met ye there, Lord Randal, my son?
An wha met you there, my handsome young man?'
'O I met wi my true-love; mother, mak my bed soon,
For I'm wearied wi hunting, an fain wad lie down.'
(Child 12A)

In this fashion, the story of how he has been poisoned is haltingly revealed, as though the tale were taking three steps forward in every verse, and two steps back again: 'lingering' here has become massively static.

When asked what he will give to his wife and children before he flees into exile, Edward's answer is succinct: 'the warldis room, late them beg thrae life, / For thame nevir mair wil I see O', and his cruel realism strikes a characteristically Scottish note. It is instructive to compare 'The Three Ravens', an English ballad, with 'The Twa Corbies' (Child 26), a counterpart from north of the Border. 'The Three Ravens' has a refrain, 'Downe a downe, hay down . . .' and it tells how a slain knight is protected from predators by his faithful hounds and his hawks, until his lady, in the symbolic form of a pregnant fallow doe, comes to bury him and then to join him in death. 'The Twa Corbies' is half the length and much less comforting. The crows have the knight to themselves:

'His hound is to the hunting gane,
   His hawk to fetch the wild-fowl hame,
His lady's ta'en another mate,
   So we may mak our dinner sweet.

'Ye'll sit on his white hause-bane,
   And I'll pike oot his bonny blue een;
Wi ae lock o his gowden hair
   We'll theek our nest when it grows bare.

'Mony a one for him maks mane,
   But nane sall ken where he is gane;
Oer his white banes, when they are bare,
   The wind sall blaw for evermair.
                  (Child 26)

The same fatalism reigns with particular force in the ballads of the supernatural.

Tales of the other world

The 'other world' in Scotland has many of its origins in Celtic lore, with tales of seal men and kelpies who delight in the downfall of poor mortals, or of the fairy folk, ruled by a beautiful queen on a milk-white horse with silver bells in its mane. The 'good people' live in mounds or under the hills, and the Eildon Hills are particularly famous as one of the doors to their kingdom. Mortals enter this realm at their peril, but they can ensure their return by leaving iron or a dirk at the gate, for the fairies are afraid of steel. (Another passport to their land is said to be the branch of an apple tree, and perhaps there is a connection here with the apples of the Hesperides, the golden fruit from the magic west that Hercules had to find in Greek myth.) The border between the natural and the supernatural is a misty one, and even the human dead can cross it as revenants from their home in *Tir nan Og* – the Isle of the Blest – which is neither Heaven nor Hell but a pagan Celtic paradise, the land of the ever-young, somewhere over the western horizon.

When the Queen of Elfland describes her kingdom to Thomas the Rhymer, it is an in-between state where magical awe meets with sexual danger, quite distinct from the after-worlds of Christian teaching:

'O see not ye yon narrow road,
   So thick beset wi thorns and briars?
That is the path of righteousness,
   Tho after it but few enquires.

'And see not ye that braid braid road,
    That lies across yon lillie leven?   lea
That is the path of wickedness
    Tho some call it the road to heaven.

'And see not ye that bonny road,
    Which winds about the fernie brae?
That is the road to fair Elfland,
    Where you and I this night maun gae.   must go

'But Thomas ye maun hold your tongue,
    Whatever you may hear or see,
For gin ae word you should chance to speak,   if one
    You will never get back to your ain countrie.'
                 ('Thomas the Rhymer', Child 37A)

Yet there are still some religious elements in the ballad, and shades of sexual guilt too, for when Thomas first sees her he mistakes the Elf Queen for the 'Queen of Heaven'. Again, during their desperate journey to fairyland – 'For forty days and forty nights, / He wade thro red blude to the knee' – Thomas is stopped just in time from picking an apple, no less than the fruit of man's first sin. Thus Christian and Celtic themes are intermingled along with hints of the romance tales, for the story of a knight abducted by the Elf Queen also features in the Arthurian cycle, which, too, contains in its turn echoes from earlier Celtic sources. (James Hogg's long poem 'Kilmeny' was to mix Christian and pagan elements in similar fashion.) Seven years pass before True Thomas returns to the Eildon Hills, although it seems but a brief time to him, and he brings back the gift of second sight – the ability to see aspects of the future.

In fact Thomas of Ercildoune seems to have been a real person, living about 1320, and various prophecies of his have been preserved, along with verses from the early fifteenth century which tell of his adventures in the first person:

Als I me wente this Endres daye,
ffull faste in mynd makand my mone,
In a merry mornynge of Maye,
By Huntle bankkes my selfe allone,
I herde the jaye, and the throstyll cokke,
The mawys menyde hir of hir songe,   thrush lamented
The wodewale beryde als a belle,   woodlark sang like
That alle the wode abowte me ronge.

The fairies might promise erotic adventure or ambiguous gifts, but it can be fatal to deal too closely with the other world. Clerk Colvill

(Child 42) dies because he has made love with a mermaid, while Tam Lin (Child 39) seduces an earthly girl while still himself under the power of the Queen of Fairies. His human lover must reclaim him by pulling him down from his fairy horse at midnight, and by holding him fast, despite the several frightening shapes he will assume. (Liz Lochhead gives this tale a contemporary and feminist spin in her poem 'Tam Lin's Lady'.) Lady Isabel manages to outwit her eerie seducer by killing him at the last minute ('Lady Isabel and the Elf-Knight', Child 4); but the 'Daemon Lover' (Child 243) is not so easily denied as he lures his former love aboard ship, only to show her 'where the white lilies grow, / In the bottom o' the sea'.

The finest of the supernatural Scots ballads deal with those moments when the other world and the everyday world come together, if only for a brief time. When the three drowned sons return to their mother in 'The Wife of Usher's Well' (Child 79), their birch-bark hats announce that they have come from the Celtic isle of the dead and, like all ghosts, they cannot stay past the dawn. When the youngest brother says goodbye to home and hearth, the simplicity of his words strikes the listener with the full force of that final, inexorable separation from the common earth and all human warmth:

> The cock he hadna crawd but once,
>   And clapped his wings at a',
> When the youngest to the eldest said,
>   'Brother, we must awa.
>
> 'The cock doth craw, the day doth daw,
>   The channerin worm doth chide;   whining
> Gin we be mist out o our place,   If
>   A sair pain we maun bide.
>
> 'Fare ye weel, my mother dear!
>   Fareweel to barn and byre!
> And fare ye weel, the bonny lass,
>   That kindles my mother's fire!'
>   (Child 79A)

The same sweetly painful grief pervades 'The Great Silkie of Sule Skerry' (Child 113), which is known in only one version collected from an old lady in the Shetlands. The 'silkies' are seal folk who can take human shape and earthly lovers, but this tale is especially poignant for its sense of the inevitable parting of all human ties, whether made with the fairy folk or not. The wider symbolic reverberations of this remarkable ballad tell how the saddest thing is not that the heart will eventually stop, but that, sooner than that, it will come to change its affections:

Now he has ta'en a purse of goud,
And he has pat it upo' her knee,
Saying, 'Gie to me my little young son,
An' tak thee up thy nourrice-fee.   nurses fee

'An' it sall pass on a simmer's day,
When the sin shines het on evera stane,
That I will tak my little young son,
An' teach him for to swim his lane.   on his own

'An' thu sall marry a proud gunner,
An' a proud gunner I'm sure he'll be,
An' the very first schot that ere he schoots,
He'll schoot baith my young son and me.'

Technical concision and grim realism meet here with insight and tender fatalism, to capture the timelessly popular poetic voice of the Scottish ballads and their many anonymous singers – a timely reminder that great art is not the exclusive property of educated or literary circles.

Robert and Francis Sempill

The energy of the oral tradition in Scots was not entirely lost to written verse, for it makes a brief appearance in the works of **Robert Sempill of Beltrees** (1595?–1665?). Robert's father was Sir James Sempill (1566–1625), the author of several pro-Presbyterian pamphlets and a satirical drama in English called *A Picktooth for the Pope, or the Packman's Paternoster*. (Sir James had been educated with James VI under George Buchanan, and he later served his king as an ambassador in London and Paris.) Robert, laird of Beltrees in Renfrewshire, was a loyalist who fought for Charles I and supported the Restoration. He did not produce much poetry, nor did his son Francis, but the Sempills represent a new class of author, drawn from the educated minor gentry, who were destined to inherit the Scots literary tradition from the clerics, scholars and courtiers who had gone before. At the same time, their resolutely colloquial spirit makes a link between Scots verse in the sixteenth century and the vernacular revival 200 years later. Robert's fame rests on the verse-form that he chose for a naïve elegy called 'The Life and Death of the Piper of Kilbarchan, or the Epitaph of Habbie Simson':

At Clark-plays when he wont to come,
His Pipe played trimly to the Drum
Like Bikes of Bees he gart it Bum,   made
   And tun'd his Reed:
Now all our Pipers may sing dumb,
   Sen Habbie's dead.

And at Horse Races many a day,
Before the Black, the Brown, the Gray,
He gart his Pipe when he did play,
   Baith Skirl and Skreed,
Now all such Pastime's quite away
   Sen Habbie's dead.

Sempill's six-line stanza with its two emphatic short lines produces a notable rhythmic effect. The scene is set and the rhyme sustained by a galloping four-stress rhythm in the opening three lines; then the pace is checked, picked up again and abruptly concluded by a second rhyme appearing in two short lines of only two strong stresses each. This second rhyme and the entire last line are repeated throughout the poem. The same delight in a tilting metre with its checks and refrains is found in the 'bob and wheel' effects of 'Christis Kirk' and 'Peblis to the Play' and they, too, seem well suited to the movement of popular dances and reels in celebration of the ordinary domestic scene. Passages with a similar rhythm – also used for satirical effect – appeared in Lindsay's *Thrie Estaitis* and in popular airs such as 'Hey Tuttie Taittie' (later sanctified in the *Gude and Godlie Ballatis*). Kurt Wittig has suggested that the pattern may owe something to Gaelic octosyllabic metres, *ochtfhoclach mór*, used for elegies, and *ochtfhoclach beag*, used for verses to dance tunes. Frank Chambers has noted a similar verse pattern in a troubadour poem by Guilhem de Peitieu and also in a medieval Latin hymn. Whatever its precursors, the stanza-form of Sempill's verses became so popular among later Scots poets that it has been known ever since as 'Standard Habbie', or sometimes, slightly varied, as the 'Burns stanza'.

'Habbie Simson' was first published in 1706 in James Watson's *Choice Collection*, and subsequently Allan Ramsay, Robert Fergusson and Burns himself were to make more of its distinctive jig-time measure than ever Sempill achieved with his naive, but touchingly direct lament for a dead piper. Fergusson and Burns found 'Habbie' particularly suited to comedy, satire and social comment, for its short lines can produce a variety of ironic, or sly or sententious effects. Sempill is usually credited with another mock elegy, called 'Epitaph on Sanny Briggs, Nephew to Habbie Simson and Butler to the Laird of Kilbarchan', but it is unlikely that either poem would be remembered had their distinctive pattern not taken fire in the hands of later and better poets.

Francis Sempill (1616?/25?–1682) is said to have shared his father's talent for vernacular verse, and 'Sanny Briggs' is sometimes attributed to him, as well as 'The Banishment of Poverty', a rather contrived account of how the poet was followed everywhere by 'poverty' – like a stray dog at his heels – until he reached the debtor's sanctuary at Holyrood and the Duke of Albany's generosity freed him. The fine song 'Maggie Lauder' is tentatively attributed to Francis, although he may only have reworked it from an earlier popular source. 'The Blythsome Wedding' is an odd and lively piece that juxtaposes a hilarious account of the grotesque guests at a country wedding with an equally extensive list of what there was to eat. The poem's vulgar and encyclopaedic zest belongs to the tradition of 'Christis Kirk' joined to that of *The Complaynt of Scotland*, and the end result is like a peasant feast recorded by Brueghel down to the last and grossest detail. If such comprehensive grotesquerie seems to be familiar in Scottish literature, it is by no means confined to the peasant world, for Sir Thomas Urquhart, knight and word-spinner extraordinary, must be its undisputed champion.

Sir Thomas Urquhart of Cromarty (1611–60)

The knight of Cromarty was a stout supporter of the Stuart crown, a flamboyant cavalier, a proud and patriotic Scot and the possessor of a uniquely eccentric mind and manner. He began his studies at Aberdeen University at the age of eleven, and, although he left without a degree, he retained fond memories and a taste for esoteric learning. During his travels abroad he describes (typically innocent of modesty) how he gained friends and 'vindicated his native county' by fighting three separate combats of honour in the lists. At home, his father refused to sign the Covenant and Thomas returned to fight for the Royalists. Despite initial successes in the north, the Cavaliers who opposed the Covenanters in the 'Bishops' Wars' were gradually dispersed. Urquhart went to London, was knighted by Charles, and produced an excruciatingly banal book, *Epigrams: Divine and Moral* (1641). His father's lack of business sense had almost ruined the estate in the far north of Scotland, and when Sir Thomas inherited it in 1642 he was quick to resume his travels. After three years abroad he returned to Cromarty determined to achieve fame as a writer, inventor, scholar and mathematician. Urquhart was an admirer of his countryman John Napier (1550–1617), the inventor of logarithms (whom the famous German astronomer Kepler regarded as the greatest mathematician of his day), and he decided to produce a treatise of his own which would help students to memorise and calculate the theorems of trigonometry. He seems to have known his subject well enough, but *The Trissotetras* (1645) is made almost completely unintelligible by a language crammed with abstract terms and neologisms. The glossary throws even more darkness on the subject: 'Amfractuosities; are taken here for the cranklings, windings, turnings, and involutions belonging to the equisoleary scheme . . . .'

Immediately after the execution of Charles I, Urquhart took part in an ill-fated Royalist uprising in the north and was declared a traitor – although he was leniently treated by the Covenanters. Within two years he was supporting Charles II's cause (in line with Covenanting policy this time) and marching south with the Scottish army that was eventually defeated by Cromwell at Worcester in 1651. Urquhart travelled with a full wardrobe and a writing-desk and many of his manuscripts and papers were looted or lost after the battle (reputedly used as toilet paper), although once more he himself was spared. After a spell in the Tower of London, he was held at Windsor Castle and, to prove his merit to his captors and avoid the confiscation of his estates, he set about the demonstration of his intellectual prowess. *Pantochronochanon* (1652) traces the descent of the Urquharts back to Adam (with Eve, too, on the female side) and promises in a future volume, if the writer is released, to explain why the shire of Cromarty alone in Britain has all its place-names derived from 'pure and perfect Greek'. Equally Greek, if not quite so pure, *Ekskybalauron, or The Discovery of a Most Exquisite Jewel* (1652) attempts to vindicate the honour of Scotland from the canting image given it by the rigid Presbyterian party. Along the way it makes another plea for its author's freedom, as well as a proposal for a universal language which will be easier to learn than any other, despite having eleven genders, ten tenses, and words which can be read just as meaningfully backwards as forwards (This seems to have been a species of code, and not quite as mad as it sounds, although Urquhart never actually perfected it.) *The Jewel* is chiefly notable for its enthusiastic account of many brave and learned Scots, in particular 'the admirable' James Crichtoun (1560–83), soldier, scholar, duellist, polyglot and lover extraordinary – a fitting hero for the knight of Cromarty.

Urquhart was paroled in 1652 and returned to Scotland only to find his creditors awaiting him. The following year saw him back in London, from where he published a many-sided diatribe against those 'stinging wasps' and another proposal for his universal language, *Logopandecteision* (1653). As always, Urquhart's prose is elaborately and relentlessly euphuistic, but it does have a manic energy and, at its best, it is the hilariously inventive and exhaustive text itself that turns out to be the main subject and hero of the piece. Even so, when faced with the cosmic grandeur of his schemes and with a style that occasionally slips into complete gobbledegook, it is difficult not to suspect that the author was a little mad.

Urquhart's peculiar genius found its true métier in 1653 with his translation of the first two books of Rabelais's *Gargantua and Pantagruel*. (A third book was published in the edition of 1694, along with Books IV and V as translated by Motteux.) Rabelais is notoriously difficult to translate, because he mixes pompous and learned diction with earthy phrases and accumulates long lists of objects, epithets and synonyms. Such a challenge might have been specially made for Urquhart, and he met it by outdoing the Frenchman, and even himself, with a 'translation' almost twice the length of the original: more compendious in its lists, more outrageous in its vulgarities and more hyperbolic in its hyperboles. When Rabelais notes the animal-noises that spoil the peace of his countryside, he manages to name the calls of dogs, wolves, lions, horses, elephants, snakes, asses, crickets and doves. Urquhart's version contains seventy-one species and their increasingly unlikely cries, including the 'drintling of turkies, coniating of storks, frantling of peacocks . . . rantling of rats, gueriet-ing of apes, snuttering of monkies, pioling of pelicans', and so on – truly a list worthy of those catalogues in *The Complaynt of Scotland*. Notwithstanding his flamboyant expansions, a good case can be made for Urquhart's essential accuracy, for his version catches the spirit of Rabelais with an immense and greasy gusto:

HOW GARGAMELLE, BEING GREAT WITH GARGANTUA, DID EAT A HUGE DEAL OF TRIPES
The occasion and manner how Gargamelle was brought to bed, and delivered of her child, was thus: and, if you do not believe it, I wish your bum-gut fall out, and make an escapade. Her bum-gut, indeed, or fundament escaped her in an afternoon, on the third day of February, with having eaten at dinner too many godebillios. Godebillios are the fat tripes of coiros. Coiros are beeves fattened at the cratch in ox stalls, or in the fresh guimo meadows. Guimo meadows are those, that for their fruitfulness may be mowd twice a year. Of those fat beeves they had killed three hundred sixty-

seven thousand and fourteen, to be salted at Shrove-tide, that in the entering of the spring they might have plenty of powdered beef, wherewith to
season their mouths at the beginning of their meals, and to taste their wine
the better.

They had abundance of tripes, as you have heard, and they were so delicious, that every one licked his fingers. But the mischief was this, that for all
men could do, there was no possibility to keep them long in that relish; for
in a very short while they would have stunk, which had been an undecent
thing. It was therefore concluded, that they should be all of them gulched
up, without losing anything.

Ezra Pound preferred Douglas's *Eneados* to Virgil and many readers
have found Urquhart's *Rabelais* equally special: it joins a select
company of translations that have achieved their own creative identity,
along with Chapman's *Homer*, Fitzgerald's *Omar Khayyam*, some of
Pound's Chinese poems, and the Authorised Version itself.

Little is known of Sir Thomas's last years. He is said to have died of
a fit of laughing when he heard of the Restoration of Charles II; and,
if that is not true, as one writer puts it, then it certainly should be.

Urquhart was not the only distinguished writer to support the Stuart
crown, for, of course, the Gaelic Highlands espoused the Catholic
cause as well, and the poet Iain Lom (who had been a friend of
Montrose's) honed the edge of his Gaelic verse to comment fiercely on
the political events of his day.

Gaelic poetry in the late seventeenth century

The second half of the century was a period of transition and renewed
activity in Gaelic verse, and, although Iain Lom was probably the most
radical and influential poet of the time, there were many others, especially among women, who composed fine songs too. The formal
patterns of bardic verse were finally changing, and syllabic metres,
high diction and learned historical allusions were giving way to a more
colloquial Gaelic with metres based on stress and strophic stanzas of
various lengths in which the last rhyme of each stanza links to its
fellows throughout the poem. This had been a gradual change, which
can be traced to the previous century, and, after all, the modes of
eulogy, elegy and bardic satire were to continue unabated into the
next. Yet the work of this period stands as a watershed between the
bardic schools and what was to become, in effect, vernacular modern
Gaelic poetry.

Niall MacMhuirich (1637?–1726)

If Iain Lom's verse looks towards modern Gaelic, then Niall stays almost entirely with the old style. This is scarcely surprising, since he and his distinguished predecessor Cathal came from a long line of MacMhuirich bards going back to the thirteenth century, and much of their poetry is in the learned tradition of elegy and panegyric for their patrons in the Clanranald branch of the MacDonalds. Niall was almost the last of the literate *filidh* school with Irish connections, and his elegy for Donald, son of John of Moidart, who died in the late 1640s, shows his clear and vigorous style and also the extreme formalism of the genre:

> The son of big-bodied spirited John of Moidart, the shortness of his life has wounded me sharply; wretched is my state now that this man is dead: that has consumed [as with fire] my flesh and my blood. . . .
>
> He was a lion in the fierceness of his exploits, but would not indulge in anything shameful, a man who was foremost in showing the way to peace, my beloved was he who gave protection to the destitute and to the learned poets.
>
> (trs. D. Thomson)

Niall's verses and his prose history of the Montrose wars (written from personal experience) were gathered, along with other pieces from the MacMhuirich bards, in a manuscript collection known as the 'Red Book of Clanranald'. (James 'Ossian' Macpherson was to see this collection in later years.) Niall wrote very little in vernacular Gaelic, but two poems do survive, both on the death of Allan of Clanranald after the battle of Sherrifmuir in 1715. He laments the passing of the traditional learning of the Gael as if he knew that the aftermath of the Jacobite risings was indeed to change their customs forever.

Roderick Morison (1656?–1714?)

Known as 'an clàrsair dall' ('the blind harper'), Morison served the MacLeod chiefs at Dunvegan and has sometimes been called (not quite accurately) the last of the old minstrel class. Tradition has it that he left Lewis to study for the ministry at Inverness, where he caught smallpox and lost his eyesight. He turned to music to survive and visited Ireland to further his craft before roving the Highlands to earn his living. In Edinburgh in 1681 he met Iain Breac MacLeod, who took him under his care at Dunvegan in Skye, although Morison was never the official bard there. Iain Breac was among the last chiefs to keep the old style of establishment, for, as well as his harper, he had a bard and a jester and his piper was the famous Patrick Og MacCrimmon himself, the roar of whose drones, according to blind Roderick, would stir the whole household into cheerful activity every morning. Morison performed the usual eulogies, but in 1688 he fell out of favour at Dunvegan and was 'banished' to Glenelg – perhaps on account of his outspoken Jacobite sympathies at a time when his chief was studiously trying to remain neutral. The harper found another patron at Talisker for a while before returning to his travels and relative obscurity.

When Iain Breac died in 1693 the blind harper composed a unique 'Song to MacLeod of Dunvegan', which begins as a lament for his former patron with a lovingly detailed picture of happy days under his roof. Then the poem turns into a scathing attack on Roderick, the son and heir who went south to live at court, spent money on gambling and clothes and ignored Skye and the old culture. The harper had cause for alarm, for in the six years before he died of consumption the young chief raised loans of £45,000 against an annual income of only £900 – 'then does the boil fester on the thigh', sings Morison, 'with its pain at the root'. The original uses rhyme in its eight-line stanzas:

> He comes out of the shop
> with the latest fashion from France,
> and the fine clothes worn on his person
> yesterday with no little satisfaction
> are tossed into a corner -
> 'The style is unmodish, not worth a plack.
> On the security of a townland or two,
> take the pen and sign a bond.'
>
> The page will not be regarded
> unless his clothes are in the current fashion;
> though it should cost a guinea a yard,
> that can be got for a mart given in lieu of rent.
> As much again in addition
> will go to the purchase of a doublet for him,
> and breeches of soft velvet
> to wrap up gusts at his rear.

(trs. W. Matheson)

A bard's satire could be fearsomely specific, but in this case it was not enough to stop young MacLeod, and many others after him, from breaking the kinship ties and becoming an absentee landlord in Edinburgh or London.

There was another bard with the MacLeods of Skye during Morison's time, although she was an unlettered and 'unofficial' one.

Màiri Nighean Alasdair Ruaidh, Mary MacLeod (1615?–1706?)

Mary MacLeod first came from Harris to be a nurse at Dunvegan, and she looked after several members of the family during her long life there. She too fell into disfavour for a while and spent some years in the Hebrides and Mull before being recalled to Skye. This may have been during young Roderick's six years as chief, or perhaps during his father's time, and so it is not certain if Mary ever met with the blind harper in the 'wide mansion' where she spent her last days as an old lady with a taste for whisky and snuff. Mary's laments and eulogies for members of the clan follow the set phrases and traditional analogies of the bardic form, but she enlivens her verse with freer stress-patterns (often in a three-line stanza) and her vernacular Gaelic is more spontaneous in feeling, music and rhythm than the old schools would have had it.

By the latter part of the century these vernacular Gaelic forms were much more common, and increasingly to be found in the mouths of women poets, too. The work of Catrìona NicGillEathain (Catherine Maclean) from Coll, for example, mixes the conventions of elegy with the more colloquial style of folksong, while the language of Mairearad Nighean Lachainn (1660?–1751) is skilful, fresh and individual, but also conservative and relatively impersonal in its genre, with much attention to panegyric, lament and the tracing of clan loyalties. In this respect her compositions, even those written in the eighteenth century, can be said to belong to an earlier tradition. Mairearad was associated on her mother's side, and also by marriage, with the Macleans of Mull. Her lament 'Gaoir nam Ban Muileach' ('The Mull Women's Cry of Woe') was composed for Sir John Maclean of Duart, who died in 1716, and speaks of the evil results of the 1715 rising: 'the West has been broken, / the heir's not come to wisdom, / this year brought destruction, / sore our loss from Mar's sudden rising.'

Sìleas na Ceapaich, Cicely MacDonald of Keppoch (1660?–1729?)

The songs of Sìleas na Ceapaich seem to date from 1700, but as with Mairearad Nighean Lachainn, her work might be said to belong to the end of the seventeenth rather than to the beginning of the eighteenth century. She was a highly literate and cultured poet, fully aware of the older Gaelic tradition, and capable, too, of political commentary. Strongly Jacobite in her sympathies, she wrote poems against the treaty of Union and poems in support of the 1715 rising: 'Scotland, arise in concert / before the English cut your throats, / since they took your credit from you, / and your goods too for gold / though your pocket's empty now.' She can strike a more personal note, too, and is especially remembered for the beautiful lament she wrote to clan chief Alasdair of Glengarry who died in 1721, only a year after Cecily's own husband, Alexander Gordon, and her daughter Anna had died:

> Alasdair of Glengarry
> you brought tears to my eyes today;
> no wonder that I am wounded,
> and that my wounds open up again;
> no wonder that my sighs are heavy,
> misfortune falls heavy on my kin;
> Death often cuts and takes from us
> the choicest and the tallest oaks.
>
> . . .
>
> You were the spouse of a precious wife,
> I'm sad that she has lost you now;
> though I must not compare myself with her
> I too have borne a bitter fate;
> let every wife who lacks a spouse
> pray that God's Son take his place,
> since He is able to give her help
> in the grief and distress that come on her.
>
> . . .
>
> ('Alasdair á Gleann Garadh', trs. D. Thomson)

Derek Thomson has suggested that it was Cecily MacDonald's personal loss that gave her later work a religious strain. The most notable and by far the most political poet at the end of the century (though he scarcely outlived it) was another bard from Keppoch.

'Iain Lom', John MacDonald (1620?–1707?)

Descended from the MacDonald chiefs of Keppoch, Iain Lom was involved in the clan feuds that grew up around Montrose's campaigns. He supported the Royalist cause passionately and was present when the Covenanters and the Campbells were defeated at the battle of Inverlochy in 1645. 'Iain Lom', as the name suggests, was a lean 'bare' man, known for his quick and scathing wit. It is said that the Campbells, all too aware of his talent for invective, offered a reward for his head. Tradition has it that he arrived at Inverary castle to claim the bounty himself and was indeed rewarded for his nerve by being entertained as a guest for a week. The Campbells had cause to fear this bard's tongue, for his account of the battle of Inverlochy shows his impressionistic and ferociously exultant verse in action – a vernacular Gaelic honed to hard, succinct and cruel images all leading to an absolutely merciless conclusion:

> Alasdair of sharp, biting blades.
> if you had the heroes of Mull with you,
> you would have stopped those who got away,
> as the dulse-eating rabble took to their heels.

> Alasdair, son of handsome Colla,
> skilled hand at cleaving castles,
> you put to flight the Lowland pale-face:
> what kale they had taken came out again.

> You remember the place called the Tawny Field?
> it got a fine dose of manure;
> not the dung of sheep or goats,
> but Campbell blood well congealed.

> To Hell with you if I care for your plight,
> as I listen to your children's distress,
> lamenting the band that went to battle,
> the howling of the women of Argyll.
>   (trs. D. Thomson)

An indefatigable Royalist, Iain Lom took Charles II fiercely to task for not claiming his kingdom – 'let not your soft tin sword / be in a fair sheath that is gilded' ('Lament for the Marquis of Huntly'). The king does not seem to have held a grudge, for with the Restoration he made Iain Lom his poet laureate in Scotland and the bard delivered a eulogy for the coronation. The poet was true to his appointment, for, when the Revolution of 1688 arrived, he did not hesitate to denounce

William of Orange as a 'borrowed king' and flayed him and his queen in the bitterest possible terms.

Vituperation was not the poet's only voice, and the 'Lament for Montrose' shows a more tender note as he describes his depression at his leader's end; and an early lament for Angus MacRanald Og of Keppoch shows his typically economical images fired with a sense of personal loss. Iain Crichton Smith's translation tries to catch this terse, bright restraint in the rhythms of the Gaelic:

I'm a goose that is plucked
without feather or brood,
or like Ossian condemned by Saint Patrick.

Or a tree that is stripped,
without apple or nut,
the sap and the bark having left it.

That raid to Loch Tay
has darkened my way:
Angus lay dead by its waters.

. . .

What wrung tears from my eyes
was the gap in your side
as you lay in the house of Cor Charmaig.

For I loved your gay face
(branched with blood and with race)
both ruthless and graceful in warfare.

The 'bard of Keppoch' also produced a number of conventional stock elegies, but his most memorable verse deals with his turbulent times and his own incisively 'ruthless and graceful' feelings. Nor did he lose his sharpness in old age, as testified by the bawdy virulence of his 'Oran an Aghaidh an Aonaidh' ('Song against the Union'), an attack on those Lowlanders who promoted the parliamentary union of 1707 for personal gain:

Lord Duplin, without delay
the vent to your throat opened,
a turbulence rose in your heart
when you heard the gold coming;
you swallowed the hiccoughs of avarice,
your lungs inflated and swelled,
control over your gullet was relaxed,
and the traces of your arse were unloosed.

(trs. D. Thomson)

Iain Lom was far from alone in his distrust of the Commissioners, but Andrew Fletcher, the most outspoken Lowland critic of the Union, would not have welcomed him or his support.

Andrew Fletcher of Saltoun (1655–1716)

As a member of parliament at the beginning of the century, Fletcher is especially remembered for his opposition to the proposed union with Westminster. Scots of all persuasions were equally disturbed. After all, the Highlands still sustained a Jacobite interest, and, as far as the Lowlands were concerned, the catastrophic failure of the Darien scheme had done little to convince Scottish businessmen of England's good faith. From an English point of view, the union of the parliaments would help to promote much-needed security for the Hanoverian succession after Queen Anne. The 'seven ill years' at the close of the century had left Scotland in terrible straits, with an acute shortage of money and resources and over a quarter of the population dead of hunger and disease. Factions both for and against Union were not slow to make the most of this failure in their arguments. In 1698 Fletcher produced *Two Discourses concerning the Affairs of Scotland*, the second of which contained a passionate denunciation of the state of affairs that had produced a permanent population of some 100,000 vagabonds, 'who have lived without any regard or subjection either to the laws of the land, or even those of God or nature'. The recent famines doubled this number and, since Fletcher believed in a citizen militia, he condemned the keeping of a standing army when such poverty was rife:

> we had more need to have saved the money to have bought bread, for thousands of our people that were starving afford us the melancholy prospect of lying by shoals in our streets, and have left behind them reigning contagion which hath swept away multitudes more, and God knows where it may end.

Although Fletcher had Highland Jacobite allies in his opposition to Union, as a stout Presbyterian he had little sympathy with their cause or their culture. No Swiss burger could have had a more vehement concern for freedom, peace and healthy trade, and the kin-based, warlike and essentially unmaterialistic nature of clan society was anathema to him. He complained that half of Scotland was occupied 'by a people who are all gentlemen only because they will not work; and who in everything are more contemptible than the vilest slaves, except that they always carry arms, because for the most part they live upon robbery.' Fletcher's patriotism looked back to the great times of the Declaration of Arbroath; and the twelve 'limitations' that he proposed to parliament in 1703 all had to do with making sure that no king could act against the interests, or without the sanction of the Estates of Scotland. He was equally passionately opposed to what he took to be the erosion of wealth and cultural identity, which a parliamentary union with England could only accelerate. To this end he wrote an essay called *An Account of a Conversation concerning a Right Regulation of Governments for the Common Good of Mankind* (1704), which includes his famous saying that 'if a man were permitted to make all the ballads, he need not care who should make the laws of a nation'. This memorable testament to the formative impact of lyric and dramatic art – as in ancient times – is a little tarnished, however, when Fletcher goes on to regret the 'unspeakable and deplorable success' of the ballad-makers of Edinburgh in corrupting rather than enlightening the people. His essay was written in the form of a Platonic dialogue in a letter to the marquis of Montrose and other Whig nationalists, and it strikes a surprisingly contemporary note to any reader familiar with the debates on devolution that took place in Scotland in the late 1970s:

> That London should draw the riches and government of the three kingdoms to the south-east corner of this island, is in some degree as unnatural, as for one city to possess the riches and government of the world. . . . And if the other parts of government are not also communicated to every considerable body of men; but that some of them must be forced to depend upon others, and be governed by those who reside far from them, and little value any interest except their own . . . I say, all such governments are violent, unjust and unnatural.

If nothing else, the contemporary recurrence of these opinions suggests that Fletcher's diagnosis of Scotland's condition was more far-sighted than the successful Unionists of 1707 could ever have realised or admitted.

5

The eighteenth century: new Athenians and the Doric

ON 28 April 1707 Chancellor Seafield concluded the last meeting of the last Scottish parliament with the words, 'Now there's ane end of ane auld sang', but these were far from the final words on the subject, for Scotland had been so deeply divided over the issue that debates and legitimate accusations of bribery and corruption raged for years. Many landowners had been in favour of what they saw as a profitable partnership, and the vested interests of Church and law had been protected by separate acts in both parliaments; but the boroughs feared a reduction in their status and the volatile urban crowds rioted at the prospect of their rulers moving to London, capital of the 'auld enemy'. It was not long before their fears were realised, agreements were broken, and even the Unionists began to have second thoughts as English businessmen denied them the expected benefits in trade and exports. Rises in taxation hit the poorer classes in Scotland much harder than their more comfortable counterparts in the south. The Kirk saw Episcopalian forms return under the new Toleration Act and the principle of lay patronage was introduced contrary to the Acts passed at the Union. Parliamentary action in far-away London was difficult and tedious to implement and the forty-five new members, and the Scottish nobility too, found themselves outnumbered and diminished when they moved to the larger stage. For a while these disappointments seemed to have little to do with the Highlanders, who expected to live in their old society much as before. Yet it was only a matter of time before disaffection with the Union and the death of Queen Anne in 1714 (after only twelve years on the throne) fanned the ashes of Jacobite hopes into a last fitful, destructive flame.

An invasion fleet planned from France in 1708 was abandoned in the face of England's naval superiority. The 1715 rising did better but was no more successful despite a fair measure of support with 10,000 men from the clans. At Braemar in September, the Catholic cause of King James VIII was declared by 'Bobbing John', the sixth Earl of Mar, a man who had lost his position as Secretary of State when Queen Anne died. Mar and the clans expected more support from France and the south than they got, for the Hanoverian succession of George I was by no means universally popular and crowds in England had rioted at the prospect. Yet Mar would not commit himself and had to be persuaded to allow 2000 of his men to join English sympathisers on the road to the capital. The Jacobites reached Preston before they were encircled by superior numbers and surrendered. By this time Bobbing John had finally brought himself to Stirling to tackle the Duke of Argyll and his Campbells, who remained loyal to the government although outnumbered two to one. The Battle of Sherrifmuir was confused and indecisive, but in effect it was a defeat for Mar, because he failed to gain access to the south and his Highlanders began to go home. In late December the Old Pretender arrived in Scotland only to return to France in little over a month, leaving money for restitution and a plea for the approaching Argyll to be merciful. In fact the disillusioned rebels were treated relatively mildly, because Scots juries were reluctant to convict Jacobites for anti-Union sentiments. Nevertheless, Lowland Scots and English prejudices against the Highlanders had been reinforced once again, and groups such as the Society for Propagating Christian Knowledge continued to link the spread of schools and Presbyterian Christianity in the north-west with the deliberate extirpation of 'heathenish customs' and the speaking of what they still called 'Irish'.

In 1719 a small force with Spanish support landed at Eilean Donan Castle but the supporting fleet was lost in a storm and the remaining Jacobite troops were defeated and dispersed at Glen Shiel in June. Garrisons were established at Fort William, Fort Augustus and Inverness, and General Wade built a network of roads that finally began to open the Highlands to trade, travel and of course the military presence of the state. At the same time soldiers were recruited from the north and the Black Watch was formed to deter the clansmen from cattle raiding and the extortion of 'black mail' – a traditional form of 'protection money'. By 1745 the new Black Watch regiment was in the Netherlands fighting bravely in the service of King George. Their absence from the home front and the French victory at Fontenoy encouraged Prince Charles Edward Stuart to revive the ambitions of the Stuart dynasty for one last throw of the dice.

The twenty-three-year-old Prince was a more daring and attractive personality than his exiled father, but he landed on the mainland near Arisaig with only a handful of followers and it took all his charm and his assurances to persuade the chiefs to join him – anti-Union sentiment was fading and the last Stuart had left the throne over forty years before. Nevertheless, moved by old loyalties or the threats of their chiefs, encouraged by an early victory at Prestonpans, or by the prospect of settling old scores against the Campbells, or even by a bad harvest at home, the clansmen gradually rallied to the Prince's cause, until by November he was on his way south with 5000 men. This time the Jacobites reached Derby and put all London in a panic before their momentum ran out and Charles's advisers persuaded him that their position was too extended and vulnerable. The army returned to Scotland, met a few French reinforcements and won another victory at Falkirk; yet its supplies were dwindling and more and more clansmen were slipping away to spend the worst of the winter at home. Meanwhile the young Duke of Cumberland was pressing north with 9000 men, an army composed of twelve English battalions supported by artillery, horse-troopers and militia, as well as three battalions of Lowland Scots and one from Clan Campbell. On 16 April 1746, and against all advice, Charles insisted on a confrontation at Culloden on the moors outside Inverness. His exhausted and outnumbered troops with their claymores, pistols and shields were torn apart by artillery and decimated again when they finally charged a modern army trained to fire its muskets in alternating volleys. Charles escaped into the west, where he was gallantly (if sometimes reluctantly) hidden from his pursuers until he could set sail for France in September; but the wounded at Culloden were killed on the field where they lay. In the savage aftermath of the battle more than 3000 men, women and children were imprisoned and shipped to the south, where 120 were executed and over a thousand more banished and transported. Even though many were eventually set free, hundreds more died in captivity of hunger, wounds or disease. Meanwhile, as a matter of government policy, 'Butcher' Cumberland began to implement the most brutal repression throughout the Highlands. Clansmen were forbidden to carry arms, to play the pipes, or to wear tartan or the kilt, on pain of death or transportation; their music, their customs and their language were reviled and the glens given over to desultory bouts of terror and killing for over five years. Charles peddled his cause around Europe to increasingly little effect and died forty-two years later, a drunken and disillusioned man whose hopes had ended with the last land battle to be fought on British soil.

In the second half of the century, Scotland began to embark on better times, with a long overdue expansion in agriculture, trade and industry and a powerful and confident middle class. Even the Highlands came to share in this prosperity as rising cattle-prices encouraged clans to keep the peace and to trade with a Lowland society whose growing appetite for fish, timber, wool and latterly kelp, to serve the soap and glass industries, meant still more wealth in the north. Highland regiments became part of the British Army tradition, and men were raised by their clan-chiefs, clad in (legal) tartan and sent out to ply their warlike skills on behalf of a government and culture scarcely less foreign to them than that of the French, Spanish or Americans they were fighting. All these factors resulted in something of a boom for the hitherto underprivileged clans, and when the potato was introduced as a staple crop in times of peace and plenty, the population began to grow dramatically. Trade was accelerated again by the Napoleonic Wars, but it left the Highlands dreadfully vulnerable when peace came in 1815 and prices dropped. Lowland Scotland was less extended: it had developed coal and industrial resources on the east coast, with the Carron ironworks (which made the famous 'carronade' guns) and linen-manufacture and trade with the Baltic, while, on the west, Glasgow was becoming a major seaport where tobacco and sugar 'barons' made their fortunes from the Americas. It seemed as if the Union was bearing fruit at last and Scotland ready to match the prosperity of her new partner to the south.

The 'golden age' of the Scottish Enlightenment began in the 1740s and lasted for a hundred brilliant years, but its origins go back long before the Union, to those more humane aspects of the Reformation that had stressed breadth, accessibility and utility in education. So it was the Kirk's hopes for learning and debate as a route to the word of God, and its emphasis on individual responsibility in one's relationships with God and others, which supported (paradoxically enough) the flowering of philosophy, economics, social theory and the secular sciences in eighteenth- and nineteenth-century Scotland. In the first half of the twentieth century it was the view of many modern historians and literary authors that the seeds of the Reformation had been wholly sterile and that it was only the Union with England that was responsible for the flowering of the Enlightenment. (In his poem 'Scotland 1941' Edwin Muir famously saw the influence of the reformed church as nothing less than 'desolation': 'Knox and Melville clapped their preaching palms / And bundled all the harvesters away'.) Contemporary critics and historians have reassessed this position, with a clearer eye for the exceptional plurality, the complexities, the cultural roots and the creative disputes and dynamism of the Scottish experience.

The old cultural tensions, paradoxes and insecurities were still there, however. From its royal foundation in 1709 to the mid-nineteenth century the Scottish Society for the Propagation of Christian Knowledge set out to supplement the parish schools and expand education throughout the Highlands. But part of their 'improving' agenda was an anxiety about Catholicism, Jacobitism and (not coincidentally) the Gaelic language, which was seen as a source of 'barbarity and ignorance' and proscribed during the school day. The similarities with British colonial policy in the next century are striking, and such an agenda was undoubtedly damaging to the cultural self-confidence of Gaelic speakers. Nevertheless, the Society's influence was not entirely malign, for a more liberal approach was adopted in 1766. In later years the Society became active in the Gaelic publication of scriptures, sermons and essays and in some parts of the country its evangelical principles led ministers to stand for the rights of the people against their often absentee landowners. The fate of the Scots language was equally complex. With first the king and then the parliament in London, Scots speech became increasingly associated with all that was 'characterful' in Scots life – rustic or antique at best, and provincial at worst. The painful ambivalence that had been felt by many over the Union was replayed in cultural terms a generation later. In the 1780s Burns's vernacular muse was ecstatically received by the Edinburgh *literati* – the very people who had made a success of two editions of a little guidebook written (anonymously) by the philosopher James Beattie called *Scoticisms, arranged in alphabetical order designed to correct improprieties of speech and writing* (1778; revised and publicly published 1787). Originally written as a guide for his own students at Aberdeen, this work was intended 'to put young writers and speakers on their guard against some of those Scotch idioms', which is to say idioms in English which are peculiar to Scots usage; it was not aimed at the use of actual Scots words, for 'the necessity of avoiding them is obvious'. In his private correspondence Beattie granted that Scots had a certain humorous expressiveness, but noted that the tongue had become 'barren' and incapable of anything but 'low humour'. He was not alone in this, for David Hume also sought to write in a purely English idiom, and yet was reported in convivial circumstances to speak with a broader accent than Robert Burns. Nevertheless, it was still the case that Scots visiting or living in London were made aware of a prejudice against their accents, and indeed their very presence in the newly united kingdom.

Visitors to the capital were made the butt of jokes against 'Sawney' and deplored for their 'Scotch' traits of meanness, ambition and lack of refinement.

So it is that there are two contrasting strains in eighteenth-century Scottish letters. The period opened with a marked revival of interest in ballads, songs and the poetry of the makars, and closed with the vernacular genius of Fergusson and Burns. In the mid century, however, the Scottish Enlightenment had also achieved a European scope and a thoroughly outward-looking critical stance which led to English-language projects such as the *Encyclopaedia Britannica* (inspired by Diderot's *Encyclopédie* of 1751) and the major literary periodicals of the 1800s. This extraordinary melting-pot produced Edinburgh as 'the Athens of the North' and it is fitting that the very fabric of the city itself should symbolise the contradictions and the creative vigour of the age, bubbling with the vulgar satirical energy of the 'Doric' to be found in the crowded streets of the old town, and cooled again with hopes for an 'Athenian' clarity and control, symbolised by the neoclassical architecture of the 'New Town'.

A vivid picture of life in mid-century Scotland can be found in the autobiography of Alexander 'Jupiter' Carlyle (1722–1805), a 'moderate' minister of the Kirk who wrote satirical pamphlets, attended the theatre, and enjoyed dancing and the company of the *literati*, much to the horror of his presbytery. In *Humphrey Clinker* Tobias Smollett acknowledges his help in introducing him to the Edinburgh intelligentsia. Among the artists of the time, John Kay produced bold likenesses of the many characters to be seen walking in the Edinburgh streets, as did David Allen – 'the Scottish Hogarth', who illustrated 'The Gentle Shepherd' and 'The Cottar's Saturday Night'. Young Allan Ramsay (1713–84), the poet's son, became a well-known painter, a contemporary of Gainsborough and an early influence on Reynolds. He travelled widely, studied in Italy and made a great success in London. His best portraits, of high and low alike, catch a luminous, individual and wholly human intelligence and they reflect his own conviction, later outlined in his *A Dialogue on Taste* (1755), that actuality and the clarity of plain observation must be the foundation of art. Ramsay's work is especially notable for his sensitive and subtle representation of women and the portraits of his first and second wives, Anne Bayne and Margaret Lindsay, are justly famous. Ramsay returned to Edinburgh in 1754 where he founded the Select Society and debated with fellow members David Hume and Adam Smith. After another visit to Italy, where he met the architect Robert Adam, Ramsay was appointed portrait-painter to the court and, in 1767, to George III.

Alexander Nasmyth (1758–1840) worked as an assistant with Ramsay during the 1770s and also travelled to Rome where he met and befriended Raeburn. Nasmyth had literary connections, too, for he produced one of the most famous likenesses of Robert Burns and designed stage sets and backdrops for the dramatisation of Scott's *The Heart of Midlothian*. Best known as a landscape artist and an influential teacher in this genre, Nasmyth's pictures often include an ancient building in a picturesque setting, but he was no rustic sentimentalist, for he made magnificent paintings of Edinburgh and the construction of Princes Street, and he was also an engineer and an inventor of note – reputed to have been aboard the maiden voyage (along with Burns, so the story goes) of Patrick Miller's steamship on Dalswinton Loch in 1788. By the end of the century Sir Henry Raeburn (1756–1823) was Scotland's best-known portraitist. His most interesting works are divided between studies of Highland chiefs, now become a new class of landowner, clad in romantic tartan and keen to see a grandiose image of themselves in oils (Macdonell of Glengarry, 1812), and more sober portraits of his Lowland friends in law, literature, Kirk and sciences (Lord Newton, 1806; Neil Gow, the great fiddle player, 1793; James Hutton, the geologist, 1782; or the three portraits of Sir Walter Scott). Raeburn's best work has a broad freedom in long brush strokes and effects of light and shade. Knighted in 1822, Raeburn was influential in promoting the case for a Scottish Academy, eventually established in 1826, now known as the Royal Scottish Academy, housed in William Playfair's neoclassical building on Princes Street, soon to be matched by another Playfair building behind it, now the National Gallery of Scotland.

The boundaries of early eighteenth-century Edinburgh had scarcely changed from two hundred years before, and so everyday life was crammed into the high tenement buildings or 'lands' which ran down the Royal Mile from the Castle to Holyrood Palace and spilled over each side of the ridge on the way. These tenements rose ten or twelve storeys high, creating ravine-deep vennels and lanes between them, darkened by overhanging gables and stinking with sewage and slops flung from the windows every evening at ten o'clock. Tenement life had long prevailed in Edinburgh, Stirling and Glasgow, producing a characteristically Scottish mixture of the classes by which elegant apartments were sandwiched among crowded attics, cellars and workshops, all linked by steep and narrow stairs. Advocates, craftsmen, beggars, butchers, porters, churchmen and academics all lived on top of one another in old Edinburgh and continued to do so until the 1780s. At first there was little in the way of formal entertainment, for the Kirk frowned on anything to do with theatre and even the richest apartments were small and cramped, so the life of society, and many professional and business transactions too, took place in the streets and, of course, in innumerable clubs and drinking 'howffs'.

A visiting Englishman remarked that Edinburgh streets were as crowded as a perpetual fair – and it was indeed a carnival of vivid contrasts, with St Giles' Cathedral and the town prison facing each other in the High Street, flanked by Parliament House and market-stalls; yet, despite the crowding, burglary, robbery and violent crime were relatively rare events, and the most common misdemeanours were drunkenness and falling into debt. Nevertheless the Edinburgh mob could be a political force to be reckoned with, as in the Porteous riot of 1736, when an army officer of that name opened fire in an attempt to disperse an unruly crowd attending an execution, only to be lynched himself; or when enraged citizens protested against the repeal of the anti-Catholic laws in 1779, by wrecking the house of the Moderator of the General Assembly and burning his library. Walter Scott compared life in these old streets and crowded rooms to 'the under deck of a ship. Sickness had no nook of quiet, affliction no retreat for solitary indulgence.' Yet there was a fierce energy to be found as well (at least for the survivors) in a milieu where everyone knew everyone else's business and where there was no room and little mercy for pretensions or class barriers. Thinking of Scotland in general, Scott noted that 'men of all ranks but especially the middling and the lower classes are linked together by ties which give them a strong interest in each others' success in life'. English visitors admired an open-mindedness about Scottish intellectuals and noted that they had a wider range of acquaintances and intimates than was common in 'polite society' and the more rarefied circles of Dr Johnson's London.

The talents of mid-eighteenth-century Scotland swung from the abstruse to the intensely practical: from divines, advocates and professors of moral philosophy to no-less-distinguished surgeons, chemists, inventors and civil engineers, many of whom came from humble origins and parish schools. By the 1760s, the School of Medicine at Edinburgh had replaced Leyden as the leading European centre for teaching and research. Glasgow too was an important centre, producing, among others, the famous Hunter brothers, who went to London to revolutionise anatomy, gynaecology and surgery. Chemistry was an equally distinguished field, with William Cullen as the first professor of Chemistry in Glasgow and one of the great teachers of the subject, as was his successor Joseph Black, who befriended and helped the young James Watt. Black's work on carbon dioxide and latent heat was followed by Rutherford's on nitrogen and Hope's on strontium. The Edinburgh mathematician David Gregory had been a friend and colleague to Newton and Halley at the beginning of the century, and James Hutton, who had studied under Gregory's successor, virtually founded modern geology. Hutton's *Theory of the Earth* (1788, book publication 1795) was hotly disputed in his day, not least because his explanation of rock formation indicated the true and frighteningly vast extent of geological time.

These were the days before the need arose for narrow specialisation in the sciences and in the traditional Scots term such men were all students of 'natural philosophy'. (In fact Hutton began his career as a student of law and then of medicine.) In applied technology James Watt is best known for his invention of the steam condenser. A merchant's son from Greenock, he had an equally learned interest in chemistry, architecture, music, law, metaphysics and language. By the mid-1770s he had founded a firm with Boulton in Birmingham to manufacture his new improved steam engines. The next decade saw paddle steamships pioneered by Millar in Dumfriesshire, experiments which bore fruit with the *Charlotte Dundas*, constructed by William Symington (1763–1831) in 1801 to tow barges on the new Forth–Clyde canal – the first practical steam vessel in the world. John Rennie from East Lothian served with Boulton and Watt for a while before becoming the most highly regarded civil engineer in the country, building harbours and canals throughout Britain; while Thomas Telford, a shepherd's son and a parish schoolboy from Dumfriesshire, made himself a household name by the end of the century, constructing over a thousand bridges and hundreds of miles of roads and canals, including the Caledonian Canal, a vast system of waterways in Sweden and the Menai suspension bridge. Men such as these founded what was to become a nineteenth-century tradition of Scottish success in engineering and the applied sciences – witness McAdam, who gave his name to an improved road surface; Mackintosh, who waterproofed cloth; and Robert Stevenson, the second in three generations of civil engineers (and the grandfather of Robert Louis Stevenson), who built twenty-three lighthouses round the Scottish coast, including one on the notoriously wave-torn Bell Rock in 1810.

Such respect for practical knowledge, and a belief that it should be available to all, was central to the Presbyterian ethic and the Scots carried it into publishing. From William and Robert Chambers, the *Chambers Cyclopaedia, or a Universal Dictionary of Arts and Sciences* appeared in two volumes in 1728. The *Encyclopaedia Britannica* started with instalments by subscription in 1768 and ran to three volumes. Nine further editions were produced in Edinburgh, under a variety of editors and publishers, expanding to over twenty volumes by 1898, before moving to Cambridge University Press in 1910 and an American publisher in 1921. In the same spirit the *Edinburgh Encyclopaedia* set out in 1810 to summarise the whole of natural science and technology, producing eighteen volumes over the next twenty years. The major educational firm of Nelson began with popular religious works published and sold by founder Thomas Nelson in the 1800s, while his contemporary William Collins, equally influential in the same field, began in Glasgow with evangelical texts. Fired by the same principles of dissemination both firms also specialised in publishing overseas.

'Auld Reekie' was becoming seriously overcrowded, even by Scottish standards, but the growth in prosperity allowed better-off families to move south to new suburbs and more spacious houses, such as the ones in the homely neoclassical style of George Square. By the 1760s plans were made to expand in the opposite direction across the Nor' Loch (now Princes Street Gardens), and the poet James Thomson's nephew, a young architect called James Craig, won a gold medal for his plan of a 'New Town' to be built in the European neoclassical manner. At last Edinburgh was to have buildings appropriate to the spirit of the Enlightenment, and the old capital, which had been so shaken by the departure of crown and parliament, could express its new-found confidence and ambition in the geometrical symmetries and the grand scale of George Street, flanked by Princes Street and Queen Street and closed by a magnificent square at each end. It did not matter that at first the site was remote and exposed to the notorious Edinburgh winds, for it soon became the most fashionable place to live. Many of the men of the Enlightenment – including David Hume, Lord Kames, Lord Monboddo, Hugh Blair and William Robertson – had been familiar figures in the Canongate, the Lawnmarket and the old High Street, but they all ended their careers in the new and more stately surroundings of 'Georgian' Edinburgh. With buildings such as Register House and the design of Charlotte Square, both done by Robert Adam, the New Town continued to expand into one of the finest neoclassical cityscapes in the world. Born in Kirkcaldy to William Adam, himself the son of a builder, Robert Adam (1728–92) trained in Rome before setting up business in London. Appointed as 'Architect of the King's Works' in 1761, his flair for neoclassical decoration made him one of the most fashionable and influential designers in the country. If literary critics in the 1920s liked to cite a combination of opposites as the feature of Scottish culture, then no more striking physical example can be found than the two faces of Edinburgh, as clearly defined today as they were in the late eighteenth century, when those spacious Palladian and Grecian symmetries were overlooked by the towering, seething, chaotic tenements and wynds of the vernacular town – new Athens and Auld Reekie, indeed.

By the end of the century egalitarian feeling was afoot once again in Scotland. Stirred by social changes, the American War of Independence and particularly the French Revolution, the newly industrialised working classes and many middle-class liberals sought to extend the franchise to all men over twenty-one. The reform movement was beginning, many 'Societies of Friends of the People' were started, and Robert Burns himself had covert connections with the Dumfries branch of this movement. The Edinburgh mob, never slow to express itself, rioted for three days after the king's birthday in 1792, to cries of 'Liberty, equality and no king!' The notorious Lord Braxfield presided over intolerant trials of freethinkers, sentencing Thomas Muir, a young advocate, to transportation for fourteen years and doing the same for three English delegates who attended a national convention in Edinburgh the following year. Outright republican sentiment gained force in Scotland, to the gradual alarm of liberal sympathisers. Tom Paine's *The Rights of Man* (1791–2) was especially sought after selling over 200,000 copies despite, or perhaps because of, a government ban, and being translated into Gaelic. The weavers – the most skilled and educated workers – were particularly active in radical circles and in the proto-revolutionary 'United Scotsmen' movement, whose Calvinist and dissenting roots went back to Rullion Green. However, the terror in France and the eventual rise of Napoleon dampened republican sympathies in the country at large and allowed the government to suppress the 'United Scotsmen' by transporting many of them to Botany Bay in His Majesty's newest colony.

'If a man were permitted to make all the ballads,' wrote Fletcher of Saltoun in 1704, 'he need not care who should make the laws of a nation.' When, despite his best efforts, the lawmakers actually went to London, Scotland was left alone with her ballads to test the truth of Fletcher's claim. The result was a revival of interest in the vernacular tongue, especially among the educated middle classes, and literary and creative ambitions began to stir again, despite the Church's puritanical attitude towards 'profane' books and plays. Between 1706 and 1711 an Edinburgh printer and bookseller called James Watson produced three separate anthologies to satisfy the literary nationalism of new readers. The first volume of Watson's *Choice Collection of Comic and Serious Scots Poems both Ancient and Modern* began with a special plea: because the book was 'the first of its nature which has been published in our own native Scots Dialect', the editor hoped that the candid reader may 'give some charitable grains of allowance if the performance come not up to such a point of exactness as may please an over nice palate'. In fact *The Cherry and the Slae* needed no such apology, but for the most part the Scots poems are self-consciously homespun pieces such as 'Habbie Simson', 'Sanny Briggs' and 'The Country Wedding'. A mock elegy by **William Hamilton of Gilbertfield** (1665?–1751) was especially influential, and when Watson published it as 'The Last Dying Words of Bonny Heck, A Famous Grey-Hound in the Shire of Fife' it sired an entire menagerie of philosophical talking animals. The convention had come from noble beginnings, and Burns was to ·rescue it again, but in the meantime the acute social observation of Henryson's animal fables had given way to pastiche and easy pathos:

'Alas, alas, 'quo' Bonny Heck,
'On Former days when I reflect!
    I was a Dog much in Respect
For doughty Deed:
But now I must hing by the Neck
    Without Remeed.'

William Hamilton was a retired army lieutenant who assisted Allan Ramsay in compiling and 'improving' songs for his *Tea Table Miscellany*. Ramsay was so impressed by the aptness of standard Habbie in 'Bonny Heck' that he adopted it forthwith and popularised it in many of his own poems, including the 'familiar verse epistles' which the two enthusiasts exchanged, thereby establishing yet another mode which was to catch on widely. It was Hamilton's 1722 edition of Blind Harry's *Wallace* that excited Burns so much with a sense of national pride, and, since the text was abridged and anglicised, the ironic implications of this say something about the times. Scots pride was evoked again by Dr George Mackenzie (1669–1725), who produced three volumes of dubious biographies – *The Lives and Characters of the Most Eminent Writers of the Scots Nation* (1708–22) – while Thomas

Ruddiman (1674–1757), a better scholar and a Jacobite sympathiser, produced and glossed an edition of Douglas's *Eneados* in 1710. A developing taste for antiquarian romance was met by Lady Elizabeth Wardlaw (1677–1727), who wrote and published 'Hardyknute' as if it were an old, anonymous ballad 'fragment' and, although her deception did not endure, the poem appeared as such in the *Ever Green* collection. In a more contemporary vein, Lady Grizel Baillie (1665–1746) chose Scots to speak to a polite audience about the love life of swains: 'Were na my heart licht I wad die'. The romance of 'ancient' poems, national pride, the vernacular comedy of common manners and rustic sentiment – these were the varied and swelling currents upon which a wigmaker in Edinburgh launched what has come to be known as the eighteenth-century revival of Scottish verse.

Allan Ramsay (1685–1758)

Sometime in his middle teens Allan Ramsay left his native Lanarkshire and arrived in Edinburgh to seek his living, encouraged by his step-father, as a maker of periwigs. In 1710 he became a burgess of the town and two years after that he was married, established as a master wigmaker, and beginning to express an enthusiasm for the world of letters. Brought up on *The Bruce*, *Wallace* and the poems of David Lindsay, he was one of the many Scotsmen of his time who felt indignant at the loss of the Scottish parliament and at what he took to be a subsequent decline in the old capital city. He determined to master English literature and make Edinburgh less provincial. Thus the emblem of his new bookshop at the Luckenbooths in 1726 was a sign with two heads on it – Drummond of Hawthornden for Scotland and Ben Jonson for England. Yet for Ramsay, as for many of his countrymen, England was still the 'auld enemy' in a sentimental sense, even if his Lowland respect for trade and 'the frugal arts of peace' could not envisage reversing the Union. Such contradictions convey the essence of the eighteenth-century Scottish condition, and to some extent they survive in the popular consciousness to the present day. Thus Ramsay and his values play a significant part in the history of Scottish culture, even although he is a much less gifted poet than either Fergusson or Burns.

In 1712 Ramsay helped to found 'the Easy Club' – a group of mild Jacobites dedicated to 'mutual improvement in conversation' and to reading the *Spectator* aloud at each meeting. By 1718 he was calling himself poet and publisher on the strength of a collection of Scots songs and a piece called 'Tartana' – English heroic couplets in praise of the humble plaid. He also published an edition of 'Christis Kirk on the Green' with two extra Scots cantos of his own – added, he said, to show 'the Follies and Mistakes of low life in a just Light, making them appear as ridiculous as they really are'. Ramsay next adopted the form and manner of 'Habbie Simson' for a lively series of Scots poems on the notables of Edinburgh street life. These early 'elegies' have a carnival vigour to them that is entirely in keeping with the Christis Kirk tradition of celebration and excess, despite Ramsay's claims to be making a moral point. His poems memorialised real people such as 'Maggie Johnston' and 'Lucky Wood', who kept low alehouses, not to mention 'John Cowper', the Kirk's watchdog on wanton girls and professional ladies. 'Lucky Spence's Last Advice' plays to another convention, with the dying words of one of the city's most famous bawds providing her girls with the benefit of long experience:

O black Ey'd Bess and mim-Mou'd Meg,	affected prim in speech
O'er good to work, or yet to beg;	Too
Lay sunkots up for a sair leg,	something
For whan ye fail,	
Ye'r face will not be worth a feg,	fig
Nor yet ye'r tail.	

  . . .

Whan e'er ye meet a fool that's fow,	drunk
That ye're a maiden gar him trow,	make him believe
Seem nice, but stick to him like glew;	
And whan set down,	
Drive at the jango till he spew,	press liquor on him
Syne he'll sleep soun.	

Whan he's asleep then dive and catch
His ready cash, his rings or watch . . .

Although the author seems to be a little in love with his own vulgar daring, there is, at least, plenty of life and good humour in such character-studies. By comparison the invocation to 'Tartana' is impossibly stilted, and, although the double entendre in the last line would be worthy of Lucky Spence, the dullness of the rest of the poem suggests that it was an accident only:

Ye Caledonian Beauties, who have long
Been both the Muse, and subject of my song,
Assist your Bard, who in harmonious Lays
Designs the Glory of your Plaid to raise.

By 1719 Ramsay and William Hamilton were exchanging elaborate compliments in the standard Habbie of their 'familiar epistles', reflecting, among other things, that

> The chiefs of London, Cam and Ox,
> Ha'e rais'd up great poetick stocks
> Of Rapes, of Buckets, Sarks and Locks,
> While we neglect
> To shaw their betters . . .

If there is a hint of insecurity in these lines, then a similar instability marks the 'Pastoral on the Death of Joseph Addison', in which Ramsay constructs a dialogue between 'Richy' and 'Sandy' – none other than 'Sir Richard Steele and Mr Alexander Pope' – discoursing like Lowland shepherds in an excruciating amalgam of broad Scots and Augustan English. Pastoral dialogue in rhyming couplets was used to better effect in 'Patie and Roger', which gains an unforced freshness from Ramsay's vernacular realism:

Last morning I was unco airly out,	very early
Upon a dyke I lean'd and glowr'd about;	wall
I saw my Meg come linkan o'er the lee,	tripping
I saw my Meg, but Maggie saw na me:	
For yet the sun was wadin throw the mist,	
And she was closs upon me e'er she wist,	
Her coats were kiltit, and did sweetly shaw	petticoats; tucked up
Her straight bare legs, which whiter were than snaw . . .	

The popularity of his poems encouraged Ramsay to produce a proper volume, and this duly appeared in 1721, pretentiously provided with a portrait of the author, dedications by other writers, footnotes, a glossary and a preface which defended the use of Scots in pastoral verse as no less appropriate than the Doric dialect used by Theocritus. Thus the language of Henryson and Dunbar was to become increasingly associated in Ramsay's mind, and in the minds of his readers, with bucolic simplicity, rustic topics and a dialect of Greek noted for its old, simple, solemn utterance. This assumption survived up to and beyond the time of Burns, and, indeed it complemented the Edinburgh intelligentsia's picture of themselves as citizens of a new Athens – urbane and educated and yet conversant, too, with what they took to be 'Doric' from the countryside beyond.

The 1721 edition was a success and Ramsay gave up wigmaking to become a full-time writer and bookseller. He started his new career by editing 'A Collection of Choice Songs' (some of them his own) and publishing them as *The Tea Table Miscellany* in 1724. Ramsay was no scholar, he did not include the music to the songs and he frequently 'improved' the originals – 'so that the modest voice and ear of the fair singer might meet with no affront'. (The first collection of airs for Scots songs appeared the following year in William Thomson's *Orpheus Caledonius*, but the first fully responsible edition of texts and music was not produced until David Herd's collection of 1769.) The *Miscellany* was popular and influential, eventually running to four volumes (including English songs) and twenty-four reprintings in the next eighty years. Ramsay promptly followed it with two volumes of older Scottish poems 'wrote by the ingenious before 1600' and culled mostly from the Bannatyne Manuscript. *The Ever Green* (1724) contained superior ballads and many fine poems by Henryson and Dunbar, but never achieved anything like the commercial success of the *Miscellany*. Once again Ramsay interfered with the texts, censoring some lines, paraphrasing others and he even added a verse prophecy of his own birth at the end of Dunbar's 'Lament for the Makaris'!

The success of 'Patie and Roger' encouraged Ramsay to produce a sequel in 1723, written from the point of view of the shepherds' girl-friends. The gentle satire of 'Jenny and Meggie' is more pointed than in the earlier piece, perhaps because Jenny's pessimism is closer to the reality of woman's lot:

> O! 'tis a pleasant thing – to be a bride;
> Syne whindging getts about your ingle-side   *whining offspring*
> Yelping for this or that with fasheous din,   *troublesome*
> To make them brats then ye maun toil and spin.   *rags*
> Ae we'an fa's sick, ane scads itsell wi broe,   *scalds; broth*
> Ane breaks his shin, anither tynes his shoe;   *loses*
> The deel gaes o'er John Wobster, Hame grows Hell, *everything falls apart*
> When Pate misca's ye war than tongue can tell.

Nevertheless, Patie's girlfriend eventually persuades Jenny to yield to romance by presenting the other side of the old coin:

> Yes, 'tis a heartsome thing to be a wife,
> When round the ingle-edge young sprouts are rife.
> Gif I'm sae happy, I shall have delight,
> To hear their little plaints, and keep them right.

These two eclogues gave birth to Ramsay's best-known work and provided him with the first two scenes of *The Gentle Shepherd* (1725) –

a dramatic pastoral comedy in five acts. The author was persuaded to add songs in 1728 and to expand it into a ballad opera, whereupon it proved very popular for the next 150 years. The text saw many editions, some of them anglicised, performed by both amateur and professional groups all over Britain, making its author wealthy and famous at last.

The Gentle Shepherd perfectly encapsulates the strengths and weaknesses of Ramsay's muse, and the divided loyalties of his countrymen. The play's rural setting is pastoral and idealised, but the plain Scots speech of the characters adds a physical conviction to the place and the people in it. Jenny's description of the woes of marriage and poverty is realistic, and yet the plot is an unashamed confection of Arcadian love-matches and hidden blue blood. Patie, the gentle shepherd, turns out to be the son of an exiled Cavalier gentleman, but still he refuses to forsake his milkmaid lover. The conflict between his lineage and his heart need not last long, for Peggy is an aristocratic foundling too, and in next to no time the shepherd and his lass are exchanging Augustan clichés in stilted Anglo-Scots, to the effect that 'Good manners give integrity a bleez [glow] / When native vertues join the Arts to please'. By this stage, not surprisingly, what vitality the play still possesses has passed to the low-life subplot, in which Bauldy seeks witchcraft to make Jenny love him instead of Roger. His energetic descriptions of the uncanny are firmly within a tradition that runs from Dunbar to Burns's 'Tam o' Shanter':

She can o'ercast the night, and cloud the moon,	
And mak the deils obedient to her crune.	devils; croon
At midnight hours, o'er the Kirk-yards she raves,	
And howks unchristen'd we'ans out of their graves;	digs
Boils up their livers in a warlock's pow.	skull
Rins wither shins about the hemlock low;	anti-clockwise
And seven times does her prayers backward pray,	
Till Plotcock comes with lumps of Lapland clay,	
Mixt with the venom of black taids and snakes . . .	toads
(II.ii)	

Notwithstanding the 'black taids', enlightenment prevails, and the poor peasant is disabused with: 'What silly notions crowd the clouded mind, / That is thro' want of Education blind!', and then he is chastised 'because he brak good breeding's laws'. Modern readers may be forgiven for preferring the imaginative force of Bauldy's fantasies to the vapid moralising of Ramsay's gentlefolk, and yet later in the century Adam Smith and Hugh Blair spoke for educated Edinburgh by decrying the passages using a 'homely' style that was 'rustic' and 'not intelligible'. 'It is the duty of a poet', opined Smith, 'to write like a gentleman', and his assumption that this was not possible in Scots was even shared at times by Burns. In this context the wide success of *The Gentle Shepherd* ensured that Scots would continue to present an exclusively bucolic face.

Ramsay moved to new premises at the Luckenbooths – a group of lockable shops near the Mercat Cross and St Giles' – and began the earliest known circulating library in Britain, from which readers could borrow books at tuppence a night. The narrow-minded took exception to such pleasures and on at least two occasions Ramsay's shop was raided by the righteous, who claimed that:

> villainous profane and obscene bookes and playes printed at London by Curle and others, are gote downe from London by Allan Ramsey, and lent out, for an easy price, to young boyes, servant weemen of the better sort, and gentlemen, and vice and obscenity dreadfully propagated.

The publisher was not to be deterred from his cultural convictions, and when his teenage son showed a talent for drawing and painting he helped to found the 'Academy of St Luke' (1729) for the graphic arts and the training of students. Much to Ramsay's satisfaction (he had hoped to be a painter himself when he was a boy) young Allan continued his studies in Italy and went on to succeed in London as one of the country's leading portrait painters.

A new collection of poems appeared in 1728, including 'The Last Speech of a Wretched Miser', in what was now a thriving genre of character monologue. ('Holy Willie's Prayer' owes something to this particular poem.) Ramsay also supported various theatrical ventures in their struggle against Presbyterian prejudice and opened a theatre of his own at Carruber's Close, only to have it threatened in 1737 by those who feared its popularity and who invoked the new Licensing Act to silence his 'hell-bred playhouse comedians' and shut the theatre down. The poet resisted for three years and gave vent to his rage in the (unpublished) 'Epistle to Mr H. S.' (1738):

> Thus whore, and bawd, doctor and pox
> The tavern and a large white ox,
> Are the whole sum for Lord or clown
> Of the diversions of our town,
> Since by a late sour-snouted law
> Which makes great heroes stand in awe
> The morall teachers of broad Truths
> Have golden padlocks on their mouths . . .

Cheerfully gratified by how far he had risen, despite a limited education, to become in his own words 'ane of the warld's wonders', Ramsay withdrew from active business at the age of fifty-five and retired to the grand new house he had built on Castle Hill. With large rooms, a stunning outlook and a Latin inscription as the 'House of the Muses', this unusual octagonal dwelling was nicknamed 'the goose pie' by irreverent locals who had to live in the teeming streets below. There were those who said that the owner himself was the goose, but Ramsay and his bookshop at the Luckenbooths had been an effective focus for the liberal arts in the early years of the century, and the cultural flowering of Edinburgh could no longer be much delayed by frosts from the pulpit. The Licensing Act, for example, was soon countered by the gambit of selling theatre tickets as 'concert' tickets followed by a 'free' play, and numerous Edinburgh lawyers – an influential new audience – supported the deception and enjoyed a night out at the show.

Pre-Romantics and others

Ramsay had committed himself and the best of his writing to the Edinburgh he loved, but other men looked elsewhere and **James Thomson** (1700–48) left for the south just two months before *The Gentle Shepherd* was completed. The son of a minister in the Borders, Thomson abandoned his career as a divinity student in favour of a literary life in London. He found a job as a tutor, joined circles in which Pope moved, and made an early reputation for himself with four poems begun in 1725 and collected as *The Seasons* in 1730. (They were to be revised quite extensively over the next sixteen years.) Thomson's neoclassical blank verse is conventional enough with poetic diction, personification and echoes of Milton's elevated tone, but a more original note is struck by his painterly eye for the play of weather and light on the landscape and a host of moral, patriotic and scientific observations, all determined to prove that the harmony of God can be shown in the natural world. Such views owe something to the Earl of Shaftesbury's writings at the beginning of the century and were promoted in Scotland by Francis Hutcheson. Thomson's 'philosophy of nature' was an untidy mixture but it proved to be a popular one, and *The Seasons* is often said to anticipate the Romantic 'discovery' of nature. With this, Thomson passes into the history of literature in England, although his descriptions of landscape were also to influence the Gaelic poetry of Alasdair MacMhaighster Alasdair. Of Thomson's later works *The Castle of Indolence* (1748) is a pleasant Spenserian pastiche; *Liberty* (1735–6) is thankfully forgotten; and *The Masque of Alfred* (1740), co-written with Malloch, is remembered only for containing the words of 'Rule Britannia'. If the author's Scottish origins can be identified in *The Seasons*, they appear in his didactic Christian rationalism and in a tendency to add more and more examples to his account of the countryside and its weather. 'Winter', published in 1726, was the first of the poems to be completed and it joins a long Scottish line – going back to Henryson and Douglas – in the poetic description of bad weather:

> At last, the muddy deluge pours along,
> Resistless, roaring; dreadful down it comes
> From the chapt mountain, and the mossy wild,
> Tumbling thro' rocks abrupt, and sounding far:
> Then o'er the sanded valley, floating spreads,
> Calm, sluggish, silent; till again constrained,
> Betwixt two meeting hills, it bursts a way,
> Where rocks, and woods o'erhang the turbid stream.
> There gathering triple force, rapid, and deep,
> It boils, and wheels, and foams, and thunders thro'.
>
> (1726 edition)

Thomson's words, punctuated with weighty pauses, establish a chain in the development of the Romantic imagination that stretches from the actuality of the Scottish Borders to Wordsworth's spirit in the Alps and the full-blown symbolism of Coleridge's sacred river.

Another small link in the evolution of a 'pre-Romantic' sensibility was contributed by **Robert Blair** (1700?–46) with the publication of *The Grave* (1743), a blank-verse meditation on mortality. (The 1808 edition was illustrated by Blake.) Blair was a Kirk minister in East Lothian, and, although the pulpit voice can be heard in most of his verse, *The Grave* enjoyed a considerable following. He featured in the so-called 'Graveyard School', along with the Englishman Edward Young, whose *Night Thoughts: On Life, Death and Immortality* (1742–4) influenced the Gaelic poet Duguld Buchanan and catered to a vogue for religiose melancholy. This genre was refined in Gray's 'Elegy' (1751) and popularised by the Gothic novel at the end of the century.

Fourteen years after Thomson, a young surgeon's apprentice called **Tobias Smollett** (1721–71) left Glasgow with a verse tragedy in his luggage (*The Regicide on the Death of James I*), and set out for London to try to get the play performed. He had little luck, and 1741 saw him enlisted in the navy as a surgeon's mate, serving in the West Indies in the war against Spain and then leaving the navy to settle in Jamaica. Five years later he was back in London with a moneyed wife (an English planter's daughter) and a not very successful practice, for surgeons were regarded as the tradesmen of the medical profession in those days. Smollett turned to journalism and satirical fiction and achieved success at last with a picaresque semi-autobiographical novel about the travels of a young Scotsman. *The Adventures of Roderick Random* (1748) assured him of an early place in the technical development of the picaresque novel in English. (Richardson's *Clarissa* appeared the same year and Fielding's *Tom Jones* the next.) The young writer happily joined the *literati* of London to become another of those Scotsmen whose noblest prospect, according to his friend Samuel Johnson, was the high road leading him to England. Yet he did not forget his native country, for in 1746 he had been prompted to write an indignant poem, 'The Tears of Scotland', against the slaughter at Culloden.

Smollett saw himself as a satirist of manners and Kenneth Simpson has associated the stylistic energy, the breadth of social vision and the Hogarthian gusto of his fiction with the spirit to be found in David Lindsay or the makars, and analogies in the prose tradition can also be found in earlier French and Spanish authors such as Alain-René Lesage's *Gil Blas* (1715–35) which Smollett translated in 1749, and Cervantes' *Don Quixote* (1606–15), also translated by him in 1755. Not far removed from the flyting tradition perhaps, Smollett's writing and pamphleteering could be intemperate, and as founder editor of *The Critical Review* in 1756 he upheld a long-running dispute with Henry Fielding, and was sentenced to jail for three months after a libel against Admiral Knowles. Equally unguarded personal references in his next novel, *The Adventures of Peregrine Pickle* (1751), which drew on his travels in France, had to be changed in the second edition. *The Adventures of Ferdinand Count Fathom* followed in 1753, anticipating a popular taste for the Gothic, while *The Life and Adventures of Sir Launcelot Greaves* (1760–2) offered the public a mad English character in the style of Don Quixote. Smollett's other publishing ventures included a translation of Voltaire's works, a seven-volume anthology of travel writing in 1756, and eight volumes of a *Complete History of England* (1757–61), which caused some controversy and sold well. In step with the *Critical Review*, he launched another Tory periodical, *The British Magazine*, in 1760, following it two years later with the short-lived *The Briton*. Increasingly troubled by consumption, Smollett travelled in Europe for two years in search of better health, reflecting on his experiences in the form of letters as *Travels Through France and Italy* (1766). Perhaps it was this perspective which led him to publish the anonymous *History and Adventures of an Atom* (1766) on his return as a fierce satirical attack on George II and the stupidity and corruption of British politics.

The sprawling structure of Smollett's novels and his taste for bawdiness, grotesquerie and caricature were seen as failings by Victorian critics, but contemporary readers have come to appreciate much more his heterogeneous style, his use of exaggeration and comic inflation and his vision of the human comedy. During his time in the navy the writer had witnessed the brutalities of service life (recounted in *Roderick Random*) as well as the follies and failings of the establishment. As a Scotsman in London in the years after Culloden he was made aware of intolerance and prejudice against differences of class, religion and nationality, and indeed *Roderick Random* cast its eponymous hero as a northern innocent abroad whose experiences throw a satirical light on the doings of the world at large. Robert Crawford sees the exploration and exposure of social prejudice as a central theme in Smollett and especially in *The Expedition of Humphrey Clinker* (1771), which is often cited, as his best and most mellow work.

Based on his own visit to Scotland on a trip of some seven months in search of health, Smollett's last novel describes a tour around mainland Britain as undertaken by Matthew Bramble, an elderly Welsh landowner, and his little party comprising his nephew and niece, his spinster sister Tabitha, a maidservant and the manservant Humphrey Clinker who joins them along the way. Their travels take them from Wales to Gloucester, Bristol, Bath, London, Yorkshire, Edinburgh, the Highlands, Glasgow, Carlisle, Manchester and back to Wales again with numerous detours, mild adventures and encounters along the way. The story is told in letter form and by the time the party returns home, various happy resolutions have been brought about, marriages contracted and the young servant Humphrey Clinker, a pedantic Methodist, is revealed as no less than Bramble's illegitimate son. But this is not the real focus of the book, nor does Clinker write any letters of his own. The main effect of the epistolary form is to offer several points of view on each place, person or incident and much in the way of indirect and direct commentary (especially from touchy old Bramble, who may well speak for the author in this regard) on the state of the nation and modern times. The letters about London paint a hectic picture of change, social confusion, tumult and hurry, stupidity and corruption, while the visit to Scotland makes an amusing commentary on the various vanities and customs of its natives while also reading at times almost like a gazetteer. In this respect Smollett's book sets out to introduce the Scots to the English and the Scots to themselves, as did the hero of *Waverley* over forty years later:

> Inverary is but a poor town though it stands immediately under the protection of the duke of Argyle, who is a mighty prince in this part of Scotland. The peasants live in wretched cabins, and seem very poor; but the gentlemen are tolerably well lodged, and so loving to strangers, that a man runs some risque of his life from their hospitality – It must be observed that the poor Highlanders are now seen to disadvantage – They have been not only disarmed by an act of parliament, but also deprived of their ancient garb, which was both graceful and convenient; and what is a greater hardship still, they are compelled to wear breeches; a restraint which they cannot bear with any degree of patience. . . They are even debarred the use of their striped stuff called Tartane, which was their own manufacture prized by them above all the velvets, brocades, and tissues of Europe and Asia. They now lounge along in loose great coats. . . and betray manifest marks of dejection – Certain it is, the government could not have taken a more effectual method to break their national spirit.

As with his first novel Smollett has once again chosen a narrative position (or positions in the case of this little group from Wales) from outside metropolitan centres and used it to offer a social and satirical commentary on the many faces and paradoxes of British society. Horace Walpole saw the novel as a scurrilous attempt 'to vindicate the Scots' but Crawford argues that the coming to terms with difference and the reconciling of prejudice in the course of the novel is nothing less than a crucial step (and a Scottish initiative) in the invention of 'Britain' and the construction of a British polity which had to be more than just a matter of the interests of London or of England and English mores.

Notwithstanding Matthew Bramble's respect for Scotland and things Scottish (including Enlightenment Edinburgh and the poetic fashion for Ossian), as editor of the *Critical Review* Smollett had fallen foul of the Scottish establishment in 1759 by criticising a long Homeric epic which had been produced by **William Wilkie** (1721–72), a Kirk minister from just outside Edinburgh. No less a man than David Hume wrote in defence of the poem, but it must be admitted that his judgement as a critic was unduly influenced by patriotism, friendship and an overdeveloped respect for classical learning done out in English heroic couplets. Nevertheless, Wilkie was a remarkable person: he came from a peasant farming family and farmed himself, while his devotion to learning and his erudition eventually gained him a chair in the sciences at St Andrews University, even if his eccentric behaviour made him equally notable as a slovenly dresser, a heavy smoker and man who insisted on piles of blankets and only dirty bed linen when he slept. Wilkie produced fables in verse, including 'The Hare and the Partan' in Scots, but his *magnum opus*, nine books on the siege of Thebes called *The Epigoniad* (1757), remains as dead as the seven heroes who razed that ancient city.

Another of Hume's enthusiasms was a blank-verse tragedy called *Douglas* by his cousin **John Home** (1722–1808), which had scored a notable success on the Edinburgh stage in 1756 before going on to London and Covent Garden. Home was a minister in Berwickshire, a lively, generous, romantic and popular man, remembered with affection by Henry Mackenzie, who wrote a biography of him. Home's next five verse tragedies were not so well received, but his namesake, the famous philosopher, still maintained that *Douglas* was better than Shakespeare and Otway because the Scots play was 'refined from the unhappy barbarism of the one, and the licentiousness of the other'. The *Douglas* tragedy is Romantic in spirit, for it concentrates on evoking wonder at the wild landscape and pity at the plight of the characters; but its structure is essentially neoclassical – elevated, stately and completely static. Notwithstanding its less-than-inflammatory style, there was scandal at the Edinburgh performance when the 'unco guid' heard that some ministers, including the liberal thinker 'Jupiter' Carlyle, had been seen in the theatre. (Indeed Carlyle had played the part of Old Norval in a private rehearsal.) It must be admitted that time has not been kind to the literary judgements of Hume and his educated friends, for most of their favourites are now forgotten, including Professor James Beattie's Spenserian imitation *The Minstrel* (1771–4) and the Augustan verses of blind Dr Thomas Blacklock (1721–91), equally praised by Dr Johnson. But fortunately Hume's taste is not the only yardstick of the man, and a closer look at his milieu and at his contemporaries from the 1720s to the 1770s will show where the real strengths of mid-century Edinburgh were to be found.

The Scottish Enlightenment

Francis Hutcheson (1694–1746) was an Irishman from County Down who went to Glasgow University and taught in Dublin before taking the chair of moral philosophy at Glasgow in 1729, where he was the first professor to teach in English instead of Latin. His thinking was developed from Shaftesbury's philosophy, which linked man's moral nature to his aesthetic responses. Hutcheson stressed individual experience and our responses to beauty and happiness, and he believed in a social, caring person whose common humane feelings, rather than any exercise of logic, would encourage them to act for 'the greatest happiness of the greatest number'. The phrase predates Bentham's more rational utilitarian system by some forty years and its spirit is totally different from the grimmer emphasis on brute survival and self-interest that had characterised Hobbes's vision of human motivation in *Leviathan* in 1651. On the contrary, Hutcheson held that the existence of this intuitive moral sense reveals the essence of mankind and the goodness of God, and more than an echo of these beliefs can be heard in Burns's call for 'Ae spark o' Nature's fire, / That's a' the learning I desire.' Indeed, the primacy of instinctive and inescapable sympathetic feeling as a gauge of morality became central to how northern writers understood themselves, the common people and the Scottish psyche in general. This tendency reached a bizarre peak of sorts with Mackenzie and degenerated into sentimentalism by Victorian times, but Burns, Scott, Hogg and Galt all testify to its healthier influence and it marked the thinking of both David Hume and Adam Smith. Given the holiness of the heart's affections in their original sense, it follows that Hutcheson, like Burns, Keats or Shelley for that matter, was against external authoritarianism, whether on the part of governments or landowners or even in the family. Indeed these seeds from Hutcheson – the seeds of intuition, empathy and a fellow feeling for others – were fundamental to the concerns for individualism, democracy and national freedom that were to characterise so many aspects of literary Romanticism and political change throughout Europe.

Professor Hutcheson was one of the first to contribute to what became known as the 'Scottish Enlightenment' and to what was to become a particularly northern exploration of moral philosophy, the nature of man and perception and hence the nature of knowledge itself. Such interests are not entirely divorced from the intellectual inheritance of Calvinism and the Reformation, with a strong tradition of individual testimony, interpretation and active debate, but the new direction was more speculative and humane, being broadly applied to society at large, and, indeed, Hutcheson was influential in the growth of a moderate party within the Church of Scotland itself.

The greatest figure of the time, however, was most certainly not a Christian moderate, for all that he was a mild and amiable man with many friends. **David Hume** (1711–76) dismissed all religion in his works and even struck at the foundations of reason itself. As a result Presbyterian reaction ensured that he never did become a university professor, despite the efforts of supporters and at least two promising opportunities at Edinburgh in 1744 and then again at Glasgow in 1751. Hume was the impecunious son of a small Berwickshire laird. He studied briefly at Edinburgh, but his enthusiasm for literature overcame his more sober intention to follow law. He then tried a post as a merchant's clerk in Bristol before escaping to France, where he lived for the next three years. There, still in his middle twenties, he completed his most important book, three volumes published in London as *A Treatise of Human Nature* (1739–40). The work had little immediate effect, however, and so on returning to his home at Ninewells in Berwickshire he produced a more accessible series of essays (1741) on moral and political issues. After another two years abroad he established himself in Edinburgh, became Keeper of the Advocate's Library and started on his monumental *History of Great Britain under the Stuarts* (1754–62). The first volume was not well received, partly because his account of the country's religious disputes treated both factions with equal contempt, but eventually the project gained favour not least because of its interest in cultural changes, and it brought him useful income over the years.

Further philosophical works appeared: the *Political Discourses* (1751) prepared the way for Adam Smith's economics, and *An Enquiry Concerning Human Understanding* (1748) and *An Enquiry Concerning the Principles of Morals* (1752) further advanced a radical critique of the age's confidence in reason. Hume's scepticism follows Locke, Shaftesbury and Hutcheson in so far as he too stresses the empirical evidence of our individual experience, but his conclusions take him much further. On the debate about the nature of morality and whether it is grounded on reason or feeling, Hume allowed both an active role, acknowledging that logical argument has an important part to play in deciding tricky cases of justice or culpability. But he then goes on to conclude that feeling – sentiment – is the true motivation towards morality and points out that every human language is replete with terms which demonstrate a clear preference for social virtues such as sociability, humanity, generosity and especially benevolence. These 'virtues' must surely correspond to some ingrained human capacity for good, even as they can also be shown to meet utilitarian requirements for serving common happiness and the common good. But in the first instance it is feeling and not argument which prompts us to act virtuously and so 'reason is, and ought only to be the slave of the passions, and can never pretend to any other office than to serve and obey them'.

Hume's scepticism is fundamental, for it dismisses all metaphysical speculation in favour of an approach firmly grounded on observation and the precise scrutiny of real-life experience. This led him to a radical reassessment of the nature of reason itself. From his earliest work in the *Treatise of Human Nature* he insists that what we call 'cause and effect' is really only based on our own psychological expectations. Thus (to invent a simplified example) when one billiard ball strikes another it always makes it move, and from repeated observation of the fact we infer certain 'laws' of physics. But Hume says that such 'laws' are only upheld by 'custom' – that is, by our supposition that the future will be conformable to the past. A statistician may assure us that colliding billiard balls have imparted motion in every recorded instance, but the only cause he has really identified is the cause of our own expectations that such events should always continue to be so. Thus Newton's 'laws of motion' depend on no less than an act of imaginative faith on our part – not so very different, after all, from a belief in miracles. Admittedly this imaginative act does not feel the same to us as, say, the idle notion that the billiard balls will turn into hedgehogs when they meet; but the apparent difference between these two expectations is simply a question of what we are used to and not a first-principles matter of reason. Therefore, according to Hume, 'logic' itself turns out to be upheld only by reference to what he calls 'custom', which is to say an experientially based sense of what is (because it always has been) likely.

Having said that, such 'custom' is not to be easily dismissed and Hume was, for example, very sceptical of Christian miracles precisely because they would contradict common experience, not to mention their dependence on unique and long-passed personal testimony which amounts, in effect, to no more than hearsay. In dismissing the possibility of confirming ancient miracles, however, he also begins to undermine the act of Christian faith in an individual, seeing it as a process 'which subverts all the principles of his understanding, and gives him a determination to believe what is most contrary to custom and experience' (*Enquiry Concerning Human Understanding*). Nor can the mind turn inwards to 'experience' or know itself, and so questions regarding the presence or otherwise of a 'soul' are 'absolutely unintelligible' to Hume. In his *Treatise* he observed calmly that 'the errors in religion are dangerous; those in philosophy only ridiculous'. It is not surprising that such 'notorious' ideas were publicly attacked in 1752 by the

General Assembly of the Kirk of Scotland. Nevertheless, Hume was well-enough received in Edinburgh circles, even by some of the more liberal churchmen. By all accounts the philosopher was a calm, genial and sociable man, whose shattering scepticism was not at all dogmatic nor in the least consonant with his comfortable girth and a face, as seen in the Allan Ramsay portrait, which has been described as that of 'a turtle-eating alderman'. And indeed in the world of practical politics he was a Tory who could see no reason why men could not organise society so that it ran quietly and efficiently.

Hume returned to France in 1763 and lived in Paris for three years as secretary to the British Embassy, where he was lionised by intellectual society and recognised as one of the most trenchant thinkers in Europe. In 1766 he returned to London with Rousseau, whom he befriended until the Frenchman's paranoia led to a parting of the ways. Two years later Hume returned to Edinburgh, where he spent his last eight years pursuing his interest in cookery and where he died calmly in the sure expectation of eternal extinction. His final demolition of Christian orthodoxy was published posthumously, and the *Dialogues on Natural Religion* (1779) show that the old man kept his wry doubts to the end.

The academic reaction to Hume's books was led by **Thomas Reid** (1710–96), an Aberdeen graduate who succeeded Adam Smith in the chair of moral philosophy at Glasgow. Reid's *Enquiry into the Human Mind, on the Principles of Common Sense* (1764) set out to refute Hume by maintaining (not entirely accurately) that his system, like Bishop Berkeley's, would reduce our certitude about the world only to a matter of internal mental sensations and ideas, claiming for example that 'there is no heat in the fire . . . the heat being only in the person that feels'. In place of this Reid invokes 'common sense' to point to the experiential difference between the idea of touching something and the actual physical act itself – or between what is really there and what we perceive. This had implications for aesthetics in that it sustained the argument that the task of artists is simply to paint what they see (as opposed to what they know), and that the quality of beauty we experience when we look at the finished work is something intrinsic to the work itself and not simply a subjective sensation in our minds alone. Such views were influential in establishing the Scottish 'common sense' school of philosophy that managed to bypass, if not to bridge, the abyss of Hume's scepticism. As a pupil and follower of Reid's thought, Duguld Stewart did much to spread the word and the common sense approach was carried to America in the work of James McCosh and especially to France, where its implications about the crucial difference between perception and objects prevailed into the nineteenth century with Victor Cousin's advocacy, later published as *La Philosophie Écossaise* (1857), aspects of which were to influence French painting and no less a person than Henri Bergson, the early modern philosopher of intuition, memory and matter.

A less searching advocate of 'common sense', but a spokesperson for conventional religious belief, was **James Beattie** (1735–1803), professor of moral philosophy at Aberdeen, a gifted teacher, a musician, a minor poet, a committed campaigner against slavery and the anonymous author of that little book against 'Scoticisms'. Beattie's *Essay on the Nature and Immutability of Truth* (1770) attacked Hume's 'sophistical arguments', seeing them as a threat to faith and morals. His defence is a popularised version of Reid's more searching work, offering in its place a somewhat inane definition of truth as that 'which the condition of our nature determines us to believe'. Beattie's defence of the truth of religion pleased Dr Johnson, whom he met in London, and struck a chord with the establishment. There were moves afoot to introduce him to orders in the English Church and he was awarded an honorary degree at Oxford in 1773.

Notwithstanding Beattie's more comfortable version of a Christian moral philosophy, Hume's clashes with the Kirk, as well as his historical writing and his interests in politics and economics, are characteristic of the Scottish scene at a time when new ideas were afoot and the study of the mind was taken to be central to an understanding of man and society. The Kirk no longer had the monopoly on such issues and was itself divided over matters of internal and external policy and doctrine. Academics such as **Dugald Stewart** (1753–1828) were influential in putting philosophy at the heart of education. Stewart saw philosophy quite simply as the science of human nature and the pursuit of understanding and analysis *per se*, and in this cause he was influential in defining the generalist approach which was to distinguish the Scottish university curriculum for the next 200 years, with its emphasis on the unity of knowledge in both the arts and sciences as a broad base of study for balanced individuals. Stewart began as a student of Thomas Reid in Glasgow but left his classes to help his ailing father, who was Professor of Mathematics at Edinburgh. He eventually succeeded to his father's chair, but returned to his first love when he followed Adam Ferguson as Professor of Moral Philosophy at Edinburgh in 1785. Stewart taught both Walter Scott and James Mill in his time and became a good friend to Robert Burns. His vision of how philosophy could contribute to the well-being of the population was outlined in the introduction to his three-volume *Elements of the Philosophy of the Human Mind* (1792–1817). Stewart contributed to the *Encyclopaedia Britannica*, wrote on the life and works of Adam Smith, Thomas Reid and William Robertson and was influential in positing a specifically 'Scottish School' of Philosophy with particular emphasis on Hutcheson, Reid and Adam Smith.

Philosophical historians followed, such as **Adam Ferguson** (1723–1816), yet another Edinburgh professor of moral philosophy, who has been called the founder of sociology. His *Essay on the History of Civil Society* (1766) proposed a comparative, almost anthropological, approach to the study of man as a being who creates social structures and moral imperatives for himself – the complete opposite of Rousseau's view of man as an isolated being who is best when least tainted by 'civilisation'. **William Robertson** (1721–93), a minister who became Principal of Edinburgh University and Moderator of the General Assembly, published a successful *History of Scotland* (1759), followed by a *History of the Reign of the Emperor Charles V* (1769) and a *History of America* (1777); next to Gibbon, perhaps, he was the most outstanding historian of his day. Unlike Hume, Robertson could see beyond the excesses of the Scottish Reformation to sympathise with the democratic impulse behind the Presbyterian ideal. He was a sociable and upright character and, although he could be forceful enough in the General Assembly, he employed his eloquence in support of the moderate cause in the Kirk. **Sir David Dalrymple, Lord Hailes** (1726–92) went to original sources to provide his *Annals of Scotland* (1776–9). A Law Lord and an antiquarian, he also collected ballads and edited the Bannatyne Manuscript. A fellow advocate and judge, **Henry Home, Lord Kames** (1696–1782), combined all the interests of philosopher, historian and literary critic. His *Historical Law Tracts* (1758) established a common historical pattern in the links between the evolution of man's institutions and his economic condition. Friend of Hume, Boswell and Benjamin Franklin, patron to Adam Smith and John Millar, Kames took an active and varied part in Edinburgh life, espousing literary criticism, crossing swords with the Kirk and then with Voltaire, publishing tracts on agricultural improvements, and all with equal panache. Kames's engagement is typical of the breadth of interest shown by professional men at the time, and they formed a 'Select Society' to provide an appropriate forum in which the only taboo subjects were religion and

Jacobitism. Also in the Select Society was **James Burnett, Lord Monboddo** (1714–99), a famously lively man of the Law, keenly interested in ancient Greek philosophy and the origins of language and primitive societies. His anthropological theories were seriously limited by his dependence on second-hand sources and by his own enthusiastic gullibility, but he is remembered now, as he was ridiculed then, for his theory that the orang-utan is a primitive member of the human species, a form of the noble savage not quite evolved enough for speech.

The philosophical study of society came to fruition in the works of **Adam Smith** (1723–90), who was a pupil of Francis Hutcheson at the University of Glasgow. By 1752 Smith had attained first the chair of logic and then of moral philosophy at Glasgow. Smith's career began as a lecturer on rhetoric (the arts of persuasion) and *belles lettres*, and indeed he founded the Select Society, along with Kames and Hume and Allan Ramsay's son in 1754, as well as contributing to the *Edinburgh Review* in its first short-lived incarnation the following year. The financial success of his first book, *The Theory of Moral Sentiments* (1759), allowed him to leave the university to travel in France as tutor and companion to the Duke of Buccleuch, who rewarded him with an annuity. Based on a concept of 'sympathy', the *Theory of Moral Sentiments* is a key text for Smith's later work as well as for the evolution of literary Romanticism and the rise of the modern democratic bourgeois state. For Smith, morality derives not from some God-given instinct, nor from abstract moral argument but from the structure of society and ordinary psychology and the balance it must strike between two fundamental human urges, namely: our own self-interest and our sympathy for others. (Smith's 'sympathy' is akin to empathy in that it has to do with our ability to put ourselves into another's shoes, and it does not imply merely sentimental feelings of pity or compassion.) This balance between self-awareness and our awareness of others is what constructs society and generates proper action: 'If we saw ourselves in the light in which others see us, or in which they would see us if they knew all, a reformation would generally be unavoidable. We could not otherwise endure the sight.' This very concept was to figure in Robert Burns's famous lines: 'O wad some Pow'r the giftie gie us / To see oursels as ithers see us! / It wad frae mony a blunder free us / An foolish notion', and indeed Burns had read the book in 1785 commenting: 'I entirely agree with that judicious philosopher Mr Smith in his excellent *Theory of Moral*

Sentiments, that Remorse is the most painful sentiment that can embitter the human bosom.' To avoid such pain, according to Smith, we will tend to act well. And even if we do not truly feel the force of this 'enlightened self-interest', we still tend to behave as if we did under general rules of conduct, or a sense of duty, or even just for the sake of appearances. Such acquiescence may not aspire to the first rank of moral sense but for all practical purposes it still promulgates good behaviour.

In 1766 Smith returned to his birthplace in Kirkcaldy to produce his *magnum opus*, *An Inquiry into the Nature and Causes of the Wealth of Nations* (1776). The modern study of political economy was virtually begun by this book, with its penetrating observations on the balance between urban and agricultural interests, on the rise of industrialisation and the need for mass education, on the duties of the sovereign and the need for an independent judiciary. Economics, the play of market forces and the division of labour all had to have a strongly moral foundation in Smith's eyes and he was particularly alert to the conflicts and balances between an individual's urge to accumulate wealth and the wider needs of society, or between the benefits of material prosperity and the needs of workers condemned to monotonous tasks. His prose is succinct and clear-eyed, just as his view of the moral case for social equity is (as with so much of his thinking) wryly practical:

> Is this improvement in the circumstances of the lower ranks of the people to be regarded as an advantage or as an inconveniency to the society? The answer seems at first sight abundantly plain. Servants, labourers and workmen of different kinds, make up the far greater part of every great political society. But what improves the circumstances of the greater part can never be regarded as an inconveniency to the whole. No society can surely be flourishing and happy, of which the greater part of the members are poor and miserable. It is but equity, besides, that they who feed, clothe, and lodge the whole body of the people, should have such a share of the produce of their own labour as to be themselves tolerably well fed, clothed, and lodged.

One of Smith's students at Glasgow went on to make his own study of class structure in a book called *Observations Concerning the Distinction of Ranks in Society* (1771). **John Millar** (1735–1801), who became Regius professor of civil law at Glasgow, was more radical than many of his fellow intellectuals, for he openly upheld the early egalitarian principles of the French Revolution and joined the Society of the Friends of the People in 1792 at a time when the establishment was bent on their suppression. Millar was a brilliant lecturer and his classes were packed with enthusiastic students.

Romanticism and the cult of feeling

By the 1770s the influence of Rousseau was making itself widely felt in the emergence of the pre-Romantic sensibility, and Adam Smith had endorsed the importance of sensibility in his *Theory of Moral Sentiments* by pleading for the power of imaginative empathy as a form of moral control. John Home's *Douglas* had invoked the heroic and the pathetic in a wild setting, and Thomas Gray struck another early chord with the Celticism of his poem 'The Bard' (1757). But it was a farmer's son from Inverness who spoke most directly to the new taste, and his 'translations' of Gaelic epic verse entranced the drawing-rooms of Britain and Europe, throwing them open to vistas from another world – Celtic, heroic, ancient and sublime.

James Macpherson (1736–96), encouraged by John Home's support, made his literary reputation in 1760 with a little book called *Fragments of Ancient Poetry Collected in the Highlands of Scotland and Translated from the Gaelic or Erse Language*. These purported to be a few love poems and battle-verses from the Ossianic tales of the third century, handed down in the Gaelic bardic oral tradition, or copied by later scribes and now translated by Macpherson. In an unsigned preface Hugh Blair announced that the young man was keen to translate still more pieces – 'if encouragement were given to such an undertaking'. The *literati* were excited by the evidence of such antique native genius and encouragement duly came in the form of a subscription. Macpherson, a handsome tutor and schoolteacher in his mid twenties, became a full-time writer and surrendered himself to fame. *Fingal* (1762) was followed by *Temora* and finally in 1765 the *Works of Ossian* were revised and collected in two volumes.

Home and Beattie were enthusiastic and in 1763 Hugh Blair, the professor of rhetoric at Edinburgh, wrote a critical dissertation in praise of 'Macpherson's Ossian'. Yet, when all is said and done, the poems were neither very good nor very authentic, although some of them were at least based on the Fenian cycle of heroic tales which came to Scotland with the Irish Gaels, and Macpherson does seem to have drawn on genuine passages, images and epithets collected in his travels or transcribed for him by others. As a boy in Inverness when the Forty-five broke out, Macpherson could speak Gaelic and he had contact with the oral tradition, as well as considerable sympathy for Highland culture. But he could never produce the manuscripts he claimed he had seen (unlikely in what was still a predominantly oral culture) and the poems remain essentially his own: a construction of a vision of a lost

age of gentle and valiant warriors. (He had already tried his hand at
sentimental heroism in 1758 with an unsuccessful poem called 'The
Highlander'.) 'Ossian's' style turns out to be a form of neoclassical
prose poetry based on Irish legend, mixing Homeric action with love,
noble pathos and a pleasingly alien landscape. Now at last the 'Athens
of the North' could lay claim, in Madame de Staël's phrase, to
'*l'Homère du Nord*':

> By the side of a rock on the hill,
> beneath the aged trees, old Ossian
> sat on the moss; the last of the race
> of Fingal. Sightless are his aged eyes;
> his beard is waving in the wind. Dull
> through the leafless trees he heard
> the voice of the North.

Dr Johnson also heard a voice from the North and promptly
denounced it as a forgery by a man who loved Scotland more than the
truth, whereupon Ossian's translator threatened to beat him with a stick
if they should meet in London. Sides were quickly drawn up so that
where Dr Johnson saw only 'Caledonian bigotry' and sought to prove
it so on his trip with Boswell, Tobias Smollett had his Highland travellers
in *Humphrey Clinker* report that 'the poems of Ossian are in every
mouth'. Indeed a sporadic debate about the authenticity of
Macpherson's work was to continue into the twentieth century.
Whether Macpherson was making a sincere act of reinterpretation for an
English-speaking audience of a sometimes despised minority culture, or
a more overtly ambitious bid for literary fame is still debatable and ultimately irrelevant, for in either case it misses the point of what made the
work so attractive to so many readers in the first place. In terms of
Scottish national identity the poems of Ossian laid claim to ancient and
noble origins, and this form of cultural patriotism was certainly one of
Professor Hugh Blair's reasons for championing the cause and collecting (not very convincing) evidence in their favour. David Hume, too,
wanted the poems to be genuine, but was bothered by their translator's
inability to show any original manuscripts and increasingly sceptical of
their survival by oral means alone. Katie Trumpener has explained this
willingness to believe in Macpherson's Ossian by pointing out that its
comfortably antique and heroic perspectives allowed contemporary
readers –and especially those south of the border – to accommodate
themselves to what was in effect a completely alien culture, and a
culture, moreover, that Enlightenment values and government policy

had done much to extirpate. Out of such ameliorations a pleasingly seamless conception of 'Britain' could lay claim to ancient roots and unity both at the same time, while Northern European readers could welcome their own alternative to the Classical tradition. Deeply imbued with the sublime, 'Ossian' joined Rousseau's 'noble savage' as a key figure in the evolution of Romanticism, from Goethe to the Gothic novel.

Johnson's scepticism could not impede the astonishing success of the poems – Burns, Scott, Byron and Hazlitt were all devotees. In America Thomas Jefferson thought Ossian 'the greatest poet that has ever existed' and Napoleon is said to have carried a copy with him everywhere. By 1860 the work had been translated into twenty-six languages. Authentic or not, Macpherson awoke public interest in the Gaelic tradition while speaking to antiquarian interests in general, and in this way his work was as influential as Bishop Percy's *Reliques* (1765 et seq.) and Lord Hailes's *Ancient Scottish Poems* (1770). Ironically, nine years before 'Ossian' appeared, the verses of the great Gaelic poet MacMhaighstir Alasdair had been banned in Edinburgh as Jacobite propaganda. The final irony is that Macpherson's popularity created a vogue among lesser Gaelic poets for compositions in its archaic style, while some of his 'fragments' in English were actually 'retranslated' into Gaelic.

The heart began to claim its own in the second half of the 'Age of Reason', and by the 1770s the novel-reading public had acquired a powerful appetite for pathos, nobility and sentiment – dampish qualities quite different from Adam Smith's more abstract and philosophical concept of 'sympathy'. Richardson's books had started the vogue in England with *Clarissa: or the History of a Young Lady* in 1747. Similar ingredients impressed the Parisians who read Rousseau's novel *Julie, où la Nouvelle Héloise* (1761) but the genre was brought to new intensities by the first novel of a young Edinburgh lawyer called **Henry Mackenzie** (1745–1831). Mackenzie was a blithe and practical person, a keen sportsman who could remember hunting for hare and ducks on the ground where the New Town had just been built, but he too in his younger years was drawn to the luxury of vicarious feeling. His novel *The Man of Feeling* (published anonymously in 1771) purports to be the biography of a sensitive youth called Harley, except that its 'manuscript' has been broken up and only odd chapters and sections remain. The pages having been used by a country curate for wadding for his gun, the supposed text begins with chapter XI. This device (intriguingly postmodern to contemporary readers) gives Mackenzie a certain ironic distance as the narrative opens, as well as an episodic freedom, for his main intention was simply to introduce 'a man of sensibility into different scenes where his feelings might be seen in their effects, and his sentiments occasionally delivered without the stiffness of regular deduction'. Indeed the 'sentiments' are regularly delivered in a whole series of affecting scenes as the hero on his first visit to London makes his way among the streets and confidence-tricksters of the metropolis. His adventures include a visit to a madhouse and a brothel, where he saves a young lady by reuniting her with her father. The key term is 'sensibility', for Harley wears his sympathies on his sleeve and Mackenzie's prose invites readers to establish their own emotional credentials by feeling for the sad lives and 'complicated misfortunes' of those he meets on his travels. (The tale is not without a certain hint of satirical irony, however, and echoes of Sterne and Goldsmith.) Harley is absent-minded and more than a little green, Candide style, yet his generous nature conveys a silent rebuke to his fellow men, who clothe their selfish interest and self-deceit in what Harley sees as a 'fabric of folly', as they pursue 'delusive ideas', which range from sexual seduction to the expansion of the British Empire. Harley is not made for this world; he retreats to his father's house, where he pines with unrequited love, catches a fever and expires with a sigh in the arms of his beloved. Eschewing 'the intricacies of a novel', the biographer is left to tell the tale of a 'few incidents in a life undistinguished, except by some feature of the heart' – an organ, it might be observed, whose tenderness kills him in the end.

There was a positive fashion for weeping over the sad passages of *The Man of Feeling*, it went through numerous editions and was translated into French, German, Italian, Swedish and Polish. Burns had two copies, calling it 'a book I prize next to the Bible'. In his turn Mackenzie praised the first collection of Burns's poems in 1786, marvelling at the 'unimitable delicacy' and the 'rapt and inspired melancholy' of the 'heaven-taught ploughman, from a humble and unlettered station'. This gentle creature scarcely sounds like the Burns we know, but it does testify to the contemporary propensity for adopting a sentimental attitude to what Adam Smith called 'the language of nature and simplicity and so forth' – a process started by Ramsay and equally in line with the European fashion for 'native genius' and the primitive. As a counterpart to Harley, Mackenzie's next book, *The Man of the World* (1773), introduced a sophisticated rake who ends in ruin. A play called *The Prince of Tunis* appeared the same year and four years later he produced an epistolary novel called *Julia de Roubigné*, after the fashion of *Clarissa*, but containing its own implied critique, as Susan Manning argues in her edition of that book, of the dangers of unfettered subjectivity.

Mackenzie's later tales and review articles were equally popular, including an essay on the taste for novels and the perils of 'the enthusiasm of sentiment', with a warning that it turned people away from 'real practical duties'. His sketches of Scottish life and character prepared the way for Galt and Scott and indeed the latter dedicated *Waverley* to him as 'the Scottish Addison'. By the late 1780s Mackenzie was a successful lawyer and a well-known figure in Edinburgh and London. He founded the *Mirror* (1779–80) and then the *Lounger* (1785–7), both periodicals in the manner of the *Spectator*, and he became an honoured and popular elder statesman in the arts, linking the age of Hume and Smith with that of Burns and Scott – the 'second generation' of the Enlightenment. As a critic Mackenzie fostered an interest in Schiller and German literature and was one of the first to appreciate Byron, Scott and Chatterton. If he welcomed Burns, mostly for the elements of sentiment in his work, his Addisonian bias led him to underestimate the broader reductive comedy of Fergusson, seeing it as somewhat tainted by 'blackguardism'. In other respects, too, he demonstrated a genteel insecurity about the essentially populist spirit of his native city, for he felt that the locals knew the author too well to credit him with wit and snobbishly confessed that the name of the Canongate seemed to him to lack the sense of 'classic privilege' conveyed by 'the Strand'.

James Boswell (1740–95) is often taken to be the quintessential example of the busy, confident Scot determined to make his name in the Strand and to ingratiate himself with the literary giants of London. Yet this picture does not do justice to a gifted and complicated writer, prey to fits of heavy drinking and plagued by depression. As the son of Lord Auchinleck, a Court of Session judge, Boswell was ordered to become an advocate in Edinburgh, but his heart was given to a life of letters and travel. While still in his twenties he had met Johnson in London (in 1763), and his appetite for fame and foreign places took him to Europe and to a somewhat contrived acquaintanceship with Rousseau and Voltaire. He produced pamphlets and articles, and a visit to Corsica in 1765 led him to champion Corsican independence three years later, when General Paoli raised his countrymen against French occupation. *An Account of Corsica* was published in 1768 and this and subsequent essays on the cause brought the young Scot a literary reputation as well as a certain notoriety (partly because of the dress he affected) as 'Corsica Boswell'. He visited the capital whenever he could, becoming the friend and confidant of Dr Johnson and eventually persuading the old man to undertake their famous trip to Scotland in 1773. *The Journal of the Tour to the Hebrides* (1785) demonstrates Boswell's talent as a gossipy and good-humoured raconteur and reveals him, despite the good doctor's frequent discouragements, as a proud Scot eager to show his country in a favourable light. From 1777 to 1783, writing as 'the Hypochondriack' (a telling pen-name), Boswell contributed many essays for the *London Magazine*. Gradually he gave himself less to Law and more to his biography of Johnson. In 1788, four years after the great man died, he moved to London to further his researches with hopes, too, for a political career that were never fully realised. Boswell's voluminous letters, notebooks, diaries and journals (occasionally scandalous and many of them available only in this century) testify to an unflagging industry as he documents absolutely everything that caught his fancy both at home and during his travels in Europe. At times he seems breathlessly naïve and tasteless, as when he pestered the dying Hume with questions about his atheism and whether he wanted to change his mind about it in the face of eternity; but his value as a writer also lies in this openness and in his ability to make even the most trivial of encounters vivid, entertaining and revealing. *The Life of Johnson* appeared in 1791, to become the most famous biography ever written, and there is a strong case for saying that the Dr Johnson so popularly known and widely quoted today was actually assembled (if not created) by Boswell's fluent, vain and paradoxically selfless talent.

Gaelic poetry: a vernacular flowering

Bardic verse declined because Highland society was changing, as the blind harper had found when his young chief set out for London. Poets still celebrated clan loyalties, of course, and still addressed their work to men who were likely to help them eat, but the old aristocratic tradition was dying and Niall MacMhuirich's elegy for Allan, chief of the Clanranald MacDonalds, fatally wounded at the Battle of Sherrifmuir in 1715, was practically the last of a line that was definitely ended by 1745. When MacDonald of Sleat made John MacCodrum his bard in 1763, it was a historical gesture rather than a cultural obligation. The new poets were writing for a more popular audience, and, as ordinary people themselves, were open to new influences and a wider range of subjects than ever before. Alasdair MacMhaighstir Alasdair produced

Jacobite poems with all the old warlike swagger, but he was impressed enough by James Thomson's *Seasons* to write poems of natural description as well. Like many of his contemporaries he called his verses 'songs', and specified, like Burns, the airs to which they could be set. From now on the term 'bard' lost its strict technical sense and came to mean simply a composer of poems. Duncan Bàn Macintyre followed Alasdair's lead in nature description; William Ross shows a familiarity with Burns and the Augustan neoclassical tradition, Eoghan MacLachlan, headmaster of Aberdeen Grammar school, wrote poems on the four seasons and translated most of the *Iliad* into Gaelic, and even Rob Donn, an unlettered man, has echoes of Pope in his poems. Comedy, satire, lampoon, Evangelical religion, everyday community life and love poems all join the Gaelic canon in the eighteenth century.

This vernacular Gaelic was much less formal than the bardic syllabic metres with their 'high style' of address, but technique was still valued. The new poems emphasise stressed rhythms – often with four stresses to a line – and internal rhymes, or assonances, are carried over from line to line throughout the verse. A brief example from John MacCodrum's 'Duan na Bainnse' ('A Wedding Rime') will show how this works, with the different rhyming vowels in bold in the Gaelic text, alternating one and two line by line:

> Chaidh mi sìos do Ph*a*ibil
>   Ann am m*a*duinn 's i ro fh*ua*r;
> Chomhdhalaich mo gh*o*istidh mi,
>   E fhéin is Lochlann R*ua*dh;
> Ghabh sinn chum na t*u*laich
>   Far 'n robh cr*u*inneachadh math sl*ua*igh:
> Ma rinn iad dearmad b*u*ideil oirnn
>   So m'*u*irsgeul dhuibh g'a l*ua*idh.

> I went down to Paible
>   One morning when 'twas very cold;
> My boon companion met me,
>   He and Lachlan Ruadh;
> We made for the knoll
>   Where there was a goodly gathering of people:
> As they missed us with the bottle
>   Here is my tale to tell of it
>   (trs. W. Matheson)

If the internal rhymes are schematised, their pattern makes two quatrains with the 'ua' sound (shown as rhyme b) appearing at the end of every second line and the other rhymes distributed as follows:

line	1	– a –
line	2	a – b
line	3	– c –
line	4	c – b
line	5	– d –
line	6	d – b
line	7	– e –
line	8	e – b

Reputed to be MacCodrum's first effort in verse, this song caused great offence in his small community by lampooning a wedding-party at which the poet got nothing to drink because he turned up as an uninvited guest.

The first-ever publication of contemporary Gaelic verse was a collection of MacMhaighstir Alasdair's work that he had printed in Edinburgh during a brief visit in 1751. Religious poems by Duguld Buchanan were next to appear in book form in 1767, and in the following year, also in Edinburgh, Duncan Bàn Macintyre's poems were copied out for him (he was unlettered) and published in the city which was now his home. Despite the immediately contemporary enthusiasm for Macpherson's *Ossian* (1760–5), the authentic genius of these poets passed relatively unnoticed in Lowland literary circles; but, as far as Gaelic speakers were concerned, the availability of work in print was a most welcome affirmation of cultural identity, and this modest growth continued, even after the Forty-five. MacMhaighstir Alasdair had already had a hand in the publication of a Gaelic-English vocabulary in 1741 (the first secular text ever published in Gaelic); Duguld Buchanan helped produce a Gaelic New Testament in 1767; Alasdair's son produced an anthology of older Gaelic verse (and some more poems of his father's) in 1776; and Macintosh's collection of Gaelic proverbs appeared in 1785. Gaelic prose, on the other hand, remained scarce and mostly confined to religious tracts, a state of affairs that lasted almost until modern times.

Alasdair MacMhaighstir Alasdair, Alexander MacDonald (1695?–1770?)

MacMhaighstir Alasdair called his collection of poems *Aiseiridh na Sean Chánain Albannaich* ('The Resurrection of the Ancient Scottish Language') as a deliberate gesture towards the widening of his art and the promotion of Gaelic. He studied bardic verse, lamenting his lack of 'chiselled stones and polished words', and wrote a praise poem to vaunt Gaelic as no less than the language of Adam and Eve which deserved to thrive 'in spite of guile / and stranger's bitter hate'. MacMhaighstir Alasdair came from an educated Episcopalian family in Moidart, where his father, 'master Alasdair', was the minister. He went to Glasgow University to study for Law or the Church, but married young and had to abandon his degree. Little else is known of his early life until 1729, when he appears as a teacher in the Highlands, working at various schools run by the Society for Propagating Christian Knowledge (SPCK). Alasdair's Gaelic–English wordbook was produced for this society, whose aim was to bring literacy, English and the Reformed Church to the north-west. His salary was little more than a pittance, but for the next sixteen years he ran a croft, became an elder of the Kirk, taught the children and composed love songs, satires and nature poems.

Alasdair's satires included scurrilous attacks on various local figures and rival bards, and the explicit imagery in these and in some of his love poems gave such offence to later collectors and editors that even today there is not a complete and unexpurgated edition of his works. Yet the spirit of his famous 'Moladh Mòraig' ('Praise of Morag') is a fine and joyful catalogue of sexual delights, rapidly delivered in an elaborate metrical imitation of pibroch, with 'ground' and 'variation', and making play with double entendres drawn from the language of piping itself.

> There's one thing that I'm certain of,
> I'd better not tell Jane of her,
> and how I've fallen headlong,
> and am going at the knees now;
> there isn't enough water
> in Loch Shiel, or snow on Cruachan,
> to cool and heal the raging fire
> that burns away within me.
>
> When I heard the melody
> played on Morag's chanter
> my spirit danced with merriment,
> an answering most joyous:
> the stately ground, most elegant,
> of her tune, with fingers tapping it,
> a music with fine setting,
> the rocks providing bass for it.
> Ah! the chanter with its grace-notes,
> a hard sharp, clean-cut music,
> sedate now, and now quavering,

or smooth, controlled, soft, tender;
a steady, stately march then,
full of vigour, grace and battle-zest,
a brisk and strutting *crunluath*
played by sportive swift-soft fingers.

                              (trs. D. Thomson)

The poem ends with the bard waking up 'on fire' beside his wife Jane
and making love to her. Fantasy or not, his jealous wife is supposed to
have prompted him to write the 'Miomholadh Mòraig' ('Dispraise of
Morag') in which, with equal extravagance, he gives his dream woman
red eyes and the face and sexual habits of a monkey.

If MacMhaighstir Alasdair's Gaelic nationalism was somewhat at
odds with his employers' preferences for English, the bawdy, sly and
passionate love songs were even more unbecoming in an elder of the
Kirk. The curious tensions and contradictions of this career came to a
head in 1744 when the SPCK noted that the schoolmaster at
Ardnamurchan was 'an offence to all Sober Well-inclined Persons as he
wanders thro' the Country composing Galick songs, stuffed with
obscene language'. In fact Alasdair's son was doing the teaching for
him by this time, and in 1745 the old man, now in his fifties, threw
over his post completely, converted to Catholicism and joined up as a
captain fighting for Clanranald in the Jacobite army.

Almost half of MacMhaighstir Alasdair's poems are dedicated to the
Jacobite cause, not just to the Prince (although he wrote many songs
to him) but to a vision of resurgent Gaeldom, free at last from the taint
of Lowland manners and values:

How I welcome the thunder of sweetly-tuned organs,
And the dazzling bonfires the streets all alighting,
While the market resounds with 'Great Charles, our own Prince!'
While each window shines with the light that is streaming
From high-burning candles fair maidens are tending,
    Every thing that is fitting to hail him with pomp!
The cannon all booming and belching their smoke-clouds
Making each country shake with the dread of the Gaels,
While we o'er-exultant, lightly, o'er-weaning,
At his heels march in order, embued with such rapture
    That no one weighs more than three fourths of a pound!
    ('Tearlach Mac Sheumas'/'Charles Son of James', trs. J. L. Campbell)

Alasdair invoked the old incitement-poetry and wrote the most
scathing and bloodthirsty verses against King George and the Clan
Campbell – those perennial enemies of the MacDonalds. He main-

tained his fervour even after Culloden, and a piece such as 'Oran Luaidh no Fucaidh' ('A Waulking Song') symbolises the exiled Prince as a beautiful girl – 'Morag of the ringlets' – and hopes for her return against the English with 'maidens' (French soldiers) 'to waulk the red cloth firmly'. Poems such as these renewed for almost the last time the old vaunting warrior-spirit of the clans, and this was why, no doubt, the unsold copies of his book are said to have been burned as seditious documents by the hangman in Edinburgh in 1752. By comparison, John Roy Stewart (1700–52) has a quieter voice as a Jacobite bard, and his two fine songs on Culloden are eloquent with pain and the sorrow of defeat.

There was a tradition of Jacobite songs in English, too, and Murray Pittock's work in this field has shown how the envisioning of Scotland as a beautiful girl and of 'Bonnie Prince Charlie' as a longed-for absent suitor, or a bold 'Highland Laddie', were common tropes in Jacobite poetry both for emotional effect and as a device to escape the censor. These songs belong to what he identifies as an erotic thread in Jacobite expression, and he proposes two further major types of song, namely the aggressive and the sacred. The aggressive mode can be seen in work such as 'Johnnie Cope' by Adam Skirving (1719–1803) with its bold first line 'Hey, Johnnie Cope are ye wauking yet?' referring to General Sir John Cope's defeat at Prestonpans in 1745, surprised in his bed by a dawn attack. The sacred metaphors, on the other hand, tend to cast Prince Charles as a Christ-like saviour, a holy martyr whose return will bring fertility and justice once more to the land. These strains can also be found in Gaelic poetry but the English language Jacobite songs, particularly by the end of the century, modulated into a much more indulgent and indeed comfortable spirit of sentimental melancholy and nostalgia.

From bardic praise poems to the 'songs' of the eighteenth-century revival, the spirit of Gaelic poetry is objective, detailed and descriptive. It responds to the physical world with such a disinterested but passionate observation of the surface of things that it positively discourages subjectivity or the symbols and philosophical reflections so favoured by the English Romantic poets. Prompted by James Thomson's *Seasons*, it was MacMhaighstir Alasdair who brought this Gaelic love of passionate catalogue to bear for the first time on poems of natural description, until he, and Duncan Bàn Macintyre after him, created some of the finest and most influential poems in the whole body of Gaelic verse.

Poems such as Alasdair's 'Oran an t-Samhraidh' ('Song to Summer'), 'Oran a'Gheamhraidh' ('Song to Winter') and 'Allt an t-Siùcair'

('Sugar Brook'), were most probably written around the early 1740s, and, although they follow Thomson's descriptive lead, they do not share his sentimental and didactic bias. Instead the Gaelic displays intellectual precision and a characteristically crystalline excitement:

> The lithe brisk fresh-water salmon,
> lively, leaping the stones;
> bunched, white-bellied, scaly,
> fin-tail-flashing, red-spot;
> speckled skin's brilliant hue
> lit with flashes of silver;
> with curved gob at the ready
> catching insects with guile.
>
> May, with soft showers and sunshine,
> meadows, grass-fields I love,
> milky, whey-white and creamy,
> frothing, whisked up in pails,
> time for crowdie and milk-curds,
> time for firkins and kits,
> lambs, goat-kids and roe-deer,
> bucks – a rich time for flocks.
>
> > ('Song to Summer', trs. D. Thomson)

The descriptive detail of nature-pieces such as these, and the fierce spirit of the later Jacobite songs come together in *Birlinn Chlann Raghnaill* (*Clanranald's Galley*), which was probably written after 1751. As MacMhaighstir Alasdair's most famous poem (and one of the longest in modern Gaelic), it is a *tour de force* among oar-songs. Attentive to the individual tasks of the crew, and all the lengthy preparations needed for a voyage to Ireland, the poem is filled with exact technical detail and inspired by the rhythms of the sea in both storm and calm. This is how the storm begins in Hugh MacDiarmid's translation of the poem (done with the help of Sorley MacLean), in which he attempts to convey something of the original metre and the impacted energy of the verse:

> Now they hoisted the speckled sails
> > Peaked and close-wrought,
> And stretched out the stubborn shrouds
> > Tough and taut
> To the long resin-red shafts
> > Of the mast.
> With adroit and firm-drawn knotting
> > These were made fast
> Through the eyes of the hooks and rings;
> > Swiftly and expertly

Each rope put right of the rigging;
  And orderly
The men took up their set stations
  And were ready.
Then opened the windows of the sky
  Pied, grey-blue,
To the lowering wind's blowing,
  A morose brew,
The sea pulled on his grim rugging   tugging (Scots)
  Slashed with sore rents,
That rough-napped mantle, a weaving
  Of loathsome torrents.
The shape-ever-changing surges
  Swelled up in hills
And roared down into valleys
  In appalling spills.
The water yawned in great craters,
  Slavering mouths agape
Snatching and snarling at each other
  In rabid shape.

If heroism still thrives in MacMhaighstir Alasdair's verse, his contemporaries John MacCodrum and Rob Donn Mackay look more to the everyday life of small communities.

Iain Mhic Fhearchair, John MacCodrum (1693?–1779)

John MacCodrum was married three times in the course of a long and quiet life on North Uist. His many songs make a wry commentary on domestic themes and local personalities – from his own problems with eager widows, to grasping tacksmen and landlords, to his last wife, who did not look after him as well as she should – at least, according to 'Gearan air a Mhnaoi' ('A Complaint about his Wife'):

'Tis no small cause of displeasure,
When I am not short of sheep,
To be buying cloth,
  Though my wife is alive;
And though it is not much to say,
I am ashamed at times
To be reduced to thigging sewing thread,
  Though my wife is alive.
                              (trs. W. Matheson)

MacCodrum was famous for the sharpness of his wit and the refrain of his complaint becomes more pointed with every repetition. Most of his poems were composed when he was in his fifties or older, and, although he was not a literate man, he belonged to an oral tradition which was capable of remarkable feats of memory. When James Macpherson arrived in Uist in 1760, MacCodrum was recommended to him as a man who could recite at length from the old Ossianic cycle, but the visitor's bad Gaelic and his bad manners evinced only a dry evasion from the bard. MacCodrum's own verses, so often based on village events, are far from Macpherson's notion of the antique sublime, as witness the descriptive comedy of such pieces as 'Banais Mhicasgaill' ('Macaskill's Wedding'), or a rhymed debate on the delights and pitfalls of drinking, 'Caraid agus Namhaid an Uisgebheatha' ('The Friend and Foe of Whisky') or 'Orain do 'n Teasaich' ('A Song to Fever') in which he characterises fever as the *cailleach* – an old crone:

> She planted confusion in my head;
> a host of men, both alive and dead,
> like those whom the Trojan Hector led,
> and Roman warriors, thronged my bed;
> that dismal, dark and hunch-backed crone,
> to scandal and lying tales too prone,
> reduced my speech to delirious moan
> and left me stripped of sense, alone.
>
> . . .
>
> Your coat has grown too big, and throws
> into relief your wrinkled hose,
> your splayed, pathetic ankle shows,
> long as a wild-cat's the nails of your toes.
>
> (trs. D. Thomson)

The poet's classical references, and his remarks on European politics in other poems, remind us that an oral culture need not be a parochial one; nor are Gaelic poets unaware of each other's work, whatever their geographical isolation. MacMhaighstir Alasdair visited MacCodrum on at least two occasions, and his poem 'The Mavis of Clanranald' was very probably composed in emulation of the Uist man's famous 'Mavis of Clan Donald'. The tradition was swift and fluid, for MacCodrum's 'Diomoladh Pioba Dhomnaill Bhain' ('Dispraise of Donald Bàn's Pipes') was his reply to another poet's extravagant praise of an inferior piper. Such interchanges were common when poems were recited and their composers valued as a part of communal experience. A skilled bard could memorise a song after only one hearing, and, indeed, MacMhaighstir Alasdair recalled two of MacCodrum's songs well enough to print them complete and without acknowledgement in his own book. Then again, Rob Donn, another unlettered poet, had such a grasp of MacMhaighstir Alasdair's 'Song to Summer' that he could produce a complex parallel to it in line after line of his own 'Song to Winter', entirely composed in his head. The tale of how MacCodrum came to be bard to the MacDonalds of Sleat also testifies to the potency of verse in an oral culture.

Tradition has it that MacCodrum satirised the itinerant tailors of Uist for being unwilling to travel to his remote house; and when they heard his lampoon ('Aoir nan Tailleirean') they retaliated by swearing to boycott him for ever more. The bard's ragged condition subsequently attracted the attention of Sir James MacDonald, who was on a visit from Skye, and when he heard the reason (and the poem) he gave MacCodrum a pension and made him his bard on Uist. The old man duly produced many praise poems and elegies on behalf of Sir James and the heroes of Clan Donald – that 'death-dealing bright company of keen blades'. Even so, the clan-system had still been irrevocably damaged at Culloden, and its close ties of kinship were breaking down at all levels.

In the 1770s the more prosperous farmers and tacksmen began to emigrate, many of them choosing to go to South Carolina. (Tacksmen used to be responsible to the chief for raising so many armed men, and they sublet their holdings to clansmen lower down the hierarchy.) When they left, their places at home were taken by strangers who did not hesitate to raise the rents until the poorer subtenants were forced to leave their crofts in turn. Thousands departed the western Highlands during these years and MacCodrum's late poem 'Oran do na Fogarraich' ('Song to the Fugitives') lamented what was happening:

'Tis a sad matter to consider,
The land is being made dearer;
Our people have swiftly left,
    And sheep have come in their place:
A weak host they and ineffective
At going into quarrel and strife,
Full of braxy and leanness,
    At the mercy of a guileful fox;
Smearing will not save you
In presence of battle on a field,
Nor will the moorland shepherd's whistle

Change your misfortune a whit;
And though you were to gather
Fifty wedders and hornless rams,
Never would one of them lift up
    An edged sword of steel.
                        (trs. W. Matheson)

In fact the 'edged sword of steel' was to be lifted again, but this time
the Highland regiments were fighting for a British cause. And among
the first of them were MacDonald troops from Skye, raised by Sir
James's successor, to fight the American 'rebellion' in 1776.

Rob Donn MacAoidh, Robert Mackay (1714–78)

Rob Donn lived in Sutherland on the far north coast of Scotland,
remote from the traumas of Culloden. He came from a humble
Presbyterian family (the Reformed Church was well established in the
north) and, like John MacCodrum, he was not lettered. Rooted in his
home community, he occasionally drove cattle to Falkirk or Carlisle,
and a brief spell as a regimental bard took him to most Scottish cities
in the early 1760s. As a boy Rob Donn ('Brown Robert') had a preco-
cious gift for rhyming, encouraged by John Mackay of Musal, who
took him under his care and gave him his first job as a herdsman. An
early failure in love is remembered with bawdy sweetness in 'Is Trom
Leam an Airigh' ('The Shieling Song'):

Fair Anna, daughter of Donald,
    If you only knew my condition,
It is unanswered love,
    That took away my reason:
It's alive in me yet
    As if you were here.
It teases and squeezes
    In my heart like a spear
        All though the day
        It's an uproar for me
        Trying to quell it
        While it grows like a tree.
                    (after a translation by I. Grimble)

The shieling was a hut in the high pastures where village boys and girls
would take the cattle for summer grazing. Many would associate the
first pangs of adolescent love with their long days at the shieling.

Rob Donn's heart survived to write other love poems, as well as verses on his passionate fondness for hunting deer, but most of his poems reflect on the events and personalities around him. He celebrated his native glen in verses that had young Isabel Mackay defend the delights of Strathmore against the attractions of Thurso, where her sister had been sent to school. When Isabel was married in 1747, her mother slighted the bard by not inviting him to the wedding. He turned up anyway with a light-heartedly bawdy lampoon on the family and their guests in which he puzzled over the fate of a supposedly missing pair of trousers. The bride's mother makes her appearance in the fourth verse of 'Briogais Mhic Ruairidh' ('MacRory's Trousers'):

Catherine, William's daughter,
Make some trousers for the lad
And don't take a penny
    In payment for them.
Who knows but it was your father
Who took them to wear?
He needed as much
    And time was when he would have done it.
                              (trs. I. Grimble)

No doubt the community enjoyed such pieces immensely, but Rob Donn also took a more general view of character, morality and politics, as with his long poem against the government ban on the wearing of the kilt. John MacCodrum's piece on the same theme had simply complained about the discomfort of trousers, and called up the old vision of a warrior in a plaid – and 'not a Saxon in the world but will blench at the sight of him'; but Rob Donn's 'Na Casagan Dubha' ('The Black Cassocks') takes a more astute and dangerous line:

So, so King George!
What a mockery of your good faith
To make new laws
That double the bondage.
But since they are fellows without honour
It would be better to strike than spare,
And there will be fewer to support you
When the same thing happens again.

If your enemy and your friend
Receive the same punishment in Scotland,
Those who rose against you
Made the better choice . . .
                              (trs. I. Grimble)

This was so politically pointed that he was called to task before the sheriff and the (Hanoverian) chief of the Mackays.

Rob Donn's verse can rise to virtuoso effects, as in 'Oran an t-Samhraidh' ('Song to Summer') or the pibroch poem to young Isabel Mackay, both of which follow the technical dazzle of MacMhaighstir Alasdair. But for the most part his muse speaks more plainly on his own and his neighbours' foibles. There is a grave, reflective quality in many of his commentaries that has been likened to the balance in Pope's couplets. In fact we know that Rob was familiar with the English poet's work through his local minister's habit of translating it into Gaelic and quoting it in his sermons. When the minister died in 1763, Rob Donn's 'Marbhrann do Mhaighstir Murchadh Macdhomhnaill' ('Elegy to Master Murdoch Macdonald') made a truly Augustan homage to the old man, if tempered with an appropriately Calvinist sternness:

> What has grieved me in spirit
> And those who loved and followed you
> Is the magnitude of your labour before you left us
> And the scantiness of its traces that remain after you.
> Some profitable lessons will flow
> From the fringes of your grace,
> That fools did not heed
> By listening to your teaching. . . .
> You made the reluctant willing
> And the ignorant wise,
> And the absolute joy of your life
> Was in imparting more light to them.
> You were gentle to those in need,
> You were generous with reasonable people,
> You were shrewd of aspect, hard
> As stone towards the miscreant,
> You were bountiful in giving,
> You were a diligent preacher,
> You gave timely advice
> And even your hostility turned to love in the end.
>   (trs. I. Grimble)

Like the poet, Macdonald enjoyed the unaccompanied singing of metrical psalms in church. These 'long tunes' are a kind of Gaelic Presbyterian plainsong, with each line chanted by the precentor and then sung at length and freely embellished by the congregation. The effect is one of wild and chilling grandeur.

The Presbyterian tradition was strong in the poet's community and in his own outlook. His verse did not hesitate to reproach Lady Reay (wife of the fifth Lord) when she tried to secure his silence over a marriage of convenience that she had forced upon two of her servants:

> With sharp command and counsel
> There was placed in my mouth a gag like a skewer
> Concerning the incident to be spoken of,
> Which did not resemble a love-affair so much as a hunt,
> Indeed I am sorry for the pair of them . . .
>
>   ('Geed a thuit mi' n car iomraill' / 'Lady Reay and her maid',
>   trs. I. Grimble)

He took morality seriously, but Ron Donn was no prude. His wry sense of humour had enjoyed singing the praises of Sally Grant – the darling of his Sutherland regiment – and his satires and lampoons, with more than a hint of flyting about them, were bluntly spoken and reinforced with a typically Highland awareness of family history:

> Your grandmother was lustful
> And bore children to twelve men,
> And your mother did not refuse
> One single man apart from her husband
>
> . . .
>
> Your mother was illegitimate
> And a great strumpet of a wench
> And she bore you a bastard
> To a lout of a fellow.
> Many a lamentable day
> They punished her on the stool of penitence,
> And you yourself got a yelping little creature
> In the usual way before you were married.
>
>   ('Tapadh leat a Bharb'ra . . .' / 'Barbara Miller', trs. I. Grimble)

Perhaps Rob Donn's most powerful poetry lies in his elegies – which were as likely to be for ordinary men as for chiefs. His wry 'Marbhrann Eoghainn' ('Lament for Ewan') compares the approaching end of an old man in a remote cottage with the reported death of a head of state – only to have the ancient revive at the last gasp in a rage at the poet for his presumption. 'Marbhrann, do Thriuir Sheann Fhleasgach' ('The Rispond Misers') uses its subjects to reflect on the uselessness of hoarding gold. In poems such as these, and in the verses to the fourth Lord Reay, Murdoch Macdonald and his old friend John Mackay (Iain Mac Eachainn), Rob Donn reshaped the Gaelic tradition of almost uncritical lament, in order to make his own commentary, sombre and hilarious by turns, on men and the times.

Dùghall Bochanan, Duguld Buchanan (1716–68)

Born and brought up in Strathyre, near the Trossachs in Perthshire, Duguld Buchanan, like Rob Donn, also came from a Presbyterian family. His mother's excessive devoutness, however, gave him morbid religious fears as a boy, and these visions marked his nature and his poetry for the rest of his life. He completed his education at Stirling and Edinburgh and spent some restless years as an apprentice carpenter for various masters. He moved from job to job as he alternated between wild escapades and the acute religious depressions that he described in his diary. He worked as an itinerant teacher before settling as schoolmaster at Kinloch Rannoch, where the General Assembly recognised his religious fervour by confirming him as a lay preacher and catechist. A later move to have him appointed as minister was frustrated by his lack of university qualifications, and by fears that his style was too inflammatory. The poems which he was beginning to write were disturbing enough – replete with images from the Book of Revelation and racked by an imaginative empathy with suffering and damnation. His most famous poem, 'Là a 'Bhreitheanais' ('The Day of Judgement'), is over 500 lines long. It describes the sublime and terrible descent of Christ on the last day, and the doom that all the sinners of history have to endure:

> On fiery chariot he sits
> with roars and thunder all around,
> calling to Heaven's outmost bounds,
> and ripping clouds tempestuously.
>
> From out his chariot's wheels there comes
> a stream of fire aflame with wrath,
> and that flood spreads on every side,
> until the world is flaming red.
>
> The elements all melt with heat,
> just as a fire can melt down wax;
> the hills and moors are all aflame,
> and all the oceans boil and seethe.
> (trs. D. Thomson)

Dante, and Robert Blair's 'graveyard school' and Young's *Night Thoughts* and the hymns and songs of Isaac Watts were undoubted influences on Buchanan and indeed Donald Meek has shown that some of Buchanan's verses are derived from lines by Watts. By the same token his poem in forty-four stanzas, 'An Claigeann' ('The Skull'), most likely borrowed its outlook from Hamlet's speech on Yorick. In these and other poems Buchanan's terse Gaelic and his visionary imagination create a special intensity. Towards the end of his life Buchanan studied in Edinburgh, where he met David Hume and compared notes with him on the sublime. He helped the Revd James Stewart produce the New Testament in Gaelic for the SPCK, and published a small collection of his own poems, *Spiritual Songs* (1767). These had a wide influence within the Evangelical movement, and many other Gaelic writers were to produce hymns and religious poems over the next hundred years.

Uilleam Ros, William Ross (1762–90)

Towards the end of the century William Ross produced a number of wryly personal and elegiac love poems. This was a new departure for the Gaelic muse, and perhaps it owes something to Ross's education in the classics and his familiarity with the poems of Burns. He was born in Skye and spent his boyhood in Strath Suardal between Broadford and Torrin, where, indeed, Dr Johnson and Boswell had stayed during their tour of the Hebrides in 1773. Ross's poem on whisky, 'Mac-na-Bracha' ('The Son of Malt') pays testimony to its effect on the good doctor, who was for once in his life 'tongue-tied', despite his English 'and his Latin and Greek speech beside'. William was sent to the grammar school in Forres on the mainland, where he excelled as a scholar. Then the family moved to Gairloch and the young man accompanied his father as travelling peddler, carrying a pack of sundry goods throughout Scotland and recording his travels in verse. After some years at this trade he returned to Gairloch to settle as the schoolmaster there. He became a popular member of the community, but died of tuberculosis at the age of twenty-eight.

Ross was more than familiar with the Gaelic tradition in poetry and some of his own pieces follow the pattern of praise poems addressed to his native glen, a Highland maiden, or to whisky, not to mention the by now almost obligatory 'Song to Summer' and an 'Elegy for Prince Charlie'. His Lowland education appears in the classical allusions that he makes in comparing his beloved to Venus or Diana, or in his references to Cupid as 'the Black Laddie' in a lightweight piece ('Oran air Cupid'), which has a priest smitten with love for a pretty cowherd. It may be that he had found something of this spirit in Burns, and certainly his 'Achmhasan an Deideidh' ('Toothache Reprimanded') looks familiar; but at the same time it is likely that vernacular Gaelic was evolving the personal lyric in its own right. (And of course Burns and Ross could draw on the folk-song tradition in each of their cultures.) Whatever their antecedents, it is Ross's love songs that are best remembered, along with the romance which grew up around his unrequited affair with a young woman called Marion Ross.

The poet must have met Mòr Ros in Stornoway during his youthful travels. He fell in love with her but she married a sea captain in 1782 and went to live with him in Liverpool. Tradition has it that she was unhappy and sent for the poet in later years. He got as far as Stirling before deciding that the affair was hopeless, and turned back only to catch the chill that killed him. His best poems do deal with this girl, and her image crops up indirectly in other verses. 'Love Song' ('Oran Gaoil') – also called 'Monday Evening' ('Feasgar Luain') – is the poet's recollection of seeing Marion at a ball in Stornoway. The formality of the occasion is matched by the verse with its classical allusions and rather highly wrought compliments. 'Oran Cumhaidh' ('Song of Lament') involves oblique references to a traditional tale of Cormac – an Irish harper who cured his love-pains with his own music. But Ross has no such consolation:

> Why was I not born sightless,
> dumb, without power to see,
> before I saw your modest face
> that dimmed a hundred's light;
> since first I ever saw you
> your virtues were renowned,
> and death to me were easier
> than to live now you are gone.
>   (trs. D. Thomson)

This poem was followed by 'Oran Eile, air an Aobhar Cheudna' ('Another Song on the Same Theme'), an even barer expression of personal anguish. The Gaelic tradition had seldom attempted such confessional force, although of course the impersonal lament was well established. The verse begins with the shocking image of a maggot hatching in the poet's chest:

> I am lonely here and depressed
> No more can I drink and be gay.
> The worm that feeds on my breast
> is giving my secret away
> Nor do I see, walking past,
> the girl of the tenderest gaze.

It is this which has brought me to waste
like the leaf in the autumn days.

Iain Crichton Smith's verse translation catches Ross's sense of desperate vulnerability very well, especially in the closing stanzas:

Ill-wishers who hear of my plight
call me a coward and worse.
They say that I'm only a poet
whose fate is as dead as my verse.
(His father's a packman. You know it.
His father, in turn, couldn't boast.)
They'd take a good field and plough it.
I cut better poems than most.

My spirit is dulled by your loss,
the song of my mouth is dumb.
I moan with the sea's distress
when the mist lies over the foam.
It's the lack of your talk and your grace
which has clouded the sun from my eyes
and has sunk it deep in the place
from which light will never arise.

I shall never praise beauty again.
I shall never design a song.
I shall never take pleasure in tune,
nor hear the clear laugh of the young.
I shall never climb hill with the vain
youthful arrogant joy that I had.
But I'll sleep in a hall of stone
With the great bards who are dead.

The oblique and brooding pain in William Ross's love poetry was to be recalled in modern times by Sorley MacLean's *Songs to Eimhir*. By comparison the last great Gaelic poet of the century composed hardly any love poems, for his work returned to the older descriptive tradition and shows no trace of introspection or personal unhappiness.

Donnchadh Bàn Mac an t-Saoir, Duncan Bàn Macintyre (1724–1812)

Duncan Bàn Macintyre lived half his life in Edinburgh, and he and his family are buried in Old Greyfriars' churchyard, but he is remembered above all Gaelic poets as a composer of songs about the remote hills and the running deer. His poems were more popular than any others and his printed collection went through two editions in his own day and three more in the following century.

Born and brought up in Glen Orchy, Duncan Bàn was unlettered and without formal education, but he could recite his own work by heart and much more again from the older Gaelic tradition. He served reluctantly in the Forty-five, for the Argyll Militia on the government side, and from 1746 to 1766 he worked as a gamekeeper for the Earl of Breadalbane and then the Duke of Argyll, walking the hills and forests of Glen Lochay, Ben Dorain and Glen Etive. His great descriptive verses were composed in these years, as well as dutiful praise poems to various members of the Glen Orchy Campbells. Duncan Bàn wrote few love poems, but his marriage to 'fair-haired young Mary' prompted a long praise poem called 'Oran d'a Cheile Nuadh-Phosda' ('Song to his Bride') as a fine and elaborately courtly compliment to Màiri Bàn Òg. Macintyre's strength as a poet lies in his observation of nature, so, while a reference to Cupid in his poem remains pretty stock stuff, some of his other similes are truly fresh and unexpected. He compares his bride's skin to white quartz, or her soft body to moor cotton-grass, or he thinks of her like a slender tree:

> I went to the wood where grew trees and saplings
>   that were radiant to view all around;
> my eyes' desire was a branch outstanding
>   in the dense growth of twigs overhead –
> a bough from top to base in blossom,
>   which I tenderly bent down:
> 'twere hard for others ever to cut it,
>   as this shoot I was destined to pluck.
>   (trs. A. MacLeod)

The other side of this coin can be found in the relentless flyting against Donald MacNaughton, a tailor who had dared to lampoon the bard – 'Oran do 'n Tàillear' ('Song to the Tailor'). The poor man paid a high price for his presumption, measured in long lines of frightful attributes, worthy of Dunbar's satire or a warlock's curse. The image of the tree is used again:

> Thou art the rotten tree, withered,
> full of decay and microbes,
> grown scraggy and stunted,
> short, hump-backed, distorted;
> a stump bound for the embers art thou,
> who didst deserve to be burned as sacrifice:

thou hast grossly neglected the gospel,
thou hast grossly neglected the gospel.
                                        (trs. A. MacLeod)

Much of Duncan Bàn's output, especially in later years, is cheerfully occasional. He loved deer hunting and he sang about what he knew and saw around him – Glen Orchy, a gift sheep, a favourite gun, an unsuccessful hunt, or, in mock elegy, a cockerel that was shot by mistake. He was an uncomplicated extrovert, unlike the fiercely touchy MacMhaighstir Alasdair; nor did he share Rob Donn's moral nature or the capacity for pain to be found in the works of Buchanan and William Ross. Nevertheless, it is with Macintyre that the Gaelic passion for objective observation reaches its highest point.

'Oran an t-Samhraidh' ('Song to Summer') is an overly formal and elaborately crafted attempt to match MacMhaighstir Alasdair, but with 'Oran Coire a' Cheathaich' ('Song to Misty Corrie') and 'Praise of Ben Dorain' ('Moladh Beinn Dòbhrain'), Macintyre is literally on his home ground and he charts it with loving detail. Verse after verse of 'Misty Corrie' moves to a measured pace, reading like some lyrically precise botanical catalogue, bringing together the life of plants and then fish, birds and deer:

Thy genial braes, abounding in blaeberries and cowberries,
    are studded with cloudberries of the round, red head,
with garlic forming pads in the angles of ledges,
    and fringed rock stacks, not a few;
the dandelion and penny-royal,
    soft, white cotton sedge, and sweet grass are there
in every part of it, from the lowest hill foot
    to the crested regions of the highest reach.

. . .

Around each spring that is in the region
    is a sombre brow of green water-cress;
at the base of boulders is a clump of sorrel,
    and sandy gravel, ground fine and white;
splashing gurgles, seething, not heated,
    but eddying from the depth of smooth cascades,
each splendid rill is a blue-tressed plait,
    running in torrent and spiral swirls.
In that rugged gully is a white-bellied salmon
    that cometh from the ocean of stormy wave,
catching midges with lively vigour
    unerringly, in his arched bent beak . . .
                                        (trs. A. MacLeod)

Such intensely focused observation is a kind of sublime transcendence, and it clearly influenced Hugh MacDiarmid, who from the 1940s came to see his later English work as a scientifically based 'poetry of fact' dedicated simply and entirely to the endless variety of the material world for its own sake. (Consider, for example, MacDiarmid's poem 'Bracken Hills in Autumn'.) The 'Song to Misty Corrie' is 'nature poetry' of the purest sort, entirely free of personal or symbolic reflection; perhaps some of John Clare's verses come close, but there is nothing else in the English tradition quite like it. The clarity of Macintyre's eye belongs to what Kenneth Jackson has called 'the high sunlight of the Celtic vision', and it is deeply ironic that within the next century the Gaelic muse would be associated – as far as Lowland culture was concerned – exclusively with glamorous shadows in a Celtic twilight.

'Praise of Ben Dorain' is based on a pipe-tune, and, like MacMhaighstir Alasdair's 'Praise of Morag', its light and lively rhythms imitate the pibroch changes between theme and variation (*urlar* and *siubhal*). In over 500 lines Duncan Bàn is attentive to the minutiae of grasses and streams on Ben Dorain's slopes; but the poem is particularly dedicated to the herds of deer that he had watched and hunted there for years. He is no sentimentalist, for, if he admires their delicate movements, he also takes delight in describing the intricacy of the flintlock on the gun that will kill them. The poem ends, moreover, with dogs pulling the deer down to die in moorland pools, and these last scenes are described by means of unstressed extra syllables in imitation of *crunluath*, the most complex movement in pibroch which marks the climax of the tune. Iain Crichton Smith's English catches something of the Gaelic's hectic excitement, and also the way the poem suddenly stops just like a pipe tune. Perhaps, like pibroch again, the effect is to bring us back to the beginning in an endless cycle:

Erratic was the veering then
and rapid in its motion
when they would go sheering on
short cuts with exertion.

Tumultuous the baying and
echo of the crying as
the hairy-coated violent
dogs would show their paces.

Driving them from summits to
lakes that are unplumbable
bleeding dying swimming and
floundering in water.

Hounds hanging to their quarries while
they sway and toss and rock and kill –
their jaws will never let them feel
their haughty style again.

The little that I've sung of them
is not enough to tell of them
O you'd need a tongue for them
of a most complex kind.

The bloody water where the deer met their end comes from the same
fresh springs praised earlier in the poem, in the quieter pace of *urlar*:

Transparent springs that nurse
the modest water cress –
no foreign wines surpass
these as drink for her.

. . .

The spotted water-cress
with forked and spiky gloss;
water where it grows
so abundantly

This is the good food
that animates their blood
and circulates as bread
in hard famine-time.

That would fatten their
bodies to a clear
shimmer, rich and rare,
without clumsiness.

It is characteristic of Duncan Bàn's muse that he should celebrate the
deer's diet with such tenderness and expertise. More than anything else,
however, his poem is full of the movement of these graceful animals, with
what Crichton Smith has called a pagan spirit that is absolutely free from
any moral dimension. Here the movement is the quicker *siubhal*:

The hind that's sharp-headed
is fierce in its speeding:
how delicate, rapid,
its nostrils,
wind-reading!
Light-hooved and quick limbèd,
she runs on the summit,
from that uppermost limit

no gun will remove her.
You'll not see her winded,
that elegant mover.
Her forebears were healthy.
When she stopped to take breath then,
how I loved the pure wraith-like
sound of her calling,
she seeking her sweetheart
in the lust of the morning.

By 1768 other men were employed on Duncan Bàn's favourite
estates and he found himself and his family in Edinburgh. With the help
of his former captain in the Argylls he joined the City Guard – a local
police force largely composed of Highlanders. As a member of what
Fergusson called 'the black banditti' he wrote songs in praise of his
halberd, his musket and whisky and brandy – those indispensable items
of company equipment. A volume of his poems was published by
subscription and sold well, but he had already done his best work. In
the 1780s he composed a series of prize-winning poems on pibroch and
Gaelic – to be recited at an annual piping competition in Falkirk as
organised by the London Highland Society. The same society gave him
a modest grant in recognition of his status as a poet. In preparation for
a second subscription volume, Duncan Bàn and his wife spent a couple
of years, sometime after 1786, touring the Highlands and islands.
Dressed in the plaid with a sword and a fox-skin cap, the bard was
widely welcomed. He left the City Guard in 1793 and served as a
soldier for six years with the Breadalbane Fencibles, although exactly
what duties were asked of a man in his seventies is not clear. His last
poems, musing on death and advancing age, adopt an untypically
moralistic tone; but a livelier note in the old vein is struck by his 'Oran
nam Balgairean' ('Song to the Foxes'), which praises them for killing
the sheep that were taking over the hillsides from his beloved deer. His
lines stand for the experience of many at the beginning of the nineteenth century, puzzled by social changes beyond their control as an
old, old way of life finally found itself in the modern world:

The villages and shielings
where warmth and cheer were found,

have no houses save the ruins,
and no tillage in the fields.

Every practice that prevailed
in Gaeldom has been altered,

and become so unnatural
in the places that were hospitable.

                                        (trs. A. MacLeod)

However painful, such changes happened along with a remarkable
flowering in Gaelic verse, and in the second half of the eighteenth
century Lowland Scotland was also about to enjoy a vernacular revival.
Clearly Gaelic culture was not unknown to Lowland Scotland but the
latter's passion for improvement seems to have led it to view the north-
west mainly as a challenging arena for economic, cultural and linguistic
'progress'. After all, this was the openly declared aim of the Scottish
Society for the Propagation of Christian Knowledge which had established 176 schools by 1758 with nearly 6500 pupils signed up for the
benefits of the Protestant faith and the English language. Duncan Bàn
was in the Grassmarket at exactly the same time as Macpherson and
Mackenzie and Fergusson and Adam Smith were the talk of Edinburgh.
He was on a poetic tour of the Highlands in 1786, the very year of
Burns's Kilmarnock edition, and yet one looks in vain to these famous
figures for any recognition of what the contemporary Gaelic literary
tradition had to offer. It is a telling reflection on the one-sided nature
of cultural hegemony that while several eighteenth-century Gaelic poets
show a fully literary awareness of Lowland culture in their allusions,
quotations and imitations, no such recognition can be found in the
work of their southern counterparts. Indeed the main impact of
Macpherson's *Ossian*, followed by the novels of Sir Walter Scott, was to
associate Highland culture with the past, or at least with what was
passing. And some of the heat generated over the authenticity of the
Ossian poems can be ascribed to a simple unwillingness to believe, on
the part of some Lowland Scots, that such work could ever have come
from a 'primitive' source.

Exemplifying an extreme case of ethnographic racism nearly thirty
years after the Ossian debate, the Scottish historian **John Pinkerton**
(1758–1826) was not entirely alone in his prejudices against Highland
culture. The two volumes of his book, *An Enquiry into the History of
Scotland Preceding the Reign of Malcolm III* (1789), went to elaborate
lengths to persuade his readers that the ancient Picts were really Goths
(admirable ancestors of the present Lowland Scots) and that they had
conquered the despicable Celts whose descendants could even now be
observed in the Highlands:

> The Lowlanders are acute, industrious, sensible, erect, free. The
> Highlanders stupid, indolent, foolish, fawning, slavish. The former in short

have every attribute of a civilised people. The latter are absolute savages: and, like Indians and Negroes, will ever continue so . . . . Had all these Celtic cattle emigrated five centuries ago, how happy had it been for the country! All we can do is to plant colonies among them; and by this, and encouraging their emigration, try to get rid of the breed.

Such was the ugly backlash to the vogue for Ossian. But while Pinkerton's references to 'Indians and Negroes' and the planting of colonies remind us that these were the years of a burgeoning British empire, we should not forget that his countryman, the philosopher James Beattie, was an early and committed opponent of slavery.

Robert Fergusson (1750–74)

If Mackenzie and his respectable Edinburgh friends had doubts about the 'classic' status of the Canongate, they were never shared by young Robert Fergusson, whose poems immortalised the vulgar intimacy of the streets in his native 'Auld Reekie'. Fergusson's parents came to Edinburgh from Aberdeenshire and 'The Farmer's Ingle' shows his familiarity with north-east Scots. As the fourth in a family of five, young Robert went to Edinburgh High School followed by a bursary to Dundee High School before going on to St Andrews University at the close of 1764, where he enjoyed a lively and irreverent under-graduate life despite poor health. While at university he wrote poems and two acts of a tragedy on Wallace which he then abandoned because he felt it was not original enough. Fergusson's sympathies were patriotically Scottish, even Jacobite, and his ambitions were set on a literary rather than an academic career. The sudden death of his father meant that he had to leave St Andrews in 1768 and find work to support the family. He ended up as a legal copying-clerk in the Commissary Office – a dull enough job, but one that kept him in Edinburgh and gave him some freedom to write for himself. He soon made friends in theatrical and musical circles by producing English words to Scots tunes, and these pieces were included in two operas performed at the Theatre Royal in 1769. In 1771 the *Weekly Magazine or Edinburgh Amusement* began to publish Fergusson's English poems, which were pastorals, mock-heroics and complaints in the prevailingly genteel Augustan manner. Fergusson continued to produce such verses for the rest of his life, but his energetic genius was only to be realised in Scots when 'The Daft Days' appeared in January 1772. This seasonal piece heralded an extraordinary two years during which Fergusson produced poem after poem in the *Weekly Magazine* – almost his entire output before he collapsed and died at the age of twenty-four. The magazine's owner, Walter Ruddiman, continued to promote his poet over the next twelve years by publishing no fewer than three editions of the collected works.

'The Daft Days' hailed the Scottish custom of celebrating the New Year with drinking and dancing. Other poems soon followed in the same vein – lamenting the decline of Scots music, laughing at the noise made by 'The Tron-kirk Bell', or praising the virtues of 'Caller Oysters' and 'Braid Claith'. All expressed in vigorous Scots and standard Habbie, these verses offered a vision of Edinburgh street life that had not been matched since Allan Ramsay or Dunbar. It was a world of lawyers, farmers, Highland porters, change-house keepers, magistrates, stall-owners, police, maids, whores, servants, men of fashion and the ubiquitous cadies (guides and errand boys), who were intimates to the whole town. The citizens were delighted to find themselves and their activities so hilariously and irreverently reflected:

On Sabbath-days the barber spark,	
Whan he has done wi' scrapin wark,	
Wi' siller broachie in his sark,	shirt
Gangs trigly, faith!	finely dressed
Or to the Meadow, or the Park,	
In gude Braid Claith.	

Weel might ye trow, to see them there,	believe
That they to shave your haffits bare,	cheeks
Or curl an' sleek a pickle hair,	
Wou'd be right laith,	reluctant
Whan pacing wi' a gawsy air	stately
In gude Braid Claith.	

. . .

Braid Claith lends fock an unco heese,	folk; considerable help
Makes mony kail-worms butterflies,	caterpillars
Gies mony a doctor his degrees	
For little skaith:	expense
In short, you may be what you please	
Wi' gude Braid Claith.	
('Braid Claith')	

Readers from Edinburgh, the Borders and Fife wrote letters to Ruddiman in praise of Fergusson's 'auld words' in a 'sonsy canty strain' and he became a well-known figure, greeted as the 'new Ramsay'. He joined the Cape Club, one of the wilder of the many drinking and debating clubs that were so popular at all levels of society. Fellow member David Herd must have encouraged his love of Scots songs, and Fergusson (unlike Burns) was known for his good voice. (Later members of the Cape included the painter Henry Raeburn and William Brodie, a respectable deacon by day and a robber by night, who was eventually hanged in 1788.) Fergusson became the very patron poet of Edinburgh tavern life:

> When big as burns the gutters rin,
> Gin ye hae catcht a droukit skin,   If; soaked
> To Luckie Middlemist's loup in,   Mistress/Goodwife; jump
>   And sit fu snug
> Oe'r oysters and a dram o' gin,
>   Or haddock lug.   ear

> When auld Sanct Giles, at aught o' clock,
> Gars merchant lowns their chopies lock,   Makes; blokes; shops
> There we adjourn wi' hearty fock   folk
>   To birle our bodles,   ring our copper coins
> And get wharewi' to crack our joke,
>   And clear our noddles.   heads
>
>   ('Caller Oysters')

No doubt the poet's rowdy pranks led him to fall foul of the City Guard, for he never misses an opportunity in his verses to satirise the 'black banditti' and their Highland accents.

Ruddiman published a collection of Fergusson's poems in 1773 and it sold moderately well, but polite literary taste had been otherwise engaged for the past fifty years and the established critics were slow to report on the work. 'Auld Reikie', which appeared separately the same year, was greeted with a similar silence, and perhaps this is why Fergusson never developed it beyond 'Canto I'. Then again, the young poet had parodied the melodrama of Henry Mackenzie's *The Prince of Tunis* by putting a highly rhetorical lament, full of 'sensibility', into the mouth of an English-speaking and neoclassically inclined pig. 'The Sow of Feeling', as he called it, would scarcely have endeared him to Mackenzie, and that influential literary figure could see little but 'coarse dissipation' in such a bohemian muse. In fact the poet's health was beginning to collapse under the pressures of late nights and heavy drinking, and his wild behaviour and unkempt appearance became ever more conspicuous. He gave up his job at the end of 1773 because of increasing physical illness and bouts of religious melancholia. It is possible that he was suffering from syphilis, and, although he made a brief recovery in the summer of 1774, a fall in which he struck his head broke his health completely and plunged him into morbid fears and virtual insanity. In the end he had to be taken from his mother's home and lodged in the Bedlam next to the Edinburgh poorhouse, where he died in a straw-littered cell in October 1774. He was buried in Canongate churchyard in an unmarked grave.

Fergusson's life was short and his poetic output relatively small, but he had considerable literary influence, not least on his successor, Robert Burns. The Ayrshire man's direct debt can be established in various specific poems, but his true inheritance comes from the integrated comic spirit of the younger writer, whose vigorous and racy tongue expressed a complete personality enlivened by an ironic eye for the pretensions of his fellow citizens. Fergusson's range is limited by the topics he chooses, but never by literary or class-conscious preconceptions, for he is not concerned with appearing genteel nor with making points about 'simple' life and pastimes. Thus Fergusson's 'dialogue' poems, such as 'Mutual Complaint of Plainstanes and Causey' and 'A Drink Eclogue', are used to make satirical reflections on the world in general, and, although the debates are personified, and the 'road' and the 'pavement', or 'brandy' and 'whisky' are revealed in speech as the broadest of Scottish characters, this alone is not Fergusson's subject. Poems such as 'Hallow Fair' and 'Leith Races' have a more local focus and they are certainly satirical and even downright impudent, but they are never condescending. In this vein Fergusson's masterpiece is 'Auld Reikie', a poem of over 300 lines in octosyllabic couplets in which he conjures up the institutions and the lively folk and the crowded, odiferous streets of his native city:

> Now some to Porter, some to Punch,
> Some to their Wife, and some their Wench,
> Retire, while noisy Ten-hours Drum
> Gars a' your Trades gae dandring Hame.   makes
> Now mony a Club, jocose and free,
> Gie a' to Merriment and Glee,
> Wi' Sang and Glass, they fley the Pow'r
> O' Care that wad harrass the Hour:
> For Wine and Bacchus still bear down
> Our thrawart Fortunes wildest Frown: obstinate
> It maks you stark, and bauld and brave,
> Ev'n whan descending to the Grave.

Fergusson's spirit is bold, ribald, cheerful or stark, but never in the least 'polite'. He lived the life he wrote about, even if 'Wine and Bacchus' did serve him sadly in that last descent.

Robert Burns (1759–96)

Thirteen years after Fergusson's death, Robert Burns commissioned a headstone in memory of a poet whom he generously acknowledged as his 'elder brother in misfortune, by far my elder brother in the muse'. At this time (February 1787) the twenty-eight-year-old Burns was newly famous after a winter season in Edinburgh literary society. The Kilmarnock edition of his poems had appeared the previous year and Henry Mackenzie in the *Lounger*, the blind poet Dr Blacklock, Hugh Blair, Professor Duguld Stewart and even 'plough boys and maid-servants' were all 'delighted, agitated, transported' by what the *Edinburgh Magazine* saw as 'a striking example of native genius burst-ing through the obscurity of poverty and the obstructions of laborious life'.

The critics underestimated Burns's education, but they were not wrong about his poverty at the time. Indeed, he had prepared the Kilmarnock collection under the most pressing need for money and, until the volume's success, had planned to emigrate to Jamaica. Things were not going well at home: he already had an illegitimate daughter by a servant girl and now his mistress Jean Armour was pregnant. Jean's father was determined that they should not marry (and she seems to have agreed with him at the time), because, with the death of his father in 1784, the poet was having to support his mother, three brothers and three sisters and his farm at Mossgiel was failing. Burns and Jean had made public repentance in church according to Kirk law and her father was seeking support for what turned out to be twins. To cap it all, in the aftermath of Jean's rejection Burns seems to have become involved with a young Highland woman called Mary Campbell, who features in some of his tenderest poems and songs but who died of a fever (perhaps in child birth) later in 1786. The details of the 'Highland Mary' affair remain conjectural, for Burns was under-standably reticent about a painful memory. Along with the other pres-sures upon him it may explain a letter written at the height of his literary fame in Edinburgh, in which he confessed to 'secret wretched-ness':

> The pang of disappointment, the sting of pride, with some wandering stabs of remorse, which never fail to settle on my vitals like vultures, when atten-tion is not called away by the calls of society or the vagaries of the Muse. Even in the hour of social mirth my gaiety is the madness of an intoxicated criminal under the hands of the executioner.

The 'heaven-taught ploughman' was a much more dynamic and complicated personality than Mackenzie's epithet implies, or than the *literati* realised in their eagerness to see Burns as the gifted offspring of Rousseau's savage and the Gentle Shepherd. Yet the time was right for Burns's success and there is no doubt that he was aware of his role as a 'rustic bard': after all, the Preface to his poems craved the reader's indulgence by assuming just such a persona. But literary and critical fashions cannot detract from his exciting debut, and the Kilmarnock edition and the 1787 Edinburgh edition that followed it reveal a young writer leaping straight to the height of his powers with astonishing assurance. Almost all of his most famous poems appeared in these collections (the exceptions are 'Holy Willie's Prayer', which was omitted; 'The Jolly Beggars', which Hugh Blair persuaded him to leave out; and 'Tam o' Shanter', which was yet to be written).

Burns's book revitalised the Scots language as a medium for verse – it had not been so potent since the days of Lindsay and Montgomerie – but at the same time its success virtually 'type-cast' poetry in Scots until modern times. His was the genius that crowned and concluded the domestic, 'Doric', vein to be found in the works of the Sempills, Hamilton, Ramsay and even in such a city poet as Fergusson. For the next hundred years and more, 'poetry in Scots' meant 'poetry like Burns's', and as late as the 1920s Hugh MacDiarmid could curse the influence of a writer whose brilliance set the mould for so many inferior imitations. These later imitators and interpreters preferred not to confront the physical and economic hardships that Burns and his class were expected to endure, nor his resentment of a social and political system that favoured inherited position or propertied landowners at every turn. Instead, subsequent generations have preferred either to sentimentalise the 'ploughman poet', or to moralise about his reputation as a supposed drinker and libertine. These contradictory and inaccurate stereotypes have survived in the popular appreciation of Burns almost to the present day.

Burns's background was genuinely close to the spirit of 'Christis Kirk on the Green', and in this sense his convivial muse belongs to the world of small farms and market towns with their local gossip and a tradition of occasional verse. On the other hand, he had also read the makars, and his vernacular approaches a standard literary Lowland Scots – he called it 'Lallans' – for he used Scots words from dialects other than his own. In 'The Vision' Burns uses an eloquent Scots, well worthy of the makars, to set the scene and to talk of his own sombre feelings. But when his muse appears as an idealised woman, it is, significantly,

English that both she and her bard adopt as the most appropriate language in which to discuss 'the dignity of Man'. Like most educated men of his day, Burns was inclined to abandon his mother tongue when he sought what he took to be a sophisticated or 'literary' voice.

Robert Burns was born the first of seven children on 25 January 1759 at Alloway in Ayrshire. His father, William Burns or Burnes, married Agnes Brown, a local woman, after coming south from Kincardineshire in search of work. But the land at Mount Oliphant farm was unproductive and at forty-four Burns senior found himself bound to a life of lonely toil until his health was damaged by the effort. By the age of fifteen Robert too was labouring in the fields, and despite his natural sturdiness he contracted a rheumatic heart-condition that was eventually to kill him. Even in hardship, Burns senior wanted a good education for his two eldest boys and so he and four of his neighbours arranged for a young tutor called Murdoch to teach their children. These arrangements were known as 'adventure schools' and meant that in areas where parish schooling was not practicable most of Scotland's rural population could still read and write. Thus Robert was introduced to English literature in selections from Shakespeare, Milton, Dryden, Addison, Thomson, Gray and Shenstone.

During the summers when he could be spared from the farm, Burns was sent away to continue his studies, and at Kirkoswald near the coast he met Douglas Graham of Shanter farm, said to be a model for Tam o' Shanter, and 'Soutar Johnnie', who was the local cobbler. He made a start at Latin, trigonometry and French, and took pride in the letters that he sent home. His commonplace book records his early rhymes and the first stirrings of what was to be a lifetime's infatuation with the female sex. The lease at Mount Oliphant expired when Burns was eighteen, and the family moved some ten miles to Lochlie farm in the parish of Tarbolton. Here Robert befriended the apothecary John Wilson, an innocent model for the fatal 'Dr Hornbook', as well as John Rankine and 'brother poet' David Sillar, who were to feature in his later epistle poems. In the company of such lively young men Burns became first president of the 'Bachelor's Club' – a debating society dedicated to the fair sex and 'honest-hearted' male friendship. The farm was failing, however. William Burns's goods were impounded to pay for back rent, and only his death in 1784 saved him from being arrested for debt. It is not difficult to explain the poet's lifelong hatred of land-lords and the kind of factor who 'thinks to knit himsel the faster / In favour wi' some gentle Master' by seeing that 'decent, honest, fawsont [seemly] folk, / Are riven out baith root an' branch, / Some rascal's pridefu' greed to quench' ('The Twa Dogs'). Robert and his brother Gilbert leased a farm less than three miles away at Mossgiel and they took the rest of the family there in 1784. This time their landlord, Gavin Hamilton, proved to be a good friend and Burns dedicated the Kilmarnock edition to him.

Now in his early twenties, Robert was set on a literary career. By this time he had read and admired *The Man of Feeling*, as well as Thomson, Sterne, Macpherson's *Ossian* and Thomas Reid, Adam Smith, Hume and Locke. Moreover, he had discovered an enthusiasm for old Scots songs and for the works of Ramsay and Fergusson. It was the latter's 'Scotch poems' in particular that encouraged him to persevere with his own verse and to 'string anew', as he put it later, his 'wildly-sounding, rustic lyre, with emulating vigour'. Accordingly, the next two years were extraordinarily full as Burns produced poem after poem and made several songs to traditional airs. No doubt the setting of words to old tunes (as well as his delight in dancing) helped to develop an early facility with strong rhythms and internal rhymes, for Burns's verse is characterised by such qualities, and the onward, reel-like thrusting of standard Habbie became such a favourite of his that it is also now known as 'the Burns stanza'. The poet's energies were more than fully engaged, for he committed himself to farming and flouted his shaky health by adopting an equally hectic social life. With his talent for friendship he was not slow in becoming well known and liked in the nearby village of Mauchline, where his landlord Gavin Hamilton worked as a lawyer and where he met Jean Armour and began an affair with her. Mauchline people went straight into his poems, and, when Hamilton's free behaviour was reprimanded by the local Kirk, Burns took his side and claimed that he would rather be damned in his friend's company than saved among such 'canting wretches'. One of the 'wretches' was an elder called William Fisher, whose vindictive hypocrisy is immortalised in 'Holy Willie's Prayer'. When Hamilton came before the Presbytery at Ayr it was 'glib tongued' Robert Aiken who demolished Holy Willie's case, and this distinguished senior lawyer became the poet's close friend and something of a patron in influential circles. (Burns dedicated 'The Cottar's Saturday Night' to him.) Burns himself appeared before the church session on more than one occasion, charged with fornication and taken to task for his affair with Jean Armour who was now pregnant and in hiding with relatives.

In this most creative period the poet's emotional life was seriously complicated: he had started an affair with Margaret Campbell, later presumed to be 'Highland Mary'; he was being sued for damages by

Jean Armour's father; Mossgiel was not flourishing, his family depended on him, and he needed money badly. One solution would be emigration to Jamaica to escape 'the holy beagles' now hot on his scent, but he could not quite make the final commitment and when Jean gave birth to twins his feelings about departure were even more mixed. In the meantime Hamilton, Aiken and others had helped to collect subscriptions for a volume called *Poems, Chiefly in the Scottish Dialect*, 612 copies of which were printed at Kilmarnock in July 1786. The immediate success of this book catapulted Burns into fame and gave him funds at last to help support Gilbert and the family. That winter Burns went to meet his reputation in Edinburgh, where plans were immediately made for an expanded 'Edinburgh' edition, which appeared in April 1787. This volume contained extra poems, including more work in English, but if his Augustan verses pleased his new literary friends, they seem merely imitative and conventional today. The most significant additions are poems such as 'The Ordination', 'The Calf' and the 'Address to the Unco Guid', which give openly satirical accounts of the Kirk and its doings. More personal attacks such as 'The Holy Tulzie' or 'The Twa Herds' were left in manuscript circulation only, and, indeed, 'Holy Willie's Prayer' did not see print until 1801.

In Burns's time it was not possible in a small community (as he and Gavin Hamilton both discovered) to ignore the Church's mandates on everyday social behaviour. Yet the Kirk was divided on several doctrinal matters, including lay patronage. The 'Moderates' were in favour of tolerating other creeds and of accepting the current law that allowed the local landowner to propose a minister for the parish. However, the minority 'Popular party', or 'Evangelicals', took a harder line and were becoming more influential in country districts. Some seceded to form a separate presbytery, and before long the seceders split and split again, reviving all the fanaticism of the old Covenanters. The history of these changing alliances, of Burghers and anti-Burghers, 'Auld Lichts' and 'New Lichts', serves to demonstrate once again the Scottish preference for theoretical or organisational disputes over what should be spiritual issues. Burns and his friends in Edinburgh regarded themselves as liberal Christians, and scoffed at the 'three mile prayers and hauf-mile graces' of the extreme faction; yet they still had to accept the Kirk's authority in a society where elders could act like moral policemen with the right of access to people's houses to ensure that the Sabbath was being kept. As a fallible lover of women, Burns had little sympathy with the 'unco guid', nor was he slow to draw attention to their hypocrisies and excesses. Thus 'The Holy Fair' satirises the annual Communion at Mauchline, a custom common in rural parishes where, in what usually became a tent show and a rowdy picnic, hundreds from different churches in the region gathered once a year in the open air to hear the preaching, to drink ale and see the sights, and – officially – to prepare for Communion:

> Here, some are thinking on their sins,
> An' some upo' their claes;   clothes
> Ane curses feet that fyled his shins,
> Anither sighs an' prays:
> On this hand sits a Chosen swatch,   sample
> Wi' screw'd up grace-proud faces;
> On that, a set o' chaps, at watch,
> Thrang winkan on the lasses   busy
>   To chairs that day.

This easy, loping verse was borrowed from Fergusson, who cast a similarly genial eye on public holidays in 'Hallow-Fair' and 'Leith Races'. The Bruegelian spirit goes back to 'Christis Kirk' and 'Peblis to the Play', but Burns's more modern eye is quicker to note the contradictions of the scene and to use the antitheses towards a wider and wittier satirical end:

> How monie hearts this day converts,
> O' Sinners and o' Lasses!
> Their hearts o' stane, gin nicht are gane   at nightfall
> As saft as ony flesh is.
> There's some are fou o' love divine;   full
> There's some are fou o' brandy;   drunk
> An' mony jobs that day begin,
> May end in Houghmagandie   fornication
>   Some ither day.

The barbed subtlety of Burns's educated punning can be more fully appreciated if the original passage from Ezekiel 36:26 is recalled: 'A new heart also will I give you, and a new spirit will I put within you: and I will take away the stony heart out of your flesh, and I will give you an heart of flesh.' And yet at the heart of the poem there is another understanding of the nature of 'communion' –the social communion of young people's courting, of meeting friends, making new friends and sharing food and drink in an entirely secular way that may in the end be no less 'holy' in the poet's eyes – or indeed more genuinely so – than the stormy sermons on damnation from the Auld Lichts.

Burns's knowledge of the Bible and his familiarity with the language of God's Presbyterian spokesmen makes 'Holy Willie's Prayer' particularly potent. Here the high-flown diction of Evangelical fervour bumps and tangles with standard Habbie and parochial Scots to lay bare the unctuous vindictiveness of the speaker:

> Lord, mind Gau'n Hamilton's deserts!
> He drinks, an' swears, an' plays at cartes,	cards
> Yet has sae mony taking arts
>   Wi' great and sma',
> Frae God's ain Priest the people's hearts
>   He steals awa.

> And when we chasten'd him therefore,
> Thou kens how he bred sic a splore,	controversy
> And set the warld in a roar
>   O' laughin at us:
> Curse Thou his basket and his store,
> Kail an' potatoes!	Cabbage

The poet dons the flesh of his enemy to explode him from within, and Willie's rolling syntax falters only when he has to confess his own failings, even if his complacency remains unmoved:

> But yet – O Lord – confess I must –
> At times I'm fashed wi' fleshly lust;	troubled
> And sometimes too, in warldly trust
>   Vile Self gets in;
> But Thou remembers we are dust,
>   Defil'd wi' sin. –

> O Lord – yestreen – Thou kens – wi' Meg –
> Thy, pardon I sincerely beg!
> O may't ne'er be a living plague,
>   To my dishonour!
> And I'll ne'er lift a lawless leg
>   Again upon her. –

> Besides, I further maun avow	must
> Wi' Leezie's lass, three times – I trow –
> But Lord, that friday I was fou	drunk
>   When I cam near her!

The characterisation is repulsively convincing, but Burns's satire begins with a wider attack on the whole system of extreme Calvinist belief which allows such a self-styled elect to set themselves apart from the majority of folk, who will be damned no matter how they behave:

O Thou that in the Heavens does dwell,
Wha, as it pleases best Thysel,
Sends ane to Heaven an' ten to Hell
  A' for Thy glory,
And no for ony guid or ill
  They've done before Thee!

I bless and praise Thy matchless might,
When thousands Thou hast left in night,
That I am here before Thy sight,
  For gifts an' grace
A burning and a shining light
  To a' this place.

Burns satirised the Auld Lichts again in 'The Ordination', and in a letter of 1788 expressed his opposition to the Calvinist doctrine that we are born 'wholly inclined' to evil. He believed instead that we come into the world 'with a heart and a disposition to do good for it', and this conviction explains his affinity with Rousseau's ideals, the Enlightenment teachings of Hutcheson and Adam Smith on 'sympathy' and his lifelong preference for 'the social, friendly, honest man / Whate'er he be' ('Second Epistle to J. Lapraik').

On a broader note, Burns enjoyed hearty companionship, like Fergusson before him, and in Edinburgh he joined a social and drinking club called the 'Crochallan Fencibles'. He goes further than his 'elder brother', however, by celebrating a Blakean faith in energy as eternal delight. The fullest expression of this anarchic, disreputable but always gloriously alive spirit comes in 'Love and Liberty – A Cantata', more familiarly known as 'The Jolly Beggars'. This sequence of poems and songs seems to have been a little too potent for his intellectual friends in Edinburgh, and Hugh Blair persuaded him to leave it out of the 1787 collection. Like 'Holy Willie's Prayer', the piece was never published in Burns's lifetime, and in fact the version that has survived may be incomplete. As so often in his work, Burns owed the initial conception to an already-established genre, for a song-sequence called 'The Happy Beggars' was featured in the *Tea Table Miscellany* and John Gay had drawn on the romance of thieves and vagabonds with his *Beggar's Opera* in 1728. Burns went further to produce an anti-pastoral (the very reverse of *The Gentle Shepherd*) that Matthew Arnold later hailed as a world of 'hideousness and squalor' and yet a 'superb poetic success' with a 'breadth, truth and power . . . only matched by Shakespeare and Aristophanes'.

Arnold's analogy with drama is appropriate, because Burns enters into the lives and voices of others as he describes a wild autumn night of merriment and song amongst a gang of wandering beggars and their doxies in Poosie Nansie's tavern. The effect of the whole is greater than any one section, for the 'Cantata' alternates between narrative passages to set the scene, and songs in which the various characters lay bare their lives and loves in a variety of stanza forms and traditional airs. The poem's diction keeps changing, too, as Burns swings from rich Scots to a cooler English and back again, so that the juxtapositions heighten the effectiveness and expand the field of his satire. The beggars, raddled, drunk, noisy and boastful, dance and fight and sing in a greasy dive; yet their antics also cast wild and telling shadows which ape the wider world outside – the world of social pretension and sexual gallantry, of political expediency, business-affairs and wars. An old soldier and his lover pledge themselves to drink and fornication, and their songs tell how he has lost an arm and a leg, while she has been through the regiment from drummer boy to chaplain; a tiny fiddler and a tinker fight over a raw-boned widow who earns her living as a pickpocket – the caird wins but the musician soon consoles himself with another lady:

The Caird prevail'd – th'unblushing fair	tinker
In his embraces sunk;	
Partly wi' LOVE o'ercame sae sair,	
An' partly she was drunk:	
Sir VIOLINO with an air,	
That show'd a man o' spunk,	spirit
Wish'd UNISON between the PAIR,	
An' made the bottle clunk	
To their health that night.	
But hurchin Cupid shot a shaft,	
That play'd a DAME a shavie -	trick
The Fiddler RAK'D her, FORE and AFT,	
Behint the Chicken cavie.	coop

Burns's diction switches contexts with a speed and irreverence that anticipates Byron's *Don Juan*. A positively Augustan epithet such as 'th'unblushing fair' is matched with abstractions such as 'LOVE' and 'UNISON' and other elements from Cupid's vocabulary. These phrases are almost serviceable, if slightly shop-soiled (entirely appropriate to the would-be sophistication of 'Sir VIOLINO'), but Burns dynamites them and all their romantic conventions with the brutality of an ugly rhyme ('drunk' / 'spunk' / 'clunk') and the outrageousness of the shaft and the shavie played out behind a hen house. These sudden heteroglossic shifts, back and fore, between English and Scots were to become one of the main features of literary Scots from now on, always evoking the mobility of the speaking voice and providing a uniquely fluid satirical and emotional resource.

The little fiddler's amour is one of three ladies in tow with a 'bard of no regard', and it is this night-town version of Burns himself who sings a closing song which shakes the rafters of Poosie Nansie's and strikes at the foundations of society's respect for property, religion and order itself. It is one of the ironies of Burns's reputation that the radical force of what his persona says in these lines has so often been overshadowed by the popular misrepresentation of the poet himself as a mere drinker and reveller.

> Here's to Budgets, Bags and Wallets!
> Here's to all the wandering train!
> Here's our ragged Brats and Callets!   children and wenches
> One and all cry out, Amen!

CHORUS
A fig for those by Law protected,
*   Liberty's a glorious feast!*
Courts for cowards were erected,
*   Churches built to please the Priest.*

The political implications of these lines are reinforced because the song and chorus are written almost entirely in English – as if the poet means to generalise.

Burns's sympathies are not just fashionably radical; they are fundamental to his background, to his optimistic and humanitarian nature and to that sense of dour pride and self-respect so important to his class. This attitude appears repeatedly in those letters and poems where he protests his independence and the honesty of his feelings with a telling and even excessive emphasis. 'The Twa Dogs' comments pointedly on the superficiality of rank in human society and the early 'Epistle to Davie' predicts another kind of democracy by insisting on the primacy of the heart and its affections.

> It's no in titles nor in rank;
> It's no in wealth like Lon'on Bank,
>   To purchase peace and rest;
> It's no in makin muckle, mair: much, more
> It's no in books; it's no in lear,   learning
>   To make us truly blest:
> If Happiness hae not her seat
>   And centre in the breast,
> We may be wise, or rich, or great,
>   But never can be blest.

The terms may be hedonistic but the spirit of these lines is not far removed from that of Presbyterian dissent (substitute 'Grace' for 'Happiness' in the seventh line); and Burns is certainly speaking from a tradition of sturdy independence within his own milieu of crofters, tenant farmers and 'bonnet lairds'. The same dignity is at the heart of the world-famous song, 'Is there for honest poverty' ('A Man's a Man for A' That'):

> What though on hamely fare we dine,
>   Wear hodden grey, and a' that.
> Gie fools their silks, and knaves their wine,
>   A Man's a Man for a' that.
> For a' that, and a' that,
>   Their tinsel show an' a' that;
> The honest man, though e'er sae poor,
>   Is king o' men for a' that.
>
> Ye see yon birkie ca'd a lord,
>   Wha struts, and stares, and a' that,
> Though hundreds worship at his word,
>   He's but a coof for a' that:
> For a' that, and a' that,
>   His riband star and a' that;
> The man of independent mind
>   He looks and laughs at a' that.

It is not far to seek the source of Burns's sympathies with the American War of Independence and, later, with the early stages of the French Revolution. In his 'Ode for General Washington's Birthday' (1794), he deplored Britain's reactionary part in opposing 'Liberty's bold note' in both America and France, nor was he afraid to make specific political attacks against injustice nearer to home. In the excoriating lines of his 'Address of Beelzebub', he imagines the devil praising the Earl of Breadalbane and the Highland Society (of landlords) who had met in London to seek ways of stopping tenants in Applecross and Skye from emigrating to Canada 'in search of that fantastic thing – LIBERTY'. An indignant Beelzebub asks 'what right hae they / To meat, or sleep, or light o' day, / Far less to riches, pow'r, or freedom, / But what your lordships please to gie them?' and he advises the landlords to throw the would-be emigrants into prison:

> An' if the wives, an' dirty brats,
> Come thiggan at your doors an' yets,   begging; gates
> Flaffan wi' duds, an grey wi' beese,   flapping; rags; vermin
> Frightan awa your deucks an' geese;
> Get out a Horse-Whip, or a Jowler,   bull-dog

The langest thong, the fiercest growler,
An' gar the tatter'd gypseys pack
Wi' a' their bastarts on their back!

It is worth noting that although this poem refers to events of 1786, the poem did not see print until 1818, twenty-two years after Burns's death. Even so, the popular success of Burns's less overtly radical work, with its many expressions of universal brotherhood, still speaks volumes for the changes in outlook, both political and personal, which followed the Scottish Enlightenment and which also prefigure the rise of Romanticism in literature. Scottish Presbyterianism, too, had emphasised the prime obligation on individuals to interpret scripture and authority in the light of their own reason and their own good conscience. Burns was fully aware of the work of Thomas Reid and Adam Smith, and indeed he had read and admired *The Theory of Moral Sentiments* in 1785 and *The Wealth of Nations* in 1789. In basing their discussions of morality and ethical behaviour on the sentiments and interests of the ordinary person, these 'common sense' philosophers had endorsed a concern with common humanity as the proper moral yardstick for our thoughts and actions. Burns was not slow to see the democratic implications of this, and its ironic side, too:

Smith, wi' his sympathetic feeling,
An Reid, to common sense appealing.
Philosophers have fought and wrangled,
An meikle Greek and Latin mangled,
Till, wi' their logic-jargon tir'd
As in the depth of science mir'd,
To common sense they now appeal –
What wives and wabsters see and feel!   weavers
          ('Epistle to James Tennant of Glenconner')

The actual language of 'wives and wabsters' was still an issue, however, in some educated circles where Scots was seen as irredeemably vulgar. As Hogg and Noble have pointed out, the attitude of Burns's friend and early biographer Dr James Currie, who himself aspired to radical principles, was typical of this mindset. As he makes something of a special plea for Burns's use of Scots, he still cannot help observing that:

all the polite and ambitious are now endeavouring to banish [it] from their tongues as well as their writings. The use of it in composition naturally therefore calls up ideas of vulgarity to the mind. These singularities are increased by the character of the poet, who delights to express himself with a simplicity that approaches to nakedness, and with an unmeasured energy that often alarms delicacy, and sometimes offends taste. Hence in approaching him, the first impression is perhaps repulsive: there is an air of coarseness about him which is with difficulty reconciled with our established notions of poetical excellence.

Currie's biographical account of Burns's life laid great emphasis on his drinking (the good doctor was ever keen to preach the dangers of alcoholism) and this analysis created a long-standing and mistaken notion that the poet was a drunkard in later days. Gilbert Burns, Wordsworth and Hazlitt all tried to put the record straight, but conservative critics such as Francis Jeffrey of the *Edinburgh Review*, John Wilson ('Christopher North') of *Blackwoods*, and even Sir Walter Scott, all supported the line, to a greater or lesser degree, that the poet's 'vehement sensibility' was at one with his class, his radicalism and his weakness for alcohol. This dispute lasted well into the ninteenth century and still colours many people's understanding of the poet.

Burns, like many other liberal and democratic spirits in Britain, had been excited by the republican principles of the American Revolution in 1766 and then in the early 1790s, by the stirrings of political change in France. Exercising his right as an Excise Officer, he bought four carronades from a smugglers' brigantine captured off the coast of Dumfries, and arranged for the guns to be transported to France at his own cost. Liberal support for the French cause was not uncommon at the time, for diplomatic negotiations were still in hand and the two countries were not yet at war. Nevertheless, Burns's gift was intercepted by the Customs at Dover and confiscated. By 1793, however, the execution of Louis XVI made libertarian ideals increasingly dangerous at home and, like Wordsworth, Coleridge and Mary Wollstonecraft, all of whom shared his sympathies in England, Burns had to be more circumspect at a time when government informers were on the look-out for sedition. It seems certain that he contributed verses to the radical press under a pseudonym but his authorship of poems such as 'The Tree of Liberty' is still debated. ('It stands where ance the Bastile stood. / A prison built by kings, man, / When Superstition's hellish brood / Kept France in leading-strings, man.') By 1795, the Reign of Terror and the threat of invasion put revolution in a different light and Burns, like many others, became disillusioned with the French experiment. He helped to organise the Dumfries volunteers and even wrote a song for them which rather uneasily combines his hatred for authoritarian rule, whatever its origins, with British patriotism:

The wretch that would a Tyrant own,
  And the wretch, his true-sworn brother,
Who'd set the mob above the Throne,
  May they be damned together.

As far as his celebrity in Edinburgh was concerned, the poet
remained the 'man of independent mind' who refused to have his head
turned by the admiring salons. He took pleasure in meeting and corresponding with influential friends but he foresaw the day when he would
return to his 'rural shades', recognising that at least part of his fame
came from what he called the 'novelty of his character' among learned
and polite people. As 'To a Louse' and 'The Twa Dogs' testify, Burns
was too sensitively aware of social pretentiousness and class differences
to be blind to these currents at work in the tide of his own reputation:

O wad some Pow'r the giftie gie us
To see oursels as ithers see us!
It wad frae mony a blunder free us
  An foolish notion.

                    ('To a Louse')

In 'The Twa Dogs' the poet's sympathies are openly with the labouring classes, and although he does not underestimate their hardships he
allows them the satisfaction of stout hearts and simple pleasures and
feels, too, that it is their toil which supports the restless hypochondria
and the corrupt activities of their idle masters. Neither Luath, the poor
man's collie, nor Caesar, the rich man's Newfoundland, has a complete
picture of the human world, but it is not long before one emerges from
their conversation. Caesar gives a hilarious version of the propertied
classes at play abroad; but Burns has not forgotten how his father died
trying to pay rent and feed his family.

At Opera an' Plays parading,
Mortgaging, gambling, masquerading:
Or maybe in a frolic daft,
To Hague or Calais takes a waft,
To make a tour an' take a whirl,
To learn *bon ton* an' see the worl'.

  There, at Vienna or Versailles,
He rives his father's auld entails;   grabs/robs; mortgages
Or by Madrid he takes the rout,
To thrum guittares an fecht wi' nowt;   cattle (bullfights)
Or down Italian Vista startles,
Whore-hunting amang groves o' myrtles:

Then bowses drumlie German-water,   drinks muddy
To make himsel look fair an' fatter,
An' clear the consequential sorrows,
Love-gifts of Carnival Signioras.

The poet's gaiety never curdles and yet at times its ferocious intensity
hints at the pain of injustice and the pressures and resentments felt by
the labouring poor.

I've notic'd, on our laird's court-day,
An' mony a time my heart's been wae,   sorrowful
Poor tenant bodies, scant o' cash,
How they maun thole a factor's snash;   must tolerate; abuse
He'll stamp an' threaten, curse an' swear
He'll apprehend them, poind their gear;   impound; belongings
While they maun stan', wi' aspect humble,
An' hear it a', an' fear and tremble!

The coarser pleasures of Poosie Nansie's and the groaning excesses
of Evangelical fervour both bear witness to how these pressures were
so often sublimated in small Scottish communities. There are hints of
a similar strain behind the male vaunting with which Burns so often
declares his passion for the 'lasses'. Thus in 'Epistle to James Smith'
the poet makes a fine allegiance with the 'hare-brained sentimental'
'ramstam boys' and scoffs at 'douse [prudent] folk that live by
rule, / Grave, tideless-blooded, calm and cool', whose hearts 'are
just a standing pool'. Here the always potentially transgressive drive
of creativity itself is specifically associated with good company, sex
and drink and by implication, perhaps, with radical politics. (Blake
was never in any doubt about these links.) Having said that, it is less
easy, perhaps, for contemporary readers to admire the 'Epistle to
John Rankine', a favourite poem of his, in which he tells how he was
fined for 'poaching' Elizabeth Paton like a partridge, leaving her
pregnant because 'ae night lately, in my fun, / I gaed a rovin wi' the
gun':

The poor wee thing was little hurt;
I straiket it a wee for sport,
Ne'er thinkan they wad fash me for't . . .   bother

As soon's the clockin-time is by,   hatching
An' the wee pouts begun to cry,   young partridges
Lord, I'se hae sportin by an by,
    For my gowd guinea . . .

In contrast to his coarser moments, which were deplored, Burns's taste for sentiment was predictably more popular in Henry Mackenzie's sophisticated circle. 'The Cottar's Saturday Night' was praised by contemporaries for giving Augustan dignity and 'the true flavour of natural tenderness' to rustic life; but modern readers may find the poem slightly condescending and prone to moralise, as well as marked by a sometimes uneasy mixture of broad Scots and formal English eulogy. Burns wanted to depict the virtues of artless, common folk and to this end his descriptive passages are more successful than has sometimes been allowed, but the barer, sterner language of Wordsworth's 'Michael' (1800) succumbs less to the sentimental side of the cult of feeling and makes a better job of the same subject. The Scot achieved an even-toned and successful combination of natural tenderness and moral reflection with 'To a Mouse'; but the very similar 'To a Mountain Daisy' contains a hint of self-pity, easy sentiment and that use of the Scots diminutive that was to multiply like frogspawn in so many luckless imitations. Nevertheless, the poem was highly regarded, not least by Mackenzie and the poet himself. A more robust comic talent finds expression in 'To a Haggis' and especially in 'Address to the Deil', where Milton's fallen archangel has to endure Burns's cheery familiarity and sceptical good wishes. Satan seems to have been something of a crony of Scottish poets since at least Dunbar's time, and Calvinist hell-fire has obviously done nothing to curb their presumptions:

An' now, auld Cloots, I ken ye're thinkan,	
A certain Bardie's rantin, drinkin,	
Some luckless hour will send him linkan,	tripping along
To your black pit;	
But faith! he'll turn a corner jinkan,	dodging
An' cheat you yet.	

The same irreverent spirit is directed at Death in 'Death and Dr Hornbook' and finds its high point in 'Tam o'Shanter', written three years later.

Burns's life was unsettled after the triumph of his first winter in Edinburgh. He left two lovers behind him and returned to Mauchline a hero; there was a reconciliation with the Armours and Jean became pregnant again, although he still did not want to marry her (he was nursing an affection for Peggy Chalmers, another new friend in Edinburgh, but she married someone else the next year). The 'Edinburgh edition' appeared in April 1787 and thereafter Burns took various tours through Scotland, being awarded the freedom of Dumfries and visiting relatives in the north-east. Creech, his Edinburgh publisher, was always slow in paying royalties, but the prospects were good and the poet arranged for half the profits to go to Gilbert and the family. Still, he was not sure how he should live and that winter saw him back in the city again. His arrival was not the social sensation it had been in 1786. He found himself involved with the beautiful Nancy M'Lehose, a married lady separated from her husband, and they conducted an impassioned and sentimentally spiritual affair, mostly through their many letters to each other as 'Sylvander and Clarinda'. Burns's literary commitment was now entirely given to songs, for he had begun to help James Johnson with *The Scots Musical Museum*, which appeared in six volumes from 1787 to 1803. Burns became the literary editor of three of these books, although he refused payment for the work, collecting and altering old songs and writing completely new ones to old airs and fiddle-tunes. He was very enthusiastic about the task and before his death he had created over 200 songs of his own, best appreciated when set to their fine and soaring melodies.

Leaving Edinburgh in the spring of 1788, Burns returned once more to Mauchline. Jean had borne him twins for the second time but the two little girls died within weeks. The poet arranged to lease a new farm at Ellisland and finally married the woman who had endured more from him, and for him, than ever Clarinda had. But it was never to be a marriage of minds and he had other affairs, including one with Anne Park, who bore him a child. Jean produced a second and then a third son and Burns was given a post at last with the Excise. He did well in the service and worked hard at his tasks, but the long miles he had to ride did not help his health.

Burns's last literary poem was 'Tam o'Shanter', written in the winter of 1790. It is a brilliant and coruscating summation of all the vigour, local comedy, satirical irreverence and the driving technical virtuosity that he had inherited from the tradition and made even more his own. The poem incorporates the mock heroic, the gothic, the bawdy and the tender; it relishes a local ghost story well told and presents a 'proper' eighteenth-century moral conclusion with a poker face; it focuses on domestic rural life with convincing realism, only to leap to the grotesquerie of a hallucinatory encounter with diabolism and most especially with unfettered sexuality. 'Tam o'Shanter' is a unique poem in European culture, for it straddles literary and cultural gulfs by combining an earthy peasant *joie de vivre* with an Enlightenment sense of irony, both of which then have to confront the more rarefied possibility of individual imaginative transport: in it 'The Miller's Tale', Smollett and the world of 'Kubla Khan' come together in a wholly unexpected amalgam.

When Ellisland eventually failed at the end of 1791 (not through lack of effort on Burns's part) the poet fell back on his Excise appointment and moved to Dumfries with his family, being appointed as acting supervisor for Dumfries in 1794. Jean gave him a daughter and he brought Anne Park's little girl into the household as his own. Here, despite uncertain health and official suspicion about his radical views, he found the energy to continue his commitment to old songs and song writing. The popular appetite for songs, whetted by Ramsay's *Tea Table Miscellany*, had been fed by many writers. Among the best known were two men from Aberdeenshire, Alexander Ross (1699–1784), a schoolmaster who produced lively pieces such as 'The Rock and the Wee Pickle Tow' and 'Woo'd and Married an' A''; and John Skinner (1721–1807), an Episcopalian minister whose racy, reeling 'Tullochgorum' was held by Burns to be 'the best Scotch song ever Scotland saw'. Burns's own editorial work for *The Scots Musical Museum* was not unscholarly, but David Herd (1732–1810) was more exacting and published fragments without embellishment. Herd's *Ancient and Modern Scots Songs* (1769; 1776) includes some of the first printings of the old ballads, and, although Burns had copies of the book, the ballads rarely influenced him in his own songs, which concentrate on tender love lyrics, drinking-verses such as 'O Willie Brew'd a Peck o' Maut', and sturdy airs such as 'Scots Wha Hae', 'Is there for honest poverty' and (refined from several originals) 'Auld Lang Syne'.

The love songs and their beautiful tunes are particularly memorable. 'The Lea Rig' and 'Corn Rigs are Bonie' celebrate the bitter-sweetness of first assignations and the joys of sexual meeting, while 'Mary Morison', 'Ae Fond Kiss' and 'Highland Mary' are songs of parting and death suffused with the poet's sense of mortality. These intimations of inevitable ending invade love lyrics such as 'A Red, Red Rose' and 'O wert thou in the cauld blast', while others (such as 'Whistle O'er the Lave o't') take a bolder, gayer note, and an old and bawdy complaint about fading potency was rewritten as an expression of simple companionship between ageing lovers – 'John Anderson my Jo'. Even with optimistic words, the plangent tunes chosen by Burns give the force of a lament to songs such as 'The Young Highland Rover' and 'Where braving angry winter's storms'. The latter was set to a fiddle tune by Neil Gow and so, like several of Burns's airs, it provides the singer with a fairly severe challenge to his or her vocal range. Later writers, such as Scott and Stevenson, felt that Burns's songs were a lesser achievement than his early poems, but modern critics have come to emphasise the high level of their musical success. Indeed, his best Scots poems were never far removed from the rhythms of popular dancing and the traditions of sentiment and humour in song.

By 1793 Creech's second 'Edinburgh' edition – with some additional poems – was published, and on top of his contributions to the *Musical Museum* Burns was also sending songs to George Thomson's *Select Scottish Airs*. Thomson's tastes were more 'refined' than Johnson's. Unlike Johnson's, his volumes were large and expensively produced and he favoured anglicising the texts to more metrically regular and complex musical settings, while Burns preferred to stay closer to folk tradition with its direct and simple utterance. The correspondence between them tells us much about how Burns saw his art and his preference for a 'wild-warbling cadence' over a more 'tamely methodical' style. (The poet's private collection of Rabelaisian verses, later known as *The Merry Muses of Caledonia*, was undoubtedly sung and circulated among the Crochallan Fencibles, but never intended for publication.) Burns kept up his editorial tasks until a few weeks before his death at the age of only thirty-seven. He was worn out, weakened by poor health, an already fragile heart, and quite possibly the well-meant administrations of his doctor. He could not have foretold the international fame that was to come, nor the ambiguous influence which his work was to have on Scottish life and culture for the next hundred years.

Burns's affinity with the age's taste for honest sentiment is seen at its clearest in his songs but he was by no means the only writer to work in the genre. As a popular art form such work, and especially the work of songsmiths other than Burns, tended to be closer to pastoral conventions in its moods and expression than it was to the oral traditions of the folk tale and the ballads. Lady Grizel Baillie pointed the way at the beginning of the century when her sentimental piece 'Werena my heart licht I wad die' appeared in Ramsay's *Tea Table Miscellany*. She was followed by other educated women who wrote and adapted material to their view of humble life. These include Jean Elliott (1727–1805) and 'The Flowers o' the Forest' most probably reworked from a now lost original; Lady Anne Lindsay (1750–1826), 'Auld Robin Gray'; John Hamilton (1761–1814), 'Up in the Mornin' Early'; Joanna Baillie (1762–1851), 'Tam o' the Lin'. From early in the next century Lady Nairne's 'The Land o' the Leal', 'Caller Herrin'' and 'Will Ye No' Come Back Again' are sung to this day. Such pieces were usually touching, sometimes comic and always decorous. By this time, too, the Jacobite songs to be found in early and mid century use, with their coded references to beautiful girls and a 'Highland Laddie' had become increasingly subject to sentiment and nostalgia: a small cloud, no bigger than a man's hand, signalling developments yet to come.

6
The nineteenth century: history, industry, sentiment

In Scottish cultural history the writers of the late eighteenth and early nineteenth century contribute to a remarkable period of change and creative activity. Walter Scott made Scotland and its past famous throughout Europe, periodical literature flourished in the capital, and there was a massive expansion of cities and industry. The population of Edinburgh doubled, with a powerful middle class to confirm its supremacy in law, medicine, the Church, banking, brewing and publishing. Farming and fishing were equally well established, on the east coast, along with heavier industries in coal, textiles, paper and especially the manufacture of linen. Great streets and houses in London were built with Aberdeen granite, and the finest American clippers were matched by sailing-ships from yards in the north-east.

The north's most significant export was people, and the economic and cultural life of the area was dominated by emigration to Canada and America. Estate owners and clan chiefs had been enclosing the land from the 1770s, and the ancient runrig style of strip cultivation, with its emphasis on subsistence farming shared by the community, had finally begun to disappear. Sheep-farming made a profitable appearance in the south-west, where there was plenty of grazing and urban markets close to hand, but in the Highlands, where the poorer land could no longer support an expanding population, the arrival of sheep only added to their problems. Landowners in search of grazing encouraged tenants to leave their crofts by offering them new jobs or assisted passage and emigration. In the second decade of the century the vast Sutherland estate set about 'improvement' in this manner, planning to resettle families on the coast, where the herring industry was enjoying a boom. (Neil Gunn's novel *The Silver Darlings* is set in this period.) The Countess of Sutherland intended these developments for the best, but old customs and loyalties could not be uprooted without pain. The evictions carried out by her agents, and the particular cruelty of Patrick Sellar in the small glen of Strathnaver, made the Sutherland 'Clearances' and Sellar's name notorious. Many Gaelic poems were written about the pains of eviction, and the small crofters conceived a hatred of sheep and the English language alike:

> Not sweet the sound that waked me from slumber,
> coming down to me from the mountain tops:
> the Lowland shepherd whose tongue displeases,
> Shouting there at his lazy dog.
>   (Iain MacLachlainn, 'Och, och mar tha mi' / 'Alas my State'
>   trs. D. Thomson)

The use of Gaelic in Highland schools was officially permitted, but in practice the Education Act of 1872 set up a system of national control and inspection that inevitably favoured English. For the most part the Highlanders offered only passive resistance to changes forced upon them; but there were outbursts from time to time between evicted crofters and the police, the militia and even the army. Women often joined in these skirmishes, and their leading part in the famous 'Battle of Braes' in Skye in 1882 gained the support of public opinion and helped to bring about the Crofters' Act, which finally offered secure tenure and controlled rents. Not the least effective in this campaign were the songs and poems of Mary Macpherson of Skye, who spoke out fearlessly on behalf of the old culture and land reform.

For the first half of the century, however, the poorer parts of the north-west Highlands had no protection from the demands of capital and the burgeoning of market forces elsewhere. When wool prices declined, or when the demand for kelp[1] collapsed in the face of cheaper imports, workers lost their livelihood, many old families went bankrupt and landownership fell into new, perhaps less caring, hands. The pattern of clan obligations had not survived the aftermath of the 1745 rising, and many chieftains now regarded themselves as landowners in the capitalist mould, spending their time and their money elsewhere. When the potato crop failed in 1846 there was no government relief for famine in the north, and thousands of impoverished Highlanders

---

1   Kelp seaweed was collected on the shore and burned to produce potash and soda, used to make glass and soap. Cheaper chemical imports from Germany eventually put an end to the home business, but it did well during the wars with France when trade was difficult. Gathering kelp on the tide line was hard, cold, raw work.

went abroad or came in search of work, like their Irish fellows, to the Lowland cities of Scotland. Little wonder that many Gaelic verses of the period, composed in Glasgow or in the settlements of Nova Scotia, are steeped in nostalgia for the communities, customs and girls left behind in the 'homeland'. Yet it is difficult to imagine how even the most enlightened of policies could have solved all the problems of the Highlands, in the face of their limited resources and a growing population.

If the brash and confident heart of the industrial nineteenth century belongs to any one area of Scotland, it belongs to Paisley, Greenock, Glasgow and the south-west. The groundwork was done by many small merchants who had invested in the weaving of cotton imported from the Americas. Their business had begun as a scattered rural industry with hand-looms for linen and cotton; next it developed with water-powered mills as in New Lanark near the Falls of Clyde, a model village developed by Robert Owen at the beginning of the nineteenth century. Owen had a far-sighted vision of the industrial community, setting up a nursery, a school, a concert hall and a church along with the workshops, dwelling places and of course the cotton mills, all in one beautiful location. Many of the workers came from the Highlands, and at its height the village contained about 2500 people. Such sites were rare, however, as was Owen's philanthropy and, with the development of steam power, factories with large work forces were concentrated nearer the cities. This led to an increased demand for coal, more industrialisation and higher wages for the miners, who had only recently been emancipated from virtual slavery on the estates of mine-owners.

Iron foundries began to produce more and more steam engines to pump the mines and power the mills. Chemical works developed new techniques in bleaching and dyeing for the textile trade, and the production of coal-tar and gas brought advanced lighting to many factories and towns. The Industrial Revolution saw Glasgow's population increasing faster than that of any other town in Britain. Thousands of labourers arrived from Ireland and the Highlands, and under such pressure the old fabric of the city could not cope. By the 1850s half the children born in Glasgow died before the age of five, and there were outbreaks of cholera until the new Loch Katrine water supply was brought into service ten years later. The Scottish Act of the great Reform Bill of 1832 was welcomed by everyone, but gradually it became apparent to the new labourers that their lot had hardly improved at all. The Chartist movement's demand for universal male suffrage found ready support in industrial Scotland, and its struggles in the 1840s confirmed a radical sensibility in the south-west and a sense of solidarity among the working class. But early attempts to gain better wages when times were hard had failed. In later years unions such as the Coal Miners' Association did better for their members, but it was 1867 before most workers got the vote and the Factory Act afforded some protection and a limit to the hours worked by women and children.

After the expansion of the railways in order to transport coal and then manufactured goods and passengers, the second half of the century saw an astonishing growth in heavy industry. Blast furnaces, fuelled by cheap coal and ore, supplied the raw material for engineering and shipbuilding. For twenty years after 1850 nearly three-quarters of all the iron vessels launched in Britain came from Clydeside, and the developing British Empire ensured that these ships, locomotives, boilers, pumps, marine engines, and the engineers themselves, went into service all around the world. 'Clyde-built' became synonymous with advanced technology and durability. Glasgow was called the 'second city of the Empire'; middle-class ironmasters and shipbuilding families made their fortunes and beautiful new terraces and parks were created in the city. But a shortage of housing for the proletariat meant that social problems got worse and worse. In 1880 a quarter of the city's families lived in one-room apartments, and many took lodgers as well. New tenements in the Scottish style were erected, and life in these crowded buildings had a special sense of community. But they were also subject to overcrowding and decay, until by the end of the century the slums of Glasgow were among the worst in Europe, breeding-grounds of violence, drunkenness and vice. Yet the booming city bred a native resilience in its people, and if the influx of families from Ireland led to religious prejudices between Protestants and Catholics, it also contributed a unique humour and vitality to the working population, not to mention a healthy scepticism about the British establishment.

As far as the Kirk was concerned, the old Presbyterian principles were once again in arms against centralised government control and patronage by landowners, while fundamentalist Evangelical preachers were coming to the fore, especially in the crowded cities, where there was a fear of Catholic emancipation. Ten years of wrangling between the state and various Church factions came to a head at the General Assembly of 1843, when nearly 40 per cent of the establishment broke away from the 'Auld Kirk' on a matter of principle and formed the Free Church, claiming to represent the true values of Presbyterianism. The 'Disruption' caused considerable hardship to the rebel congregations

and their ministers, for in the early days they were harried by their landlords and forced to worship on the open hillside. They survived,
however, to form a General Assembly and a parallel organisation of
their own, even down to schools and overseas missions. The Free Kirk
was particularly successful in the Highlands, much to the dismay of the
landowners, and its radical tendency immediately made itself felt in
votes for the Liberal Party that unseated many established Tory
members. In other respects, however, the Protestant ethic was entirely
in tune with the pursuit of profit and the age's materialistic belief that
every man should make his way by dint of personal initiative,
'respectability' and hard work. Thousands of Scots took this course by
leaving home, and skilled, unskilled, Highland and Lowland alike, they
spread throughout the British Empire to become a byword – both
loved and hated for their ambition, hardiness and ingenuity.

By the 1880s Scotland was indisputably part of British Victorian
industrial society, yet the Scots' own sense of their cultural differences
from England had not died out. Thus, when the country's prosperity
was most fully centred on heavy industry in the urban areas, there grew
up a vogue for 'cabbage-patch' literature – backward-looking and
sentimentally rustic tales extolling simple 'Scotch' folk, pawky humour
and 'honest' feeling. When Queen Victoria built Balmoral in 1855, it
confirmed an English vogue for tourism, tartan and turrets in the
north, and 'Scottish baronial' architecture in the same style appeared
throughout the country in a rash of railway stations and hotels. A
monument to Wallace towered over the plain at Stirling; the new
railway station at Edinburgh was called 'Waverley', and the Scott
monument commanded Princes Street like a mislocated cathedral spire.
Burns had his monument in Auld Reekie too, and Burns Associations
were formed throughout the world to promulgate his works and to
consume a ritual supper each year on the anniversary of his birth. The
typical 'canny Scotsman' began to appear in the press with a famous
Punch cartoon in 1860 along the lines of: 'I hadna been in London
mair than half-an-hour, when bang! went saxpence!' This northern
counterpart to John Bull – staid, bewhiskered and famously cautious
with his money – has more in common with his petit bourgeois
Victorian inventors than he has with an older, prouder and more
volatile Scottish spirit.

Not all was tartan ribbons and bardolatry, however, and national
feeling took a political dimension too, for the Association for the
Vindication of Scottish Rights was formed in 1853, and, of course, the
Disruption of the Kirk had already served to remind folk of old Scottish

values. When those crofters on Skye resisted eviction by physical force, they were aware that similar action had made nationalism a potent political issue in Ireland, and so the Highland Land League was formed along Irish lines to press for reform. In the face of the 'Irish question' to the west and the so-called 'Crofters' War' to the north, the Liberal government was pleased to make concessions by passing the Crofters' Act. When the government fell after the failure of the Irish Home Rule Bill in 1886, Liberal and nationalist opinion in Scotland was further stimulated and an all-party Home Rule Association was formed to promote political independence. Their case did not have the urgency or the violence of the Irish movement, but it contained a separatist and a nationalist feeling which has played a part in Scottish politics ever since.

Although the century began in Scotland with Walter Scott's verse romances, there was no poet to match the achievement of Burns, nor was there any Scottish equivalent to the English Romantic poets, unless, of course, **George Gordon, the sixth Lord Byron** (1788–1824) is seen as a Scottish writer. This claim is not as eccentric as it may seem, for Byron's early childhood was spent in Scotland – he attended Aberdeen Grammar School and his mother was Elizabeth Gordon of Gight, an unstable member of an unstable family from Donside. He himself claimed to be 'half a Scot by birth and bred / A whole one' (*Don Juan*), and T. S. Eliot believed there was a particularly Calvinist element in his delight in posing as a damned creature. Gregory Smith identified Byron's mercurial temperament with the 'clean contrair' spirit of the Scottish sensibility, and it must be admitted that the poet's swift transitions from pathos to mockery, or from moral satire to self-deflating parody, scarcely correspond to an English conception of literary decorum. Not that his origins helped him when the pontifical *Edinburgh Review* reported on his collection of poems *Hours of Idleness* in 1808, to note a flatness in his verses 'as if they were so much stagnant water'. Within a year Byron had retaliated with his lengthy satire *English Bards and Scotch Reviewers* in which he lambasted the editor Francis Jeffrey, his magazine and almost every other author in Britain – including Walter Scott whom he accuses of foisting his 'stale romance' on public taste. Byron's complex relationship with Scotland can be developed at greater length, but for present purposes his career must be left to the realm of English letters, where he came to prominence with *Childe Harold's Pilgrimage* in 1812 to join Walter Scott, no less, as one of the most famous writers in Europe.

Notwithstanding Byron's fame and Scott's early success in verse, the medium of the age in Scotland was undoubtedly prose, and the spread of literacy, of circulating libraries and the book-buying habit created an enormous appetite for books and periodicals of all sorts. Writers came to depend on the periodical scene to make their living, and, of course, many novels appeared there in serial form. Edinburgh became a most influential publishing centre, largely due to Archibald Constable and William Blackwood, whose presses, along with the *Edinburgh Review* and *Blackwood's Magazine*, made them household names throughout the kingdom. The phenomenal popularity of Scott's fiction was intimately bound up with Constable's firm and it exactly matches the expansion of what was coming to be known as 'the reading public' – a new critical conception and a new market.

Scott, Hogg, Galt, Ferrier, Lockhart and Moir were all writing at the same time, and this talented 'Blackwood's' group played a large part in the growing status of prose fiction throughout urban Britain. Yet their work is curiously divided, not least because they rarely deal with city life. Susan Ferrier brings English and Scottish society together, and town and country, too, for the purposes of mutual satirical comparison. Scott and Hogg look to an earlier and still potent Romantic or Gothic tradition; while Galt and Moir, with their sharp novels of small town or rural society, foreshadow the petit bourgeois provincialism of late-Victorian Scottish culture. In fact the essence of this latter vision had first appeared as early as 1806 in the work of the painter David Wilkie (1785–1841). In that year Wilkie, a son of the manse from Fifeshire, made his reputation at the Royal Academy in London with a picture called 'Village Politicians'. He produced genre paintings in similar vein for the next two decades – all distinguished by a novelistic desire to imply a story and to portray humour, pathos and sturdy 'Scottish' character-types, rather in the manner of 'The Cottar's Saturday Night' or Wordsworth's poems about Cumbrian folk. When Galt and Moir wrote for *Blackwood's* they confirmed a whole country's view of its own nature in terms that were not essentially different from Wilkie's genre painting. This is not to undervalue Galt's keen documentary eye and his sense of comedy, character and irony, but in the hands of lesser men and women the inheritance became 'provincial' in the worst sense of the word, leading to the 'Kailyard' at the end of the century, with its vision of Scotland as a charming rustic backwater.

Unaware of these future developments, Scott's contemporaries felt themselves to belong to the 'second generation' of the Scottish Enlightenment. That hater of the Gael, John Pinkerton (1758–1826), had tried to repair the public neglect of poets such as Barbour and Dunbar with his collection of *Ancient Scotish Poetry* (1786), and the

Revd Dr John Jamieson (1759–1838) produced his *Etymological Dictionary of the Scottish Language* (1808, 1825) a work that remained a substantial scholarly reference until modern times. As antiquarians, Sibbald, Irving and Laing wrote biographies and literary histories, and Scott founded the Bannatyne Club in 1823 to publish rare historical texts. In the field of moral philosophy, Duguld Stewart (1753–1828) succeeded Adam Ferguson as professor at Edinburgh, and, while Stewart was not an original thinker, being content to follow Thomas Reid's 'common sense' school, his personality, eloquence and liberal views influenced a whole generation. Most prominent among his peers were Henry Thomas Cockburn (1779–1854), and his friend Francis Jeffrey (1773–1850), two middle-class lawyers who played a part in establishing the Reform Bill and went on to become Whig law lords. Cockburn's *Life of Jeffrey* (1852) and his own various memoirs, published posthumously, give an attractive account of his life and times.

Francis Jeffrey started the *Edinburgh Review* in 1802 with the support of Henry Brougham and the English clergyman and wit Sydney Smith – former pupils of Duguld Stewart – and the new quarterly immediately made a name for itself. Within ten years the *Review* had a circulation of over 13,000 and its publisher Constable could attract the best writers in the country with astonishing fees of up to 20 guineas a sheet for anonymous reviews and £1000 or more for a single poem or article. Cockburn wrote on matters of law, and during the 1820s and 1830s Macaulay and Carlyle contributed regularly with some of their most famous essays.

The Edinburgh Review was never more successful than during its early years. Jeffrey was sympathetic to the literature of feeling, but it had to be supported by formal style and moral content, so that Burns, for example, was criticised for espousing 'vehement sensibility' without 'decency and regularity'. In this sense Jeffrey's values are neoclassical and it is not surprising that he began a famous review of Wordsworth's *The Excursion* on a typically proscriptive note – 'This will never do.' The *Review* was celebrated for the scathing and superior tone of its criticism, and, while it allowed Wordsworth and the English 'Lake School' to have 'a great deal of genius and of laudable feeling', it did not hesitate to chastise the poets for 'perverseness and bad taste'. Scott's *Marmion* was pruned with equal rigour, as if the task were an irksome duty – 'because we cannot help considering it as the foundation of a new school, which may hereafter occasion no little annoyance both to us and to the public'. Little wonder that Byron satirised Jeffrey and his 'critic clan' by referring to them as the 'bloodhounds of Arthur's Seat'!

It was not long before Scottish Tories lost patience with the dominance of the *Review* and its Whiggish politics. Walter Scott helped to found the (London) *Quarterly Review* in 1809, but Jeffrey's periodical did not meet its match until 1817, when William Blackwood, Constable's rival in publishing, produced the *Edinburgh Monthly Magazine*, which was soon changed to *Blackwood's Edinburgh Magazine*. The revised 'Maga' or 'Ebony', as it came to be known, was edited by John Gibson Lockhart and John Wilson, two young lawyers determined to make their mark on the cultural scene. This they did without delay, helped by James Hogg, in a mock biblical 'Translation from an Ancient Chaldee Manuscript', which satirised the 'war' between Constable and Blackwood and provided malicious caricatures of their Whig enemies and literary rivals. There was an immediate scandal, the October issue sold out, new readers were left panting for more, and the (anonymous) authors found it expedient to leave town. Over the next two years the publisher had to pay out £1000 in damages, but he stood by his 'wild fellows' and *Blackwood's* flourished, to be published without a break until 1980. Under Wilson and Lockhart, and an Irishman William Maginn, 'Maga' continued to make a stir, particularly in its wholehearted opposition to the poetry of Leigh Hunt, Shelley and Keats, motivated, perhaps, by the fact that Francis Jeffrey had greatly praised Keats in the *Edinburgh Review*. Whatever the reason, *Blackwood's* roasted 'the Cockneys' with a vituperative glee virtually indistinguishable from snobbish and personal spite. Of course, Keats's fiery mind was not 'snuffed out' by any such 'article', as Byron has it in *Don Juan*, nor was he the only writer to suffer from the critical hostilities declared between Constable and Blackwood. Wilson and Lockhart were not above petty lies and libels and political prejudices and old scores were settled forcefully on all sides. Nevertheless, *Blackwood's* supported many fine writers and serious articles, showing a particular interest in Gothic fiction with a famous series of 'Tales of Terror'. (Walter Scott's review of *Frankenstein*, for example, was very favourable – except he thought it was really written by Percy rather than Mary Shelley.)

John Wilson (1785–1854) continued as contributing editor to *Blackwood's*, and as 'Christopher North' he produced many of the 'Noctes Ambrosianae' (1822–35), a long-running series of essays in the form of conversations or monologues supposedly overheard by the scribe. (They were published in four volumes in 1885.) These often featured a version of his friend James Hogg somewhat broadly sketched as the 'Shepherd', a bibulous and loquacious countryman, spokesperson for common sense, but given to tall tales or sudden flights of philosophising:

> *Tickler*: James, would you seriously have North to write dramas about the loves of the lower orders – men in corduroy breeches, and women in linsey-woollen petticoats –
>
> *Shepherd*: Wha are ye, sir, to speak o' the lower orders? Look up to the sky, sir, on a starry nicht, and, puir, ignorant, thochtless, upsettin' cretur you'll be, gin you dinna feel far within, and deep down your ain sowl, that you are, in good truth, ane o' the lower orders – no, perhaps, o' men, but o' intelligences! and that it requires some dreadfu' mystery, far beyond your comprehension, to mak' you worthy o' ever in after life becoming a dweller in those celestial mansions. Yet think ye, sir, that thousan's, and tens o' thousan's o' millions, since the time when first God's wrath smote the earth's soil with the curse o' barrenness, and human creatures had to earn their bread wi' sweat and dust, haena lived and toiled, and laughed and sighed, and groaned and grat, *o' the lower orders*, that are noo in eternal bliss, and shall sit above you and Mr. North, and ithers o' the best o' the clan, in the realms o' heaven!
>
> *Tickler*: 'Pon my soul, James, I said nothing to justify this tirade.

The 'Noctes' proved very popular, and other writers, most notably Lockhart and Hogg, contributed, while De Quincey featured as a character in them and wrote for *Blackwood's* in his own right. (Wilson had befriended him and Wordsworth during a stay in the Lake District in his earlier years.)

Sir Walter Scott (1771–1832)

Scott's career belongs to the nineteenth century but his sympathies start with the earlier Edinburgh of Burns and Mackenzie, and it was his interest in ballads and Romantically 'medieval' adventure-poems that led him to prose fiction and the virtual invention of the 'historical novel'. He was born in a house in College Wynd among the crowded, disease-ridden streets of Old Edinburgh, where only six of his parents' twelve children survived infancy. Walter was the third of three healthy boys, but at eighteen months a bout of infantile paralysis left him weak with his right leg permanently lamed. His next eight years were spent at his grandfather's farm in the Borders, where he regained his health and acquired a taste for tales and ballads and stories of the Jacobite rebellion. He never did lose his lameness, but he thrived among doting elders, turning into a robust lad, forthright and full of confidence. Back with the family at a new house in George Square, he attended the old

High School in Edinburgh and read Shakespeare, Macpherson's *Ossian*, Pope's Homer, Ramsay's *Ever Green* and Spenser, all of which developed his appetite for 'the wonderful and the terrible', as he put it – 'the common taste of children . . . in which I have remained a child even unto this day'. Little wonder that he came to admire the Stuart cause, with the Cavaliers and Montrose and his Highlanders, and yet his private tutor was a Whig and a Presbyterian and so their amicable wrangles ensured that Scott also heard about the history of the Kirk and the sufferings of the Covenanters. Summer holidays were still spent in the Borders, where he discovered Bishop Percy's *Reliques* and the 'historical incidents and traditional legends' associated with the ruins of castles and abbeys all around.

Apprenticed as a copy-clerk to his father's law practice in 1786, he learned to produce hundreds of pages of legible manuscripts to short order, and business travels to Perth and the Trossachs (once with an escort of armed soldiers) gave him tales and settings enough for his later fiction. The young clerk attended the theatre and mixed with literary people, leaving a memorable description of Robert Burns, whom he met briefly in the home of Professor Adam Ferguson.

> His person was strong and robust: his manners rustic, not clownish; a sort of dignified plainness and simplicity . . . I would have taken the poet . . . for a very sagacious country farmer of the old Scotch school . . . There was a strong expression of sense and shrewdness in all his lineaments; the eye alone, I think, indicated the poetical character and temperament. It was large and of a dark cast, and glowed (I say literally *glowed*) when he spoke with feeling or interest.

In due course it was decided that Walter should follow his father's profession, so he graduated as a qualified advocate in 1792, although his studies did not preclude him from the city's convivial drinking habits, nor from joining various clubs and debating societies. Despite his withered leg, Scott had matured into a strong, raw-boned man who could ride, walk or drink with the hardiest farmer or sportsman. When French invasion threatened in 1797, he joined the Royal Edinburgh Volunteer Light Dragoons, delighting in the uniform and the dashing practice with horse and sabre on the sands of Portobello.

A predilection for boisterous, manly company was characteristic of his class and countrymen, and Scott was equally typical in his more sentimental longings. For five years in the early 1790s he had nursed passionate feelings for Williamina Stuart-Belsches of Fettercairn, a young and beautiful heiress whom he called the 'lady of the green mantle' – the model for a character of the same name in *Redgauntlet* and for several more of his gentle and rather pallid heroines. Williamina married someone else in 1797, but within the year Scott had met and fallen for Charlotte Margaret Charpentier, of French extraction, a lively and witty person who became his loyal and affectionate wife until her death in 1826.

The young advocate harboured literary ambitions and under the spur of the Romantic Gothic craze he translated Gottfried Bürger's 'Lenore' and 'Der Wilde Jäger'. In fact the German poet had already been influenced by ballads in Percy's *Reliques*, and so Scott's versions brought the wheel of fashionable influence full circle. A meeting with 'Monk' Lewis led to a translation of Goethe's *Götz von Berlichingen* – the essence of Romantic medievalism – and a visit to London to see the volume published in 1799. Scott's links with the Borders were renewed when he was appointed Sheriff-depute of Selkirkshire, shortly after his father's death in 1799, and he needed no further encouragement to roam among the hills and rivers of Ettrick, Tweed and Yarrow. In a sense he had been preparing all his life for such a collection as *The Minstrelsy of the Scottish Border* (3 vols, 1802–3), and it seems equally inevitable that he should have followed its success by writing poems of his own, inspired by German literature's interest in national identity and suffused with the romance of antique battles in a benevolent wilderness.

As an editor Scott was inclined to collate what he regarded as the 'best' text from several different versions (he later recognised the scholarly limitations of this approach) but he also collected from oral sources and sought the help of better scholars and local people too, including the redoubtable James Hogg and his mother, whom he met in the summer of 1802. The *Border Minstrelsy* was an immediate success, beautifully printed by his old friend James Ballantyne, with an enthusiastic introduction and footnotes full of history and quaint details. A third volume was projected for the following year and the work was reprinted several times thereafter, to become a milestone in the Scottish literary world's rediscovery of its own past.

Scott contributed to the newly founded *Edinburgh Review*, encouraged Hogg in his hopes of being published and received William and Dorothy Wordsworth on their Scottish tour. He persuaded James Ballantyne to move to Edinburgh and entered into a secret partnership that ensured that Ballantyne got plenty of printing commissions for legal work, as well as Scott's own books and other antiquarian projects from various different publishing houses. Scott lent money, took a

share of the profits and thought it a good scheme, although it put him
in an ambiguous position on occasion, and eventually went badly
wrong. At first, however, business thrived and Archibald Constable
took a commercial interest as well. Preferring to leave the Bar, Scott
managed to get appointed as one of the clerks of Session who sit below
the judge in the High Court at Edinburgh. His duties as Sheriff of
Selkirkshire encouraged him in 1804 to set up a house at Ashestiel in
that county, and henceforth he spent half the year sitting at the Court
of Session and the rest of the time in travel, or living happily by the
Tweed as a 'rattle skulled half-lawyer, half-sportsman' surrounded by
his children, his dogs and various family retainers.

Prompted by the Countess of Dalkeith's enthusiasm for a local story
of supernatural mischief, *The Lay of the Last Minstrel* was originally
intended as an imitation ballad for the third volume of the *Minstrelsy*.
It grew considerably, however, under Scott's compulsion to spin a tale
of love, magic and chivalry, with English and Scottish armies in
conflict, and many descriptions of Border lore and 'scenery and
manners'. Whatever he learned from the ballads, it was not concision,
and the poem is a typically Romantic confection of that glamorous
'medieval' world already familiar from the poems of Spenser,
Chatterton and Coleridge. (Scott acknowledged a metrical debt to
'Christabel', which he had heard recited in 1802, long before it was
published in 1816, and he used much the same pattern of octosyllabic
iambic couplets for his other long poems.) The *Lay* was an unprecedented popular success throughout Britain in 1805, with several
editions and over 21,000 sales in the first four years, rising to almost
44,000 copies by the time the collected poems appeared in 1830.
Francis Jeffrey gave it an enthusiastic review, although he felt that it was
too 'local', and opined that 'Mr Scott must either sacrifice his Border
prejudices, or offend his readers in the other parts of the empire' – a
revealing point of view from the leading critic in 'the Athens of the
North', and completely blind to what made Scott's poem special. The
author's literary ambitions were thoroughly aroused and he started on
a novel that was to deal with Highland life of sixty years earlier. But
public acclaim demanded another metrical romance, and so Scott put
away prose fiction and set to work on *Marmion*, which was promptly
purchased by Constable – unseen and still unfinished – for 1000
guineas.

The *Lay* was essentially an old legend, but *Marmion* (1808) is closer
to a novel in conception. Set in 1513 as 'a tale of Flodden field', it visualises the melancholy end of James IV and his army in rather the same

spirit as Malory describes the fate of Arthur's Round Table. Marmion is an English knight, an anti-hero with a complicated and treacherous love life. His peace mission to the Scottish court fails just as his private affairs catch up with him disastrously, and he dies on the battlefield with 'repentance and reviving love'. The melodrama is relieved by a wealth of geographical and historical detail, drawn from Scott's own youthful memories and his reading of the chronicles of Froissart and Pitscottie. He never did take Jeffrey's advice to eschew the 'local', and there are striking set descriptions of the abbey at Lindesfarne, or the battle at Flodden, or Marmion's first sight of Edinburgh. It was another huge success. After working on Dryden, Scott accepted a further contract with Constable to produce an edition of Swift which was to take him six years to complete. He was unpretentious enough to compare such editorial labour to a good cash crop of 'turnips and peas', but a growing dissatisfaction with the Whig politics of the *Edinburgh Review* led to a split with Constable. Scott had Ballantyne form his own publishing house under the name of his younger brother John, an entertaining but somewhat dilettante character, who was also to act as Scott's agent. The rival business did not last much beyond 1813, for the principals were not good enough judges of what would sell, but it did produce Scott's best and most popular poem.

The Lady of the Lake (1810) takes place in the reign of James V, some twenty-five years after Flodden, and it turns on the king's habit of travelling incognito among his people. (Popular legend refers to him as 'the Gaberlunzie man' – a travelling beggar.) Here the Gothic furniture of knightly chivalry is abandoned in favour of the excitements of stag-hunting, and the real romance of the tale lies with the beauty of the wild countryside around Loch Katrine and 'the ancient manners, habits and customs' of the Highlanders. Scott was sensitive to trends in popular taste and he knew that Anne Grant's *Highland Memoirs* (1806) and *The Cottagers of Glenburnie* (1808), a novel by Elizabeth Hamilton, had already stirred an urban interest in Highland life. He was no expert in Gaelic culture, however, despite a liking for talking to old Jacobites, and it is an oddly bitter reflection that when he was visiting the country around Loch Katrine, convinced that 'the old Scottish Gael' was a subject 'highly adapted for poetical composition', Duncan Bàn Macintyre, one of the greatest Gaelic poets of the eighteenth century, was far from his beloved Ben Dorain and passing the last years of his life virtually unknown to polite Edinburgh as a retired member of the City Guard in the narrow streets of the old town. Yet Scott's 'discovery' of the 'aboriginal race by whom the Highlands of Scotland were inhabited' took lowland Britain and Europe by storm. In fact his romantic and selective view of the clansmen as a warrior class, volatile, proud, loyal to their own and cruel to others, still prevails in the popular consciousness. In a confrontation between Roderick Dhu and the disguised King James, Scott has the Highlander justify his clansmen's raids in exactly the same terms as a Native American Indian chief might have used when speaking to the white man, and indeed a Canadian academic has noted that the parallels were close enough at the time for *The Lady of the Lake* to be translated into the Mohawk tongue in 1814. And by the 1820s Fenimore Cooper had come to be known as 'the American Scott' for his leatherstocking novels that proposed a very similar vision of Native Americans living in the wilderness:

> These fertile plains, that soften'd vale,
> Were once the birthright of the Gael;
> The stranger came with iron hand,
> And from our fathers reft the land.
> Where dwell we now? See, rudely swell
> Crag over crag, and fell o'er fell. . . .
> Pent in this fortress of the North,
> Think'st thou we will not sally forth,
> To spoil the spoiler as we may,
> And from the robber rend the prey?
> Ay, by my soul! While on yon plain
> The Saxon rears one shock of grain,
> While of ten thousand herds there strays
> But one along yon river's maze,
> The Gael of plain and river heir,
> Shall with strong hand redeem his share.
>
> (V.vii)

In another striking scene, 'Black Roderick' only has to give a whistle and the bare hillside comes alive with armed men, springing up like Satan's minions in *Paradise Lost*:

> And every tuft of broom gives life
> To plaided warrior arm'd for strife . . . .
> As if the yawning hill to heaven
> A subterranean host had given.
> Watching their leader's beck and will,
> All silent there they stood, and still.
> Like the loose crags, whose threatening mass
> Lay tottering o'er the hollow pass.
>
> (V.ix)

These are not the only Miltonic aspects that Scott ascribes to James's fierce antagonist, for earlier in the poem the 'waving of his tartans broad' and his 'darken'd brow' had, indeed, made him seem like the 'ill Demon of the night', and even on his death-bed he is described with an epic simile worthy of the fallen angel:

As the tall ship, whose lofty prore
Shall never stem the billows more,
Deserted by her gallant band,
Amid the breakers lies astrand
So, on his couch, lay Roderick Dhu!

(VI.xiii)

Thus the chieftain is revealed as a Romantic anti-hero in the Satanic/Byronic mould – arrogant, intractable and yet honourable according to his own lights. Nevertheless, Roderick must die to leave the way clear for a bitter-sweet reconciliation between Lowland lords – the exiled Douglas, whose daughter Ellen is the 'Lady of the Lake', and the stag-hunting 'Fitzjames', now revealed as an enlightened and forgiving monarch. The future is clearly theirs.

The poem concludes somewhat in the spirit of *A Winter's Tale* as identities are revealed and the opposing values of country and court set aside (if not reconciled) with the promise of a noble marriage and a happy ending. Another Shakespearean analogy is suggested by the way Scott intersperses ballads and songs throughout the poem – a device he was to use to even greater effect in the novels. Scott's octosyllabic measure is not markedly better than in his previous verses, but for once the plot avoids Gothic elaboration, and so the hunt-scenes and the beautiful landscapes are given room to stand forth as swiftly paced and effectively unified symbols of freedom and daring, to convey a strikingly ritualised, almost balletic vision of heroic conflict: as if war, too, were sport on the shores of Loch Katrine – a remote Arden in the north.

The Lady of the Lake was Scott's greatest success to date. A few critics, and Coleridge in particular, continued to dislike his loping couplets ('prose in polysyllables'), but the public had no doubts and bought over 20,000 copies within the year. Even Jeffrey changed his tune about 'local subjects' and hoped in the *Edinburgh Review* that the poet would turn to 'a true Celtic story':

There are few persons, we believe, of any degree of poetical susceptibility, who have wandered among the secluded valleys of the Highlands, and contemplated the singular people by whom they are still tenanted – with their love of music and of song – their hardy and irregular life, so unlike the unvarying toils of the Saxon mechanic – their devotion to their chiefs – their wild and lofty traditions – their national enthusiasm – the melancholy grandeur of the scenes they inhabit – and the multiplied superstitions which still linger among them – without feeling that there is no existing people so well adapted for the purposes of poetry, or so capable of furnishing the occasions of new and striking inventions.

We are persuaded, that if Mr Scott's powerful and creative genius were to be turned in good earnest to such a subject, something might be produced still more impressive and original than even this age has yet witnessed.

Scott's poem and Jeffery's newfound enthusiasm show how strongly a Highland version of 'Scottishness' seized the popular imagination. Here at last was the formula for a national identity uncomplicated by the rigours and the old pains of Presbyterianism, and most gratifyingly separated from the everyday political and commercial facts of the Union. At last 'Scottishness' could be glamorous and noble and fashionable – and 'safe'. Before the publication of *The Lady of the Lake*, Loch Katrine and surrounding hills were little known and virtually inaccessible. After 1810, thousands of visitors flocked to the Trossachs to see the place for themselves, and innkeepers and pony-hirers never knew such trade. As if inspired by his own subject, the author himself set out on a trip through the Hebrides to collect more old customs and 'legends of war and wonder'.

Scott felt that he could now afford a home of his own in the Borders, and so he bought a little farmhouse called Cartley Hole situated on the Tweed between Melrose and Galashiels. Builders were engaged to add to it, and the famous poet and his family, his horses, dogs and fishing rods, arrived in the summer of 1812. He renamed it Abbotsford and spent the next twelve years buying property, planting trees and developing the building until it grew into a huge mansion – a maze of wings and towers filled with antiques, ancient arms and armour. In order to finance these baronial ambitions, Scott took on heavier and heavier commitments, borrowing, mortgaging and spending advances on books not yet written. The laird of Abbotsford was not ashamed of financial success – indeed, he saw it as a merit – yet, when the Waverley novels first appeared, he kept his authorship secret, and, although it was a well-known secret for years, he did not publicly acknowledge them until 1826. Scott's sense of honour and his material ambitions brought him much heartache in the end, but his generous temperament remained unspoiled. In the early hours of every morning he worked hard at his desk – scorning 'artistic' affectations and taking pride in his capacity for workmanlike, profitable toil. Later in the day he was an outgoing host to many friends and famous visitors – the very image of a sporting country laird and a spokesperson for the culture of romantic Scotland.

Rokeby, a poem of the Civil War, appeared at the beginning of 1813 but it could not match the economy and force of *The Lady of the Lake*. Besides, Byron had burst on the scene with the first two cantos of *Childe Harold's Pilgrimage* – a publishing-sensation scarcely less glamorous than its young creator. The elder poet recognised *Childe Harold* as 'a piece of most extraordinary power', and he and Byron entered into an amicable and respectful correspondence, despite the public's desire to see them as bitter rivals. They met each other frequently in London during two months in 1815 and parted good friends. Byron's romances, such as *The Giaour* (1813), *The Bride of Abydos* (1813) and *The Corsair* (1814), owe something to the genre created by Scott, but his settings were even more wildly exotic, and the modern misanthropical psychology of Childe Harold quite overtook the antiquarian romance and the chivalric code of the 'last minstrel'.

Scott recognised that his vogue was over, and later verse romances – *The Bridal of Triermain* (1813), *Harold the Dauntless* (1817) and *The Lord of the Isles* (1815) – were never to recapture his early triumphs. 'Well, well, James, so be it', he remarked to Ballantyne with typically pragmatic modesty; 'but you know we must not droop, for we can't afford to give over. Since one line has failed, we must just stick to something else.' 'Something else' was prose fiction, with the resumption of *Waverley*, a novel he had worked on in 1808 and again in 1810 and never finished. At the age of forty-three Scott embarked on an entirely new creative career.

In a 'postscript which should have been a preface' the author of *Waverley* explained his point of view, giving notice, in effect, of the themes that were to inspire and guide him in all the later novels. He felt that the most extreme historical and social changes had taken place in the Highlands and Lowlands during the last two generations, as if the sixteenth century had led straight to the nineteenth century, so that 'the present people of Scotland [are] a class of beings as different from their grandfathers as the existing English are from those of Queen Elizabeth's time'. Scott thought that he had come to terms with these changes, but his feelings were crucially ambivalent. As a Lowland Tory and a Unionist, he was half in love with a warlike Stuart cause. As a man of aristocratic prejudices, and a lifelong opponent of the Reform Bill, he delighted in the oral tradition and the sturdy independence of common Scots folk. These are the conflicting claims at the heart of his novels, in which he places ordinary people at a time of violent change. His young heroes, whose inheritance is progress and the United Kingdom, learn to accept what Scott calls 'the prose of real life', but it seems colourless by comparison with the old ways and the 'poetry' of a lost Scotland.

Conflicts between 'emotional' and 'rational' responses to the Union had been manifest in Ramsay's time; but their sublimation in Scott's novels raised what might otherwise have been adventure fiction to a penetrating exploration of loyalty and historical change. It is as if the author's own contradictory feelings were being replayed through his account of the characters and events of the past, and the difficulties of his position may well be reflected in the nature of his young protagonists. Thus it is that a typical Scott hero seems rather passive: he is often cast as a stranger and an observer from 'outside' who is caught up in events, so that the scenes and actions of the novel are introduced to the readers in just the same way as they are introduced to him. This allows the author to describe at length the landscape and manners of his native country in what amounts to an act of recognition, translation and explanation – not just for his readers, but for himself too. Edward Waverley in the novel of that name is a young Englishman whose father is a Whig interested in commercial and political advancement in the city of London, but whose uncle is a Tory cavalier of the old aristocratic school. Young Captain Waverley despises his father's values, and when he is posted to Scotland and visits Baron Bradwardine he becomes involved in the freebooting life of the Highlands, falls in love with a Highland girl, is cashiered from the army and ultimately joins the Jacobite rising of the Forty-five. (He returns to the fold in the end, however, and is granted a pardon.) In Waverley's case it is psychologically convincing that his sentimental and romantic nature should have been stirred by the charm of Charles Edward Stuart and his cause, just as he was fascinated (like his creator) with the clansmen, so strange and fierce in their loyalties and wild as the countryside they inhabit.

Of course, Scott's glamorous settings are part of the popular Romantic taste for the 'picturesque', but they also touch on the wellsprings of his inspiration, for he frequently makes his landscapes play a part in the workings of plot and denouement, and they relate to his understanding of mood and character too. A chapter from *Waverley*, 'The Hold of a Highland Robber', perfectly displays the author's talent for combining the awesomely picturesque with detailed observation and a lively sense of contrast:

The party preserved silence, interrupted only by the monotonous and murmured chant of a Gaelic song, sung in a kind of low recitative by the steersman, and by the dash of the oars, which the notes seemed to regulate, as they dipped to them in cadence. The light, which they now approached more nearly, assumed a broader, redder, and more irregular splendour . . . . As he saw it, the red glaring orb seemed to rest on the very surface of the lake itself, and resembled the fiery vehicle in which the Evil Genius of an Oriental tale traverses land and sea. They approached nearer, and the fire sufficed to show that it was kindled at the bottom of a huge dark crag or rock, rising abruptly from the very edge of the water; its front, changed by the reflection to dusky red, formed a strange and even awful contrast to the banks around, which were from time to time faintly and partially illuminated by pallid moonlight. . . .

The principal inhabitant of this singular mansion . . . came forward to meet his guest, totally different in appearance and manner from what his imagination had anticipated. . . . Waverley prepared himself to meet a stern, gigantic, ferocious figure, such as Salvator would have chosen to be the central object of a group of banditti.

Donald Bean Lean was the very reverse of all these. He was thin in person and low in stature, with light sandy-coloured hair, and small pale features, from which he derived his agnomen of *Bean*, or white, . . . He had served in some inferior capacity in the French army, and in order to receive his English visitor in great form, and probably meaning, in his way, to pay him a compliment, he had laid aside the Highland dress for the time, to put on an old blue and red uniform, and a feathered hat, in which he was far from showing to advantage, and indeed looked so incongruous, compared with all around him, that Waverley would have been tempted to laugh, had laughter been either civil or safe.

Waverley, or 'Tis Sixty Years Since (1814) was an immediate success and it remains one of Scott's best-known novels. Critics and readers admired the colourful minor characters and enthused about the use of 'Daft Davy Gellatly' as a kind of Shakespearean fool. They expressed enlightened relief that the pains of discord and civil war were now in the past, and the author (often surmised as Scott) was congratulated on his portrayal of a northern race that was assumed without question to have 'vanished from the face of their native land . . . within these few years'. Here and in succeeding novels the reading public found action, adventure and morality tied to outdoor places and 'real' historical events – a significant change from the contrived settings and over-heated horrors of the prevailing Gothic school.

Maria Edgeworth's Irish novels, such as *Castle Rackrent* (1800), had pioneered the use of regional settings, and Scott acknowledged their influence on him, but his version of the Highlands was even more intriguing for a growing urban readership in Scotland and

England alike. On top of this, his many colourful secondary characters provide a comedy of manners less fine than Jane Austen's, but
broader and more various, for Scott delights in robust contrasts
between Highlanders and Lowlanders, Englishmen and Scotsmen,
young and old, rich and poor, noble and devious, all to great effect.
By comparison, the love interest in these novels is a more conventional thing and his heroes and heroines are not without a flavour of
the juvenile lead. Even so, the 'passive hero' so familiar in Scott's
fiction does allow him to concentrate on the pressure of events and
on how social, political or religious influences manifest themselves. In
the last analysis these influences, and Scott's evocation of travel, landscape and local history all drive the novels along just as effectively as
any more unique or dominant hero could. Indeed, the reader may
find it easier to empathise with a protagonist who is caught up in
events in the same way that he, or she, is caught up in reading the
book. This sort of empathy is common to many popular novels, then
as now, and no doubt it was yet another factor in the extraordinarily
wide appeal of the 'wizard of the North'. *Waverley* went through four
editions in as many months and sold 40,000 all over again when the
complete 'Waverley Novels' edition appeared with notes in 1829.
Scott returned from a tour of the Northern Isles to find himself
famously suspected of being 'the Great Unknown', although his first
public admission of authorship was not to be made until 1827. He
now gave himself up to fiction with a complete concentration of his
remarkable energies.

Constable published *Guy Mannering* in 1815 and *The Antiquary* in
1816, both 'by the author of Waverley', as well as *Paul's Letters to his
Kinsfolk* (1816), which appeared under Scott's own name as an
account of his visit to Europe and the battlefield of Waterloo. In the
same year two more novels, called *The Black Dwarf* and *Old Mortality*,
from a series to be called 'Tales of my Landlord', were published by
Blackwood as apparently collected and retold by an old schoolmaster
named Jedediah Cleishbotham. It seems to have been John Ballantyne
who persuaded Scott to go to another publisher with this scheme. In
the face of this prolific output Scott explained how the first three
Waverley novels were to fit together:

> The present Work completes a series of fictitious narratives, intended to
> illustrate the manners of Scotland at three different periods. *Waverley*
> embraced the age of our fathers, *Guy Mannering* that of our youth, and *The
> Antiquary* refers to the last ten years of the eighteenth century.
>
> (Introduction to *The Antiquary*)

Compared to *Waverley*, *Guy Mannering or the Astrologer* is something of a disappointment to the modern reader; being closer to a conventional romance of its day, it lent itself well to stage adaptation, with a lost heir, supernatural agencies and a happy ending. Yet the novel still gains from its setting and its evocation of country life in the Borders, and characters such as the lawyer Pleydell, Dandie Dinmont and the wild old crone Meg Merrilies – a fated instrument of fate herself – give it life and charm. *The Antiquary*, more nearly contemporary, is Scott's best comedy of manners. It involves a melodrama – also about a lost heir – but the elaborations of this plot about unsung noble birth and its eventual discovery are the least important elements in a novel rich with sympathetic humour and charged with topographical, psychological and social details. As with many of Scott's novels, it is possible to trace originals for some of the more entertaining characters: Jonathon Oldbuck, the eccentrically enthusiastic 'antiquary', owes something to old George Constable, a friend from the author's boyhood, and Edie Ochiltree the travelling beggarman had a real counterpart too. These figures are not isolated creations, however, for they fit into a wider portrait of a small Scots coastal community of fishermen, modest gentlemen and landed aristocrats, and Scott drew on his own upbringing to show that the spirit of such a place belongs most enduringly with the common folk. They are the ones who transmit the tales and legends from old times; they meet poverty and bereavement with strength and dignity and their opinions, prejudices and sufferings are a sturdy yardstick against which we measure the unlikely Gothic entanglements of the better born, or the enthusiasms and hobbyhorses of the better educated. Among his many novels it was Scott's own favourite.

While such figures as Edie Ochiltree are drawn with a generosity that rescues them from caricature, Scott is not, on the whole, a novelist who explores the psychological depths of motivation and introspection; nor do his characters evolve much or stray from their original casting in the course of his books. Yet, if he does not seek a directly analytical depth, he still achieves subtlety by the telling juxtaposition of events, scenes and characters. When the Earl of Glenallan, for example, has to face error, cruelty and shame in his own past, he hears of it in a fisherman's cottage from the mouth of old Elspeth, a singer of ballads and one time lady's maid to his mother. She spins a complicated tale of hatred, intrigue, suicide and a posthumous baby heir since lost. Glenallan is plunged into frozen gloom. By direct and deliberate contrast, the fisher family has just lost its eldest boy to the sea, and old Saunders

Mucklebackit, stiff and grim with grief, stands on the beach repairing the shattered boat that drowned his son – even as Glenalmond hears how his own mother arranged to kill the baby daughter he never knew he had. The sentimental Gothicism of these tangled webs is highly contrived, to say the least, but Scott manages it by having it told by a storyteller who is herself implicated in guilt and half-crazed with age, and it is distanced again by comparison with the silent, clumsy pain of Saunders as he fumbles blindly with his repairs:

> 'And what would ye have me to do,' answered the fisher gruffly, 'unless I wanted to see four children starve, because ane is drowned? It's weel wi' you gentles, that can sit in the house wi' handkerchers at your een when ye lose a friend; but the like o' us maun to our wark again, if our hearts were beating as hard as my hammer.'

Scott has a dramatist's grasp of how to use such juxtapositions to sustain powerful effects in pathos and in comedy too, and he may well have learned it from his early love of Shakespeare. Indeed Edie Ochiltree, the garrulous and dignified old beggar who links the various strands of the plot together, is a truly Shakespearean creation. Licensed by his age and humble station, he moves between cottage and manor like some unlikely, interfering Prospero whose native wit, tricks and compassion are all mobilised to help the other characters, and the author himself, to achieve a proper resolution:

> what wad a' the country about do for want o' auld Edie Ochiltree, that brings news and country cracks fae ae farm-steading to anither, and ginger-bread to the lasses, and helps the lads to mend their fiddles, and the gudewives to clout their pans, and plaits rush-swords and grenadier caps for the weans, and busks [dresses] the laird's flees [fishing flies], and has skill o' cow-ills and horse-ills, and kens mair auld sangs and tales than a' the barony besides, and gars ilka body laugh wherever he comes? Troth, my leddy, I canna lay down my vocation; it would be a public loss.

The final factor in Scott's realisation of comedy and drama is to be found in his selective use of the spoken vernacular. This sinewy and lively idiom (never too dense for the average reader) varies the narrative and illuminates character and society with such impact that the author hardly needs to comment more. For thousands of delighted readers, it was Scott rather than Wordsworth who revealed the democracy of plain values and common sense among humble folk, and reaffirmed, not least in Scotland itself, a sense of native character with all its strengths – and its terrible blind spots too.

For the theme of *Old Mortality* (1816) Scott returned to civil strife, this time between Cavalier and Covenanter in the late seventeenth century. The novel, from the 'Tales of my Landlord' series, is a much plainer and grimmer work than *The Antiquary* and it was Scott's first attempt in prose to recreate an historical past quite beyond living memory and his own boyhood roots. True to his muse, he seizes on the voices and features of the commons to measure his vision of the divided times, so that it is the old widow Mause Headrigg, expelled from her house and out on the hillside with the open-air conventicles, who speaks for the pride of ordinary folk, keeping to the harsher demands of their faith despite all consequences. Her son Cuddie is less convinced, however, and his hopes for a comfortable life are constantly and comically frustrated by his mother's insatiable need to testify, at the drop of a Bible, against 'popery, prelacy, antinomianism, erastianism, lapsarianism, sublapsarianism, and the sins and snares of the times'. 'Hout tout, mither', he complains as he drags her away from yet another confrontation, 'ye preached us out o' our canny free house and gude kale-yard . . . sae ye may haud sae for ae wee while, without preaching me up a ladder and down a tow.' We enjoy the exchange and yet in this novel it is likely that Scott's tendency to equate passionate principles with comic or grotesque characters goes some way towards defusing, disguising and ultimately aiming to deny the important and fundamental divisions that caused so much unhappiness in seventeenth-century Scotland.

Old Mortality works well enough as a warning against extremism, or as an adventure among the Covenanters, but despite Scott's researches in the writing of it and his ironic distance from the protagonists, its historical and philosophical insight is limited. Undoubtedly he intended to make a case for moderate Presbyterianism, for his hero Henry Morton comes from dissenting stock and when circumstances make him a leader in the Covenanters' camp he stands by the cause, even when his sympathies are divided because his sweetheart, Edith Bellenden, and some of his friends are Royalists from old families. He retains his humanity and disowns the men of perpetual violence, such as the daemonic Balfour of Burley, a historical character and one of the murderers of Archbishop Sharp of St Andrews. Yet Morton remains unconvincing because he never expresses intellectual conviction about his religious or political principles, and Scott surrounds him instead with a host of wild and curious figures with such names as Habakkuk Mucklewrath – a fanatical madman – or Poundtext, Kettledrummle and Macbriar, all of whom are satirical figures who expatiate on their cause in endlessly pedantic or comic fashion. Like Waverley before him,

Morton is pardoned for his beliefs and reconciled with conventional authority in the end. He marries Edith Bellenden and the book ends happily, even if the more truly revolutionary issues of these times were never to be so easily reconciled or dismissed.

Scott's next novel, *Rob Roy*, published in December 1817, returned to the Highlands, to revisit, and indeed to rethink the themes of *Waverley*. Although set around the 1715 rising, the book is not so much a paean to the rise of Great Britain (and an elegy on the demise of Highland society) as was its precursor, but rather an exploration of the conflicting forces that were very much at large in Scott's own time. Starting with a quarrel between young Englishman Frank Osbaldistone and his merchant father in London, the novel plays the Enlightenment values of Adam Smith, with their emphasis on the pragmatism of commerce, prosperity, law and common social progress against the equally powerful spirit of Romantic individualism, cultural difference and tribal loyalty, realised in the somewhat shady figure of the outlaw Rob Roy MacGregor. Yet the two sides of the equation are reimagined in less clear-cut terms than this suggests, with a now familiar Shakespearean delight in characterful and colourful creation, often on the edge of comedy, as with the unforgettable Bailie Nicol Jarvie, that most garrulous and pragmatic of Glasgow traders, or indeed in the mysterious and elusive comings and goings of Rob Roy MacGregor, who has his own notion of what honour is in a novel whose discourse (taking its tone from Frank's father) is often steeped in the vocabulary of narrow accountancy.

The tale is told in Frank's own words, looking back on the adventures of his youth, and we recognise him as another of Scott's rather unreliable and naïve young men as he takes us on a trip that will reveal his own limitations, while problematising, if not actually challenging, the values of a new and would-be united kingdom with its burgeoning mercantile class and an expanding imperial project with markets in North America and round the world. In such a context Rob Roy is as alien to the Lowland Scot Nicol Jarvie as he is to the young narrator, yet it is Frank's fate to be haunted by MacGregor, just as the Bailie must admit to his own hidden kinship – for in fact he is Rob Roy's blood cousin. Scott stirs the pot still further by seeing a parallel to these tensions in the contentious relationship between Frank and his father – in what will become a familiar trope in Scottish culture in various future fictional accounts of patriarchal severity and filial resistance.

The novel is not particularly well constructed but Scott compensated by creating a host of memorable characters, and it proved to be one of his most successful books, going into three editions within the year, and becoming a hugely popular stage adaptation for decades to come. It is no accident, perhaps, that Bailie Nicol Jarvie should have stolen the show on stage, for Rob Roy himself remains an intriguingly ambiguous and liminal character in the book. He seems a decent man, yet he is associated with savagery and married to a frighteningly cruel and unforgiving wife; he represents cultural difference and an older Scotland, yet moves across social and political borders with deceptive ease; he is a shadowy hero who carries some sort of symbolic freight for Frank Osbaldistone, and yet he is an outlaw in his own country. Old Andrew Fairservice is given the last word on this enigmatically protean figure – all too symbolic perhaps of Scott's own divided feelings – in that he sees the Highlander as 'ower bad for blessing, and ower gude for banning'. Only six months after *Rob Roy*, despite severe stomach pains due to gallstones, Scott completed the book that many critics hold to be best of all his novels.

The Heart of Midlothian (1818) is set in the Edinburgh of 1736, the year of the Porteous riots, and its central theme is the moral and physical journey which Jeanie Deans undertakes to save her pretty young half-sister from the death penalty. Eighteen-year-old Effie is accused of murdering her illegitimate baby – it has, indeed, disappeared – and in the absence of an infant body the complicated case against her depends on the fact that she kept her pregnancy secret from everyone because her lover, implicated in the killing of Captain Porteous, has had to flee and leave her unsupported. She does not know it, but she is innocent of the child's death, for it was stolen away from her while she was in a fever. Even so, she would probably be acquitted if only her sister Jeanie would testify that she had told her she was pregnant, for this is the key point in a law intended to stop heartless infanticides. But Jeanie, the daughter of 'Douce David Deans', a stern and moral old Covenanter, cannot tell a saving lie, despite the agony it brings to them all. It is a classical conflict between two kinds of good – the inviolable nature of truth as opposed to family love and natural justice. In this case stern Kirk morality and the unshakable strictness of the letter of the law are shown to be equally absolute and inescapable imperatives – a very Scottish pairing. The truth prevails and Effie is condemned to death. Jeanie sets out on an epic walk to London and has to experience several adventures and setbacks along the way before she succeeds in winning clemency for her sister at the court of Queen Caroline.

Jeanie Deans is quintessentially Scottish but there is no trace of the colourful 'Scotch character' about her, and at last Scott has created a positive hero, central to the novel, who makes things happen and takes responsibility firmly into her own hands. Indeed, Jeanie and her father embody the Presbyterian strengths and the moral seriousness that Scott had failed or chosen not to evoke in Henry Morton and the Covenanters of *Old Mortality*. The central debate between law and conscience is pursued and renewed at many levels, not least in setting it against the Porteous riots and the Tolbooth prison – the so-called 'Heart of Midlothian' itself. The issues are discussed again at a comic level in the inspired gobbledegook of Bartoline Saddletree, a harness-maker with legal pretensions, while the novelist's talent for wild and touching scenes creates Madge Wildfire, a demented creature who dies singing 'Proud Maisie' and acts as an instrument of fate in the same mould as old Elspeth or Meg Merrilies. Madge too is caught up in the theme of accusation and compassion, for the poor creature is charged with witchcraft and subjected to the 'justice' of a mob near Carlisle.

Scott continues the tale of Effie and her lover beyond the more obvious conclusion, which would seem to have arrived with her pardon. The unhappy pair are eventually reunited and return to high society as 'Sir George and Lady Staunton'. Sir George meets a violent end at the hands of a wilful young bandit whom he comes upon by accident in the Highlands, without ever knowing that he is Effie's lost child and the son he has, himself, so long sought. This latter part of the book is often criticised for slipping into melodrama and it is usually accepted that Scott was under pressure to make the novel long enough for four volumes. This is not the whole story, however, for the conclusion does try to continue the unifying theme of guilt, mercy and justice, a topic that Scott pursues far more consistently in this book than any other theme in his other novels. He was not often so single-minded and was given to dismissing the extent of his labours and the importance of unity in them. 'I am sensible', he wrote in his journal, 'that if there be anything good about my poetry or my prose either, it is a hurried frankness of composition, which pleases soldiers, sailors and young people of bold and active dispositions.' Beneath his bluff disclaimers he was genuinely clear-sighted about the strengths and weaknesses of his art. He could make complicated plans for the structure and evolution of his novels, but characters and incidents seemed to lead him astray of their own accord:

> When I light on such a character as Bailie Jarvie, or Dalgetty, my imagina-
> tion brightens, and my conception becomes clearer at every step which I
> make in his company, although it leads me many a weary mile away from the
> regular road, and forces me to leap hedge and ditch to get back into the

route again. If I resist the temptation, as you advise me, my thoughts become prosy, flat, and dull; I write painfully to myself, and under a consciousness of flagging which makes me flag still more; the sunshine with which fancy had invested the incidents, departs from them, and leaves everything dull and gloomy. I am no more the same author, than the dog in a wheel, condemned to go round and round for hours, is like the same dog merrily chasing his own tail, and gambolling in all the frolic of unrestrained freedom.

(Introductory Epistle, *The Fortunes of Nigel*)

Scott was to provide plenty more sunshine in his novels, but the image of that dog condemned to toil for hours was to become all too grimly apposite to his later creative life. In the meantime he continued to be extraordinarily productive and, despite a severe illness that only slowly retreated, he turned out two and sometimes three multi-volume novels a year. The manuscripts show virtually no signs of revision or hesitation, and in 1819 the most part of *The Legend of Montrose*, *The Bride of Lammermoor* and *Ivanhoe* were actually dictated during convalescence. Thus he managed, once more, to pay various debts and bonds, even if the expenses of Abbotsford more than kept pace with his considerable earnings. He wrote essays and reviews and took part in the launching of *Blackwood's*, through which he made friends with John Wilson and John Gibson Lockhart, his future biographer and son-in-law. He was made a baronet in 1818 and his place in established society was confirmed when he was asked to organise King George IV's visit to Scotland in 1822 in what became something of a tartan pageant of constructed Scottishness. Still Scott poured out books – 'let us stick to him', wrote Constable's partner, 'let us dig on and dig on at that extraordinary quarry'.

For southern readers *Ivanhoe* (1819) was the greatest success yet, and although its history is faulty it opened a whole new seam of picturesque romance in a 'medieval' English setting. Yet this is no minstrel's 'lay', for the novel sustains the feeling for internal conflict that had marked Scott's Scottish books, as he describes an England divided between Normans and Saxons and compounds these complexities and prejudices by imagining a love triangle between the eponymous hero, the Saxon princess Rowena and the beautiful Jewess Rebecca. Scott's determination to deal with the rape of Rebecca and the novel's exposure of anti-Semitism make this historical invention a seriously moral and surprisingly modern text. *The Monastery* and *The Abbot* (both 1820) returned to sixteenth-century Scotland, while *The Pirate* (1821) drew on earlier visits to the Shetlands, and *Kenilworth*, from the same year, took readers to the English court of Queen Elizabeth. Scott's daughter Sophia had married Lockhart in 1820, and, when young Walter married five years later, his father made a will that settled the whole of Abbotsford on his favourite son and his bride. These were happy and varied years for 'the Great Unknown', now in his fifties and recovering something of his former strength. He had become the most celebrated writer in Britain and a famously generous host at Abbotsford, where he entertained guests in a setting which brought Gothic interiors together with the most modern of gadgets, including pneumatic bells and gas lighting.

The Fortunes of Nigel (1822) was followed a year later by *Peveril of the Peak*, *Quentin Durward*, set in fifteenth-century France, and *St Ronan's Well*. Jacobite themes returned once more with *Redgauntlet* (1824), which is set in the 1760s to tell the story of another failed rising – one last throw of the dice by Charles Edward Stuart. The first half of the novel takes epistolary form before the action takes over, and its mixing of letters, journals, tales and reported narratives gives the text an interestingly partial, not to say relative set of perspectives. Thus it is that different characters and different narrative and moral positions, not to say different languages – formal and informal, English as well as Scots – all play against each other. (The novel is especially notable for 'Wandering Willie's Tale', a *tour de force* of the supernatural told in broad Scots, which is often published as if it were a separate short story.) These differing perspectives and registers give Scott's art a degree of subtlety that has often been overlooked, and one that responds well to close critical reading. In fact he had often chosen to frame his narratives within other frames, even as 'Jedediah Cleishbotham' had introduced the novels in the 'Tales of my Landlord' sequence. That old schoolmaster was only the first of a family of crusty and testy *personae* whom Scott recruited to deliver his fiction as correspondents, interlocutors, fallible editors or introducers. The last of them, the lawyer Chrystal Croftangry from *The Chronicles of the Canongate*, has a more than autobiographical flavour; nevertheless the device does show that Scott – especially with his own love of tales and the oral tradition – is fully aware that 'history' may be somewhat more fluid in the recounting than historians like to admit, and indeed his young protagonists, like Frank Osbaldistone in *Rob Roy*, are often shown to be unreliable narrators of their own adventures.

The Middle Ages featured once again in a lesser novel set in Wales, *The Betrothed*, and in the adventures of *The Talisman* (both 1825) where Scott admires the dignity of the Saracens compared to the prejudices and the petty squabbles of the Crusaders. He also began a lengthy nine-volume *Life of Napoleon Bonaparte*, not published until 1827. Despite his industry, however, his financial affairs were finally and disastrously overextended. For years now, Constable the publisher, Ballantyne the printer and Scott, that 'extraordinary quarry', had erected an ever-more-complex tower of mutually supportive credit, guarantees and bills of exchange. In the meantime Constable's London agent had been speculating on the volatile money market of the day, and when he was finally swept away by the general recession of 1825 the financial backwash brought down the Edinburgh partners as well. Scott was faced with private debts of £30,000 and a further call for over £96,000 owed through Ballantyne, Constable and various other parties. Not even his closest friends knew of his financial involvement with these businesses, and so the news of his ruin at the beginning of 1826 fell on Edinburgh, in Cockburn's words, like a thunderbolt: 'if an earthquake had swallowed half the town, it would not have produced greater astonishment, sorrow and dismay. . . . How humbled we felt when we saw him – the pride of us all, dashed from his honourable and lofty station, and all the fruits of his well-worked talents gone.' Even so, Scott refused to accept bankruptcy, just as he resisted the various subscriptions that were proposed to help him. A trust was formed for his creditors; he took lodgings and sold his Edinburgh house. He was allowed to live at Abbotsford rent-free, however, for he had already bequeathed it to his son, although he had only recently remortgaged the estate for a further £10,000 in a futile attempt to help Constable just before the crash.

So Scott, bound by his sense of honour in the matter, set about the massive task of clearing his debts by the further labours of his pen. At first his spirits were stimulated by the immediate controversy that surrounded his *Letters of Malachi Malagrowther* (1826), a lively pamphlet in opposition to the government's plan to do away with the distinctive paper currency of the Scottish banks. Such emblems of national identity were important to him, and he felt equally strongly about threats to the unique character of Scots law, just as he had revered the old Scottish regalia when they were discovered in 1818. The Malagrowther letters carried the day, but Scott was becoming increasingly isolated. The splendid years were over and the establishment at Abbotsford much reduced. Lady Scott died in the early summer of 1826, leaving her husband shaken with grief and melancholy. He had just begun a private journal and this intimate work provides a unique record of his last years. Bothered with rheumatism and palpitations of the heart, he seemed almost to welcome the routine of endless writing. He completed *Woodstock* in 1826 and the next year produced his *Life of Napoleon*, a set of short novels called 'Chronicles of the Canongate', and the first series of *Tales of a Grandfather* – a retelling of Scottish history for children, written for his frail grandson, who had only four more years to live. Three further volumes in this series appeared between 1828 and 1830, along with *The Fair Maid of Perth* (another of the 'Chronicles'), and what he called his 'Opus Magnum', a complete new edition of the Waverley novels furnished with introductions and notes. After *Anne of Geierstein* (1829) a serious stroke finally broke his strength. He retired as clerk of the Court of Session, but refused to give up writing, although he was sorely extended by his *Letters on Demonology and Witchcraft* (1830), and by two further short novels, *Count Robert of Paris* and *Castle Dangerous*, both from 1831. Scott was uncertain about the quality of these books and critics in the past have tended to discount them as work from a failing hand. Yet modern scholars have found a then contemporary parable in his vision of betrayal, confusion and final moral renewal set against a declining Byzantine empire in the eleventh century (*Count Robert*). Scott's all-too-limited energies were further expended by more Malachi letters against the various Reform Bills that were dividing parliament and country in those years. The redistribution of political seats and the extension of franchise were long overdue, but the old novelist could only see anarchy and an end to the values he loved, and even his more conservative friends thought his views were intemperate. They persuaded him to burn the Malachi manuscript, but they could not stop him from speaking for the Tory candidate at an election in Jedburgh, where he was shouted down and his carriage stoned.

By now Scott was markedly frail and prematurely old. Ironically, perhaps, it was a Whig government that helped the novelist to escape from a Scottish winter, by arranging for a frigate to take him to Malta and Naples. He saw the sights and struggled with another novel, to be called *The Siege of Malta*, as if the old dog could not give up the wheel to which he had been bound so long. But his mind was fading and his main anxiety was to get back to Abbotsford before the end. Another stroke threw him into a coma, but he gained a few days of clarity by Tweedside in the early autumn, before dying at the age of sixty-one on 21 September 1832. He is buried among cloisters in the ruins of Dryburgh Abbey.

The 'wizard of the North' was one of the best-loved and most famous writers in Europe and America – a figure along with Goethe and Byron who dominated the literary scene of his day, moving and influencing thousands of readers and dozens of writers who were to be famous in their turn. He was the first novelist to engage at length with how the broad forces of history impinge on the lives of common people, while also allowing them scope for their own emotional or moral dramas. His attachment to Scotland and to what made Scotland different from England led him to highlight the many cultural and historical differences between the two countries at a time when Enlightenment values and the imperatives of Union and Empire were ready to deny all such diversity. Often accused of having invented the 'tartan' Scotland of modern tourism, his true achievement may have been to sustain a sense of cultural difference, even of cultural nationalism (however partial and politically conservative), that might otherwise have withered away. Yet the years to come belong to Dickens, Balzac, Flaubert, Tolstoy or Dostoevsky, for Scott strikes an older balance between the robust and rational world of the Enlightenment and a Romantic love for the fabric of Scotland and her people. Conservative and yet nationalistic, a sentimental antiquarian, and yet practical and down to earth, his spirit, and the contradictions within it, belongs to the Edinburgh of the late eighteenth century – divided as always between a United Kingdom and the call of an 'auld sang'.

Scott's own life became part of that song too, largely owing to his son-in-law Lockhart's massive biography, *The Life of Sir Walter Scott* (1837–8). This long and entertaining study made full use of Scott's journals and thousands of letters and has earned a place in all subsequent studies despite being somewhat partial in places, as for example in its account of James Hogg, which was coloured by personal dislike and a recent quarrel. Educated at Glasgow and Oxford, **John Gibson Lockhart** (1794–1854) was another of those advocates who took to literature in Edinburgh. He wrote a somewhat genteel life of Burns in 1828 and so the book on Scott was not his first biography. After the scandal of the 'Chaldee Manuscript' in his youth, *Peter's Letters to his Kinsfolk* (1819) was a much more illuminating, although still scathing, series of sketches on the intelligentsia and Scottish manners. Lockhart's contributions to 'Maga' included many poems, and in the early 1820s he began writing novels. *Valerius* and *Reginald Dalton* have less to commend them than *Adam Blair* (1822) and *Matthew Wald* (1824), which manage to hint at darker psychological tensions in northern society. Adam Blair is a Presbyterian minister who eventually makes love to a married cousin, a girl who enters his life after his wife's death. Blair is tormented by what they never doubt to be a sin, most especially against the cloth, and he can find peace again only through public atonement and long suffering. *Matthew Wald* is a less satisfactory novel, but a similar involvement with crime and the Presbyterian conscience reminds us that Hogg's *Justified Sinner* was not the only book to explore this aspect of the country's psyche. Lockhart's early success with *Blackwood's* in Edinburgh was followed by his editorship of the *Tory Quarterly Review*, a post he held in London from 1825 until the year before his death.

It is not surprising that Scott should have dominated the literary scene at this time both in terms of his own production and his critical reception then and in later years. Nevertheless, there were a number of well-known women writers of the period who enjoyed wide readerships and lively contemporary reputations, even if the genres that some of them espoused have since fallen out of favour with modern readers. The influence of contemporary feminist criticism has had much to do with a reassessment of these authors as well as the genres within which they worked. Contemporary literary theory has also analysed the cultural expectations under which they laboured in their time—for better or for worse – as 'lady' writers. Modern scholarship's reassessment of the literature of travel and personal memoir has also rescued these authors from the shadow of Walter Scott and from being, in the ironic words of a recent critic, the other 'great unknowns'.

Anne Grant of Laggan (1755–1838) wrote poetry but is best remembered for her *Letters from the Mountains* (1806) which impressed the Wordsworths with a sense of the romance of Scotland, while her *Essays on the Superstitions of the Highlanders of Scotland, with Translations from the Gaelic* (1811) did much to explore the cultural differences between Highland and Lowland society. The daughter of an army man, Grant had spent her childhood and teenage years in pre-revolutionary North America and Canada and in *Memoirs of an American Lady* (1808) she gives a fascinating account of her time there, including a sympathetic portrait of how the Native American tribes had been debased by the white man. Grant is one of several Scottish women writers who share a sense of cultural difference and disparity that may well have been prompted by their experience in Scotland and given a further nuance, perhaps, by their awareness of their own subaltern status as members of the 'weaker sex'. Such was the case with **Elizabeth Hamilton** (1758?–1816), who was no political radical, but still resented the fact that the supposed physical weakness of women was used by men to deny them mental equality. She wrote poetry, essays and instructive treatises on education, religion, morals and sensibility as well as three novels, the first of which, *Translation of* *the Letters of a Hindoo Rajah* (1786), describes the education of its protagonist under imperial rule and his subsequent visit to Britain. While this traveller's tale in reverse is supportive of the imperial project, it does also appreciate cultural difference and uses its cross-cultural theme to cast an occasionally searching and critical light on British mores and on the role of women in both cultures. (The same comparative approach was to serve Susan Ferrier's novels well, without leaving the British Isles.) Hamilton's second novel satirised the feminism of Godwin and Mary Wollstonecraft but her third book was the most popular. *The Cottagers of Glenburnie* (1808) is remembered best for the vivid dialogue of its Scots-speaking peasantry and for Hamilton's concern with social conditions in the Highlands, by which a governess, Mrs Mason, gradually brings hygiene and enlightenment to a slovenly village. It is not irrelevant that Hamilton's heroine is physically handicapped, having been burned while rescuing her charges from a fire. For all its moral earnestness, *The Cottagers of Glenburnie* brought the challenges of cultural and social difference in the Highlands to the public eye in ways that anticipate Scott. Born in Ireland of a Scottish father but brought up in Stirlingshire, Hamilton deplored the decline of the Scots language and regretted that so many speakers could scarcely read it. Nevertheless, as was to be the case with Scott, her upper-class characters use English, as does the narrative voice itself. She settled in Edinburgh, became a friend of Scott and Anne Grant and had her portrait painted by Sir Henry Raeburn. (She was opposed to the effects of drinking tea and coffee, but judging by her portrait, she seems to have favoured snuff.)

The theme of historical, cultural and national difference can be found again in the writing of **Jane Porter** (1776–1850), who is sometimes acclaimed as a precursor to Scott, who knew her mother and must have met Jane when she was a child. Born in Durham to a Scottish mother but brought up in Edinburgh, Porter came from a highly creative family, for her brother Robert Ker Porter (1777–1842) was a noted historical painter and traveller (his two-volume *Tales of Other Realms* was published in 1809), and she shared her literary talent and two books with her even more prolific sister Anna Maria (1780–1832). Often cited as one of the earliest historical novels, Jane's *Thaddeus of Warsaw* (1803) was based on the Polish struggle for independence in the 1790s and the real-life exploits of the nationalist General Kosciusko. Set first in Poland and then in England, *Thaddeus* was a considerable popular success at home and abroad (Kosciusko wrote to her in praise of it) with translations being made and over a dozen editions. It has little interest, however, in the otherness of Poland and the past and, especially in its English episodes, it remains an unashamedly romantic tale of emotional entanglements, financial hardship, hidden identities and family reunion, all to be resolved in the end. Closer to home, if set in a much more distant period, *The Scottish Chiefs* (1810) revived the epic heroism of Ossian in the context of the Scottish wars of independence. For Porter, Wallace is never less than a noble hero-martyr, spurred to action by the cruel murder of his wife in a scene taken from Blind Harry and eerily reminiscent of *Braveheart*. As with *Thaddeus*, however, this is not really a historical novel so much as a violently patriotic adventure narrative that is surprisingly bloody in its action scenes, considering its author's quiet and thoughtful personality, and her nickname, Il Penseroso. This book, too, went through nine reprints in Porter's lifetime; it was translated into French and Gaelic and has proved popular with younger readers in various editions right into the twentieth century.

Mary Brunton (1778–1818) chose contemporary settings for her novels. Her first book, with the rather daunting title of *Self-Control* (1810–11), was dedicated to Joanna Baillie with the intention to instruct and 'improve' her readers. A woman of strong and independent mind, Brunton was interested in the 'common sense' philosophy of Thomas Reid (an interest she shared with her minister husband) and in later years she started to learn Gaelic. Her emphasis on discipline and self-control commends those stereotypically masculine virtues to her fictional heroines as a form of self-empowerment and as a critical comment on popular fiction's preference for more passive creatures. (The heroine of *Self-Control*, surrounded by weak men and pursued by a rake, is interested in mathematics, and when she is kidnapped in Canada she escapes by shooting the rapids in a canoe.) There is a strongly Christian agenda in Brunton's writing but she also has a firm grasp of the economic realities of life for many people, not least in the poorer sections of society, and an ironic awareness of the conventions of her genre. In a metatextual moment, for example, the protagonist of her second novel, *Discipline* (1814), observes that the 'heroines of romance often show a marvellous contempt for the common necessaries of life; from whence I am obliged to infer that their biographers never knew the real evils of penury'. *Discipline* is indeed a romance with incidents of love, jealousy, sexual predation and suicide; yet it also has a particular sympathy for the sufferings of the poor, the horrors of slavery and the degradation of the contemporary madhouse. At every turn, whatever the difficult odds, it emphasises the importance of maintaining independence and dignity. Set in London and Scotland, its Highland locations were produced independently of Scott's *Waverley* (published in the same year) and signal a tendency in so much of the popular fiction that was to come, to see rural Scotland as the home of common decency and natural virtue.

Joanna Baillie (1762–1851) was an admirer of Jane Porter and had some success as a poet and songwriter – not unconnected with a contemporary vogue for the 'female author' as the very model of the Christian gentlewoman, although of course this taste tended to dictate what themes were 'appropriate' for such a paragon. (This was something that Hamilton and Porter also had to contend with.) Baillie produced a patriotic 'Metrical Legend of William Wallace' in 1821, inspired by the success of Scott's ballads, and as a songwriter she operated in a largely domestic and popularly characterful 'Scottish' genre by which older and sometimes rawer songs were reworked with a more genteel audience in mind. The death of her minister father and family circumstances brought her mother, her sister and a teenage Joanna to live in London, where she was to stay from the 1780s until her death, sustaining her connections with Scotland through her writing and occasional visits north. An ironic note about the power of feminine wiles can be identified in the Scots language of her version of 'Woo'd and Married and a'', but for the most part these verses fulfil what a largely patriarchal society preferred to expect of a 'poetess'. However Baillie's reputation was first established, she was most praised for her plays, and these were made of sterner stuff. Her first volume, *A Series of Plays in which it is attempted to delineate the stronger passions of the mind*, was published in 1798 and the first work to be staged from it, *De Montfort*, was done at Drury Lane in 1800 with Mrs Siddons in the lead role. Well received by the critics of the day, it is tragic drama in blank verse with a psychological focus. Baillie went on to produce several volumes of plays and her critical success (not without dissent from Francis Jeffrey in the *Edinburgh Review*) was an inspiration to many other women writers of her time. Scott was an admirer of her work and she came to visit him in Edinburgh. They became good friends, and the novelist helped to promote the Edinburgh production of *The Family Legend* in 1810, a melodrama of clan warfare and high romance much enlivened by its spectacular stage effects and Gothic overtones. Nevertheless, Baillie considered the value of her work to lie in her use of blank verse to explore human psychology –preferably on a smaller stage than was then popular – and in her programmatic depiction and analysis of the passions. It is a mode that has rather lost its charm for modern readers, but her proto-feminist attempt to theorise the psychology of passion and to trace its roots to the domestic arena rather than to the world of men, politics and affairs has caught the interest of contemporary critics.

Scott was also known to **Elizabeth Grant of Rothiemurchus** (1797–1885), best remembered for the fascinating recollections of a long and full life in *Memoirs of a Highland Lady* written for her children and not published until 1898 – and then only in an edition slightly censored and abridged by her niece Lady Strachey. (The Canongate edition of 1988, edited by Andrew Tod, is the most complete yet produced.) Grant gives a lively account of life in Edinburgh, Oxford, London and her father's Highland estate on Speyside. A woman of Whig sympathies, strong opinions and wide contacts, she greatly disapproved of Scott's wife parading around Edinburgh in her new carriage and had little time for *Waverley*: 'the hero contemptible, the two heroines unnatural and disagreeable, and the whole idea given of the highlands being so utterly at variance with truth.' Not exactly susceptible to hero-worship, she also remembers meeting the young Shelley: 'slovenly in his dress, neither wearing garters nor suspenders, nor indeed taking any pains to fasten any of his garments with a proper regard to decency'. The memoirs of **Mary Somerville** (1780–1872) are equally notable from this period as an account of the life and times of a remarkable woman who became one of the most respected and honoured scientific writers of her age. (Somerville College in Oxford is named after her.) Born in Jedburgh and brought up in Musselburgh, Mary's interest in mathematics led her to translate Laplace's *Mécanique céleste* in 1831. Her book on *The Connexion of the Physical Sciences* (1834) explicated all the latest developments in physics and astronomy and this was followed by further accounts of physical geography, molecular and microscopic science. Somerville's memoirs were published after her death as *Personal Recollections, from Early Life to Old Age, of Mary Somerville* (1873) and republished by Canongate as *Queen of Science* (2001). The original title scarcely does justice to a lively and entertaining account of contemporary society which includes memories of supper parties in Edinburgh, the theatre of the day, personal reminiscences about Walter Scott, Maria Edgeworth and Joanna Baillie, and many travels abroad, including revolution in Italy and the eruption of Vesuvius.

The best of the women novelists whose works appeared during Scott's reign is **Susan Edmonstone Ferrier** (1782–1854), who looks to the novel of manners in the vein of Jane Austen or Maria Edgeworth. Ferrier was one of a large family born to an Edinburgh Writer to the Signet and her novels – the first two of which were taken up by Blackwoods and published anonymously – contain memorable characters, or caricatures, the Edinburgh originals of which her readers were much exercised to identify. She knew both Henry Mackenzie and Scott, visiting the latter in Ashestiel and Abbotsford on more than one occasion. He encouraged her writing and admired her talents in conversation, 'simple, full of humour, and exceedingly ready at repartee, and all this without the least affectation of the blue stocking'. In his later years, according to Hogg, she was tactful about his lapses in memory. Ferrier's themes were established from the first in *Marriage* (1818), probably her best novel, in which her satirically comic social observation is used to explore the circumscribed roles of young women within the marriage market – a not unfamiliar theme. The book proved a bestseller, being later translated into French and Swedish. In Ferrier's work (*The Inheritance* followed in 1824) she sets the fashionable world of London or Bath against the provincial life of Scotland, where her heroines have to meet an entirely different culture in a series of confrontations which make their own telling points against both sides. Ferrier is not Romantic about the north, for she gleefully satirises the Edinburgh bourgeoisie, while some of the Highlanders are seen as comic grotesques and the clan chiefs who appear in her work from time to time are often represented as weak and unworthy men. Having said that, her sympathies do come to rest with the common Scottish people and their virtues of piety and common sense, even if their behaviour and broad accents – well caught in her prose – are finally judged to be uncultivated. Ferrier's last work had a Highland heroine, and while *Destiny, or The Chief's Daughter* (1831) has a darker vision with a more overt moral agenda, it still sustains its author's critically intelligent and satirical eye for the shallowness and foolishness of men and women in polite society and the inequalities of gender, class and rank. After *Destiny* she wrote no more novels. She joined the Free Church following the Disruption of 1843 and her religious convictions led her to disapprove of her early work. No such qualms ever occurred to James Hogg, her fellow *Blackwood's* writer, whose roots were inextricably bound to the oral tradition of the common people of Scotland, the vernacular vigour of the Scots language, and a complex vision of the interface between the natural and the supernatural world.

James Hogg (1770–1835)

When Hogg's father's sheep-farm failed, his seven-year-old son was obliged to leave school and go to work. As a shepherd in his teens the boy taught himself to play the fiddle and laboured to develop his rudimentary grasp of reading and writing. One employer, a Mr Laidlaw of Blackhouse, gave Hogg access to his library, and the shepherd stayed with him for ten years, befriending his son William, who was later to be steward of Scott's estate at Abbotsford. At the age of twenty-seven, 'ravished', as he put it, by 'Tam o' Shanter', Hogg resolved to be a poet like Burns, and before long his 'Donald MacDonald', a war song against Napoleon, became well known throughout the country. His *Scottish Pastorals* appeared in 1801 – a small collection of songs and poems in the style of Ramsay's *Gentle Shepherd* – 'sad stuff, although I judged them to be exceedingly good'. In 1802 Scott's *Border Minstrelsy* inspired Hogg to set old tales into rhyme, and his friend William Laidlaw was instrumental in introducing Hogg's mother to Scott as a source of further traditional material. The 'Ettrick Shepherd' and the Sheriff of Selkirkshire became friends.

Hogg was never to be a successful farmer, and when a plan to run sheep on Harris came to nothing he lost his savings and had to turn again to shepherding in the Borders. His ballad-imitations were published as *The Mountain Bard* (1807), prefaced by a romantic account of his humble origins, but a treatise on the diseases of sheep proved more profitable. By 1810 he was finally out of work and came to Edinburgh to try his luck as a writer. Constable was persuaded to publish *The Forest Minstrel* (1810), an unsuccessful anthology – 'but the worst of them are all mine', as Hogg reflected later with characteristic self-mockery. He started a weekly paper in the style of *The Spectator* called *The Spy*, mostly written by himself, which lasted for a full year before closing. Disappointed at his inability to emulate Burns's success, Hogg used the last issue of his paper to publish a piece on the Spy's 'real character and the difficulties he has had to encounter', which noted the snobbery he had to endure from his middle-class literary advisers and encouraged the popular image of himself as the Ettrick Shepherd – an illiterate native genius who 'ran away from his master' to seek his fortune in the arts 'with his plaid wrapt round his shoulders, and all at once set up for a connoisseur in manners, taste and genius'. He lived to regret this role, but for the moment he was at the mercy of his insecurity, and his responses to the educated society that he longed to join could be naïve, vain or aggressive by turns, though not without some justification. (He had copied essays by Addison and Johnson into his own hand to show to his advisers, only to hear them pronounce 'his' work dull and coarse with incorrect grammar.)

The popularity of Scott's narrative verse was at its height and Hogg determined to try a long poem in the same style, choosing a framework that allowed him to offer several different poems as 'recited' by bards in a competition before Mary Queen of Scots at Holyrood in 1561. *The Queen's Wake* finally appeared in 1813 and it was successful enough to be compared with Byron and Scott and for Blackwood to take it onto his lists. The poem allows Hogg to adopt different poetic forms and voices over three nights of the competition, many of them in the vein of romantic minstrelsy. Two of the best and most popular 'songs' were 'The Witch of Fife', a Scots ballad full of grotesque misadventures, somewhat in the spirit of 'The Gyre-Carling'; and 'Kilmeny', a supernatural lay originally written in a heavily 'antique' Scots but later anglified. Both poems are enlivened by Hogg's familiarity with folk tales and the uncanny, but 'Kilmeny' makes something more original and disturbing out of its account of how a young virgin is spirited away, perhaps to Heaven, by the fairies and given an allegorical vision of the future. Hogg adds a chaste eroticism and a spiritual idealism to the bare bones of the ballad, and the result, with echoes from Ramsay's 'The Vision', is prophetic of the mystical other realms that would much later appear in the fiction of George MacDonald.

'O, bonny Kilmeny! free frae stain,
If ever you seek the world again,
That world of sin, or sorrow and fear,
O, tell of the joys that are waiting here;
And tell of the signs you shall shortly see;
Of the times that are now and the times that shall be.'

They lifted Kilmeny, they led her away,
And she walked in the light of a sunless day:
The sky was a dome of crystal bright,
The fountain of vision, and fountain of light:
The emerald fields were of dazzling glow,
And the flowers of everlasting blow.
Then deep in the stream her body they laid,
That her youth and beauty never might fade.
And they smiled on heaven, when they saw her lie
In the stream of life, that wandered bye.
(1819 version)

The Queen's Wake was a success in its time (especially in Edinburgh) and Hogg was encouraged to develop it into a longer version in 1819. But its narrative links are weak and Hogg was satisfied in later years to acknowledge Scott's supremacy in 'the school o' chivalry'. But he would not relinquish his own claim to be 'the king o' the mountain an' fairy school', and his poem 'Superstition' (1814) testifies to the impact of folklore on his young imagination.

At last the poet had 'arrived', and the Duke of Buccleuch was so impressed that he gave Hogg Altrive Lake Farm, rent-free for the rest of his life. He was introduced to Wordsworth in Edinburgh and toured with him in the Borders before visiting Rydal Mount to join John Wilson, and De Quincey too. The little gathering was not without its tricky moments, as Hogg later recalled in typical style. The party was viewing a meteor in the night sky when Hogg ventured a pretty remark to Dorothy:

> 'Hout, me'm! it is neither mair nor less than joost a treeumphal airch, raised in honour of the meeting of the poets.'
> 'That's not amiss. – Eh? Eh – that's very good', said the Professor [Wilson], laughing. But Wordsworth, who had De Quincey's arm, gave a grunt and turned on his heel, and leading the little opium-chewer aside, he addressed him in these disdainful and venomous words: – 'Poets? Poets? – What does the fellow mean, – Where are they?'

Hogg produced further long poems in English over the next two years, but they offered only derivative romance or contrived philosophising. *The Poetic Mirror* (1816), however, did show his considerable talent for imitating his famous contemporaries, including Scott, Byron, Coleridge and – sweet revenge – Wordsworth, whom he hilariously parodied in 'The Flying Tailor'.

These volumes had a mixed reception, but the 'Ettrick Shepherd' was established as a kenspeckle figure, even if it is difficult not to suspect a certain condescension among his friends when they refer to their 'good honest shepherd' and his 'quaint originality of manners'. The *Blackwood's* connection encouraged Hogg to return to prose with essays and tales for this and other periodicals. He needed the money, for his verse was flagging and *Dramatic Tales* (1817) for the stage had been a failure. Accordingly *The Brownie of Bodsbeck and Other Tales* appeared in 1818 as a book whose oral style of narration touches the taproots of Hogg's imagination by linking folk superstitions with tales of the Covenanters. *The Brownie of Bodsbeck* is set after the Battle of Bothwell Brig, telling how a shepherd is arrested for secretly helping Covenanters to escape from Claverhouse, and how his daughter, suspected of conniving with evil spirits, is denounced by the local curate, who has his own designs upon her. Even the father himself comes to fear that his Katherine is in league with the shambling 'Brownie' before it is revealed that the 'spirit' is really an injured Covenanter and that the odd happenings have been owing to her tending the wounded at night. Yet Hogg's evocation of the uncanny has been so successful that the possibility of magic survives his realistic 'explanation'. He was to use this double vision again.

As a stout Presbyterian, brought up on the sufferings of the just under 'bloody Clavers', Hogg was bound to differ from Scott's more gentlemanly and Tory preferences in *Old Mortality*. The Shepherd claimed that his manuscript predated Scott's novel (published at the end of 1816) and defended it against the great man's displeasure. Hogg was no liberal – 'the great majority o' shepherds are Conservatives', according to his alter ego in 'Noctes', 'no to be ta'en in by the nostrums o' every reformer'. But on the issue of religion, his sympathies belonged with the common people and the folk history of their persecution by the establishment – a theme he was to return to in later stories such as 'The Edinburgh Baillie', 'A Tale of Pentland' and 'A Tale of the Martyrs' and *Tales of the Wars of Montrose* (1835). Such a position was far from the genteel tastes of educated Edinburgh, however, and Hogg's ventures into prose were not without their critics, more accustomed to the novel of manners than to work stemming from an oral narrative tradition. Still, it was at this time that he joined the 'Blackwood's' set with the founding of the magazine in 1817. No doubt his experience with *The Spy* was reckoned to be of value in this context, but when the magazine came to review his own prose fiction it was still wont to find 'coarseness' in his work.

Hogg married in 1820 and took a nearby farm at Mount Benger for nine years until the lease expired and his finances failed again. In the meantime he edited collections of his own and other stories, produced a collection of Jacobite songs, *Jacobite Relics* (1819, 1821) and worked on his most ambitious novel yet, *The Three Perils of Man: War, Women and Witchcraft* (1822). The subtitle does indeed set the main topics for this ramshackle, picaresque book, mobilising allegory, fantasy, historical romance, coarse comedy and mock epic in a series of adventures in which knights and border reivers rub shoulders and tangle with wizards, magic and old-fashioned skulduggery. It includes a set of tales told by characters within the tale – each in an appropriate style – and it is all set against Robert II's determination to besiege the English in Roxburgh castle in the fourteenth century. The book is lively, savage and long-winded by turns, and its anachronistic history draws from the ballads and the oral tradition rather than from conventional scholarship. Pressed by Scott to try for 'a little more refinement, care and patience' in his work, Hogg admitted that he was inclined to let his imagination sail on 'without star or compass', although this is to be too modest about the novel's enthusiastic and often infectious energy. The *Blackwood's* circle did not appreciate the wild vigour of such inspiration, however, and in the face of their gentility, Hogg's next book, *The Three Perils of Woman, or Love, Leasing and Jealousy* (1823), rashly attempted the novel of manners and emotional entanglement. Written 'as if in desperation' and utilising multiple narratives in 'a series of domestic Scottish tales', it was roundly condemned by the critics who did not understand that Hogg's subversive agenda was to question, or indeed to trample on all considerations of 'decorum' in describing social and sexual manners as a circus of vanity, deceit and foolishness. Dealing with the lower as well as the upper classes, mixing the mood from comedy to disgust and not afraid to mention prostitution and venereal disease, Hogg's assault on good taste backfired hugely and later editions of his work left it out altogether.

Chief among the novel's critics was John Wilson ('Christopher North'), whose 'Noctes Ambrosianae' had just begun to caricature Hogg in the role of an aboriginal worthy, to the delight of thousands of *Blackwood's* readers. There is a telling irony in the fact that a man on the point of writing one of European literature's earliest masterpieces of the divided psyche should have been so caught up in the doings and sayings of 'the Shepherd', or 'the Caledonian Boar' – his own familiar, vulgar and profitable *doppelgänger*. The tensions in Scottish cultural identity, already felt by Ramsay and Scott, were about to take a stranger, darker twist.

The Private Memoirs and Confessions of a Justified Sinner (1824) was published anonymously because its author was particularly concerned that his identity be kept from his friends at the 'Maga'. He need scarcely have worried, for it made very little critical impact and the *Westminster Review* took him to task for 'uselessly and disgustingly abusing his imagination'. Yet it is a novel of extraordinary force, economically written and darkly modern in its psychological insights, so that some readers, more familiar with the 'Noctes' perhaps, have wondered whether Hogg actually wrote it at all, as if the garrulous Shepherd were suddenly revealed as Dostoevsky. Yet the book contains so many thematic and stylistic elements already used in Hogg's earlier work – however imperfectly – that his authorship is not in serious doubt, even if it does contain echoes of the psychological *doppelgänger* from Hoffmann's novel *The Devil's Elixir* (1815–16) or from Lockhart's novels of religious anguish. Hogg's friend Robert Pearse Gillies published a translation of Hoffmann, under Blackwood's imprint in June 1824 (the same month that Hogg's novel appeared) and, as Peter Garside notes in his edition of the *Sinner*, it is very possible that the two men talked together about their different projects. Louis Simpson has also noted a possible documentary seed in the real confessions of a religious-minded murderer called Nicol Muschet, which were published in Edinburgh in 1818.

The Justified Sinner is told in three parts: the 'editor's' narrative; the sinner's confession; and finally a brief account of how the editor and his friends had a hand in recovering the middle part of the tale from the sinner's grave. The book opens as a curious story of rival brothers at the very beginning of the eighteenth century, told by an enlightened editor in the early nineteenth century. The brothers' parents are mismatched, for the father is an easy-going conservative sensualist and his wife is a narrow-minded Presbyterian, much under the influence of the Revd Robert Wringhim, a fanatically Calvinist minister. The elder son is called George Colwan, but his father disowns the younger boy, Robert, because he suspects him to be the natural son of Wringhim. Cut off from his inheritance, Robert is brought up by the minister and even baptised as a Wringhim. He is more intelligent and intense than George, whom he hardly ever sees, but his mother and the minister educate him to hate his father and his brother, and they fill him with extreme antinomian doctrines. This creed takes Calvinist predestination a step further by arguing that, since good works and faith alone are not enough to get to Heaven (for that would be like purchasing salvation), then good works may not even be necessary for the 'justified' – like Burns's Holy Willie – who are already chosen for heaven. Still more startling is the possibility that sins committed by the justified may not be sins at all, but merely a part of God's higher plan.

Fired by a mission to chastise the unbelievers, young Robert begins to haunt his brother like a dark counterpart to George's dim, cheerful, generous and athletic nature – a political counterpart too, for, whereas Wringhim looks to the Covenanters, old Colwan is a Tory MP given to sentiments in favour of the Cavaliers. The turning point between the two brothers comes early one morning on the hill known as Arthur's Seat that overlooks Edinburgh. George has gone for a walk on the cliffs and is admiring the brilliant morning when a huge threatening shadow appears in the mist. He turns away in panic only to stumble into Robert, who is right behind him, and George strikes him in the ensuing confusion. Robert soon recovers his usual disdainful composure and prosecutes George for attempted fratricide, but he loses the case when his habit of following George everywhere is revealed in court. George goes off to celebrate with his boisterous friends, but quarrels with a Highlander called Drummond, and is found stabbed later that night. Drummond flees. The bad news kills George's father and Robert inherits everything. The first half of the novel ends when eyewitnesses to George's death are tracked down and persuaded to tell how it was Robert who stabbed him in the back while his brother was duelling with another figure, who only *resembled* Drummond. The Highlander's name is cleared, but now Robert cannot be found.

The second part of the novel is Robert's 'confession', recovered from his grave, in which the events already described are told all over again to show him in a noble and righteous light. The unbalanced intensity of this narrative inspires the novel and draws the reader into another world, utterly alien to the comfortable and shallow assumptions of young bloods such as George and his companions. We discover that Robert has a friend and religious mentor called Gil-Martin – a 'brother' in the revealed truth – who haunts him just as he himself has pursued George. Gil-Martin instructs him in godly doctrine at every step and it is he who encourages and aids Robert in seeking justified vengeance on sinners and on George in particular. The reader soon suspects that Gil-Martin is the Devil. On the other hand, Robert's state seems strangely alienated, and in a fit of illness he feels himself to be two people, Gil-Martin and his brother, between whom he has somehow lost himself. The extreme subjectivity of Robert's tale would certainly suggest that he is deluded, except that Hogg produces independent witnesses to testify to Gil-Martin's actual physical presence at crucial times. Robert may profit through his shadowy companion, but his mental state deteriorates. He conceives a mortal fear of Gil-Martin until, alcoholic, amnesiac and still raving in his belief that he is one of the elect, he publishes his confession as a moral pamphlet and ends it with a promise to take his own life. The novel concludes with how the editor tracked down the author's grave from an essay published in *Blackwood's* in which James Hogg (no less) had given an account of an unknown suicide and strange events associated with his burial site in the country. The editorial party seeks the aid of the Shepherd himself, but he proves unhelpful and too busy to 'houk up hunder-year-auld banes'. It is left to the editor to exhume the text and to republish *The Private Memoirs and Confessions*. Full of confidence in his own and his age's capacity for reason, he explains it as an 'allegory', born out of 'dreaming or madness', in which the unfortunate author came to believe that he was his own fictional character. This is the final sophisticated twist to the novel's capacity to set tales within tales, as different narrators come up with different explanations for the same events.

Hogg's discovery of the mirror mazes of subjectivity takes him beyond these merely relative differences, however, and his use of 'the double' anticipated Dostoevsky's Golyadkin by more than twenty years to give dramatic and psychological depth to a study of obsession and madness. On the other hand, Gil-Martin's role as the Devil suggests an unearthly rather than a psychological explanation, and it is not easy to choose between them, for the book provides evidence for both points of view, allowing Hogg to reconcile his domestic realism with a penchant for the supernatural and the grotesque. This combination becomes especially potent given the Presbyterian Church's historical obsession with witchcraft and demonology and the paradox that puritanism has always been prone to imagining the personifications of temptation and evil. In this case the 'shadow' may throw light on the 'substance' of all such religious convictions based on fear. Yet there are no easy answers, for in the face of such mysteries George's complacent Tory rationality is almost as unattractive as Robert's fanaticism and both are bound together in a complicity of unhappiness. The novel can be called a moral and cultural allegory as well as a supernatural tale or a study of psychotic delusion, for it offers a searching analysis of the nature of the Scottish psyche as it engages with its own religious history, divided loyalties and lost inheritance. More than that, it deals with political and class divisions within society and the clash of competing discourses – not least in the challenge it poses to those who would uphold the Enlightenment's insistence on empirical practice: 'We have nothing on earth but our own senses to depend upon: if these deceive us, what are we to do.' Hogg's book goes far deeper into such matters than the author of *Old Mortality* could comprehend; yet it was neither a critical nor a commercial success. He was never to achieve its like again and as far as literary Edinburgh was concerned, he returned to his role as 'Maga's' favourite Shepherd.

Hogg turned back to poetry but when *Queen Hynde* eventually appeared in 1825, as a long romantic poem of Scottish pre-history, it was judged to be a lengthy failure and Hogg settled for more sketches and tales, including the notable 'Brownie of the Black Haggs' (1829), for a number of different periodicals including *Chamber's Edinburgh*

Journal, the *Edinburgh Literary Journal, Fraser's Magazine* and, of course, *Blackwood's*. This work was later collected as *The Shepherd's Calendar* (1829), *Songs* (1831), and *A Queer Book* (1832). He visited London for three months in 1832 and was a considerable social success while organising a collected edition to be called *Altrive Tales*, only one volume of which ever appeared. Two years later he produced essays on good manners and *The Familiar Anecdotes of Sir Walter Scott*, which Lockhart found so very offensive because Hogg dared to recall his old friend's undignified end, and remarked on Scott's 'too strong leaning to the old aristocracy of the county' – namely those families descended from 'old Border Barbarians'. 'In Wilson's hands the Shepherd will always be delightful', wrote Lockhart, putting the Chaldee manuscript and his old collaborator firmly behind him, 'but of the fellow himself I can scarcely express my contemptuous pity'. Undaunted by the quarrel, Hogg continued to select and revise his prose, and a three-volume collection of previously unpublished stories appeared as *Tales of the Wars of Montrose* in the spring of 1835. That November he died of a liver disease at the age of sixty-five. *The Tales and Sketches of the Ettrick Shepherd* were published two years later, but Hogg had abridged the *Justified Sinner* to 'The Confessions of a Fanatic' and his greatest novel was not printed again until 1895, nor appreciated by literary critics until at least the 1920s. The French novelist André Gide set the book in a European perspective with an enthusiastic preface to the edition of 1947, and this started the modern revaluation of Hogg's work which began to understand that the unstable tone and the mixed modes and the conflicting and erratic narratives of his work showed an original and challenging intelligence at work in the written medium, and a man with his roots in an oral tradition, rather than a naïve author who did not understand literary decorum and the 'proper' genres.

John Galt (1779–1839)

Although it was *Blackwood's Magazine* that serialised his early novels, John Galt did not seek out or belong to the Edinburgh milieu of Scott, Hogg and Ferrier. He was born in Irvine on the coast of Ayrshire and brought up in Greenock, the seaport to the west of Glasgow where his father was a shipmaster to the West Indies. Galt left for London when he was twenty-five, but by 1809 his business plans in the capital had foundered and he took a two-year tour through the Mediterranean and the Near East, befriending the young Lord Byron along the way (and eventually publishing a biography of him in 1830). Back in London he wrote about his travels and produced a biography of Cardinal Wolsey and a volume of five tragedies. He turned to writing full-time after his marriage in 1813, and offered Constable a book looking back to an old-fashioned Scotland to be called *Annals of the Parish*. The publisher turned it down as too local and too Scottish, but the success of *Waverley* was soon to change such assumptions. Galt drew on his voyages again for a book of poems and an equally unsuccessful novel called *The Majolo* (1816), and he persevered with a variety of articles and projects, including textbooks, further biographies and two more novels. But these were dull, hard years and critical success eluded him until he entered his forties and *Blackwood's* began to serialise *The Ayrshire Legatees* in 1820. Galt may have taken his pattern from Lockhart's *Peter's Letters to his Kinsfolk*, or from Smollett's *Humphrey Clinker*, for the work comprises a series of letters in which an Ayrshire family tells their friends at home all about their visit to London. The exchanges are full of topical details, and the Scots family – naïve and level-headed by turns – is used as an affectionately comic and ironic touchstone for the sophistication of London. The epistolary form also allows Galt to present the same incidents from several different points of view, recognising the relativity of all internal experience. This was to be a key element in his own understanding of human nature and in his technique as a writer. The *Legatees* series (which was presented anonymously) proved very popular. William Blackwood made it into a book in 1821 and asked Galt for more. The author sent him *Annals of the Parish* and this time it was published straight away.

Galt did not consider these books to be true novels, preferring to call them sketches, observations or 'theoretical histories' that outlined the manners and the changes in provincial society, often through the voice of a single character. The *Annals* purport to be the chronicles of the country parish of Dalmailing from 1760 to 1810, as recorded in the Revd Micah Balwhidder's journal. Its companion volume *The Provost* (1822) reminisces about small-town politics and public events over the same period, all recounted in the revealingly opportunistic and blithely unselfconscious tones of Provost James Pawkie. ('Pawkie' in Scots means artful, with suggestions of country cunning.) These ironic 'auto-biographies' owe their success to Galt's capacity for sympathy with his narrators, even while he uses their voices to cast indirect reflections on their own failings. 'What happened in my parish was but a type and index to the world', Balwhidder assures us serenely, and no doubt Galt's urban readers allowed themselves a smile at his parish-pump priorities:

> The Ann. Dom. 1763, was, in many a respect, a memorable year, both in public and in private. The king granted peace to the French, and Charlie Malcolm, that went to sea in the *Tobacco* trader, came home to see his mother.

Yet Galt has the eye of a social historian, and these amusing chronicles accumulate a host of minor but significant details in fashion, economics, manners and politics as the old ways of speaking and living gradually changed during the second half of the eighteenth century. Galt's intention was to chart the recent past just as Scott claimed to have done with *Waverley, Guy Mannering* and *The Antiquary*, and it can be argued that his diaristic approach allowed him to do a better job without (apparently) imposing his own voice on that of his characters. In this respect Galt, like Hogg, shows a clear interest in plural voices and limited and multiple narratives. The autobiographical style also suited Galt's strengths as a writer because it allowed him to use the distinctive rhythms of Lowland speech (in Scots or English) as his central narrative medium, with plenty of scope for broad Scots and proverbial expression. He uses a denser dialect than Scott allowed himself – amounting to a *tour de force* in the case of Lady Grippy in *The Entail* – and this oral flow, with its encapsulation of regional and national attitudes, lies at the ironic heart of Galt's understanding of how 'voice' reveals character, and how that 'local' voice can be used to make double-edged social comments on the wider world of his more sophisticated readers.

The Entail (1823) completes Galt's sequence of major Scottish books and it is closer to a conventional novel in that it abandons the autobiographical mask and follows the fortunes of a single family over three generations and a forty-year period. As a study of the ties of property, avarice and affection in the rise and fall of a self-made man, and in the legal disputes within the family after his death, *The Entail* has been seen as a forerunner in the line of Balzac, Dickens, Zola, Hardy and Galsworthy. It has a claim to be Galt's most powerful novel, if less fully realised than *Annals*; yet, while Scott, Byron, Coleridge and Jeffrey had all admired the Scottish series, there were also complaints about the latest book's 'sordidness' and its impenetrable dialect. It was not reprinted in the author's lifetime. Galt stepped up his output of fiction with four more novels using Scottish settings and three historical novels all within four years of 1822, but, not surprisingly, these works seem hastily written and were less successful than their precursors.

Ringan Gilhaize (1823), however, is notable as another imaginative autobiography, this time in a grim and tragic mode. It was written to vindicate the Covenanting spirit, 'hugely provoked', in Galt's words, by *Old Mortality* and by what he felt to be Scott's ridicule of the defenders of the Presbyterian Church and their sufferings over more than three generations. This time Galt immersed himself totally in the mind and voice of his narrator – full of long phrases, ringing with biblical rhythms and echoes, as he asserts, 'I have not taken up the avenging pen of history, and dipped it in the blood of martyrs, to record only my own particular woes and wrong.' There is no hint of comic or ironic distance in Ringan's savage experiences and in his ultimately successful quest to shoot Claverhouse down. Galt's achievement is to let that iron-hard, obsessive nature speak for itself, without apology and without entirely forfeiting the reader's sympathy. He was particularly proud of this technique of what he called imaginative 'transfusion', but it was not fully understood by readers and the novel got little credit for a serious attempt to come to terms with some of the most painful themes in the Scottish inheritance.

Galt's success was on the wane and his best books were behind him. Between 1825 and 1829 he worked in Ontario as superintendent for the Canada Company, but his health was poor and problems with the board of directors led to resignation, bankruptcy, and a spell in debtors' prison in London. He continued to write, but a series of strokes in his mid-fifties left him an invalid, and in 1834 he returned to Greenock, where he died five years later.

Perhaps the popularity of Galt's early Scottish novels obscured the subtleties of his approach to imaginative biography, and the importance of sympathy in the chain of ironic distances that he established between author, 'narrator' and reader. His successors settled for much broader effects, almost exclusively in the vein of domestic comedy. The first step in this direction was taken by **David Macbeth Moir** (1798–1851), a friend and biographer of Galt's and a doctor in Musselburgh near Edinburgh. Moir contributed regularly to *Blackwood's* with both prose and poetry under the *nom de plume* of 'Delta', or Δ. His best-known book, *The Life of Mansie Wauch, Tailor of Dalkeith* 'written by himself', began as a series for the magazine in 1824 and was published as a book four years later. These small-town 'memoirs' were dedicated to Galt, but they lack the older man's sense of perspective and social irony. The result is closer to genre literature, and the pattern was set for the 'Kailyard' and a Victorian vogue in Scottish 'worthies'.

Sentimentalists and Spasmodics

By the 1850s nationalism had become a revolutionary force in Europe, but once the social and political unrest of the 1820s had passed, Lowland Scottish culture was to remain remarkably complacent for the rest of the century. The British Empire was thriving, after all, and many Scots were its beneficiaries and its active agents both at home and abroad. And if Scott's novels had a patriotic appeal, they had always been romantic, conservative and Unionist in the end. On the other hand, Patrick Fraser Tytler's *History of Scotland* (1823–43) gave scholarly support to a popular understanding of how the nation had evolved and defended its frontiers, while the Disruption had done much the same for the old values of the Kirk, and movements such as the Association for the Vindication of Scottish Rights were formed to attack the centralisation of government around Westminster interests. Yet somehow these scholarly, religious and political stirrings never came together to achieve any truly effective cultural or political expression. With poetry in particular, the distinctively Scottish tradition seems to have completely lost its way.

Carolina Oliphant, Lady Nairne (1766–1845), disguised as 'Mrs Bogan of Bogan', had written and adapted many Scots songs for *The Scottish Minstrel* in the early 1820s. Her work is genteel and pastoral or suffused with the nostalgic parlour Jacobitism which Hugh Millar memorably characterised as 'a sort of laughing gas', agreeably exciting to the feelings. 'Will ye no' come back again?', 'Caller Herrin'', 'The Hundred Pipers' and 'The Land o' the Leal' are still sung today. The various *Whistle-Binkie* anthologies from 1832 to 1890, subtitled 'A Collection of Songs for the Social Circle' have lasted less well (with the possible exception of 'Wee Willie Winkie') and the title has provided a generic label for all such milk-and-water vernacular verse, in a sentimental, complacent and utterly trivialised notion of what poetry might be. On the other hand, the only alternative seemed to be the sub-Miltonic rhetoric of epics such as *A Life-Drama*, which appeared in 1851. Its author, **Alexander Smith** (1830–67), a working-class lace-pattern-maker from Kilmarnock, was immediately hailed by the critics for the portentous ambition of his English verse, although he was accused of plagiarising from Tennyson after his second collection, *City*

Poems, appeared in 1857. His early literary efforts secured him a post as secretary to the University of Edinburgh in 1854, but he was to die relatively young. Smith also wrote essays, most notably the collection *Dreamthorp* (1863), susceptible to the beauty of the world and haunted by the fleeting nature of human life in the manner of his admired Montaigne. He also produced personal reminiscences of Skye in *A Summer in Skye* (1865) and a novel. He is best remembered today for his poem 'Glasgow', which tackles the reality of urban life in central Scotland, recognising the pains of industrial labour for many thousands, but seeing a hellish glory and a 'sacredness of love and death' in the city's 'noise and smoky breath':

> In thee, O City! I discern
> Another beauty, sad and stern.
>
> Draw thy fierce streams of blinding ore,
> Smite on a thousand anvils, roar
>   Down to the harbour-bars;
> Smoulder in smoky sunsets, flare
> On rainy nights, with street and square
>   Lie empty to the stars.
> From terrace proud to alley base
> I know thee as my mother's face.
>
> When sunset bathes thee in his gold,
> In wreaths of bronze thy sides are rolled,
>   Thy smoke is dusky fire;
> And, from the glory round thee poured,
> A sunbeam like an angel's sword
>   Shivers upon a spire.
> Thus have I watched thee, Terror! Dream!
> While the blue Night crept up the stream.
>
> The wild Train plunges in the hills,
> He shrieks across the midnight rills;
>   Streams through the shifting glare,
> The roar and flap of foundry fires,
> That shake with light the sleeping shires;

Smith's vein of extravagantly heated expression had a certain vogue, however, even if it was prone to occasionally turgid lines, self-important solemnity and a second-hand Romantic inflation. This was a failing shared by his English contemporaries, Philip Bailey and Sydney Dobell, so that they all came to be known as the 'Spasmodic school'.

The 'Spasmodics' were christened and parodied by **W. E. Aytoun**

(1813–65), yet another Tory Edinburgh lawyer, son-in-law to John Wilson, a friend of Alexander's and a prolific contributor to 'Maga'. Aytoun became professor of Rhetoric at Edinburgh in 1845 and was noted as a very popular lecturer. He supported the Scottish Rights Association and wrote solemn poems on national topics such as 'Edinburgh after Flodden' and 'The Execution of Montrose'. He is best remembered for humorous short stories and his satirical verse parodies. The prose of 'How We Got Up the Glenmutchkin Railway and How We Got Out of It' gives a humorously cynical account of the investment craze for stocks and shares in public transport. The mock-tragical verses of *Firmilian; or The Student of Badajoz: a Spasmodic Tragedy* (1854) tells us enough about the Spasmodics to justify their oblivion, although some readers took it for the real thing, despite lines such as 'Firmilian, Firmilian / What have you done with Lilian?' The *Bon Gaultier Ballads* (1855), a collaboration with Theodore Martin, developed Ayton's penchant for parody still further, mocking Highland romance with 'The Massacre of the Macpherson' and Tennyson's 'Locksley Hall' with 'The Lay of the Love-lorn' and producing what J. H. Millar called the best-ever parody of the old Scots ballads in an account of Queen Victoria's visit to France, which has her lamenting her hosts' taste for 'thae puddock-pies'. As with James Hogg's parodies, Aytoun's humour depends on a good critical ear, but it is closer to burlesque than to any more pointed satire. There is one indisputably great writer of this period, however, who would have nothing to do with parody, rustic sentiment or the likes of Mansie Wauch, and he came from a small village in Dumfries whose name might have been invented for the pages of *Whistle-Binkie*.

Thomas Carlyle (1795–1881)

Born in Ecclefechan, about ten miles from the Border, Carlyle came from a strongly Presbyterian family, and this early theological discipline, along with his philosophical disposition and an intense Romantic idealism combined to make him one of the most complicated and intransigent thinkers and cultural critics in Victorian Britain. Carlyle lived and worked in London after the age of thirty-nine, yet his roots were deeply Scottish; he kept in touch with family and home through regular visits and correspondence, and before he died in February 1881 he declined a place in Westminster Abbey and asked that his body be returned to Ecclefechan in the plainest of coffins.

Carlyle's father was a stonemason-builder, a grim and taciturn man who was largely self-educated. He and his family belonged to the 'Burghers', a branch of the secession Church which had condemned the Church of Scotland for lax doctrine, and so his son grew up with a creed which stressed the power of preaching and solemn exposition, and the importance of individual acts of will and judgement in the face of eternity. Inevitably destined for the Church, Carlyle set off for Edinburgh University in 1809. He was excited by science and mathematics, but became disillusioned with university life just as his faith in the religious doctrine of his childhood began to falter, along with his health. He supported himself by working as a tutor and teacher – which he hated – and made abortive plans to study law. He learned German, undertook translations and reviews and corresponded with Goethe. The German Romantics made a deep impression on his idealistic, mandarin and uncouth temperament. Dyspeptic, sleepless and prone to depression, he seems to have undergone something of an existential crisis at this time, later described in *Sartor Resartus* as a sense of the 'Everlasting NO':

> To me the Universe was all void of Life, of Purpose, of Volition, even of Hostility: it was one huge, dead, immeasurable Steam-engine, rolling on, in its dead indifference, to grind me limb from limb.

He was not the only Victorian to be so haunted.

By the mid-1820s his translations and his life of Schiller were gaining Carlyle a place in the world of letters, and he had met, and clumsily wooed, a doctor's daughter called **Jane Welsh** (1801–66), a witty and beautiful middle-class girl who became his lifelong companion. Jane's *Letters and Memorials* (1883), published after her death, provide a fascinating insight into their liaison, and the complete collection of her correspondence (more than 3000 letters have survived) is an extraordinary record of her life and times, when she talked and corresponded with the intelligentsia of the day on equal terms. The couple married in 1826 and had two happy years in Edinburgh before financial constraints took them to remote Dumfriesshire. Their life was isolated at Craigenputtock and Jane had to cope with Carlyle's intense, restless and hypochondriac nature, which required absolute silence as he struggled with his thoughts, his journal and his highly wrought prose style. Among the essays of this period, 'Signs of the Times', which appeared in the *Edinburgh Review* in 1829, launched a prophetic attack on the evils of contemporary materialism and the cool calculation inherent in Utilitarian ideas. In the 1830s Carlyle continued to develop a complex and transcendental analysis of his own relationship with the world in what was to be his first major work.

The elaborate and ponderously mannered prose of *Sartor Resartus* was serialised in 1833, but it did not appear as a book until an American publisher took the risk in 1836, and it was a further two years before it was published in London. The title – literally, 'The Tailor Retailored' – refers to an elaborate disquisition on the philosophy of clothes, or of 'appearances', supposedly edited from the life and scattered writings of 'Herr Teufelsdröckh' ('Devil's dung' / cast-off) a fictional German philosopher and mystic. The alter ego of Teufelsdröckh, and his peculiar brand of pedantic whimsy (as much a Scottish failing as a German one), allows Carlyle to air his transcendental views in an unashamedly prophetic style. 'Rightly viewed,' he tells us (in a sentence which sums up his creator's hopes for his own vocation), 'no meanest object is insignificant; all objects are as windows, through which the philosophic eye looks into Infinitude itself.' Under this apparent concern with 'clothes' as the appearance of things, Carlyle constructs what he called a 'symbolic myth' that is no less than a forerunner of semiotic study and modern-day cultural criticism. The fact that he had lost faith in the personal God of his childhood did not mean that Carlyle had lost the need for faith itself, and he set about constructing what amounts to an existentialist answer to the crisis that had first come upon him as the 'Everlasting NAY'. His answer was a commitment to work in tones that would have pleased any Calvinist preacher: 'Up! Up! Whatsoever thy hand findeth to do, do it with thy whole might. Work while it is called Today; for the Night cometh, wherein no man can work' (*Sartor*, 'The Everlasting Yea'). Carlyle's 'work' was to be the critical analysis of society and its values as they can be decoded in all their manifestations – the 'old clothes' of old ideas in their grandest and meanest forms. He warns against the snares of received opinion and even of language itself: ' . . . are not the tatters and rags of superannuated worn-out symbols (in this Rag-fair of a world) dropping off everywhere, to hoodwink, to halter, to tether you; nay if you shake them not aside, threatening to accumulate, and perhaps produce suffocation?' (*Sartor*, 'Symbols').

Carlyle used the strange rhetoric of his symbolic myth to try to understand the relationship between the human spirit and the material world, seeing the world as nothing less than the product of that spirit: from cities to arsenals to tilled fields and books. And these manifestations are all that we can ever leave behind: 'compress the threescore years into three minutes: what else was he, what else are we? Are we not

Spirits, that are shaped into a body, into an Appearance; and that fade-away again into air and Invisibility? That is no metaphor, it is a simple scientific *fact* . . .' (*Sartor*, 'Natural Supernaturalism').

The couple moved to London in 1834 and set up house in Chelsea. Carlyle wrote with difficulty, and his sentences are highly crafted and rugged at the same time, full of biblical echoes, repetitions, allusions and antitheses. At his best this method of address is bold, jagged and direct as he seeks to persuade the reader by the very passion of his own conviction, using tones of intimacy, irony or open scorn as he seeks to achieve rapport, agreement or downright surrender. Here is his lively defence of the transcendental, but it is not an argument in any sense of the word at all:

> Thou wilt have no mystery or mysticism; wilt live in the daylight (rushlight?) of truth, and see the world and understand it? Nay, thou wilt laugh at all that believe in a mystery; to whom the universe is an oracle and temple, as well as a kitchen and cattle stall? *Armer Teufel!* Doth not thy cow calve, doth not thy bull gender? Nay, peradventure, doest not thou thyself gender? Explain me that, or do one of two things: retire into private places with thy foolish cackle; or, what were better, give it up and weep, not that the world is mean and disenchanted and prosaic, but that thou are vain and blind.
>
> Is anything more wonderful than another, if you consider it maturely? I have seen no men rise from the dead; I have seen some thousands rise from nothing. I have not force to fly into the sun, but I have force to lift my hand, which is equally strange.
>
> (*Early Life*, II, 1830)

There is something that anticipates Walt Whitman's celebration of the physical world in these lines, as when the American poet cries in 'Song of Myself' that 'the narrowest hinge in my hand puts to scorn all machinery, / And the cow crunching with depress'd head surpasses any statue, / And a mouse is miracle enough to stagger sextillions of infidels.'

Carlyle's historical writing is haunted by this sense of the oncoming of 'Night' – a poignant sense of the 'pastness' of the past – and a furious sympathy for the unsung plight of the common people who remain in the shadows while the same few aristocrats strut in the lime-light of posterity's attention: figures such as 'Mary Stuart, a Beauty, but over light-headed; and Henry Darnley, a Booby who had fine legs'. Like his contemporary Macaulay, a fellow contributor to the *Edinburgh Review* and equally fierce in his opinions, Carlyle preferred what would now be called social history and he looked for moments of what he took to be evolutionary change in the spirit of the times. The

Reformation was such a moment, when 'all Scotland is awakened to a second, higher life . . . convulsed, fermenting, struggling to body itself forth anew'; or the turmoil in France, which threw new ideals and a new fanaticism into the world. For the writing of *The French Revolution* (1837) Carlyle's research drew on the memoirs of other men, but it is supremely his own imagination and his rhetorical use of the present tense that transforms his material to the atmospheric immediacy of an eyewitness account. 'History, after all, is the true Poetry', he had proposed in 1832. 'Reality, if rightly interpreted is grander than Fiction; nay, that even in the right interpretation of Reality and History does genuine Poetry consist.' Some critics were puzzled by the outstandingly dramatic style of *The French Revolution*, but for most it established Carlyle as a major writer and historian, one of the most sought-after intellectual figures in London. As 'the sage of Chelsea', he became friends with J. S. Mill, Emerson, Browning, Arnold, Tennyson and Dickens. Mill called *The French Revolution* the 'truest of histories . . . not so much a history as an epic poem', and its author was pleased to concur.

With *Chartism* in 1839, and in *Past and Present* (1843), Carlyle once more brooded angrily on *laissez-faire* economics and the plight of the poor and the working classes; and showed bitter contempt, too, at the inadequacies of Reform, which could only tinker with a rotten system. Yet sympathy for the oppressed did not make Carlyle a democrat. He mistrusted the emancipated masses and, when he extolled new directions and a new humanity in the evolving spirit of the times, he looked for them to be manifested in 'heroic' individuals. These thoughts were taken further with *On Heroes and Hero Worship* (1841), which began as a set among his many public lectures. The 'forerunners of history', according to Carlyle, included Odin, Mahomet and Napoleon; and his Scottish bias appears in his choice of Burns and Rousseau and in his respect for the authority of Luther, Knox and Cromwell. Such heroes, like the Calvinist elect, were chosen above others to lead or to show the way.

As he grew older, however, Carlyle's bracing prophesies of needful transformation and turmoil gave way to fears of anarchy and led him to equate heroic authority with control as a bulwark against change. He spent the latter part of his life working on an exhaustive and sterile act of homage with a *History of Frederick the Great* (1858–65), and the gross insistence of such pieces as *The Nigger Question* (1853) caused controversy and offence by maintaining that slaves (in the spiritual as well as the literal sense) are deemed slaves by the 'Supreme Powers' and should remain so. The harsh prophetic urgency of his early voice had become strained, hysterical and intolerant of all but its own views. Like the pattern of the Reformation in his native land, it is as if Carlyle's philosophy moved from an iconoclastic striving of the highest spirit, to a death grip of the most rigid and gloomy sort. In the obituary that he wrote for Carlyle, Walt Whitman proposed him as the 'representative author' of modern times: 'no man else will bequeath to the future more significant hints of our stormy era, its fierce paradoxes, its din and its struggling parturition periods . . .'

Hugh Millar (1802–56)

Hugh Millar never aspired to Carlyle's stature, but he came from a similar background and was an influential figure, by precept and example, in his own right. Essayist, journalist and geologist, he embodies the independence and the didacticism of the Scottish dissenting tradition. A self-educated stonemason from Cromarty, near Inverness, he became a local journalist and entered the national lists with a pamphlet letter against Church patronage. On the strength of this he was brought to Edinburgh to edit the *Witness*, the newspaper that became the voice of the Free Church after the Disruption. Millar was a moderate in Free Kirk circles and played a worthy part in their concern to bring education, self-advancement and self-expression to the labouring classes. He and his newspaper roundly condemned the clearances in Sutherland, for example, and protested against landowners who would not allow the Free Kirk – with its radical overtones – to build on their land. Atheist John Maclean and the Independent Labour Party workers of the next century were to lay similar emphasis on the education of the working classes as the route to social justice, but Millar's sturdy Presbyterian respectability was never revolutionary. He opposed Chartism and the formation of unions as too violent a step for the times, even although his own lungs had been damaged by stoneworkers' silicosis in his youth. In the end his health did collapse, and exhausted and depressed, he took his own life, with a gun. Among his books, the succinct prose of *The Old Red Sandstone* (1841) is something of a geologist's classic, even if he did try to reconcile the biblical account of creation with his scientific observations in a later work called *Footprints of the Creator* (1849). *Scenes and Legends of the North of Scotland* (1835) and an autobiography called *My Schools and Schoolmasters* (1854) testify to the life of the times and his constant interest in the landscape around him. Carlyle commended Millar as a genial fire 'tempered down into peaceful radical heat' and described the natural stateliness of his prose as 'luminous, memorable, all wholesome, strong and breezy' – an image of the man himself that outlasted his poor end.

William Alexander (1826–94)

The Disruption was a major historical and personal event in the life of Millar and thousands like him in parishes throughout the country. It revived communal ideals and redefined, if only through opposition, the traditional centres of authority in village life, balanced as they were between minister, schoolteacher and laird. The dialect novel *Johnny Gibb of Gushetneuk* (1871) describes just such a community. Its author, William Alexander, worked on farms in Aberdeenshire until an accident in his twenties cost him one of his legs and he turned to journalism as a career. He became editor of the *Aberdeen Free Press* and published his memoirs and the collection *Sketches of Life among my Ain Folk* (1875), both dedicated, like his novel, to preserving a record of the life, manners and speech in the countryside of his birth. Then, as now, he spoke to a potent sense of pride and regional identity in his north-east readers. Alexander uses formal English for passages of objective narrative and comment, and this tends to distance him from his creation, but the true life of the novel comes from the density of its dialect speech – a repository of wit, scorn, gossip and common wisdom. This oral inheritance is the social and moral focus of the book – weighty, considered and dryly alert to pretension, it is the voice by which a community knows and guides itself.

Alexander's tendency to explain his characters at every turn was part of his documentary intention, for he was looking back some thirty years and his little community already seems frozen in time. Of course, change did not come equally to the remoter parts of Scotland, and even when it did, few writers seemed able to manage more than nostalgia at the prospect. This was particularly evident in the Highlands, where continuing and considerable changes failed to produce literature that was equal to the occasion, although some poets did manage political commitment and a fine rage in their verse. Perhaps new forms were needed to respond to the times, and most Gaelic poets were still loyal to the old communities and the old ways of looking at the world.

Gaelic literature

In search of opportunity, faced with rising rents, or simply cleared off their lands, thousands of Highlanders set sail for America in the opening years of the century. The oral treasury of Gaelic verse, music and tale-telling went with them and the old propensity for elegy and lament found new scope in their leave-taking. The homeland verses from the Gaelic-speaking settlements of Nova Scotia, South Carolina or the cities of Lowland Scotland all speak of exile, parting lovers, childhood and a simplified past. Popular songs poured out on these themes – typified by the 'Canadian Boat Song' in a translation sent back to *Blackwood's Magazine* by John Galt in 1829:

> From the lone shieling of the misty island
>   Mountains divide us and the waste of seas;
> Yet still the blood is strong, the heart is Highland,
>   And we in dreams behold the Hebrides.
> **Chorus**
> Fair these broad meads – these hoary woods are grand;
> But we are exiles from our fathers' land.

There were many competent voices singing in these nostalgic pastures, but there were almost no poets to equal those of the previous century.

In the very years when so many Gaels were leaving for America, tartan was breaking out like a rash, thanks to the 'wizard of the North', all over Britain and France. Fashionable society endured a craze for extravagantly formal 'Highland dress', and McIan's (still popular) clan prints, or the formal, plaid-ridden portraits of Raeburn all testify to the glamour of the kilt. The uniform dress of the Highland regiments was gradually adapted to civilian purposes and mill-owners and chieftains got together to define 'recognised' clan tartans and to associate them with Lowland families so that any Scot with any surname could be told to which clan he or she 'belonged'. The respectability of the kilt and all things tartan was finally assured when Queen Victoria sojourned at Balmoral and Prince Albert, that worthy Hanoverian, bared his knees and appeared in public as a Jacobite pretender.

In the meantime native Gaelic speakers were coming to terms with life in modern urban society. The Free Church, the Society for Propagating Christian Knowledge, and the rise of Evangelical Christianity all played a part in promoting literacy and the publishing of hymns and religious verses in Gaelic as well as homilies and sermons in prose. Yet the true fluency and power of Gaelic prose was largely unrecorded, for it came from the extempore oral tradition of the Free Church pulpit, and the passionate address of these sermons was to influence later Gaelic poets even if they were not church-goers or Christians. Prose fiction, on the other hand, remained almost unknown and indeed the market had little chance of developing for as long as Gaelic speakers lacked the leisure, the spending-power or the literacy to read novels in their own language. Songs and poems were published successfully, however, because they had the strength of the oral tradition behind them; and for the same reason folk stories and proverbs were collected in books such as John F. Campbell's four-volume *Popular Tales of the West Highlands* (1860–2). Gaelic periodicals were also established to speak to the growing Highland communities in Glasgow and the west of Scotland. The **Revd Norman Macleod** (1783–1862), called 'the friend of the Gael', was an influential editor and contributor to these magazines. He worked tirelessly on Gaelic education and produced a Gaelic dictionary (1831) and composed the beautiful song 'Farewell to Fiunary'. His short essays and dialogues were particularly widely appreciated and were collected posthumously in a volume called after him – *Caraid nan Ghàidheal* (1867). A prose piece such as his 'Long mhór nan Eilthireach' ('The Emigrant Ship') extracts the maximum pathos from the leave-taking of the young who crossed the Atlantic and the grief of the elderly left behind.

On the other side of the Atlantic, **Iain MacIlleathain, John MacLean** (1787–1848), a native of Tiree and one-time bard to the Laird of Coll, found himself in Nova Scotia, describing the hardships of that first settlement in a strange land, even if things were later to improve:

> When summer comes, and the month of Maytime,
> the heat of the sun will leave me weak;
> it will put vigour in every creature
> which, in all the holes, has been asleep;
> the beastly bears, they too will waken
> to go through the herd, causing massive loss,
> and the taloned insect, poisonous and snouty,
> will wound me profusely with its sharp-tipped lance.
>
> It will make my face come up lumpy,
> I'll not see the world, I will be blind;
> ('Oran do dh' Ameireaga'/'Song to America' , trs. D. Meek)

As the century progressed, the poetry of exile and in particular the songs of exile became more and more sentimental, painting an increasingly idealised picture of the lost homeland. Donald Meek has pointed out that the poets who moved to the Lowland cities of Scotland were particularly prone to this and it was there, too, that they found their most appreciative audiences. **Niall MacLeòid, Neil MacLeod** (1843–1913), who came to Edinburgh to work for a tea merchant, was particularly prolific and influential in this vein, and his sweet and melodiously sentimental songs, such as 'An Gleann san robh mi Og' ('The Glen where I was Young') gave rise to many imitators:

> When we would waken in the morning
> dew would be on grassy tips;
> the cuckoo would be calling
> in the close thicket of the nuts;
> the young calves would leap with joy,
> taking romps across the fields;
> but there is no sign of that at this time
> in the glen where I was young.
>
> In the glen where I was young,
> in the glen where I was young,
> it were my wish to be at that time
> in the glen where I was young.
>   (trs. D. Meek)

The prevailing theme of such work is one of childhood innocence in which leaving the homeland becomes nothing less than an expulsion from Eden. (The Gaelic rockgroup Runrig was to invoke the same themes to great popular success in the 1980s with albums such as *Recovery* and *Heartland*.) The Lowland Scots tradition had a similar appetite for nostalgic songs and poems about an idealised and rustically pious Scotland, and many writers of the so-called 'Kailyard' school reached their largely urban readership through the Evangelically directed *British Weekly,* edited by the Revd William Robertson Nicoll.

By the end of the century anthologies and collections of Gaelic poems were being published, popularised and translated by journalists such as Henry Whyte ('Fionn', 1852–1914) who was particularly keen on the song tradition. From 1909 into the 1920s Marjory Kennedy-Fraser produced *The Songs of the Hebrides* in several volumes, although she was inclined to 'improve' her folk sources to meet what she felt to be more refined standards of taste. In a more scholarly project Alexander Carmichael spent the last forty years of the century collecting the vast storehouse of anonymous Gaelic tales, songs, hymns and incantations that was finally published in six invaluable volumes as *Carmina Gadelica* (1900–69). Highland societies flourished in

Glasgow and Inverness, while Gaelic churches, ceilidhs, concerts and shinty-matches all established themselves as part of Scottish city life. Under the same stimulus amateur dramatic societies performed short Gaelic plays, and An Comunn Gaidhealach was formed to promote Highland culture and music. The first National Mod was held in 1893, and before long regular competitions were arranged, with Gaelic choirs assembled and an official 'bard' crowned as if to bring respectability and concert-hall status to the informality of the old oral ways.

Gaelic literature was not entirely given over to sentiment and respectability, however. **Uilleam MacDhunléibhe, William Livingstone** (1808–70) looked back to a heroic past and wrote battle-poems dramatising old conflicts against the Norse or the wars of independence against England. A self-educated man with a fierce hatred for everything English, he brought his rage to bear on the problem of depopulation in the Highlands. In 'Fios thun a'Bhàird' ('A Message to the Bard') he paints a loving picture of his native Islay and then upsets the convention by crying out against the absence of people in the scene. His refrain 'carry this clear message / as I see it, to the Bard' comes to seem increasingly bitter as the poem progresses.

Iain Mac a' Ghobhainn, John Smith (1848–81) composed lampoons and humorous verses about village life in Lewis, but his best poems are directly political. 'Oran Luchd an Spòrs' ('Song for Sportsmen') attacks the Scots themselves for allowing their lands and their heritage to fall into the hands of sportsmen and industrialists, and its scathingly radical outlook is prophetic of Hugh MacDiarmid's later disgust for the 'pickle makers' who had come to own the hills.

> Some of them trafficked in opium,
> they gathered a great deal of riches,
> their vice made the Chinamen suffer,
> their people destroyed by the poison;
> men without kindness or mercy,
> who were hard to prick in the conscience;
> in payment for all of their plunder
> they deserved to be stabbed with a whinger.   short sword
> (trs. D. Thomson)

Smith was thinking of James Matheson, a native of Sutherland who had made his fortune in the disgraceful opium trade with China and purchased the whole island of Lewis in 1844. He and his factors were not popular, most especially Donald Munro, whose autocratic rule (he held almost every official post on the island) earned him the local title of 'the Shah'. The poet recognised that the poor man can be arrogant, too, and he mocks the 'unco guid' of the Free Church in 'Spiorad an Uamhir' ('The Spirit of Pride'). But his finest rage is reserved for the world of social injustice and misused privilege. Among other lines in favour of *caritas*, 'Spiorad a' Charthannais' ('The Spirit of Kindness') speaks on behalf of the Highland regiments at Waterloo to make a complaint which Scotland, and Lewis in particular, was to hear again at the end of the First World War:

> What solace had the fathers
> of the heroes who won fame?
> Their houses, warm with kindliness,
> were in ruins around their ears;
> their sons were on the battlefield
> saving a rueless land,
> their mothers' state was piteous
> with their houses burnt like coal.
>
> While Britain was rejoicing
> they spent their time in grief.
> In the country that had reared them,
> no shelter from the wind;
> the grey strands of their hair were tossed
> by the cold breeze of the glen,
> there were tears upon their cheeks
> and cold dew on their heads.

Smith reminds his oppressors that death is a landlord who comes to us all, but he saves his most vehement hatred for the factor Munro:

> The wriggling worm will praise you then
> for your flesh's enticing taste,
> when it finds you placed before it
> on its table, silent now,
> saying 'This one's juicy flesh
> is good for earthy worms,
> since he made many hundreds thin
> to feed himself for me.'
>
> (trs. D. Thomson)

Smith's images are strong, concrete and uncomfortably savage, with something of the spirit of Iain Lom in place of the nostalgia that prevails in so many of the 'homeland' verses.

On the other hand, there was a strong tradition of military service in the Highland regiments, and this too was covered in Gaelic verse, as for example in the poem 'Saighdear Gàidhealach' ('A Highland Soldier') by

Iain Caimbeul, John Campbell (1823–97), whose warlike fervour is all the more incongruous for being sung by the trooper's beloved:

> Lift high the banner, my own people's kindreds,
> raise it in victory, with the shout of your conquest;
> your forebears bequeathed that true blood, unsullied,
> which could uphold us in each struggle and hardship.
>
> (trs. D. Meek)

The warlike virtues of *brosnachadh* proved to be eminently transferrable skill and Scotland's Highland regiments have a long and distinguished record in defence of the British Empire. From the French and Indian wars in Canada to the 'thin red line' of Colin Campbell's troops at Balaclava, from the Indian Mutiny to the siege of Khartoum, the rebels of 1745 became national heroes, with their once proscribed pipes and kilts striking terror into the hearts of the colonised as the very symbols of Imperial power.

There were some, however, who were less susceptible to unthinking loyalty and it was the struggle for land reform in Skye in the 1880s that motivated many of the poems of **Màiri Nic a' Phearsain, Mary Macpherson** (1821–98). Màiri Mhór lived latterly in Inverness and Glasgow, and some of her songs, such as 'Soraidh leis an Nollaig ùir' ('Farewell to the New Christmas'), and 'Nuair bha mi òg' ('When I was young') evoke longing for the island of her youth:

> I call to mind all the things I did there
>   that will not fade till my story's end,
> walking in winter to prayer or wedding,
>   my only lantern a peat in hand;
> the splendid youngsters, with song and dancing . . .
>   Gone are the days now and sad the glen;
> now Andrew's croft under shrouding nettles
>   brings back to mind how our days were then.
>
> (trs. W. Neill)

But Mary was no sentimentalist and her popular songs in support of land reform made her something of a legend; she became well known for her outspoken and earthy expression, made doubly impressive by her energy and her huge size. Imprisoned at Inverness on what she insisted was a false charge of shoplifting, she explained in 'Na dh'fhuiling mi de dh'fhòirneart' ('The Oppression I Suffered') that the injustice of the experience was what turned her talents to verse. In the cause of land reform she listed the movement's heroes in 'Oran Beinn-Lì' ('Song of Ben Lee'); and she composed 'Brosnachadh nan Ghàidheal'

('Incitement of the Gaels') on behalf of the reform candidates at the elections of 1885. In these verses she recalled the boatload of soldiers and policemen that had been sent to Uig to suppress unrest the previous year:

If the language here is blunt,
    truth is often sore to speak,
they send warships and armed men
    to guard and save their law of land.

When the landlords gathered round
    assembled in the county town,
'twill be recalled in every age,
    the tricks they practised to deceive us.
                                    (trs. W. Neill)

It is entirely fitting that 'Big Mary of the songs' should have become one of the heroes herself, for it was the womenfolk of the crofts, after all, who had driven off the police in the 'battle of Braes' on Skye in 1882.

Margaret Oliphant (1828–97)

In complete contrast to Mary Macpherson, the many books of Margaret Oliphant return us to the Lowlands and to a politer provincial scene. Born near Edinburgh and brought to live in Liverpool as a girl, Mrs Oliphant's sympathies remained with small dissenting communities and her northern origins. The heroine of her first novel, *Margaret Maitland* (1849), encapsulates all the Scottish Victorian spinsterly virtues of piety, good sense, reticence and industry. The author herself had to draw on these strengths soon enough, for she was widowed while scarcely in her thirties and had to turn to writing to support herself, her family and an alcoholic brother as well. Her career in England spans forty-five years of extraordinary industry during which time she produced innumerable articles and reviews for 'Maga' as well as biographies, criticism, literary histories, an autobiography, a history of *Blackwood's* and over sixty two- and three-volume novels. She prided herself on being a *Blackwood's* author, as well she might, but her life's work did not make her particularly rich or famous. Margaret Oliphant wrote several Scottish novels, including *Merkland* (1851), *Katie Stewart* (1853) – an historical piece – and *Kirsteen: A Story of a Scottish Family Seventy Years Ago* (1890). Oliphant was an admirer of

Walter Scott's work and the eponymous heroine of *Kirsteen* is not unlike Jeanie Deans in *The Heart of Midlothian* – or indeed Oliphant herself. After Kirsteen's fiancé is killed while serving the empire in India, she determines to support her often unworthy parents, brothers and sisters and sets out, the very model of an indomitable Scottish woman, to make a fortune on her own despite many setbacks along the way. The novel is remarkable in that it sets a very strong-minded heroine against her own father, the Laird of Drumcarro, a man who made and lost a fortune in the slave trade, and a patriarchal bully (and a murderer) in what will become an increasingly familiar Scottish type. Kirsteen shows that her own true grit and business acumen can win through and save the family in the end, without concessions to her sex and without the need for male support or marriage.

Not all Oliphant's heroines are as determined as Kirsteen and many of her novels are concerned with the more mundane tribulations of provincial life and manners. Q. D. Leavis has cited the novels in this vein as a useful link between the worlds of Jane Austen and George Eliot, and indeed Oliphant's *Miss Marjoribanks* (1866) may have been a direct influence on *Middlemarch* (1871–2). (George Eliot was suspected of being the author of *Miss Marjoribanks* because it was serialised in *Blackwood's*, where her own *Scenes of Clerical Life* had first appeared.) *Miss Marjoribanks* belongs to a series of novels and stories set in England that were collected as 'The Chronicles of Carlingford' (1863–6) after the style of Trollope's 'Barchester' books and Mrs Gaskell's 'Cranford' sketches. By the end of the 1860s, however, Oliphant had to support another of her brothers and his family, and her increased literary output led to a decline in quality for the rest of her life as a professional author. Even so, she was a respected friend of Carlyle's, and Barrie, Robert Louis Stevenson and Henry James admired her best work for the potential they saw in it, just as they acknowledged her good humour and her indomitable spirit.

Oliphant is probably best remembered today for her supernatural fiction, which she described as her 'stories of the seen and the unseen'. These were all written in the last twenty years of her life, and she seems to have taken more care with them, noting in her uncompleted autobiography that she could 'produce them only when they come to me'. Like so many Victorians of her time, and perhaps in response to her own grief at the death of three of her young children, she was haunted by the possibility of supernatural or theosophical intimations of a realm of spirits beyond death. Her novella *A Beleaguered City* (1880) tells the story of a provincial French town whose inhabitants are forced out of their homes by a strange and oppressive darkness. The mayor of the town records these eerie events and the growing confusion of the population, but in the end it is the womenfolk who come to realise what has been happening. They have been besieged by the shades of the dead who have come back to remind their materialistic relatives that compassion and things of the spirit are more important than the getting and spending of wealth. When they finally recognise what is happening the townsfolk can re-enter their houses and pick up their lives again – more fully appreciative, if only for a short while, of their human blessings.

In this as in her other supernatural writing, Oliphant is gripped by a sense that the borderline between the realms of being and non-being is thinner and more permeable than we like to think. 'The Open Door' (1882) evokes just such a portal while its Scottish setting recalls old tales and ballads of the supernatural. 'The Library Window' (1896), on the other hand, anticipates the psychological complexity of Henry James's *The Turn of the Screw* (1898) in an entirely realistic domestic setting. A young woman staying with her old aunt gradually begins to discern a room beyond a library window in a building opposite – except that there may be no window there at all and the effect merely a *trompe-l'oeil*. Nevertheless as her long summer days pass she comes to see more and more clearly into the room beyond, until what is happening there – and the mysterious figure of a man at a desk – comes to seem more real to her than the world around her, and certainly more fascinating than the routinely dull social round of her aunt and her aunt's friends. There is a certain sexual charge in the air, and a sense of the unnamed heroine's own suspension and uncertainty – leading to an epiphanic moment of strange intensity that will survive the mundane recognition that the window does not exist, and that nothing in her life to come, neither her marriage nor her children, will ever quite match:

> I watched him with such a melting heart, with such a deep satisfaction as words could not say; for nobody could tell me now that he was not there, – nobody could say I was dreaming any more. I watched him as if I could not breathe – my heart in my throat, my eyes upon him. He looked up and down, and then he looked back to me. I was the first, and I was the last, though it was not for long: he did know, he did see, who it was that had recognised him and sympathised with him all the time. I was in a kind of rapture, yet stupor too; my look went with his look, following it as if I were his shadow; and then suddenly he was gone, and I saw him no more.

Almost the last story that Oliphant wrote, 'The Library Window' is one of the finest supernatural stories in English. An earlier piece, 'The Land of Darkness' (1885), is a more conventionally phantasmagorical tale in which she imagines the otherness of a strangely hellish underworld in terms of the industrial cities of late Victorian Britain – crowded, polluted and driven by greed and selfishness:

> I could by glimpses perceive a low horizon all lurid and glowing, which seemed to sweep round and round. Against it in the distance stood up the outline, black against that red glow, of other towers and house-tops, so many and great that there was evidently another town between us and the sunset, if sunset it was. . . . The distant town rose against it, cutting the firmament so that it might have been tongues of flame flickering between the dark solid outlines; and across the waste open country which lay between the two cities, there came a distant hum like the sound of the sea, which was in reality the roar of that other multitude.

There were scenes very like these in our next writer's poetry, and they will appear again in the 'Unthank' of Alasdair Gray's *Lanark* in the century still to come.

James Thomson (1834–82)

Among the other Scots working in London at this time, James Thomson was to make a grimmer indictment of late-Victorian life and belief than even Carlyle had attempted. Thomson's father was a merchant seaman in Port Glasgow until a stroke paralysed him when James was six. The family moved to London, but Thomson's mother died within two years and he went to an asylum for the children of poor Scottish servicemen. With his limited means he joined up as an army schoolmaster, but after eight years his drinking led to dismissal and in 1862 he found himself back in London looking for a new livelihood. He turned to literature and journalism, having published some poems and articles while he was still in the army, and eventually gained a post with the *National Reformer* – a periodical directed at freethinkers who wanted to keep up with the views of Darwin, Spencer and Huxley. Thomson's mother had been an Irvingite and no doubt he assimilated some of her passionate Christianity along with a youthful enthusiasm for Shelley and Novalis, the late-eighteenth-century German Romantic poet. (Thomson used 'BV' – Bysshe Vanolis – as a pseudonym for his verses.) Early poems and articles suggest a struggle between idealistic and mystical beliefs and a conviction that the profit-motive and the old ways of worship have corrupted and enslaved mankind. He attacked Christianity for ignoring the vital present in favour of rewards and punishments in an afterlife, and proposed a kind of pantheism in which each man's duty is to realise the true freedom of his spirit before it returns to the infinite, impersonal, evolutionary flow of matter. Thomson gradually came to atheism and a philosophical pessimism that recognised the disparity between human hope and man's imperfectability, and he published these views in the *National Reformer*. He also produced a memoir of the Italian pessimist Giacomo Leopardi and translated his dialogues and discourses.

Thomson's drive to show 'the bitter, old, and wrinkled truth, stripped naked' culminates in *The City of Dreadful Night*, published in parts during 1874 and as a book in 1880. The poem is often cited as a 'modern' vision of the city as nightmare, but it is essentially a Dantesque allegory, a symbolic rather than a realistic visit to a cold Inferno of streets, squares and graveyards in some archetypal city located, perhaps, in metaphysical space, rather like Margaret Oliphant's later story 'The Land of Darkness'. (In fact earlier poems such as 'Sunday up the River' and 'Sunday at Hampstead', from 1865, are markedly more 'realistic' and more modern in their use of colloquial English. They also show London in a cheerful and sunny mood, to remind us that Thomson was not entirely given over to gloom.) Even so, *The City of Dreadful Night* does look forward to T. S. Eliot's vision of London as a wasteland, and Thomson's empty squares have a strange and menacing calm, which seems to anticipate surrealism and the modern paintings of De Chirico. For the most part, however, the echoes are of Dürer and Shelley, and the poet's atheism is suffused with a melancholy that might have been drawn from Fitzgerald or even Drummond of Hawthornden:

And now at last authentic word I bring,
Witnessed by every dead and living thing;
    Good tidings of great joy for you, for all:
There is no God; no Fiend with names divine
Made us and tortures us; if we must pine,
    It is to satiate no Being's gall.

. . .

This little life, is all we must endure,
The grave's most holy place is ever sure,
    We fall asleep and never wake again;
Nothing is of us but the mouldering flesh,
Whose elements dissolve and merge afresh
    In earth, air, water, planets, and other men.
                                    (XIV)

On the other hand, there are realistic passages in the poem that undoubtedly catch the spectral nature of modern cities at night:

> I sat forlornly by the river-side
> And watched the bridge-lamps glow like golden stars
> Above the blackness of the swelling tide,
> Down which they struck rough gold in ruddier bars;
> And heard the heave and plashing of the flow
> Against the wall a dozen feet below.
>
> Large elm-trees stood along that river-walk;
> And under one, a few steps from my seat,
> I heard strange voices join in stranger talk,
> Although I had not heard approaching feet . . .
>   (VI)

Even the readers of the *National Reformer* were startled by the sustained threnody of Thomson's 'comfort', and, although he received encouraging letters from George Eliot and Meredith, most reviewers accused the poem of insincerity or heresy or both, and they preferred the other pieces in the 1880 collection. Thomson despaired of finding favour with the prestigious literary periodicals, and a break with his editor saw him reduced to writing reviews and biographical essays for *Cope's Tobacco Plant* – a journal subsidised by a Liverpool tobacco firm.

Increasingly given to bouts of excessive drinking, the poet's health and morale declined until a particularly destructive episode killed him in June 1882. He had achieved a modest reputation, but *The City of Dreadful Night* spoke more clearly to a later generation. If its images of despair look rather romantic to readers used to Eliot and Kafka, we can still sympathise with his courageous attempt to face the material indifference of the universe without flinching. At least he felt that poetry should tackle serious philosophical issues, and in this he shared his idealism, and a preference for evolutionism too, with John Davidson. Hugh MacDiarmid's later poetry can also be seen to have a place in this company, going back to Carlyle himself, in what amounts to a school of Scottish writers who have married a 'metaphysical' inclination to a polemical urgency.

By comparison, the desperate plight of poetry in Scotland may be judged by the continuing success of the *Whistle-Binkie* anthologies and the vogue that grew up for the verse of **William McGonagall** (1825?–1902), 'poet', 'tragedian' and public performer from Dundee. McGonagall himself was sincere (or deluded) in his ambitions to be a great poet, but his audiences came mostly to laugh. Nevertheless, he undertook poetry readings throughout Scotland and even visited London and New York. His naïve verses on all the issues of the day – preferably 'tragedies' such as the Tay Bridge disaster in 1879 – do demonstrate a positive genius for the banal, stuffed with prosaic details and hilariously contrived rhymes and constantly repeated kennings 'most beautiful to see', if not to hear. He is not quite so easily dismissed, however, as the 'world's best bad poet', even although he almost certainly is. To begin with, he is operating in the already familiar oral tradition of the broadside ballad, selling his wares to comment on the events of the day. And some readers have noted that these comments are more subversively satirical than might be thought at first glance, painting, even if indirectly, a comically horrendous picture of the self-satisfied complacency of small-town Scottish life. (Dundee endures the stain of his greatness to this day with mixed feelings of pride and abjection.) It seems inconceivable that he was unaware of the fact that his audiences were laughing at him, and the absurdly grotesque outfits that he wore in the street as well as on the stage, suggest a man who has chosen to live the role to the hilt. The accounts of his acting several Shakespearean parts at once, of his refusal to die as Macbeth (his favourite role), of his clearing the stage, the orchestra pit and the front stalls with his violent swordplay suggest a talent for deadpan comedy – consciously or unconsciously realised – that recalls the manic seriousness of a Buster Keaton. If the fruit and flour-bombs were flying about his head, at least it was a living for an old handloom weaver at a time when the machines were taking over. The contemporary poet W. N. Herbert has called McGonagall 'indisputably Scotland's first Dadaist: he drew out from all levels of the population their essential mistrust of poetry, and crystallised this philistinism in his totally anarchic performances', concluding that perhaps 'the most radical thing we can say about McGonagall is that he was awful because Scotland – wee sleekit, shortie-slurping bourgeois North Britain – was awful too.' Nevertheless, the old man's *Poetic Gems* (1890) have never been out of print – a reflection that would have given poor Thomson little comfort – and they have been translated (with what result one can only wonder) into Russian, Bulgarian, Romanian, Japanese, Thai and Chinese.

Robert Louis Stevenson (1850–94)

James Thomson's confrontation with the problems of modernity, urban despair and scientific materialism, scarcely features in the fiction of

Robert Louis Stevenson, whose best-known books belong to an extrovert tale-telling tradition that looks back to Scott. He was not alone, and for the rest of the century the preferred modes of Scottish novelists will be Stevensonian romance, symbolic fantasy or nostalgic rusticism. While these forms undoubtedly represent a reaction to the materialistic face of the contemporary world, they cannot be said to deal with it directly. It would be wrong to accuse Stevenson of escapism, however, for his mercurial personality had a most complicated relationship with Scotland and his own Scottishness. Critical and nostalgic by turns, he wrote about his homeland from exile in the South Seas, seeking to express a vision shaped by the rigours of Calvinism and yet self-consciously dedicated to the free life of art and the imagination. Such internal divisions fuel the best of Stevenson's fiction, as if he were replaying in psychologically ambiguous terms Walter Scott's own conflict between Unionist stability and Jacobite romance. He had scarcely begun to fulfil his deepening grasp of these old themes when a brain haemorrhage ended his life at the age of forty-four.

Stevenson's health was perpetually at the mercy of acute lung troubles and tuberculosis, and the damp and windy climate of Edinburgh plagued his boyhood with coughs and chills that put him to bed for weeks of fever and sleepless nights. As an only child, he would not have survived if he had not come from a well-off and caring family, for his father was a harbour engineer and lighthouse-builder, like his grandfather, who had constructed the 'impossible' light on Bell Rock. Stevenson senior was a devout and conservative man, whose sense of duty had led him in his father's footsteps to be a civil engineer, despite his own rather intense and imaginative nature. He was fond and affectionate with his son and encouraged his youthful writing. So often confined to bed, the boy thrived on escapist tales and delighted to create plots with cut-out figures from his toy theatre – a pastime he recalled in his essay 'A Penny Plain and Two Pence Coloured' (1883). Many of his poems in *A Child's Garden of Verses* (1885) – assembled while he was convalescing as an adult – relate to this imaginative life of bedside dreams and games on the counterpane, and he dedicated the collection to Alison Cunningham, the devoted young nurse of his childhood whom he never forgot as 'My second Mother, my first Wife'. 'Cummie' came from strict Presbyterian stock and, although she disapproved of plays and novels, she still fired her charge's imagination with stories of the Covenanters and tales of righteousness.

Stevenson entered Edinburgh University at the age of seventeen, but his studies in civil engineering (to please his father) took second place to new friends, new books and the bohemian life. He declared a romantic preference for the low life of Edinburgh – 'the lighted streets and the swinging gait of harlots' – so excitingly different from a New Town background in middle-class bourgeois respectability. When engineering failed to enthuse him he attempted law, but growing differences with his father came to a head over his professed agnosticism and his bohemian friends – notably his lively cousin Bob Stevenson. Louis's parents (his name was pronounced 'Lewis' by the family) were disproportionately frightened and dismayed by their son's loss of grace and he was made to feel extremely guilty. Life at home became tense, and a very early story only recently published – 'The Edifying Letters of the Rutherford Family' – deals with this crisis. The young man found relief in intimate letters to Mrs Francis Sitwell, an older woman whom he had met at a cousin's house in Suffolk. She believed in his talent, and she and Sidney Colvin – later her husband – helped him to make London contracts in journalism and publishing. The following year saw something of a reconciliation with the family, who never ceased to support him financially, and he was back in Edinburgh studying Scots law again. His father gave him £1000 when he finally became an advocate in 1875, but had to accept that his son's career was henceforth to be a literary one. Stevenson duly began his peripatetic adult life with regular visits to London and the continent, especially to the forest of Fontainebleau, where his cousin Bob spent the summers painting in congenial artistic company, away from the cold winds and the sterner expectations of the North.

A few essays and book reviews had already appeared under Stevenson's name, including a piece on what he took to be John Knox's two-faced attitude to women. At Edinburgh Infirmary he met the English poet W. E. Henley, who had come to have the tubercular bones of his foot treated by Joseph Lister. Stevenson based Long John Silver's better qualities on his rumbustious friend, and they wrote four plays together in the 1880s, without much stage success. The two writers remained close for thirteen years until a quarrel over a slight to Stevenson's wife parted them. Neither gave in to their ailments, and both seemed determined to pursue an actively physical life. Indeed, Louis's first book, *An Inland Voyage* (1878), describes a canoe holiday he took through the canals of Belgium in the summer of 1876. Later that year at a hotel in Fontainebleau he met the woman he was to marry.

Fanny Osbourne was an American in Europe with her children, where she intended to study painting and make a break from her husband. Stevenson was struck by this resourceful and intelligent lady, ten years his senior, and she was intrigued by his physical frailty combined with an extraordinarily vital and volatile personality. They became lovers, but Fanny's money finally ran out and she had to return to America. That autumn Stevenson set out on a twelve-day mountain-walking tour in the south of France, travelling alone with his pack, his notebook, a revolver and a donkey called Modestine. By now his delight in France and the free life had produced a study of François Villon and a short story featuring him – 'A Lodging for the Night' (1877) – as well as 'The Sire de Malétroit's Door' (1878). He had made friends with Andrew Lang and Edmund Gosse and produced a number of essays for Henley's *London*, later collected in *Virginibus Puerisque* (1881). In the winter he completed *Edinburgh: Picturesque Notes*, and in June 1879 *Travels with a Donkey in the Cévennes* became a minor classic among travel books. His literary career was under way at last.

Then Stevenson received a cable from Fanny Osbourne in California and, to the absolute consternation of friends and family, he decided to go to Monterey to join her, though she was not yet divorced. Excited by the prospect of America, he expected to meet the energy and opti-mism that he had found in the works of Walt Whitman; but the rigours of the journey and the strain of his arrival nearly killed him. *Across the Plains* (1892) and *The Amateur Emigrant* (1895) give a rawly realistic account of the sufferings he shared with his fellow voyagers, but neither piece appeared in his lifetime. Louis's fiction was more successful, and 'The Pavilion on the Links' (1880) was published as an atmospheric short story set on the bleak sands of the Scottish east coast – full of convincing detail, mysterious doings at night and the lore of tides and winds. His youthful visits to lighthouses with his father had not been forgotten, and many later works show the same delight in shores, islands, harbours and coastal inns.

Stevenson and Fanny were married in May 1880. With limited means, but tough and resourceful in her own way, Fanny took her husband into the mountains for the sake of his health, and their expe-riences in an abandoned shack at an old silver-mine produced *The Silverado Squatters* (1883). Fences were mended with Edinburgh and by August the new couple and twelve-year-old stepson Lloyd Osbourne were in Heriot Row, where Fanny succeeded in befriending Louis's parents and friends. As ever, the approach of a Scottish winter drove them abroad, but the following summer saw them back in Pitlochry and Braemar, and Stevenson began to write again, using

Scots for the first time as a major narrative voice. 'Thrawn Janet' (1881) is a gripping account of supernatural possession with its roots in the oral tradition – not unlike Scott's 'Wandering Willie's Tale'. It tells how the Revd Murdoch Soulis is forced to recognise the power of the Devil, although as a college-educated and liberal young minister he used to scoff at such superstition and to chide the locals for their cruelty to Janet, the local witch. The community's beliefs are vindicated when Janet is found to be a reanimated corpse and, on the imaginative level at least, Stevenson joins Hogg in accepting the intimate proximity of the Devil and all his works. Fired by his theme and its native setting, Stevenson followed it with 'The Body Snatcher' and then 'The Merry Men' (1882) as a tale of Cameronian piety and guilt among the shipwrecks on an elemental Scottish coast in the eighteenth century. Not far from the spirit of Hawthorne and Poe (whom he had read and admired), 'The Merry Men' is made into a subtler and more profound tale by Stevenson's mastery of atmospheric description and an existential sense of the world balanced on the edge of a chaotic and indifferent universe, just as his characters find themselves battered by storms on the edge of a cliff above a 'charnel ocean'.

Stevenson's fascination with shores and his memories of the California coast came to fruition when he began to write *Treasure Island*. Conceived in Braemar and finished in Switzerland, where they wintered again, 'The Sea Cook' began as a tale around a map drawn for young Lloyd's amusement. It followed a genre already established by Captain Marryat (1792–1848) and popularised by a fellow Edinburgh writer, **R. M. Ballantyne** (1825–94), whose dozens of books include *Martin Rattler*, *The Coral Island* (both 1858) and *The Gorilla Hunters* (1861). Yet *Treasure Island* (1883) was more than another adventure serial in *Young Folks*, for Stevenson had uncovered a theme that spoke to his life experience and his imagination with equal force. Indeed, its psychological and moral patterns were to reappear in all his mature works. The typical Stevenson hero is an untried young man faced with formative experience: Jim Hawkins is a teenager, while the protagonist of 'The Merry Men' and David Balfour of *Kidnapped* are scarcely older – lads of university age at a time when studies started young. Archie Weir also fits this pattern, although he is less typical in other respects. On leaving home, or travelling, these young heroes are freed from the security of convention and routine, much as the author himself threw over Heriot Row in favour of Fontainebleau and Silverado. Impressions of the world are heightened in such new surroundings – an effect that the readers share – and the protagonists have to make judgements on people and events entirely from their own resources. Having lost their fathers (a motif of interest to the psychoanalytical critic), the heroes look to friends for guidance instead, or to charismatic strangers or distant uncles, only to be shocked by what they find. The world of their elders, like the elders themselves, is not what it seemed to be from the security of childhood. Nevertheless, when Jim Hawkins finally realises that Silver is a lot less than the 'best of shipmates', he still cannot condemn him. Dr Livesey, Squire Trelawney and Captain Smollett belong to the world of gentlemen – the world Jim will enter after these rites of passage – but it is Silver who strikes a strange note of sympathy and complicity with the boy, and it is Silver, like a dangerous mixture of Iago and Falstaff, who dominates the stage with his power to charm. Thus Jim and Long John, like David Balfour and Alan Breck, or the two Duries in *The Master of Ballantrae*, or the two sides of Dr Jekyll, represent opposed tendencies in a shifting balance between stability and adventure, or social responsibility and individual freedom. If Walter Scott proposed a similar polarity, he always ended with the status quo, but for Louis the condition is psychological and less easily resolved – a struggle within the hearts and minds of his heroes, who are still haunted by the booming surf, or by nights on the bare hillside, even after they have accepted a settled future. In this way Stevenson transcends the adventure novel by using its uncomplicated lines to say some rather complicated things about the tensions between imagination and convention, and the changes that take place, for better and for worse, between youth and maturity.

When Stevenson chooses the past – and almost all his stories do – it is imaginative freedom that he is choosing, as if the past were another kind of exotic location, more appropriate for such deeds and dilemmas than late-Victorian Edinburgh. A moment's comparison with Dostoevsky or James will show his limitations in this respect, yet the landscapes of *Treasure Island* or *Kidnapped* are so vividly realised, and the reader is so involved with the physical immediacy of vicarious experience, that all is made contemporary again. Despite his favourite eighteenth-century settings, Stevenson is not a historical novelist at all, certainly not in the style of Scott or Galt, who were so keen to explore the differences between 'then' and 'now'. Nevertheless, Louis was sensitive about his standing as a conscious and serious artist. He explained his theories about fiction and defended prose romance in an essay called 'Gossip on Romance' (1882), and again in 'A Humble Remonstrance' (1884), which was offered as a reply to Henry James's essay 'The Art of Fiction'. The Scot maintained that truth to life was not enough in fiction, for life is inchoate, while the novelist's job is to construct order by subsuming character, setting and incident to an overriding creative conception. At the same time he must meet the challenge to convey a sense of 'real' and dazzling experience in his prose. This concern with style and the writer's craft gave him common ground with James, and the two men met and corresponded and became admirers of each other's work.

Further collections of essays and short stories and the book publication of *Treasure Island* brought critical status and much-needed royalties; but Stevenson's health forced him abroad again, where he completed a lesser romance, *Prince Otto* (1805), and began *The Black Arrow* (1888). After a year, the family returned to Britain for what was to be their last sojourn, settling in Bournemouth at 'Skerryvore', where Stevenson wrote 'Markheim' and the novels *Kidnapped* and *Jekyll and Hyde*, both of which appeared in 1886.

As a novel of travel and the Scottish landscape *Kidnapped* has few equals, yet its fascination comes as much from character as from action, although its main protagonists need to be considered together to realise the author's theme in this respect. David Balfour is the canny heir to Walter Scott's Lowland, Presbyterian, Unionist world, while Alan Breck Stewart epitomises the wilful courage and Jacobite romance of the Highlands – still potent five years after Culloden. Yet, even although David is carried along by events, rather like a Scott hero, Breck's loyal, vain and dangerous spirit seems to echo something within himself. When their escapade is over, Alan Breck must go into exile in France and David must turn to the gentlemanly responsibilities of his inheritance. This is symbolised by his passing through the doors of the British Linen Bank at the end of the adventure, and all the time 'there was a cold gnawing in my inside like a remorse for something wrong'. The remorse is not unlike J. M. Barrie's regret for the loss of boyhood symbolised by Peter Pan's kingdom of ruthless innocence and amoral imaginative freedom. Peter Pan crows like a cock at the defeat of his enemies, with just the same untrammelled spirit as Alan Breck does when he claims staid and earnest Balfour for his own:

He came up to me with open arms. 'Come to my arms!' he cried, and embraced and kissed me hard upon both cheeks. 'David,' said he, 'I love you like a brother. And O, man,' he cried in a kind of ecstasy, 'am I no' a bonny fighter?'
Thereupon he turned to the four enemies, passed his sword clean through each of them, and tumbled them out of doors one after the other. As he did so, he kept humming, and singing, and whistling to himself . . .

Such is the 'brother' David must learn to leave behind, but his call is felt from within and it cannot be denied without that feeling of 'remorse for something wrong'.

Stevenson had already realised that duality was the true and underlying theme of his fiction, for he had just given an overtly psychological focus to it in *Strange Case of Dr Jekyll and Mr Hyde* (1886). Its origins as a Gothic 'shilling shocker' are obvious and Louis had already written a play about the good Deacon Brodie's secret career of crime in Edinburgh. But this novel's interest in the unconscious and interior nature of good and evil give it a more serious moral dimension, just as it also symbolises a social truth about Victorian society and the anonymity of its great cities, where depravity and respectability rub shoulders. Although the tale is set in London, it has deeply Scottish roots, and true to the ethos of the *Justified Sinner* it shows the principle of evil as a kind of double being that threatens the upright personality from within. Jekyll's experiments were originally intended to remove this unworthy self, but they released him instead, and it is the experience of pleasure that subverts the doctor's Calvinist ideal of 'a life of effort, virtue and control'. At first he rejoices in his new ability to slip off 'genial respectability', as he puts it, like a schoolboy who sheds his clothes to 'spring headlong into the sea of liberty'. But he discovers that he cannot escape from his freer and darker side without killing himself. The novella's closing insights into the nature of human subjectivity go beyond the more usually understood concept of duality, for Stevenson attacks the concept of the unified self (that Victorian 'fortress of identity' and probity) by proposing, in Jekyll's words, that 'man will be ultimately known for a mere polity of multifarious, incongruous and independent denizens'. It is interesting to note that one of the 'blasphemous' tricks that Hyde plays on Jekyll is to destroy the portrait of his father, and indeed Jekyll thinks of Hyde as an unruly son. For Stevenson the normal tensions between fathers and sons are never very far away from Calvinist dread. This patriarchal/patricidal theme will appear again in his work with *Weir of Hermiston*, as it will in later Scottish novels, such as George Douglas Brown's *House with the Green Shutters* and William McIlvanney's *Remedy is None*.

Stevenson's long and complicated relationship with his father – resentful, affectionate and dependent by turns – finally came to an end when the old man died, and the writer decided to leave Britain once and for all with his mother, Fanny and Lloyd in 1887. They went to the Adirondacks near the Canadian border, where he could attend a TB clinic. His American royalties alleviated his perpetual money problems at last, until wanderlust and a longing for the sun took them all to California, where they chartered a schooner for an extended cruise in the South Seas. *The Master of Ballantrae* (1889) was completed in Hawaii, shortly after the New Year.

This time Stevenson symbolised the divisions of eighteenth-century Scotland in the lifelong struggle between two brothers. Staid and worthy Henry Durie is briefed to support the Hanoverian cause, while his younger brother James – a charming and amoral character – becomes a Jacobite adventurer. Their father's plan is that the house should survive, whatever the outcome of the rising. Here the differences between a Balfour type and a Breck type are exacerbated by rivalry in love, moral obsession and fraternal betrayal. At first our judgement of the two brothers is biased because the major part of the tale is told by Ephraim Mackellar, an educated and dogmatic servant, jealous on behalf of his 'Mr Henry' and prone to see things from his point of view. Mackellar is a limited narrator worthy of Galt, and the quality of the novel is much enhanced by his distinctive voice. Thus we only slowly come to realise that young James is neither a Byronic chevalier in exile, nor the Devil incarnate, although the Durie family casts him in both roles. The rather colourless and pious Henry is obsessed with his 'Satanic' brother, but it is his own sense of grievance, justification and wounded pride that takes over his sanity and ruins him. In the end, the old religious fears and the old Stuart romances have killed them both.

The Master of Ballantrae can be seen as a more mature examination of the adventure elements in *Kidnapped* and *Treasure Island,* now revisited and reappraised as a theatre of ineptitude, hypocrisy and delusion. Even that old Scottish stand-by, the demonic double, is reappraised in terms that have a much more modern and nihilistic turn to them, as we see when Mackellar confronts James Durie in terms that are prophetic of T. S. Eliot's 'hollow men' and Conrad's *Heart of Darkness*:

> I had moments when I thought of him as a man of pasteboard – as though, if one should strike smartly through the buckram of his countenance, there would be found a mere vacuity within.

It is significant – and existentially challenging – that chance should play such a large part in the motivation of the main characters. The toss of a coin decides which of the two brothers should join the Jacobite uprising and who should stay at home; and that same coin is flung through the family crest in a stained glass window, making its own point about the hollowness of honour and tradition. And when he is lost in the wilderness the Master tosses a coin once more, in a passage that clearly symbolises the ultimate emptiness behind the devilishly Byronic façade of this adventurer: 'He suddenly plucked out his coin, shook it in his closed hands, looked at it, and then lay down with his face in the dust.' The final mystery of the enmity between the brothers and their 'cause- less duplicity' is signalled when James refers to his brother Henry as 'Jacob', referring to the rivalry between Esau and Jacob in Genesis 25 – a rivalry without meaning, ordained from the start by God, just as the Calvinist doctrine of the elect tells us that some are saved and some are damned regardless of merit or their deeds. The passage from Genesis is a key text in the doctrine of Calvinist predestination, but the force of Stevenson's insight is to reinterpret it – via what seems to be only an 'adventure' novel – in a what amounts to a recognition of existential blankness.

Andrew Lang found 'a very modern gloom' in the book while W. E. Henley thought that it left 'an impression of unreality . . . as if you had been awakened from a sinister dream', concluding that the novel 'is a romance which differs from the romances of Sir Walter [Scott] as a black marble vault differs from a radiant palace'. Despite the adventurous travels and trappings to be found within its pages, *The Master* makes a new and challenging point about Scottish character and history and its author's earlier engagement with these themes. More than this, Stevenson's vision has taken a much wider philosophical perspective when his story, which he subtitled 'A Winter's Tale', confronts final absurdity to end, as it does, with a double death in a trackless wilderness.

The Stevenson family found itself on another sea trip, on a trading- schooner through the Gilbert Islands, and these voyages on the fringes of respectable commerce provided the material for the author's best South Sea stories. In his fortieth year he was making a growing commit- ment to life in the Pacific, and when they came to Samoa again they bought a large estate at Upolu and built a house there. Thinking to visit Britain just one more time, they travelled to Sydney in 1890, but Louis's health collapsed, and collapsed again even after another conva- lescence. The little party returned to Vailima, where they remained for the last four years of the author's life. Slowly the estate established itself, and Stevenson became a respected figure in the community as a cham- pion of native rights and a 'Tusitala' – a storyteller.

Louis's thoughts turned to Scotland, which he never expected to see again. He corresponded with J. M. Barrie and invited him to Samoa, longing to talk to a fellow Scot; and he began *Weir of Hermiston*. Faced with more immediate demands for money, he fell back on David Balfour and wrote *Catriona* (1893) as a sequel to *Kidnapped*, substituting moral complications and a love interest for the topographical brilliance of the earlier book. Further adventure stories were in order, so he worked on *St Ives* about a French prisoner of war in England (finished by Quiller-Couch in 1897) and started books on the Covenanters and Prince Charlie.

In the meantime, the South Seas featured in a selection of tales and fables called *Island Night's Entertainments* (1893), which included 'The Beach at Falesa', a completely different kind of story describing the sordid activities of white traders in what Stevenson called 'the first realistic South Sea story; I mean with real South Sea character and details of life'. The first publication of this story in the *Illustrated London News* was bowdlerised for fear of offending its readers and Stevenson had to fight to stop the publishers making further cuts to the book version – not always successfully. A modern edition has restored the original. A novel called *The Ebb-Tide* followed with an even grimmer picture of moral decay and the seamy side of island existence. It is ironic that Stevenson was so resolutely unromantic about his exotic surroundings while the Kailyard school was reinventing Scotland as a homespun Eden for the sentimental delectation of exiled Scots around the globe. But Stevenson's experience of the European colonial presence in the Pacific had led him to reassess the part that was being played by Europeans – including those sentimental Scots – in undeveloped countries throughout the world.

Shared with Lloyd Osborne in its initial conception, but finally written and revised by Stevenson himself, *The Ebb-Tide* (1894) is one of the author's finest works. It can stand comparison with Conrad's *Heart of Darkness* – published only eight years later – as both an exposé of colonialism and a masterpiece of modernity and existential horror – the same blankness that *The Master of Ballantrae* had touched on and that Hannah Arendt would later call 'the banality of evil'.

The novel traces the exploits of three men who find themselves 'on the beach' without jobs and without prospects. Herrick is an educated idler who has known better times, his countryman Huish is a vicious and vulgar Cockney and Captain John Davis is an American skipper who ruined his career with drink. All three have been known by different names, all three are acquainted with failure and shame. Penniless, sick and starving, they seize the chance to crew a schooner that no other white men will touch since an outbreak of yellow fever on board. They plan to hijack the ship and its load of champagne, but not before they break into the hold and start drinking the cargo – only to discover after a while that the most part of it is water. They soon find themselves lost at sea with insufficient food – a sham crew with a sham cargo – until they come to a strangely spectral island unmarked on any map. This turns out to be a pearl station run by William John Attwater, a striking figure under the Union Jack, dressed in immaculate white drill: tall, suave, commanding, organised and educated – with a Winchester rifle. But the strangely deserted station is not quite what it seems. Attwater quickly identifies the three miscreants as 'vulgar wolves' out to rob him and they find themselves in his power as he wines and dines them. They are simultaneously horrified and fascinated by the 'silken brutality' of his amoral intelligence and the rapturous assurance, not to say the Calvinist conviction, with which he quotes scripture and rules his island: '"religion is a savage thing, like the universe it illuminates; savage, cold, and bare, but infinitely strong."' Their attempts to escape his influence will not come to a good end. Attwater is one of Stevenson's most memorable creations, but the true power of the story lies in the strangely unstable world it evokes, where nothing is what it seems and the names of men and ships are changed to escape past history, on an unmapped island, where the beach and the gravestones are as white as the ship's figurehead mounted on the headland – a terrible and finally unknowable symbol: 'a woman of exorbitant stature . . . beckoning with uplifted arm' as white as snow.

At the end of 1894 Louis was working once more on *Weir of Hermiston*, excited by its exploration of the doomed relationship between an overbearing father and his sensitive son. It was his practice to read passages aloud to the family at the end of each day, but on 3 December he suffered a sudden cerebral stroke and died in the evening with the story unfinished.

Weir of Hermiston (1896) might have turned out to be Stevenson's greatest Scottish novel but what survives is still a magnificent beginning in which the author's fascination with the duality of character and the mysterious influences of inheritance and history are expressed as a conflict between father and son, with the very spirit of Calvinist authority set against the frailer virtues of imagination and empathy. Loosely based on the real Lord Braxfield, Judge Adam Weir is an unforgettable fictional creation. A brutally plain-spoken Lord Advocate of the early nineteenth century, he faces harsh truths about the world with a cruel relish for absolute exposure. He cares for his son Archie, but is suspicious of his own tenderness as if it were a weakness to be despised. Yet Stevenson manages to make us thrill to the savage flair and the awkward, granite integrity of his crushing and grim humour: '"Weel it's something of the suddenest"', he comments when he hears of his ineffectual wife's unexpected death, '"But she was a dwaibly body from the first. . . . It was a daftlike marriage." And then, with a most unusual gentleness of tone, "Puir bitch," said he, "puir bitch!"'

Weir fears that his son will take after his weak mother, and certainly the young man's excitable, imaginative and sentimental nature is as yet unformed and untried. Stevenson was setting a green version of his own impulsive sensibility against archetypal Scottish mores, whose fascination and whose kinship he could not deny, even from the distance of Samoa. Could these two elements ever be at peace with each other, or within one nature? The stage is set for a terrible confrontation, which will come about when the son has to be sentenced by his own father for the murder of the man who betrayed him with his girl. The psychological drama of the Weirs, father and son, is set against the remoter backdrop of oral tradition associated with the Weaver's Stone, which is where the lovers meet; where a Covenanter was once brutally murdered; and where murder will be done again. This ballad-like sense of community history and inevitable fate is emphasised by Stevenson's narrative distance and the ironic compassion with which he treats the sweetly foolish love-games of the young people. Archie and Christina are infatuated with the idea of being in love, and Frank Innes, the rival suitor, toys with their affections and his own impulses like a cruel boy. Their sentimental idyll at Archie's country home will come to a bad end, and Archie will soon have to face his father in a suddenly and tragically adult world.

The violent folk-history of the Borders and a symbolic model of Scottish society are brought together in the four 'black Elliott' brothers – a businessman, an improving farmer, a radical weaver and a poet – who rode down the robbers who killed their father in years past. It is likely that Stevenson would have had them ride again to free Archie for the sake of their niece, but we cannot tell whether this would have led to a melodramatic rescue or a more mature and less predictable outcome. Stevenson was not immune to the dangers of romance, but the ironic 'folk-historical' distance of his narrative style in *Weir of Hermiston* suggests a new control in his treatment of it. If the novel had come to show the limitations of swashbuckling solutions (which would have been wholly in line with *The Master of Ballantrae* and *The Ebb-Tide*, after all), it might, indeed, have been his greatest work.

Stevenson's talent for telling a tale gained him a considerable popular audience, and in this respect his skills were shared by his compatriot

Arthur Conan Doyle (1859–1930). Both writers, incidentally, admired the stories of Emile Gaboriau, the inventor of the French detective-novel in the 1860s. Conan Doyle, who was born in Edinburgh nine years after Stevenson, took a medical degree in 1881 and turned to writing to help his finances as a struggling doctor at Southsea near Portsmouth. Sherlock Holmes was introduced to the world in *A Study in Scarlet* (1887) and thereafter on the pages of a new periodical, the *Strand Magazine*, throughout the 1890s. (His deductive talents were based on those of the austere Dr Joseph Bell, one of Doyle's teachers at Edinburgh and a pioneer of forensic medicine.) Conan Doyle produced more than sixty books during his career, including historical novels, such as *Micah Clarke* (1889) and *The White Company* (1891), as well as a very successful series about the exploits and adventures of a young French cavalry officer set in the Napoleonic wars. (The *Brigadier Gerard* stories were collected in 1896 and 1903.) He wrote novels about a modern-day explorer and adventurer called Professor Challenger, who is best remembered for *The Lost World* (1912), as well as non-fictional studies of the Boer War, the First World War and, latterly, of spiritualism. Conan Doyle enjoyed great success as a popular writer; his support for the Boer War earned him a knighthood in 1902 but he also used his fame in support of divorce, medical education for women and Irish home rule. It is Holmes and Watson, however, who remain his best-loved and best-known creations, forever associated with the atmospheric streets of late-Victorian London. Those very streets provide a symbolic undercurrent to the Holmes genre that goes beyond our astonishment at the great detective's deductive powers. Holmes's London has its own intimations of modernity – along with Thompson and Oliphant – in that we get an uncomfortable sense in story after story of the great metropolis as a maze of streets and rooms teeming with uncontainable mystery, diversity, injustice and horror. In the face of such fears, Holmes's ability to discern logical order in a world of violence and confusion was well suited to reassure the middle-class readers of the *Strand*. (John Buchan's fiction was to offer similar reassurances by virtue of his heroes' fundamental decency and gentlemanly pluck.) In the light of the Scottish fascination with divided and unstable selves, it is interesting to reflect on how Holmes and Watson operate as a complementary and redemptive pair, although Holmes himself is doubled by his brilliant brother Mycroft and then again by Professor Moriarty, his evil *alter ego*.

Conan Doyle's interest in spiritualism – he wrote several books on the topic in the 1920s – was sadly linked to the death of his son through illness exacerbated by wounds in the aftermath of the First World War, and indeed the grief of many thousands of families led to a widespread vogue for such belief at the time. Even so, the late-Victorian age had already seen many similar reactions to a prevailing sense that established religion had somehow failed to give comfort in the face of scientific materialism, industrialisation, and the anonymity of the great cities. This urge to restore the primacy of the imagination and the spirit manifested itself in the Oxford Movement or in the Evangelical fervour of the 'Irvingites', who encouraged 'speaking in tongues' at their meetings. There was a wide interest in theosophy, while William Morris's fantasy novels and the Pre-Raphaelite artists all speak to the public's longing for other realms and modes of being. One of the most striking literary exponents of this tendency was a large dandified Scot with a black beard, whose mythopoeic novels and fairy stories prompted G. K. Chesterton to declare him the most original writer of his age.

George MacDonald (1824–1905)

Brought up on an Aberdeenshire farm, MacDonald went to King's College at his home university, where he graduated with an MA in 1845. Unable to afford a medical career, he worked in London as a tutor for three years, until, encouraged by his future wife, he became a minister of the Congregational Church – a moderately Calvinist dissenting body, more numerous in England than in the north. He was invited to take the pulpit at Arundel in 1850 and married in the spring of the following year, despite a severe lung haemorrhage. MacDonald was to be haunted by the spectre of tuberculosis all his life: it had killed his beloved mother when he was eight, his father lost a leg to it, his brother and a half-sister died young and his wife shared the condition too. Not surprisingly, perhaps, he conceived an early interest in Novalis, who had died of TB at twenty-nine and held a mystical conception of death as the doorway to another existence – a doorway his fifteen-year-old fiancée had already passed through. Before long, MacDonald's unorthodox views in this regard, not least his conviction that no God of love could go along with Calvinist damnation, forced him to resign from the ministry, and he set about establishing himself in the world of journalism and letters. He became a popular lecturer in the Manchester area, and a rather 'spasmodic' blank-verse drama, *Within and Without* (1855), achieved a modest success and was admired by Tennyson. A collection of poems was completed in 1857 after a winter in Algiers for the sake of his health, and the following year saw the publication of his first novel – 'a faerie romance for men and women'.

The hero of *Phantastes* (1858) is called Anodos ('pathless'), and the book follows his dream-fantasy journey into fairyland. MacDonald's imagination shows the influence of Novalis, Hoffman, Dante, Spenserian allegory, Celtic lore and Victorian sentiment, but in the end this eclectic realm is a place of his own devising. The book is suffused with a search for maternal love along with an almost erotic surrender to death and, in a startlingly Freudian world of dream-like transformations, mysterious prohibitions and stifled sexual longings, it is difficult to be sure that the author is in full control of his imagination. Yet later readers have praised MacDonald's intuitive grasp of the inner logic of dreams, and this aspect of his work has taken his reputation into the twentieth century, with a direct influence on such writers as C. S. Lewis, Charles Williams and David Lindsay.

Still much in demand on the popular lecturing circuit, MacDonald moved to London in 1859 to take up a professorship of English at Bedford College. He made friends with many writers and started another novel and several fairy stories. *David Elginbrod* (1863) was the first of three novels to be set in the author's native Aberdeenshire. Poorly constructed and inclined to preach, it has many faults but MacDonald used it to reassess his own background and to argue for the need for every man to rediscover human and divine love, free from false sophistication and free from the strictures of Calvinism. MacDonald himself had been persuaded of this by F. D. Maurice – a controversially popular Christian socialist – and had joined the Church of England. The same search occupies *Alec Forbes of Howglen* (1865), perhaps his best book on this theme and his most consistent picture of regional society. The third novel in the series, *Robert Falconer* (1868), is less unified and more didactic, but all of these books are marked by MacDonald's commitment to using broad Scots reported speech and a determination to find timeless themes in local life.

MacDonald continued to publish fairy stories, ostensibly for children, during the 1860s, and these 'Works of Fancy and Imagination' were collected in ten volumes in 1871. One story in particular, 'The Golden Key' (1867), has a rare imaginative power. Much more coherent than *Phantastes*, it is probably MacDonald's best work, with disturbing images of search and fulfilment through death in some other world. *The Princess and the Goblin* (1872) and its sequel *The Princess and Curdie* (1883) are still popular with young readers, while *At the Back of the North Wind* (1871) was an even more successful children's novel about the 'land of everlasting dream' once visited, as the boy hero discovers, by James Hogg's fated girl Kilmeny. MacDonald balanced these mystical experiences with social realism and a concern for reform, a cause close to his heart, all fuelled by vicarious descriptions of the sufferings of poor children. This very Victorian taste for a mild sentimental sadism can be disturbing to the modern reader, and episodes of abasement and whipping feature rather too vividly in some of MacDonald's later adult novels. It is difficult not to suspect several such unhealthy tensions in Victorian fantasy literature in general, and MacDonald's Scottish inheritance left him uneasily balanced between sentimental realism and mystical idealism, always with the harsher shadows of Calvinist authority in the background.

By the late 1860s MacDonald had become a well-known figure in nonconformist and spiritualist circles and he was the friend and confidant of Ruskin, Arnold, Carlyle, Browning, Tennyson, Kingsley and Lewis Carroll. (It was MacDonald who persuaded Carroll to publish *Alice*.) He made a lecture tour of America in 1872 and dazzled his audiences with charismatic eloquence and a taste for cloaks, white suits, or the kilt and plaid – not exactly the expected dress for a farm boy from Aberdeen. His American friends included Emerson and Mark Twain. During the rest of his career MacDonald produced a further eighteen novels – ten of them with Scottish settings – but they tend to cover already-established themes in somewhat sentimental 'kailyard' modes. The best of them, *Sir Gibbie* (1879), drew on his memories of Aberdeen and is still popular in Christian bookshops as an inspiring tale of a street urchin's moral progress and eventual worldly success, although there are elements in it that are scarcely less fantastic than his tales of magic. Such novels were never far from an improving agenda and MacDonald admitted that he saw them as a popular substitute for preaching. His last book, however, is notable because it returns once more to darker modes of dream fantasy.

Lilith (1895) offers a strange other-dimensional world that is grimmer and more frightening than his earlier versions of fairyland. This realm, a place without tears or rain, lies beyond a looking-glass in the house of the first-person narrator 'Mr Vane' and he visits it several times in an attempt to understand why skeletons slowly regrow their flesh there, or why lost babies turn into rapacious giants. The land is terrorised by Lilith, a beautiful vampire demon princess who kills children and assumes the shape of a spotted leopardess. MacDonald's metaphoric images are strange and cruel, or sweet and sickly sentimental – for example, the lisping baby talk of 'the little ones' – and the author's mystical optimism is juxtaposed with morbid visions of horror and pain. It becomes increasingly difficult for the reader to track the moral import of writing that seems both allegorical and deeply opaque at the same time, and yet this is part of its fascination and we are left, like the protagonist, strangely disturbed:

> Now and then, when I look round on my books, they seem to waver as if a wind rippled their solid mass, and another world were about to break through. Sometimes when I am abroad, a like thing takes place; the heavens and the earth, the trees and the grass appear for a moment to shake as if about to pass away; then, lo, they have settled again into the old familiar face! At times I seem to hear whisperings around me, as if some that loved me were talking of me; but when I would distinguish the words, they cease, and all is very still. I know not whether these things rise in my brain, or enter it from without. I do not seek them; they come, and I let them go.

MacDonald was never afraid to give his imagination free reign, and perhaps in this book above all it took its colouring from a life experience in which tuberculosis had returned to kill his favourite grandchild and five of his own children. His own disease was arrested, but that was small consolation. The last eight years of his life were spent in virtual silence after a stroke, waiting for the death he had thought to welcome in his younger days.

Towards the Celtic twilight

MacDonald was not alone in his desire to find imaginative worlds to counter narrow determinism and a society based on industrial capitalism. Matthew Arnold proposed 'culture' as a weapon against the spiritual sterility of the times, and in the 1860s he had identified a 'Celtic' spirit as the antithesis of narrow materialism. William Morris and Ruskin advocated a new art and utopian socialism in the 1870s, while the more aesthetic bias of the 1890s, with Dowson, Lionel Johnson, Symons and Yeats, looked to French Symbolism or the hermeticism of the 'Golden Dawn' as yet another alternative to materialism. The Irish Celtic revival sought a renewal of poetic force and imagination in myth and legend and, from a more conventional academic direction, two Scots scholars did much to further this new interest in mythology and primitive societies: Andrew Lang and J. G. Frazer.

Andrew Lang (1844–1912) from Selkirk and St Andrews University, and a classics don at Oxford, was one of anthropology's pioneers with his studies of myth and comparative religion. His major work on *Myth, Ritual and Religion* (1887) proposed a profound stratum of subtle belief that is common to so-called primitive myth systems around the world, seeing echoes of such beliefs beneath the surface of folklore and fairy tales. Thus Lang took mythic belief and popular folklore seriously, without seeing it, as J. G. Frazer and his followers were wont to do, as only one stage towards higher forms of knowledge. A versatile and eclectic man, Lang also worked at poetry, fiction, history, biography and literary journalism, and his Fairy Books, published under various colours, are still enjoyed by children today.

J. G. Frazer (1854–1941), a Glasgow man who became a fellow in classics at Cambridge, began his monumental study *The Golden Bough* in the 1890s and this work, which expanded from two volumes at its first appearance to twelve by 1915, was to make an extraordinary impact on intellectual life in the twentieth century. Frazer's work offered insights into the primitive mind that laid the foundations of social anthropology and comparative religion. Furthermore, his observation that powerful myths of fertility, death and renewal can be discerned beneath the cultural surface of various civilisations was to have an enormous influence on the thinkers and artists of early modernism, not least in the images of sacrifice and sterility that haunt T. S. Eliot's *The Waste Land*, and ultimately in the mythopoeic and symbolic histories adopted by writers such as Grassic Gibbon and Neil Gunn, with their emphasis on the timeless land or the sea, or on the quest and rites of passage.

There was a vogue for Celticism in Scotland, with a self-conscious preference for France rather than England and an interest in Breton and Belgian cultural minorities. This outward-looking nationalism was supported by **Patrick Geddes** (1854–1932), a polymath biologist, botanist and architect who established the Outlook Tower in Edinburgh in 1892 as a focus for his new ideas in sociology, ecology and culture. Geddes was born in Ballater, educated in Perth and travelled to London to study as a biologist under Thomas Huxley. When his vision was damaged on a research trip to Mexico, Geddes could no longer use the microscope so he turned his scientific training to the study of man in his environment, arguing that just like plants and animals we flourish best in sympathetic surroundings. Living and working in Edinburgh he lectured on biology there and at Dundee

University, while he began to envision a human habitat in which education, industry, ecology, culture, gardening, housing and public health were all part of the same ecosystem. His plans to restrain industry and to bring affordable housing, gardens and a respect for creativity into the urban landscape make him the father of social science and city and environmental planning, even if his views were to be more influential in America and Europe than in his home country. (The Ramsay Gardens flats on Edinburgh's Royal Mile were one of his projects.) He was equally idealistic in his plans for culture, envisaging a 'Scottish Renascence' in literature and the arts that would be true to the native spirit of Scotland, and especially to what he took to be the spiritual side of Celtic culture. Based at the Outlook Tower, he and his friends set out to publish 'Celtic' work by establishing *The Evergreen* periodical and an associated 'Celtic Library' series in an attempt to match the Irish revival. This was very much in the spirit of the times, for the 1890s saw a new outburst of 'Ossianism' in craft and design, with art-nouveau style and organic abstractions of a decoratively 'Celtic' sort being produced in Glasgow by the Macdonald sisters, Herbert MacNair and the brilliant young architect and designer Charles Rennie Mackintosh (1868–1928).

Scottish Celticism never produced a writer to compare with Yeats, but its purest exponent was **William Sharp** (1855–1914), whose self-consciously musical prose is not unlike the cadences of Synge in *Riders to the Sea*. Sharp was born in Paisley and cut short a degree in Glasgow University to go to London to work as a journalist, biographer, art critic and essayist. His dashing bohemian looks and nervous intensity gained him admission to the Rossetti circle, where he espoused the Pre-Raphaelite cause and met most of the writers of the day, including Browning, Swinburne, Morris and Holman Hunt, as well as Walter Pater, who impressed him greatly, and the young Yeats, with whom he shared an interest in spiritualism and the occult. He was informed about the art and literature of many countries and travelled widely all his life, spending short spells in Europe, the Middle East and America. As a cosmopolitan journalist and a lively, dandyish figure, Sharp had a curious relationship with his own identity, for he came to perceive a sensitive, secret and feminine side to his personality, coloured by hints of a mystical Catholicism quite different from his Presbyterian roots in Paisley. He associated this side of his nature with visits to the Highlands and psychic experiences from childhood, and he identified his sense of passive poetic fatedness with what he took to be a Celtic inheritance. Eventually this persona entered his writing under the name of 'Fiona

MacLeod', whom he pretended was a cousin of his and something of a recluse. *Pharais* ('Paradise') appeared in 1894, *The Mountain Lovers* and *The Watcher of the Ford* in the following year. These books dealt with timeless and archetypal patterns of love and death in remote Highland settings and sold well. Sharp became an adviser to the Celtic Library as planned by Patrick Geddes in Edinburgh, and the Outlook Tower published *The Sin Eater* (1895) as yet another book from his feminine *alter ego*. Further novels, essays and short stories appeared in the next ten years as 'Fiona MacLeod' gradually took over literary production from William Sharp. This was more than a successful pseudonym, and Sharp took elaborate steps to maintain the fiction of Fiona's existence and dreaded exposure and the disillusionment of his readers.

Sharp's Celticism lacked the linguistic, political and nationalistic direction that fuelled the Irish movement. His ideal was to seek a mystical expression of the eternal feminine that would add a much-needed leaven to Anglo-Saxon pragmatism and the Presbyterian work ethic. But he belongs to the 'Celtic twilight' because his world of hills and islands is sentimentally charged by the conviction that it is already passed or doomed to pass. He paints a 'golden age' that never existed in Gaelic culture, and its popular appeal is almost wholly aesthetic, depending on the fact that it is far indeed from industrialisation and the gaslights and tenements of Glasgow streets. The habitual association between Scottish Celticism and the feminine is equally telling, for the spiritual values so associated with this construction of the Gael – as well as his or her unworldly and even impractical character – are regularly associated with what is taken to be the female sensibility. In one sense this links the movement to the liberal advances being made at the time on suffrage and the 'woman question' and even to a new psychological understanding of the unconscious forces that drive us. On the other hand, the feminisation of the Celt, and his association with a lost golden age, means that such an identity is forever disenfranchised from the practical world of politics and historical change. Even so, a similar search for spiritually and archetypally native values is very marked in the work of Edwin Muir, Lewis Grassic Gibbon, Neil Gunn and George Mackay Brown. These writers from the next century could be said to form a distinctively Scottish school of 'mythopoeic realism' whose origins go back to the cultural and anthropological insights of Andrew Lang and J. G. Frazer and the search for spiritual values that, at least in the 1890s, had taken the form of a 'Celtic' ideal.

Apart from Stevensonian romance or symbolic Celtic fantasy, Scottish fiction ended the century with a vision of itself which was parochial, sentimental and almost entirely given over to nostalgia. Late-Victorian readers seem to have refused to countenance the industrial and urban growth around them, and, although the prolifically popular novelist 'Sarah Tytler' (Henrietta Keddie, 1827–1914) touched on the poverty and disease of Glasgow in *St Mungo's City* (1884), the theme was not central to her tale of a self-made businessman who learns charity and recovers his holdings. For most other novelists the honourable tradition of domestic realism had not advanced beyond the hearthside piety of 'The Cottar's Saturday Night'. Fiction in just this vein by J. M. Barrie, S. R. Crockett and Ian Maclaren achieved widespread success in the 1890s, as if Lowland Scots were longing, like their Gaelic-speaking compatriots, for their own 'homeland' literature of childhood memories and maternal security.

The kailyard

The term comes from the verse epigraph to a collection of tales published by Ian Maclaren in 1894:

> There grows a bonnie brier bush in our kail-yard,
> And white are the blossoms on't in our kail-yard.

Within a year W. E. Henley's *New Review* attacked the genre as cabbage-patch – 'kailyard' – writing, and J. H. Millar, the critic in question, renewed the assault in 1903 in his *History of Scottish Literature*. Perhaps the most scathing comments over the years have been made by other modern authors, such as the novelist George Blake, who blasted *Barrie and the Kailyard School* in 1951. Indeed, critics and writers in the early twentieth century found it especially difficult to say anything positive about these tales, determined to clear the ground for their own vision of Scottish identity and to deny their precursors under what Harold Bloom has called the anxiety of influence. There's no doubt that the literary vogue for a rustically characterful Scotland, like the Victorian appetite for tearful death-scenes, has passed away. Yet the case of the Kailyard reveals much about the complicated nature of Scottish cultural identity, going back at least as far as the genteel insecurities of Alan Ramsay.

The best works of Scott, Hogg, Galt and Stevenson were derived from the passions of the past, the difficulties of change, or from their authors' grasp of psychological or moral tensions. But the most striking feature about the Kailyard is that it was largely against change, and when it looks to the past – usually one generation back – it describes a timeless stasis of isolated rural communities whose dramas revolve around the doings of the minister or the dominie, tracing arrivals, departures, weddings, funerals and the pitfalls of petty presumption. It must be admitted, of course, that these themes do indeed belong within the Scottish tradition of feeling and domestic realism, even if it was dwindling to a sentimentalised subgenre. Thus the contemporary critical debate has begun to reassess the kailyard writers – for all their failings – by finding a new interest in the wider context of their literary production and by recognising their place in the evolving history of Scottish writing. Their chosen themes and settings are not so very alien, after all, to those of Grassic Gibbon's *Sunset Song*, or later novels such as Jessie Kesson's *The White Bird Passes*.

As *Blackwood's* was the forum for so many influential writers earlier in the century, so the *British Weekly* and a number of liberal Presbyterian ministers were the patrons of the Kailyard. This Evangelical periodical was edited in London by the **Revd William Robertson Nicoll** (1851–1923). Born and educated in the north-east, Nicoll trained as a Free Church minister like his father before him, and from him he inherited a vast library and a voracious appetite for books. He served as a minister for twelve years before moving to London to establish a career in journalism with Hodder and Stoughton, one of the Kailyard's principal publishers. He founded the *British Weekly* in 1896, aimed at a nonconformist market where Christian doctrine was leavened by humorous sketches and articles on moral issues such as the 'temptations of London'. On literary subjects *The Bookman* followed in 1891 and *Woman at Home* (1893) spoke to married women with fashion-notes, advice and popular fiction-serials. Nicoll championed the young J. M. Barrie and persuaded Ian Maclaren to take up writing. Anne S. Swan (1859–1943), the redoubtable creator of innumerable romantic stories, was an early contributor and became the mainstay of *Woman at Home*, subtitled 'Annie S. Swan's Magazine'. The *British Weekly* and the *Christian Leader* – a Baptist weekly from Glasgow – were particularly responsive to Kailyard fiction, in which sentimental piety was so conveniently packaged. On the strength of this market Ian Maclaren toured America with lectures and sermons in 1896, followed by Nicoll and J. M. Barrie, who were well received in their turn by large audiences in Boston and New York.

J. M. Barrie (1860–1937)

Only the initial stages of Barrie's career properly belong to the Kailyard
school, but his sketches of village life in 'Thrums', most of which
appeared in the *St James's Gazette* and the *British Weekly*, were among
the earliest and most successful publications in the genre. Barrie came
from a large working-class family in Kirriemuir, where his father was a
linen-weaver, operating the loom from his own home. The children –
five daughters and three sons – (two more died as infants) were all
brought up in the Free Kirk, although their mother Margaret Ogilvy
came from a more puritanical sect called the 'Auld Lichts', who
objected to hymns, religious music and even to written prayers and
sermons. True to type, the family was determined that the boys should
gain advancement through education, so the eldest son became a
teacher and David, Mrs Barrie's favourite, was destined for the
ministry. But David was killed in a skating-accident at the age of thirteen and his mother fell into an obsessive grief that entirely excluded
her youngest son. Wracked with jealousy, sympathy and guilt, James
Matthew Barrie, scarcely seven years old, tried very hard to take
David's place in his mother's heart. He spent long afternoons with her,
telling stories and listening to tales and memories from her own childhood, and the pair grew very close. When eventually she died Barrie
was compelled to relive their intimacy publicly in a loving memoir
published the following year as *Margaret Ogilvy and Her Son* (1896).
His complicated feelings for this emotionally smothering and puritanical little woman almost certainly led to the failure of his marriage, and
it is tempting to find the roots of his affection for children, his fear of
ageing and his fascination with death in the overwhelming nature of
this early relationship.

Barrie graduated with an MA from Edinburgh in 1882 and set his
mind on a literary career. He reviewed plays and worked as a journalist
in Nottingham for two years before moving to London, where he
placed articles with the *St James's Gazette* and various other periodicals
(sometimes using the name 'Gavin Ogilvy') and made friends with W.
E. Henley and Robertson Nicoll. A light novel called *Better Dead* was
published at his own expense in 1886, but his sketches of 'Scotch' life
for the magazines were so popular that he was encouraged to assemble
them in book form. *Auld Licht Idylls* appeared in 1888 and *A Window
in Thrums* was ready the following year. Both derive from his mother's
recollections of an isolated community of farmers and nonconformist
weavers, a world of parish-pump politics, proud, pious and obsessed

with keeping up appearances. The stories also do much to recognise the central role played by women in many Scottish families – an insight shared by later playwrights in the working-class dramas that became popular in the 1930s and the 1990s. Barrie's descriptive prose is well realised, his use of Scots dialogue – especially for vituperation – is powerful and dense and his observant and cutting humour can rise to bleak irony, for he remembered enough about Kirriemuir to know that 'Thrums' was by no means entirely idyllic. Yet he 'miniaturises' its society in a way that Scott or Galt would not have done, and in place of a changing social scene he writes a series of brief vignettes and invites us to eavesdrop upon them. As vignettes do, these depend on single moments of pathos or comic discomfiture, and Barrie's complex tone can be ambiguously and simultaneously patronising and ironic.

If these sketches have any wider scope, it comes from Barrie's awareness of change and mortality – we have already been told that such communities died away in the last fifty years – and the opening piece of *A Window in Thrums* evokes Jess McQumpha's cottage, now empty and fallen into disrepair. Hers is the window where she sat 'for twenty years or more looking at the world as through a telescope'. In the narrator's reminiscences we share this window with Jess, but the telescope is the wrong way round, and what we really see is Barrie's sense of his own lost childhood, suspended in time, and ever so far away. Thrums exists like Shangri-La in a charmed circle and Barrie is overcome by pathos whenever characters have to leave it, for in this light, death or just a departure for London seem equally final; and any hint of the outside world would certainly be fatal. Barrie's talent as a writer and the psychological complexity of his imagination in this vein make these stories much more interesting to the modern reader than the many inferior imitators that followed them. Here, as in *Peter Pan*, Barrie offers us a symptomatic insight into the disturbingly death-haunted nature of nostalgia and, by implication, the consequences for a culture that becomes too dependent on it.

The Thrums books were popular and even Stevenson admired them (although the folk at Kirriemuir were not so sure), but Barrie's greatest success in the mode came with two later novels. *The Little Minister* (1891) was originally serialised in the *British Weekly* as the improbable tale of a minister's love for a gipsy girl (it was later filmed with Katherine Hepburn in the starring role). *Sentimental Tommy* (1896) draws on Barrie's childhood with rather more psychological insight, not to say considerable self-awareness, to describe how his character's intensely sensitive and imaginative inner life simultaneously fits him for artistic creativity and prevents him from achieving maturity. This auto-biographical focus was continued in *Margaret Ogilvie* published in the same year, and became still more pointed in the novel *Tommy and Grizel* (1900), which dared to raise the question of marriage. By this time the author had been married for six years, but he found it easier to work in his study for hours, or to visit his club, than to share his thoughts or his physical affections with Mary Ansell, his beautiful actress wife.

Following the success of the Thrums stories and his novels Barrie made a triumphal visit to America with Robertson Nicoll. In 1897 he adapted *The Little Minister* for the stage, and it was such a hit on both sides of the Atlantic that he was persuaded to turn all his considerable energies to the theatre, producing twenty-nine more plays in the next twenty-four years. These brought him a knighthood, wealth and public status, yet he remained a complicated and withdrawn personality, reclusive, hard-working, small of stature and intensely shy. Barrie had made friends with Shaw – a vigorous supporter of Ibsen and 'Ibsenism' at the time – but the Scotsman's witty social comedies rarely attempted Shaw's didactic challenge, and they settled, like *The Admirable Crichton* (1902), for comfortable endings within the status quo. Thus *What Every Woman Knows* (1908) proposed that a briskly competent and managing wife – his ideal woman – is the real power behind a success-ful man; but the point is painlessly made and in flattering both sexes the play entertained large audiences who were not quite ready for *A Doll's House*. Later dramas that took a more sceptical look at manipulative female charms, such as *The Adored One* (1913), were less well received.

Barrie never allowed his own wife to share his inner life or his phys-ical attentions (the marriage seems to have been unconsummated) and she left him for a more generous man in 1909. He was still in emotional bondage to an unrecoverable past and some of his best later plays, such as *Dear Brutus* (1917), *Mary Rose* (1920) and the fine novella *Farewell Miss Julie Logan* (1932), are full of hints of death, loss, eternal childhood, and the poignant divisions between inevitable age (or maturity) and carefree youth. Innocent of Freud and psychoanaly-sis, Barrie, like George MacDonald, is still remarkably open to insights of genuinely disturbing symbolic power, and perhaps it is exactly this unguardedness that makes such work so startling for the modern reader. Barrie's most famously enduring achievement in this vein was, of course, *Peter Pan*.

The theme sprang from a friendship which he had formed with the neighbouring Llewelyn Davies family and their three (later five) sons.

It was as if this famous little writer, with his gruff manner and an unpre-possessing pale face, had adopted another man's family – somewhat to the consternation of his own wife, not to mention Arthur Llewelyn Davies. The fantasy stories told to 'David' by a thinly disguised version of himself in the novel *The Little White Bird* (1902) mark the origins of 'Peter Pan' and remain the first and most disturbing exploration of the topic. (We should remember, not without a certain chill, that the great god Pan is essentially indifferent to human life and that David was the name of the dead brother whom Barrie could never replace in his mother's affections.) When it appeared as a play no one was really sure at first if *Peter Pan, or The Boy Who Never Grew Up* (1904) was intended for adults or children, but it was a huge success in either case and went on to become a family Christmas treat for years to come. Even so, its dreamlike evocation of flight, the plight of the 'lost boys', the motherly comfort offered by a child, and the Oedipal tensions about paternal authority – burlesqued as the mutilated 'Captain Hook' – seem like hints of a deep fable from the unconscious. Most memo-rable of all is the relationship between Peter and Wendy, in which her motherly, fussy and yet loving character hopes for some deeper bond, only to be betrayed in the end by the innocently cruel forgetfulness of Peter's eternally immature nature. Barrie's earlier novels *Sentimental Tommy* and *Tommy and Grizel* had shown that he understood some-thing of this betrayal in his own innermost being. And in symbolic terms this theme also hints at profound truths – even if unconsciously realised – that neither an individual life nor a nation's culture can stand still, and that a backward-looking desire for fixity and the past is nothing less than a longing for death.

Prose versions of the play soon followed with *Peter Pan in Kensington Gardens* (1906) and *Peter and Wendy* (1911). The first of these was derived from the stories told in *The Little White Bird*, but its effect is much more anodyne without the framing story of the lonely adult narrator and – to contemporary eyes at least – his discon-certingly tender relationship with the little boy. The playwright's connections with the Llewelyn Davies family were deepened when Arthur died in 1907, and became closer still when Barrie's marriage broke up. Within three years Sylvia Llewelyn Davies died as well and Barrie became guardian and unofficial father to 'my boys', paying for their education at Eton and taking a great interest in their careers. Nevertheless, he could not avoid Wendy's fate, for the Davies boys, and then other young friends, inevitably matured and left him behind. Viewed in this light Sir J. M. Barrie seems a rather lonely figure, and although he continued to write successful plays for years, few of these later works have been worth reviving. He died in 1937, but by then developments in Scottish literature had long left him behind – almost from the moment of his early theatrical success in London.

'Thrums' renewed a vogue for pawky Scotchness and what *The Times* admired as 'unstrained pathos'. The **Revd John Watson ('Ian Maclaren'**, 1850–1907), was a Free Kirk minister who was persuaded to recount his experiences of Perthshire for Robertson Nicoll's magazine. Henceforth the collections *Beside the Bonnie Brier Bush* (1894) and *The Days of Auld Lang Syne* (1895), along with the village of 'Drumtochty' and the name 'Ian Maclaren', all became very widely known. Watson was a minister in Liverpool when he began writing and produced as many religious works as fiction. He also helped to found the University of Liverpool and Westminster College, Cambridge, and was much in demand as a public speaker and preacher. A Drumtochty novel called *Kate Carnegie and those Ministers* appeared in 1896, and other collections followed in the next six years, including the sketches in *St Jude's* (1907), set in the Glasgow where he had preached for three years before 1880.

The Drumtochty tales came from three happy years at a church in Glen Almond, and they are suffused with longing for a country life left behind. Not surprisingly, perhaps, the narratives revolve around the kirk and many of the stories focus on either man's chief end (to glorify God) or man's mortal end:

> 'Ye can hae little rael pleasure in a merrige,' explained our gravedigger, in whom the serious side had been perhaps abnormally developed, 'for ye never ken hoo it will end; but there's nae risk about a "beerial".'

In this, and indeed in general, the author shares the views of the community for, unlike Barrie, Maclaren writes from within its values and does not erect the former's affectionately satirical distance between his creatures and himself. On the other hand, his prose is often weak and sentimental and his piety has an untried, naïve air, especially when it is exercised over the frequent deaths that occur in the tales. Like most Kailyard fiction, it is as if all the more profane human passions which Presbyterianism was so intent on stifling could be rechannelled and respectably expressed only through vicarious grief at one fictional death after another. Such green pathos cannot appeal to modern readers, but in its day the evocation of Drumtochty as another lost Eden proved to be extraordinarily popular – especially in the United States, where over

500,000 copies were sold in the first few years. Maclaren died in America during his third tour of readings and lectures.

Samuel Rutherford Crockett (1859–1914) was yet another Free Church minister, although he gave up his charge in 1895 once his success seemed assured and became a productive best-seller with over forty novels and adventure romances in the mode of Stevenson. The Kailyard sketches from his native Galloway first appeared in the *Christian Leader* and were collected in 1893 as *The Stickit Minister*. Crockett's descriptive style is ambitious in its evocation of place and atmosphere, and at its best the narrative energy of a story such as 'The Lammas Preaching' makes the 'idylls' of Maclaren's Drumtochty seem naïve in execution. But most of Crockett's tales are too obviously designed to move his readers to laughter, or pity and horror, although they always manage to come to a comforting conclusion. To this end he mobilises sentimentality with ruthless insistence. In 'The Tragedy of Duncan Duncanson', a drunken schoolmaster, once a minister himself, strikes one of his pupils with a poker – quite forgetting that he had it in his hand. But the wounded boy protects him, for love of his young daughter, and swears that he hurt himself in a fall. 'Oh, Flora but yer e'en are terrible bonny!' the lad whispers as he regains consciousness. In another tale an old spinster who aspires to be a poet dies with tears of happiness in her eyes just as she sees her work mentioned in the newspaper. She does not know that the review was a savage one concocted by a smart young reporter. 'God is more merciful than man', intones Crockett at the end of 'The Heather Lintie'. Such is his preferred method: to evoke pain and then to 'kiss it away' with anodyne conclusions. The device is especially noticeable in *Cleg Kelly, Arab of the City* (1896), although this novel does at least recognise the harshness of Victorian Edinburgh; but an insistently idyllic sentimentality entirely overwhelms the love story behind *The Lilac Sunbonnet* (1894). Crockett's talent for vigorous description does much better with his later historical romances such as *The Raiders* (1894) and *The Men of the Moss Haggs* (1895). If these lack the psychological tensions of Stevenson's work, they still remain well-written and popular adventure fiction.

The factory yard

Crockett's *Cleg Kelly* reminds us that not all the popular literature of this time depended on idealised villages in a rural hinterland and

William Donaldson's agenda-changing studies of periodical literature in Victorian Scotland have drawn attention to how many social issues of the day were tackled by popular authors who produced their novels in serial form rather than seeking literary respectability with hardcover publishers. Newspapers such as *The North Briton*, *The People's Friend* and *The People's Journal* commanded huge readerships, especially among the working classes. The now almost completely forgotten author **David Pae** (1828–84), for example, was the founding editor of *The People's Friend* and a prolific writer who syndicated over fifty serial stories to journals throughout Scotland. His most popular production was *Lucy, the Factory Girl*, which ran for a year in weekly instalments in *The North Britain* from Edinburgh between 1858 and 1859. Donaldson recognises that there is a Cinderella-like theme in this story, but he also notes how passionately it preaches against the prevailing materialism of the times. As with Crockett's *Cleg Kelly*, it is a characteristic of this fiction to seek sentimental and affecting – even if tragic – resolutions. Nevertheless, along the way such writing did much to lay bare the grim conditions of labour and the plight of the urban poor in the great cities of a British Empire dedicated to industrial production and material profit. The Dundee periodical publishers John Leng and latterly D. C. Thomson (founded in 1905) supplied popular fiction to a huge working-class market in dozens of weekly and daily journals, and it is to be expected, after all, that some of this output should reflect the experience, the language and the daily lives of their readers. The most prolific and well-known vernacular Scots commentator of the time, for example, was William D. Latto (1823–99) whose prose epistles under the pen name 'Tammas Bodkin' appeared in *The People's Journal* for over twenty years.

One of these working-class readers and the original 'factory girl' was **Ellen Johnston** (1835?–74?), who started as a power loom weaver in Dundee at the age of ten with an appetite for Walter Scott's novels and ambitions to be a writer and an actress. Suffering abuse at home and seeking to support herself and her illegitimate child (born when she was seventeen), Johnston submitted poems to the weekly journals and made a name for herself under the *nom de plume* 'the Factory Girl'. Her poems combine moral earnestness with patriotic feeling and radical sentiment – a not uncommon combination to be found in the popular Dundee press of the time. Nor is Johnston entirely critical of her industrial experience, for she values the support of friends and foremen on works outings and sees the factory floor as a dynamic environment preferable to the domestic drudgery that faces more 'respectable' women. Even so, she did not hesitate to write poems in support of the Unions against miserly wage settlements ('Lines. On Behalf of the Boilermakers and Boatbuilders of Great Britain and Ireland'), and sentimental verses in Scots about the sufferings of the poor:

> Our merchants and mill-masters they wad never want a meal
> Though a' the banks in Scotland wad for a twalmonth fail;
> For some o them hae far mair gowd than ony ane can see.
> What care some gentry if they're weel though a' the puir wad dee?
>
> ('The Last Sark')

Johnston had some success with her poems, but after a spell of ill health she returned to work in the mills of Glasgow, Belfast and Manchester before coming home to Dundee in 1861. A second edition of her verses appeared in 1867 as *Autobiography: Poems and Songs of Ellen Johnston, the 'Factory Girl'*, prefaced by an account of her own hard life, whose romantically literary style speaks with a certain pathos of her wide reading and her hopes for authorial respectability. However, her poems, like the work of so many other writers who published in the weekly press, were soon lost to the canon and dismissed as ephemeral, until contemporary critics began to value them as alternative voices – male and female, radical and conservative – whose work is so expressive of working-class urban and industrial experience in the nineteenth century. One of the first tasks that the contemporary poet Tom Leonard set himself when he was appointed writer in residence at Paisley Public Library was to trawl the archives for the hundreds of radical poems that had been published in newspapers from the eighteenth to the twentieth century, collecting them in his anthology *Radical Renfrew* (1990).

Though neither school is a stranger to sentiment, it is true to say that such writing from the factory yard, so to speak, does something to offset the rustic kailyard's failure to engage with the urban realities of modern Scotland. It is fitting that this volume should end with the Scottish writer who did most to find a voice for modernity and the coming century.

John Davidson (1857–1909)

Davidson was a contemporary of William Sharp, and, although the two Scots were very different in outlook, they both came to prominence in the London of the 1890s. Davidson contributed early lyrics to the

Yellow Book, mixed with the Rhymers' Club at the Cheshire Cheese and had some of his novels illustrated by Beardsley. He made friends with Max Beerbohm, Richard Le Gallienne and Edmund Gosse, and he crossed swords with Yeats on one occasion. As a writer, however, he did not really belong to their circle. Outwardly conservative in appearance and manners, he was often contemptuous of his bohemian friends, preferring to see himself as a more truly intellectual rebel.

As the son of an Evangelical minister, Davidson was brought up in Glasgow and Greenock. He was an enthusiastic reader and soon tried his hand at poetry, but had to leave school early to earn a living, first as a laboratory assistant and then as a pupil teacher. He went to Edinburgh University in 1876, but his student career, or his money, or perhaps his patience, lasted only a year. He returned to teaching, with a post in Glasgow, where he met John Nichol, professor of English at the university, a friend of Swinburne's and a freethinker. Davidson's absolutist nature and his impatience with his father's creed responded to the Carlylean fervour of Nichol's mind, and his literary ambitions must have been greatly stimulated when Swinburne admired his youthful verses and pronounced him poet. After getting married in 1884 he worked for a while as a clerk, but soon found himself teaching again, although he did not enjoy it. During these years in Glasgow, Perth and Crieff, his output of prose, verse and drama received very little recognition, but he nevertheless decided to commit himself to journalism and set out for London in 1888 with his young son and his pregnant wife.

His first collection of poems, *In a Music Hall* (1891), made little impact, but the next two, *Fleet Street Eclogues* (1893) and *Ballads and Songs* (1894), were rather well received. Sadly, he was never to regain this early success, although he produced further collections of eclogues and ballads in the next five years. His impressionistic poetic sketches of cityscape and country scenes are not untypical of their time, with Kiplingesque ballads and 'ninetyish' mood pieces with titles such as 'Nocturne'. Yet some of the ballads strike a new note of barely suppressed rage at the futility and humiliation of daily urban life as suffered by Britain's equivalent of Gogol's clerks and the 'superfluous persons' of Russian fiction. 'In a Music Hall' reflects his own experiences as a clerk in Perth and it catches the fevered and sleazy excitements of popular entertainment as seen from both sides of the footlights. 'Thirty Bob a Week' is equally animated by a ferociously ironic spirit raging at the material difficulties of making ends meet on a pittance in a tiny apartment:

. . .

> Three rooms about the size of travelling trunks.
> And we cough, my wife and I, to dislocate a sigh,
> When the noisy little kids are in their bunks.

Yet these poems are not merely 'social realism', for they offer a vision of the individual spirit – a spirit capable of a metaphysical destiny – somehow trapped and sullied in the ordinary world. The effect is startling, as if Kipling were suddenly to speak like Shelley, or Carlyle:

> A little sleeping seed, I woke – I did, indeed –
> A million years before the blooming sun.

> I woke because I thought the time had come;
> Beyond my will there was no other cause;
> And everywhere I found myself at home,
> Because I chose to be the thing I was;

During the early 1890s Davidson wrote several light novels somewhat in the manner of Beerbohm or Chesterton. *Baptist Lake* (1894), for example, lampooned the pretensions of aristocrats and aesthetes alike and there are moments in some of his books when the writer's humour can seem disconcertingly sadistic or ironically wild, rather like the later satire of Huxley or Wyndham Lewis. Since he always wrote slowly and with difficulty, Davidson found the demands of journalism particularly exhausting. Yet he needed the work, for he had to support his mother in Edinburgh as well as his wife, children and a younger brother too, whose alcoholism and irrational violence had brought him to an asylum. Towards the end of the century he tried his luck with adaptations and plays for the London theatre, with only short-lived success. His *New Ballads* (1897) were given bad reviews in the *Athenaeum*, and his spirits and general health (he suffered from chronic bronchitis) began to decline. He particularly resented his lack of poetic success, yet the rough-hewn and ambitious scope of a poetry so full of abstruse ideas could never have appealed to popular taste and his critics began to call it chopped-up journalistic prose. Even so, despite their imperfections, these verses were his most original achievement.

Davidson was beginning to evolve a vitalist philosophy of how the universe and consciousness emerge out of matter as if driven by an evolutionary will. He linked a growing fascination with scientific materialism with the romantic spirit of assertion to be found in Carlyle and especially in Nietzsche. This was his answer to the Victorian crisis of faith and his own bouts of terrible depression. Thus he celebrates the crystalline structure and the 'purpose' of a snow-flake, which is to achieve form for its own sake ('Snow'); or he commands his soul to do the same by casting off bourgeois values and conventional notions of good and bad in favour of being 'haughty, hard, / Misunderstood' ('The Outcast'). There can be harsh inconsistencies in voice and craft in some of Davidson's verses, but an awkwardly powerful and original poetry does emerge from the assertive violence and confusion of his metaphysics. In the last ten years of his life he pursued this vision into longer and longer blank-verse poems, knotted with argument and ideas, increasingly idiosyncratic, increasingly unsuccessful with the public.

'The Crystal Palace' (1908), one of Davidson's last poems, was constructed – like several others – from an article he had already written in prose. It is a long, low-key, Browningesque monologue on the urban crowd as it throngs through the Victorian age's most famous monument to modernity. The juxtaposition it makes between aristocratic cultural values and vulgar entertainment anticipates something of the spirit of Pound and Eliot:

> A dense throng in the central transept, wedged
> So tightly they can neither clap nor stamp,
> Shouting applause at something, goad themselves
> In sheer despair to think it rather fine:
> 'We came here to enjoy ourselves. Bravo,
> Then! Are we not?' Courageous folk beneath
> The brows of Michael Angelo's Moses dance
> A cake-walk in the dim Renascence Court.

T. S. Eliot admitted to being influenced by 'Thirty Bob a Week' as well as by the poet's eye for 'dingy urban images', for Davidson was one of the few poets of his generation (along with Thomson, whose work he admired) to portray the squalor, despair and grim beauty of the modern city:

> Now wheel and hoof and horn
> In every street
> Stunned to its chimney-tops,
> In every murky street –
> Each lamp-lit gorge by traffic rent
> Asunder,
> Ravines of serried shops
> By business tempests torn –

In every echoing street,
From early morn
Till jaded night falls dead,
Wheel, hoof and horn
Tumultuous thunder
Beat
Under
A noteless firmament
Of lead.

('Yuletide', 1905)

Davidson shares something of this innovative free-verse structure with some of the *Sospiri di Roma* poems that William Sharp had privately printed in 1891, and W. E. Henley, whose recurrent visits to Edinburgh for treatment of the tubercular bones in his foot led him to write his ' In Hospital' poems (1873–5). The Scot also wanted poetry to 'certify the semi-certitudes of science', and he brought the very stuff of the sciences into his verse. The result was not always successful but there are original and striking passages too:

The other atoms, as the planets cooled,
Became; and all the elements, how much
So ever differing in appearance, weight,
Amount, condition, function, volume (gold
From iodine, argon from iron) wrought
Of the purest ether, in electrons sprang
As lightning from the tension filling space.
Forms of the ether, primal hydrogen,
Azote and oxygen, unstable shapes,
With carbon, most perdurable of all
The elements, forthwith were sifted out
To be the diverse warp and woof of life,
The lowest and the highest, louse and man.

(*The Testament of John Davidson*, 1908)

Hugh MacDiarmid acknowledged a debt to this aspect of Davidson's vision, and his own later world-language poems are equally laden with esoteric scientific ideas. Davidson's long monologues and dialogues, darkly Spasmodic poetic tragedies and his polemic testaments – there were five of them – were his last achievements. They can be disturbingly desperate. *The Testament of a Vivisector* (1901), for example, revels in images of sadomasochistic pain, and yet manages to convey, too, the author's sensitive anguish at the material plight of our bodies. The poet's sense of isolation was not helped by a move to Penzance in 1907. When *The Testament of John Davidson* appeared the following year, he became angry and depressed at the incomprehension and hostility of the critics, and in the belief that he had contracted cancer he took a revolver and disappeared from home in March 1909. His body was recovered from the sea after six months. Hugh MacDiarmid's poem 'Of John Davidson' was to remember the report of that suicide and the poet's 'small black shape by the edge of the sea, / – A bullet-hole through a great scene's beauty, / God through the wrong end of a telescope.'

Uneven as they are, passages from Davidson's later works did genuinely enlarge the subject matter of poetry as Davidson pushed his vision and his grasp well beyond the comfortable and accepted limits of his day. Ezra Pound and D. H. Lawrence knew his work and the inclusive ambition of his long poems, so determined to engage with philosophical and scientific ideas, marks him as a significant precursor of modernist poetry in English. His death marks the end of an extraordinary century of intellectual achievement in Scottish literature and heralds an even more remarkable one to come.

Chronological table

Abbreviations: A = autobiography; B = biography; C = cinema;
D = drama; F = fiction; P = prose; V = verse; *d.* = dies; *r.* = reigned.

Date	Author	Event
500		Scoti established in Dalriada
c.600	*Gododdin* (V)	Battle between Welsh and Angles at Catterick
1058		Malcolm III Canmore (*r.* 1058–93)
1066		Norman Invasion
1086		The Domesday Book
1093	*Duan Albanach* (V)	
1124		David I (*r.* 1124–53)
1168		Oxford University founded
1200	Scottish Gaelic bardic poetry well established	University of Paris founded
1215		Magna Carta
1249	The 'golden age'	Alexander III (r. 1249–86)
1253		University of Sorbonne founded
1286		Disputes over Scottish succession
1297		Wallace; Battle of Stirling Bridge. The War of Independence (1296–1328)
1305		Wallace executed in London. Papal seat moves to Avignon.
1306		Bruce kills Comyn; crowned king (r. 1306–29)
1314		Battle of Bannockburn Famine in Europe (1314–17)
1320		Declaration of Arbroath Dante dies (1321). Bruce dies (1329)

Date	Author	Event
1332–57		Further war as John Balliol makes a bid for the throne of Scotland with Edward III's support
1337		Start of the Hundred Years War
1347–53		The Black Death
1374–5	Barbour, *The Bruce* (V)	
1378		Pope returns to Rome. Rival 'Antipope' sustained in Avignon until 1414
1381		Peasant's Revolt in England
c.1385		Chaucer, *Troilus and Criseyde*
1387		Chaucer begins Prologue to *Canterbury Tales*
1394		James I (*r.* 1394–1437)
1400		Chaucer *d.*
1406		James I captured by English
1411	Lachlann MacMhuirich, *Harlaw Brosnachadh* (V)	Battle of Harlaw
1412		University of St Andrews founded
1415		Battle of Agincourt
c.1424	James I, *The Kingis Quair* (V)	James IV freed from English captivity. Joan of Arc burned at stake (1431)
1437		James II (*r.* 1437–60)
1440		Gutenberg uses moveable type
c.1450	Holland, *Buke of the Howlat* (V)	
1451	Sir Gilbert Hay, *The Buke of Armys* (P)	University of Glasgow founded. End of Hundred Years War and fall of Constantinople (1453). Wars of the Roses (1455–85)
1460	Corcadail, 'O rosary that recalled my tear' (V)	James III (*r.* 1460–88)
c.1460	Henryson, *The Morall Fabillis* and *Testament of Cresseid* (V)	
1470		Malory, *Morte d'Arthur*
c.1477	Blind Harry, *Wallace* (V)	
1478		Caxton prints *Canterbury Tales*

Date	Author	Event
1485		Botticelli, 'The Birth of Venus'
1488		James IV (*r.* 1488–1513)
1492		Columbus in San Salvador
1495	Dunbar, poems at court	First record of monastic production of Scots whisky (1494). Aberdeen University founded at King's College. Erasmus at Oxford
1509		Henry VIII takes throne of England. Michelangelo paints Sistine Chapel (1508–12)
1512	Book of the Dean of Lismore (collection of Gaelic verse)	
1513	Gavin Douglas, *Eneados* (V)	Battle of Flodden James V (*r.* 1513–42)
1515	Asloan MS of Scottish poetry (V)	
1520		Luther, 'On Christian Freedom'; Papal ban
1533	Bellenden translates Boece's *History and Chronicles of Scotland* (1527) into Scots (P)	Henry VIII breaks from Church of Rome (1534)
1536		Calvin's *Institutes of Christian Religion*
1542		Mary Queen of Scots (*r.* 1542–87). Copernicus, *De Revolutionibus* (1543)
1549	*The Complaynt of Scotland* (P)	
1552	Sir David Lindsay, full performance of *The Thrie Estaits* (D)	
1557	George Buchanan, *Jephtha* (Latin D)	
1558	Knox, *First Blast* . . . (P)	Elizabeth I takes throne of England
1560	Knox et al., *First Book of Discipline* (P)	Treaty of Edinburgh. Reformation Parliament
1567	Wedderburn brothers, *Gude and Godlie Ballatis* (V)	James VI (*r.* 1567–1625). Bruegel, 'The Peasant Wedding'
1568	Bannatyne Manuscript (V)	
1570		Donald Mor MacCrimmon born: family piping-dynasty established in Skye

Date	Author	Event
c.1575	Robert Lindsay of Pitscottie, *History and Chronicles of Scotland* (P)	Holinshed, *Chronicle* (1577). Drake circumnavigates the world (1577–80)
1580s	James VI and 'Castalian band' at court (V). Poems of Alexander Scott. Maitland Folio (V); Maitland Quarto (1586) (V)	University of Edinburgh founded (1582). Montaigne, *Essais*
1588		Spanish Armada; Marlowe, *Dr Faustus*
1597	Montgomerie, *The Cherry and the Slae* (V)	Shakespeare, *Merchant of Venice* Honourable East India Company chartered (1600)
1603		**Union of Crowns** James VI goes to London. Shakespeare, *Othello*
1604	James IV, *A Counterblaste to Tobacco* (P)	
1605		Bacon, *Advancement of Learning.* Shakespeare, *King Lear;* Jonson *Volpone* (1606). Gunpowder plot foiled
1611		King James Bible. Shakespeare, *The Tempest.* Galileo discovers moons of Jupiter
1614	Drummond, *Poems* (V)	Cervantes, *Don Quixote* (1615). Donne, *Songs and Sonnets* (1617)
1620		*Mayflower* sets sail for America
1623	Drummond, *Flowers of Sion* (V) and *A Cypresse Grove* (P)	
1625		Charles I (*r.* 1625–49). Harvey on circulation of blood (1628)
1637–8		Riot in St Giles': National Covenant. Descartes, *Discourse on Method*
1639		Civil War (1639–49)
1643		Solemn League and Covenant. Milton, *Areopagitica* (1644). Whisky production taxed (1644)

Date	Author	Event
1649–52		Charles I executed; Montrose hanged. Commonwealth established. Charles II crowned at Scone. Scotland subdued under Monck
*c.*1650	Robert Sempill, 'Habbie Simson' (V)	Hobbes, *Leviathan* (1651)
1653	Urquhart translates Rabelais (F)	Walton, *Compleat Angler*; Cromwell dissolves parliament and becomes Lord Protector
1660	Gaelic poetry on Montrose wars and exhortations to Charles, by Iain Lom	Restoration of Charles II (*r.* 1660–85). Royal Society established. Pepys starts to keep a diary
1666		Covenanters march on Edinburgh; Battle of Rullion Green. 'The Killing Times'
1667		Milton, *Paradise Lost*
1679		Covenanters defeated at Battle of Bothwell Brig
1685		James VII and II (*r.* 1685–1701)
1687		Newton, *Principia Mathematica*
1688		'The Glorious Revolution'; James dethroned. Battle of Killiecrankie (1689). William and Mary (*r.* 1689–1702)
1690		William defeats James at Battle of the Boyne. Locke, *On Human Understanding*
1692		Massacre of Glencoe. Witch trials in Salem
1695	Martin Matin, *A Description of the Western Isles of Scotland* (P)	
1698		Darien scheme: financial disaster
1701	Gaelic poems by Niall MacMhuirich and Morison ('An clàrsair dall')	James II dies: his son the 'Old Pretender' recognised by Louis XIV as heir to British throne
1704	Fletcher of Saltoun opposes Union (P)	Queen Anne (*r.* 1702–14) Newton, *Opticks*

Date	Author	Event
1707		**Union of Parliaments**
1706–11	Watson (ed.), *Choice Collection* (V)	Pope, *Essay on Criticism.* Shaftesbury, *Characteristics of Men, Manners* (1711)
1714		Pope, *The Rape of the Lock*
1715		George I (*r.* 1714–27). Jacobite rising for Old Pretender
1717		Handel, *Water Music*
1719		Abortive Jacobite landing at Loch Duich with Spanish support
1721	Ramsay, *Poems* (V)	The South Sea Bubble (1720). Walpole becomes first (de facto) prime minister
1722		Bach, *Well-tempered Clavier*
1724	Ramsay (ed.), *Tea Table Miscellany* and *The Ever Green* (V)	Swift, *Drapier's Letters.* Defoe, *A Tour Thro' the Whole Island of Great Britain* (1724–27). Wilson's of Bannockburn established
1725	Ramsay, *The Gentle Shepherd* (D)	General Wade starts building roads in Highlands; Vivaldi, *The Four Seasons*
1726		Swift, *Gulliver's Travels*
1727		George II (*r.* 1727–60). Newton *d.*
1729		Swift, *A Modest Proposal*
1730	James Thomson, *The Seasons* (V)	
1736	'The Scottish Enlightenment'	Porteous riots in Edinburgh. Ramsay opens theatre at Carruber's Close
1739–40	Hume, *Treatise of Human Nature* (P)	Richardson, *Pamela.* Black Watch regiment formed from Wade's Highland companies
1742	Hume, *Essays Moral and Political* (P)	Handel, *Messiah*
1745		Jacobite rising for Charles Edward Stuart
1746		Battle of Culloden
1747		Disarming Act: wearing tartan banned (repealed 1882)

Date	Author	Event
1748	Hume, *An Enquiry Concerning Human Understanding* (P); Smollett, *Adventures of Roderick Random* (F)	Richardson, *Clarissa*
1751	Gaelic poems of MacMhaighstir Alasdair published in Edinburgh	Gray's *Elegy*. General Turnpike Act and toll roads
1756	Home, *Douglas* (VD)	Johnson's *Dictionary* (1755)
1757		Highland regiments in North America as part of the seven years' war between Britain and France
1759	Adam Smith, *Theory of Moral Sentiments* (P)	Voltaire, *Candide*. Sterne, *Tristram Shandy* (1759–67)
1760s	'Gaelic vernacular revival' Poetry of Rob Donn	
1760	James Macpherson, *Fragments of Ancient Poetry* ('Ossian') (V)	George III (*r.* 1760–1820)
1761		Rousseau, *Julie, ou la Nouvelle Héloise*
1764–5		Walpole, *Castle of Otranto*. Percy's *Reliques*. Trent and Mersey Canal begun (1766)
1767–8	Gaelic poems by Duncan Bàn Macintyre and Duguld Buchanan published in Edinburgh. Gaelic poems of MacCodrum	Forth and Clyde Canal begun (1768)
1769	David Herd, *Ancient and Modern Scots Songs* (V)	
1770		Watt's steam condenser; Industrial Revolution under way. Rousseau, *Confessions*
1771	Henry Mackenzie, *The Man of Feeling* (F); Smollett, *Humphrey Clinker* (F); *Encyclopaedia Britannica* published in Edinburgh	
1773	Fergusson, *Poems* (V)	Goethe, *Werther* (1774) Priestley discovers oxygen. The Boston Tea Party.

Date	Author	Event
		Boswell and Johnson tour Highlands, Johnson's *Journey to the Western Islands of Scotland* published (1775)
1776	Adam Smith, *Wealth of Nations* (P)	American Declaration of Independence; Bentham, *A Fragment on Government*
1777		Case of Joseph Knight at Edinburgh declares slavery against basic human rights
1780s	Gaelic poems of Ross	Kant, *Critique of Pure Reason* (1781); Galvanic current observed. Highland 'improvement' and population shift
1783		Royal Society of Edinburgh founded. Britain recognises US Independence, revolutionary war ends
1785	Boswell, *Tour of the Hebrides* (P)	
1786	Burns, *Poems, Chiefly in the Scottish Dialect*, Kilmarnock edn (V)	
1787–1803	Burns (ed.), *Scots Musical Museum*	Mozart, *Don Giovanni* (1787).
1788	James Hutton, *Theory of the Earth* (P)	Kant, *Critique of Practical Reason*. Charles Edward Stuart dies
1789		French Revolution. Blake, *Songs of Innocence*. Bentham, *Principles of Morals and Legislation*
1790		Forth and Clyde Canal opened
1791	Boswell, *Life of Johnson* (P)	Mozart, *The Magic Flute*. Paine, *Rights of Man* (1791–2). De Sade, *Justine*. Successful black slave revolution in Haiti
1792		Wollstonecraft, *Vindication of the Rights of Woman*. Start of Revolutionary and Napoleonic Wars. Louis XVI and Marie Antoinette executed (1793)
1798		Wordsworth and Coleridge, *Lyrical Ballads*

Date	Author	Event
1800	Baillie, *De Montfort* (D)	Napoleon in power; Beethoven, *First Symphony*. Owen at New Lanark (1800–28). Macadam designs new road surface
1802	Jeffrey et al. start *Edinburgh Review*; Sir Walter Scott (ed.), *Border Minstrelsy* (3 vols, 1802–3)	Telford builds roads in Highlands. Steam canalboat tug *Charlotte Dundas* on the Forth and Clyde canal
1803	Grant, *Letters from the Mountains* (P)	Caledonian Canal begun
1805	Scott, *Lay of the Last Minstrel* (V)	Battles of Trafalgar and Austerlitz. Mungo Park in Africa
1808	Hamilton, *Cottagers of Glenburnie* (F)	Parliament prohibits slave trade (1807). Beethoven, Symphonies 5 and 6. Byron, 'English Bards and Scotch Reviewers'
1810	Scott, *The Lady of the Lake* (V)	
1811		Luddite riots. Austen, *Sense and Sensibility*. The Great Comet
1812		Byron, *Childe Harold, I* and *II*
1813	Hogg, *The Queen's Wake* (V)	Austen, *Pride and Prejudice*
1814	Scott, *Waverley* (F)	Austen, *Mansfield Park*
1815		Battle of Waterloo
1816	Scott, *The Antiquary* and *Old Mortality* (F)	
1817	*Blackwood's Magazine* founded	Keats, *Poems*
1818	Scott, *The Heart of Midlothian* (F)	Shelley, *Frankenstein*
1819	Scott, *Ivanhoe* (F)	'Peterloo Massacre'. Schopenhauer, *The World as Will and Idea*. Byron, *Don Juan* (1819–24). Wilson's of Bannockburn pattern book of 100 tartans
1820		George IV (*r.* 1820–30)
1821	Galt, *The Ayreshire Legatees* and *Annals of the Parish* (F)	Constable, *The Hay Wain*. De Quincey, *Opium Eater*; Napoleon *d.*
1822		George IV visit to Scotland. Mill and Utilitarianism
1823	Galt, *Ringan Gilhaize* (F)	Babbage's 'difference engine'

Date	Author	Event
1824	Hogg, *Confessions of a Justified Sinner* (F); Ferrier, *The Inheritance* (F); Lockhart, *Matthew Wald* (F); Scott, *Redgauntlet* (F)	Pushkin, *Boris Godunov* (1825) Stephenson's Stockton and Darlington railway opens (1825)
1826		Cooper, *Last of the Mohicans*
1829		Stephenson's 'Rocket' set speed record at Rainhill Trials
1830		William IV (*r.* 1830–7). Stendhal, *Le Rouge et le Noir*. Liverpool and Manchester passenger service heralds explosion of rail transport. Pushkin, *Eugene Onegin* (1831)
1832	*Whistle-Binkie* anthologies (V) (1832–90)	First Reform Bill; emancipation of slaves in British colonies (1834)
1835		Donizetti, *Lucia de Lammermoor*. De Tocqueville, *Democracy in America* (1835–40)
1836	Carlyle, *Sartor Resartus* (P)	Dickens, *Pickwick Papers*
1837	Carlyle, *The French Revolution* (P); Lockhart, *Life of Scott* (P)	Victoria (*r.* 1837–1901); Dickens, *Oliver Twist* (1838)
1841	Carlyle, *On Heroes and Hero Worship* (P)	Poe, 'Murders in the Rue Morgue'. Edinburgh–Glasgow railway line opens (1842). Livingstone in Africa
1843		Disruption of the Church of Scotland. United Free Church formed
1845		Poe, *The Raven and Other Poems*. Wagner, *Tannhauser*; Dumas, *Count of Monte Cristo* (1846). Potato blight and famine in Ireland. Thomson patents inflatable tyre
1847		J. Y. Simpson uses chloroform
1848		'Year of Revolutions' in Europe. Marx–Engels, *Communist Manifesto*
1849	Oliphant, *Margaret Maitland* (F)	Dickens, *David Copperfield*; Marx in London
1840–60	Gaelic poetry of Livingstone	Tennyson, *In Memoriam* (1850). Browning, *Sonnets from the Portuguese*. Hawthorne, *The Scarlet Letter*. Melville, *Moby Dick* (1851).

Date	Author	Event
		Crimean War (1854–6). Whitman, *Leaves of Grass* (1855)
1856	Cockburn's *Memorials*	Wagner, *Die Valküre*
1857	Smith, *City Poems* (V); Livingstone, *Missionary Travels* (P)	Baudelaire, *Les Fleurs du Mal*. 'Indian mutiny' at Lucknow
1858	George MacDonald, *Phantastes* (F)	Ballantyne, *Coral Island*
1859	*Chambers Encyclopaedia*	Darwin, *Origin of Species*. Wagner, *Tristan und Isolde*. Mill, *On Liberty*
1861		American Civil War (1861–5). Eliot, *Silas Marner*
1865	MacDonald, *Alex Forbes* . . . (F)	Tolstoy, *War and Peace* (1865–9)
1866	Oliphant, *Miss Marjoribanks* (F)	Arnold, 'On the Study of Celtic Literature'; *Culture and Anarchy* (1869). Marx, *Das Kapital*
1870s	Gaelic poetry of John Smith	Eliot, *Middlemarch* (1871). J. C. Maxwell, *Electricity and Magnetism* (1873)
1879	Stevenson, *Travels with a Donkey* (P)	Ibsen, *A Doll's House*. Tay Bridge disaster
1880–1	James Thomson, *City of Dreadful Night* (V) Oliphant, *A Beleaguered City* (F)	Dostoevsky, *The Brothers Karamazov*. James, *Portrait of a Lady*
1882	Gaelic poetry of Mary Macpherson	The 'battle of Braes' on Skye. Highland Land league
1883	Stevenson, *Treasure Island* (F)	Renan, *Souvenirs d'enfance et de jeunesse*. Nietzsche, *Thus Spoke Zarathustra*. Edison invents light bulb
1886	Stevenson, *Dr Jekyll and Mr Hyde* and *Kidnapped* (F)	Daimler Benz motor car. Seurat, 'La Grande Jatte'. English translation of *Das Kapital*
1887	Lang, *Myth, Ritual and Religion* (P)	Dunlop develops pneumatic tyre
1888	Barrie, *Auld Licht Idylls* (F)	Scottish Labour Party formed with Keir Hardie and Cunninghame Graham
1889	Stevenson, *The Master of Ballantrae* (F) Barrie, *A Window in Thrums* (F)	Yeats, *The Wanderings of Oisin*. Carnegie endows libraries

Date	Author	Event
1890	MacGonagall, *Poetic Gems* (V); Oliphant, *Kirsteen* (F) Frazer, *The Golden Bough* (P)	Forth rail bridge completed
1891	Conan Doyle, Sherlock Holmes stories (F)	Geddes founds the Outlook Tower in Edinburgh (1892)
1893	Davidson, *Fleet Street Eclogues* (V) Crockett, *The Stickit Minister* (F)	
1894	Maclaren, *Beside the Bonnie Brier Bush* (F) Sharp, *Pharais* (F)	*The Yellow Book*. Debussy, *L'Apres-midi d'un faune*
1895	George MacDonald, *Lilith* (F) Sharp, *The Mountain Lovers* (F)	Trial of Oscar Wilde. Yeats, *Poems*. Marconi and wireless; Lumiere shows film of a train in Paris
1896	Stevenson, *Weir of Hermiston* (F); Barrie, *Margaret Ogilvie* (B); Munro, *The Lost Pibroch* (F)	
1898	Buchan, *John Burnet of Barns* (F)	Boer War (1899–1902). Wilde, 'Ballad of Reading Gaol'. Zola, 'J'accuse'
1900	Charles Murray, *Hamewith* (V) Cunninghame Graham, *Thirteen Stories* (F)	Freud, *Interpretation of Dreams*. Sibelius, *Finlandia*. Chekhov, *Uncle Vania*. Strindberg, *Dance of Death*.
1901	George Douglas Brown, *The House with the Green Shutters* (F); Bell, *Wee McGregor* (F)	Edward VII (*r.* 1901–10). Kipling, *Kim*
1904	Barrie, *Peter Pan* (D) Geddes, *City Development* (P)	Rennie Mackintosh designs Willow Tea Rooms in Glasgow. Synge, *Riders to the Sea*. Einstein, *Theory of Relativity* (1905)
1907		Picasso, 'Les Demoiselles d'Avignon'. Bergson, *Creative Evolution*. Kipling wins Nobel prize
1908	Davidson, *Testament of John Davidson* (V)	

Select Bibliography and Further Reading

Literary history

Craig, Cairns (General Editor), *The History of Scottish Literature* (Aberdeen: Aberdeen University Press, 1987–8):
  Volume One *(Origins to 1660),* ed. R. D. S. Jack (1988).
  Volume Two *(1660–1800),* ed. Andrew Hook (1987).
  Volume Three *(Nineteenth Century),* ed. Douglas Gifford (1988).
  Volume Four *(Twentieth Century),* ed. Cairns Craig (1987).
Craig, David, *Scottish Literature and the Scottish People, 1680–1830* (London: Chatto & Windus, 1961).
Daiches, David (ed.), *A Companion to Scottish Culture* (London: Edward Arnold, 1981).
Findlay, Bill (ed.), *A History of Scottish Theatre* (Edinburgh: Polygon, 1998).
Gifford, Douglas and McMillan, Dorothy (eds), *A History of Scottish Women's Writing* (Edinburgh: Edinburgh University Press, 1997).
Gifford, Douglas, Dunnigan, Sarah and MacGillivray, Alan (eds), *Scottish Literature in English and Scots* (Edinburgh: Edinburgh University Press, 2002). [Contains over 200 pages of an outstandingly extensive and detailed bibliography of primary and secondary texts and further reading.]
Hart, Francis, *The Scottish Novel* (London: John Murray, 1978).
Henderson, T. F., *Scottish Vernacular Literature*, 3rd rev. edn (Edinburgh: John Grant, 1910).
Lindsay, Maurice, *History of Scottish Literature* (London: Robert Hale, 1977; 1992).
MacLean, Magnus, *The Literature of the Highlands* (London & Glasgow: Blackie, 1925).
Millar, J. H., *A Literary History of Scotland* (London: Fisher Unwin, 1903).
Royle, Trevor, *The Mainstream Companion to Scottish Literature* (Edinburgh: Mainstream, 1993).
Smith, G. Gregory, *Scottish Literature, Character and Influence* (London: Macmillan, 1919).
Speirs, John, *The Scots Literary Tradition* (1940) rev. edn (London: Faber, 1962).
Thomson, Derick, *An Introduction to Gaelic Poetry* (London: Gollancz, 1974).
Thomson, Derick (ed.), *A Companion to Gaelic Scotland* (Oxford: Blackwell, 1983).
Walker, Marshall, *Scottish Literature since 1707* (London: Longman, 1996).
Wittig, Kurt, *The Scottish Tradition in Literature* (Edinburgh: Oliver & Boyd, 1958).

Literary and Cultural Criticism

Ascherson, Neal, *Stone Voices: The Search for Scotland* (London: Granta Books, 2002).
Ash, Marinell, *The Strange Death of Scottish History* (Edinburgh: Ramsay Head Press, 1980).

Bell, Eleanor and Miller, Gavin (eds), *Scotland in Theory: Reflections on Culture and Literature* (Amsterdam: Rodopi, 2004).

Beveridge, Craig and Turnbull, Ronald, *The Eclipse of Scottish Culture* (Edinburgh: Polygon, 1989).

Brown, Terence (ed.), *Celticism* (Amsterdam: Rodopi, 1996).

Carruthers, Gerald, Goldie, David and Renfrew, Alastair (eds), *Beyond Scotland: New Contexts for Twentieth-Century Scottish Literature* (Amsterdam: Rodopi, 2004).

Chapman, Michael, *The Celts: The Construction of a Myth* (New York: St Martin's Press, 1992).

Craig, Cairns, *Out of History: Narrative Paradigms in Scottish and British Culture* (Edinburgh: Polygon, 1996).

Craig, Cairns, *The Modern Scottish Novel: Narrative and the National Imagination* (Edinburgh: Edinburgh University Press, 1999).

Crawford, Robert, *Devolving English Literature* (Clarendon Press, 1992).

Davie, George Elder, *The Democratic Intellect* (Edinburgh: Edinburgh University Press, 1964).

Davie, George Elder, *The Crisis of the Democratic Intellect* (Edinburgh: Polygon, 1986).

Devine, T. M. and Finlay, R. J. (eds), *Scotland in the 20th Century* (Edinburgh: Edinburgh University Press, 1996).

Donnachy, Ian and Whatley, Christopher (eds), *The Manufacture of Scottish History* (Edinburgh: Polygon, 1992).

Ferguson, William, *The Identity of the Scottish Nation* (Edinburgh: Edinburgh University Press, 1998).

Fielding, Penny, *Writing and Orality: Nationality, Culture and Nineteenth-Century Scottish Fiction* (Oxford: Clarendon Press, 1996).

Gonda, Caroline (ed.), *Tea and Leg-Irons: New Feminist Readings from Scotland* (London: Open Letters, 1992).

Hook, Andrew, *From Goosecreek to Gandercleugh: Studies in Scottish-American Literary and Cultural History* (East Linton: Tuckwell Press, 1999).

Hunter, James, *A Dance Called America: The Scottish Highlands, the United States and Canada* (Edinburgh: Mainstream, 1994).

Manlove, Colin, *Scottish Fantasy Literature: A Critical Survey* (Edinburgh: Canongate Academic, 1994).

McCrone, David, *Understanding Scotland: The Sociology of a Stateless Nation* (London: Routledge, 1992).

McCrone, David, Morris, Angela and Kiely, Richard, *Scotland – The Brand: The Making of Scottish Heritage* (Edinburgh: Edinburgh University Press, 1995).

MacDougall, Carl, *Painting the Forth Bridge: A Search for Scottish Identity* (London: Aurum Press, 2001).

MacDougall, Carl, *Writing Scotland: How Scottish Writers Shaped the Nation* (Edinburgh: Birlinn, 2004).

Muir, Edwin, *Scott and Scotland: The Predicament of the Scottish Writer* (London: Routledge, 1936).

Pick, J. B., *The Great Shadow House: Essays on the Metaphysical Tradition in Scottish Fiction* (Edinburgh: Polygon, 1993).

Pittock, Murray H., *The Invention of Scotland: The Stuart Myth and the Scottish Identity, 1638 to the Present* (London: Routledge, 1991).

Scott, Paul H., *Scotland: A Concise Cultural History* (Edinburgh: Mainstream, 1993).

Whyte, Christopher (ed.), *Gendering the Nation: Studies in Modern Scottish Literature* (Edinburgh: Edinburgh University Press, 1995).

Bibliography

Aitken, William R., *Scottish Literature in English and Scots* (Detroit: Gale Research, 1982).

Burgess, Moira, *The Glasgow Novel: A Survey and Bibliography*, 3rd edn (Glasgow: Scottish Library Association, 1999).

Crawford, Robert, *Literature in Twentieth-Century Scotland: A Select Bibliography* (London: British Council, 1995).

Scheps, Walter and Looney, Anna J., *Middle Scots Poets: A Reference Guide to James I of Scotland, Robert Henryson, William Dunbar and Gavin Douglas* (Boston, MA: G. K. Hall, 1986).

General history

Campbell, R. H., *Scotland since 1707* (Oxford: Blackwell, 1965).

Devine, T. M., *The Scottish Nation, 1700–2000* (London: Allan Lane, 1999).

Devine, T. M., *Scotland's Empire, 1600–1815* (London: Allan Lane, 2003).

Dickinson, W. C., *Scotland from the Earliest Times to 1603* (Edinburgh: Edinburgh University Press, 1965).

Donaldson, Gordon (General Editor), *The Edinburgh History of Scotland* (Edinburgh: Oliver & Boyd, 1978):

Volume 1, *Scotland: The Making of the Kingdom*, ed. Archibald A. M. Duncan (1978).

Volume 2, *Scotland: The Later Middle Ages*, ed. Ranald Nicholson (1978).

Volume 3, *Scotland: James V-James VII*, ed. Gordon Donaldson (1978).

Volume 4, *Scotland: 1689 to the Present*, ed. William Ferguson (1978).

Fry, Michael, *The Scottish Empire* (Edinburgh: Birlinn, 2001).

Harvie, Christopher, *Scotland and Nationalism: Scottish Society and Politics, 1707–1994* (London: Routledge, 1994).

Harvie, Christopher, *Fool's Gold: The Story of North Sea Oil* (London: Allan Lane, 1994).

Harvie, Christopher, *No Gods and Precious Few Heroes: Twentieth-Century Scotland* (Edinburgh: Edinburgh University Press, 1998).

Hechter, Michael, *Internal Colonialism: The Celtic Fringe in British National Development with a new introduction and a new appendix by the author* (New Brunswick and London: Transaction Publishers, 1999).

Kermack, W. R., *The Scottish Highlands: A Short History, 1300–1746* (Edinburgh: Johnston & Bacon, 1957).

Lenman, Bruce, *An Economic History of Modern Scotland, 1660–1976* (London: Batsford, 1977).

Lynch, Michael, *Scotland: A New History* (London: Century, 1991).

Marr, Andrew, *The Battle for Scotland* (London: Allan Lane, 1992).

Nairn, Tom, *The Break-Up of Britain: Crisis and Neo-Nationalism* (London: NLB, 1977).

Smout, T. C., *A History of the Scottish People, 1560–1830* (London: Collins, 1969).

Smout, T. C., *A Century of the Scottish People, 1830–1950* (London: Collins, 1986).

Scottish culture

Cameron, David Kerr, *The Ballad and the Plough: A Portrait of the Life of the Old Scottish Farmtouns* (London: Gollancz, 1978).

Cameron, David Kerr, *Willie Gavin, Crofter Man: Portrait of a Vanished Lifestyle* (London: Gollancz, 1980).

Carter, Ian, *Farm Life in North East Scotland: The Poor Man's Country* (Edinburgh: Birlinn, 2003).

Carter, Jennifer and Withrington, Donald (eds), *Scottish Universities: Distinctiveness and Diversity* (Edinburgh: John Donald, 1992).

Collinson, F. M., *The Traditional and National Music of Scotland* (London: Routledge & Kegan Paul, 1966).

Dick, Eddie (ed.), *From Limelight to Satellite: A Scottish Film Book* (London: Scottish Film Council, BFI, 1990).

Douglas, Sheila (ed.), *The Sang's the Thing: Voices from Lowland Scotland* (Edinburgh: Polygon, 1992).

Dunbar, John Telfer, *Highland Costume* (Edinburgh: William Blackwood, 1977).

Fyfe, J. G. (ed.), *Scottish Diaries and Memoirs, 1550–1746* (Stirling: Eneas Mackay, 1928).

Fyfe, J. G. (ed.), *Scottish Diaries and Memoirs, 1746–1843* (Stirling: Eneas Mackay, 1942).

Gardiner, Michael, *Modern Scottish Culture* (Edinburgh: Edinburgh University Press, 2005).

Graham, Henry G., *The Social Life of Scotland in the Eighteenth Century* (London: A. & C. Black, 1909).

Hay, George, *Architecture of Scotland* (Northumberland: Oriel Press, 1977).

Keay, John and Julia (eds), *Collins Encyclopaedia of Scotland* (London: Harper Collins, 1994).

McArthur, Colin (ed.), *Scotch Reels: Scotland in Cinema and Television* (London: BFI Publishing, 1982).

MacLean, Calum I., *The Highlands*, foreword by Sorley MacLean (Edinburgh: Mainstream, 1990). [1st edition 1959.]

MacMillan, Duncan, *Scottish Art, 1460–2000* (Edinburgh: Mainstream, 2000).

MacNeill, Seumas, *Piobaireachd* (Edinburgh: BBC, 1968).

McNeill, F. Marian, *The Silver Bough*, 4 vols (Glasgow: William Maclellan, 1957–68).

Millman, R. N., *The Making of the Scottish Landscape* (London: Batsford, 1975).

Purser, John, *Scotland's Music* (Edinburgh: Mainstream, 1992).

Ross, Anne, *Folklore of the Scottish Highlands* (London: Batsford, 1976).

West, T. M., *A History of Architecture in Scotland* (London: University of London Press, 1967).

Scots and Gaelic

Aitken, A. J. and McArthur, T. (eds), *Languages of Scotland* (Edinburgh: Chambers, 1979).

Corbett, John, *Language and Scottish Literature* (Edinburgh: Edinburgh University Press, 1997).

Kay, Billy, *Scots: The Mither Tongue* (Edinburgh: Mainstream, 1986).

McClure, J. Derrick, *Language, Poetry and Nationhood: Scots as a Poetic Language from 1878 to the Present* (East Linton: Tuckwell Press, 2000).

McClure, J. Derrick (ed.), *Scotland and the Lowland Tongue: Studies in the Language and Literature of Lowland Scotland* (Aberdeen: Aberdeen University Press, 1983).

MacKinnon, Kenneth, *Gaelic: A Past and Future Prospect* (Edinburgh: Saltire Society, 1991).

MacLennan, Malcolm, *A Pronouncing and Etymological Dictionary of the Gaelic Language: Gaelic–English, English–Gaelic* (Edinburgh: Acair & Mercat Press, 1995).

Murison, David, *The Guid Scots Tongue* (Edinburgh: William Blackwood, 1977).

Robinson, Mairi (ed.), *The Concise Scots Dictionary* (Aberdeen: Aberdeen University Press, 1985).

Anthologies

Bateman, Meg and Crawford, Robert (eds), *Scottish Religious Poetry: An Anthology* (Edinburgh: St Andrews Press, 2000).

Black, Ronald (ed.), *An Tuil* (Edinburgh: Polygon, 1999). Twentieth-century Scottish Gaelic verse.

Burgess, Moira (ed.), *The Other Voice: Scottish Women's Writing since 1808* (Edinburgh: Polygon, 1987).

Clancy, Thomas (ed.), *The Triumph Tree: Scotland's Earliest Poetry, AD 530–1350* (Edinburgh: Canongate Classics, 1998).

Craig, Cairns and Stevenson, Randall (eds), *Twentieth-Century Scottish Drama* (Edinburgh: Canongate Classics, 2001).

Crawford, Robert and Imlah, Mick (eds), *The New Penguin Book of Scottish Verse* (London: Allan Lane, 2000).

Dunn, Douglas (ed.), *The Faber Book of Twentieth-Century Scottish Poetry* (London: Faber, 1993).

Kerrigan, Catherine (ed.), *Scottish Women Poets* (Edinburgh University Press, 1991).

Leonard, Tom (ed.), *Radical Renfrew: Poetry from the French Revolution to the First World War* (Edinburgh: Polygon, 1990).

MacAulay, Donald (ed.), *Modern Scottish Gaelic Poems* (Edinburgh: Canongate Classics, 1995).

McCordrick, David (ed.), *Scottish Literature: An Anthology*, 3 vols (New York: Peter Lang, 1996, 2002).

MacDougall, Carl (ed.), *The Devil and the Giro: Two Centuries of Scottish Stories* (Edinburgh: Canongate Classics, 1991).

MacLaine, Allan H. (ed.), *The Christis Kirk Tradition: Scots Poems of Folk Festivity* (Glasgow: Association for Scottish Literary Studies, 1996).

McMillan, Dorothy and Byrne, Michel (eds), *Modern Scottish Women Poets* (Canongate Classics, 2003).

Meek, Donald (ed.), *The Wiles of the World/Caran An T-Saoghail* (West Lothian: Barbour Books, 2003). Nineteenth-century Scottish Gaelic poetry.

O Baoill, Colm (ed.), *The Harp's Cry/Gàir nan Clàrsach* (Edinburgh: Birlinn, 1994). Seventeenth-century Gaelic poems.

O'Rourke, Daniel (ed.), *Dream State: The New Scottish Poets* (Edinburgh: Polygon, 1994; 2002).

O'Rourke, Daniel and Whyte, Hamish (eds), *Across the Water: Irishness in Modern Scottish Writing* (Glendaruel: Argyll, 2000).

Scottish Texts Society, Most of the major older Scottish poets and MS collections are available in these often multi-volume scholarly editions.

Scottish Gaelic Texts Society, The works of almost all the older Gaelic poets, usually with translations and helpful introductions, can be found in this series.

Tasioulas, J. (ed.), *The Makars: The Poems of Henryson, Dunbar and Douglas* (Edinburgh: Canongate Classics, 1999).

Thomson, Derek (ed.), *Gaelic Poetry in the Eighteenth Century* (Aberdeen: Association of Scottish Literary Studies, 1993).

Watson, Roderick (ed.), *The Poetry of Scotland: Gaelic, Scots, English, 1380–1980* (Edinburgh: Edinburgh University Press, 1995).

Watson, W. J. (ed.), *Bàrdachd Ghàidhlig: Specimens of Gaelic Poetry, 1550–1900* (Glasgow: An Comunn Gaidhealach, 1959).

Scotnotes

For school and college teaching, *Teaching Scottish Literature: Curriculum and Classroom Applications*, ed. Alan MacGillivray (Edinburgh: Edinburgh University Press, 1997) is a detailed professional package, while the ASLS *Scotnotes* series offers a useful collection of student study guides to individual authors and texts.

Baird, Gerald, *The Poems of Robert Henryson*.

Blackburn, John, *The Poetry of Iain Crichton Smith*.

Burgess, Moira, *Naomi Mitchison's **Early in Orcadia**, **The Big House** and **Travel Light***.

Carruthers, Gerard: *Robert Louis Stevenson's **Dr Jekyll and Mr Hyde**, **The Master of Ballantrae** and **The Ebb-Tide***.

Dickson, Beth, *William McIlvanney's **Laidlaw***.

Jack, Ronald D. S., *The Poetry of William Dunbar*.

McCulloch, Margery Palmer, *Liz Lochhead's **Mary Queen of Scots Got Her Head Chopped Off***.

MacGillivray, Alan, *Iain Banks's **The Wasp Factory**, **The Crow Road** and **Whit***.

MacGillivray, Alan, *George Mackay Brown's **Greenvoe***.

MacLachlan, Christopher, *John Buchan's **Witch Wood**, **Huntingtower** and **The Thirty-Nine Steps***.

Petrie, Elaine, *James Hogg's **The Private Memoirs and Confessions of a Justified Sinner***.

Riach, Alan, *The Poetry of Hugh MacDiarmid*.

Robb, David S., *Muriel Spark's **The Prime of Miss Jean Brodie***.

Simpson, Kenneth, *Robert Burns*.

Smith, Iain Crichton, *Robin Jenkins's **The Cone-Gatherers***.

Smith, Iain Crichton, *George Douglas Brown's **The House with the Green Shutters***.

Thomson, Geddes, *The Poetry of Edwin Morgan*.

Watson, Roderick, *The Poetry of Norman MacCaig*.

Young, Douglas, *Lewis Grassic Gibbon's **Sunset Song***.

1   The beginnings of Scotland: two cultures

Bannerman, John, *Studies in the History of Dalriada* (Edinburgh: Scottish Academic Press, 1974).

Barrow, G. W. S., *Robert Bruce and the Community of the Realm of Scotland* (Edinburgh: Edinburgh University Press, 1988).

Barrow, G. W. S., *Kingship and Unity: Scotland, 1000–1306* (Edinburgh: Edinburgh University Press, 2003).

Duncan, Archibald A. M. (ed.), *John Barbour, The Bruce* (Edinburgh: Canongate Classics, 1997, 2000).

Henderson, Isabel, *The Picts* (London: Thames & Hudson, 1967).

Laing, Lloyd and Jenny, *The Picts and the Scots* (Stroud: Allan Sutton, 1993).

Powell, T. G. E., *The Celts* (London: Thames & Hudson, 1958).

2   The fifteenth century: the flowering

Bawcutt, Priscilla, *William Dunbar* (Oxford: Clarendon Press, 1992).

Jack, R. D. S. (ed.), *The Mercat Anthology of Early Scottish Literature, 1375–1707* (Mercat Press, 1997).

Lyall, Roderick J. and Riddy Felicity (eds), *Proceedings of the Third International Conference on Scottish Language and Literature (Medieval and Renaissance), 1981* (Glasgow: University of Stirling, 1981).

Mapstone, Sally and Wood, Juliette (eds), *The Rose and the Thistle: Essays on the Culture of Late Medieval and Renaissance Scotland* (East Linton: Tuckwell Press, 1998).

McKim, Anne (ed.), *Blind Harry, The Wallace* (Edinburgh: Canongate Classics, 2003).

McQueen, John (ed.), *Ballatis of Luve: The Scottish Courtly Love Lyric, 1400–1570* (Edinburgh: Edinburgh University Press, 1970).

McQueen, John, *Robert Henryson: A Study of the Major Narrative Poems* (Oxford: Clarendon Press, 1967).

Tasioulas, J. (ed.), *The Makars: The Poems of Henryson, Dunbar and Douglas* (Edinburgh: Canongate Classics, 1999).

3   The sixteenth century: John the Commonweill

Cowan, Ian B., *The Scottish Reformation: Church and Society in Sixteenth-Century Scotland* (London: Weidenfeld & Nicolson, 1982).

Edington, Carol, *Court and Culture in Renaissance Scotland: Sir David Lindsay of the Mount* (East Linton, Tuckwell Press, 1995).

Jack, R. D. S., *The Italian Influence on Scottish Literature* (Edinburgh: Edinburgh University Press, 1972).

Jack, R. D. S., *Alexander Montgomerie* (Edinburgh: Scottish Academic Press, 1985).

Lyall, Roderick (ed.), *Sir David Lindsay, Ane Satyre of the Thrie Estaitis* (Edinburgh: Canongate Classics, 1989).

Macdonald, Alasdair A., Lynch, M. and Cowan, Ian B. (eds), *The Renaissance in Scotland: Studies in Literature, Religion, History and Culture* (Leiden: Brill, 1994).

Shire, Helena M., *Song, Dance and Poetry at the Court of Scotland under James VI* (Cambridge: Cambridge University Press, 1969).

4   The seventeenth century: crown and Covenant, the ballads

Bold, Alan, *The Ballad* (London: Methuen, 1979).

Buchan, David, *The Ballad and the Folk* (London: Routledge & Kegan Paul, 1972).

Child, Francis James (ed.), *English and Scottish Popular Ballads*, 5 vols: *1882–98* (Boston & New York: Dover, 1965).

Cowan, Ian B., *The Scottish Covenanters, 1660–1688* (London: Gollancz, 1976).

Fogle, F. R., *A Critical Study of William Drummond of Hawthornden* (New York: 1952).

Larner, Christina, *Enemies of God: The Witch-Hunt in Scotland* (Oxford: Blackwell, 1981).

Lyle, Emily (ed.), *Scottish Ballads* (Edinburgh: Canongate Classics, 1994).

MacKenzie, Annie M. (ed.), *Orain Iain Luim, Songs of John MacDonald Bard of Keppoch* (Edinburgh: Scottish Gaelic Texts Society, 1973).

Matheson, William (ed.), *The Blind Harper (An Clarsar Dall). The Songs of Roderick Morison and his Music* (Edinburgh: Scottish Gaelic Texts Society, 1970).

Muir, Willa, *Living with Ballads* (London: Hogarth Press, 1965).

O Baoill, Colm (ed.), *The Harp's Cry/Gàir nan Clàrsach* (Edinburgh: Birlinn, 1994). Seventeenth-century Gaelic poems

O Baoill, Colm (ed.), *Bàrdachd Shìlis na Ceapaich, Poems and Songs by Sìleas MacDonald* (Edinburgh: Scottish Gaelic Texts Society, 1972).

Smout, T. C., *A History of the Scottish People, 1560–1830* (London: Collins, 1969).

Watson, J. Carmichael (ed.), *Gaelic Songs of Mary MacLeod* (Edinburgh: Scottish Gaelic Texts Society, 1982).

5 The eighteenth century: new Athenians and the Doric

Allan, David, *Virtue, Learning and the Scottish Enlightenment* (Edinburgh: Edinburgh University Press, 1993).

Bold, Alan, *A Burns Companion* (London: Macmillan, 1991).

Broadie, Alexander, *The Tradition of Scottish Philosophy: A New Perspective on the Enlightenment* (Edinburgh: Polygon, 1990).

Broadie, Alexander (ed.), *The Scottish Enlightenment: An Anthology* (Edinburgh: Canongate Classics, 1997).

Campbell, R. H and Skinner, A. S., *The Origins and Nature of the Scottish Enlightenment* (Edinburgh: John Donald, 1982).

Carswell, Catherine, *The Life of Robert Burns* (Edinburgh: Canongate Classics, 1990).

Chitnis, Anand, C., *The Scottish Enlightenment: A Social History* (London: Croom Helm, 1976).

Colley, Linda, *Britons: Forging the Nation, 1707–1837* (New Haven, CT: Yale University Press, 1994).

Crawford, Thomas, *Burns: A Study of the Poems and Songs* (Edinburgh: Canongate Academic, 1960; 1994).

Crawford, Thomas, *Society and the Lyric: A Study of the Song Culture of Eighteenth-Century Scotland* (Edinburgh: Scottish Academic Press, 1979).

Crawford, Thomas, *Boswell, Burns and the French Revolution* (Edinburgh: Saltire Society, 1990).

Daiches, David, *The Paradox of Scottish Culture* (London: Oxford University Press, 1964).

Daiches, David, *Robert Burns* (London: Deutsch, 1966).

Daiches, David, *Scotland and the Union* (London: John Murray, 1977).

Daiches, David, *Literature and Gentility in Scotland* (Edinburgh: Edinburgh University Press, 1982).

Daiches, David, *Robert Fergusson* (Edinburgh: Scottish Academic Press, 1982).

Donaldson, William, *The Jacobite Song: Political Myth and National Identity* (Aberdeen: Aberdeen University Press, 1988).

Ferguson, J. De L and Roy, Ross (eds), *The Letters of Robert Burns*, 2 vols (Oxford: Clarendon Press, 1985).

Gaskill, Howard (ed.), *Ossian Revisited* (Edinburgh: Edinburgh University Press, 1991).

Graham, Henry G., *The Social Life of Scotland in the Eighteenth Century* (London: A. & C. Black, 1909).

Grimble, Ian, *The World of Rob Donn* (Edinburgh: The Edina Press, 1979).

Kinsley, James (ed.), *The Poems and Songs of Robert Burns*, 3 vols (Oxford: Clarendon Press, 1968).

Lenman, Bruce, *The Jacobite Cause* (Glasgow: Richard Drew, National Trust for Scotland, 1986).

Low, Donald A. (ed.), *Robert Burns: The Critical Heritage* (London: Routledge & Kegan Paul, 1995).

McGuirk, Carol, *Robert Burns and the Sentimental Era* (East Linton: Tuckwell Press, 1997).

McIlvanney, Liam, *Burns the Radical: Poetry and Politics in late Eighteenth-Century Scotland* (East Linton: Tuckwell Press, 2002).

MacLachlan, Christopher (ed.) *Before Burns: Eighteenth-Century Scottish Poetry* (Edinburgh: Canongate Classics 2002).

MacLeod, Angus (ed.), *The Songs of Duncan Ban Macintyre* (Edinburgh: Scottish Gaelic Texts Society, 1952).

McMillan, Dorothy (ed.) *The Scotswoman at Home and Abroad: Non-Fictional Writing, 1700–1900* (Glasgow: Association for Scottish Literary Studies, 1999).

MacQueen, John, *The Enlightenment and Scottish Literature: Progress and Poetry* (Edinburgh: Scottish Academic Press, 1979).

MacQueen, John, *The Rise of the Historical Novel: The Enlightenment and Scottish Literature* (Edinburgh: Scottish Academic Press, 1989).

Miller, Karl, *Cockburn's Millennium* (London: Duckworth, 1975).

Noble, Andrew and Hogg, Patrick Scott (eds), *The Canongate Burns* (Edinburgh: Canongate Classics, 2003).

Rendall, Jane, *The Origins of the Scottish Enlightenment* (London: Macmillan, 1978).

Simpson, Kenneth, *The Protean Scot: The Crisis of Identity in Eighteenth-Century Scottish Literature* (Aberdeen: Aberdeen University Press, 1988).

Smart, Alastair, *Allan Ramsay: Painter, Essayist and Man of the Enlightenment* (New Haven, CT: Paul Mellon, Yale University Press, 1992).

Snyder, Franklyn Bliss, *The Life of Robert Burns* (Hamden, Conn.: Archon, 1968). First published 1932.

Stafford, Fiona, *The Sublime Savage: James Macpherson and the Poems of Ossian* (Edinburgh: Edinburgh University Press, 1988).

Thompson, Harold W., *A Scottish Man of Feeling: Some Account of Henry MacKenzie Esq. of Edinburgh and of the Golden Age of Burns and Scott* (London: Oxford University Press, 1931).

Thomson, Derek (ed.), *Gaelic Poetry in the Eighteenth Century* (Aberdeen: Association of Scottish Literary Studies, 1993).

6 The nineteenth century: history, industry, sentiment

Anderson, W. E. K. (ed.), *The Journal of Sir Walter Scott* (Edinburgh: Canongate Classics, 1998).

Birkin, Andrew, *J. M. Barrie and the Lost Boys* (London: Constable, 1979).

Blake, George, *Barrie and the Kailyard School* (London: Arthur Barker, 1951).

Burgess, Moira, *Imagine a City: Glasgow in Fiction* (Glendaruel: Argyll Publishing, 2004).

Calder, George (ed.), *Gaelic Songs by William Ross* (Edinburgh: Scottish Gaelic Texts Society, 1937).

Calder, Jenni, *RLS: A Life Study* (Glasgow: Richard Drew, 1990).

Campbell, Ian, *Kailyard: A New Assessment* (Edinburgh: Ramsay Head Press, 1981).

Campbell, Ian, (ed.), *Nineteenth-Century Scottish Fiction* (Manchester: Carcanet, 1979).

Campbell, Ian, *Thomas Carlyle* (Edinburgh: Saltire Society, 1993).

Chapman, Malcolm, *The Gaelic Vision in Scottish Culture* (London: Croom Helm, 1978).

Cockshut, Anthony O.J., *The Achievement of Walter Scott* (London: Collins, 1969).

Daiches, David, *Sir Walter Scott and His World* (London: Thames & Hudson, 1971).

Donaldson, William, *Popular Literature in Victorian Scotland: Language, Fiction and the Press* (Aberdeen: Aberdeen University Press, 1986).

Donaldson, William (ed.), *The Language of the People: Scots Prose from the Victorian Revival* (Aberdeen: Aberdeen University Press, 1989).

Furnas, J. C., *Voyage to Windward: The Life of Robert Louis Stevenson* (London: Faber & Faber, 1952).

Gifford, Douglas, *James Hogg* (Edinburgh: Ramsay Head Press, 1976).

Gordon, Ian A., *John Galt. The Life of a Writer* (Edinburgh: Oliver & Boyd, 1972).

Grant, Elizabeth, *Memoirs of a Highland Lady* (Edinburgh: Canongate Classics, 1988).

Hayden, John O. (ed.), *Scott: The Critical Heritage* (London: Routledge & Kegan Paul, 1970).

Herdman, John, *The Double in Nineteenth-Century Fiction* (London: Macmillan, 1990).

Jack, R. D. S., *The Road to the Never Land: A Reassessment of J. M. Barrie's Dramatic Art* (Aberdeen: Aberdeen University Press: 1991).

Johnson, Edgar, *Sir Walter Scott: The Great Unknown* (London: Hamish Hamilton, 1970).

Leonard, Tom, *Places of the Mind: The Life and Work of James Thomson* (London: Cape, 1993).

Letley, Emma, *From Galt to Douglas Brown: Nineteenth-Century Fiction and Scots Language* (Edinburgh: Scottish Academic Press, 1988).

Lockhart, John Gibson, *The Life of Sir Walter Scott*, intro. W. M. Parker, abridged (London: Everyman, 1957).

Lockhart, John Gibson, *Peter's Letters to His Kinsfolk* (London: Nelson, 1952).

Lownie, Andrew, *John Buchan: The Presbyterian Cavalier* (London: Constable, 1995).

Mack, Douglas (General Editor), *The Stirling South Carolina Research Edition of the Collected Works of James Hogg* (Edinburgh: Edinburgh University Press, 1995 ff.). These volumes contain invaluable introductions and critical apparatus.

Mack, Douglas, *Scottish Fiction and the British Empire* (Edinburgh: Edinburgh University Press, 2006).

Meek, Donald (ed.), *The Wiles of the World/Caran An T-Saoghail* (West Lothian: Barbour Books, 2003). Nineteenth-century Scottish Gaelic poetry.

Miller, Karl, *Doubles: Studies in Literary History* (Oxford: Oxford University Press, 1987).

Millgate, Jane, *Walter Scott: The Making of a Novelist* (Toronto: Toronto University Press, 1981).

Prebble, John, *The King's Jaunt: George IV in Scotland, 1822* (London: Collins, 1988).

Prebble, John, *The Highland Clearances* (London: Secker & Warburg, 1963).

Sandison, Alan, *Robert Louis Stevenson and the Appearance of Modernism* (Basingstoke: Macmillan, 1995).

Shaw, Harry E. (ed.), *Critical Essays on Sir Walter Scott: The Waverley Novels* (London: Prentice-Hall, 1996).

Simpson, Louis, *James Hogg: A Critical Study* (Edinburgh: Oliver & Boyd, 1962).

Smout, T. C., *A Century of the Scottish People, 1830–1950* (London: Collins, 1986).

Trumpener, Katie, *Bardic Nationalism: The Romantic Novel and the British Empire* (Princeton, NJ: Princeton University Press, 1997).

Index